T0233799

Communications
in Computer and Information Science 595

Commenced Publication in 2007
Founding and Former Series Editors:
Alfredo Cuzzocrea, Dominik Ślęzak, and Xiaokang Yang

More information about this series at http://www.springer.com/series/7899

Isidoro Gitler · Jaime Klapp (Eds.)

High Performance Computer Applications

6th International Conference, ISUM 2015
Mexico City, Mexico, March 9–13, 2015
Revised Selected Papers

 Springer

Editors
Isidoro Gitler
CINVESTAV-IPN
ABACUS Centro de Matemáticas Aplicadas
  y Cómputo de Alto Rendimiento
La Marquesa
Mexico

Jaime Klapp
Instituto Nacional de Investigaciones
  Nucleares
La Marquesa
Mexico

ISSN 1865-0929   ISSN 1865-0937 (electronic)
Communications in Computer and Information Science
ISBN 978-3-319-32242-1   ISBN 978-3-319-32243-8 (eBook)
DOI 10.1007/978-3-319-32243-8

Library of Congress Control Number: 2016935218

Printed on acid-free paper

This Springer imprint is published by Springer Nature
The registered company is Springer International Publishing AG Switzerland

Preface

Supercomputing is rapidly being recognized as more than an essential tool and instrument for contemporary science and technology. It has turned out to be, together with the development of basic theory and experimentation, the third crucial pillar for the improvement of our understanding of nature, the analysis of society, and technological advancement. Nowadays, current research in applied mathematics, physics, biology, engineering, medicine, and environmental sciences relies more and more on supercomputing, allowing us to expand basic research and experimentation in areas such as astrophysics, cosmology, fluid dynamics, elementary particle physics, medicine, and life sciences. Supercomputing has proven to be equally essential for developing and understanding a wide range of advanced science and technology topics that are directly related to our daily lives, including scientific global warming forecasting, simulations of natural disasters that help minimize the damage from events such as earthquakes, tsunamis, torrential rains, and typhoons among others. Other areas benefiting from supercomputing are genome analysis for gene therapy and protein analysis for drug design, the development of new devices and materials, car crash simulations, jet engine design, and many more. High-performance computing (HPC) enables the design of models and running computer simulations of phenomena before passing through an experimental phase, with great economic savings, but more importantly allowing us to provide results within days or weeks when months or even years were required in the past.

Technology today is more than computers; modern applications combine networks, visualization, data storage, data mining, remote instruments, sensors, supercomputers, servers, laptops, etc. Science is increasingly driven by data (large and small). Data come from everywhere: scientific instruments, experiments, sensors, new devices, and are used by everyone: scientists, technologists, consumers, educators, and the general public. We find strong parallels between genomics today and astronomy 20 years ago, similarities between turbulence/CFD, N-body, ocean circulation, and material science, and on the future exascale everything will be a big data problem. Progress in supercomputing has become an everyday challenge for human endeavors.

The 6th International Conference on Supercomputing in Mexico — ISUM 2015 — was held in Mexico City, during March 9–13, 2015. The organization was a joint effort of various research institutions and universities in Mexico City and the State of Mexico: the Centro de Investigación y Estudios Avanzados (CINVESTAV), the Universidad Nacional Autónoma de México (UNAM), the Universidad Autónoma Metropolitana (UAM), the Instituto Politécnico Nacional (IPN), the Instituto Nacional de Investigaciones Nucleares (ININ), the Universidad Autónoma del Estado de México (UAEMEX), la Corporación Universitaria para el Desarrollo del Internet (CUDI), and the Consejo Nacional de Ciencia y Tecnología (CONACYT).

Building on the success of the five previous ISUM Meetings, the 2015 edition was held in Mexico City, where most research centers, universities, enterprises, government agencies, and businesses in the country are found. This is the most important event in

Mexico organized to discuss progress, problems, and challenges at a national and international level regarding the future of supercomputing. The objectives of ISUM, in its various editions, have been about upgrading technology and information exchange among leaders of major projects (both domestic and foreign), linking actions capable of enhancing existing infrastructure, and increasing the number of people trained in HPC.

The main objective of the 2015 ISUM edition was to make the conference a world-class forum through the exchange and dissemination of new ideas, research, and expertise in HPC. The ISUM Conference is organized every year over a period of five days. During these days, it features internationally and nationally renowned speakers from both academia and industry, concurrent sessions holding frontier research and new ideas in both scientific and industrial applications, as well as poster sessions, workshops (keeping in mind the importance of training human resources), and discussion panels on key issues in the future of HPC. The ISUM Conference also organizes an exhibition floor and an exhibitor's forum where attendees can see and learn about the latest innovations in HPC, hardware, software, applications, networking, storage, and related technologies available in distinct fields of the supercomputing industry. The exhibition attracted groups of scientists, researchers, department managers, laboratory directors, decision makers, and vendors from all corners of the HPC community and networking industry involved in the HPC development in Mexico. ISUM 2015 was attended by roughly 350 participants; among them, a considerable number were researchers, academics, engineers, graduate, and undergraduate students.

ISUM 2015 came across with new conditions for the HPC environment in Mexico. New laboratories for HPC are up and working. Furthermore, Mexico is now back in the Top 500 list of the 500 most powerful supercomputers in the world. The ISUM 2015 conference was hosted by ABACUS, the recently created Centro de Matemáticas Aplicadas y Cómputo de Alto Rendimiento (Centre for Applied Mathematics and High-Performance Computing) of CINVESTAV, which from early 2015 has hosted one of the largest supercomputers in Latin America, where scientists and engineers in Mexico and other countries are able to develop computational projects that require very large HPC facilities.

It is worth noting that Mexico has significant experience in the use of supercomputers, beginning in 1991, when UNAM installed a Cray YMP supercomputer. Afterwards, Mexico appeared in the Top 500 supercomputing list several times: the case of the oil industry (Top 83, Top 84, and Top 85 in the list of November 2003). A few years later, UNAM and UAM placed computers in slots 126 (2006) and 225 (2008), respectively. Other outstanding projects in Mexico are the National Laboratory for High-Performance Computing in Mexico City (UNAM-UAM-CINVESTAV), the National Supercomputing Center of San Luis Potosi within the Instituto Potosino de Investigación Científica y Tecnológica (IPICYT), the Grids National Laboratory, the National Supercomputing Laboratory of the Southeast, and ABACUS-CINVESTAV, which recently placed its supercomputer ABACUS-I in the 255 slot of the top 500 list of June 2015.

Although we have a platform and experience in supercomputing, it is still very scarce for the needs of a country like Mexico. Hence the importance of ISUM 2015, where we had the opportunity to discuss the currently installed platforms and defined some of the possible growth policies regarding the acquisition and use of these technologies.

The topics of interest included, but were not limited to: use of high-performance computing systems to solve complex problems in academic and scientific research fields, applications for science and engineering, scientific visualization, simulation and modeling, parallel processing, algorithms and techniques, GPU, Xeon Phi and other accelerators, cluster, grid, and cloud computing, tools and environments for high-performance system engineering, software tools, programming tools, virtualization, architectures, component technologies, infrastructure, emerging and new technologies for HPC, big data, advance networking, petascale/exascale technologies, high-performance technical and business computing (HPTC/HPBC), energy, cooling/green computing, resource provisioning and optimization, HPC in health, education, and government, HPC for the oil and gas industry, and innovation and development of HPC technologies in Mexico.

The plenary lectures were given by directors and researchers from major supercomputing centers: "Words of Data Science in the Presence of Heterogeneous Computing Architectures" by Ilkay Altintas, San Diego Supercomputer Center (SDSC), USA, "The State of the Art in 3D Seismic Imaging" by José M. Cela Espín, Barcelona Supercomputing Center (BSC), Spain, "Taming Big Data" by Ian Foster, University of Chicago, USA, "Energy Efficiency in Embedded System Design" by Jean Luc Gaudiot, University of California – Irvine, USA, "The Future of the Message-Passing Interface" by William Gropp, University of Illinois Urbana-Champaign, USA, "HPC in Japan: More in Application and Utilized in Production Design in Industries" by Ryutaro Himeno, Advanced Center for Computing and Communication (ACCC), RIKEN, Japan, "Supercomputing for the European Human Brain Project" by Thomas Lippert, Forschungszentrum Jülich, Germany, "Towards Exascale Machines" by Philippe Olivier Alexandre Navaux, Federal University of Rio Grande do Sul, Brazil, "The Data-Enabled Revolution in Science and Society: A Need for (Inter)National Data Services and Policies" by Edward Seidel, National Center for Supercomputing Applications, USA, "Runtime Aware Architectures" by Mateo Valero, Barcelona Supercomputing Centre (BSC), Barcelona, Spain, "Efficiency of Exascale Supercomputer Centers" by Vladimir Voevodin, Moscow State University, Russia, and "The XSEDE Extended Collaborative Support Program: 3 Years of Highlights and Lessons" by Nancy Wilkins Diehr, San Diego Supercomputing Center, USA.

ISUM 2015 also had eight technological plenary lectures: "Addressing Challenges of Exascale Systems Usability" by Lim Goh, Silicon Graphics, "Programmability for HPC Is the Key" by James Reinders, Intel Corporation, "Interconnect Your Future" by Scot Schultz, Mellanox, "Technologies, Cloud and HPC Systems and Solutions" by Robert Anderson, Seagate, "Transformational technologies of the new style of IT" by Javier Flores, HP, "Trends in Processing and Storage Solutions" by Guillermo Sandoval García, CADGRAFICS, "Benefits of the Cloud to Virtualize HPC Environments" by Eduardo Marin Grijalva, VMware, and "RHEL and Supercomputing. The Value of Community" by Rolando Cedillo, RedHat.

In addition to the plenary and technological lectures, over 100 contributions were presented in oral parallel sessions. A very important activity during ISUM 2015 were the 10 workshops offered: (1) Introductory course to parallel computing with MPI and CUDA, Frédéic Massets, UNAM; (2) A Practical Introduction to Numerical Hydrodynamics, Alejandro Esquivel, ICN-UNAM; (3) Centralized HPC Cluster Management with CFEngine, Eduardo Ortega and Yolanda Flores, DGTIC-UNAM; (4) Distributed

High-Performance Scientific Computing, Sergio Nesmachnow, Universidad de la República, Uruguay; (5) Management of NWChem in HPC Infrastructures, Marcos Rivera Almazo, UAM-I; (6) Parallel Programming with Intel Cluster Studio XE 2013, Carlos Antonio Sánchez Sevilla, UAM-I; (7) Building a Lustre Storage System, Luis Arturo Nuñez Pablo, UAM-I; (8) HPC Applications Development assisted by Eclipse for Parallel Application Developers, Apolinar Martínez Melchor, UAM-I; (9) Understanding Performance in Modern High-Performance Computers, Irving Álvarez, Julio César Clemente, José Luis Gordillo and Leobardo Itehua, DGTIC-UNAM; (10) Development and Visualization Training Using CUDA, Carlos Jaime Barrios Hernández, Industrial University of Santander, Colombia.

This book contains selected contributions presented during the ISUM 2015 conference and includes plenary and other contributions. The book contains three parts. In Part 1, we have included four contributions on perspectives in supercomputer infrastructure and applications, two of which describe previous experience on how to build an adequate networking environment so that people in HPC can further collaborate and add on work already done with emphasis on the Mexican case. Also, it offers two more papers, which give an overview on current collaborative support programs as well as a glimpse of some relations between an exascale supercomputing system and education.

In Part 2, the contributions focus on parallel algorithms and optimization for both CPUs and GPUs. GPU computing was introduced to HPC users in 2007. Since then the technology has advanced rapidly, largely driven by HPC practitioners looking for greater performance and improved energy efficiencies. Performance has been a fundamental driver in the HPC market since its inception, while energy efficiency is a more recent demand that has come about as a result of the breakdown of Dennard scaling. GPUs are able to offer a better performance and performance-per-watt compared with CPUs on parallel software thanks to their throughput-optimized design and considerable floating point capability if certain conditions are fulfilled. As a result, accelerators are now found in nearly half of all new HPC systems deployed, thus having a profound impact on the implementation of parallel algorithms, particularly for those looking for optimal solutions for a given problem. We have included several contributions that use CPUs and/or GPUs architectures.

In Part 3, we have included contributions in HPC applications and simulations. Nowadays, as a consequence of the growth in supercomputer performance, there is an increase in the development of data-intensive predictive science as a solution to scientific problems via simulations that generate large amounts of data. Generally, the problems that are studied are multiscale and multidisciplinary simulations such as: digital engineering, rocket engine design, electrical energy storage, solar energy fixation, fusion, genome networks, human body simulations, hemodynamics, protein function analysis, protein folding, protein control, virus, anti-cancer drugs, nano-devices and nano-science modeling and fragmentation, material design, astrophysical simulations, cosmological simulations, disaster prevention, volcano simulations, earthquake wave propagation, cloud analysis, climate prediction, high-resolution atmospheric circulation, melted rock simulations, engineering, non-steady flow, compressible flow, large eddy simulation, and structural analysis, among many others.

For many of these simulations, we find fluid dynamics in their core, which is a highly developed branch of science that has been subject to continued and expanding research activity both theoretically and experimentally since more than a century and a half ago. Mexico has a strong and active community in this area. At ISUM 2015, a wide variety of fluid dynamics topics were presented that included: asymptotic methods in fluids, convection, computational methods for biological systems, interfacial fluid dynamics, colloidal dispersion, and flow in fractured porous media.

The book is aimed at senior undergraduate and graduate students, as well as scientists in the fields of HPC, computer sciences, physics, biology, mathematics, engineering, and chemistry who have interest in the solution of a large variety of problems that make use of supercomputers. The material included in this book is adequate for both teaching and research.

The editors are very grateful to the institutions and people that made possible the realization of the 6th International Conference on Supercomputing in Mexico — ISUM 2015, especially Julia Tagüeña Parga and Elías Micha Zaga from CONACYT, Felipe Bracho Carpizo from UNAM, Luis A. Villa Vargas from IPN, José Mustre de León from CINVESTAV, Lydia Concepción Paredes Gutiérrez and Federico Puente Espel from ININ, Axel Aviles Pallares from UAM, and Carlos Casasús López Hermosa and Salma Leticia Jaliffe Villalón from CUDI.

The following individuals were instrumental in organizing the ISUM 2015: ABACUS-CINVESTAV: Ruslan Gabbasov, Francisco Ortiz Arango, Alejandro Flores Méndez, Juan Antonio Vega, Olivia Lazcano, Daniel Ortiz, Omar Nieto, Estela Hernández, Adriana Aranda, Alberto Trejo; ININ: Jorge Luis Cervantes Cota, Estela Mayoral Villa; UNAM: Alfredo Santillán, Fabián Romo, José Luis Gordillo, José de Jesús Cruz, Liliana Hernández; IPN: René Luna García, Juan Carlos Chimal; UAM: Apolinar Martínez Melchor, Luis Arturo Núñez Pablo, Juan Carlos Rosas Cabrera; UAEMEX: Luis Enrique Díaz, Roberto López Rendón; CUDI: Salma Leticia Jaliffe Villalón, Hans Ludwing Reyes, Martha Ávila.

ISUM 2015 was organized by the following institutions: ABACUS-CINVESTAV, CONACYT, CUDI, ININ, IPN, UAM, UNAM, LNS-SURESTE, CICESE, LANGEBIO-CINVESTAV, CIMAT, UAEMEX, UAEM, CNS-IPICYT, UCOL, UDG, UNISON, UV, and The National Committee ISUM; it was sponsored by: SGI, Fujitsu, Intel, HP, Cray, Dell, ATOS, Seagate, Mellanox, Huawei, B-CAUSE, Penguin Computing, Red Hat, Enter, VMware, ENLACE, and CADGRAFICS.

We acknowledge the help of the Edition Committee for their important and valuable contribution to the final manuscript, in particular Ruslan Gabbasov, Salvador Galindo Uribarri, Julian Becerra Sagredo, Nathan Weinstein, Leonardo Di G. Sigalotti, Alejandro Aviles Cervantes, and Carlos Jaime Barrios Hernández.

We thank Estela Hernández Juárez and Adriana Aranda for their valuable contribution to the production of this book.

February 2016   Isidoro Gitler
                                                                Jaime Klapp

Acknowledgments

The production of this book was sponsored by the Consejo Nacional de Ciencia y Tecnología (Conacyt), the Consejo Mexiquense de Ciencia y Tecnología (Comecyt), the Instituto Nacional de Investigaciones Nucleares (ININ), and the Centro de Matemáticas Aplicadas y Computo de Alto Rendimiento of the Centro de Investigación y de Estudios Avanzados of the Instituto Politécnico Nacional through the "ABACUS" CONACyT grant EDOMEX-2011-C01-165873.

Contents

HPC Applications and Simulations

Contributors

Alma Y. Alanis CUCEI, Universidad de Guadalajara, Apartado Postal 51-71, Col. Las Aguilas, 45080 Zapopan, Jalisco, Mexico, e-mail: `almayalanis@gmail.com`

Jay Alameda University of Illinois at Urbana-Champaign, National Center for Supercomputing Applications, 1205 W. Clark St., MC-257, Room 1008, Urbana, IL 61801, USA, e-mail: `alameda@illinois.edu`

Betrand J. Almeida Arrieta Unidad Azcapotzalco, Universidad Autónoma Metropolitana, Mexico City, Mexico, e-mail: `al208200282@alumnos.azc.uam.mx`

Oscar Alvarado-Nava Unidad Azcapotzalco, Universidad Autónoma Metropolitana, Mexico City, Mexico, e-mail: `oan@correo.azc.uam.mx`

Carlos E. Alvarado-Rodríguez División de Ciencias Naturales y Exactas, Universidad de Guanajuato, Noria Alta, Guanajuato, Mexico; "ABACUS" Centro de Matemáticas Aplicadas y Cómputo de Alto Rendimiento, Departamento de Matemáticas, Centro de Investigación y de Estudios Avanzados (CINVESTAV-IPN), Carretera México-Toluca Km 38.5, La Marquesa, 52740 Ocoyoacac, Estado de México, Mexico

Omar S. Areu-Rangel Instituto Politécnico Nacional, ESIA, UZ, Miguel Bernard S/N, Edificio de posgrado, 07738 Mexico, D.F., Mexico

Guillermo Arreaga-García Departamento de Investigación en Física, Universidad de Sonora, Hermosillo, Sonora, Mexico, e-mail: `garreaga@cifus.uson.mx`

Eduard Ayguadé BarcelonaTECH, Universitat Politècnica de Catalunya, Barcelona, Spain; Barcelona Supercomputing Center, Barcelona, Spain

Juan Pablo Balarini Centro de Cálculo, Facultad de Ingeniería, Universidad de la República, Montevideo, Uruguay, e-mail: `jpbalarini@fing.edu.uy`

Héctor Barrios-Piña Instituto Tecnológico de Monterrey, Zapopan, Jalisco, Mexico, e-mail: `hector.barrios@itesm.mx`

Eduardo Basurto Departamento de Ciencias Básicas, Universidad Autónoma Metropolitana-Azcapotzalco, Av. San Pablo 180, 02200 Mexico, D.F., Mexico, e-mail: `ebasurto@correo.azc.uam.mx`

Gustavo Bautista-Carbajal Academia de Matemáticas, Universidad Autónoma de la Ciudad de México, 07160 Mexico, D.F., Mexico

Julián Becerra-Sagredo "ABACUS" Centro de Matemáticas Aplicadas y Cómputo de Alto Rendimiento, Departamento de Matemáticas, Centro de Investigación y de Estudios Avanzados (CINVESTAV-IPN), Carretera México-Toluca Km 38.5, La Marquesa, 52740 Ocoyoacac, Estado de México, México, e-mail: juliansagredo@gmail.com

Alexandre Bekstein Universidad Nacional Autónoma de México, Instituto de Ciencias Físicas, PO Box 48-3, 62251 Cuernavaca, MOR, Mexico

Rosanna Bonasia CONACyT, Instituto Politécnico Nacional, ESIA, UZ, Miguel Bernard S/N, Edificio de posgrado, 07738 Mexico, D.F., Mexico, e-mail: rosannabonasia017@gmail.com

Salvador Botello-Rionda Departamento de Ciencias Computacionales, A.C., Centro de Investigación en Matemáticas, Jalisco S/N, Col. Valenciana, 36240 Guanajuato, GTO, Mexico, http://www.cimat.mx, e-mail: botello@cimat.mx

Uriel Cabello Department of Computer Science, Center of Research and Advanced Studies (Cinvestav), Mexico City, Mexico, e-mail: jcabello@computacion.cs.cinvestav.mx

Victor E. Cardoso Departamento de Ciencias Computacionales, A.C., Centro de Investigación en Matemáticas, Jalisco S/N, Col. Valenciana, 36240 Guanajuato, GTO, Mexico, http://www.cimat.mx, e-mail: victorc@cimat.mx

Juan C. Catana-Salazar Posgrado en Ciencia e Ingeniería de la Computación, Universidad Nacional Autónoma de México, Mexico, Mexico, e-mail: j.catanas@uxmcc2.iimas.unam.mx

John Cazes Research Office Complex 1.101, J.J. Pickle Research, Campus, Texas Advanced Computing Center, Building 196, 10100 Burnet Road (R8700), Austin, TX 78758-4497, USA, e-mail: cazes@tacc.utexas.edu

José María Cela Computer Applications in Science and Engineering, Barcelona Supercomputing Center, Jordi Girona 29, 08034 Barcelona, Spain, e-mail: josem.cela@bsc.es

Hilda M. Chablé Martínez Unidad Azcapotzalco, Universidad Autónoma Metropolitana, Mexico City, Mexico, e-mail: hmcm@correo.azc.uam.mx

Joaquín Collado Automatic Control Department, Cinvestav, IPN 2508 Ave, 07360 Mexico, D.F., Mexico, e-mail: jcollado@ctrl.cinvestav.mx

Lonnie Crosby National Institute for Computational Sciences, University of Tennessee, Knoxville, PO BOX 2008 MS6173, Oak Ridge, TN 37831-6173, USA, e-mail: lcrosbyl@utk.edu

Oscar Cruz-Castro CONACyT Research Fellow Facultad de Ingeniería, Universidad Autónoma del Estado de México, Mexico, Mexico, e-mail: oscruc@gmail.com

Abraham Cuevas-Otero DEPFI-UNAM, Mexico City, Mexico, e-mail: abraham.esiaz@gmail.com

Josep de la Puente Computer Applications in Science and Engineering, Barcelona Supercomputing Center, Jordi Girona 29, 08034 Barcelona, Spain

Irene de Teresa Department of Mathematical Sciences, University of Delaware, Newark, DE 19716, USA

Jaime de Urquijo Instituto de Ciencias Físicas, Universidad Nacional Autónoma de México, PO Box 48-3, 62251 Cuernavaca, MOR, Mexico

Edmundo del-Valle-Gallegos Instituto Politécnico Nacional, ESFM – Departamento de Física, Zacatenco, Mexico City, Mexico

J.M. Domínguez Environmental Physics Laboratory (EPHYSLAB), Universidad de Vigo, Vigo, Spain

Bernabé Dorronsoro Universidad de Cádiz, Cádiz, Spain

Alexander Yu. Drozdov Moscow Institute of Physics and Technology, Moscow, Russia, e-mail: alexander.y.drozdov@gmail.com

J. Félix Laboratorio de Partículas Elementales, Departamento de Física, Universidad de Guanajuato, León, Guanajuato, Mexico, e-mail: felix@fisica.ugto.mx

Miguel Ferrer Computer Applications in Science and Engineering, Barcelona Supercomputing Center, Jordi Girona 29, 08034 Barcelona, Spain

Daniel Frascarelli Universidad de la República, Montevideo, Uruguay

Ruslan Gabbasov Centro de Investigación en Tecnologías de Información y Sistemas, Instituto de Ciencias Básicas e Ingeniería, Universidad Autónoma del Estado de Hidalgo, Carretera Pachuca-Tulancingo Km. 4.5, Cd. Universitaria, 42090, Mineral de la Reforma, Hidalgo, Mexico, e-mail: ruslan.gabb@gmail.com

Armando Gama Goicochea Tecnológico de Estudios Superiores de Ecatepec, Av. Tecnológico s/n, Ecatepec, 55210, Ecatepec de Morelos, Estado de México, Mexico, e-mail: agama@alumni.stanford.edu

Godofredo R. Garay Camagüey University, Camagüey, Cuba, e-mail: godofredo.garay@reduc.edu.cu

Isidoro Gitler "ABACUS" Centro de Matemáticas Aplicadas y Cómputo de Alto Rendimiento, Departamento de Matemáticas, Centro de Investigación y de Estudios Avanzados (CINVESTAV-IPN), Carretera México-Toluca Km 38.5, La Marquesa, 52740 Ocoyoacac, Estado de México, Mexico, e-mail: igitler@math.cinvestav.edu.mx

Armando M. Gómez-Torres Instituto Nacional de Investigaciones Nucleares, Ocoyoacac, Estado de México, Mexico

Ramón González Centro de Investigación en Dinámica Celular, Instituto de Investigación en Ciencias Básicas y Aplicadas, Universidad Autónoma del Estado de Morelos, 62209 Cuernavaca, Morelos, Mexico, e-mail: rgonzalez@uaem.mx

Adán Guerrero Laboratorio Nacional de Microscopía Avanzada, Universidad Nacional Autónoma de México, 62210 Cuernavaca, Morelos, Mexico; Instituto de Biotecnología, Universidad Nacional Autónoma de México, 62210 Cuernavaca, Morelos, Mexico, e-mail: adanog@ibt.unam.mx

Natalia Gutiérrez Computer Applications in Science and Engineering, Barcelona Supercomputing Center, Jordi Girona 29, 08034 Barcelona, Spain

Mauricio Hanzich Computer Applications in Science and Engineering, Barcelona Supercomputing Center, Jordi Girona 29, 08034 Barcelona, Spain

Catalina Haro-Pérez Departamento de Ciencias Básicas, Universidad Autónoma Metropolitana-Azcapotzalco, Av. San Pablo 180, 02200 Mexico, D.F., Mexico

Benjamín Hernández Oak Ridge National Laboratory, Oak Ridge, TN, USA

Haydee O. Hernández Laboratorio Nacional de Microscopía Avanzada, Universidad Nacional Autónoma de México, 62210 Cuernavaca, Morelos, Mexico; Instituto de Biotecnología, Universidad Nacional Autónoma de México, 62210 Cuernavaca, Morelos, Mexico, e-mail: hoha@ibt.unam.mx

Rubén Hernández Pérez Centro de Investigación en Tecnologías de Información y Sistemas, Instituto de Ciencias Básicas e Ingeniería, Universidad Autónoma del Estado de Hidalgo, Carretera Pachuca-Tulancingo Km. 4.5, Cd. Universitaria, 42090, Mineral de la Reforma, Hidalgo, Mexico, e-mail: rub3n.hernandez.perez@gmail.com

J.D. Hernández Velázquez CICFIM, UANL, San Nicolás de los Garza, Nuevo León, Mexico

Paloma Hidalgo Instituto de Biotecnología, Universidad Nacional Autónoma de México, 62210 Cuernavaca, Morelos, Mexico; Centro de Investigación en Dinámica Celular. Instituto de Investigación en Ciencias Básicas y Aplicadas, Universidad Autónoma del Estado de Morelos, 62209 Cuernavaca, Morelos, Mexico, e-mail: hopr@ibt.unam.mx

Santiago Iturriaga Universidad de la República, Montevideo, Uruguay, e-mail: siturria@fing.edu.uy

Salma Leticia Jalife Villalón Corporación Universitaria para el Desarrollo de Internet, A.C., Red Nacional de Investigación y Educación de México, Mexico, Mexico, e-mail: salmajalife@cudi.edu.mx

Javier Jimenez-Escalante Institute for Neutron Physics and Reactor Technology, Karlsruhe Institute of Technology, Karlsruhe, Germany

Jaime Klapp Departamento de Física, Instituto Nacional de Investigaciones Nucleares, La Marquesa S/N, Ocoyoacac, Estado de México, Mexico; "ABACUS" Centro de Matemáticas Aplicadas y Cómputo de Alto Rendimiento, Departamento de Matemáticas, Centro de Investigación y de Estudios Avanzados (CINVESTAV-IPN),

Carretera México-Toluca Km 38.5, La Marquesa, 52740 Ocoyoacac, Estado de México, Mexico, e-mail: jaime.klapp@inin.gob.mx

Dzmitry Kliazovich University of Luxembourg, Luxembourg, Luxembourg, e-mail: Dzmitry.Kliazovich@uni.lu

Jean Kormann Computer Applications in Science and Engineering, Barcelona Supercomputing Center, Jordi Girona 29, 08034 Barcelona, Spain, e-mail: jean.kormann@bsc.es

Jorge López Departamento de Ciencias Computacionales, A.C., Centro de Investigación en Matemáticas, Jalisco S/N, Col., Valenciana, 36240 Guanajuato, GTO, Mexico, http://www.cimat.mx, e-mail: jorge.lopez@cimat.mx

Manuel Guillermo López Buenfil Departamento de Ciencias Computacionales, Centro de Investigación en Matemáticas, A.C., Jalisco S/N, Col., Valenciana 36240 Guanajuato, GTO, Mexico, http://www.cimat.mx, e-mail: manuel.lopez @cimat.mx

Carlos Casasús López Hermosa Corporación Universitaria para el Desarrollo de Internet, A.C., Red Nacional de Investigación y Educación de México, Mexico, Mexico, e-mail: ccasasus@cudi.edu.mx

Roberto López-Rendón Laboratorio de Bioingeniería Molecular a Multiescala, Facultad de Ciencias, Universidad Autónoma del Estado de México, Av. Instituto Literario 100, 50000 Toluca, Mexico

Alberto Lorandi Instituto de Ingeniería, Universidad Veracruzana, Boca del Río, Veracruz, Mexico

Carlos Málaga Departamento de Física, Facultad de Ciencias, UNAM, Ciudad Universitaria, 04510 Mexico, D.F., Mexico

Francisco Mandujano Departamento de Física, Facultad de Ciencias, UNAM, Ciudad Universitaria, 04510 Mexico, D.F., Mexico

E. Mayoral Departamento de Física, Instituto Nacional de Investigaciones Nucleares, La Marquesa, s/n, Ocoyoacac, Estado de México, Mexico

S. Mejía-Rosales CICFIM, UANL, San Nicolás de los Garza, Nuevo León, Mexico

Itza Mendoza-Sanchez Instituto Politécnico Nacional, ESIA, UZ, Miguel Bernard S/N, Edificio de posgrado, 07738, Mexico, D.F., Mexico

Amilcar Meneses-Viveros Department of Computer Science, Center of Research and Advanced Studies (Cinvestav), Mexico City, Mexico, e-mail: ameneses@cs.cinvestav.mx

Vanessa Miranda CICESE Research Center, Ensenada, B.C., Mexico, e-mail: vanessa.vsphinx@gmail.com

J. Alejandro Morales Universidad de Guadalajara, CUCEI, Apartado Postal 51-71, Col. Las Aguilas, 45080 Zapopan, Jalisco, Mexico, e-mail: `ergo_horro@hotmail.com`

Edgar Nathal Instituto Nacional de Neurología y Neurocirugía Manuel Velasco Juárez, Insurgentes Sur No. 3877, Tlalpan, La Fama, 14269 Mexico, D.F., Mexico, e-mail: `enathal@yahoo.com`

Iris Neri Facultad de Ingeniería, Universidad Veracruzana, Boca del Río Veracruz, Mexico

Sergio Nesmachnow Centro de Cálculo, Facultad de Ingeniería, Universidad de la República, Montevideo, Uruguay, e-mail: `sergion@fing.edu.uy`

Sergey V. Novikov Moscow Institute of Physics and Technology, Moscow, Russia, e-mail: `serg.v.novikov@gmail.com`

Gerardo Odriozola Departamento de Ciencias Básicas, Universidad Autónoma Metropolitana-Azcapotzalco, Av. San Pablo 180, 02200, Mexico, D.F., Mexico, e-mail: `godriozo@azc.uam.mx`

Silvio Oreste Topa EESA Num. 1, Tornquist, Pcia. de Buenos Aires, Argentina

José Luis Oropeza Rodríguez Computing Research Center, National Polytechnic Institute, Juan de Dios Batiz s/n, P.O. 07038, Mexico, Mexico, e-mail: `joropeza@cic.ipn.mx`

Jorge L. Ortega-Arjona Departamento de Matemáticas, Facultad de Ciencias, Universidad Nacional Autónoma de México, Mexico, Mexico, e-mail: `jloa@-ciencias.unam.mx`

Gerardo M. Ortigoza Facultad de Ingeniería, Universidad Veracruzana, Boca del Río Veracruz, Mexico, e-mail: `gortigoza@uv.mx`

Karla Gisela Pedroza-Ríos Hospital Regional de Alta Especialidad de Ixtapaluca, Km. 34.5 Carretera Federal México-Puebla, Pueblo de Zoquiapan, 56530 Ixtapaluca, Mexico, e-mail: `drakarlapedroza@gmail.com`

Hugo Pérez Universitat Politècnica de Catalunya, BarcelonaTECH, Barcelona, Spain; Barcelona Supercomputing Center, Barcelona, Spain, e-mail: `hperez@bsc.es`

Marlon Pierce Indiana University, 2709 East 10th Street, Bloomington, IN 47408, USA, e-mail: `marpierc@iu.edu`

Jesús Ponce-Palafox Universidad Autónoma de Nayarit, Tepic, Nayarit, Mexico, e-mail: `jesus.ponce@usa.net`

Miguel Ramírez Automatic Control Department, Cinvestav, IPN 2508 Ave, 07360 Mexico, D.F., Mexico, e-mail: `mramirez@ctrl.cinvestav.mx`

Hermilo Ramírez-León Instituto Mexicano del Petróleo, Mexico City, Mexico, e-mail: `hrleon@imp.mx`

José Francisco Reyes Saldaña Computing Research Center, National Polytechnic Institute, Juan de Dios Batiz s/n, P.O. 07038, Mexico, Mexico, e-mail: jfreyes0114@gmail.com

J.M. Riesco-Ávila Departamento de Ingeniería Mecánica, Universidad de Guanajuato, Carretera Salamanca-Valle de Santiago Km 3.5+1.8 Km. Comunidad de Palo Blanco, 36885 Salamanca, GTO, Mexico, e-mail: riesco@ugto.mx

José Rodríguez Department of Computer Science, Center of Research and Advanced Studies (Cinvestav), Mexico City, Mexico, e-mail: jrodriguez@cs.cinvestav.mx

Juan Esteban Rodríguez Computer Applications in Science and Engineering, Barcelona Supercomputing Center, Jordi Girona 29, 08034 Barcelona, Spain

Clemente Rodríguez-Cuevas Faculty of Engineering, UASLP, San Luis Potosí, Mexico, e-mail: clemente.rodriguez@uaslp.mx

Andrés Rodríguez-Hernandez Instituto Nacional de Investigaciones Nucleares, Ocoyoacac, Estado de México, Mexico, e-mail: andres.rodriguez@inin.-gob.mx

Eduardo Rodríguez-Martínez Universidad Autónoma Metropolitana, Unidad Azcapotzalco, Mexico City, Mexico, e-mail: erm@correo.azc.uam.mx

Braulio Rojas Instituto de Ciencias Físicas, Universidad Nacional Autónoma de México, PO Box 48-3, 62251 Cuernavaca, MOR, Mexico

Ralph Roskies Pittsburgh Supercomputing Center, 300 South Craig Street, Pittsburgh, PA 15213, USA, e-mail: roskies@psc.edu

Isaac Rudomín Barcelona Supercomputing Center, Barcelona, Spain

Victor H. Sanchez-Espinoza Institute for Neutron Physics and Reactor Technology, Karlsruhe Institute of Technology, Karlsruhe, Germany

Sergiu Sanielevici Pittsburgh Supercomputing Center, 300 South Craig Street, Pittsburgh, PA 15213, USA, e-mail: sergiu@psc.edu

Manuel-H. Santana-Castolo Universidad de Guadalajara, CUCEI, Apartado Postal 51-71, Col. Las Aguilas, 45080 Zapopan, Jalisco, Mexico, e-mail: msantana.castolo@gmail.com

J. Serrano-Arellano División de Arquitectura e Ingeniería en Energías Renovables, Instituto Tecnológico Superior de Huichapan, ITESHU-TecNM-SEP., Dom. Conocido S/N, El Saucillo, 42411 Huichapan, HGO, Mexico, e-mail: jserrano@iteshu.edu.mx

Leonardo Di G. Sigalotti Área de Física de Procesos Irreversibles, Departamento de Ciencias Básicas, Universidad Autónoma Metropolitana-Azcapotzalco (UAM-A), Av. San Pablo 180, 02200 Mexico, D.F., Mexico; Centro de Física, Instituto Venezolano de Investigaciones Científicas, IVIC, Apartado Postal 20632, Caracas 1020-A, Venezuela

Joel Suárez Cansíno Centro de Investigación en Tecnologías de Información y Sistemas, Instituto de Ciencias Básicas e Ingeniería, Universidad Autónoma del Estado de Hidalgo, Carretera Pachuca-Tulancingo Km. 4.5, Cd. Universitaria, 42090 Mineral de la Reforma, Hidalgo, Mexico

Sergio Suárez Guerra Computing Research Center, National Polytechnic Institute, Juan de Dios Batiz s/n, P.O. 07038, Mexico City, Mexico, e-mail: ssuarez@cic.ipn.mx

Gonzalo Tancredi Universidad de la República, Montevideo, Uruguay

Andrei Tchernykh CICESE Research Center, Ensenada, B.C., Mexico, e-mail: chernykh@cicese.mx

Ketzasmin A. Terrón-Mejía Laboratorio de Bioingeniería Molecular a Multiescala, Facultad de Ciencias, Universidad Autónoma del Estado de México, Av. Instituto Literario 100, 50000 Toluca, Mexico

Dante Tolentino Instituto Politécnico Nacional, ESIA, UZ, Miguel Bernard S/N, Edificio de posgrado, 07738 Mexico, D.F., Mexico

Franklin Torres-Bejarano Universidad de la Costa, Barranquilla, Colombia, e-mail: ftorres4@cuc.edu.co

Sulema Torres-Ramos Universidad de Guadalajara, CUCEI, Apartado Postal 51-71, Col. Las Aguilas, 45080 Zapopan, Jalisco, Mexico, e-mail: sulema7@hotmail.com

Nico Trost Institute for Neutron Physics and Reactor Technology, Karlsruhe Institute of Technology, Karlsruhe, Germany

Carlos A. Vargas Departamento de Ciencias Básicas, Universidad Autónoma Metropolitana-Azcapotzalco, Av. San Pablo 180, 02200 Mexico, D.F., Mexico

J. Miguel Vargas-Felix Departamento de Ciencias Computacionales, Centro de Investigación en Matemáticas, A.C., Jalisco S/N, Col. Valenciana, 36240 Guanajuato, GTO, Mexico, http://www.cimat.mx, e-mail: miguelvargas@cimat.mx

Victor E. Vladislavlev Moscow Institute of Physics and Technology, Moscow, Russia, e-mail: victor.vladislavlev@gmail.com

Vadim Voevodin Research Computing Center, Moscow State University, Leninskie Gory, 1, bld. 4, 119234 Moscow, Russia, e-mail: vadim@parallel.ru

Vladimir Voevodin Research Computing Center, Moscow State University, Leninskie Gory, 1, bld. 4, 119234 Moscow, Russia, e-mail: voevodin@parallel.ru

Nathan Weinstein "ABACUS" Centro de Matemáticas Aplicadas y Cómputo de Alto Rendimiento, Departamento de Matemáticas, Centro de Investigación y de Estudios Avanzados (CINVESTAV-IPN), Carretera México-Toluca Km 38.5, La Marquesa, 52740 Ocoyoacac, Estado de México, Mexico

Nancy Wilkins-Diehr San Diego Supercomputer Center, University of California, San Diego, 9500 Gilman Dr., La Jolla, CA 92093-0505, USA, e-mail: `wilkinsn@sdsc.edu`

Christopher D. Wood Laboratorio Nacional de Microscopía Avanzada, Universidad Nacional Autónoma de México, 62210 Cuernavaca, Morelos, Mexico; Instituto de Biotecnología, Universidad Nacional Autónoma de México, 62210 Cuernavaca, Morelos, Mexico, e-mail: `chris@ibt.unam.mx`

Francisco Javier Zaragoza Martínez Universidad Autónoma Metropolitana, Unidad Azcapotzalco, Mexico City, Mexico, e-mail: `franz@correo.azc.uam.mx`

Perspectives in Supercomputer Infrastructure and Applications

An Overview of the XSEDE Extended Collaborative Support Program

Nancy Wilkins-Diehr[1(✉)], Sergiu Sanielevici[2], Jay Alameda[3], John Cazes[4],
Lonnie Crosby[5], Marlon Pierce[6], and Ralph Roskies[2]

[1] San Diego Supercomputer Center, University of California, San Diego, 9500 Gilman Dr.,
La Jolla, CA 92093-0505, USA
wilkinsn@sdsc.edu
[2] Pittsburgh Supercomputing Center, 300 South Craig Street, Pittsburgh, PA 15213, USA
{sergiu,roskies}@psc.edu
[3] National Center for Supercomputing Applications, University of Illinois at Urbana-Champaign,
1205 W. Clark Street, MC-257, Room 1008, Urbana, IL 61801, USA
alameda@illinois.edu
[4] Texas Advanced Computing Center, Research Office Complex 1.101, J.J. Pickle Research,
Campus, Building 196, 10100 Burnet Road (R8700), Austin, TX 78758-4497, USA
cazes@tacc.utexas.edu
[5] University of Tennessee, Knoxville, PO BOX 2008 MS6173,
Oak Ridge, TN 37831-6173, USA
lcrosby1@utk.edu
[6] Indiana University, 2709 East 10th Street, Bloomington, IN 47408, USA
marpierc@iu.edu

Abstract. The Extreme Science and Engineering Discovery Environment (XSEDE) is a flagship cyberinfrastructure project funded by the US National Science Foundation (NSF). XSEDE's Extended Collaborative Support Services (ECSS) program is a significant component of the XSEDE effort, dedicated to extended engagements with our user community which transform their research. We describe the organization, operation and some highlights of the program in this submission.

1 Introduction

The Extreme Science and Engineering Discovery Environment (XSEDE) [1] is a flagship cyberinfrastructure project funded by Computer and Information Science and Engineering (CISE) directorate of the US National Science Foundation (NSF). XSEDE delivers allocation services, integrated user support, software and operations services, and education and outreach activities. These not only support the NSF's investments in high end computing but are designed to encourage development of a wider ecosystem through interoperability efforts with campuses and other cyberinfrastructure (CI) environments.

XSEDE's mission is to substantially enhance the productivity of a growing community of scholars, researchers, and engineers through access to advanced digital

© Springer International Publishing Switzerland 2016
I. Gitler and J. Klapp (Eds.): ISUM 2015, CCIS 595, pp. 3–13, 2016.
DOI: 10.1007/978-3-319-32243-8_1

services that support open research; and to coordinate and add significant value to the leading cyberinfrastructure resources funded by the NSF and other agencies.

One of the largest components of XSEDE is the Extended Collaborative Support Service (ECSS). ECSS pairs members of the user community with expert ECSS staff members for an extended period, to work together to solve challenging problems through the application of CI. With the increase in the digital aspects of research, most users are challenged to be not only experts in their fields, but also experts in the rapidly expanding elements of CI.

Comprising roughly one third of the XSEDE budget (~ $7 M per year, 2016-2021), the ECSS program is of sufficient size to consist of staff with a wide variety of expertise. Our goal, often exceeded, is 50 ECSS projects and 50 training events per year. Our organizational structure and the activities within each area are described further below.

While most ECSS staff members come from sites who have also received NSF grants to operate large scale resources (and so have deep expertise on these platforms), ECSS does include staff members from other institutions who bring in valuable expertise in areas such as digital humanities, workflows and science gateways. We find this expertise increasingly necessary as the domain areas, the programming methods and the advanced CI resources allocated by XSEDE continue to diversify.

We find that the extended interactions made possible by ECSS give research teams the support they need to tackle difficult problems but also give them an opportunity to learn new computational techniques that may help with further development. Most ECSS staff members have advanced degrees in scientific fields, as well as technology expertise, and thus speak the language of the researchers. Our domain expertise includes areas tradition-ally associated with high end computing –astrophysics, computational fluid dynamics, computational chemistry, climate modeling, engineering, molecular dynamics and physics to name a few– and also in newer areas where demand has grown - genomics, digital humanities, machine learning, phylogenetics and statistics. This combination of domain plus technology expertise allows staff to contribute in deep ways.

Just as domain areas using advanced CI have been diversifying, so too has the programming expertise needed to solve today's problems. Historically, extended support has been focused on improving code performance on supercomputers – perform-ance analysis, petascale optimization, debugging, the use of specific computing archi-tectures and visualization among others. Today, the expertise of ECSS staff members extends to science gateway development and workflow systems, the use of R, Java, and MATLAB, database optimization, cloud computing, data mining and more.

In the XSEDE program, ECSS assistance is requested through the same mechanisms that CPU, data and other resources are requested. This coordinated access makes it plain that expertise and resource access can go hand in hand. Researchers can think about areas where they will need specific assistance at the same time that they are planning their computational objectives, but ECSS can also be requested at any point in an allo-cation lifecycle as needs develop. ECSS collaborations can last from weeks up to one year. Renewals are also possible.

ECSS is divided into two areas. ECSS Projects, where work is done primarily with individual research groups, and ECSS Communities, where work benefits larger communities. The areas work very closely together and staff members, projects and activities often span and shift back and forth between the two areas.

ECSS projects are true collaborations between XSEDE staff and allocated XSEDE researchers. An important component of all ECSS projects is a well-documented work plan. These are developed collaboratively by ECSS staff and the research team. They name contributors and their time commitments, both from ECSS and the research team. They outline goals and include quarterly tasks toward those goals. Work plans are critically important for a number of reasons. They establish expectations appropriately for everyone involved and help promote productive collaboration that is balanced and incorporates the strengths and expertise of both the XSEDE staff members and researchers. Work plans set goals and allow collaborators to understand when the defined work has been completed or needs to be changed. For example, it can be difficult to outline specific optimization paths before profiling a code. Work plans also routinely involve several different ECSS staff members allowing for an increased representation of expertise. However, a single lead consultant will direct the work and serves as a single point of contact for the research team.

Continued training of our own staff is a high priority for ECSS as the need for diverse expertise expands. One way of addressing this is our monthly web-based symposium, at which one or two presenters discuss lessons learned from ongoing projects or provide an introduction to new capabilities that are being planned for XSEDE. The symposium series is advertised publically so these lessons can be shared more broadly as well. We also sponsor workshops targeted specifically at our staff including topics such as new resources and capabilities available within XSEDE.

ECSS staff also serve as reviewers for the XSEDE allocation process, reviewing hundreds of requests of varying sizes per year and in this way maintaining a close connection to the research being done on XSEDE resources.

Many staff are also involved in projects beyond XSEDE. Some are principal investigators or staff members on NSF-funded software, data and science gateway projects. Others are funded to conduct research using the very largest of the NSF computing system, Blue Waters. Some are involved in site-specific activities. We find that while juggling multiple activities can be a distraction, the benefits in terms of broad expertise and access to top notch personnel greatly outweigh the costs.

The sub areas of ECSS Projects and ECSS Communities are described below.

2   ECSS Projects

The ECSS Projects area consists of two sub groups, ESRT (Extended Support for Research Teams) and NIP (Novel and Innovative Projects). Through these project-based interactions with research groups, we both encourage new communities and advance existing communities in their use of XSEDE resources and digital services, furthering and transforming the groups' scientific research goals.

2.1   Extended Support for Research Teams

An Extended Support for Research Teams (ESRT) project is a collaborative effort between an XSEDE user group and one or more ECSS staff members, the goal of which is to enhance the research group's capability to transform knowledge using XSEDE-allocated resources and related technologies. At present, these projects comprise approximately 60 % of all ECSS projects. ESRT projects take a variety of forms. They might include the optimization and scaling of application codes to use large scale parallelism, new architectures or interconnect technologies; aggregating petabyte databases from distributed heterogeneous sources and mining them interactively; or implementation of new libraries, methodologies, or workflows within scientific computations.

The best examples of ESRT projects emphasize the collaborative nature of the researcher-staff interaction. Although ECSS staff members possess varied expertise and are highly trained and motivated to solve researchers' problems, the collaborative interaction between researcher and staff member can add an extra level of understanding, investment, and impact to the ESRT project. Beyond delivering optimized application code, scripts, capabilities, and tools, ESRT projects with sufficient levels of collaboration can deliver scientific impact. An example of such a project was entitled "Gender and Social Dynamics: A Large-Scale, Cross-Platform Study of Social Behavioral patterns in Massively-Multiplayer Online Games". Dr. Cuihua Shen at the University of California at Davis led a team that performed analysis on data sets, game logs, from "EverQuest II" and "Chevalier's Romance 3" to obtain information on players' online behaviors. Using analytical tools supported on Gordon and advanced parallel computing, Dora Cai, an ESRT consultant from NCSA, constructed and maintained the needed database for the project, trained the UC Davis project team in its use, and provided an R script that executes needed data analysis in parallel. This work has resulted in both publications led by the ESRT consultant [2] and by the researcher [3].

2.2   Novel and Innovative Projects

The mission of the Novel and Innovative Projects (NIP) team is to proactively seek out and mentor sustained projects by non-traditional (to high performance computing and advanced CI) users and communities. Activities range from initial contact to the development and execution of successful projects, including the development and execution of ECSS work plans. The scope of NIP includes disciplines whose practitioners have not traditionally used HPC/CI resources. Examples include bioinformatics, economics, the social sciences, arts and humanities. It also includes the promotion of demographic diversity among XSEDE users by working with minority and women researchers and educators and with those based at minority serving institutions and at institutions in historically underserved geographic regions. NIP collaborated with the XSEDE Outreach team to set up the Domain Champions program, which enrolls successful and influential users as volunteers to explain to colleagues in their field how they too can productively use XSEDE and other advanced CI resources, and to advise ECSS on how to address specific challenges that arise in their community. For sample NIP projects, see Sect. 4 below, "ECSS Areas Working Together".

3 ECSS Communities

Extended Collaborative Support for Communities focuses efforts on collaborative projects that benefit larger user communities rather than individual research groups. The Communities area has three components—Extended Support for Community Codes (ESCC); Extended Support for Science Gateways (ESSGW); and Extended Support for Training, Education and Outreach (ESTEO).

3.1 Extended Support for Community Codes

Extended Support for Community Codes (ESCC) efforts are aimed at deploying, hardening, and optimizing software systems necessary for extensive research communities to create new knowledge using XSEDE resources and related technologies. In addition to optimization of already installed community codes, ESCC staff also explore software that might be appropriate for installation on XSEDE resources.

Examples include work on codes such as Gadget [4], Trinity [5], Allpaths-LG [6, 7], P3DFFT [8], Enzo [9], OpenFOAM [10], and Amber [11]. Although most ESCC projects are the result of requests from researchers, ECSS management occasionally creates internal projects to support a common request or to address a gap in the community software installed on XSEDE resources. Examples of internal projects are support for optimizing Trinity-Allpaths, Amber, and OpenFOAM.

There are many benefits to optimization of community codes. Since many of these codes are heavily used on XSEDE systems, optimizing them not only saves CPU hours for the groups using the codes, but also frees up time that can be allocated to others. Even more valuable though is when these changes are accepted back into a code base that is widely deployed - on local clusters, campus clusters, large scale computing facilities funded by other agencies, etc. Now the optimization benefits can extend far beyond XSEDE.

One example of ESCC support was a project with John Wise at the Georgia Institute of Technology to improve a component of Enzo [9]. ESCC supporter Lars Koesterke (TACC) assisted Wise and team on their project entitled *The First Galaxies Throughout Cosmic Time*. Enzo is a widely used adaptive mesh astrophysics community code used in this project to simulate the formation and evolution of dwarf galaxies. Over the course of the project, Koesterke assisted Wise with the optimization of the radiative transfer component of Enzo, profiling the code and identifying hotspots. Several different strategies were considered to optimize the performance, including techniques from the visualization community. After assessing different solutions, such as Xeon Phi acceleration and pre-computation of the ray tracing, Wise and Koesterke settled on creation of separate loops around the exp() function to allow the compiler to easily vectorize the computation over different energy groups. These changes improved the performance of the module by 20 %. Future enhancements will include a custom exp function call and more asynchronous MPI communication to gain even more performance. This exemplifies the type of support provided by ESCC.

3.2   Extended Support for Science Gateways

Science gateways are community-designed and supported interfaces (often web-based) that provide a user-friendly interface to many services   [12]. Depending on the community, these might include data collections, user work spaces, collaboration spaces, and computation and visualization capabilities. Gateways enable entire communities of users associated with a common discipline to use cyberinfrastructure resources, national, international and local, through an interface that is configured for optimal use. Researchers who use gateways are able to focus on their scientific goals and less on assembling the cyberinfrastructure they require. Gateways can also foster collaborations and the exchange of data and ideas among researchers.

The primary mission of the Extended Support for Science Gateways (ESSGW) group is to provide Extended Collaborative Support to existing and new scientific communities that would like to use XSEDE resources through gateways. ESSGW does not directly develop and support gateways but instead supports science gateway operators with tasks such as integration with XSEDE resources and choice of technologies. Work can involve the integration of high-end resources into gateways, help with user-requested projects, and work on infrastructure tasks that benefit all gateways such as testing and assisting with the integration of gateway identity assertion mechanisms that associate gateway-provided identities with job executions that use community accounts.

ESSGW also acts as a community resource, organizing presentations on topics of community-wide interest and hosting community forums to get requirements and other feedback from gateway community members.

Solutions for one gateway are often very applicable to a gateway in an entirely different domain. ESSGW also works closely with ESTEO and other XSEDE training, education and outreach efforts as well as the XSEDE Campus Champions program to promote the use of science gateways by new users, particularly those at Minority Serving Institutions. Campus Champions are non-XSEDE-funded local university representatives who are knowledgeable about XSEDE resources and who engage large numbers of researchers, educators, and students among their campus community.

ESSGW also is the home for support for the use of scientific workflow tools, which are closely related technologies to science gateways. ESSGW does not directly support the development and production integration of scientific workflow tools but instead acts as a community broker, matching researchers with workflow problems to existing workflow tools and tool developers, and assisting with the use of these existing tools on XSEDE. ESSGW maintains a Web site (https://sites.google.com/site/xsedeworkflows/) and dedicated login node with community-supported workflow tools pre-installed that allows XSEDE users to explore and evaluate these technologies on their own without having to install the software themselves.

Through the mutual efforts of science gateway operators and ESSGW support staff, over 4,000 unique users per quarter used XSEDE resources to execute computational experiments during the October through December 2015 reporting period. This outnumbers users accessing XSEDE resources through the traditional command line interface during that same period (2,605). There were 14 gateways actively submitting jobs.

ESSGW thus plays a key role XSEDE's strategy to scale up the number of users that it supports through science gateways.

3.3   Extended Support for Training, Education and Outreach

Diffusion of ECSS expertise into the community is an important part of the work we do. Many ECSS staff contribute a portion of their time to XSEDE's training, education and outreach efforts and in fact supply much of the person-power, expertise and technical content for activities directed by other parts of the program, for example the training component of user services as well as outreach efforts, such as those to underrepresented communities. Additional activities supported by this area include presentation of conference papers, development of tutorials, delivery of training both remotely and in person, as well as mentoring students visiting their institutions and at events such as the International HPC Summer School.

Lessons learned through ECSS projects are passed along in several ways. ECSS staff present at the monthly ECSS symposium. Project final reports identify lessons learned and advanced topic documentation or tutorials for others that would be beneficial.

ESTEO and Training staff survey existing online training materials delivered by all service providers and identify new areas where materials would benefit the community. They create new material where needed, review existing documentation and training modules and test sample codes related to these efforts. This just-in-time training is increasingly popular with the user community when both time and travel budgets are limited.

ESTEO staff present at dozens of events each year, including "train-the-trainers" events, onsite classes requested by Campus Champions, conferences and summer schools (national and international). One ongoing success has been the ESTEO collaboration on regional workshops with the Underrepresented Community Engagement (URCE) effort in XSEDE. ESTEO staff participate in the 6-month planning process for each workshop, including identifying trainers and tailoring content in an effort to meet the needs of the institution and community we are engaging at the workshop. The collaboration continues after the workshop, to ensure connections are made between participants and ECSS staff, especially through allocation requests made by participants which could include requests for ECSS support.

As mentioned earlier, as the diversity of XSEDE resources, user interests and technology all continue to expand, the need for staff training is paramount. ESTEO constantly surveys the need and works with content specialists to develop in depth, hands on training specifically designed for ECSS staff. We have begun using face-to-face opportunities at the annual conference for more in depth training.

ESTEO also provides support for teams using XSEDE systems for education. For example, ECSS staff have supported the Small Private Online Courses hosted by XSEDE and the University of California-Berkeley, in which we work with the course teaching assistants to ensure that the homework problems work as expected on the XSEDE resources, as well as ensure that issues encountered by the students are addressed promptly by the appropriate staff.

Finally, the Campus Champions Fellows program is a significant component of ESTEO. Campus Champions, local experts on XSEDE resources, apply annually to become Fellows. Fellows engage in an intensive one-year collaboration with an ECSS staff member on user projects where ECSS support has been requested. The ultimate goal is to strengthen the user support fabric that is being woven throughout the country via the Champions initiative.

4   ECSS Areas Working Together

To illustrate how the organizational areas of ECSS interoperate to enable scientific advances, especially by multidisciplinary teams dealing with complex technological challenges unprecedented in their fields, we briefly discuss two examples.

The *Galaxy* genomics analysis system was created in 2008 by a collaboration of researchers at Emory and Penn State [13]. ECSS-Projects director Roskies became aware of the rapidly increasing popularity of this system at a conference in January 2011, and referred information about it to the NIP team which was just then being formed in anticipation of the official start of the XSEDE project. Over the next few months, close contacts between ECSS and the *Galaxy* teams were established, also prompted by requests from prospective users to ECSS-Communities director Wilkins-Diehr, that instances of *Galaxy* that they had begun to run in their own genomics labs be enabled to send large analysis tasks to XSEDE resources. The *Galaxy* team itself, faced with tens of thousands of end-users of the small "Galaxy-Main" server they were hosting at Penn State, requested the assistance of ECSS and the XSEDE community in developing and deploying a scalable solution. The XSEDE partners and service providers PSC, TACC and SDSC, as well as our partner CI project NCGAS (National Center for Genome Analysis Support) led by Indiana University, joined the ECSS collaboration with the *Galaxy* team.

With help from the XSEDE networking group, the end-to-end data transfer performance between Penn State, PSC and TACC was optimized. But since *Galaxy* was initially designed to run analysis jobs local to the hosting site, and relied on a shared filesystem between the web server and the backend computational resources that ran the analyses, it was not yet possible to offload user jobs to remote XSEDE systems. With help from ESSGW and NIP, the *Galaxy* team has now decoupled the web front end from the computational resources, enabling *Galaxy* to submit jobs to remote resources and perform the necessary data migration. They have built a scheduling and messaging system to interface with a wide variety of backend compute resources [14]. The main server, http://usegalaxy.org, is now hosted on a cluster at TACC and is able to send a running job to the *Stampede* system (transparently to the end user) if its execution time reaches the limit allowed on the main cluster. The team is now finishing work on enabling routing of *de novo* transcriptome assembly jobs to the large shared memory nodes of the *Greenfield* and forthcoming *Bridges* systems at PSC. This is made possible by previous work under an ESCC project to deploy and optimize the *Trinity* software [5] on HPC systems, in collaboration with its developers at the Broad Institute and with

NCGAS. The XSEDE domain champion for bioinformatics, Brian Couger of Oklahoma State University, was an important contributor to this effort.

This collaboration has enabled the main public Galaxy analysis website to support more than 50,000 genomics researchers performing hundreds of thousands of analysis jobs every month, a portion of which run on XSEDE resources.

Our second example is the *Paleoscape Model of Coastal South Africa During Modern Human Origins*, an international cross-disciplinary effort uniting knowledge and scientists from paleoanthropology, behavioral ecology, botany, ecology, cultural anthropology, geology, geography, marine geophysics, oceanography, paleo-oceanography, climate modeling, and climatology [15]. Its goal is to better understand the origins of modern humans by simulating the climatic conditions and distribution of natural resources available to humans during the critical time period 50,000 to 130,000 years ago, during which our ancestors survived near-extinction due to adverse environmental conditions and developed modern cognitive abilities and strategies in the process. The geographic focus is the southern Cape region of South Africa, which was rich in natural resources for hunter-gatherer groups including edible plants, shellfish, animals, and raw materials.

This large-scale computational project was initiated by a fortuitous meeting between Curtis Marean of the Institute of Human Origins at the University of Arizona, who is directing excavations at the Pinnacle Point site in South Africa, and ECSS NIP manager Sergiu Sanielevici, who visited the site on vacation in 2012. When introduced to the capabilities of XSEDE and ECSS, Marean requested a startup allocation of computing resources and ECSS assistance, initially to adapt and run the CCAM climate model used by his colleagues in South Africa at the resolution required to study the climate in the region of interest under a variety of interglacial and glacial climate states. We assigned this project to the community codes area of ECSS, ESCC, because we anticipated that its results could be applicable to a broader community of researchers, including those interested in studying regional implications of global climate change. Shortly after its launch, the project was joined by ECSS Campus Champion Fellow Eric Shook of Kent State University. Working closely with ESCC expert David O'Neal (PSC) and with Marean's team, Shook took the lead in expanding the technical scope of the project to develop efficient HPC versions of an agent based model used to simulate the behavior and decision making of hunter-gatherers given the caloric resources available in their environment.

As a result of the progress achieved to date, the *Paleoscape* team (which now includes Shook as a co-PI) has developed an ambitious project to couple the climate model results to two complementary vegetation models that will generate the resource landscape within which the NetLogo ABM Workflow System (NAWS) [16] developed with ESCC support will simulate multiple foraging and mobility decisions by humans during a 6-hour work day before returning to share resources at their camp. The results of these simulations, mapped to the actual geography of the southern Cape Region, will be amenable to verification by archeological field work.

5   Challenges

Although ECSS has been very successful, it continues to evolve in order to better serve a wide range of researchers on a growing diversity of resources in the XSEDE ecosystem. ECSS co-directors conduct exit interviews with every principal investigator (PI) receiving ECSS support. We ask whether communication with the research team was timely and effective, about the satisfaction with and impact of the ECSS contributions, whether ECSS staff suggested new directions for the work or rose to a level where they were co-authors on publications, among other topics. We have found these exit interviews to be invaluable for the insights they provide not only for the ECSS program, but for other areas of XSEDE as well.

The cyberinfrastructure landscape for research changes continually. Recent NSF hardware acquisitions introduce new technologies and operating modes (e.g. virtual machines, persistent database services, flash storage), increased use of XSEDE resources by non-traditional communities, and new programming modes such as those necessary for data analytics and informatics. ECSS continues to adapt by either training existing staff members in new technologies or swapping staff members at XSEDE sites to bring in needed expertise.

A second concern is simply managing ECCS itself, which is a virtual organization with close to 70 different individuals from all over the United States, and matching the expertise of particular staff members to the ECSS requests. Inevitably, some valuable staff members are already fully committed, while there may not be sufficient requests for collaboration for others. ECSS staff who are not committed for the moment are assigned other tasks such as developing or vetting training material, or reviewing smaller requests for access to XSEDE resources.

A third issue is that it is sometimes hard for project PIs who request ECSS assistance to treat the ECSS staff as collaborators rather than simply as a helping hand who can be assigned tasks not appropriate to their expertise. This requires continued education of the user community.

Finally, despite our best efforts to date, a great number of XSEDE users and potential users remain unaware of the availability of ECSS resources. We are addressing this by continually improving our web presence, including ECSS in XSEDE outreach and training materials and presenting to community groups such as the XSEDE Campus Champions.

References

1. Towns, J., Cockerill, T., Dahan, M., Foster, I., Gaither, K., Grimshaw, A., Hazlewood, V., Lathrop, S., Lifka, D., Peterson, G.D., Roskies, R., Scott, J.R., Wilkins-Diehr, N.: XSEDE: Accelerating scientific discovery. Comput. Sci. Eng. **16**(5), 62–74 (2014). doi:10.1109/MCSE.2014.80
2. Cai, Y.D., Ratan, R.R., Shen, C., Alameda, J.: Grouping game players using parallelized k-means on supercomputers. In: Proceedings of the 2015 XSEDE Conference: Scientific Advancements Enabled by Enhanced Cyberinfrastructure, p. 10. ACM (2015)

3. Shen, S., Ratan, R., Cai, Y.D., Leavitt, A.: Do men perform better than women? Debunking the gender performance gap in two massively multiplayer online games. Journal of Computer-Mediated Communication (2015, submitted)
4. Springel, V.: The cosmological simulation code GADGET-2. Month. Not. R. Astron. Soc. **364**(4), 1105–1134 (2005)
5. Grabherr, M.G., Haas, B.J., Yassour, M., Levin, J.Z., Thompson, D.A., Amit, I., Adiconis, X., Fan, L., Raychowdhury, R., Zeng, Q., Chen, Z., Mauceli, E., Hacohen, N., Gnirke, A., Rhind, N., di Palma, F., Birren, B.W., Nusbaum, C., Lindblad-Toh, K., Friedman, N., Regev, A.: Full-length transcriptome assembly from RNA-seq data without a reference genome. Nat. Biotechnol. **29**(7), 644–652 (2011). doi:10.1038/nbt.1883. PubMed PMID: 21572440
6. Gnerre, S., MacCallum, I., Przybylski, D., Ribeiro, F., Burton, J., Walker, B., Sharpe, T., Hall, G., Shea, T., Sykes, S., Berlin, A., Aird, D., Costello, M., Daza, R., Williams, L., Nicol, R., Gnirke, A., Nusbaum, C., Lander, E.S., Jaffe, D.B.: High-quality draft assemblies of mammalian genomes from massively parallel sequence data. Proceed. Natl. Acad. Sci. USA **108**(4), 1513–1518 (2011)
7. Ribeiro, F., Przybylski, D., Yin, S., Sharpe, T., Gnerre, S., Abouelleil, A., Berlin, A.M., Montmayeur, A., Shea, T.P., Walker, B.J., Young, S.K., Russ, C., MacCallum, I., Nusbaum, C., Jaffe, D.B.: Finished bacterial genomes from shotgun sequence data. Genome Res. **22**, 2270–2277 (2012)
8. Pekurovsky, D.: P3DFFT: a framework for parallel computations of Fourier transforms in three dimensions. SIAM J. Sci. Comput. **34**(4), C192–C209 (2012)
9. Bryan, Greg L., et al.: ENZO: an adaptive mesh refinement code for astrophysics. Astrophys. J. Suppl. Ser. **211**(2), 19 (2014)
10. Jasak, H.: OpenFOAM: open source CFD in research and industry. Int. J. Naval Arch. Ocean Eng. **1**(2), 89–94 (2014). doi:10.2478/ijnaoe-2013-0011. ISSN: 2092-6782
11. Case, D.A., et al.: The amber biomolecular simulation programs. J. Comput. Chem. **26**(16), 1668–1688 (2005)
12. Wilkins-Diehr, N.: Special issue: science gateways—common community interfaces to grid resources. Concurrency Comput. Pract. Experience **19**(6), 743–749 (2007)
13. Goecks, J., Nekrutenko, A., Taylor, J.: Galaxy: a comprehensive approach for supporting accessible, reproducible, and transparent computational research in the life sciences. Genome Biol. 11(8) (2010). R86
14. https://github.com/galaxyproject/pulsar
15. Shook, E., Wren, C., Marean, C.W., Potts, A.J., Franklin, J., Engelbrecht, F., O'Neal, D., Janssen, M., Fisher, E., Hill, K., Esler, K.J., Cowling, R.M., Scheiter, S., Moncrieff, G.: Paleoscape model of coastal South Africa during modern human origins: progress in scaling and coupling climate, vegetation, and agent-based models on XSEDE. In: Proceedings of the 2015 XSEDE Conference: Scientific Advancements Enabled by Enhanced Cyberinfrastructure, St. Louis, MO doi:10.1145/2792745.2792747
16. https://github.com/HPCGISLab/naws

Efficiency of Exascale Supercomputer Centers and Supercomputing Education

Vladimir Voevodin[✉] and Vadim Voevodin

Research Computing Center, Moscow State University,
119234, Leninskie Gory, 1, bld. 4, Moscow, Russia
{voevodin,vadim}@parallel.ru

Abstract. The efficient usage of all opportunities offered by modern computing systems represents a global challenge. To solve it efficiently we need to move in two directions simultaneously. Firstly, the higher educational system must be changed with a wide adoption of parallel computing technologies as the main idea across all curricula and courses. Secondly, it is necessary to develop software tools and systems to be able to reveal root causes of poor performance for applications as well as to evaluate efficiency of supercomputer centers on a large task flow. We try to combine both these two directions within supercomputer center of Moscow State University. In this article we will focus on the main idea of wide dissemination of supercomputing education for efficient usage of supercomputer systems today and in the nearest future as well as describe the results we have reached so far in this area.

1 Introduction

Computing technologies quickly evolve penetrating constantly to new areas of our life. A very illustrative example is science. Until recently, science was founded on two components: theory and experiment, but now many scientists hardly will do their research without numerical experiments, which have become the third pillar of the science. Computing experiments are everywhere and more and more researchers start using benefits of computer sciences in their everyday scientific work. This is especially true in large supercomputer centers, which attract large groups of users from different areas of the science.

Performance of the best supercomputers in the world is measured in Petaflops providing unprecedentedly powerful scientific instruments for research. At the same time, the efficient usage of all opportunities offered by modern computing systems represents a global challenge. Using full potential of parallel computing systems and distributed computing resources requires new knowledge, skills and abilities. Most users did not get a proper education in computer architecture, numerical methods and parallel programming technologies therefore efficiency of their applications and entire supercomputer centers is critically low.

This is a common serious problem, which is typical for all large supercomputer centers. To solve it efficiently we need to move in two directions simultaneously. Firstly, the higher educational system must be changed with a wide adoption of parallel

I. Gitler and J. Klapp (Eds.): ISUM 2015, CCIS 595, pp. 14–23, 2016.
DOI: 10.1007/978-3-319-32243-8_2

computing technologies as the main idea across all curricula and courses. But this cannot be done immediately or quickly. Simultaneously with the transformation of education it is necessary to develop software tools and systems to be able to reveal root causes of poor performance for applications as well as to evaluate efficiency of supercomputer centers on a large task flow during any period of time.

We try to combine both these two directions within supercomputer center of Moscow State University. Currently the supercomputer center includes two flagship supercomputers with peak performance of 1.7 and 2.5 Petaflops, which are used by more than 700 scientific groups from MSU, institutes of the Russian academy of sciences and Russian universities. Fast development of software tools suite ensuring efficiency of the supercomputer center goes with active incorporation of supercomputer education ideas into the education process of the university.

The importance of education in the area of parallel, distributed and supercomputer technologies is understood by the international education community. A number of large-scale projects can be cited which try to elaborate on and structure this area of education, offering recommendations on preparing teaching materials and providing examples of training courses. These projects include:

- the Russian Supercomputing Education national project [1, 2], where the Moscow State University was the principal coordinator,
- activities related to developing a computer science curricula (Computer Science 2013) by the ACM and IEEE-CS international societies [3],
- The Curriculum Initiative on Parallel and Distributed Computing project, supported by NSF/IEEE-TCPP [4].

Important recommendations in this area are given as part of the SIAM-EESI project for developing education and research in the area of Computational Science and Engineering [5].

To ensure the efficiency of large supercomputing centers, we use an approach based on a suite of interrelated software systems, technologies and instruments. It is designed for a coordinated analysis of the entire hierarchy of a supercomputing center: from hardware and operating system to users and their applications. This analysis requires going through both system level (CPU-related data, network performance, I/O operations, memory subsystem, etc.) and the upper level of entire supercomputing center (users, applications, queues, task flows, supercomputer sections, etc.).

In this article all software systems mentioned above will be shortly described. And at the same time, we will explain why supercomputing education is tightly connected with all these systems. It should be specially mentioned that the paper is written in a quite untraditional manner. There is no "related works" section, there is no description of future plans. It was made intentionally. In the present short communications we tried to focus on the main idea of wide dissemination of supercomputing education for efficient usage of supercomputer systems today and computing systems in the nearest future.

2 Software Tools and Efficiency of Supercomputers

Most of the systems use system-level data which is collected by *the total monitoring system*. We call it "total monitoring" since we need to know almost everything about dynamic characteristics of supercomputers to be sure in their efficiency at each time point. Ensuring the efficient functioning of a supercomputing center requires monitoring absolutely everything that happens inside the supercomputer, and that task alone requires sifting through tons of data. Even for the relatively small "Lomonosov" supercomputer at the Moscow State University (1.7 Pflops peak, 100 racks, 12 K nodes, 50 K cores) [6], the necessary data arrive at the rate of 120 Mbytes/s (about 30 different metrics analyzed for each node, measured at the frequencies of 0.01–1.00 Hz). It means 3+ Pbytes for 365 days of a year. This is an incredibly large amount of data which must be collected with a minimum impact on application performance. Nevertheless, a total monitoring system can be built by reaching a reasonable compromise on two key issues: what data must be stored in the database, and when should it be analyzed.

The monitoring system gives us very useful and detailed information about features of applications and about the supercomputers as well. For example, Fig. 1 presents an average CPU_load parameter across entire 6000-core supercomputer "Chebyshev" for a particular period of time. At the same time, Fig. 2 shows the same CPU_load parameter, but for a particular application. Information from the Fig. 1 is very important for system administrators. To reveal reasons of low efficiency sysadmins should fulfill a root cause analysis what is a serious problem since so many hardware and software components can directly or indirectly be involved and influent system efficiency.

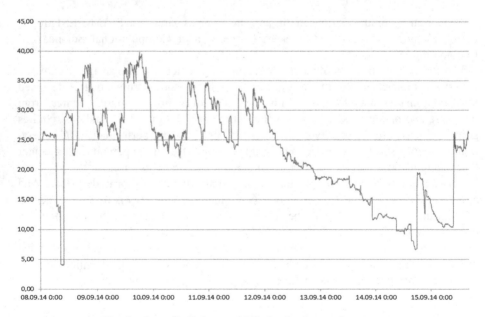

Fig. 1. Overall efficiency of "Chebyshev" supercomputer.

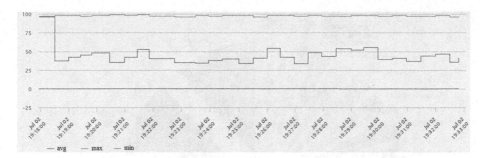

Fig. 2. CPU load timeline graph for an application.

Figure 2 represents one of the most important parameters of an application and is intended for a user. An average CPU load is very unbalanced varying from 0 to 100 % across all the cores during runtime. To improve efficiency of the application the user need to fulfill a supercomputing co-design analysis starting from optimization of the code up to possible redesign of an algorithmic approach. Practice shows that this is a tough problem for users and the reason of this situation is clear. How many of students around you have seen dynamic parameters of their parallel codes? How many of them are familiar with the notion of supercomputing co-design? This is really a question of supercomputing education, since if we examine existing curricula in computer science of the most universities we won't find much about parallel computing, efficiency, scalability, etc.

A modern supercomputing center is not only about managing supercomputers per se – this function has been studied well enough already – but about efficiently organizing a multitude of related issues: managing software licenses, user quotas, project registration and maintenance, technical support, tracking warranty and post-warranty service and repairs, monitoring of software components usage and many other tasks. All these issues are closely linked to one another and, given the huge number of components, it is clear how hard it is to efficiently organize work flows and maintain the entire supercomputing center in an up-to-date condition.

The OctoShell system combines data on all critical components for efficiently operating a supercomputing center, describing their current state and connections between components: the hardware and software components being utilized, users, projects, quotas, etc. Can this information be used to improve efficiency of large supercomputer centers? Yes, in can be used in many ways. Figure 3 presents current statistics on different software components usage for "Lomonosov" supercomputer. It should immediately draw attention of sysadmins and management of the supercomputer center due to at least two reasons. Firstly, the most popular packages and libraries must be carefully installed and highly optimized (FFTW, Intel MKL, BLAS, etc....). Secondly, tutorials and trainings on highly demanded packages in specific areas should be provided (Gromacs, VASP, etc....) otherwise efficiency of the supercomputer will certainly be low. Again, practice shows lack of proper education, even for experienced users, so continuous education is a must for advanced users as well as diverse educational activities is a must for large supercomputer centers.

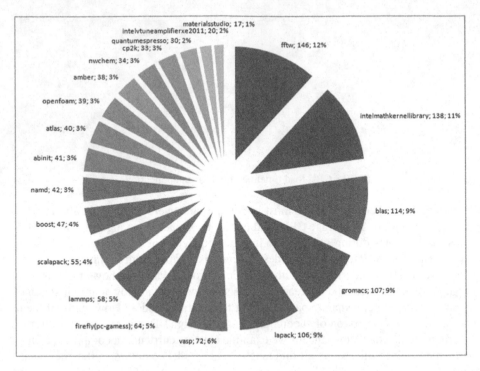

Fig. 3. Top used software components for "Lomonosov" supercomputer.

The practice of supercomputing center maintenance defines a set of strict technology and tool requirements for supporting the functioning of supercomputer systems. This includes maintaining high performance for the supercomputing infrastructure, constant monitoring of potential emergencies, continual performance monitoring for all critical software infrastructure modules, automatic decision-making on eliminating emergency situations and increasing the performance of supercomputer operations, guaranteed operator notification about the current status of the supercomputer and actions taken by the automatic maintenance system, and others. Until all these requirements are met, neither the efficient operation of a supercomputing center, nor the safety of its hardware can be guaranteed.

The goal of *the Octotron project* is to design an approach that guarantees the reliable autonomous operation of large supercomputing centers. The approach is based on a formal model of a supercomputing center, describing the proper functioning of all its components and their interconnections. The supercomputer continually compares its current state with the information from the model. If practice (monitoring data of the current supercomputer state) deviates from theory (the supercomputer model), Octotron can perform one of the predefined or dynamically selected actions, such as notifying the operator via email and/or SMS, disabling the malfunctioning device, restarting a software component, displaying an alert on the systems administrator screen, etc. No human is capable of monitoring millions of components and processes inside a supercomputer, but the supercomputer itself can do this. Importantly, this approach guarantees not only reliable operation of the existing fleet of systems at a supercomputing center, but also ensures maintenance continuity when moving to a new generation of machines. Indeed, once an emergency situation arises, it is reflected in the model, along with the root causes and symptoms of its existence, and an adequate reaction is programmed into the model. It may never happen again in the future, but if it does, it will immediately be intercepted and isolated before it has any effect on the supercomputer operation.

The thesis similar to "no human is capable to control computing systems" certainly should be reflected in modern curricula. Courses on computer architectures, operating systems, system programming, and parallel programming technologies should clearly explain high complexity of computing systems. This is important today but it will be much more important in the future [7]. Like supercomputers, mobile devices are already slightly parallel today but they will be highly parallel in several years becoming more and more complex. What we see in supercomputing area today forces us to change computer education in general to make our students well prepared for living in the hyper-parallel computer world in the future.

The main purpose of *the Situational screen* is to give system administrators full and prompt control over the state of the supercomputing center. The screen provides detailed information on what is happening inside the supercomputer, and provides updates on the status of hardware and system software, task flow, individual user activity and/or the performance of individual supercomputing applications. The situational screen and its underlying instruments are designed to meet a number of strict requirements: the need to reflect all key performance parameters of the supercomputing systems, grant of complete control over their status, scalability, expandability, configuration and minimization of the impact of the situational screen on the supercomputer performance.

Based on many years of experience in administrating supercomputer systems, we can point out the most important components which the situational screen must reflect:

- supercomputer hardware: computing modules, hosts, secondary servers, storage, networks, engineering infrastructure elements. Here it is important to know both the overall characteristics and the status of individual components;
- system software: the status for the entire supercomputer and individual nodes, conducting audits with specified criteria for any number of nodes;
- user task flows: tasks queued, tasks being executed, current and historical data, statistics on various partitions of the supercomputer, statistics on application package usage;
- activity of a particular user: what is being executed now, what is queued, overall performance over a recent time period, etc.;
- status of any working application: statistics on performance, locality, scalability and system-level monitoring data.

The OctoStat statistics collection system provides highly valuable information on the performance of supercomputing systems with regards to the flow of tasks queued for execution. Task queue length, waiting time before execution, the distribution of processors needed for applications of different classes, statistics by partitions of the supercomputer, by users or application packages, intensity of application flow for execution at different times… All of this – and many other metrics – need to be analyzed and used to optimize quotas, priorities and strategies for distributing valuable super-computing resources. Moscow State University supercomputing center uses OctoStat to generate daily statistics on the supercomputer usage, enabling prompt decision-making.

One key issue when analyzing the efficiency of supercomputing centers is the user application runtime performance analysis. Today this is a crucial question (and it always was). According to our estimates only a few percent of users are able to analyze properly efficiency of their applications, and most often they do not think about efficiency at all. Performance of a supercomputer on real-life applications today is quite low, amounting to just a small percentage of the peak performance characteristics. As parallelism increases, this figure is bound to decline. There are a multitude of reasons for this decline in efficiency, and we use supercomputing system hardware and software monitoring data to identify them. A lot of data is required for the analysis: CPU load, cache misses, flops, number of memory references, Loadavg, IB usage, I/O usage, etc. This data is used to build a runtime profile for each application, which is presented as a set of timeline graphs demonstrating the changes in monitoring data during the application execution. This profile, along with a number of aggregate system characteristics (we call it *JobDigest of an application*) gives a good first estimate of the application performance and its features. If any issues are observed with the application overall performance, additional analysis of the monitoring data is performed to identify the causes. Particular attention is paid to analyzing application properties such as efficiency, data locality, performance, and scalability, which are extremely important for the supercomputing systems of the future.

But no matter how rich the set of tools we use, high performance is not achievable in principle with some applications. The reason is that the structure of these applications do not correspond to the specific architecture of the computational platform. From the standpoint of supercomputing resource efficiency, a lot depends on the properties of algorithms used by these applications. What are these properties? What should be discovered and expressed explicitly in existing algorithms when a new parallel architecture appears? How to ensure efficient implementation of an algorithm on a particular parallel computing platform? The idea of deep a priori analysis of algorithm properties and their implementations forms the grounds for a web-oriented system: *AlgoWiki, an open encyclopedia of algorithm features* [8], and this encyclopedia is intended to answer this sort of questions. The main purpose of AlgoWiki is to present a description of fundamental properties of various algorithms, giving a complete understanding of both their theoretical potential and the particular features of their implementations for various classes of parallel computing systems.

A description of algorithm properties and features in AlgoWiki consists of two parts. The first part describes the actual algorithms and their properties, while the second one is dedicated to a description of their implementation features on various software and hardware platforms. This distinction is intentional, to single out machine-independent properties of various algorithms, which determine the quality of their implementation on parallel computing systems, and describe them separately from a number of issues related to the subsequent stages of algorithm programming and program execution.

At first sight, the idea of such an encyclopedia seems simple, but it is a daunting and non-trivial task in reality. Three stages of the implementation process need to be analyzed for each item: (a) studying the properties of algorithms, (b) studying the properties of the resulting programs, and (c) comparing the identified properties with the hardware features. Throughout the process – all three stages – two principal properties which determine implementation quality need to be considered: resource of parallelism and data usage. Additional complexity is introduced by the fact that these two properties need to be studied in continuity between the stages and coordinated during each stage.

One issue of utmost importance is to ensure a complete description of the implementation process, determining control over the efficiency of both new parallel programs and those ported from one computing platform to another. In other words, all principally important issues affecting the efficiency of the resulting programs must be reflected in the description of an algorithm properties and structure.

AlgoWiki provides an exhaustive description of an algorithm. In addition to classical algorithm properties such as serial complexity, AlgoWiki also presents complementary important information, which together provides a complete description of the algorithm: its parallel complexity, parallel structure, information graph (data dependency graph), determinacy, data locality, performance and scalability estimates, communication profiles for specific implementations (for distributed memory machines), and many others. As an example, Fig. 4 presents the performance depending on the number of processors and the problem size and Fig. 5 shows a memory access profile for a specific sparse matrix algorithm.

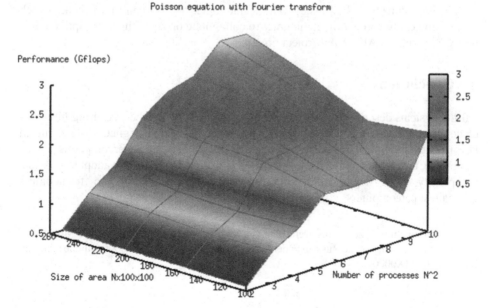

Fig. 4. Performance distribution over number of processors and problem size.

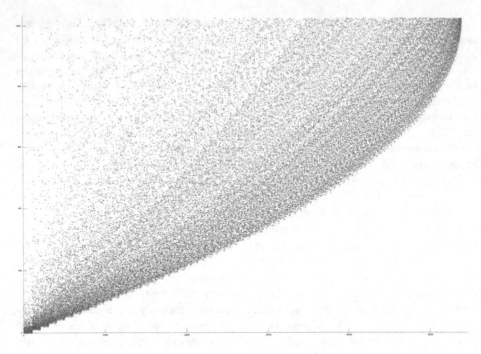

Fig. 5. Example of memory access profile.

The encyclopedia is built using Wiki technologies and is open to everyone, which enables the entire computing community to collaborate on algorithm descriptions. It is freely available at: AlgoWiki-Project.org/en.

3   Conclusions

All the systems described above are closely linked to one another, ensuring high efficiency for large supercomputing centers. Of course, they were designed while taking all key aspects of maintenance and usage into account for existing supercomputers. At the same time, the architecture of these systems was designed to be able to adopt large scale, complexity, high degree of parallelism and performance of the forthcoming exascale supercomputers.

Acknowledgments. The results were obtained with the financial support of the Ministry of Education and Science of the Russian Federation, Agreement N 14.607.21.0006 (unique identifier RFMEFI60714X0006).

References

1. Supercomputing education in Russia. Final report on the national project "Supercomputing Education", supercomputing consortium of the Russian Universities (2012). http://hpc.msu.ru/files/HPC-Education-in-Russia.pdf
2. Voevodin, Vl.V., Gergel, V.P.: Supercomputing education: the third pillar of HPC. In: Computational Methods and Software Development: New Computational Technologies. vol. 11, no. 2, pp. 117–122. MSU Press, Moscow (2010)
3. Computing curricula computer science (2013). http://ai.stanford.edu/users/sahami/CS2013
4. NSF/IEEE-TCPP curriculum initiative on parallel and distributed computing. http://www.cs.gsu.edu/~tcpp/curriculum/
5. Future directions in CSE education and research. Report from a Workshop Sponsored by the Society for Industrial and Applied Mathematics (SIAM) and the European Exascale Software Initiative (EESI-2). http://wiki.siam.org/siag-cse/images/siag-cse/f/ff/CSE-report-draft-Mar2015.pdf
6. Sadovnichy, V., Tikhonravov, A., Voevodin, Vl., Opanasenko V.: "Lomonosov": supercomputing at Moscow State University. In: Contemporary High Performance Computing: From Petascale toward Exascale (Chapman and Hall/CRC Computational Science), pp. 283–307. CRC Press, Boca Raton (2013)
7. Dongarra, J., et al.: The international exascale software roadmap. Int. J. High Perform. Comput. **25**(1), 3–60 (2011). ISSN 1094-3420
8. Antonov, A., Voevodin, V., Dongarra, J.: AlgoWiki: an open encyclopedia of parallel algorithmic features. J. Supercomput. Front. Innovations **2**(1), 4–18 (2015)

The Role of National Research and Education Networks Providing Connectivity and Advanced Network Services to Virtual Communities in Collaborative R&E Projects. CUDI: The Mexican Case

Part 1

Salma Leticia Jalife Villalón[✉]
and Carlos Casasús López Hermosa[✉]

Corporación Universitaria para el Desarrollo de Internet, A.C.,
Red Nacional de Investigación y Educación de México,
Mexico City, Mexico
{salmajalife, ccasasus}@cudi.edu.mx

Abstract. This paper describes the role of National Research and Education Networks (NRENs) and their aim to provide a seamless, large scale, high-speed, low-latency network to accelerate scientific and education discovery for national, regional or global collaborative projects that are dependent on the use of modern high performance distributed computing systems (HPDCS) to process mathematical models, produce new knowledge and drive innovation when resolving complex problems. NRENs have become the mainstream of communication and collaboration to integrate the efforts of large geographically distributed teams of Virtual Communities (VC) that - train, teach and learn-, -create, use and share- knowledge, data, information and communications technology resources (e.g. computer and information systems, middleware, tools, instruments, data sets, repositories, applications and services) building e-infrastructures necessary to meet the collaborative projects' goals. The paper focuses on the current status of the Mexican NREN: CUDI, its future organization and political support, necessary to provide seamless, large scale, high-speed, low latency and secure national backbone and international links providing connectivity, advanced network services and technical support to VCs and their e-infrastructures in collaborative R&E projects within the country, the LAC region and worldwide.

Keywords: National Research and Education Networks · NREN · HPDCS · Grid computing · High Performance Computing · Cloud computing · e-infrastructures

© Springer International Publishing Switzerland 2016
I. Gitler and J. Klapp (Eds.): ISUM 2015, CCIS 595, pp. 24–47, 2016.
DOI: 10.1007/978-3-319-32243-8_3

1 Introduction

1.1 National Research and Education Networks

The term "National Research and Education Network" or NREN was originated around the decade of the 80s in the United States (US), whose current NREN is operated by Internet2[1]. Its initial aim was to interconnect the main advanced computing sites within the country with a gigabit-like bandwidth, for the development of advanced technologies by the research and academic community and the improvement of the Internet. Europe and other regions of the world rapidly adopted this approach and extended the purpose to allow the implementation of R&E projects in the different domains of science.

NRENs are open to the private and public research and higher education communities of the country and run on a non-for-profit basis. In most of the countries, NREN members pay small contributions to the cost of production services according to their affiliation, while governments fund their longer-term expansion, innovation, upgrades and international connectivity[2]. NRENs are generally founded with the support of one or more government bodies such as ministries of science and technology, education and communications. To facilitate international connectivity, only one network per country is recognized as an NREN. They interconnect with each other to form a global R&E network infrastructure.

NRENs respond to new ways of education and research using high-speed fiber optic links and advanced heterogeneous computing resources that interconnect with other instruments and tools to provide innovative services. Through NRENs, researchers and educators are able to access, compute, simulate, visualize, store, collect or send data or information, to support different virtual communities, generally interacting with high performance distributed computing systems (HPDCS)[3], national laboratories, data centers, networks of sensors, etc. within the country, or in other global facilities located abroad. NRENs are an essential infrastructure for data intensive collaborative projects where expensive instruments such as the Large Hadron Collider at CERN can be shared by thousands of researchers, processing particle accelerator experiments in grid computing sites at hundreds of institutions and laboratories interconnected worldwide to resolve complex problems. NRENs add value to isolated specialized instruments and large-scale computers when connected to the global community.

Today, there are more than 120 NRENs operating worldwide[4]. They are generally organized in regional consortia such as GÉANT in Europe, NORDUNET in the Scandinavian region, CLARA in Latin America, CKLN in The Caribbean, APAN and TEIN in Asia, Ubuntunet in East & South Africa, WACREN in Central Africa, and ASREN in the Mediterranean region connecting the Arab States.

---

[1] http://www.internet2.edu/.

[2] The Case of National Research and Education Netowrks, John Dyer, Terena 2009.

[3] The term HPDCS was taken from the article "A Survey of Load-Balancing in High-Performance Distributed Computing Systems", Z.F. El-Zoghdy, S. Ghoniemy that includes cluster, grid and cloud computing systems.

[4] https://en.wikipedia.org/wiki/National_research_and_education_network.

As R&E play an important role in economic growth, NRENs in developed countries have become essential infrastructure (i.e. public good) for governments and policy makers. NRENs are capable of increasing domestic, regional and global cooperation in the different domains of science and education that are consequently transformed into national social and economic benefits. Figure 1 shows the current inter-regional collaboration of NRENs.

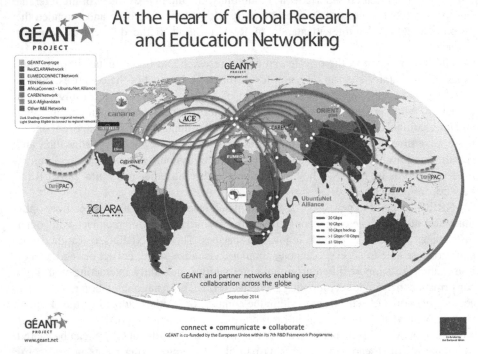

Fig. 1. World NRENs and regional Consortia (Europe is a strong promoter on the development of regional NRENs consortia. www.geant.net) https://blogit.realwire.com/New-high-speed-15000km-international-link-seamlessly-connects-African-radio-astronomers-to-Europe-through-GEANT-and-UbuntuNet (Color figure online)

Developing countries are replicating developed NRENs' best practices worldwide, to provide science and education communities as well as technical groups, with an advanced and stable computer and communications network environment. Altogether the network, the instruments, the computing resources, tools and applications are able to improve the quality of local R&E and increase the ability to innovate. As a result, NRENs consolidate the power of networking, both from the technical and community perspectives.

1.2 NRENs and High Performance Distributed Computing Systems

NRENs worldwide are the highways for scientific and technological innovation. High Performance Distributed Computing Systems (HPDCS) have been tested using NRENs and afterwards implemented commercially. The latest three innovative HPDCS – grid computing, cluster (or HPC) computing and cloud computing – are currently being used in global R&E collaborative projects using NRENs worldwide.

The sum of NRENs and HPDCS provide researchers and educators with modern platforms, tools, services and applications for their daily work and mission-critical applications. Together these facilities are generally known as e-infrastructures and they are used for different purposes commonly guided by virtual communities' needs.[5] For scientists and educators collaborating nation-to-world wide, these e-infrastructures are essential for data management, storage, analysis and collection, repositories, simulations, tools for visualization, tools for implementing massive training and learning systems, tools for support in relation to methods or analysis, as well as remote access to, and manipulation of, large-scale instruments.

Sections 1.2.1, 1.2.2 and 1.2.3 describe how different virtual R&E communities have used HPDCS and NRENs to resolve complex problems implemented by collaborative projects.

1.2.1 Grid Computing

Grid Computing (GC) is highly dependent on network reliability and inter-regional cooperation because it supports global scientific and education communities that interact as Virtual Organizations (VO). VOs use shared GC, ICT and human resources (e.g. data, software, expertise, CPU, storage space, network, visualization) regardless of geographical location, under a set of rules and conditions, ranging from administrative tools, middleware and political organization.

The High Energy Physics Virtual Community or HEP (VO) uses the largest Grid Computing System in the world. It supports the four main particle acceleration collaborative projects (ATLAS, ALICE, CMS and LHCb) of the Large Hadron Collider (LHC) at the European Council for Nuclear Research or CERN. Its 4 Tier hierarchical network architecture is supported by national and regional NRENs that provide access to more than 8,000 LHC physicists worldwide.

Tier0 is the Main Data Center at CERN. LHC GC System uses 10–50 Gbps fiber optic links to connect Tier0 to each of the thirteen Tier1 GC sites. In Europe, seven Tier1 SG sites use GÉANT as the transport network and the European Grid Infrastructure (EGI) to monitor regional GC sites. In North America, three Tier1 GCs use Internet2 and Canarie (Canadian NREN) as the transport networks and the Open Grid Science e-infrastructure to monitor GC sites. In Asia, the two remaining Tier1 GC sites use APAN and TEIN as the transport networks as well as TWGrid and EU-India Grid to monitor the GC sites. The 155 medium GC sites located in Universities and Research

---

[5] http://www.eresearch2020.eu/eResearch%20Brochure%20EN.pdf e-Infrastructures can be defined as networked tools, data and resources that support a community of researchers, broadly including all those who participate in and benefit from research. Following this definition, the term e-Infrastructure comprises very heterogeneous projects and institutions within the scientific community.

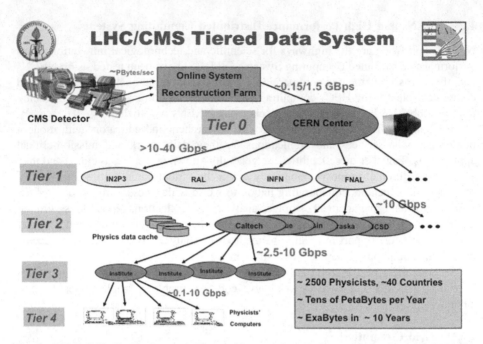

Fig. 2. LHC Grid Computing – 4 Tier architecture http://pcbunn.cithep.caltech.edu/sc2005/ Bubble_Diagram_SC05.gif

Centers are connected through 1 Gbps fiber optic links to their NRENs in 41 countries. Tier3 are the sites or individual computers where users access the LHC GC system represented in Fig. 2.

The LHC GC system is supported by Regional Operation Centers (ROCs) connected to NRENs. ROCs' main task is to monitor distributed GC sites located in their region ROCs functionality encompasses authentication and authorization, monitoring, user and operational support, management of Service Level Agreements (SLA), helpdesks, etc. Countries with longstanding expertise in grid computing systems have created National Grid Infrastructures (NGI) to support their R&E communities locally. Countries that are unable to implement NGIs, rely on the "Catch All" task implemented in the ROC to provide them with NGI type services. ROCs were initially created to monitor the global HEP VOs. However, as other domains are becoming regular users of GC facilities, non-HEP VOs are being integrated to ROCs services, thus providing an efficient use of the e-infrastructure.

1.2.2 High Performance Computing

High Performance Computing (HPC) communities also understand the power of networking. HPC R&E demand fast-growing computing power, currently in the order of PetaFlops, although rapidly migrating to the ExaFlop scale, to resolve complex problems. HPC also generates very high volumes of data (Big Data) that need to be computed, analyzed, simulated, visualized, transported and stored for different purposes. In turn, highly specialized human resources, scientists and engineers, can interact locally or

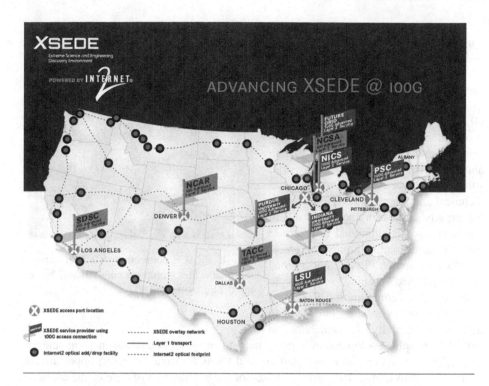

Fig. 3. XSEDE connectivity via Internet2 https://www.internet2.edu/media/medialibrary/2014/07/01/xsede-internet2-maps.pdf (Color figure online)

distributed to accomplish specific tasks. Two recent (2010) successful HPC collaborative initiatives XSEDE (Extreme Science and Engineering Environment)[6] in the United States and PRACE (Partnership for Advanced Computing in Europe)[7] use the power of NRENs to accomplish extremely complex projects using regionally distributed HPC resources and human capacity building strengths (Fig. 3).

XSEDE supports 17 supercomputers and high-end visualization and data analysis resources across the US, it integrates these resources and services via Internet2 the US NREN. It provides renewable one-year access to computing, visualization and storage resources as well as support services to researchers and educators (faculty). A US principal investigator (PI) researcher or educator from a US public or private higher education institution or research center applies for allocation of service units (SU) according to the Resource Allocation System (XRAS) via the XSEDE User Portal: https://www.xsede.org/web/xup#/guest. Other rules apply for training or education purposes and to create science gateways. Its governance relies on a Resource Allocation Committee (XRAC) that meets quarterly to review requests based on merit and then award available SUs. XSEDE also has a strong support team to assist users and for training purposes.

---

[6] www.xsede.org.

[7] http://www.prace-ri.eu.

PRACE integrates six Tier0 super-computer systems provided by 4 members from different countries: BSC in Spain, CINECA in Italy, GCS in Germany and GENCI in France. The HPC centers are interconnected vía GÉANT. Contrary to XSEDE, PRACE provides allocation of resources to any scientist and researcher from academia and industry from around the world, subject to a Peer Review Process, with technical and scientific reviews. Technical experts and leading scientists evaluate the proposals submitted in response to the bi-annual calls. http://www.praceri.eu/how-to-apply/. PRACE has a broad educational and training schedule to assist users and communities (Fig. 4).

Fig. 4. PRACE connectivity GÉANT https://thatsmaths.files.wordpress.com/2013/02/prace.jpg (Color figure online)

Both initiatives are intended to increase productivity of researchers and educators to solve socio-economic problems and maintain competitiveness in science and technology. At the same time XSEDE and PRACE provide ongoing opportunities to increase skills of engineers and scientists for the exploitation of state of the art large scale heterogeneous advanced computing resources and e-infrastructures. Europe and the US understand that it is extremely expensive and requires high expertise to use leading supercomputing infrastructure efficiently. Both have established collaborative strategic policies that strengthen the operation of XSEDE and PRACE in the long term. For the interoperability of these HPDCS, Internet2 and GÉANT, in their respective regions, have become an essential component of the ecosystem.

1.2.3 Cloud Computing

The most recent HPDCS is Cloud Computing (CC). CC is also dependent on reliable networking as servers are located remotely. Resources (hardware and/or software) are delivered on demand to end-users using scalable and elastic capabilities. CC promotes three types of services Infrastructure as a Service (IaaS, hardware), Platform as a Service (PaaS, hardware and software), and Software as a Service (SaaS, software). CC main objective is to abstract users from maintaining or managing hardware and/or software. Scientists and educators need increasing flexibility and simplicity to access/use heterogeneous e-infrastructures. Scientists and educators are currently more dependent on readily available large data sets and repositories in their R&E activities that may result in innovative scientific discoveries as well as new learning and training tools used in a CC environment.

In 2014, The NSF CISE Research Infrastructure: Mid-Scale Infrastructure - NSFCloud program, announced new science and technology public policies aiming to finance two CC testbeds called "Chameleon" and "CloudLab", for R&E to experiment with new cloud architectures and produce new applications to revolutionize the science and engineering of CC systems[8]. At the same time, the European Cloud Partnership (ECP) research activities were supported by an initial budget of €10M under the EU's Research Programme, which set up the Cloud for Europe project.[9]

1.3   Virtual Communities for R&E

Virtual Communities is the way distributed researchers and educators throughout nations and worldwide group themselves, develop projects, exchange expertise, share data resources and instruments and collaborate in common interest topics of specific domains using e-infrastructures, to resolve complex problems. In the beginning of NRENs, Virtual Communities were integrated by members of a single-domain of science and education (Fig. 5).

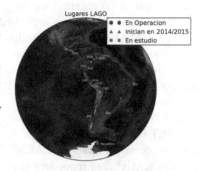

Fig. 5. LAGO sites http:// documents.ct.infn.it/record/580/files/ CHAIN-REDS-D4.5_v06.pdf (Color figure online)

An example of a modern multi-domain Virtual Community (VC) is derived from a collaborative project named *The Latin America Giant Observatory*[10] (LAGO - previously known as Large Aperture Gamma Ray Observatory). Ten Water Cherenkov Detectors (WCD) very specialized instruments that have been installed in 8 Latin American countries, Mount Chacaltaya (Bolivia), Sierra Negra (Mexico), Pico Espejo (Venezuela), Marcapomacocha (Peru), and low altitude detectors in Argentina, Colombia, Guatemala and Ecuador forming a network of 34 institutions sharing their experiments, experience, computing resources and data produced by this network of detectors. The LAGO VC operates a distributed e-infrastructure interconnected to NRENs of the 9 participating LA countries (Brazil included), regionally connected via RedCLARA. LAGO VC integrates more than 80 Latin American researchers currently collaborating with European research groups of IN2P3 (France), INFN (Italy), and CIEMAT (Spain). The interconnection between regional e-infrastructures is accomplished using a fiber optic submarine cable that runs from Brazil to Portugal, in points of presence of RedCLARA and GÉANT, thus reaching the three European participating institutions.

As part of its e-infrastructure, the LAGO Virtual Community has built a data repository located in Bucaramanga, Colombia that collects registered and simulated

---

[8] http://nsf.gov/news/news_summ.jsp?cntn_id=132377 Suzi Iacono, acting head of the National Science Foundations's Directorate for Computer and Information Science and Engineering (CISE). Chameleon and CloudLab projects were financed with $10 M USD each.

[9] Digital Agenda for Europe. http://ec.europa.eu/information_society/digital-agenda/index_en.htm.

[10] http://lagoproject.org/.

data of cosmic rays phenomena in the energy range [~ 2 GeV, ~ 100 TeV]. Data is preserved on DSpace[11].

LAGO runs curated data simulations using MAGCOS[12], CORSIKA[13] and GEANT4[14], software installed at the Universidad de Santander Supercomputing Center (Colombia), the SUMO cluster at The Atomic Center of Bariloche (Argentina) and the other clusters in CEDIA (Ecuador's NREN). Other smaller clusters control a visualization wall of 16 monitors of 24 inches, capable of generating a 32 MP resolution, which are used for analysis and visualization of astronomical and astrophysical data.

The LAGO data repository has become part of the Knowledge Base and the Semantic Search Engine developed by the CHAIN-REDS project, incorporating authorship to the curated data sets using combinations of PID for data and ORCID for authors. LAGO will use the DART methodology proposed by this same project, to address its data preservation directives. The CORSIKA-GRID version will use EGI and ROC-LA infrastructures to support LAGO's project and VO configured in 4 sites (GRNET in Greece, UNAM in Mexico, CIEMAT in Spain and UIS in Colombia) and will be accessible via the SCALAC Science Gateway developed by FESC-UNAM.

The LAGO data repository is of interest to the following scientific and education virtual communities:

a. Gamma Astronomy: The LAGO WCD installed at high altitude sites are sensitive to detect the effects of gamma rays such as those produced during the Gamma Ray Bursts.

b. Space Weather: LAGO activities relate to the physics of low-energy cosmic rays, to solar activity and to space weather phenomena. It is crucial to study these effects because it may establish levels of radiation in the atmosphere and near-Earth space environment.

c. Ecologists/Climate Change: Study high altitude environments to correlate them with possible climate change and global warming effects using the environmental sensors at LAGO WCDs.

d. Ultra-High and High Energy Astroparticles: LAGO can form an ecosystem with HAWC and Auger communities in Latin America.

e. Higher Education Professors and Students: First, virtual seminars every 2 weeks about tools and techniques in astroparticles[15] and meetings of 40 academic hours/school every year. Second, training students using real environments of

---

[11] http://www.dspace.org/ DSpace is open source software for digital repositories. DSpace preserves and enables easy and open access to all types of digital content including text, images, moving images, mpegs and data sets.

[12] http://cosray.unibe.ch/ ~ laurent/magnetocosmics.

[13] https://web.ikp.kit.edu/corsika (Cosmic Simulations for KASKADE) a program for detailed simulation of extensive air showers initiated by high-energy cosmic ray particles. Protons, light nuclei up to iron, photons, and many other particles may be treated as primaries.

[14] http://geant4.cern.ch.

[15] Seminario CAE Colaboración LAGO https://www.youtube.com/watch?v=3U3ra_7Pm9o.

LAGO. First year university students are introduced to Data Science using real research tools, techniques and environments[16].

2 Backgrounds

2.1 CUDI – The Mexican NREN

In 1999, with the support from the federal government, infrastructure donated by long distance operators and equipment manufacturers, as well as, membership fees from academic, corporate and institutional partners, the Mexican NREN was established under the name of Corporación Universitaria para el Desarrollo de Internet, A.C. (CUDI) a non-for-profit organization. The Mexican NREN started operations using a 155 Mbps fiber optic national backbone shown in Fig. 6. It remained for 12 years with the same network architecture and bandwidth, unable to own and upgrade its network because of the lack of government funding to address the long-term needs.

CUDI immediately celebrated international agreements with different NRENs to interconnect its national backbone and start scientific and education collaborations using e-infrastructures. It started with three points of interconnection in Tijuana, Ciudad Juarez and Reynosa to reach the US national backbone and one international link to connect with its Latin American partners of CLARA.

With the aim to support more institutions doing collaborative e-science both nationally and internationally, in 2008 CUDI started promoting the importance of the Mexican NREN with the office of the e-Mexico National System located in the Ministry of Communications and Transport (SCT). CUDI proposed to SCT the enhancement of the Connectivity Agenda[17], through the participation of Higher Education Institutions and Research Centers in its implementation, supporting SCT with its current backbone (infrastructure) and membership (capacity building).

In return, the Mexican NREN expected to get support from the government to use bandwidth from the fiber optic backbone owned by the public electricity entity (CFE) to increase its bandwidth and expand its network to the rest of the country. With this support, CUDI would also be able to strengthen the Mexico City, Guadalajara, and Monterrey delta backbone with redundant paths. In the following two years, the e-Mexico National System became the Coordinaton for the Information and Knowledge Society (CSIC) at SCT and the Connectivity Agenda was transformed into the "**Red N**acional de **I**mpulso a la **B**anda **A**ncha" initiative (RedNIBA), a high bandwidth transport backbone for multiple public policy purposes.

In June 23rd, 2010 CUDI and CSIC-SCT signed an agreement to allow the Mexican NREN and its members to use RedNIBA's infrastructure without having to pay a fee. CUDI and CSIC established a schedule to implement a 39 hotels backbone

---

[16] See Exposición Temprana de Nativos Digitales en Ambientes, Metodologías y Técnicas de Investigación en la Universidad H. Asorey, L.A. Núñez and Christian Sarmiento-Cano http://arxiv.org/abs/1501.04916.

[17] Connectivity Agenda (Agenda de Conectividad 2008) was an initiative announced by the government (SCT) as a public policy to reduce the digital divide in Health and Education.

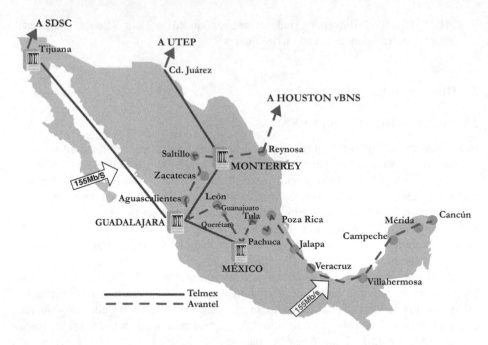

Fig. 6. CUDI 2003 backbone. http://www.cudi.edu.mx

(Points of Presence to connect to the backbone) using the CFE fiber optic network, with links of up to 1 Gbps to each of the State Capitals and three 10 Gbps links between Mexico City, Guadalajara and Monterrey. After a three year implementation the topology of the Mexican NREN offered a more robust national backbone. The topology expected to be ready by the end of 2015 is shown in Fig. 7. Today, RedNIBA, Axtel, Bestel, Telmex (RI3) and CUDI (proprietary) links integrate the Mexican NREN backbone.

In 2012, the Higher Education Institutions were granted $50M Mexican Pesos by the Congress, as seed money to connect public universities to Red CUDI's backbone via RedNIBA's infrastructure. These resources have been used to buy 31 last mile fiber optic IRUs (Indefeasible Rights of Use)[18] links and 5 SDN (Software Defined Networks) routers (level 3), 20 switches and 40 access routers to connect public universities to the 39 hotels. With this connectivity universities will have more flexibility to increase their bandwidth access to the Mexican NREN's backbone.

CUDI provides operational services such as networks monitoring/status, traffic control/load and traceroute/ping analysis on all the backbone except for those links controlled by CFE. It also provides information, security and user support services through its Network Operation Center (NOC-CUDI) and its Network Development Committee (CDR).

---

[18] Long-term lease (temporary ownership) of a portion of the capacity of a fiber optic cable it may include electronic equipment.

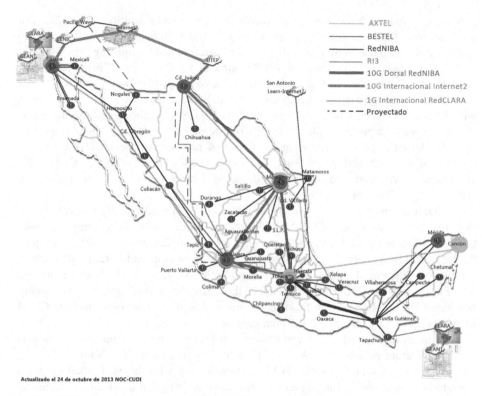

Fig. 7. CUDI 2015 projected backbone. http://www.cudi.mx/conexion/backbone (Color figure online)

2.1.1 Public Policies and Sustainability of CUDI, the Mexican NREN

From 1999 to 2009 CUDI was able to sustain a modest backbone and operation office, from its associate membership fees mainly provided by the 18 largest and most important public and private universities and from 2 research centers of CONACYT (CICESE and IPICYT) as well as from CONACYT central offices representatives, occupying two seats in CUDI's Directive Council. Affiliate membership fees were provided by smaller universities who are not part of CUDI's Directive Council. CUDI's budget during this period fluctuated between $6–9M Mexican Pesos.

During this period, telecom carriers donated most of the backbone, NSF in the North financed a few cross-border links and others were owned by CUDI. There were no public policies on the long term to allow CUDI to expand its backbone nationwide and to increase its bandwidth at the same pace of demand to be able to support mission critical and global complex projects. CONACYT central offices' fees (approximately $2–3M Mexican Pesos) were used as seed money for national calls to CUDI members on the creation of unpretentious applications using the Mexican NREN.

In 2010, after an internal crisis, CUDI realized it was fully dependent on the telecom carriers' infrastructure. With this concern CUDI approached the government to explain the role NRENs play in R&E, and show how in most countries, particularly in

Europe, government funds were fundamental to achieve sustainability of the NREN in the long term (update, expansion, interconnection and innovation on infrastructure) while membership fees were generally used for operation and monitoring. The Ministry of Communications and Transport (SCT) allowed CUDI to use CFE's backbone, through RedNIBA. SCT made an important move on public policy for the Mexican NREN by recognizing it in the National Digital Agenda and by signing agreements with CFE and another with CUDI to expand the NREN's backbone and extend access to all the main capitals of the 32 States of Mexico as well as 7 other important cross-border cities. Thus, increasing the points of presence of the backbone and the number of research and institutions able to access CUDI's backbone. CUDI-SCT agreements have been updated and modified in three opportunities: November 30, 2012, May 20, 2013 and April 28, 2014.

CUDI also renegotiated its agreements with CONACYT. Originally fees came from two research centers and CONACYT's central office. After reviewing the case, CONACYT ordered CUDI to apply for CAI funds[19], under a work program project, that included international interconnections, e-infrastructure, and paradigmatic applications on different domains of science and technology, as well as, dissemination activities. Since 2012 CONACYT and CUDI celebrate annual agreements ranging between $8M to $10 Mexican Pesos each year[20]. The new agreements include CUDI membership of all CONACYT research centers.

In August of 2014, the Mexican Congress approved the new Telecommunications and Broadcasting Federal Law. Article 213 of the law states that "The National Science and Technology Council [CONACYT], in coordination with the SCT, shall establish the administrative and technical mechanisms necessary to grant financial and technical support required by higher education and research public institutions for the interconnection of their networks, with sufficient capacity to form a National Research and Education Network, as well as the interconnection of such NREN with the academic specialized international networks"[21].

This is an important step on public policy to recognize the role of government in the long-term sustainability model for the Mexican NREN, in order to consolidate a seamless, large scale, high-speed, low-latency network to accelerate scientific and education discovery for national, regional or global collaborative projects that are dependent on the use of modern high performance distributed computing systems. Three main government authorities are currently addressing the implementation of Article 213: science and technology (CONACYT), higher education (Ministry of Education, SEP,

---

[19] http://www.conacyt.mx/index.php/fondos-y-apoyos/apoyos-institucionales.

[20] 2012–2014 Annual Reports of the CONACYT-CUDI agreement can be found in www.cudi.edu.mx.

[21] *Ley Federal de Telecomunicaciones y Radiodifusión de México, Artículo 213*. El Consejo Nacional de Ciencia y Tecnología, en coordinación con la Secretaría, establecerá los mecanismos administrativos y técnicos necesarios y otorgará el apoyo financiero y técnico que requieran las instituciones públicas de educación superior y de investigación para la interconexión entre sus redes, con la capacidad suficiente formando una red nacional de educación e investigación, así como la interconexión entre dicha red nacional y las redes internacionales especializadas en el ámbito académico.

Subsecretaría de Educación Superior) and communications (SCT, Subsecretaria de Comunicaciones).

In May 2015, CUDI was granted a concession on the category of "Social Use" by IFT, the independent regulatory authority of telecommunications and broadcasting. This concession allows CUDI to provide telecommunications and broadcasting services on non-commercial terms and conditions. As a non-for-profit entity, it brings CUDI membership an opportunity to become the operative branch and trusted independent expertise entity on the development of national R&E public policy with respect to ICT networking and connectivity.

2.2   CUDI and Its International Connectivity

2.2.1   The European Commission (EC) Infrastructure Funding
to Support CLARA's R&E Collaboration

ALICE Project. In 2003, CUDI was globally recognized as the Mexican NREN, through its participation in the project "América Latina Interconectada Con Europa" (ALICE and ALICE2) supported by the Ministers of Science and Technology of Europe and Latin America and the announcement of the EU-LA Heads of State summit in Madrid approving €62.5M to address Information Society initiatives (@lis Alliance for the Information Society). The European Commission designated €10M to DANTE[22] to lead the ALICE project, with the aim to interconnect European and Latin American researchers as well as to support the creation of the regional consortium of NRENs in Latin America named CLARA (Consorcio Latino Americano de Redes Avanzadas) an institution to manage and operate the regional network (Fig. 8).

CUDI participated as one of the six Latin American NRENs that cooperated with €2.5M to support the ALICE project. By the end of the first stage of the project in 2008, CLARA had connected 11 Latin American NRENs to include more than 700 academic institutions into the global advanced academic network.

ALICE2 Project. ALICE2 project became the second phase for RedCLARA with a €12M budget co funded by EC and the LA NRENs (€6M + €6M). This model was based on a widely adopted cost-distribution system and on a solid financial administration to develop a funding model for its stability and long-term sustainability. Fourteen Latin American countries (Argentina, Bolivia, Brazil, Chile, Colombia, Costa Rica, Ecuador, El Salvador, Guatemala, Mexico, Panama, Peru, Uruguay and Venezuela, all of them beneficiaries of @LIS2), and four European countries (Spain, France, Italy and Portugal) represented by their respective NRENs participated. From 2008 to 2012, ALICE2 gave continuity to the Latin American expansion of NRENs based on long-term IRUs or indefeasible right of use contracts for the use of dark fiber and wavelengths in order to ensure low recurrent costs, improving connectivity between Latin American and European researchers (Fig. 9).

---

[22] DANTE plans, procures, builds and operates large-scale, advanced high-speed networks for global research and education, including the pan-European GÉANT network. http://www.dante.net/Pages/default.aspx.

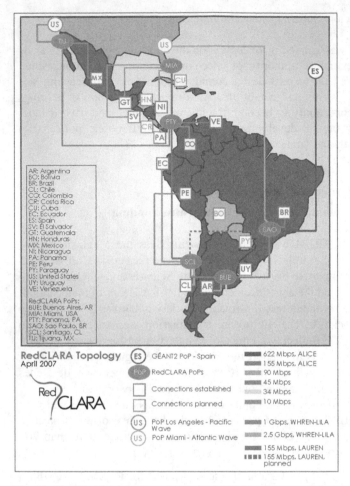

Fig. 8. RedCLARA topology by April 2007 http://www.redclara. net/index.php/en/network-and-connectivity/topologia (Color figure online)

During this phase closer collaboration of Virtual Communities such as that of Astronomy was feasible. Interconnection of e-infrastructures in Europe: ESO Astronomical Observatories and Latin America: the Pierre Augier Observatories was accomplished. ALICE2 also helped in disseminating the potential of RedCLARA's use by creating Virtual Communities that helped to reach the Millennium Development goals agreed by UN Member States. All the goals were accomplished.

Since 2013, partners' fees provide RedCLARA's operations and management sustainability, a not for profit international organization based in Uruguay. Latin American NRENs are Innova-Red (Argentina), ADSIB (Bolivia)[23], RNP (Brazil), REUNA (Chile), RENATA (Colombia), RedCONARE (Costa Rica), CEDIA (Ecuador), RAICES (El Salvador), RAGIE (Guatemala), UNITEC (Honduras)[24], CUDI (Mexico), RENIA (Nicaragua) (see Footnote 24), RedCyT (Panama), ARANDU (Paraguay) (see Footnote 23), RAAP (Peru), RAU (Uruguay) and REACCIUN (Venezuela). Six existing NRENs were co-funders of the ALICE Project (Argentina, Brazil, Chile, Costa Rica, Mexico and Venezuela), eight were created during the ALICE Project (Colombia, Ecuador, El Salvador, Guatemala, Panama, Peru, and Uruguay) and three were created in the ALICE2 Project (Honduras,

---

[23] *Not connected.

[24] +Not partner.

Nicaragua and Paraguay). Red CLARA currently has 15 members, 13 of which are connected and 2 have not finalized their internal NREN process yet. RedCLARA's infrastructure is based on 6,000 km of dark fiber, with DWDM equipment to light up to 20 lambdas of 10 Gbps, 3,000 km of length waves (2.5–10 Gbps) and international links to Europe (622 Mbps) and the US (5 × 1 Gbps).

CUDI has chaired the CLARA's Director's Council twice. Its Network Operating Center, NOC-CUDI is currently responsible for regional NOC activities both in LA and the Caribbean. CUDI recently re-located its international interconnection point of presence to CLARA from Tijuana to Tapachula, Chiapas (a city located in the south border with Guatemala), increasing its international fiber optic link from 45 Mbps to 2.5 Gbps, while strengthening Central America pathway to the CLARA backbone.

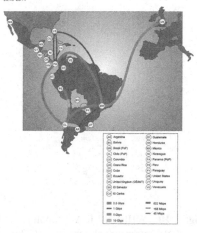

Fig. 9. RedCLARA topology by June 2014. http://www.redclara.net/index.php/en/network-and-connectivity/topologia (Color figure online)

2.2.2 The US National Science Foundation (NSF) Infrastructure Funding to Support CUDI and CLARA R&E Collaborations

The Center for Internet Augmented Research and Assessment, at the Florida International University (CIARA, FIU) has been a key player in integrating different partners in the participation of NSF funded projects through the International Research Network Connections (IRNC) calls such as WHREN/LILA, AMPATH IXP, AmLight and AtlanticWave to the enhancement of continental R&E collaboration between North America, Central and South America linking NRENs.

WHREN/LILA. A five year (2005–2010) cooperative agreement funded by the NSF ($5M USD) made possible the interconnection of key points of aggregation to build a continental loop providing operation and production infrastructures from the Western Hemisphere Research and Education Networks (WHREN) to RedCLARA via the Links Interconnecting Latin America (LILA). FIU as leader of the project accomplished different collaborative agreements to build a continental ring. CANARIE, the Canadian NREN, as well as regional US network initiatives were able to agree on international exchange points and peering capabilities to include the LA NRENs in the continental loop, while LILA aimed to improve connectivity in the Americas through the establishment of new inter-regional links. WHREN/LILA powered participants' network resources to increase discovery in research and enhance education across the Americas, several Virtual Communities have benefited from this high-bandwidth connectivity. Figure 10 shows the topology of the WHREN/LILA connectivity and the networks involved.

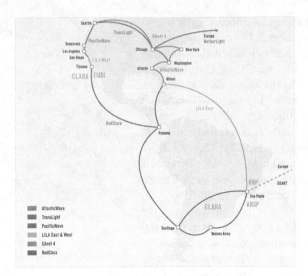

Fig. 10. WHREN/LILA topology 2008 http://www.internet2.edu/presentations/fall08/20081015-international-ibarra.pdf (Color figure online)

WHREN: In the east coast of the US, Atlantic Wave (NY-Washington-Atlanta-Miami) helped to extend distributed exchange services from the US international points to Sao Paulo, Brazil (RNP) a 10 Gbps distributed service to facilitate international peering between North and South America as well as with other regions/countries.

To connect the west infrastructure with the east international points using Layer 2 services, CANET4 (NY-Chicago-Seattle-Vancouver) and TransLight (Washington-Chicago-Seattle) helped close the east-west path using StarLight operated by Northwestern University and University of Illinois at Chicago, supporting U.S. Central international R&E exchange. Finally, PacificWave operated by CENIC and PNWGP provided Layer 2 services and R&E peering to Red CUDI and Red CLARA in the area of the Pacific Rim (Seattle-SFBay area-Los Angeles-San Diego) to close the loop. In this point, CUDI is able to peer with NRENs shown in Fig. 11.

LILA: the 2 × 1 Gpbs links connecting Los Angeles (PacificWave) to Tijuana, Mexico (CUDI) known as LILA West, and the 2.5 Gbps circuit-connecting Miami (Ampath) to Sao Paolo, Brazil (RNP) known as LILA East. The WHREN-LILA initiative has been an important resource for continental and transcontinental collaborations.

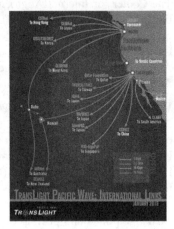

Fig. 11. Translight Pacific Wave International Links, Jan 2015 (Color figure online)

AMPATH. AMPATH is an international exchange point located at the NAP of the Americas in Miami, Florida. It facilitates peering as well as network research and services between the US, Latin America and The Caribbean NRENs. It provides access such as Internet2, Florida LambdaRail and Energy Science networks, Layer2 transport services between NRENs using AtlanticWave infrastructure, IXP connectors and peers, commodity Internet, settlement free peering to Content Distribution Networks (CDN) and collocation.

AMLIGHT. The Americas Lightpaths (AmLight) project supports WHREN/LILA in the engineering of network services and technologies necessary to meet the high demanding and evolving needs of VCs throughout the continent, particularly those of the HEP and Astronomy VCs. Five new or enhanced links have been coordinated to increase bandwidth, reliability and connectivity to international exchange points to support current e-science projects in the region. AmLight East: Miami-Sao Paulo links 2×10 Gbps connecting end-to-end circuits and routed IP connections from AMPATH to RedCLARA and co funded by NSF, FAPESP and RNP. AmLight West: Tijuana-Los Angeles link 2×1 Gbps end-to-end circuits and routed IP connections from PacificWave to Red CUDI and co funded by NSF, CICESE, UNAM and CUDI-CONACYT. AmLight Central: San Antonio-Mexico City link 1 Gbps connecting LEARN to Red CUDI and co funded by NSF, LEARN and CUDI-CONACYT. AmLight Andes: Sao Paulo-Santiago 1 Gbps connecting RNP with REUNA and co funded by NSF, AURA, ANSP and CLARA. The latest two links have multiple Layer 2 and 3 paths providing hybrid-networking services such as diversity, predictability and production quality. Steering, Research Advisory, Engineering and other committees govern the service provision, implementation of new technologies and uses as well as management of lightpaths (Fig. 12).

3 Searching for CUDI's Sustainable Model

CUDI has only been able to collect as much as $21.6M Mexican Pesos in the year 2014, the rest of the years the budget has not reached more than $18M Mexican Pesos. This budget currently is provided by membership fees, and since 2012, from the CONACYT-CUDI agreement. Approximately One fourth of its budget is dedicated to international interconnections and CLARA's membership, half of the budget in personnel, administrative matters and mobility, the last fourth of the budget is dedicated to support virtual communities projects/activities, e-infrastructure implementations and applications.

In order to resolve CUDI's sustainability and the implementation of Article 213 of the Federal Law of Telecommunications and Broadcasting, it is considered pertinent to analyze the Brazilian NREN's sustainable model, as it is the best connected and well positioned NREN in Latin America in terms of collaborative R&E networking. However, other NRENs may as well be included in the analysis. The findings will provide the participating authorities with factual elements to consider when implementing Article 213 of the telecommunications and broadcasting federal law.

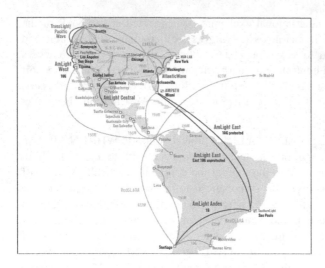

Fig. 12. AmLight topology 2013 http://ciara.fiu.edu/ downloads/AmLight_FLYER.pdf (Color figure online)

RNP, the Brazilian NREN, with the support of the government, has been successful not only in the implementation of a state of the art, seamless, high-speed, secure network and services, but also on the integration of virtual R&E communities using HPDCS to build e-infrastructures for e-science and e-education. "With a long-term commitment from the government to support R&E networking, RNP has enjoyed increased stability and has been able to improve the quality and variety of the services provided to the academic community in Brazil… the continued support of MCT, which has made available significant funding to permit investments, in network infrastructure and equipment, RNP has been able to seek opportunities for collaboration with owners of telecommunications infrastructure… and has been able to build its own optical metro networks in capital cities, and increasingly, in non-capital cities."[25]

A summary of the main aspects of RNP's contract with the Ministry of Science and Technology are listed below:

- Dedicated R&E networking model with advanced services (increased bandwidth, reduced latency, increased availability, secure communication, HPDCS, high capacity data repositories, more research centers connected, improved access to commercial networks via RNP-IXPs)
- The creation of an administrative council with representation from the Ministry of Science and Technology; the Ministry of Education; the Brazilian Computing Society; the Laboratory of Computer Networks and Architectures (LARC); RNP-IXPs, its members and users. The Law of Social Organizations is the legal framework for the integration of representatives of the public sector, the civil society, members and users.
- RNP Annual Budget $198MReais the equivalent to $51.07MUSD or $848M Mexican Pesos[26] (CUDI's largest annual budget, $21.6M MPesos in 2014)

---

[25] Michael Stanton et al., RNP a brief look at the Brazilian NREN, pages 20–21. Accessed on 2015/10/13 http://www.researchgate.net/publication/228525420_RNP_a_brief_look_at_the_Brazilian_NREN.

[26] 1 USD = 16.6036 Mexican Pesos = 3.8771Reais http://portalweb.sgm.gob.mx/economia/es/tipos-de-cambio/brl-usd/437-tablas-real-brasileno-us-dolar.html accessed on 2015/10/15.

- RNP as a social organization is committed to:
  - An annual five-year budget projection
  - A Work Program including obligations, responsibilities and goals
  - Specific conditions for its execution: performance indicators (reviewable) and criteria to accept results
  - Strategic objectives for the development of high impact projects using NRENs
  - Accountability and supervision
- RNP personnel is approximately 200 (CUDI personnel 16)
- RNP serves around 300 organizations, including 130 universities and 30 public and private research centers with a total of 600 sites connected[27] (CUDI serves 266 institutions[28], 246 sites connected[29]).

RNP has been able to upgrade more than 4 times its network and associated equipment to keép up with technological evolution and the ICT network and connectivity needs of R&E collaborative projects. With the possibility to control directly its own backbone, RNP has also put in production several network services such as VoIP and Advanced VoIP, QoS, Middleware, Monitoring, Reliable Multicast, Network Storage, Virtual Community Grid, Directories in Higher Education, Public Key Infrastructure for Education, Digital Video, Digital TV, etc. for the benefit of its members and users. The government has relied in RNP's expertise to increase the number of research centers using advanced networks particularly extending this benefit to the Ministries of Health (MS), Defense (MD) and Development, Industry and Commerce (MDIC). The integration of the SINAPAD project (distributed HPC Centers) to RNP connected via high-speed links from the Brazilian NREN has opened new opportunities for different science domains to become part of collaborative projects using HPDCS and NRENs.

With the new legal framework, the Mexican NREN could sign an agreement with CONACYT and SCT to ensure resources on annual basis but with a five-year prospective; identify strategic projects; set performance/goal indicators; become accountable. CUDI has identified the following strategic projects for the 2016–2020 timeframe that could benefit using the Mexican NREN:

- National Supercomputing System to collaborate with PRACE and XSEDE as well as with SCALAC[30] in Latin America and the Caribbean
- National Laboratories System
- Second phase: Connectivity of the CONACYT Research Centers System
- Astronomic Observatories System
- HEP Observatories, collaboration with regional initiatives such as ALICE and AUGER forming an ecosystem
- Chetumal Satellite Station for Satellite Image Repositories

---

[27] http://www.researchgate.net/publication/228525420_RNP_a_brief_look_at_the_Brazilian_NREN accessed on 2015/10/13.

[28] http://www.cudi.edu.mx/acerca-de-cudi/lista-miembros accessed on 2015/10/13.

[29] http://www.cudi.edu.mx/conexion/instituciones-conectadas accessed on 2015/10/14.

[30] Servicios de Cómputo Avanzado para América Latina y el Caribe (SCALAC) is a regional initiative to provide HPDCS services using infrastructure from the participating members and CLARA NRENs. SCALAC also aims to provide training an support to its members.

- CiiMar GOMC System for Marine Sciences R&E
- Langebio connectivity for Genomics collaboration with the US
- Tier 1 Laboratory CERN – LHC in ICN UNAM
- Consolidate the Mexican Grid and Cloud Academic Infrastructures
- National Research and Training Health System
- National Videoconference System
- National IXP network
- REMERI: National Institutional Repositories System
- Conricyt identity federation, storage and connectivity.

These projects are described in Part 2 of this article.

4 Conclusions

NRENs should be viewed as public goods not as a competition to commercial telecom providers as they only serve R&E communities' specific needs. The also provide the R&E communities with economies of scale in the use of very expensive instruments and e-infrastructures.

CUDI, the Mexican NREN has been an active NREN in the national, regional and international levels. CUDI has promoted international interconnections with the US and CLARA to allow R&E collaborations worldwide for specific R&E communities and projects. CUDI has been regionally active in the consolidation of CLARA and has chaired twice its Directive Council. NOC-CUDI personnel have been responsible for the operation of the Regional Network Operation Centers of CLARA and C@ribNET because of their expertise, commitment and highly qualified technical support to both regions.

In its sixteen years of existence, the Mexican NREN has experienced a non-existent long-term financing environment and a reduced short-term budget provided by membership fees. CUDI has been dependent in the good faith of telecommunications carriers donating selected routes of the national fiber optic backbone to build a very basic infrastructure for R&E, with regular speeds and limited coverage, in its first 10 years.

Despite its modest budget and limited functionalities, since the beginning, CUDI has promoted the development of virtual communities and e-infrastructures supporting e-science and e-education projects[31], but has not been able to consolidate its own seamless, large scale, high-speed, low latency and secure national backbone that responds to the growing demand of national and international collaborative R&E projects dependent on HPDCS and NRENs.

CUDI encountered in the CSIC-SCT agreement a palliative to stop its first 10 years of infrastructure stagnation (as shown in Fig. 6). This agreement provided CUDI's backbone expansion and bandwidth upgrades to reach the capital cities of the 32 Mexican States where many of the R&E centers and institutions are located. The delta ring: Mexico City-Guadalajara-Monterrey was upgraded from 155 Mbps to 10 Gbps with redundant links (telecom carrier links + CFE links) to reach equivalent bandwidths

---

[31] A detailed description of the results of national and international collaboration of virtual research and education communities as well as e-infrastructure projects is covered in **Part 2** of this article.

of comparative NRENs in other parts of the world. Current capital cities and selected new cities were upgraded up to 1 Gbps.

Notwithstanding the improvement in the NREN's backbone topology and bandwidths, as shown in Fig. 7, CUDI is still fully dependent on third parties' decision-making (CSIC-SCT and CFE) to manage, operate and control advanced network services and e-infrastructures. One of its main concerns is to be able to provide efficient response times to its members on special scalable network requirements as well as to monitor, identify and correct failures in a timely manner. From the HPDCS e-infrastructure perspective, exa-scale and big data R&E requirements need to be based on an integral operational model that includes all significant network flows, desirably managed by the Mexican NREN.

The recent approval of Article 213 of the Federal Law of Telecommunications and Broadcasting can change CUDI's long-term stability for good. However, a serious analysis by the participating authorities on how to implement it will be needed, to help the Mexican NREN respond to specific goals and objectives without having to depend on third parties decision-making and donations. The analysis should take into account best practices, such as those obligations and rights agreed in the contract signed by MTC and RNP in Brazil to make efficient use of government funding in R&E using ICT advanced networks and connectivity. The Brazilian case shows positive results in terms of R&E innovation and productivity as well as international collaboration on high impact projects.

A pragmatic perspective may lead to two scenarios arising from the current legal framework to resolve the Mexican NRENs' infrastructure constraints, based on the fact that CUDI owns a social concession:

(1) To grant full access to CFE's infrastructure by allowing the Mexican NREN to own and control a pair of fiber optic cables nationwide exclusively for R&E.
(2) To celebrate a direct contract with the entity[32] controlling CFE's fiber optic backbone to eliminate third parties, whose main objectives differ from those of R&E advanced networks.

Commercial ISPs and telecomm operators should not see this as a threat, nor see NRENs as competitors, as the latest provide differentiated services from those of commodity Internet. In fact, all can jointly collaborate in piloting innovative network and ICT services using the power of the NRENs' constituency. In return, NRENs can adopt best industry practices in their network operations.

The increasing participation of Mexican R&E Virtual Communities and their associated institutions in national and international high impact collaborative projects, demands that the Mexican NREN be understood as a public good that provides access to expensive instruments and e-infrastructures by its constituencies. The academic sector through its NREN could also be viewed as a collective purchasing power to allow for economies of scale.

---

[32] The Mexican Constitution and the Federal Telecommunications and Broadcasting Law of 2014 indicate that CFE will give its title to provide public telecommunication services to the public entity, Telecomunicaciones de México.

References

1. Dmitry, G., Maarten, L.: Delft University of Technology, Netherlands, National Research and Education Networks: Analysis of Management Issues. https://www.isoc.org/inet99/proceedings/3h/3h_1.htm. Accessed 15 Aug 2015
2. http://www.internet2.edu/. Accessed 16 Aug 2015
3. Dyer, J.: The Case of National Research and Education Networks. Terena (2009)
4. https://en.wikipedia.org/wiki/National_research_and_education_network. Accessed 10 Sept 2015
5. http://www.geant.net. Accessed 9 Sept 2015
6. http://www.eresearch2020.eu/eResearch%20EN.pdf. Accessed 25 Aug 2015
7. http://www.xsede.org/. Accessed 28 Aug 2015
8. http://www.prace-ri.eu/. Accessed 15 Aug 2015
9. http://nsf.gov/news/summ.jsp?entn_id132377. Accessed 20 Sept 2015
10. http://ec.europa.eu/information_society/digital-agenda/index_en.htm. Accessed 19 Sept 2015
11. http://lagoproject.org/. Accessed 20 Aug 2015
12. http://www.dspace.org/. Accessed 20 Aug 2015
13. http://cosray.unibe.ch/laurent/magnetocosmics. Accessed 20 Aug 2015
14. https://web.ikp.kit.edu/corsika. Accessed 20 Aug 2015
15. http://geant4.cern.ch. Accessed 20 Aug 2015
16. https://www.youtube.com/watch?v=3U3ra_7Pm9o. Accessed 20 Aug 2015
17. http://arxiv.org/abs/1501.04916. Accessed 20 Aug 2015
18. http://www.cudi.edu.mx/conexion/backbone. Accessed 10 Aug 2015
19. http://www.conacyt.mx/index.php/fondos-y-apoyos/apoyos-institucionales. Accessed 17 Sept 2015
20. http://www.cudi.edu.mx. Accessed 10 Oct 2015
21. http://www.diputados.gob.mx/LeyesBiblio/ref/lftr/LFTR_orig_14jul14.pdf. Accessed 9 Sept 2015
22. http://www.dante.net/Pages/default.aspx. Accessed 26 Sept 2015
23. http://www.redclara.net/index.php/network-and-connectivity/topologia. Accessed 9 Sept 2015
24. http://www.internet2.edu/presentations/fall08/20081015-international-ibarra.pdf. Accessed 14 Sept 2015
25. http://www.ciara.fiu.edu/downloads/AmLight_FLYER.pdf. Accessed 10 Sept 2015
26. http://www.researchgate.net/publication/228525420_RNP_a_brief_look_at_the_Brazilian_NREN. Accessed 13 Oct 2015
27. http://www.cudi.edu.mx/acerca-de-cudi/lista-miembros. Accessed 13 Oct 2015
28. Casasús, C.: CUDI: Situación Actual y Perspectivas, 7 May 2013. Presentation to Julia Tagüeña, Deputy Director for Research, Conacyt
29. Hüsing, T. (ed.) Empirica GmbH: The Role of e-Infrastructures in the Creation of Global Virtual Research Communities, European Commission. Information Society and Media (2010). http://www.eresearch2020.eu/eResearch%20Brochure%20EN.pdf
30. The worldwide LHC Computing Grid. CERN (2015). http://home.web.cern.ch/about/computing/worldwide-lhc-computing-grid
31. The Grid a System of Tiers. CERN (2015). http://home.web.cern.ch/about/computing/grid-system-tiers

32. AmLight: Enhancing Research and Education in the Americas, NSF International Research Network Connections (IRNC) Kickoff Meeting, Arlington, VA, 13 July 2010. Presentation by Julio Ibarra, PI, FIU, Heidi Alvarez, Co-PI, FIU, Chip Cox, Co-PI, FIU, Jim Dolgonas, Co-PI, CENIC
33. International Research Network Connections WHREN-LILA Project Status and Plans, presentation by Julio Ibarra, Executive Director, CIARA, FIU http://www.internet2.edu/presentations/fall08/20081015-international-ibarra.pdf
34. IRNC-ProNet: Americas Lightpaths: Increasing the Rate of Discovery and Enhancing Education across the Americas, award #0963053

CUDI: The Mexican National Research and Education Network. A Look into the Past Helps Build a Better Future

Part 2

Salma Leticia Jalife Villalón[✉]
and Carlos Casasús López Hermosa[✉]

Corporación Universitaria para el Desarrollo de Internet, A.C.,
Red Nacional de Investigación y Educación de México, Parral, Mexico
{salmajalife, ccasasus}@cudi.edu.mx

Abstract. Part 1, *"The Role of National Research and Education Networks (NRENs) providing connectivity and advanced network services to Virtual Communities in collaborative R&E projects. CUDI: The Mexican Case"*, provides a general introduction to NRENs and explains the case of the Mexican NREN, its current infrastructure and policy status by 2015, and proposes actions to implement Article 213 of the Federal Telecommunications and Broadcasting Law to strengthen CUDI and e-infrastructures. This paper, describes how CUDI, throughout its 15 years of existence, has supported its members in their participation in different R&E collaborative projects using the NREN connected to High Performance Computing Distributed Systems (HPCDS), hardware and software tools and even remote instruments to implement different e-science applications by Virtual Communities (VCs). It extracts the positive aspects of previous collaborative R&E projects and identifies opportunities necessary to build the sustainable future Mexican NREN. That is, a robust national advanced network infrastructure with seamless, large scale, high-speed, low-latency characteristics aimed to accelerate scientific and education discovery on identified R&E collaborative projects using e-infrastructures for the short term (2016–2020).

Keywords: CUDI · The mexican national research and education network · NREN · e-infrastructures

1 Introduction

Advanced Networks have had a slow to develop in Mexico and Latin America because of the lack of telecommunications infrastructure in the region except for Brazil. Part 1 of this article, described how the US AMPATH and WHREN-LILA projects and the European ALICE and ALICE2 projects gave stimulus for advanced research and education connectivity inside each Latin American country, enhancing the academic infrastructure already promoted by the governments of Argentina (RETINA), Brazil (RNP), Chile (REUNA) and Mexico (CUDI) to create their NRENs, and promoting the

© Springer International Publishing Switzerland 2016
I. Gitler and J. Klapp (Eds.): ISUM 2015, CCIS 595, pp. 48–75, 2016.
DOI: 10.1007/978-3-319-32243-8_4

creation of new NRENs in the rest of the Latin American countries, though, with clearly differentiated business models. This stimulus motivated collaborative projects within the LA region and among regions, mainly with US and Europe.

In Mexico, early after the creation of CUDI in 1999 and the implementation of its fiber optic backbone, several Mexican Higher Education Institutions and Research Centers became CUDI members. The participating institutions were interested in resolving national problems through their research groups benefiting from the economies of scale proposed by a NREN infrastructure. Different purposes were to be accomplished such as, testing telemedicine applications; building access to digital libraries and repositories; creating new models and learning objects for long distance education; translating computer simulations on different domains of science into advanced visualization; operating virtual labs; manipulating specialized scientific instruments; building middleware for the operation of distributed clusters and supercomputing centers; as well as, using videoconference on demand services. These institutions started using the NREN to participate in a series of national and international initiatives addressing different types of inter-institutional collaboration on e-infrastructures for e-science, e-education and e-health.

From an engineering perspective, in the beginning CUDI needed to consolidate its national and international connectivity. Collaboration was mainly focused on the establishment of a seamless, large scale, high-speed, low-latency network. CUDI in 2000 accomplished to setup the ATM-IPv6 protocol backbone at 155 Mbps, in the main cities where academic research and education is currently concentrated.

CUDI celebrated agreements for the use of 4,000 km of fiber optic telecom infrastructure provided by Telmex and another 4,000 km of fiber optic telecom infrastructure provided by Avantel, two public telecommunications carriers operating in Mexico. The international connectivity was the result of collaborative agreements to different points of presence of the US-NSF academic network. Europe initiated an aggressive project with the Latin American NRENs to form the regional consortium CLARA. In the meantime, CUDI expanded its agreements with other National and Regional RENs: UCAID and CENIC (US), CANARIE (Canada), REUNA (Chile), RETINA (now InnovaRed), RedIris (Spain), CLARA (Latin American Consortium) and CEDIA (Ecuador).[1]

In 2012 CUDI complemented its backbone by signing and agreement with CSIC-SCT to use CFE's national fiber optic infrastructure and in a period of 3 years CUDI increased the main links to up to 1 and 10 Gbps. With the support of CIARA-FIU, CENIC, Internet2 and CLARA, CUDI has also been able increase its number of points of presence in the border to connect its network to other NRENs.

UCMEXUS is a Mexico-US initiative established in 1980 contributing to promote collaborative bi-national research and academic + exchange programs. In the year 2000, ten projects were approved to start using NRENs in collaborative bi-national projects listed in the Table 1. The identification of research and education projects lead to understand the needs of connectivity, bandwidth and special technical support to build virtual environments and e-infrastructures easy to use for educational and research purposes.

---

[1] http://www.cudi.edu.mx/acervos/convenios.

Table 1. The projects approved for using NRENs in collaborative bi-national projects

	Approved Project UCMEXUS-CONACYT Program for the Year 2000	USA	Mexico
1	A pilot Internet project based distance learning course on Agroecology involving 5 Mexican Agricultural Universities	UCB	UAY
2	Virtual Collaboration in the Californias	UCSD	CICESE
3	The MexLinks Consortium for Technology Access and Educational Advancement: applying Internet2	UCSB	BUAP
4	QoS of network multiservice for virtual campus	UCSC	IPN
5	Client Server Discrete Event Simulation Over Very Large Communications Networks (Internet2 and CUDI)	UCI	CICESE
6	Internet Assisted Remote Experiments in Teaching Food and Biochemical Engineering	UCD	UDLAP
7	Parallel Algorithms for solving propositional satisfiability using the high bandwidth of Internet2 and CUDI	UCSC	ITESM
8	MIRO: Adaptive Middleware for a mobile Internet robot	UCI	ITAM
9	Bioinformatics Network for Education and Research	UCI	IPN-CBG
10	A collaborative engineering environment for global integrated product development	UCB	ITESM

With the connectivity in place, virtual communities (VCs) have developed complementary e-infrastructures using NRENs for different purposes. In the beginning, the main activities regarding e-infrastructures were done by building grid computing infrastructures, authentication and authorization infrastructures (AAI) as well as training and capacity building. Fifteen years later, the needs remain the same, but the orders of magnitude in bandwidth, computer power and the diversity of computing distributed platforms for different purposes have evolved significantly. A summary of the most relevant initiatives where Mexican research and education institutions have participated is described in Sect. 2 and summarized in Box 1.A, Box 1.B, Box 2 and Box 3. These four boxes are representing a timeline of e-infrastructure projects using CUDI, VCs and HPCDS in collaboration with national and international entities.

Finally, Sect. 3 identifies a set of relevant projects that need to be accomplished in Mexico that will provide educators and researchers with a more robust connectivity and access to distributed computing, simulation, visualization and storage resources for the increasing need of data and network intensive solutions to national, regional and international problems.

With the historic information of relevant collaborative R&E projects using NRENs and e-infrastructures and the identification of relevant projects to be developed from 2016 to 2020, we have concluded that all the positive aspects found may become opportunities to build a better future for the Mexican NREN.

2   Timeline of the Evolution of Selected National and International Collaborative R&E Projects Using HPCDS, Red CUDI and VCs in e-science

The first collaborative e-infrastructure initiative recorded in CUDI's repositories is GRAMA (Mexican Academic Grid). An interinstitutional, heterogeneous, shared distributed experimental infrastructure interconnected through RedCUDI with the participation of CICESE, CINVESTAV, NOC-CUDI, UAM, UDG and UNAM telecommunications and computers teams. The GRAMA project integrated a total of 435 processors and approximately 300 GB of RAM and the installation of a library MPICH-G2 to convert parallel programs into grid jobs. UAM allocated in its Supercomputing and Visualization Lab a donation of six nodes with two processors Itanium 2 at 1.4 GHz, a 4 GB RAM memory per node and a computing performance of 72 Gflops. The donors were Intel and Lufac, two companies interested in the development of Grid Computing. Training was an important aspect of the project. Participants gained expertise in networks, middleware, security, applications and organization. Globus Toolkit2 was the selected middleware used to authenticate users, computer equipment and services. The CICESE team became the certification authority. The UNAM team administered the participating grid resources and provided monitoring services. A live demonstration of the project took place on the third quarter of 2004. The objective was the renderization of an image, the computing processes took place in the resource centers of UNAM and CICESE, and the output of the image, was provided by a third computer.

GRAMA fulfilled its objectives and reached the following conclusions:

- The heterogeneous hardware installed in all 5 institutions allowed participants to understand the different processes to setup resource centers with specific characteristics to become a node of the grid architecture and operate as a single system.
- The different teams gained expertise in the implementation, put in production, monitoring and operation of grid infrastructures.
- **Insufficient bandwidth** became a problem in the communication of processes and file transfer for certain institutions, the information obtained when evaluating connectivity could serve to **propose modifications to the RedCUDI**, increasing performance of grid computing applications.
- It would be desirable to continue implementing a national grid infrastructure.
- The current tools are not yet as developed as they would have wanted, to be able to provide seamless coordinated use of heterogeneous resources, and a balanced workload of jobs in the distributed resource centers.
- GRAMA can issue certificates of centralized information of resources, centralized monitoring of resources and its different modes of interaction.

Boxes 1.A and 1.B. The most relevant initiatives implemented in the period of 2008–2010.

BOX 1.A. List of national and international collaborative inter-institutional initiatives on Grid Computing and related topics using NRENs (1999-2009)		
PROJECT NAME	**DESCRIPTION**	**SCOPE**
PRAGMA (2003-2005) *Pacific Rim Application and Grid Middleware Assembly* Funded by NSF sustained collaborations and advance the use of grid technologies in apps in the Pacific Rim http://goc.pragma-grid.net	Collaboration US (CaliT2) - Mexico (CICESE) - Korea (KISTI) to migrate the MM5/Mpich-Gx to a Grid environment, abiding by PRAGMA operating principles and procedures. Image of the Climate in the Baja California Peninsula using the three sites computing power	
GRAMA (2004-2005) *Grid Académica Mexicana* Partners CICESE, CINVESTAV, CUDI, UAM, UDG and UNAM Financed by CONACYT-CUDI www.grama.cudi.edu.mx	A joint collaboration of 6 institutions that implemented a distributed grid computing architecture to share resources and provide the first e-infrastructure for e-science using the Mexican NREN RedCUDI and Resource Centers in each of the 6 institutions	
HELEN (2005-2008) *High Energy Physics for the Latin American-European Networks* Participating countries in LA are AR, BR, CH, CO, CU, MX, PE, VZ Financed by EU www.roma1.infn.it/exp/helen	Physicists from 22 Universities/Research Centers of 8 Latin American countries participate in HEP projects and experiments at CERN, DESY, Gran Sasso and Pierre Auger laboratories, building their own HEP Grids locally to provide a model for Latin America	
RINGrid (2006-2007) *Remote Instrumentation in Next Generation Grid* 12 institutions from 12 countries PO, AU, GR, BU, MX, IT, BR, UY, CH, UK, RO Financed by EU www.ringrid.eu	Synergy among remote instrumentation and NextGen Grid between 7 European countries and 4 Latin American countries Mexico (UNAM) identified the following instruments - Gas Cromograph Varian 38000 - Atomic absorption Varian AA800 - Varian Cary 1EuV-Vis Spectrometer - ICP-Mass spectrometer	

BOX 1.B. List of national and international collaborative inter-institutional initiatives on Grid Computing and related topics using NRENs (1999-2009)		
PROJECT NAME	**DESCRIPTION**	**SCOPE**
EELA (2006-2008) *E-infrastructure shared between Europe and Latin America* Partners 21 institutions from Europe and LA (UNAM and CLARA) Financed by FP6-EC www.eu-eela.eu	EELA benefited from the mature state of the ALICE project and RedCLARA. EELA created a collaboration network for training in Grid technologies (Epikh grid school) and of the deployment of a pilot Grid infrastructure for e-science apps in biomedicine, HEP, e-education, climate and vulcanology	
EELA-2 (2008-2010) *E-science grid facility for Europe and Latin America* Partners 78 institutions from 16 countries (UNAM, CUDI, CLARA) Financed by FP7-EC www.eu-eela.eu	Close to 60 Applications from 5 different scientific domains (Life Sciences, Earth Sciences, High Energy Physics, Astronomy & Astrophysics, Engineering and Fusion) covering 24 scientific areas are supported by a bi-regional grid e-infrastructure	
OPTIPUTER (2008-) *Optical Portal* Partners CICESE and CALiT2, CENIC and CUDI Financed by NSF-CONACYT http://optiputer.cicese.mx	Connect optiportals with a 1 Gbps fiber optic link between Ensenada and San Diego upgraded to 10GbE, to share a visualization wall that allows, among others, environmental modeling and simulation fed by real-time sensors for different applications	

IBM in 2005 sponsored a Latin American initiative on Grid Computing (LAGrid) operating in Mexico, Argentina and Puerto Rico; its main objective was to link faculty, students and researchers to the T.J. Watson IBM Research Center, to collaborate with the industry on innovative grid applications on Health, Biotechnology and Hurricane Mitigation.

The HELEN project in 2005 aimed to foster Grid technology transfer in Latin America, Grid infrastructures were developed in each of the 8 participating LA countries. As a result, the HEP Virtual Community created the ROC-LA (Regional Operating Center – Latin America: https://roc-la.org) and consolidated its operation in 2009, as a joint initiative involving three research institutions in Latin America: the Brazilian Center for Research in Physics (CBPF, Brazil), the Institute of Nuclear Science of UNAM (ICN-UNAM, Mexico) and Universidad de los Andes (Uniandes, Colombia) to support Latin American Virtual Communities representing the four experiments at CERN: ALICE, ATLAS, CMS and LHCb, ROC-LA agreed to expand its tasks and resources to support other Latin American Virtual Communities from non-HEP domains. Today ROC-LA provides support for: (a) the administration of resources, (b) users, (c) the development of applications, and (d) training. It manages Virtual Organizations' (VO) needs in the LA region under the name of *prod.vo.eu-eela.eu*.

In 2006 under the 6th Framework Program for Research, Technological Development and Demonstration of the European Commission (FP-6) a bi-regional consortium was approved to establish collaborative human and infrastructure networks, to share grid e-infrastructures in Europe and Latin America on different applications such as High Energy Physics (HEP), Biomedicine, Education and Climate. The consortium named EELA included the participation of the Mexican institution UNAM and the Mexican NREN, CUDI as a member of CLARA. EELA was successful in providing training in Grid technologies and of the deployment of a pilot Grid infrastructure for e-science applications. The HEP group in the Institute of Nuclear Sciences at UNAM benefited from this project. EELA's Grid Infrastructure was implemented on 16 Resource Centers (RCs) with over 730 CPU cores and 60 Terabytes of storage space.

In 2008 EELA-2 became the second phase of the project. It was intended to consolidate and expand to 30 RCs, mobilizing 3000 computing nodes and 700 Terabytes of storage to increase in 20 % its computing power and 15 % its storage power. This e-infrastructure was built on GÉANT2 regional network of European NRENs and RedCLARA network of LA NRENs. The main purpose was to ascertain the conditions of the durability of the e-infrastructure, beyond the project duration to provide the full set of Grid services needed by all types of applications in their scientific environment.

After the end of the EELA-2 project a Joint Research Unit for Mexico on Grid infrastructure (JRU-Mx) was proposed and approved by CONACYT, to collaborate in e-infrastructure initiatives, particularly focused in Grid Computing. CUDI, CICESE, UNAM, ITESM, IPN, IPICYT, UAEMorelos, USON and UMSNH became part of this consortium supported by CONACYT. The JRU-Mx used CUDI's Grid Community as its work and dissemination platform. Participating institutions intended to create, manage and maintain the National Grid Initiative (NGI) and expand it to other research and higher education institutions, A second goal would be to create a regional initiative, the Latin American Grid Initiative (LAGI) to collaborate with EGI, its European counterpart in projects such as GISELA, CHAIN and CHAINREDS to support Virtual Communities in both regions.

In 2008, after its participation in PRAGMA (Pacific Rim Grid Middleware Applications) CICESE became interested in collaborating with CalIT2 in advanced visualization labs. The dedicated 1 Gbps optical fiber collaboratory where remote researchers from CalIT2 and CICESE are analyzing complex data is known as the OPTIPUTER project. The interaction of computing and data collection tools such as sensors, networks, storage, computing and visualization involves a new way for researchers to analyze data, simulations or experiments. CENIC and CUDI helped upgrade the cross border link to 10 Gbps to connect this visualization sites in both countries.

CUDI's Grid community gained technical and scientific experience participating in collaboration with national and international institutions when building e-infrastructure for e-science and e-education purposes. The acquired knowledge led to design new collaborative projects with emphasis on strengthening both the national and regional advanced computing resource infrastructures using NRENs.

In 2010, the top three largest High Performance Computing (HPC) centers of Mexico, UNAM, CINVESTAV and UAM proposed the creation of a National HPC Laboratory building a delta HPC grid metropolitan architecture connecting with fiber optic its supercomputer nodes, the project was authorized and funded by CONACYT. This is the first Mexican initiative designed to share distributed HPC resources. The three institutions have participated in the interconnection of their resources. However, there is no evidence that these institutions have put in place a collaborative process to allocate computing, storage or visualization resources so researchers or educators of any other academic institution can access the LANCAD infrastructure seamlessly, in the way it has been established by XSEDE or PRACE initiatives.

For the same call, other members of CUDI's GRID Community also proposed a project named Grid Supercomputing National Laboratory: e-infrastructure for e-science. The project was authorized but could not be accomplished because of the difficulties to align the legal frameworks of the 7 participating institutions in order to share advanced computing resources. All participating institutions are members of the JRU-Mx and understood the importance of collaboration on the build out of e-infrastructures for researchers and educators. These institutions together with other CUDI members decided to create a National Committee to issue the first International Supercomputing Mexico Conference (ISUM). This initiative has become the means for disseminating the work on supercomputing and related topics. Mexican and International scientists and engineers have been participating in its six editions. ISUM has gained relevance for the Mexican HPC and advanced computing communities as it issues annually the conference proceedings that include a selection of the most innovative research conducted nationwide. It is also relevant for the International HPC and advanced computing community to share knowledge on relevant collaborative projects and training seminars.

GISELA and CHAIN projects were funded by the EC and were complementary to EELA and EELA-2 as their intention was to work on the Grid Infrastructures of Europe

Box 2. List of the most relevant initiatives implemented in the period of 2010–2012.

BOX 2. List of national and international collaborative inter-institutional initiatives on Grid Computing, HPC and related topics using NRENs (2010-2012)		
PROJECT NAME	**DESCRIPTION**	**SCOPE**
GISELA (2010-2012) *Grid Infrastructure Services for Europe and Latin America* Partners 31 institutions from 15 countries (UNAM, CUDI, CICESE, IPN-CIC, USON) Financed by FP7-EC www.gisela-grid.eu	Long-term Sustainability Model for Advanced Computing Services (ACS) implemented by CLARA, LA NRENs and Institutions to Support Virtual Research Communities with e-Infrastructure and Application-related Services, such as Science Gateways, to enhance research	
LANCAD (2010-) *Delta Metropolitana de Cómputo de Alto Rendimiento (Demecar)* Partners CINVESTAV, UAM and UNAM. Financed by CONACYT	The HPC National Laboratory is metropolitan delta grid architecture to connect with fiber optic the three largest HPC centers of Mexico City	
ISUM (2010-) *International Supercomputing Mexico* Partners ISUM National Committee Seed financial support from CUDI-CONACYT www.isum.mx	A yearly International Conference that congregates internationally and nationally renown speakers from both academia and industry, presenting frontier research and new ideas in both scientific and industrial applications, courses, workshops as well as discussion panels on key issues on the future of HPC and related topics	
CHAIN (2010-2012) *Coordination and Harmonization of Advanced e-Infrastructures* Partners LA CLARA Financed by FP7-EC *https://www.chain-project.eu/*	Strategy and definition of instruments to ensure coordination and interoperation of the European Grid Infrastructure with those emerging in other regions of the world. Promoted the uptake of the Science Gateway paradigm in cooperation with other projects and the CHAIN Application Database (http://www.chain-project.eu/applications) has evolved into a "gateway" to the existing Science Gateways.	

and Latin America, to support Virtual Research Communities (VRC) such as WeNMR, WRF4G, jModelTest, DC-NET/INDICATE and DECIDE, that were already participating in previous projects, and to include new VRCs from Climate Change and SuperB (High energy Physics) and other domains such as Agriculture and Health (LSGC) to provide them with innovative HPDCS services, with the aim to expand and harmonize the e-infrastructure and applications in both regions.

UNAM under the GISELA project developed a VRC-driven Science Gateway upon a model discussed within CHAIN. It is a web 2.0 environment designed to fully exploit the e-infrastructure services by users, through a normal web browser. Access is given using a username/password provided by an Identity Provider (Identity Federation System) to submit applications filling web formats (components include authentication and authorization). Since 2010, the LA region has been introducing Identity Federations in NRENs and the participation in eduGAIN, a simple authentication mechanism adopted worldwide; users are able to run selected high-impact applications in an easy way.

The GISELA Science Gateway connects many different services including virtual resources, infrastructure, network provisioning and customized applications for different user communities. In the GISELA project, the Science Gateway has been proposed to provide sustainability to the e-infrastructure in Latin America, as it is an innovative way of attracting a larger number of Latin American scientific and education communities to the use of GC.

By the end of the project, GISELA Science Gateway offered 4 VRC-specific Science Gateways and 7 applications.

1. VRC **Cultural Heritage**:
   a. Application 1 **ASTRA**: aims to reconstruct the sound or timbre of ancient instruments using archaeological data as fragments from excavations, written descriptions, pictures;
2. VRC **Industry**:
   a. *Application 2* **Industry@Grid**: gridify JobShop Scheduling and Supply Chain models using techniques based on heuristics and branch and bound methods, focusing on SMEs that are able to use GC as a leading-edge tool for their internal planning process;
3. VRC **Life Sciences**:
   a. *Application 3* **ClustalW**: it is a tool for aligning multiple protein or nucleotide sequences;
   b. *Application 4* **GATE**: is advanced opensource software developed by the international OpenGATE collaboration and dedicated to the numerical simulations in medical imaging. It currently supports simulations of Emission Tomography (Positron Emission Tomography - PET and Single Photon Emission Computed Tomography - SPECT), and Computed Tomography (CT);
   c. *Application 5* **Phylogenetics** (MrBayes): it is a program for the Bayesian estimation of phylogeny;
4. VRC **Mathematics**:
   a. *Application 6* **Octave**: GNU Octave is a high-level interpreted language, primarily intended for numerical computations. It provides capabilities for the

numerical solution of linear/nonlinear problems, and for performing other numerical experiments. Octave language is equivalent to Matlab, most programs are easily portable;

b. *Application 7* **R**: is a free software environment for statistical computing and graphics. It can be used for different seismotectonic settings.

In the GISELA-CHAIN Conference held in Mexico City in 2012, one of the outcomes was the regional agreement to support the sustainability of the existing e-infrastructure in LA. Mexico, Ecuador and Colombia signed the first regional agreement to continue the e-infrastructure's operation in order to make it available for researchers and educators advanced computing resources, networks and services. The NRENs CEDIA (Ecuador), CUDI(Mexico) and RENATA (Colombia), as well as, Universidad de Los Andes (Uniandes - Colombia) and Universidad Nacional Autónoma de México (UNAM - Mexico), committed to expand opportunities for different virtual research communities and find financial and organizational mechanisms for Latin America to undergo a process of consolidation and sustainability of the e-infrastructure in the region.

The CHAIN-REDS project has promoted worldwide the need for standards-based interoperability of HPDCS using NRENs. The project has collected information from Open Access Document Repositories (OADR), Data Repositories (DR) and Open Access Educational Repositories (OAER) worldwide. CHAIN-REDS widened the scope of the previous CHAIN Knowledge Base (KB)[2] to Data Infrastructures.

Tools provided by CHAIN-REDS[3]:

– Science Gateways that interface different types of Distributed Computing Infrastructures.
– Creation of Identity Federations, granting secure and easy access to online services.
– An Interoperation Model between Europe and other regions of the world, based on the creation of Regional Operation Centres.
– The uptake of standards and technical guidelines for Clouds interoperability across continents and the use of PIDs (Permanent Identifiers).
– Thematic workshops and training events worldwide.
– The aforementioned CHAIN-REDS Knowledge Base that provides useful information on
  • Grid infrastructures worldwide
  • Open document, data and, recently, educational repositories.
– DART (Data Accessibility, Reproducibility and Trustworthiness) - an integrated methodology for better accessing, sharing, reusing and manipulating scientific data.
– DART challenge, which allows a user to easily find repositories containing data associated to a specific term (metadata), use it as an input in an application running on the Science Gateway in order to either reproduce a previous experiment or perform a new one, obtain and retrieve the final results and, if required so, upload them in a public repository with Persistent Identifiers assigned (PID).

---

[2] CHAIN Knowledge Base (KB), available at http://www.chain-project.eu/knowledge-base.
[3] CHAIN-REDS project http://www.chain-project.eu/.

Complementary to the different initiatives with Latin America and Europe, CUDI has also promoted new initiatives to better understand the specific requirements needed by R&E communities from NRENs to fulfill the US-Mexico scientific and education discovery. The Big Data, Big Networks (BDBN) conferences/workshops have been organized mainly, to raise awareness of research and education communities aiming to collaborate, and to identify new needs from those communities already collaborating with, their counterparts in cross-border scientific and education projects between Mexico and the US that are highly dependent on advanced computing and network infrastructures and services.

The *Big Data, Big Network: Big Opportunities for Collaboration between Mexico and the United States* first workshop was supported by CICESE and CUDI-CONACYT, as Mexican partners and by NSF under the AmLight project leaded by FIU, CalIT2 @UCSD, CENIC, as US partners. CENIC and CUDI-CONACYT have sponsored the second and third conferences/workshops respectively as new initiatives have been increasing the portfolio of collaborative projects between Mexico and the US. The celebration of these BDBN conferences/workshops is guided by the following goals:

1. To increase understanding of the challenges and issues of conducting network-enabled cross-border science research and education collaborations;
2. To create an environment that will stimulate discussion and facilitate knowledge sharing; and
3. To identify short-term and long-term objectives for stimulating network-enabled cross-border Big Data science and education collaboration.

The report issued by the BDBN Program Committee[4] provided recommendations for the short term (6 months to 24 months) and the long term (three to five years) describing relevant aspects to be accomplished. In the report a summary of domains and focus areas reflecting existing and future cross-border collaborations can be found. It shows the relevance and role played by the e-infrastructure where NRENs are participating such as the AmLight links as well as the CUDI and CLARA complementary links that provide full connectivity to the cross-border research and education when promoting joint efforts. These findings are valuable information for both governments and could lead to identify where cyberinfrastructure can be leveraged by joint investments (Fig. 1).

The Latin American initiative SCALAC (Servicio de Computacion Avanzada America Latina y el Caribe) was formally established in March 2013 with the Bucaramanga Declaration, signed at the Industrial

Fig. 1. SCALAC Science Gateway

[4] BDBN Workshop Report, Program Committee Members, 2014.

Box 3. List of the most relevant initiatives implemented in the period of 2012–2015.

BOX 3. List of national and international collaborative inter-institutional initiatives on Grid Computing, HPC and related topics using NRENs (2013-2015)		
PROJECT NAME	DESCRIPTION	SCOPE
CHAINREDS (2012-2014) *Coordination and Harmonization of Advanced e-Infrastructures for Research and Education Data Sharing* LA Partner CLARA by CUDI and UNAM Co-financed by FP7-EC	Intercontinental cooperation to develop scientific data and e-infrastructure tools addressing existing and emerging VRCs ACS needs (e.g. Earth Science, Climate Change, Genomics, etc.) with pragmatic approaches impacting their daily work in federated and AA environments	
BDBN (2013-) *Conference/Workshop Big Data Big Networks* Partners US-Mexico NREN member institutions Financed by NSF-CICESE-CUDI-CONACYT	Twice a year invited researchers from Mexico and the US meet to discuss their Advanced Computing and Networking needs on collaborative projects	
SCALAC (March 2013-) *Advanced Computing Services for Latin America and the Caribbean* Partners Institutions from AR, BR, CH, CO, CR, EC, MX, UY, VZ Seed financial support from CUDI-CONACYT	An initiative to consolidate a regional e-infrastructure, human resources expertise and applications for the region with the support from NRENs, RedCLARA, c@ribNET and HPC Higher Education Institutions and Research Centers of the region	
RISC (2013-2014) *Red Iberoamericana de Supercómputo* Partner Universidad Veracruzana (UV)	Multinational and multi-stakeholder community in the participating countries to facilitate strategic R&D cooperation EU and LA in HPC. ISUM institutions participated	
Guanajuato State Supercomputing Network (2014-2016) Partners CIMAT, CINVESTAV/LANGEBIO, CIATEC, CIO, ITESI, CEMER, UDEGy PTSM Financed CONCYTEG-GG	The State of Guanajuato aims to connect 8 facilities to strengthen its supercomputing resources and benefit the industry located in the region with HPC services CUDI advisor on network issues	
RedMexSu (2014-2016) *Red Mexicana de Supercómputo* Partners Financed by CONACYT	Human networking platform, where people as well as institutions collaborate in training, e-infrastructure and studies to resolve problems using HPC	
LNS (2104-) *Laboratorio Nacional de Sureste* Partners BUAP, INAOE, UDLA Financed by CONACYT	The southeastern region of Mexico has implemented the largest Supercomputing Laboratory with a performance of 200 Tflops using 6528 cores Haswell, Intel Xeon E5-2680 v3 http://lns.org.mx/equipamiento/	

University of Santander, in Bucaramanga, Colombia. RedCLARA had originally supported the SCALAC initiative. CUDI and UNAM are the Mexican partners. SCALAC was inspired by other initiatives in the region as well, GRID computing projects such as GISELA, EELA and EELA-2. The operational center of SCALAC is a distributed system installed in the three major participants premises: Mexico, Colombia, and Brazil (ROC-LA). In addition, Costa Rica and Ecuador provide small-scale services. The Barcelona Supercomputing Center (BSC) and the Center of Research in Energy, Environment and Technology (CIEMAT) in Spain provide international support. The institutions participating as of today are:

Argentina, University of Buenos Aires (UBA), Brazil, SINAPAD, UFRGS, Chile, NLHPC, UFSM, Colombia, SC3UIS, UniAndes, Costa Rica, CNCA, UCR, Ecuador, CEDIA, Mexico, CUDI, UNAM, CINVESTAV-ABACUS, Uruguay, UDR, Venezuela UC, International RedCLARA

SCALAC integrates HPC human resources in a regional network of collaborations. The team support academic activities, forming HPC specialists at different levels (technical, specialized, scientific). Their institutions allocate supercomputing platforms for applied and basic research projects. SCALAC aims to support HPC technology transfer and use of HPC platforms for projects focused on the most important needs of the region (climate, health, and security). Dissemination so far has been provided in regional events such as: ISUM, CARLA (CLCAR + HPCLATAM), SCCAMP, RIOHPC. During this year SCALAC has promoted HPC in Latin America at ISC2015 (Frankfurt/July), SC15 (Austin/November) to attract other partners to the region. RedCLARA and the LA NRENs play an important role in the consolidation of a regional HPC infrastructure. Seed money from CUDI-CONACYT has been used to create the science gateway to access HPC infrastructures. Also collaboration with PRACE and XSEDE as well as with COMPUTE Canada has been explored with the aim to build a continental partnership and exchange of human resources expertise, technical support and services to provide LA researchers and educators with powerful HPC tools.

The AMERICAS project implemented during 2012–2013 with EU-FP7 funding (Latin America-Europe ICT Cooperation Advanced Strategies) created the Special Council for e-infrastructures of Mexico (CEeI), to support political dialogue of ICT and to foster cooperation for R&D. It was officially launched on May 25, 2012 during the CUDI's Spring Meeting. Its main objectives are:

- To build a map of e-infrastructures in Mexico
- To identify existing and potential Research Virtual Communities (VRCs) as intensive users, providers and developers of e-infrastructures
- To promote the benefits of existing e-infrastructures
- To foster collaboration with existing VRCs using e-infrastructures
- To prioritize areas using e-infrastructures on education, research and technological development
- To organize dissemination and information conferences, workshops, etc.
- To provide visibility for national and international e-infrastructures
- To close the gap between public and private e-infrastructures through collaborative projects on R&D

CUDI's 2013 Autumn Meeting, held the first CEeI Conference, where the Special Council coordinated by CUDI, ITESM and UEMEXCYT(CONACYT), shared the views of its members related to Human Networks (AMCAV, Red-TIC, PNC-TIC), Industry (CANIETI, AMITI, AMIPCI, PMT) Academia (UNAM, CINVESTAV, UAM, CICESE) and invited speakers from international projects where Latin American researchers and academics are participating in the implementation of e-infrastructures for e-science.

In 2013, The RISC (Red Iberoamericana de Supercómputo) project was financed by the EU and coordinated by the Barcelona Supercomputing Center (BSC) of Spain. The Iberoamerican Supercomputing Network selected a group of institutions in different countries to diagnose the current situation of research clusters focused on fundamental HPC and Computational Science activities in the participating countries and develop a strategy to enhance research and development between regions on a research/industrial level and policy level between the EU and Latin America in key areas of mutual interest. The Universidad Veracruzana participated in this initiative as the Mexican partner. SCALAC serve as a bridge to identify groups that were not originally included in the project. In Mexico, the Grid Community of CUDI and the ISUM national committee became aware of the importance of the project, and the need to collaborate in providing information for the development of a database of HPC infrastructures and human resources. RISC identified skills gaps and proposed mechanisms for collaboration. The Centro de Investigación en Computación CIC-IPN is the first Mexican institution to accomplish a graduate academic program with the BSC. RISC prepared a Green Paper and a Roadmap that addresses the importance of HPC and how to impact and engage policymakers.[5] RISC managed to create the environment to discuss with representatives of important institutions that use HPC in Mexico from the government and the private sector. The agenda include representatives from Health Natural Resources, Energy, Natural Disasters, Environment and Finances from ISSSTE, CUDI, SEP, SEDESOL, CFE, PEMEX, IMP and Banco de México.

The State of Guanajuato Supercomputing Network aims to strengthen the research and education institutions and their human resources and infrastructures located in the State of Guanajuato to collaborate in the solution of industrial problems using HPC for established companies in the same State. CUDI is advising this group on network technology issues. The Guanajuato Supercomputing Network is also collaborating in the integration of its supercomputing power with the rest of the regional initiatives recently being developed in different zones of Mexico through the ISUM and Red-MexSu collaboration.

After 12 years of collaborations in different initiatives, CUDI's Grid Community decided to create the Mexican Association for Advanced Computing (AMCAV) with the following purposes:

- Promote technical development and cooperation among its members
- Promote collaboration with the scientific, academic and technological communities
- Contribute to the support of public policies for the development of advance computing initiatives

---

[5] http://www.risc-project.eu/publication_type/green-papers/.

- Dissemination of best practices, creation and innovation on the design, development and information of HPC, supercomputing and advanced computing
- Research
- Exchange of experiences and methodologies within multidisciplinary and multi-institutional working groups
- Build a national e-infrastructure that puts researchers on the frontier of e-science using NRENs worldwide
- Build a networks of specialized human resources in advanced computing and related areas

The same group, in 2014 promoted the creation of the Red Mexicana de Super-cómputo (RedMexSu), a thematic network sponsored by CONACYT, whose aim is to pursue the same objectives. RedMexSu has expanded the number of participating institutions and scientific and technical groups originally involved in AMCAV.

RedMexSu[6] has formally gathered 46 researchers and academics from 17 institutions. The thematic network promotes high level training of human resources, the development of infrastructures, advanced networks, applications and services for advance computing used to strengthen scientific research, technological innovation and support to industry development. RedMexSu's goals are:

- Foster collaboration among its members
- Prepare the State of the Art in Supercomputing
- Diagnose national supercomputing inventories, infrastructure, applications, human resources, advanced communication networks (connectivity), last mile connectivity and collaboration networks
- Promote infrastructure development for Mexico's HPC needs
- Create National Supercomputing Centers for different purposes (tier 0, tier 1 and tier 2) taking into account the results of the diagnosis.
- Design academic programs both for pre-graduate and graduate studies to build capacity on HPC and related areas
- Promote human resources specialization on HPC and related areas through workshops Develop PC services and access interfaces
- Disseminate RedMexSu's work and increase membership
- Promote the internationalization of RedMexSu
- Foster publications of its members in scientific and engineering periodicals
- Protect the production of the member's intellectual property work and patents

One of the latest initiatives has been the implementation of a new supercomputing site, the LNS, located in Puebla at the Benemérita Autonomous University of Puebla, with the collaboration of INAOE and UDLA and financed by CONACYT to provide services to the southeastern R&E institutions. LNS and CUDI are collaborating to bring high-speed fiber optic reliable connectivity from this supercomputing and data center site in Puebla to the Sierra Negra Volcano where the Great Millimeter Telescope (LMT/GMT, @ 4600 m) and the High Altitude Water Cherenkov Observatory (HAWC, @4100 m) are located. HAWC acquires around 1.5 Terabytes of data per day.

---

[6] http://www.redmexsu.mx/Miembros.

Data are sent by road to HAWC data center at ICN-UNAM and mirrored at UMD, Sierra Negra Internet connection used for HAWC monitoring and communications. Sierra Negra connection also has to support LMT/GTM data transmission as well as other administrative users. Data needs to be sent to Maryland through one of CUDI's international cross-border links and needs at least 10 Gbps bandwidth throughout its operating sites.

3   Identified Strategic R&E Projects for 2016–2020 Using e-infrastructures the Mexican NREN and Its International Connectivity

CUDI is known for its strong relationship with the US, Canada, Europe and Latin America in R&E. More recently it has been actively participating with the Asian and African regions participating in multinational projects such as MAGIC with its Technical Working Groups and with the TEMDEC project created by the University Hospital of Kyoshu in Japan with the Health Community of Asia and Latin America.

The experience gained in the past 15 years on R&E collaborative funded projects mainly by the US and Europe, has served to understand when, where and how NRENs become the necessary infrastructure that leverages resources to reach out a larger number of communities of interest that are increasingly using existing research networks; supercomputing, grid and cloud computing facilities as well as visualisation, storage and data centres.

In terms of the need of large-scale networks, connectivity and big data CUDI has identified the following 15 projects to be accomplished in the short term, to be able to respond to R&E immediate needs.

1. **National Supercomputing System to collaborate with PRACE and XSEDE as well as with SCALAC in Latin America and the Caribbean.**

   - It is known that more R&E domains of science are using distributed systems to analyze, simulate, store, process, visualize and manipulate large data volumes. Some data may be sensitive for national purposes and thus, may need to be stored and processed within the national territory. A robust infrastructure of advanced computing services is needed in Mexico, but it is advisable to include advanced networking and connectivity to other national and regional initiatives such as PRACE and XSEDE, to gain expertise on how these two initiatives are providing high quality and secure services to their constituents.
   - From a regional point of view, the gained expertise of the Mexican Super-computing communities and infrastructure together with those of Brazil, Colombia, Chile and Argentina can help the Latin American region to develop SCALAC with the aim to provide advanced computing services regionally, while increasing the R&E knowledge and HR expertise on this area through the region. RedCLARA is the vehicle to connect these resource centers regionally and LA NRENs the vehicles to support networking services for the advanced computing systems.

- RedMexSu could become an important player to provide national cohesion, and a natural bridge to help SCALAC develop further.

2. **National Laboratories Program**[7].

- CONACYT has approved 65 National Laboratories in different domains of science in different cities of Mexico. Most of them are not connected to the Mexican NREN and some are not located in the main 200 cities where telecom infrastructure is available. It may be true that all of them collaborate with compatible R&E international institutions that use services they provide or data generated by the instruments they own. In order to extend the benefit of the work being developed in this national laboratories, or to take advantage of the services provided by this laboratories, they should be connected to the NREN soon. They could find economies of scale when connecting to the NREN versus using increasing commercial Internet international links that may be still very expensive.
- In general, connectivity issues are not part of the proposals when submitting applications to become National Laboratories. A structured and strategic public policy to accomplish National Laboratories connectivity with a reasonable and increasing bandwidth using the NREN, could be one of the topics to be included in the annual work plans presented by CUDI and approved by CONACYT, if the implementation of Art. 213 of the law takes place in the near future.

3. **Second Phase: Connectivity of the CONACYT Research Centers System**[8].

- CONACYT funds 27 public research centers, they are located in different cities of the Mexican territory an grouped in three great subsystems. Exact and Natural Sciences (10 centers) Social Sciences and Humanities (8 centers); Technological Development and Services (8) and the last one dedicated to finance graduate studies. A few have been connected and participating in the Mexican NREN's activities since the beginning. Their activities increasingly need connectivity to reach databases, instrumentation and computing power in different scales. The same opportunities and benefits apply to these research centers as those being described for National Laboratories.

4. **Astronomic Observatories System**.

- The first Big Data Big Networks Conference, included a presentation of the connectivity and projects of the Institute of Astronomy at Ensenada, the San Pedro Mártir observatory and its collaborative projects with China, Arizona State University and Mexico City (UNAM). To get data from San Pedro Mártir UNAM rents a 2 Mbps microwave link. The telescope works through a robot and produces 22Gbytes of data. Each night 4Tbytes of data need to be transferred to different

---

[7] The link provides information of each of the 65 National Laboratories approved and financed by CONACYT http://www.conacyt.mx/index.php/el-conacyt/desarrollo-cientifico/programa-de-laboratorios-nacionales.

[8] http://www.conacyt.mx/index.php/el-conacyt/centros-de-investigacion-conacyt.

locations in the US and Mexico, and information is increasing in at least one order of magnitude, higher throughput networks need to reach the Astronomy Community in Mexico and to its collaborating partners. Access to supercomputers is also necessary for theoretical astronomers analyzing millions of images captured by the telescope. CISESE plays a key role for the access to supercomputing power and connectivity in Baja California and CUDI's can project growth of the cross border links to China and Arizona via Internet2 points of presence. Data repositories are also needed. CUDI's backbone needs to be upgraded at least to 1 Gbps in the Tijuana-Hermosillo link, it is currently operating at 100 Mbps.

- CONACYT has recently approved a proposal to enhance the Institute of Astronomy telecom infrastructure, it appears to be an independent network from those links already operated by CUDI. Economies of scale and greater collaboration and sharing of scarce resources could be accomplished if CONACYT is aware of the different network and infrastructure needs, R&E institutions are requiring to be able to plan for the long term a robust NREN with high capacity and flexibility to grow at the same pace of demand.

5. **HEP observatories, collaboration with regional initiatives such as ALICE and AUGER forming an ecosystem (for example LAGO).**

- The HEP Virtual Community LAGO was described in Part 1 of this article. The physicist working on different R&E activities throughout the LA region have been experiencing the need for processing data models, storing data collected from sensors in open access repositories to be used by multidisciplinary R&E virtual communities. SCALAC may serve as a collaboratory (virtual resources, customized applications, etc.) to seamlessly access HPC, Grid or Cloud computing resources, to process data originated and produced in its different observatories. RedCLARA may provide network services and the local NRENs could support its participating R&E members of each LA country involved.
- The SCALAC science gateway and other Science Gateways that were described in the BDBN Report may as well serve as gateways to use underlying infrastructure needed to accomplish LAGO regional operation with seamless network connections, HPCDS and instrumentation.
- LNS has become an important HPC and storage node for HAWC and GTM initiatives, very large bandwidth, both nationally and internationally is needed to maintain the rhythm of data acquisitions gathered daily for the different experiments being developed at the Sierra Negra Volcano.
- The MINERvA collaboration involves 7 countries with 22 participating institutions (Universidad de Guanajuato and Fermilab) with circa 100 physicist collecting neutrino-nucleus data with MINERvA detector since 2010. By the end of 2016 it will collect around 150 Terabytes of raw unformatted data and will require 600 TB of Monte Carlo unformatted data from simulations of neutrino nucleons inside MINERvA detector. The project needs computational technology, storage, communication, data acquiring, data curing, transferring analyzing and processing, as well as data mining experts. They use a grid

architecture between Leon and Guanajuato cities. There is an increasing need to have a high speed connection with Fermilab laboratories in the USA. It is also necessary to improve human skills in different big data areas.

6. **Tier 1 Laboratory CERN-LHC in ICN-UNAM (Mexico City)**

- In 2014, CERN and UNAM signed an agreement to upgrade the HEP grid of Mexico into a Tier 1 Laboratory. It means ICN-UNAM is increasing its activities and obligations with the LHC project and will generate larger volumes of data and processes. It also means that this laboratory will require at least 10 Gbps link form UNAM to CERN as part of the e-infrastructure demanded by the global HEP Grid architecture.
- The HEP Grid Infrastructure operates ROC-LA for the use of grid resources worldwide. It would be very important to introduce long-term support to upgrade, monitor and operate the National Grid Infrastructure as well.

7. **Chetumal Satellite Station for Satellite Image Repositories**

- The Mexican Space Agency (AEM) has indicated that the space infrastructure for an early warning system needs a National Storage and Data Processing System for Geomatics, Space and Astrophysicists Information; Connectivity; and Applications.
- The Mexican Space Agency is building a state-of-the-art storage facility in Merida for a data flow of more than 1.5 Petabytes of satellite images.
- Together with the Colégio de la Frontera Sur (Ecosur), AEM is preparing a scientific program to take advantage of the Satellite Information acquired by the Earth Station located in Chetumal (ERIS-Chetumal) using satellite applications. Multiple government, industry and academic institutions may benefit from this information in real time. Thus, a very high-speed connectivity needs to reach the storage facilities, with a very high standard of security.

8. **CiiMar GOMC (Consorcio de Instituciones de Investigación Marina del Golfo de México y del Caribe) System for Marine Sciences R&E**

- CiiMAR encompasses 25 Mexican R&E institutions and more than 100 US diverse, strategic, and connected universities for the sustainability of the Gulf of Mexico contributing to the best management practices and sustainable development of the region by providing science and knowledge and regional public policies to improve the ecosystem health condition and economic wealth of this region. Its main areas of interest are pollution, living marine resources, marine ecosystem health, climate change, socioeconomic impact and public policies. Science groups such as Gulf Of Mexico Alliance, Northern Gulf Institute, Gulf of Mexico Universities Research Collaborative, Gulf of Mexico Costal Ocean Observing System and other US federal government entities such as NOAA, NASA, IOOS, EPA, and USGS.
- The Gulf of Mexico participating institutions need regional connectivity to build a strong network of innovative high tech oceanographic solutions to maintain a healthy marine ecosystem away from anthropogenic and natural

hazards. It is also important to connect this region, with other regions of the world to be able to understand their relationship as well as the economic value and sustainable exploitation of marine resources.

- Data acquired serve to understand the implications of the climate change scenario, networks of sensors and high frequency radars (HFR) connected to a HPCDS to produce numerical models and share them through NRENs to reach participating R&E institutions to study sea level rises provoking floods, storm surges marine transgression, pollution, Hypoxia, Marine debris, erosion, sediment management ocean acidification, invasive species and hurricanes. This information in turn provide social and economic benefits if it is used to provide healthy seafood, clean beaches, renewable energy sources, stable fisheries, ecotourism and biodiversity, etc.

9. Langebio connectivity for Genomics collaboration with the US Scripps Research Institute at La Jolla

- Biology has advance since computer power has become an essential tool for R&E in this field. The biomolecular lab at Leon, Guanajuato studies molecular mechanisms of cellular processes at atomic levels. Their researchers need access to the main international repositories for NextGen sequencing results. Metadata downloads is in the order of 22 Gbytes and sequences (compressed raw data) are in the order of 650 Tbytes. A large metadata analysis for a determined experiment may require tens or hundreds of Tbytes of raw data. To study complex relationships between molecular structures, dynamics and functions of diverse cellular machinery there is an increasing need of interdisciplinary collaboration such as spectroscopy, mathematics, HPC, informatics and software engineering, big networks, molecular biology, biophysics and molecular modeling, these groups of multidisciplinary domains may work virtually. This lab needs high-speed reliable connectivity as it depends on sources of data stored globally; it requires HPC and storage when generating new data.

10. National Research and Training Health System

- The University of Kyushu, Japan invited CUDI's Health Community and Multicast Technical Group to participate in the Telemedicine Development Center of Asia (TEMDEC) initiative leaded by Dr. Shuji Shimizu in Japan and by Dr. Miguel Tanimoto of the National Institute of Nutrition.
- Several live events took place during 2013 and 2014 with Medical Associations of different specialties to share with doctors of different countries of Latin America, Japan and Korea, knowledge on techniques while observing live endoscopies in both regions through the videoconference system of the NRENs. These live endoscopies need very high bandwidth, low latency and secure networking through the intervention to the patient. Doctors in different countries can communicate to share their knowledge and learn from different techniques.

- This training by videoconference has proved to be very efficient in National and Regional Medical Conferences. Public government health institutes are increasingly participating with the School Hospitals at Universities in different training and research programs for the personnel of the hospital: nurses, instruments personnel and doctors.
- A National Research and Training Health System will benefit from the international collaboration through its integration to the NREN.

11. Consolidate the Mexican Grid and Cloud Academic Infrastructures

- Most of the participating institutions in the different e-infrastructure projects described in Sect. 2, have been improving their grid and cloud architectures. There is an increasing demand for Grid and Cloud HPCDS to process, analyze and store collected data. In order to provide high quality grid and cloud academic infrastructures, it is desirable to consolidate previous isolated efforts into virtual regional or national services for R&E institutions using the NRENs.

12. National Videoconference System

- Videoconference has become one of the most useful networking tools in the past 20 years. Videoconference systems have evolved dramatically, becoming a Web RTC service. The NRENs are able to provide this service seamlessly to R&E communities so they can communicate in an independent way through any mobile communications equipment. This type of service may require flexible bandwidths to allow for Full HD interaction of multiple sites and virtual live events supported by videoconference, worldwide.
- CUDI's Virtual Communities use videoconference in their daily activities as well as in seminars, workshops, live events, etc. CUDI has built a standardized video repository with all the events being organized by its community for the past 16 years in collaboration with the Community of the Red Mexicana de Repositorios (REMERI) that gathers specialists on library science, information databases, video databases, data mining, data acquisition, data curing, data storage, etc.

13. National Network of IXPs

- CUDI promoted the creation of the first Internet Exchange Point in Mexico. This infrastructure is necessary to maintain local exchange of data – locally. Universities and Research Centers are natural generators of billions of data and information and they are increasingly exchanging data and research information. There is an increasing need to install points of presence with IXP functionalities in different cities of Mexico, to access caches with this information where a critical mass of institutions could benefit from economies of scale, on sharing the cost of peering to access the Internet and low latencies to access important academic resources and databases as well as other services that are already in Internet, such as google search.

14. REMERI: National Institutional Repositories

- The Mexican Law of Science and Technology was modified in the second quarter of 2014 to include a Chapter on Open Access for Research Work. This legal framework provides an opportunity to disseminate the public work of researchers and educators to more individuals.
- CUDI's Community: Red Mexicana de Repositorios Institucionales (REMERI) anticipated to this initiative, creating a strategy to provide Mexican institutions with support and training activities to create their own institutional repositories, and at the same time building a federated network of open access repositories with the aim to integrate, disseminate, preserve and grant visibility to the scientific, academic and document production of Mexican institutions. REMERI uses standardized metadata and protocols agreed by the 9 participating countries of LA REFERENCIA, a LA initiative of Federated Repositories of Scientific Documents, operated by CLARA with the support of the participating NRENs and the corresponding LA Science and Technology authorities. REMERI has currently 123 repositories of 70 Mexican Institutions with a total of 472, 266 documents.
- CONACYT recently published the guidelines to build institutional repositories. REMERI can support CONACYT in expanding this initiative rapidly and efficiently through the use of the NREN.

15. AMP BACKBONE: AmLight - Mexico Pathways

- In 2014 FIU, LEARN, University of Arizona, and CENIC presented a project before the NSF related to the IRNC call of that year. The purpose is to build a supplementary cross-border network infrastructure to the current AmLight topology. The goals of the project are:
  (1) To establish strategic (demand driven) cross-border network connections;
  (2) To extend the Internet2 Innovation Platform into Mexico with the aim to increase R&E collaboration seamlessly;
  (3) To enhance support for meritorious science drivers, (i.e. findings from the Big Data Big Networks final report);
  (4) To strengthen continental connectivity with RedCLARA in South and Central America and with CUDI in Mexico.
- Participating institutions from Mexico, Latin America and the US (CENIC, LEARN, University of Arizona, University of Texas El Paso (UTEP), Florida International University (FIU), Internet2, CUDI, Universidad Nacional Autónoma de Mexico (UNAM), Universidad de Guadalajara, Instituto Tecnológico y de Estudios Superiores de Monterrey (ITESM), CICESE, and RedCLARA) agreed to support this initiative. It did not get in due time the support needed from the Mexican and US R&E communities,

Table 2. Resume of positive aspects that could turn into opportunities.

	Positive aspects	Opportunities
1	More than 15 Mexican R&E Institutions have participated with CUDI and other NRENs using e-infrastructures	There is a need to democratize the use of NRENs to all communities of researchers and educators
		It is noted that opportunities to reach large instruments such as the HAWC and GMT as well as the San Pedro Mártir Telescope may lead to a more efficient use of these instruments, and to benefit from advanced technologies such as robots to manipulate at a distance instruments
2	HEP and Astronomy are the most familiarized VCs using NRENs and e-infrastructures nation, region and worldwide	There is a vertiginous growing demand of needs of high-speed low-latency seamless NRENs and e-infrastructures in other domains of R&E. For example Health, Education, Industry, Bioinformatics, Disaster Mitigation, Satellite Image Processing, etc
3	Most of the Mexican R&E Institutions listed in the above initiatives have declared HR specialization on networks and e-infrastructures as important	There is a good selection of specialized HR that could become the trainers of new HR in the different areas, however new profiles need to be analyzed to keep up to date with evolution of NRENs and e-infrastructures, HPC, Cloud, Grid, hardware and software tools, etc
4	The evolving initiatives show a stronger collaboration of R&E Institutions, and CUDI is the common denominator	Those institutions that are not participating in the Mexican NREN can benefit from economies of scale and closer collaboration with regional or international researchers and educators with common interests
The National Videoconference System can rapidly show the relevance of national, regional and global collaboration as it is already using mobile devices
5	The grid computing e-infrastructure has proved to be useful and in some cases more efficient than other e-infrastructures	There is a need to support and fund the National Grid Infrastructure as it relies on HR and Resource Centers as well as middleware upgrades to provide seamless services
6	HPC, storage, visualization, simulation are already e-infrastructures highly demanded by researchers and educators	The Mexican NREN needs to interconnect the e-infrastructures available such as supercomputing facilities, national labs, scientific

(Continued)

Table 2. (*Continued*)

	Positive aspects	Opportunities
		instruments (telescopes, microscopes, etc.) to make an efficient and collaborative use of these scarce resources.
		Examples in the US (XSEDE) and Europe (PRACE) show this is highly efficient and reliable
7	HR and Resources Centers have been growing with a certain degree of regionalization	The Mexican NREN can strengthen regions and connectivity between them to provide Regional or National Services and make efficient use of the international connectivity when collaboration extends to foreign NRENs and R&E institutions
		Big Data is integrating more R&E collaborations
8	Mexico's participation in regional (Latin American) collaboration has a strong position The Mexican NREN operates the regional NOC of CLARA and CaribNET Mexican HPC infrastructure and Human Resources in the LA region can benefit pertaining to SCALAC and using CLARA as the networking vehicle	The Mexican NREN has strengthen its connectivity with the US and Latin America however, to keep up with the pace of growth in collaborative projects, it needs a more stable budget and strategic planning for medium and long term network commitments to be able to support R&E collaboration regionally and worldwide
		A Cyber-infrastructure or e-infrastructure annual budget, similar to the one established in other countries could be used to build, operate, upgrade and monitor the QoS, performance and security of the Mexican NREN while providing seamless connectivity to participating institutions in collaborative projects. Article 213 of the Federal Telecom and Broadcasting Law, supports the creation of this initiative. RNP, the Brazilian NREN could be a functional agreement to follow in the government-NREN relationship
9	ISUM, AMCAV and RedMexSu can join efforts to accelerate the implementation of e-infrastructures using HPCDS and NRENs	A strategically planned system of e-infrastructures is desirable to make efficient use of computing and network resources

(*Continued*)

Table 2. (*Continued*)

	Positive aspects	Opportunities
		Part of the annual work plan of the NREN could include the engineering of e-infrastructures and network architectures that fulfill national communications and computing demands
10	CEeI represents academia, government, industry	Reactivate this Council to work for the benefit of the NREN and e-infrastructures with different perspectives and solutions to national, regional and global problems
		Several institutions participate in different projects they may share NREN's network and HPCDS e-infrastructures. However coordination and collaborative support for the availability of computing and network resources in a seamless, large scale, low latency and secure manner, needs to be accomplished to benefit from this infrastructure sharing

4 Conclusions

More than 17 R&E collaborative initiatives on a national or international basis have been described for the purpose of understanding the importance of NRENs and their relationship with e-infrastructures using HPCDS and instrumentation. While analyzing the different collaborative initiatives, we noted positive aspects and opportunities to reduce the gap of researchers and educators that do not use NRENs and e-infrastructures in their current R&E projects and may be lacking the benefits (less processing time, better performance, different ways of representing experiments, better manipulation of big data sets, etc.) they may obtain when using these valuable resources. In the analysis we also find that not only the infrastructure deployed is relevant for R&E collaborative projects, the need for specialization of human resources in different areas related to new hardware and software as well as integrated systems make the difference on how we impact in providing utility computing and network services to larger communities of researchers and educators.

We consider NRENs have not been used as extensively as they should in some countries; such is the case of Mexico. We may find more reasons than those expressed in the Table 2 below of why this is true, however, we have centered our analysis in the use of NRENs when building e-infrastructures using HPCDS on collaborative R&E initiatives.

We found at least 10 positive aspects that could turn into opportunities if, proper actions are taken by the government, the research centers and higher education institutions participating as CUDI members (and those who are not). Little participation of the industry is evident in the timeline of initiatives presented.

Through the Special Council on e-infrastructures a more active role may be accomplished, to involve the industry in promoting the implementation of a robust NREN as well as the e-infrastructures, and the training of Human Resources. CUDI has already implemented some actions and proposes other actions mentioned in Sect. 3 of this article.

References

1. http://www.cudi.edu.mx/acervos/convenios. Accessed 15 October 2015
2. SCALAC, Un servicio de Computación Avanzada para América Latina y El Caribe para la Era Exascale. C.J. Barrios Hernández, G.J. Díaz Toro, R. García Mayo, R. Ramos Pollan, J. Cruz, A. de la Ossa, L. Giraldo, S. Jalife, A. Tadeu Gomes, P. Navaux, Javier Torres, A. Stolk, H. Castro, J. Chacón, L. Núñez y M. Valero
3. Reporte Final sobre la construcción de una Grid Interinstitucional en México con la red CUDI. José Luis Gordillo Ruiz, UNAM, José Luis Briseño Cervantes CICESE; Carmen Rodríguez Armenta UdG, Juan Carlos Rosas Cabrera UAM, Arturo Pérez Díaz CINVESTAV. http://www.cudi.mx/sites/default/files/CUDI/convocatorias/2003_noviembre/proyectos/grid/reporte_final_construcion_grid.pdf. Accessed 29 October 2015
4. BDBN Workshop Report. Program Committee Members, 2014 and presentations of the 1st, 2nd, and 3rd BDBN Conferences/Workshops found at www.cudi.edu.mx/videoteca. Accessed 15 October–30 November 2015
5. http://www.conacyt.mx/index.php/el-conacyt/desarrollo-cientifico/programa-de-laboratorios-nacionales. Accessed 15 November 2015
6. http://www.conacyt.mx/index.php/el-conacyt/centros-de-investigacion-conacyt. Accessed 15 November 2015
7. Luis, A., Rodríguez, T.: (ITESM) José de Jesús Cruz Guzmán (UNAM), Carmen Heras Sánchez (USON), José Lozano Risk (CICESE) Salma Jalife Villalón (CUDI) 15. Cómputo Grid y de alto desempeño en México. Antecedentes, estado actual y nuevos retos, págs. 161–177. e-book CUDI Internet Avanzado: Red Nacional de Educación e Investigación. Unión de visiones y vinculación Institucional (2013)
8. Helen Site http://www.roma1.infn.it/exp/helen/. Accessed 20 November 2015
9. PRAGMA Grid Applications Site http://goc.pragma-grid.net. Accessed 2007 and reproduced via the presentation Latin American Grid Initiatives, Carlos Casasus, May 14, 2007 the site is no longer available. This presentation can be found on www.cudi.edu.mx
10. GRAMA project site http://www.grama.cudi.edu.mx. Accessed 20 November 2015
11. RINGRID project site http://www.ringrid.eu. Accessed 2007 and reproduced via the presentation Latin American Grid Initiatives, Carlos Casasus, May 14, 2007 the site is no longer available. This presentation can be found on www.cudi.edu.mx
12. EELA and EELA-2 Site http://www.eu-eela.eu. Accessed 16 November 2015
13. OPTIPUTER project site http://optiputer.cicese.mx. Accessed 20 November 2015
14. GISELA project site http://www.gisela-grid.eu. Accessed 20 November 2015
15. ISUM site http://www.isum.mx. Accessed 20 November 2015, to access a specific year please use ISUMxx, where xx is the numbers of the year

16. CHAIN AND CHAINREDS site https://www.chain-project.eu/. Accessed 20 November 2015
17. CHAIN Knowledge Base (KB). http://www.chain-project.eu/knowledge-base. Accessed 20 November 2015
18. CHAIN-REDS project http://www.chain-project.eu/. Accessed 20 November 2015
19. http://lns.org.mx/equipamiento/. Accessed 20 November 2015
20. http://www.risc-project.eu/publication_type/green-papers/. Accessed 20 November 2015
21. http://www.redmexsu.mx/Miembros. Accessed 20 November 2015

Parallel Algorithms and Optimization

Multiobjective Energy-Aware Workflow Scheduling in Distributed Datacenters

Sergio Nesmachnow[1][✉], Santiago Iturriaga[1], Bernabé Dorronsoro[2], and Andrei Tchernykh[3]

[1] Universidad de la República, Montevideo, Uruguay
sergion@fing.edu.uy
[2] Universidad de Cádiz, Cádiz, Spain
[3] CICESE Research Center, Ensenada, Mexico

Abstract. This article presents a multiobjective approach for scheduling large workflows in distributed datacenters. We consider a realistic scheduling scenario of distributed cluster systems composed of multi-core computers, and a multi-objective formulation of the scheduling problem to minimize makespan, energy consumption and deadline violations. The studied schedulers follow a two-level schema: in the higher-level, we apply a multiobjective heuristic and a multiobjective metaheuristic, to distribute jobs between clusters; in the lower-level, specific backfilling-oriented scheduling methods are used for task scheduling locally within each cluster, considering precedence constraints. A new model for energy consumption in multi-core computers is applied. The experimental evaluation performed on a benchmark set of large workloads that model different realistic high performance computing applications demonstrates that the proposed multiobjective schedulers are able to improve both the makespan and energy consumption of the schedules when compared with a standard Optimistic Load Balancing Round Robin approach.

1 Introduction

Datacenters are large supercomputing facilities hosting computing resources that provide multiple services, including computing power, networking, storage, etc. in different application domains, including science, industry and commerce [29].

New paradigms for computation that propose using geographically distributed infrastructures to deal with complex problems (i.e. *grid* and *cloud* computing) have gained notorious interest due to the emergence of modern datacenter facilities and parallel computing methodologies and libraries. Indeed, a federation of distributed datacenters provides a significantly large amount of computing power to be used in modern supercomputing applications. Each datacenter in a federation is typically composed by a large number of computational resources, including high performance clusters, large storage systems, and/or components of large grids or cloud systems [30].

Energy efficiency has become a major issue when using large computing infrastructures. The energy consumption of datacenters should be kept as low

© Springer International Publishing Switzerland 2016
I. Gitler and J. Klapp (Eds.): ISUM 2015, CCIS 595, pp. 79–93, 2016.
DOI: 10.1007/978-3-319-32243-8_5

as possible, for both economic and environmental reasons. However, energy efficiency is in conflict with the performance of the system, since increasing the performance requires using more energy, and reducing the energy consumption will negatively affect the Quality of Service (QoS) that the computing system provides to the users. Thus, a multi-objective analysis is needed for finding accurate solutions of the datacenter planning problem, providing different trade-offs between energy consumption and performance.

Different techniques for reducing the energy consumption in datacenters have been proposed, ranging from ad-hoc hardware solutions to more general software methods adapted for specific infrastructures [1,24,25,28].

This article presents a hierarchical multi-objective approach for energy-aware scheduling of large workloads into a federation of distributed datacenters, composed by a number of clusters that might be geographically distributed, which is indeed the architecture of modern high performance and distributed computing systems, including big supercomputers, high performance computing centers, and cloud infrastructures, among others. We extend the greedy list scheduling heuristic approach for multi-core heterogeneous computing systems presented in our previous works [6,17] to consider: (i) a hierarchical model that uses two levels for assigning jobs to resources; (ii) the scheduling of large workflows having tasks with dependencies; and (iii) the utilization of a mutiobjective evolutionary algorithm to decide the best assigning of jobs to distributed cluster nodes.

The hierarchical two-level approach [7,20,21] divides the scheduling problem into a number of simpler and smaller sub-problems to be solved in each component of the datacenter infrastructure, and a specific ad-hoc backfilling heuristic based on combining the makespan, the energy consumption, and the QoS of solutions is presented for scheduling within each cluster. In this work, we measure the QoS of each schedule using a simple metric that accounts for the jobs whose deadlines are not met.

The experimental evaluation of the studied schedulers is performed over a benchmark set of 75 workloads with large jobs that model typical high performance computing applications over realistic distributed infrastructures. Three classes of workloads are considered: Series-Parallel, Heterogeneous-Parallel, and Mixed. Each problem instance contains 1000 jobs, with up to 132 tasks each, to be scheduled in a federation of datacenters with up to 1500 computational resources. The experimental results demonstrates that accurate solutions are computed by the best performing schedulers, allowing the planner to achieve improvements of up to **17.9** % in makespan, **20.7** % in energy consumption, and **36.4** % in deadline violation penalization over a traditional optimistic load balancing round-robin strategy.

The article is organized as follows. The problem formulation and review of the related work are presented in Sect. 2. The scheduling approach and the proposed methods ares described in Sect. 3. The experimental evaluation is reported in Sect. 4, including a comparison against a traditional optimistic load balancing round robin approach. Finally, Sect. 5 formulates conclusions and main lines for future work.

2   Energy-Aware Scheduling in a Federation of Datacenters

This section introduces the problem model and discusses the related work about energy-aware scheduling in datacenters.

2.1   Problem Model and Formulation

The energy-aware scheduling problem addressed in this article considers the following elements:

- A distributed infrastructure (datacenter federation) formed by k heterogeneous *Cluster Nodes* (the datacenters) $CN = \{CN_0, CN_1, \ldots, CN_k\}$. Each CN is a collection of NP_r multi-core processors, which is characterized by five values $(NP_r, ops_r, c_r, E^r_{IDLE}, E^r_{MAX})$, defining the number of processors, their performance (in FLOPS) and number of cores, and the energy consumption of each processor at idle and peak usage, respectively.
- A set of n independent heterogeneous jobs $J = \{j_0, j_1, \ldots, j_n\}$. Each job j_q has an associated deadline D_q. Each job j_q is a parallel application that is decomposed into a (large) set of tasks $T_q = \{t_{q0}, t_{q1}, \ldots t_{qm}\}$ with dependencies among them. Typically, each task has different computing requirements.
- Each task $t_{q\alpha}$ is characterized by two values $(o_{q\alpha}, nc_{q\alpha})$ defining its length (number of operations), and the number of resources (cores) required for the parallel execution, respectively.

Each job is represented as a *Directed Acyclic Graph* (DAG), i.e. a precedence task graph $j_q = (V, E)$, where the set of nodes V contains each task $t_{q\alpha}$ ($0 \leq \alpha \leq m$) of the parallel program j_q. The set of (directed) edges E represents the dependencies between tasks, a partial order $t_{q\alpha} \prec t_{q\beta}$ that models the precedence constraints: an edge $e_{\alpha\beta} \in E$ means that task $t_{q\beta}$ cannot start before task $t_{q\alpha}$ is completed. We consider negligible communication costs, as they only occurs between servers within the same CN.

We are dealing with large workloads, so the problem instances are composed of thousands of jobs (this means hundreds of thousands of tasks) to be scheduled onto a number of CN (hundreds to thousands computing resources).

The described scheduling scenario is modeled with the multi-objective problem min (f_M, f_E), that proposes the simultaneous optimization of the *makespan* f_M and the *energy consumption* f_E.

The makespan evaluates the total time to execute a set of jobs, according to the expression in Eq. 1, where x represents an allocation, k is the number of available cluster nodes, and CT_r is the completion time of cluster node r (CN_r). The *energy consumption* function for a set of jobs executed in certain cluster nodes is defined in Eq. 2, using the energy model for multi-core architectures by Nesmachnow et al. [17], where f_1 is the higher-level scheduling function, and f_2 is the lower-level scheduling function. Both the energy required to execute the tasks assigned to each computing resource within a CN, and the energy that each resource consumes in idle state are taken into account. The deadline violation penalization is defined in Eq. 3. A penalty function $Penalty_q(F_q)$ is associated with every application j_q, where F_q is the additional amount of time required to finish the execution of j_q after its deadline D_q is met. If j_q is finished before its deadline, then F_q is 0. Three different penalization functions are used in this work, a simple identity function $(Penalty_q(F_q) = F_q)$, a square root function $(Penalty_q(F_q) = \sqrt{F_q})$, and a square function $(Penalty_q(F_q) = F_q^2)$.

$$f_M(x) = \max_{0 \leq r \leq k} CT_r \tag{1}$$

$$f_E(x) = \sum_{r \in CN} \sum_{\substack{j_q \in J: \\ f_1(j_q)=CN_r}} \sum_{\substack{t_{qi} \in T_q: \\ f_2(t_{qi})=p_j}} EC(t_{qi}, p_j) \\ + \sum_{p_j \in CN} EC_{IDLE}(p_j) \tag{2}$$

$$f_P(x) = \sum_{j_q \in J} Penalty_q(F_q) \tag{3}$$

In this article, we study the optimization problem from the point of view of the computing system (i.e. the infrastructure administration), thus we use two system-related objectives. Additionally, we consider a QoS-related objective such as the number of job deadlines violated, taking into account the point of view of the customer/user in the problem formulation.

2.2   Related Work

Many works in the literature have dealt with energy-aware scheduling in computing systems. Two main optimization approaches are established: independent and simultaneous. In the *independent* approach, energy and performance are assumed independent, so scheduling algorithms that optimize classic performance metrics are combined with a slack reclamation technique, such as dynamic voltage scaling (DVS)/dynamic voltage and frequency scaling (DVFS) [3,22]. In the *simultaneous* approach, performance and energy are simultaneously optimized, and the problem is modeled as a multi-constrained, bi-objective optimization one. The algorithms are oriented to find Pareto optimal schedules; where no scheduling decision can strictly dominate the other ones with better performance and lower energy consumption at the same time.

In this article, we follow the simultaneous approach. Below we briefly review the main related works about simultaneous optimization of energy and performance metrics.

Khan and Ahmad [9] applied the concept of Nash Bargaining Solution from game theory for scheduling independent jobs, simultaneously minimizing makespan and energy on a DVS-enabled grid system. Lee and Zomaya [11] studied several DVS-based heuristics to minimize the weighted sum of makespan and energy. A makespan conservative local search technique is used to slightly modify scheduling decisions when they do not increase energy consumption for executing jobs, in order to escape from local optima. Later, Mezmaz et al. [15] improved the previous work by proposing a parallel bi-objective hybrid genetic algorithm (GA) for the same problem, using the cooperative island/multi-start farmer-worker model, significantly reducing the execution time of the scheduling method. Pecero et al. [18] proposed a two-phase bi-objective algorithm based on the Greedy Randomized Adaptive Search Procedure (GRASP) that applies a DVS-aware bi-objective local search to generate a set of Pareto solutions.

Kim et al. [10] studied the priority/deadline constrained scheduling problem in ad-hoc grids with limited-charge DVS-enabled batteries, and proposed a resource manager to exploit the heterogeneity of tasks while managing the energy. Luo et al. [14] showed that batch mode dynamic scheduling outperforms online approaches, though it requires significantly more computation time too.

Li et al. [12] introduced a MinMin-based online dynamic power management strategy with multiple power-saving states to reduce energy consumption of scheduling algorithms. Pinel et al. [19] proposed a double minimization approach for scheduling independent tasks on grids with energy considerations, first applying a MinMin approach to optimize the makespan, and then a local search to minimize energy consumption. Lindberg et al. [13] proposed six greedy algorithms and two GAs for solving the makespan-energy scheduling problem subject to deadline and memory requirements.

In our previous work [17], we introduced an energy consumption model for multi-core computing systems. Our approach did not use DVS nor other specific techniques for power/energy management. Instead, we proposed an energy consumption model based on the energy required to execute tasks at full capacity, the energy when not all the available cores of the machine are used, and the energy that each machine on the system consumes in idle state. We proposed twenty fast list scheduling methods adapted to solve a bi-objective problem, by simultaneously optimizing both makespan and energy consumption when executing tasks on a single cluster node. Using the same approach, Iturriaga et al. [8] showed that a parallel multi-objective local search based on Pareto dominance outperforms deterministic heuristics based on the traditional Min-Min strategy.

In [8,17], we tackled the problem of scheduling independent Bag-of-Tasks (BoT) applications. In this article, we extend the previous approach to solve a more complex multi-objective optimization problem, by considering large jobs, whose tasks have precedences, modeled by DAGs. In addition, here we propose a fully hierarchical scheduler that operates in two levels for efficiently planning large jobs in distributed datacenters.

3 The Proposed Hierarchical Energy-Aware Schedulers for Federations of Datacenters

We propose a hierarchical two-level scheduling approach, which fits properly to our problem model and the considered nowadays distributed infrastructures.

The higher-level scheduler (executing in a service front-end) applies a cluster assignment optimization, adapting a combined heuristic from our previous work [17], in order to distribute jobs to cluster nodes. Within each cluster node, the lower-level scheduler applies a local scheduler specifically conceived for multi-core architectures and managing idle times (we called them *holes*) due to core availability. Both methods are described in the next section.

3.1   Lower-Level Scheduler

The proposed low-level scheduling heuristics are based on the Heterogeneous Earliest Finish Time (HEFT) strategy [27]. HEFT is a successful scheduler for DAG-modeled applications that works by assigning priorities to tasks, taking into account the *upward rank* metric, which evaluates the expected distance of each task to the last node in the DAG (the end of computation). The upward rank is recursively defined by $UR_i = t_i + \max_{j \in succ(i)} c_{ij} + UR_j$, where t_i is the execution time of task i in the computing resources, *succ* is the list of successors of task i, and c_{ij} is the communication cost between tasks i and j. After sorting all tasks of the job by taking into account the upward rank metric, HEFT assigns the task with the highest upward rank to the computing element that computes it at the earliest time.

The proposed heuristic for low-level scheduling in datacenters is *Earliest Finish Time Hole* (EFTH). It follows the schema of HEFT, using a backfilling technique and adapting the algorithm to work with multi-core computing resources, by taking into account the "holes" that appear when a specific computing resources is not fully used by a single task.

EFTH sorts the tasks according to the upward rank values, then gives priority to assign the tasks to existing holes rather than using empty machines in the CN. When a given task fits on more than one hole, the heuristic selects the hole that can complete the task in the earliest time, disregarding the hole length or other considerations. As a consequence, this variant targets the reduction of deadline violations and the improvement of the QoS for the users of the datacenter. When no holes are available to execute the task, the heuristic chooses the machine with the minimum finish time for that task.

The rationale behind this strategy is to use available holes and left unoccupied large holes and empty machines for upcoming tasks. Ties between holes as well as between machines are decided lexicographically, as the method searches sequentially (in order) both holes and machines.

3.2   Higher-Level Scheduler

The higher-level scheduler assigns jobs to cluster nodes. In this work, we study two algorithms: a specific version of the two-phase combined heuristic MaxMIN [17] and a multiobjective evolutionary algorithm, NSGA-II.

MaxMIN. The class of combined heuristics is a set of specific greedy list scheduling methods, which combine the makespan and energy consumption optimization criteria for scheduling in multi-core computers. Originally proposed to schedule independent tasks following the Bag-of-Task model [17, 26], in this work we extend the greedy approach in order to schedule large workflows having tasks with dependencies. MaxMIN operates in two phases. First, it builds a set of pairs (job, cluster node), by associating every job to the cluster node that can complete it with less energy use, taking into account all previous assignments already performed for each CN. After that, among all these pairs, it chooses the one with the maximum completion time among feasible assignments (i.e., the servers of the cluster node have enough cores to execute the job). Therefore, larger tasks are allocated first in the most suitable cluster nodes and shorter tasks are mapped afterward, trying to balance the load of all cluster nodes and making use of available results. When deciding where to assign a given job, MaxMIN first checks which CNs are able to execute the job, meaning that their servers have enough number of cores to execute any task in the job. In order to guide the search of the MaxMIN scheduler, we use heuristic functions to estimate the execution time and the energy required to execute each jobs. We approximate the completion time of a job in the assigned CN as the sum of the expected time to compute all tasks in the job, if they were executed sequentially, divided by the total number of cores available in the CN. To estimate the energy consumption when executing the job j_q in CN_r, we multiply the execution time estimation by the number of processors in CN_r and the energy consumption of such processors at peak power, and add it to the time the CN_r remains idle after finishing its assigned jobs until the last CN executes all jobs (i.e., the makespan value).

NSGA-II. Evolutionary algorithms (EAs) are non-deterministic methods that emulate the evolution of species in nature to solve optimization, search, and learning problems [2]. In the last thirty years, EAs have been successfully applied for solving many high-complexity optimization problems. Multiobjective evolutionary algorithms (MOEAs) [4,5] have been applied to solve hard optimization problems, obtaining accurate results when solving real-life problems in many research areas. Unlike many traditional methods for multiobjective optimization, MOEAs are able to find a set with several solutions in a single execution, since they work with a population of tentative solutions in each generation. MOEAs must be designed taking into account two goals at the same time: (*i*) approximating the Pareto front, usually applying a Pareto-based evolutionary search and (*ii*) maintaining diversity instead of converging to a reduced section of the Pareto front, usually accomplished by using specific techniques also used in multimodal function optimization (sharing, crowding, etc.).

In this work, we apply the *Non-dominated Sorting Genetic Algorithm, version II* (NSGA-II) [5], a popular state-of-the-art MOEA that has been successfully applied in many application areas. NSGA-II includes features to deal with three criticized issues on its predecessor NSGA, to improve the evolutionary search: (*i*) an improved non-dominated elitist ordering that diminishes the complexity of the dominance check; (*ii*) a crowding technique for diversity preservation; and (*iii*) a new fitness assignment method that considers the crowding distance values. Next we present the main characteristics of the proposed NSGA-II algorithm.

Solution Encoding. Each solution is encoded as a set of lists of integers. Each list represents the job execution queue for each data center and contains the identifiers of its assigned jobs. The execution order of the jobs in each data center is given by the order of the job identifiers in each list.

Fitness Function. The fitness function is computed using the EFTH algorithm. Given a higher-level schedule, EFTH computes the lower-level scheduling and calculates the makespan, energy consumption, and violation penalization metrics.

Population Initialization. The initial population is created randomly using an uniform distribution function.

Selection Operator. Selection is performed using the binary tournament method. This method randomly selects two solutions from the population. If one of the selected solutions is dominated, then it is discarded and the non-dominated solution is selected. If both solutions are non-dominated, then the solution which is in the most crowded region is discarded and the remaining solution is selected.

Crossover Operator. The well-known Partially Matched Crossover (PMX) method is used as the crossover operator. To apply this method, a single job list is constructed for each parent by concatenating the job list of every data centres. Two jobs are randomly selected from this list as cutting points. All jobs in between these two points are swapped. The remaining jobs are rearranged using position wise exchanges, maintaining its original ordering information. Finally, the resulting list is disaggregated to reconstruct a job list for each data centre.

Mutation Operator. A simple exchange method is used as the mutation operator. This method works by randomly selecting a job and swapping it with another randomly selected job from any job list.

Repair Operator. This special operator repairs an infeasible solution turning it into a feasible solution. It is applied right after the Crossover and Mutation operators in order to repair any infeasibility introduced by these operators.

3.3   Baseline Scheduler for the Comparison

In order to compare results computed by the proposed schedulers, we consider a typical scenario as a baseline reference, applying a load balancing method and a backfilling technique such as the ones traditionally used in current cluster, grid, and cloud management systems.

Both methods are described next:

- In the higher-level, *Optimistic Load Balancing Round Robin* (OLB-RR) [6] assigns every job to a cluster node trying to balance the load between them. If the job can not be executed in the selected cluster node (because some task in it requires more cores than the number of cores of the servers in the cluster node), then the heuristic continues the iteration to the next ones until a suitable cluster node is found.

– In the lower-level, *NOUR Best Fit Hole* (NOUR) [6] applies a "best fit hole" strategy, i.e. selecting the hole with the closest length to the execution time of the task, but without taking into account the task sorting using the upward rank metric. Instead, the heuristic simply sorts the list of tasks lexicographically (from task #0 to task #N), but it obviously takes into account the precedence graph. This heuristic is intended to produce simple and compact schedules by not sticking to the importance given by the upward rank metric.

4 Experimental Analysis

This section reports the experimental analysis of the proposed hierarchical scheduling methods.

4.1 Problem Instances

A benchmark set of 75 different workflows batches was generated for the experimental evaluation of the proposed energy-aware hierarchical scheduler. The number of tasks in workflows ranges from 3 to 132. Workflows were generated using the SchMng application [23].

We use three different workflow models to consider different problem scenarios: (1) *Series-Parallel* (2) *Heterogeneous-Parallel*, and (3) *Mixed*. The Series-Parallel model represents jobs that can be split into concurrent threads/processes running in parallel. Heterogeneous-Parallel represent a generic job composed of non-identical computational tasks with arbitrary precedences. The Mixed workflow category combines Series-Parallel, Heterogeneous-Parallel and single-task jobs. Figure 1 shows the overall shape of the different workflow types, aimed to reflect real high performance computing applications. Each block represents a computational task, the execution time of a task is represented by the height of the block, and the number of cores is represented by the width of the block. Dependencies are represented by the edges in the graph.

In the benchmark set of 75 batch of workflows, 25 correspond to 1000 Series-Parallel workflows (25000 workflows altogether), 25 are composed of 1000 Heterogeneous-Parallel workflows (25000 workflows altogether), and the remaining 25 are Mixed, including a combination of different workflow types (300 Heterogeneous-Parallel workflows, 300 Series-Parallel workflows, and 400 Single-Task applications). A total number of **75000** workflows are studied in the experimental analysis. The benchmark set of workflows is publicly available at https://www.fing.edu.uy/inco/grupos/cecal/hpc/EAWSDD-2015.tar.gz.

Regarding the computational infrastructure, we consider scenarios with five cluster nodes, with up to 100 processors each. We take into account combinations of nowadays Intel processor with one to six cores, listed in Table 1.

4.2 Development and Execution Platform

Both proposed schedulers (higher- and lower-level) were implemented in the C programming language, using the stdlib library and the GNU gcc compiler.

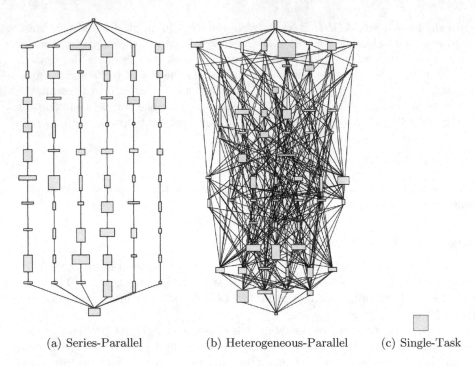

(a) Series-Parallel   (b) Heterogeneous-Parallel   (c) Single-Task

Fig. 1. Workflow types used in the experimental evaluation of the proposed energy-aware hierarchical scheduler

Table 1. Characteristics of the processors considered for the CN infrastructures

Processor	Frequency	Cores	GFLOPS	E_{IDLE}	E_{MAX}	GFLOPS/core
Intel Celeron 430	1.80 GHz	1	7.20	75.0 W	94.0 W	7.20
Intel Pentium E5300	2.60 GHz	2	20.80	68.0 W	109.0 W	10.40
Intel Core i7 870	2.93 GHz	4	46.88	76.0 W	214.0 W	11.72
Intel Core i5 661	3.33 GHz	2	26.64	74.0 W	131.0 W	13.32
Intel Core i7 980 XE	3.33 GHz	6	107.60	102.0 W	210.0 W	17.93

The experimental evaluation was performed on a Dell Power Edge server, Quad-core Xeon E5430 processor at 2.66 GHz, 8 GB RAM and Gigabit Ethernet, from the Cluster FING high performance computing facility (Universidad de la República, Uruguay, website http://www.fing.edu.uy/cluster) [16].

4.3 NGSA-II Parameter Configuration

We configured a number of 100 solutions for the NSGA-II population. The crossover operator is applied with a probability $p_c = 1.0$ and the mutation operator with a probability of $p_m = 0.2$. Finally, for the stopping condition, we considered a fixed number of 20000 fitness function evaluations, which provides an adequate convergence behaviour for the population of solutions.

4.4 Results and Discussion

Table 2 reports the best, average, and standard deviation values for the makespan and energy consumption objectives, obtained in 25 executions of the proposed scheduler for different batches of each workflow type. We compare the MaxMIN-EFTH results with those computed by two schedulers combinations: MaxMIN-NOUR and RR-NOUR. This way, we study the capability of the proposed scheduler to improve the results in both (higher and lower) scheduling levels.

Table 2. Makespan and energy comparison for the studied schedulers

	MaxMIN-NOUR			MaxMIN-EFTH			RR-NOUR		
	Series-Parallel workflows								
metric	f_M	f_E	f_P	f_M	f_E	f_P	f_M	f_E	f_P
avg.	8782.7	70998.9	1.11×10^8	**7658.0**	**62003.4**	8.73×10^7	8847.6	71351.8	**6.56$\times10^7$**
σ	237.4	1881.0	0.97×10^7	203.6	1603.4	0.72×10^7	230.8	1833.4	0.71×10^7
best	8457.3	68393.3	9.29×10^7	7352.8	59680.2	7.38×10^7	8452.7	68291.2	5.19×10^7
	Heterogeneous-Parallel workflows								
metric	f_M	f_E	f_P	f_M	f_E	f_P	f_M	f_E	f_P
avg.	5060.9	50305.1	3.45×10^7	**4616.7**	**45940.3**	2.91×10^7	5130.1	50774.8	**2.21$\times10^7$**
σ	148.0	1412.2	0.41×10^7	124.2	1176.3	0.34×10^7	152.9	1519.7	0.25×10^7
best	4842.4	48300.2	2.54×10^7	4407.6	43966.7	2.20×10^7	4881.5	48296.4	1.63×10^7
	Mixed workflows								
metric	f_M	f_E	f_P	f_M	f_E	f_P	f_M	f_E	f_P
avg.	3112.6	28722.0	9.71×10^6	**2961.6**	**28535.7**	8.68×10^6	3607.0	32855.9	**6.05$\times10^6$**
σ	747.6	5160.5	5.73×10^6	601.8	3804.6	4.52×10^6	641.1	4240.1	3.50×10^6
best	2381.3	22998.0	5.35×10^6	2288.0	23458.6	4.89×10^6	2677.0	25633.9	3.09×10^6

The Kruskal-Wallis statistical test was applied to study the statistical confidence of the results, by analyzing the distributions of the results computed by each scheduler for each problem instance class. The best results for each metric and problem instance are marked in bold (gray background) in Tables 2 and 3 when the p-value computed in the correspondent pair-wise Kruskal-Wallis test is below 10^{-2} (meaning a statistical confidence of the results greater than 99 %).

The results in Table 2 demonstrate that the proposed MaxMIN-EFTH scheduler computes the best makespan and energy results for all problem classes. Overall, MaxMIN-EFTH computes the best makespan values in all **75** scheduling scenarios, and the best energy values in **58** out of 75. Although its accuracy regarding the makespan and energy objectives, the penalization is neglected by MaxMIN-EFTH. This is shown in Table 2 where the RR-NOUR baseline schedulers are able to compute the best penalization values for all the problem classes.

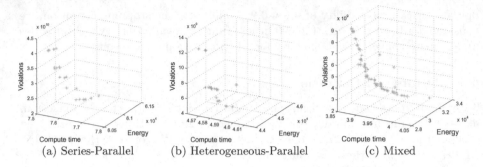

(a) Series-Parallel   (b) Heterogeneous-Parallel   (c) Mixed

Fig. 2. Example Pareto fronts computed by NSGA-II-EFTH when solving a Series-Parallel, a Heterogeneous-Parallel, and a Mixed problem instance.

Next we evaluated the NSGA-II-EFTH algorithm considering a total of 30 independent executions for each problem instance. Figure 2 presents the Pareto front computed by a single NSGA-II-EFTH execution when solving a problem instance of each workload class.

To compare the schedules computed by NSGA-II-EFTH and RR-NOUR, we chose from each Pareto front computed by NSGA-II-EFTH the *compromise solution*, i.e. the *closest* to the one computed by RR-NOUR for each instance using a normalized Euclidean distance Table 3 presents the average improvements of the solutions computed by MaxMIN-NOUR, MaxMIN-EFTH, and the compromise solution computed by NSGA-II-EFTH, over the reference baseline schedulers for each workload class and objective function.

Table 3. Average makespan, energy consumption, and penalization improvements over RR-NOUR

workflow type	MaxMIN-EFTH			NSGA-II-EFTH		
	f_M	f_E	f_P	f_M	f_E	f_P
Series-Parallel	13.4%	13.1%	*-33.0%*	13.8%	13.7%	**36.4%**
Heterogeneous-Parallel	10.0%	9.5%	*-31.4%*	10.5%	**11.8%**	**34.2%**
Mixed	17.9%	13.1%	*-43.5%*	17.2%	**20.7%**	**19.3%**

The results demonstrate that MaxMIN-EFTH computes better schedules than RR-NOUR in terms of makespan and energy consumption, but RR-NOUR computes better penalization improvements than MaxMIN-EFTH. This is because MaxMIN considers makespan and energy consumption but not task's deadlines, while RR does not consider any objective but favors meeting deadlines by evenly distributing tasks among datacenters. NSGA-II-EFTH is able to compute more accurate schedules than MaxMin-EFTH for nearly all objectives and all problem instances, improving RR-NOUR schedules on all objectives. MaxMIN-EFTH computes competitive solutions when considering the makespan objective,

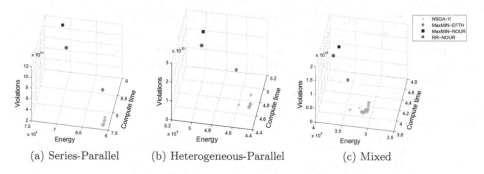

(a) Series-Parallel   (b) Heterogeneous-Parallel   (c) Mixed

Fig. 3. Example solutions computed when solving a Series-Parallel, a Heterogeneous-Parallel, and a Mixed problem instance.

but it is outperformed by NSGA-II-EFTH in the remaining objectives. NSGA-II-EFTH computes up to a **7.6 %** improvement in energy consumption, and up to **69.4 %** improvement in the penalization function over MaxMIN-EFTH. On the other hand, the execution time of NSGA-II-EFTH ranges from 12 h when solving problem instances of the Heterogeneous-Parallel and Mixed workload classes, up to 45 h when solving problem instances of the Series-Parallel workload class. These execution time requirements turn NSGA-II-EFTH unsuitable for tackling online scheduling problems.

Figure 3 graphically shows the solutions computed by RR-NOUR, MaxMIN-NOUR, MaxMin-EFTH, and a single NSGA-II-EFTH execution when solving a problem instance of each workload class.

5   Conclusions and Future Work

We introduced a multiobjective formulation of a two-level scheduling problem in datacenters using multi-core computers and considering makespan, energy consumption, and deadline violation penalization. The EFTH backfilling-oriented scheduler is used as a lower-level algorithm to schedule tasks locally within each cluster, while the MaxMIN heuristic and NSGA-II metaheuristic are both adapted to work with distributed datacenters and used as higher-level schedulers.

The experimental evaluation of the MaxMIN-EFTH and NSGA-II-EFTH schedulers compares the makespan, energy, and deadline violation penalization results against those computed by a traditional RR, and the MaxMIN heuristic both combined with a simple backfilling technique. The evaluation is performed over a set of 75 instances consisting of 1000 jobs each considering a total of 30 independent executions. From the experimental results, we conclude that MaxMIN-EFTH is able to obtain significant improvements in makespan and energy consumption objectives over the references baseline schedulers, but sacrificing accuracy in the deadline violation penalization objective. On the other hand, NSGA-II-EFTH obtains improvements in all three objectives while sacrificing efficiency by requiring execution times not suitable for online scheduling.

MaxMIN-EFTH is a promising shceduler for modern distributed datacenter infrastructures. Nevertheless, the results computed by NSGA-II-EFTH show that the solutions computed by MaxMIN-EFTH could be greatly improved specially for the deadline violation penalization objective.

The main lines for future work are focused on improving the scheduling approach by studying different combinations of higher-level heuristics and lower-level backfilling schedulers.

References

1. Ahmad, I., Ranka, S.: Handbook of Energy-Aware and Green Computing. Chapman & Hall/CRC, Boca Raton (2012)
2. Bäck, T., Fogel, D., Michalewicz, Z.: Handbook of Evolutionary Computation. Oxford University Press, New York (1997)
3. Baskiyar, S., Abdel-Kader, R.: Energy aware DAG scheduling on heterogeneous systems. Cluster Comput. **13**, 373–383 (2010)
4. Coello, C., Van Veldhuizen, D., Lamont, G.: Evolutionary Algorithms for Solving Multi-objective Problems. Kluwer, New York (2002)
5. Deb, K.: Multi-Objective Optimization using Evolutionary Algorithms. Wiley, Chichester (2001)
6. Dorronsoro, B., Nesmachnow, S., Taheri, J., Zomaya, A., Talbi, E.G., Bouvry, P.: A hierarchical approach for energy-efficient scheduling of large workloads in multicore distributed systems. Sustain. Comput. Inf. Syst. **4**(4), 252–261 (2014)
7. Hirales-Carbajal, A., Tchernykh, A., Yahyapour, R., González-García, J., Röblitz, T., Ramírez-Alcaraz, J.: Multiple workflow scheduling strategies with user run time estimates on a grid. J. Grid Comput. **10**(2), 325–346 (2012)
8. Iturriaga, S., Nesmachnow, S., Dorronsoro, B., Bouvry, P.: Energy efficient scheduling in heterogeneous systems with a parallel multiobjective local search. Comput. Inf. J. **32**(2), 273–294 (2013)
9. Khan, S., Ahmad, I.: A cooperative game theoretical technique for joint optimization of energy consumption and response time in computational grids. IEEE Trans. Parallel Distrib. Syst. **20**, 346–360 (2009)
10. Kim, J.K., Siegel, H., Maciejewski, A., Eigenmann, R.: Dynamic resource management in energy constrained heterogeneous computing systems using voltage scaling. IEEE Trans. Parallel Distrib. Syst. **19**, 1445–1457 (2008)
11. Lee, Y., Zomaya, A.: Energy conscious scheduling for distributed computing systems under different operating conditions. IEEE Trans. Parallel Distrib. Syst. **22**, 1374–1381 (2011)
12. Li, Y., Liu, Y., Qian, D.: A heuristic energy-aware scheduling algorithm for heterogeneous clusters. In: Proceedings of the 15th International Conference on Parallel and Distributed System, pp. 407–413 (2009)
13. Lindberg, P., Leingang, J., Lysaker, D., Khan, S., Li, J.: Comparison and analysis of eight scheduling heuristics for the optimization of energy consumption and makespan in large-scale distributed systems. J. Supercomputing **59**(1), 323–360 (2012)
14. Luo, P., Lü, K., Shi, Z.: A revisit of fast greedy heuristics for mapping a class of independent tasks onto heterogeneous computing systems. J. Parallel Distrib. Comput. **67**(6), 695–714 (2007)
15. Mezmaz, M., Melab, N., Kessaci, Y., Lee, Y., Talbi, E.G., Zomaya, A., Tuyttens, D.: A parallel bi-objective hybrid metaheuristic for energy-aware scheduling for cloud computing systems. J. Parallel Distrib. Comput. **71**, 1497–1508 (2011)

16. Nesmachnow, S.: Computación científica de alto desempeño en la Facultad de Ingeniería, Universidad de la República. Revista de la Asociación de Ingenieros del Uruguay 61, pp. 12–15 (2010). (text in Spanish)
17. Nesmachnow, S., Dorronsoro, B., Pecero, J.E., Bouvry, P.: Energy-aware scheduling on multicore heterogeneous grid computing systems. J. Grid Comput. 11(4), 653–680 (2013)
18. Pecero, J., Bouvry, P., Fraire, H., Khan, S.: A multi-objective grasp algorithm for joint optimization of energy consumption and schedule length of precedence-constrained applications. In: International Conference on Cloud and Green Computing, pp. 1–8 (2011)
19. Pinel, F., Dorronsoro, B., Pecero, J., Bouvry, P., Khan, S.: A two-phase heuristic for the energy-efficient scheduling of independent tasks on computational grids. Cluster Comput. 16(3), 421–433 (2013)
20. Quezada-Pina, A., Tchernykh, A., González-García, J.L., Hirales-Carbajal, A., Ramírez-Alcaraz, J.M., Schwiegelshohn, U., Yahyapour, R., Miranda-López, V.: Adaptive parallel job scheduling with resource admissible allocation on two-level hierarchical grids. Future Gener. Comput. Syst. 28(7), 965–976 (2012)
21. Ramírez-Alcaraz, J., Tchernykh, A., Yahyapour, R., Schwiegelshohn, U., Quezada-Pina, A., González-García, J., Hirales-Carbajal, A.: Job allocation strategies with user run time estimates for online scheduling in hierarchical grids. J. Grid Comput. 9(1), 95–116 (2011)
22. Rizvandi, N., Taheri, J., Zomaya, A.: Some observations on optimal frequency selection in DVFS-based energy consumption minimization. J. Parallel Distrib. Comput. 71(8), 1154–1164 (2011)
23. Taheri, J., Zomaya, A., Khan, S.: Grid Simulation Tools for Job Scheduling and Datafile Replication in Scalable Computing and Communications: Theory and Practice. Wiley, Hoboken (2013). Chap. 35, pp. 777–797
24. Tchernykh, A., Lozano, L., Bouvry, P., Pecero, J., Schwiegelshohn, U., Nesmachnow, S.: Energy-aware online scheduling: ensuring quality of service for iaas clouds. In: Proceedings of the International Conference on High Performance Computing Simulation, pp. 911–918 (2014)
25. Tchernykh, A., Lozano, L., Schwiegelshohn, U., Bouvry, P., Pecero, J., Nesmachnow, S.: Bi-objective online scheduling with quality of service for iaas clouds. In: Proceedings of the 3rd International Conference on Cloud Networking, pp. 307–312 (2014)
26. Tchernykh, A., Pecero, J.E., Barrondo, A., Schaeffer, E.: Adaptive energy efficient scheduling in peer-to-peer desktop grids. Future Gener. Comput. Syst. 36, 209–220 (2014)
27. Topcuouglu, H., Hariri, S., Wu, M.Y.: Performance-effective and low-complexity task scheduling for heterogeneous computing. IEEE Trans. Parallel Distrib. Syst. 13(3), 260–274 (2002)
28. Valentini, G., Lassonde, W., Khan, S., Min-Allah, N., Madani, S., Li, J., Zhang, L., Wang, L., Ghani, N., Kolodziej, J., Li, H., Zomaya, A., Xu, C.Z., Balaji, P., Vishnu, A., Pinel, F., Pecero, J., Kliazovich, D., Bouvry, P.: An overview of energy efficiency techniques in cluster computing systems. Cluster Comput. 16(1), 3–15 (2013)
29. Zomaya, A., Khan, S.: Handbook on Data Centers. Springer, New York (2014)
30. Zomaya, A.Y., Lee, Y.C.: Energy Efficient Distributed Computing Systems. Wiley-IEEE Computer Society Press, New York (2012)

Domain Segmentation of Meshes Suited for FEM Using Parallel Computing

Jorge López$^{(\boxtimes)}$, Victor E. Cardoso, and Salvador Botello

Departamento de Ciencias Computacionales,
Centro de Investigación en Matemáticas, A.C., Jalisco S/N, Col. Valenciana,
36240 Guanajuato, GTO, Mexico
{jorge.lopez,victorc,botello}@cimat.mx
http://www.cimat.mx

Abstract. The Finite Element Method is widely used in the industry, how is mentioned in [4]. In this method most of the analysis require huge meshes to discretize the geometry into finite elements. Such meshes are processed slowly in a single modern computer due to the limits on memory and processing units. The problem is tackled by dividing the mesh into several sub-meshes with an algorithm similar to the mentioned in [2], this procedure is known as domain segmentation and it is considered a complex problem by itself, because the segmentation requires to maintain a balanced number of nodes for each sub-domain, while minimizing the number of edges in the boundaries of such domains like in [3]. This is made in order to decrease the intercommunication of process when solving FEM problems in a distributed memory scheme. In this work we parallelize the spectral bisection algorithm proposed in [1]. The output of this algorithm could be used for two purposes, *(1)* to segment the domain and *(2)* to enumerate the nodes of the mesh in order to reduce the fill-in of the LU decomposition, this enumeration is also know as labelling.

Keywords: Parallel computing · Domain segmentation · Labelling · FEM · Spectral bisection

1 Introduction

The use of meshes to perform simulations is a remarkable technique to analyze and optimize particular products such as cars, bikes, doors, etc. FEM meshes are the discretization of an object and many companies analyze this object to reduce the material used, or to design another geometry that produces a best durability, that supports more weight, or any other optimization. Most of the computer aided engineering packages (CAE) perform analysis and optimization using huge meshes and a serial implementation of the FEM solver, it takes a long time to solve the problem. An adequate segmentation of the mesh can accelerate the computing time.

© Springer International Publishing Switzerland 2016
I. Gitler and J. Klapp (Eds.): ISUM 2015, CCIS 595, pp. 94–103, 2016.
DOI: 10.1007/978-3-319-32243-8_6

The parallel scheme exploits the sparse nature of the matrix by using efficient data structures and a shared memory scheme with OpenMP. We test our parallel implementation using three triangular meshes of a circle in order to obtain statistics about the performance, such as the speed-up and the efficiency.

2   Spectral Bisection Algorithm

The spectral bisection is an heuristic to solve the problem of partitioning a mesh, this partition is optimal when the number of edges which connect separated groups is minimal, and the number of nodes in each group is the same. The implementation of this algorithm requires finding the smallest non-trivial eigenvector of the *Laplacian* matrix associated to the mesh created. This matrix has important features, is sparse, symmetric and positive definite and its size is the same that the number of nodes in the mesh.

All meshes can be represented as graphs using a sparse matrix. For this point of view the graph should be partitioned into sub-graphs which will be processed by distinct *cores* in the CPU, and each one of the sub-graphs must be of similar size (similar number of nodes) in order to maintain a good load balance. Furthermore the number of edges connecting the sub-graphs have to be minimized to decrease the communication between the *cores*.

To execute the algorithm, the information required is the connectivity matrix of the mesh as non directed graph G given by (1), where V is the set of vertices, v_i and E is the set of edges denoted by (v_i, v_j) in G. The algorithm creates disjoint sub-graphs P_i defined by (2), and the sub-graphs satisfy the restriction of maximizing the load balance and minimizing the connectivity between groups.

$$G = (V, E) \tag{1}$$

$$\begin{cases} P_i = (V_i, E_i) \\ V = \cup_i V_i \qquad V_i \cap V_j = \emptyset \quad if \quad i = j \end{cases} \tag{2}$$

To optimize the load balance the variance of the number of vertices contained in the partitions must be minimized, this value is given by (3), where $|V_i|$ is the number of vertices in P_i and $\bar{V}$ is the average number of vertices in the sub-graphs. To optimize the connectivity between sub-groups the number of edges that were cut by the partition must be minimized using (4).

$$min \ Var = \sum_i (|V_i| - \bar{V})^2 \tag{3}$$

$$min \ \sum_{i,j} |C_{i,j}| \quad where \quad C_{i,j} = \{(v, w) \mid v \epsilon V_i, w \epsilon V_j\}. \tag{4}$$

3   Problem Solution

First, the *Laplacian* matrix is created using the mesh connectivity. This matrix is given by $L(G) = l_{i,j}$, where each element is defined by (5).

$$L(G) = \begin{cases} -1, & if \quad (v_i, v_j) \; \epsilon \; E. \\ deg(v_i), & if \quad i = j. \\ 0, & other \; cases. \end{cases} \tag{5}$$

Where $deg(v_i)$ is the number of incident edges to vertex v_i. The smallest eigenvalue of the *Laplacian* matrix is 0 and has associated an eigenvector which contains only ones; furthermore, if G is connected, the second smallest eigenvalue is positive and its eigenvector contains important directional information about the graph. The last eigenvector mentioned is called the *Fiedler* vector and its components are weights corresponding to the vertices of the graph G. Sorting elements of *Fiedler* vector, the vertices of the graph are sorted too, keeping near vertices together.

The domain segmentation obtained is a good approximation to the optimal solution.

To solve the problem the inverse power with deflation algorithm is applied to the *Laplacian* matrix to find the *Fiedler* vector and obtain the sub-domains of graph G. Using the inverse power algorithm, first eigenvalue and its eigenvector do not have to be calculated because they are known, and the deflation of the *Laplacian* matrix to find the second smallest eigenvalue and eigenvector, neither needs to be calculated because first smallest eigenvalue is $\lambda = 0$, so then the deflated *Laplacian* matrix is the same as before. Equation (6) shows how the deflated matrix is calculated.

$$\tilde{A} = A - \lambda x y^t \tag{6}$$

Where:

1 $\tilde{A}$: Is the deflated matrix.
2 A: Is the original matrix.
3 $\lambda x y^t$: Is the deflation applied to the matrix.

4   Parallelization

Before finding the *Fiedler* vector, an algorithm is used to relabel the vertices in order to obtain a *Laplacian* matrix in which most of its elements are located near its diagonal. By relabelling the vertices, an efficient sparse matrix factorization is achieved in order to calculate the *Fiedler* vector. For an efficient memory usage the sparse matrix is stored in a structure and the second minimum eigenvector is found using the inverse power with deflation algorithm parallelized with *OpenMP* using a shared memory scheme [5]. Sub-domains are created after finding and sorting the *Fiedler* vector.

With this parallelized algorithm an output file is created which contains information about the domain segmentation. The file format used is: `Vertex-Group-Xcoordinate-Ycoordinate`, where:

```
Vertex:         Is the number of vertices.
Group:          Is the number of group of the vertex.
Xcoordinate:    Is the position X of the vertex.
Ycoordinate:    Is the position Y of the vertex.
```

5   Numerical Results

The inverse power algorithm requires a linear system solver to find the smaller eigenvalues. For this parallelized algorithm three different solvers were used, two direct and one iterative. The idea of use these solvers is to compare which is the faster to solve the problem, and analyze if the direct and iterative solvers obtain similar results in the sub-domains.

Table 1 shows the information about the execution time using LU decomposition to find the *Fiedler* vector, with meshes that have 5000, 35000 and 99999 vertices.

The information contained in Table 1 is the execution time using a different number of *cores* and creating just two groups. The execution time shown in Table 1 corresponds to the factorization because this is the parallelized function that spends most time in the algorithm. The results displays statistics about the domain segmentation performed, from the point of view of the execution time the results were not good, because the efficiency decreases with respect to the number of *cores*.

In Table 2 the results of *Cholesky* factorization are shown, and comparing the direct methods used, it is observed that *Cholesky* factorization is the best if we consider the execution time in a serial way, but using parallel computing, LU decomposition is the best.

The results of the direct solvers are shown in Fig. 1, that correspond to the mesh with 35,000 nodes. In this figure is plotted the number of *cores vs execution time* for the two direct methods used.

In Figs. 2 and 3 some results of the algorithm using direct solvers are shown, (Using any direct solver the domain segmentation is the same). The results are good in all meshes, the domain segmentation obtained is well defined using any number of sub-domains. To compare the results obtained using direct solvers with results obtained using an iterative solver, in Table 3 the information about the execution time with iterative solver is shown. In this case the iterative solver used is the Conjugate Gradient, and the results are given with 1×10^{-16} precision. Analyzing results from Table 3, it can be observed that the iterative solver uses less time than direct solvers, but produces bad quality results, producing unconnected elements within a sub-group, even with more precision were not achieved best results for some meshes.

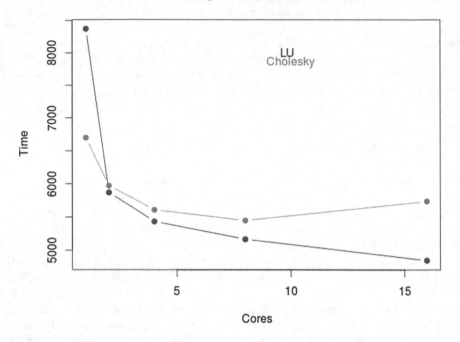

Fig. 1. Execution time for *LU* and *Cholesky* methods.

Table 1. Results with *LU* decomposition

5000 vertices				35000 vertices			99999 vertices		
Cores	Time	Speed-up	Efficiency	Time	Speed-up	Efficiency	Time	Speed-up	Efficiency
1	19.18	1.0000	1.0000	8371.69	1.0000	1.0000	133988.66	1.0000	1.0000
2	14.66	1.3083	0.6541	5868.49	1.4265	0.7132	102187.48	1.3112	0.6556
4	12.22	1.5695	0.3923	5434.25	1.5405	0.3851	92117.220	1.4545	0.3636
8	11.31	1.6958	0.2119	5166.27	1.6204	0.2025	86442.055	1.5490	0.1936
16	11.19	1.7140	0.1071	4844.61	1.7280	0.1080	84076.217	1.5936	0.0996

Table 2. Results with *Cholesky factorization*

5000 vertices				35000 vertices			99999 vertices		
Cores	Time	Speed-up	Efficiency	Time	Speed-up	Efficiency	Time	Speed-up	Efficiency
1	19.18	1.0000	1.0000	8371.69	1.0000	1.0000	133988.66	1.0000	1.0000
2	14.66	1.3083	0.6541	5868.49	1.4265	0.7132	102187.48	1.3112	0.6556
4	12.22	1.5695	0.3923	5434.25	1.5405	0.3851	92117.220	1.4545	0.3636
8	11.31	1.6958	0.2119	5166.27	1.6204	0.2025	86442.055	1.5490	0.1936
16	11.19	1.7140	0.1071	4844.61	1.7280	0.1080	84076.217	1.5936	0.0996

Cholesky, 5000 vertices, 8 groups

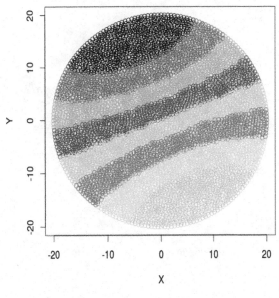

(a) Cholesky, 5000 vertices, 8 groups

Cholesky, 35000 vertices, 8 groups

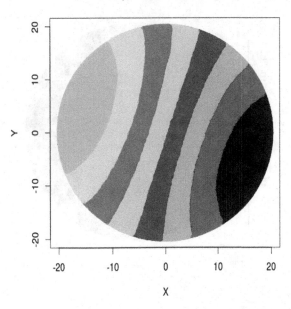

(b) Cholesky, 35000 vertices, 8 groups

Fig. 2. Results obtained using Cholesky direct solver.

LU, 5000 vertices, 16 groups

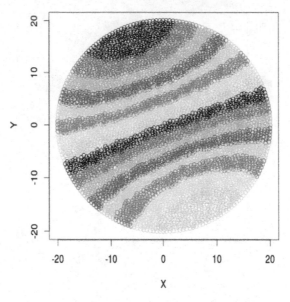

(a) LU, 5000 vertices, 16 groups

LU, 35000 vertices, 2 groups

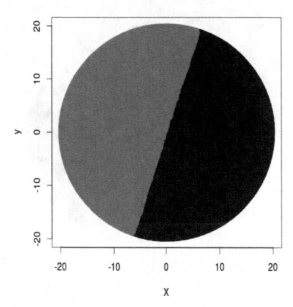

(b) LU, 35000 vertices, 2 groups

Fig. 3. Results obtained using LU direct solver.

Conjugate Gradient, 5000 vertices, 4 groups

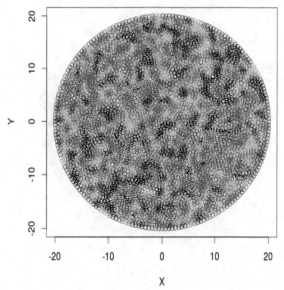

(a) Conjugate Gradient, 5000 vertices, 4 groups, precision 1×10^{-16}

Conjugate Gradient, 5000 vertices, 8 groups

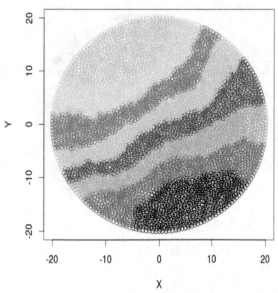

(b) Conjugate Gradient, 5000 vertices, 8 groups, precision 1×10^{-16}

Fig. 4. Results obtained using Conjugate gradient iterative solver.

Conjugate Gradient, 35000 vertices, 16 groups

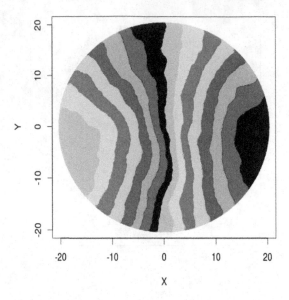

(a) Conjugate Gradient, 35000 vertices, 16 groups, precision 1×10^{-16}

Conjugate Gradient, 99999 vertices, 4 groups

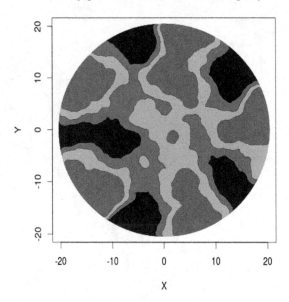

(b) Conjugate Gradient, 99999 vertices, 4 groups, precision 1×10^{-16}

Fig. 5. Results obtained using Conjugate gradient iterative solver.

Table 3. Results with *Conjugate Gradient*

5000 vertices				35000 vertices			99999 vertices		
Cores	Time	Speed-up	Efficiency	Time	Speed-up	Efficiency	Time	Speed-up	Efficiency
1	1.00	1.0000	1.0000	57.58	1.0000	1.0000	741.24	1.0000	1.0000
2	0.63	1.5873	0.7963	30.98	1.8586	0.9293	339.77	2.1815	1.0907
4	0.41	2.4390	0.6097	16.26	3.5412	0.8853	179.48	4.1299	1.0324
8	0.57	1.7504	0.2192	17.22	3.3437	0.4179	146.97	5.0434	0.6304
16	0.93	1.0752	0.0672	13.68	4.2090	0.2630	153.11	4.8412	0.3025

Finally, in Figs. 4 and 5 are shown some results obtained with the iterative solver and in some cases the domain segmentation is not well defined as is observed in the last graph. An iterative solver can be used for domain segmentation, in that case it must be checked if the domain segmentation is acceptable. We prefer the implementation with direct solvers.

6   Conclusions

The parallelization of the spectral bisection algorithm uses a shared memory scheme implemented with OpenMP.

The inverse power iteration requires a linear system solver to find the smaller eigenvalues; we use two kinds of linear system solvers, (*1*) direct solver (*Cholesky* and *LU* decomposition) and (*2*) iterative solver (*Conjugate Gradient*), these methods were compared and the results are qualitatively acceptable and are obtained in a relatively short time, but the program scalability can be improved.

To enhance the results, we are going to research how to compute faster the *Fiedler* vector using only direct solvers.

This algorithm will be used to segment meshes suitable to solve FEM problems or any other technique which requires similar discretizations.

References

1. Barnard, S.T., Simon, H.D.: A fast multilevel implementation of recursive spectral bisection for partitioning unstructured problems. Concurrency pract. experience **6**(2), 101–117 (1994). Ames Research Center
2. Kincho, H.L.: Graph Partitioning Algorithms. Stanford (2005)
3. Van Driessche, R., Roose, D.: An improved spectral bisection algorithm and its application to dynamic load balance. Parallel Computing **21**(1), 29–48 (1995). Elsevier B.V
4. Hsien, S., Paulino, G.H., Abel, J.F.: Recursive spectral algorithms for automatic domain partitioning in parallel finite element analysis. Comput. Methods Appl. Mech. Eng. **121**(1–4), 137–162 (1995). Elsevier B.V.
5. Regusa, J.C.: Application of multi thread computing and domain decomposition to the 3-D neutronics FEM code cronos. In: International Conference of Supercomputing in Nuclear Applications (2003)

Parallelized 3D Inverse Kinematics with Multiple Objectives

Manuel Guillermo López Buenfil$^{(\boxtimes)}$, Víctor E. Cardoso, and Salvador Botello

Centro de Investigación en Matemáticas A.C. (CIMAT), Jalisco S/N,
36240 Valenciana, Guanajuato, Mexico
{manuel.lopez,victorc,botello}@cimat.mx

Abstract. A strategy of parallel computing (HPC) is proposed to solve the problem of inverse kinematics in 3D with multiple objectives using the damped least squares method, also known as the Levenberg-Marquardt method.

The program solves the problem of moving one or more end-effectors of a robot to a desired target position by manipulating its joints, which are the degrees of freedom. The HPC strategy consists in parallelizing the motion calculations required to accomplish the different objectives.

Tests were conducted with a simulation of a ping-pong game using multiple balls. Robots are placed at each end of a table, the movement of the balls is predicted integrating its position numerically, and the robots' end-effectors are moved to hit the balls. The amount of end-effectors correspond to the number of balls, with priorities assigned to each of them.

Keywords: Inverse kinematics · Damped least squares method · Levenberg-Marquardt · HPC

1 Introduction

A robot is comprised of a set of rigid segments linked together by joints, which can be revolute (rotational) or prismatic (translational). We only consider the ending points on the ending segments as end-effectors. These end-effectors can be moved to their corresponding target positions. The problem of inverse kinematics (IK) consists in determining the joints configuration required to realize such an operation, as can be seen in Fig. 1.

There are several techniques to solve the IK problem. In this paper, we cover differential kinematics, which finds the relationship between the velocities, linear and/or angular, of the joints and end-effectors. We are going to focus on the case of redundant mechanisms, where the number of joints is bigger than the minimum needed to reach the target positions, which means that there are multiple solutions for the IK problem. We are interested in finding good solutions even when the objectives are out of reach of the end-effectors, in which case the end-effector should be moved as close as possible to its target position. We use the Levenberg-Marquardt method to solve a damped version of the linear system arising from differential kinematics.

© Springer International Publishing Switzerland 2016
I. Gitler and J. Klapp (Eds.): ISUM 2015, CCIS 595, pp. 104–115, 2016.
DOI: 10.1007/978-3-319-32243-8_7

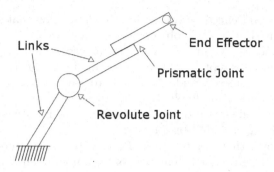

Fig. 1. Components of a robot

A parallelized implementation is proposed, which allows us to calculate the movement of each end-effector in separate threads, to later combine them in a single final motion. To test our implementation, a simulation of a ping pong game is used, in which a robot must hit multiple balls by handling an equal number of end-effectors.

2   Related Works

Previous proposals of parallelized inverse kinematics are focused on the case of a single objective. For example, [1,2] consider a robot with n degrees of freedom. The Jacobian matrix J is first calculated in every thread, and then its SVD decomposition is approximated in parallel using $n/2$ processors, taking as starting point the approximation for the previous time step. Finally, this decomposition is used to solve Eq. 1. This technique differs in that it is optimized to solve for a single objective, while the proposed method is designed for m objectives with m processors, which means that each objective is calculated in parallel, and then combined.

Another technique is included in [3], which represents a kinematic chain using a continuous "backbone curve", which represents a robot's macroscopic geometric features. This curve is optimized using calculus of variations (minimizing bending, twisting, rolling and extension/contraction of the curve), and then it is adapted to the original robot using a "fitting procedure", which maps the backbone curve to joint configurations. Optimizing the backbone curve is a $O(1)$ operation, while the fitting procedure is $O(n)$, but can be parallelized to be $O(1)$ using n processors. However, this method also parallelizes over the degrees of freedom, and not the objectives.

Another alternative is presented in [4], where each degree of freedom is represented as an agent. A supervisor computes the goal matrix for each agent, and then each agent computes a "satisfaction coefficient" with the goal matrix. These coefficients are collected by the supervisor, and the agent with the highest satisfaction is then asked to move. This means that the degree of freedom which can best move the end effector towards its target position makes a movement. Again, this is focused on a single objective.

Another approach is used in [5,6], which use a genetic algorithm in the following way: An individual is represented by the configuration of the joints. On each step, u individuals are chosen, and m threads are used to generate $\frac{m}{u}$ estimated Jacobian matrices for each individual (using added white-noise). The fitness is evaluated as a weighted sum of the space error and orientation error for the end effector after applying each Jacobian matrix.

In [7], it is shown that, for the case of parallel manipulators, it is possible to solve the problem of inverse kinematics for each manipulator in parallel. Furthermore, the problem of inverse dynamics can almost completely be solved in parallel.

Finally, in the case when there is a closed-form solution for the inverse kinematics problem, and the desired trajectory for each joint is known, [8] has proposed a method which calculates the new configuration for each joint by using an approximation of the configuration of the other joints, which allows updating all of them in parallel. In our case, this information is not known, and we do not have a closed-form solution.

3   Inverse Kinematics

A robot is composed of links and joints, where the joints represent the degrees of freedom of the robot. Each of these links can be represented as a segment between two points P_1 (located at the beginning of the link) and P_2 (the end of the link). V is determined as the unitary vector in direction $P_2 - P_1$, which indicates the link's orientation.

First, the Jacobian matrix J is calculated, which consists of 6 rows representing the position and orientation of an end-effector, and n columns indicating the relationship between the joint velocities and the end-effector linear and angular velocities. Given the target position F_p and orientation F_w of the end-effector, along with its current position E_p and orientation E_w, the Jacobian matrix is constructed as follows:

1. For the prismatic joints (which allow translation), the corresponding column is $[V, \mathbf{0}]^T$.
2. For the rotational joints, the corresponding column is $[V \times (E_p - P_2), V]^T$.
3. If a joint is not in the end-effector's kinematic chain, then its corresponding column is zero.

Having the matrix J, the vector $F = [E_p - F_p, d_w(F_w, E_w)]$ is calculated, which represents the end-effector's desired change, where the function $d_w(F_w, E_w)$ calculates the angle difference along the shortest trajectory from E_w to F_w. This results in the following system of equations:

$$J\dot{q} = F \qquad (1)$$

where $\dot{q}$ is a $n \times 1$ vector representing the change we must apply to the joints. This system in general is not square, and it may not have a unique solution. In this paper, we are going to focus on the case of redundant robots, which have a big number of degrees of freedom, and results in a potentially infinite number of solutions for the previous equation. In particular, this means that $n > 6$, which means that there are more degrees of freedom than needed. It could be solved using the pseudo-inverse of J, also known as the *Moore-Penrose* pseudo-inverse: $J^T(JJ^T)^{-1}$, which finds the solution with minimum magnitude $||\dot{q}||^2$. In case the system has no solution, this method obtains the vector which minimizes $||J\dot{q} - F||^2$. However, the *Moore-Penrose* pseudo-inverse has stability problems in close vicinity of singularities, which could correspond to motion directions which are not reachable. To solve this, the method *Damped least squares*, also known as *Levenberg Marquardt*, is used. Instead of obtaining the value of $\dot{q}$ with minimum norm, we now try to minimize the following:

$$||J\dot{q} - F||^2 + k||\dot{q}||^2 \tag{2}$$

where k is a regularization constant. The solution is obtained as follows:

$$\dot{q} = (J^T J + kI)^{-1} J^T F \tag{3}$$

which is equivalent to:

$$\dot{q} = J^T (JJ^T + kI)^{-1} F. \tag{4}$$

The advantage is that now the matrix to invert has size 6×6 instead of $n \times n$. This will be our pseudo-inverse:

$$J^\dagger = J^T (JJ^T + kI)^{-1}. \tag{5}$$

The solution to the problem is:

$$\dot{q} = J^\dagger F. \tag{6}$$

Additionally, the pseudo-inverse has the property that $(I - J^\dagger J)$ performs a projection to the null space of J. This means that we can set the movement to:

$$\dot{q} = \dot{q}_1 + (I - J^\dagger J)\dot{q}_2 \tag{7}$$

where $\dot{q}_1$ is a primary objective and $\dot{q}_2$ is a secondary objective, which means that the movement performed to fulfill $\dot{q}_2$ does not interfere with the primary objective movement performed by $\dot{q}_1$. The matrix $(I - J^\dagger J)$ represents the redundancy, reserving the degrees of freedom that we can use for other objectives. We can continue to aggregate objectives recursively, if we set $\dot{q}_1$ or $\dot{q}_2$ to be itself the combination of another primary and secondary objective. In this case, this can be applied to create a robot with several arms, with each arm having a different priority. The result is that the secondary objectives with less priority try to move to their target positions only after the arms with higher priority, which means that sometimes the secondary objectives cannot be satisfied.

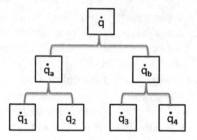

Fig. 2. Motion hierarchy

4   Parallelization Scheme

We are going to focus our attention on Eq. 7. As an example, suppose our resulting motion $\dot{q}$ is composed of two other motions, $\dot{q}_a$ and $\dot{q}_b$, with $\dot{q}_a$ having bigger priority. The motion $\dot{q}_a$ is composed of $\dot{q}_1$ and $\dot{q}_2$ (with $\dot{q}_1$ having bigger priority), and the motion $\dot{q}_b$ is composed of $\dot{q}_3$ and $\dot{q}_4$ (with $\dot{q}_3$ having bigger priority). This is illustrated in Fig. 2.

$\dot{q}_a$ has a bigger priorities than $\dot{q}_b$, which implies that both $\dot{q}_1$ and $\dot{q}_2$ have bigger priority than $\dot{q}_3$ and $\dot{q}_4$. This means that, in this case, the priorities of the movements $\dot{q}_i, i = 1 \ldots 4$ coincide with their indices. In general, the resulting movement will give the leaves the ordering of an in-order traversal, which means that any tree in which the leaves are visited in the same order will have equivalent priorities. An equivalent tree is shown in Fig. 3.

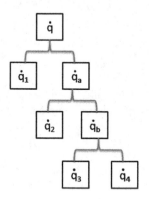

Fig. 3. Equivalent motion hierarchy

The advantage of the first arrangement is that every branch of this hierarchy can be computed in parallel. By maximizing the number of nodes at the same level, we further parallelize this calculation. The disadvantage is that it needs to calculate the matrix which performs a projection to the null space of both children of the left node (e.g. in Fig. 2, the node $\dot{q}_a$ needs the matrix which performs a projection to the null space of $\dot{q}_1$ and $\dot{q}_2$, which is calculated as $(I - J_1^\dagger J_1)(I - J_2^\dagger J_2)$). This requires an additional matrix product, which is a heavy operation and affects the usefulness of the tree shown in Fig. 2. The advantage of the tree shown in Fig. 3 is that it does not need to calculate any extra projection matrices, which means that the workload for each internal node is minimized. Its disadvantage is that, after processing the leaves, the rest of the tree is practically executed serially. However, the proportion of work to be executed by the internal nodes is very small compared to the leaves (as shown in the next paragraph), which means that this tree is still very efficient.

We will now examine the complexity of the merging operation described in Eq. 7. In order to perform this operation, we need to store the matrix $(I - J^\dagger J)$ to perform the product $(I - J^\dagger J)\dot{q}_2$, which has a quadratic complexity on the number of rows of $\dot{q}_2$ (which in this case is 6), and then perform an addition with $\dot{q}_2$, which has linear complexity on the number of rows of $\dot{q}_2$. By comparison, finding the solutions $\dot{q} = J^\dagger F$ has a cubic complexity, which means that the work performed at every leaf is heavier than the merging operation. It is also possible to calculate the matrix $(I - J^\dagger J)$ in the leaf nodes, further reducing the workload in the internal nodes. This is convenient because the leaves can all be executed simultaneously, but the internal nodes need to wait for their descendants to finish, which means that the program becomes increasingly less parallelized as we move up the tree. However, after the leaves have finished, the remaining amount of work to do is relatively small, which alleviates this problem.

5   Numerical Tests

Two robots are created, along with a table and a set of n balls, represented as particles. Each robot is equipped with n rackets, each assigned to one ball.

To obtain the desired position (F_p, F_w) of each end-effector, the trajectory of its corresponding ball is predicted for a certain amount of steps in the future, and in particular, the point in which it intersects a plane that separates the table from the robot.

Every time the ball collides with an obstacle, a prediction of its movement is performed, and if this movement intersects the "action plane" of a robot (which is defined as the vertical plane over the table border at the robot's side), then the intersection point is set as the target for the robot's end-effector. If this point is very distant from the robot (e.g. too high above the robot), then it is ignored, and the target position is reset to the center of the action plane.

To make the robots' job easier, two guiding walls were added at the sides of the table, to prevent the ball from leaving through the sides. This can be seen in Fig. 4. Figure 5 shows two robots with two end-effectors playing with two balls, which shows the way in which more objectives and end-effectors can be added.

If a robot misses the ball and it falls from the table, then the ball is reset to the center of the table, and its velocity is randomly assigned to move towards one of the robots.

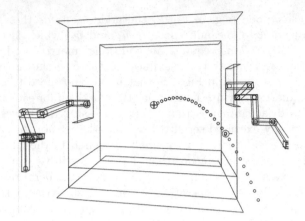

Fig. 4. Prediction of the ball movement. The intersection with the action plane corresponding to the right robot is drawn.

5.1   Particle System

The balls are implemented as particles. Each particle is represented with a state which is composed of position and velocity:

$$p = \begin{bmatrix} \mathbf{x} \\ \mathbf{v} \end{bmatrix} = \begin{bmatrix} x \\ y \\ z \\ v_x \\ v_y \\ v_z \end{bmatrix} = \begin{bmatrix} x \\ y \\ z \\ x' \\ y' \\ z' \end{bmatrix}. \tag{8}$$

Its derivative consists of velocity and acceleration, respectively:

$$p' = \begin{bmatrix} \mathbf{x'} \\ \mathbf{v'} \end{bmatrix} = \begin{bmatrix} \mathbf{v} \\ \mathbf{a} \end{bmatrix} = \begin{bmatrix} \mathbf{v} \\ \mathbf{f}/m \end{bmatrix} = \begin{bmatrix} x' \\ y' \\ z' \\ f_x/m \\ f_y/m \\ f_z/m \end{bmatrix} \tag{9}$$

where $\mathbf{f}$ is the force applied to the object (gravity), and m is its mass. This state can be integrated numerically using Runge-Kutta.

The applied force is different from the gravity when the particle collides with a wall (such as the table or one of the rackets). We consider a simple impulse response force, in which the component of the velocity in the direction normal to the collision surface is reflected instantly. In cases like this, when we want to apply a velocity $\mathbf{v}_2$ to the particle, we apply the following force:

$$\mathbf{f} = m(\mathbf{v}_2 - \mathbf{v}_1)/h. \tag{10}$$

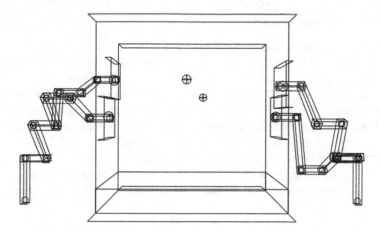

Fig. 5. Robots with 2 end-effectors trying to hit 2 balls. Additional end-effectors and balls are added in a similar fashion.

A wall is defined as a rectangular cuboid of size $[2w, d, 2h]$. Starting with a wall located in the origin which spans the space from $[-w, -d, -h]$ to $[w, 0, h]$, we apply a rotation R and a translation c, such that a point x on the wall becomes $x' = c + Rx$. We will only consider collisions with the side of the wall which originally pointed upwards. In order to check if a particle collides with a wall, we perform the opposite transformation: $x = R^{-1}(x' - c) = R^T(x' - c)$, which uses the fact that R is a rotation matrix to obtain $R^T = R^{-1}$. Once the particle has been "projected" to the original wall's frame of reference, it is simple to check if it is in collision (it suffices to check if its coordinates are in the original interval spanned by the wall). If so, it is reflected, which involves changing the direction of the velocity component which is normal to the plane, and also adjusting its position to prevent it from entering the wall. This position adjustment can be done by taking the absolute value of the particle's y coordinate, due to the horizontal orientation of the wall. This is illustrated in Fig. 6.

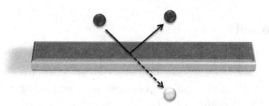

Fig. 6. In a collision, the velocity component normal to the plane is reflected. To ensure that the particle position is outside of the wall, and because we are only interested in collisions with its upper side, it suffices to take the absolute value of the y coordinate, since in this frame of reference the wall spans the vertical interval $[-d, 0]$ which means that any position with a positive y coordinate is outside the wall.

5.2   Parallelization Results

A shared memory scheme was implemented in C++ with OpenMP. The results
shown were obtained running on a server with processors Intel Xeon E5-2620 v2
at 2.1 GHz (2 sockets, 6 cores per socket of a total of 12 cores, and 2 threads
per core for a total of 24 threads). Three experiments were performed: Fig. 7
shows the results obtained with 16 objectives in which the speed-up increases
until 8 threads, at which point it starts to decrease. At this point, the cost of
thread management exceeds the benefits of having more threads. Figure 8 shows
the results with 48 objectives, in which the speed-up is maximum when using
16 threads. Finally, Fig. 9 shows the results using 240 objectives, in which the
speed-up only starts to decrease at the very end, when we reach 24 threads.

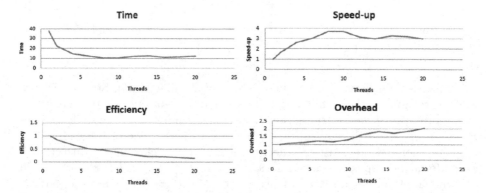

Fig. 7. Results with 16 objectives. An optimum speed-up is achieved close to 8 threads.
This can be interpreted as every thread handling exactly 2 objectives. Adding more
threads increases the overhead without speed improvements, since some threads will
handle more objectives than others. When we have 16 threads, there is again a small
improvement in speed-up and overhead, but by this point the cost of thread management has become too high.

5.3   Related Results

In order to place the performance of the algorithms presented in this paper in
a broader context, we present an analysis of the work presented in [1]. It is
parallelized in the SVD decomposition of the Jacobian matrix, and the solution
calculated using that decomposition. Two experiments are performed: the first
one solves for one objective, which is combined with a second known objective. It
presents a speed-up of 3.61 with 4 threads (ignoring the time for calculating the
Jacobian, which is performed in each thread separately, and the time to transfer
data between threads). The second experiment solves for 2 objectives. It has a
speed-up of 3.17 with 4 threads (ignoring the same steps).

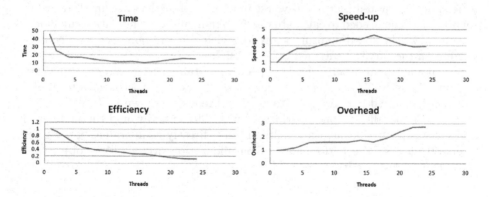

Fig. 8. Results with 48 objectives. The maximum speed-up is obtained with 16 threads. Adding more threads results in a bigger overhead, due to thread management.

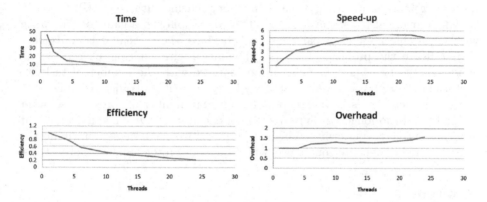

Fig. 9. Results with 240 objectives. The speed-up almost always increases, and only starts to decrease at the very end. Having more objectives, the maximum speed-up obtained is also higher, and a smaller overhead is obtained, which increases more slowly.

Table 1. Speed-up with 4 threads, using processors Intel Xeon E5-2620 v2 at 2.1 GHz

Objectives	16	48	72	96	240
Speed-up	2.667007	2.730069	3.114098	3.126279	3.166282

Table 2. Speed-up with 4 threads, using processors Intel Xeon E5502 at 1.87 GHz

Objectives	16	48	72	96	240
Speed-up	2.824007	3.007781	3.085249	3.099509	3.144625

It should be noted that in our work, numerous objectives are handled. Additionally, the time needed to calculate the Jacobian, and transfer data, is included. Table 1 shows the speed-up using 4 threads, with different numbers of objectives, running on the server mentioned in Sect. 5.2.

As an additional experiment, the speed-up obtained on a server with processors Intel Xeon E5502 at 1.87 GHz (2 sockets, 2 cores per socket for a total of 4 cores, and 1 thread per core for a total of 4 threads) is shown in Table 2.

Since the parallelization is performed in a different way, and the number of objectives is not the same, the results are not directly comparable, but it gives a general idea for the performance of parallelization over multiple objectives, which can represent advantages in some problems.

6   Conclusions

In this work the problem of inverse kinematics is efficiently solved using Levenberg-Marquardt, using a shared memory scheme with OpenMP.

The numerical tests, which include two robots playing a game of ping-pong with a variable number of balls and rackets, have shown that it is convenient to parallelize the problem of inverse kinematics with multiple objectives. As expected, the benefits of parallelization increase with the number of tasks to perform, and display a better scalability when the number of objectives increases. A consequence of this is that there is an optimal number of cores to use, after which there is no longer an improvement in execution time. This indicates that it is important to perform a previous performance analysis to determine the optimal number of processors to use, which depends on the number of objectives.

References

1. Maciejewski, A.A., Reagin, J.M.: A parallel algorithm and architecture for the control of kinematically redundant manipulators. IEEE Trans. Robot. Autom. **10**, 405–414 (1992)
2. Braun, T.D., Maciejewski, A.A., Siegel, H.J.: A parallel algorithm for singular value decomposition as applied to failure tolerant manipulators. In: IPPS/SPDP, pp. 343–349. IEEE Computer Society (1999)
3. Chirikjian, G.S., Burdick, J.W.: Kinematically optimal hyper-redundant manipulator configurations. IEEE Trans. Robot. Autom. **11**(6), 794–806 (1995)
4. Regnier, S., Duhaut, D.: Parallel resolution of the inverse kinematics. In: 1994 IEEE International Conference on Systems, Man, and Cybernetics, 1994. Humans, Information and Technology, vol. 1, pp. 599–604, October 1994
5. Farzan, S., DeSouza, G.N.: From D-H to inverse kinematics: a fast numerical solution for general robotic manipulators using parallel processing. In: 2013 IEEE/RSJ International Conference on Intelligent Robots and Systems (IROS), pp. 2507–2513, November 2013
6. Farzan, S., DeSouza, G.N.: A parallel evolutionary solution for the inverse kinematics of generic robotic manipulators. In: 2014 IEEE Congress on Evolutionary Computation (CEC), pp. 358–365, July 2014

7. Gosselin, C.M.: Parallel computational algorithms for the kinematics and dynamics of planar and spatial parallel manipulators. J. Dyn. Syst. Meas. Control **118**, 22–28 (1996)
8. Zhang, H., Paul, R.P.: A parallel inverse kinematics solution for robot manipulators based on multiprocessing, linear extrapolation. IEEE Trans. Robot. Autom. **7**(5), 660–669 (1991)

Study of Particle Swarm Optimization Algorithms Using Message Passing Interface and Graphical Processing Units Employing a High Performance Computing Cluster

Manuel-H. Santana-Castolo, J. Alejandro Morales, Sulema Torres-Ramos, and Alma Y. Alanis[✉]

Universidad de Guadalajara, CUCEI, Apartado Postal 51-71, Col. Las Aguilas, C.P., 45080 Zapopan, Jalisco, Mexico
almayalanis@gmail.com

Abstract. Particle Swarm Optimization (PSO) is a heuristic technique that have been used to solve problems where many events occur simultaneously and small pieces of the problem can collaborate to reach a solution. Among its advantages are fast convergence, large exploration coverage, and adequate global optimization; however to address the premature convergence problem, modifications to the basic model have been developed such as Aging Leader and Challengers (ALC) PSO and Bio-inspired Aging (BAM) PSO. Being these algorithms parallel in nature, some authors have attempted different approaches to apply PSO using MPI and GPU. Nevertheless ALC-PSO and BAM-PSO have not been implemented in parallel. For this study, we develop PSO, ALC-PSO and BAM-PSO, through MPI and GPU using the High Performance Computing Cluster (HPCC) Agave. The results suggest that ALC-PSO and BAM-PSO reduce the premature convergence, improving global precision, whilst BAM-PSO achieves better optimal at the expense of significantly increasing the algorithm computational complexity.

Keywords: ALC-PSO · BAM-PSO · CUDA · GPUs · HPCC · MPI · Parallel algorithms · Particle swarm optimization · PSO

1 Introduction

Particle Swarm Optimization (PSO) has been used to solve many problems as [1–3]. Among its advantages are rapid convergence speed, high capacity for exploration in difficult problems, and satisfactory global search ability. Many implementations and modifications have been made to the main algorithm, as an Aging Leader and Challengers model (ALC-PSO) [4], and Bio-inspired Aging Model (BAM-PSO) [5]. The main disadvantage of PSO is that it has been addressed from a serial perspective despite of its parallel nature, resulting in the use of many computational resources for more complex problems.

© Springer International Publishing Switzerland 2016
I. Gitler and J. Klapp (Eds.): ISUM 2015, CCIS 595, pp. 116–131, 2016.
DOI: 10.1007/978-3-319-32243-8_8

Multiple approaches in parallel implementation, using Message Passing Interface (MPI), have been done by [6–10]. Using Compute Unified Device Architecture (CUDA), and it's implementation on graphical processing units (GPU), have been carried out by [11–14].

These implementations have in common that they can address problems of a wide range of dimensions, from as low as 2, up till 200 [6,11–13]. It is well known that as the dimensionality increases, the performance declines due to the use of more computational resources to solve the problem. In fact, it is common to find problems with high dimensionality which are addressed with High Performance Computing Cluster (HPCC) systems using tens, hundreds or even thousands of processors. In order to reduce the computational time in the solution of these problems, we make a HPCC implementation of the PSO algorithm and two variants (ALC-PSO and BAM-PSO). Our implementation are programmed with MPI and CUDA, varying the amount of particles, number of iterations, and the amount of cores in the case of MPI. All the implementations were tested with known functions of benchmark which are Griewank, Sphere, Rastrigin and Rosenbrock, tests are performed and the results are presented, to make a comparative study between implementations. It is important to note that the implementation of the ALC-PSO and BAM-PSO algorithms have not been previously done in parallel.

2   Particle Swarm Optimization

PSO is a stochastic optimization technique, originally proposed and developed by Kennedy and Eberhart in 1995 [15]. This technique takes inspiration in the behavior and the collective intelligence of flocks of birds or fish shoals, where all the group is called swarm and each individual element is named particle, having speed and position within the search space.

In PSO a population of particles is initialized with random positions and velocity $V = 0$. Each particle moves through a n-dimensional search space based in the best position found by the swarm ($gBest$), and its own historical best position ($pBest$). Each particle is a possible solution of the optimization problem in each t iteration, which eventually converges to the best point found by the swarm.

The velocity and position update rules of the PSO are:

$$v_{ij}(t+1) = w \cdot v_{ij}(t) + c_1 \cdot r_1 \cdot (pBest_{ij}(t) - x_{ij}(t)) + c_2 \cdot r_2 \cdot (gBest_j(t) - x_{ij}(t)) \quad (1)$$

$$x_{ij}(t + 1) = x_{ij}(t) + v_{ij}(t) \quad (2)$$

where $v_{ij}(t + 1)$ and $x_{ij}(t + 1)$ are vectors of velocity and position of each ith particle, respectively, in $t + 1$, iteration and $j(j = 1, 2, \ldots, n)$ the jth dimension of search space. c_1 and c_2 represent the social and cognitive parameter, r_1 and r_2 are two random values uniformly distributed in the interval $[0, 1]$. The value w was introduced by [16]; it represents the inertia weight used to control the local and global search in the search space and it's value lays in the interval $[0, 1]$.

3   PSO with Aging Leader and Challengers (ALC-PSO)

The ALC-PSO raises the proposal to include aging in the original PSO, to represent living organisms. The authors in [4] suggest that aging is an important and useful feature for evolution because it provides a mechanism to encourage beneficial properties of organisms and increases the diversity of species. The incorporation of such characteristic benefits that younger and stronger organisms have opportunities to replace leaders who have aged. This promotes better guidance to the whole swarm.

In the original PSO, the *gBest* could be considered as the leader of the swarm. When a leader is positioned in an optimal local site, it can cause a premature convergence; so, ALC-PSO uses a leader with a limited life time. The particles continue to learn from the leader, but if its lifetime is over, new particles emerge to challenge and replace the leader. Thus, promoting the diversity and exploration of the algorithm. If a leader has a strong ability to lead the swarm to better positions for a period of time, then their lifespan will be lengthened. If instead it fails to find better positions, its lifetime will be reduced.

To differentiate the leader in ALC-PSO, it will be defined as **Leader**. And the velocity update rule is

$$v_{ij}(t+1) = \omega \cdot v_{ij}(t) + c_1 \cdot r_1(t) \cdot (pBest_{ij}(t) - x_{ij}) + c_2 \cdot r_2 \cdot (\textbf{Leader}^j(t) - x_{ij}(t)) \quad (3)$$

After updating the positions and velocities of each particle, the algorithm updates the lifespan of the **Leader** through the lifespan controller. Based on its leadership, the lifespan is increased or decreased. When the **Leader** reaches its lifespan, the algorithm will generate a challenger based on the characteristics of the current **Leader**, using it to lead the swarm for a limited number of iterations. If the challenger is better than the current **Leader**, the latter will be replaced with the challenger. Otherwise, the old **Leader** leading the swarm will remain unchanged. Then the algorithm continues.

4   PSO with Bio-Inspired Aging Model (BAM-PSO)

Desirable traits for PSO such as the ability to solve premature convergence and better error approximation have been reached by ALC-PSO, where an aging factor for the leader is used [4]. In [5] a model called Particle Swarm Optimization with Bio-inspired Aging Model (BAM-PSO) is presented, which is similar to ALC-PSO, but it differs in the fact that it uses a mathematical model describing the dynamics of aging to adjust the lifespan on each particle.

BAM-PSO uses the dynamics of telomeres (the final portion of chromosomes), and is based on a mathematical model based on experimental observations. The model presented in [17] is used to model the dynamics of telomeres with the equation

$$\frac{dT}{dt} = \alpha(p^* - T)N \quad (4)$$

where T is the remaining number of divisions that telomeres can reach per cell, α is consumption rate of the cell, $p*$ is the telomere capacity of the cell, and N is the number of cells. It's important to mention that adding the aging mechanism to all particles will help the exploration without affecting convergence and provides a measure of premature convergence in real time [5]. This is done in order to discard useless particles and to improve the swarm search, as well as the accuracy in numerical results. In Fig. 1 we show the flowchart of the three PSO techniques mentioned above.

5   Methodology

PSO, ALC-PSO and BAM-PSO were tested in three different implementations: serial, MPI, and CUDA. And they will be detailed below.

Some parameters are shared by all PSO algorithms, namely $c1$, $c2$ and w. The assigned values for these parameters were taken from Kenedy [18] as the standard values for PSO, and remained constant throughout the experiments (see Table 1). ALC-PSO and BAM-PSO have the additional parameters $Lifespan$ and $Tries\ Challenger$ and all the experiments were also performed with their respective standard values [4,5], presented in Table 1.

To analyze the performance of the implemented PSO algorithms, we tested four common benchmark functions [13,19]. They are the Griewank, Rastrigin, Sphere, and Rosenbrock functions (Table 2), the first and second functions are unimodal while the third and fourth are multimodal. All of them have already been used to test serial and parallel PSO implementations [11,20], are scalable in dimension, and have their global minima at the origin [6].

The speedup S of a parallel program [21] is defined as the relationship between the serial run-time T_{serial} and its parallel counterpart $T_{parallel}$ as

$$S = \frac{T_{serial}}{T_{parallel}} \tag{5}$$

then, its efficiency E when running in a number of cores p can be defined as

Table 1. Values employed for all PSO algorithms

Parameters	Test values
Dimension	500
Cognitive parameter (c1)	41.49618
Social parameter (c2)	1.49618
Inertia weight (w)	0.729844
Lifespan	60
Tries challenger	2
Tests by function	10

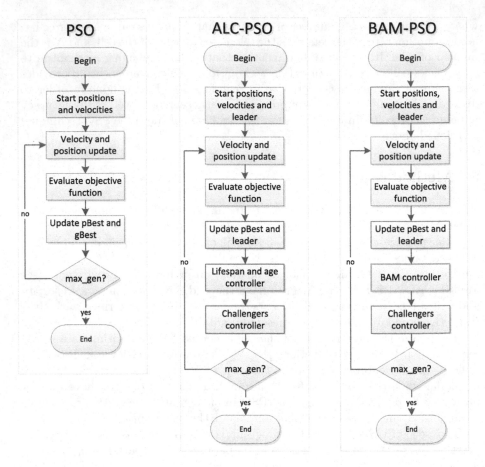

Fig. 1. Flowchart of the PSO algorithm (left), ALC-PSO algorithm (center), and BAM-PSO algorithm (right) (Changes to the original algorithm in red and green are shown in the case of ALC-PSO and BAM-PSO respectively) (Color figure online).

Table 2. Test functions

Test function	Domain	Name
$f_1(x) = \sum_{i=1}^{d} \frac{x_i^2}{4000} - \prod_{i=1}^{d} cos(\frac{x_i}{\sqrt{i}}) + 1$	$[-300, 600]$	Griewank
$f_2(x) = 10d + \sum_{i=1}^{d} [x_i^2 - 10cos(2\pi x_i)]$	$[2.56, 5.12]$	Rastrigin
$f_3(x) = \sum_{i=1}^{d} x_i^2$	$[50, 100]$	Sphere
$f_4(x) = \sum_{d=1}^{i-1} ((100 * (x_{i-1} - x_d^2))^2 + (x_d - 1)^2)$	$[-5, 10]$	Rosenbrock

$$E = \frac{T_{serial}}{p \cdot T_{parallel}} \tag{6}$$

Thus, the theoretical limit for the linear speedup is $T_{parallel} = T_{serial}/p$ and has $S = p$.

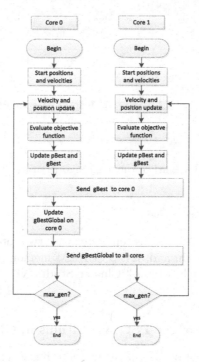

Fig. 2. Flowchart of the PSO algorithm in MPI (implementation for two cores). It can be scaled as long as cores are available.

5.1   Implementation of the PSO Algorithms in MPI

Our parallel implementation of PSO algorithms is based on the broadcast model explained in [9], also deployed in [12]. In this parallel PSO implementation, the swarm is divided into interconnected subgroups, which contain the same amount of particles. These subgroups are distributed in the available cores (a subgroup per core), so that the algorithm can be scaled as cores become available.

All subgroups share their information among them in every iteration, allowing the particles to have information from all groups, so they behave as a single swarm. Per iteration, the position and velocity vectors are updated according to rules (1) and (2), and subsequently update a local $pBest$ and a local $gBest$, afterwards, each subgroup, sends its $gBest$ to the master core, where the $gBestGlobal$ is calculated and sent to all cores. This implementation is synchronous. Finally, the stop criteria, cycle repetition, or the termination of the algorithm is verified.

The implementation of the three algorithms is done similarly, according to the individual characteristics of each one. The representation of the particles and their speed and position vectors, are equally represented as serial versions. The only difference is that the solution reported will be the $gBestGlobal$. The PSO implementation flowchart is shown in Fig. 2.

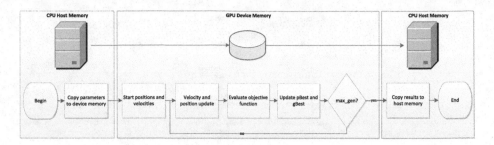

Fig. 3. Flowchart of the PSO algorithm in CUDA.

5.2   CPU Architecture

The HPCC used, named Agave, has ten nodes with two Intel® Xeon® processor E5 − 2600, eight cores each, and 32 GB of RAM memory. For compilation and execution of programs, it has Intel® Cluster Studio XE 2012, and CentOS 6.5 operating system.

5.3   Implementation of the PSO Algorithms in GPU

We based our development on [12], with the following scheme. The configuration is done in the CPU and the values are copied to the global memory on the GPU. The execution of the algorithm is done by the CPU but runs entirely on the GPU. The execution of the kernels on the GPU is done in a way that they cover the total number of particles independently executed by a thread, allowing running many threads to give flexibility to the program and reduce the latency of memory access. As on [12], the kernel to update gBest is executed with a number of threads equal to the dimension of the function to update. Once the number of iterations are completed, the CPU copies the error obtained from GPU to the main memory.

The flowchart of the parallel CUDA-PSO implementation is shown in Fig. 3. The same scheme is followed by ALC-PSO and BAM-PSO.

According to [12], this implementation is still very general and major adjustments are needed, such as maximum use of shared memory, coalescing memory access, thread divergence, and correct selection of the block size. When these changes are made to its implementation, speedup of up to 167x is achieved, compared to their serial version (Rosenbrock function, dimension size 20, and 16384 particles). This implementation may limit the extent of the problem and the number of particles used, as it depends on the hardware used and the amount of shared memory disposal. If a real application needed a change in dimensions, it would have to be adapted to suit the specific task. For this first implementation of PSO, ALC-PSO, and BAM-PSO, the algorithms are provided only with access to global memory, to address high dimensionality problems.

5.4 GPU Architecture

The experiments with GPU were performed on a NVIDIA® Tesla® K20c card, with 4800 MB of GDDR5 memory, 13 Multiprocessors with 192 cores each one, with a total number of 2496 CUDA cores, based on the NVIDIA Kepler™ Architecture. The memory of the Kepler Architecture is composed by global, constant, and texture memory spaces (we only use global memory for the implementation of all the CUDA algorithms). The card is installed on a PC that has an Intel® Xeon® CPU E5 − 2620, 2.10 GHz and 32 GB of memory RAM, and Ubuntu 14.10 operating system.

6 Experimental Results

We analyzed first, the MPI against the serial versions; second, CUDA versus serial versions; and finally, the analysis between MPI and CUDA implementations.

6.1 MPI-PSO Algorithms

The three algorithms were implemented in MPI based on Fig. 2. The first experiment exploits the potential of a HPCC using a large number of particles and increasing the amount of cores used.

In Fig. 4, we can see the execution time of the Rastrigin function with 500 dimensions, 2048 particles, 16000 iterations, and different number of cores. As expected, the calculation time decreases proportionally to the number of cores. BAM-PSO is the slowest of the three, but there is not much difference between them. On average, the difference between PSO and ALC-PSO is less than 1 %, while the PSO against BAM-PSO is approximately 38 %. The difference in execution time between PSO and ALC-PSO is consistent with the conclusions reached by the authors in [4]. The difference between PSO and BAM-PSO can not be compared with the results of the original authors as they did not present their results with common benchmark functions.

Figure 5 shows that the speedup increases as the number of processors grow; specifically, how speedup reaches up to 46x in the ALC-PSO and PSO algorithms, and almost 47x for the BAM-PSO algorithm. The geometric efficiency growth observed is generated by the nature of the algorithm. Consider Fig. 2, a part of the parallel algorithm always has to send its results to core zero, and then forward them to all cores. This part will increase communication time between cores and not allow a linear growth in the speedup. The numerical results of execution time are presented in Table 3.

As mentioned in Sect. 5.2, each node of Agave has two processors with eight cores each. A significant communication time will not be added to the execution total time while one node is used, thus using more than one node, a communication time increase is generated due to the nature of the algorithm's implementation. As shown in Fig. 6, efficiency drops as the number of cores increase, and it is greater when more than one is used.

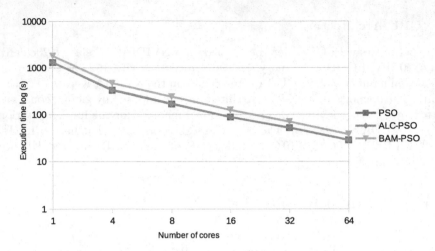

Fig. 4. Execution time for all MPI-PSO algorithms, with different number of cores (Rastrigin function, 2048 particles, 16000 generations, mean of 10 trials).

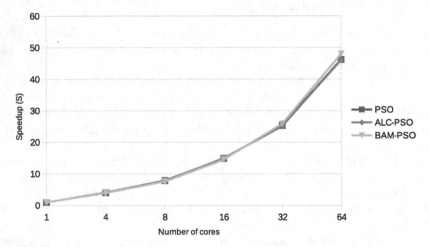

Fig. 5. Speedup for all MPI-PSO algorithms, with different number of cores (Rastrigin function, 2048 particles, and 16000 generations).

Table 3. MPI execution time results (s).

Cores	PSO	ALC-PSO	BAM-PSO
1	1,312.2	1,311.69	1,807.89
4	328.44	334.02	463.81
8	166.63	169.18	238.32
16	88.02	87.61	124.35
32	51.94	52.28	69.96
64	28.39	28.49	37.69

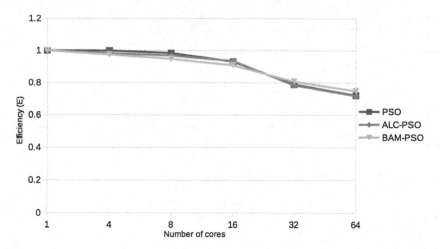

Fig. 6. Efficiency for all MPI-PSO algorithms, with different number of cores (Rastrigin function, 2048 particles, and 16000 generations).

Table 4. MPI efficiency.

Cores	PSO	ALC-PSO	BAM-PSO
1	100.00	100.00	100.00
4	99.87	98.17	97.44
8	98.43	96.91	94.82
16	93.17	93.57	90.86
32	78.94	78.40	80.74
64	72.21	71.92	74.93

A large number of particles is recommended by [10], when a large number of cores is available. This increments the probability of improving the solution. Therefore, the second experiment is designed to test the ability of convergence and exploration capability with problems of great magnitude, for which the number of processors is fixed at sixteen, while increasing the number of particles to be divided between these. All three algorithms were executed in all four selected functions. Figure 7 shows how the optimum found did not change significantly with the PSO algorithm in the four functions. This behavior is caused by a local optimum that traps all the swarm and leads to premature convergence. This behavior is what led to the develop of variants of the original PSO algorithm. As shown in Fig. 7, in ALC-PSO and BAM-PSO, the optimal its significantly improved in each function.

6.2   CUDA-PSO Algorithms

The implementation of the three algorithms in CUDA was made based on Fig. 3. In Fig. 8, we can see the speedup of the Rosenbrock function with 500 dimensions and different numbers of particles for the three CUDA algorithms. We show

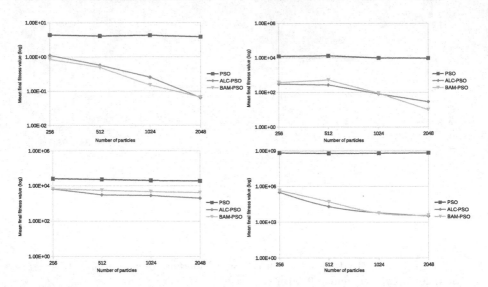

Fig. 7. Mean fitness value found in all MPI-PSO algorithms, for different number of particles. (top left) Griewank, (top right) Sphere, (bottom left) Rastrigin, and (bottom right) Rosenbrock functions (16 cores and 4000 generations).

the increase in the speedup of the algorithm, compared to their serial version. This increase, shows concordance with the results presented by the authors of [12]. They report a similar increase in speedup when increasing the number of particles. The difference in the speedup between PSO and ALC-PSO is less than 1.5 %, reaching a speed increase of nearly 20x in both algorithms. In the case of BAM-PSO the speedup achieved is smaller, because the algorithm's complexity increases compared to the original PSO and ALC-PSO. An increase of only nearly 6.5x was achieved. The difference in speedup with PSO is nearly 30 %.

Similarly, as in the case of MPI, a test is performed by increasing the number of particles and verifying the convergence of the four objective functions. Figure 9 shows the optimum found in all four functions.

The convergence behavior with the Rastrigin function, is similar to the MPI version, and slightly slower, compared with the other functions.

6.3   Comparison Between Implementations

Finally, a comparison between all implementations is performed. For this experiment, the amount of particles used incremented. The number of processors in the MPI versions was fixed to 16. Also, is used the largest number of iterations to all algorithms have a change to converge. Lastly, the Griewank function was chosen because it has local minima close to the global optimum, as the solution approaches the origin.

Figure 10 clearly shows the advantages between implementations. The MPI version provides a better alternative to the serial PSO. Still, the implementation

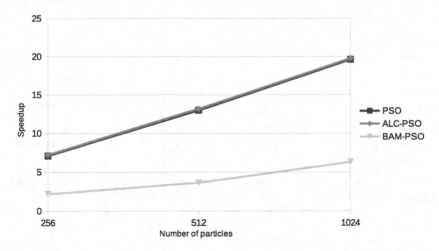

Fig. 8. Speedup for all CUDA-PSO algorithms, with different number of particles (Rosenbrock function and 16000 generations).

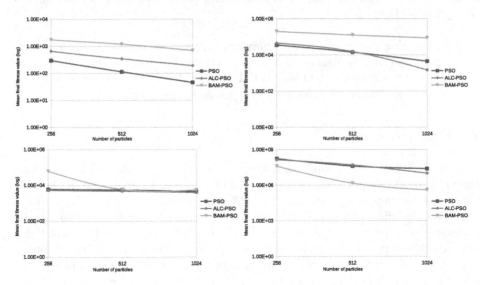

Fig. 9. Mean fitness value found for all CUDA-PSO algorithms for different number of particles. (top left) Griewank, (top right) Sphere, (bottom left) Rastrigin, and (bottom right) Rosenbrock functions (4000 generations).

in CUDA gets an acceptable improvement in execution time. In addition, between serial algorithms, it's shown that the ALC-PSO achieved slight better execution time, making it a good alternative to the original PSO to find better fitness values. All PSO versions implemented in MPI have similar execution time. Finally, in the CUDA versions, BAM-PSO got the highest time, in comparison to the other alternatives; offering possible routes for future work by improving the implementation done.

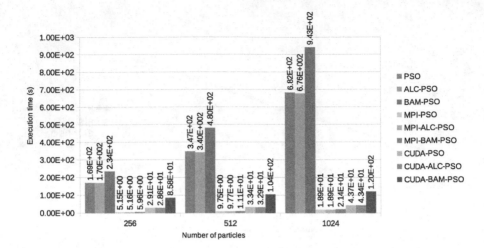

Fig. 10. Execution time of all algorithms in serial, MPI and CUDA for different number of particles (Griewank function, 16000 generations, mean of 10 trials and 16 cores in the case of MPI).

By observing the execution time between versions, we find that the behavior is similar to the already mentioned in other sections. There is not much difference in execution time between PSO and ALC-PSO; BAM-PSO always be the slowest. This applies to the three implementations made in this article.

7   Discussion

It is clear that the MPI implementation offered better results. The execution time improved, compared to serial and CUDA implementations. Also, it showed better convergence, compared to the CUDA algorithms. However, the algorithms were executed disposing of vast resources. This is the ideal scenario when a high dimensionality problem is addressed. Observing Table 4, we might think it is still possible to run the algorithms with a greater number of cores without much efficiency loss. Probably, it could still reduce execution time and improve the speedup achieved. However, a reduction in time execution can be reached, due to the communication time increase. The above mentioned, will continue to increase as we increment the number of cores used. This imposes limits when it comes to improving the algorithms' time execution. The authors of [21] indicate that it is a normal behavior. In other words, when the size of the problem increases, speedups and efficiencies increase. This explains the behavior observed in Figs. 5 and 6, when using a large dimension.

With the testing benchmark functions, it's seen that the PSO in MPI do not improve as the number of particles or iterations increase. Only variants of PSO (ALC-PSO and BAM-PSO) show a significant improvement in the performed error.

Compared with serial versions, the parallel implementations provide an alternative to using the traditional PSO. In the CUDA implementation tests, the speedup achieved was not as high as with the MPI version. This is because the execution was carried out with the GPU card installed in a workstation, using Linux compilers (version 4.8.4), unlike the HPCC that uses Intel® Cluster Studio.

This study differs from others [11–13], where we do an implementation of the three algorithms, in CUDA and MPI. Furthermore, up to our knowledge, it's the first time that ALC-PSO and BAM-PSO are implemented in parallel. In addition, we address optimization problems of greater magnitude.

8   Conclusions and Future Work

In this paper an implementation of three PSO algorithms was performed in parallel on the cluster Agave and on a workstation with a GPU card. We looked for a comparison between different versions of PSO in parallel rather than a report of the implementations made. To accomplish this, we made tests with four objective functions and different settings to corroborate its abilities to convergence, exploration, and speed. These tests showed the same features as the serial algorithms, but unlike the latter, parallel versions achieved significant improvements in execution time.

However, just as [6] uses sixteen benchmark functions problems and the authors of [4] used seventeen, additional work of this study could include a greater number of objective functions that could provide significant information for the comparison of the algorithms.

Other future work could include full comparative tests between the performance of Linux compiler and Intel® Cluster Studio XE 2012 compiler.

Future work in versions of MPI include testing in a variety of dimensions to corroborate the features listed here. Versions of GPU development could include, as proposed by fellow researchers, major adjustments and testing in a variety of both small and very high dimensions, to address problems of greater magnitude.

Although other developments in GPU have achieved higher speedup when it comes to addressing problems of small dimension, this implementation offers a clear alternative for solving large dimension problems in acceptable times without needing a HPCC.

Acknowledgements. The Authors thank the support of the Agave HPCC team at Universidad de Guadalajara, campus CUCEI, and the Science and Technology National Counsel (CONACYT) for its support to the authors by the scholarship grant CVU-555944.

References

1. Mukhopadhyay, A., Mandal, M.: A hybrid multiobjective particle swarm optimization approach for non-redundant gene marker selection. In: Proceedings of Seventh International Conference on Bio-Inspired Computing: Theories and Applications (BIC-TA 2012), pp. 205–216. Springer (2013)

2. Robinson, J., Rahmat-Samii, Y.: Particle swarm optimization in electromagnetics. IEEE Trans. Antennas Propag. **52**(2), 397–407 (2004)
3. Wang, Y., Lv, J., Zhu, L., Ma, Y.: Crystal structure prediction via particle-swarm optimization. Phys. Rev. B **82**(9), 094116 (2010)
4. Chen, W.-N., Zhang, J., Lin, Y., Chen, N., Zhan, Z.-H., Chung, H.S.-H., Li, Y., Shi, Y.-H.: Particle swarm optimization with an aging leader and challengers. IEEE Trans. Evol. Comput. **17**(2), 241–258 (2013)
5. Rangel, E., Alanís, A.Y., Ricalde, L.J., Arana-Daniel, N., López-Franco, C.: Bio-inspired aging model particle swarm optimization neural network training for solar radiation forecasting. In: Bayro-Corrochano, E., Hancock, E. (eds.) CIARP 2014. LNCS, vol. 8827, pp. 682–689. Springer, Heidelberg (2014)
6. Deep, K., Sharma, S., Pant, M.: Modified parallel particle swarm optimization for global optimization using message passing interface. In: 2010 IEEE Fifth International Conference on Bio-Inspired Computing: Theories and Applications (BIC-TA), pp. 1451–1458. IEEE (2010)
7. Omkar, S., Venkatesh, A., Mudigere, M.: MPI-based parallel synchronous vector evaluated particle swarm optimization for multi-objective design optimization of composite structures. Eng. Appl. Artif. Intell. **25**(8), 1611–1627 (2012)
8. Koh, B.-I., George, A.D., Haftka, R.T., Fregly, B.J.: Parallel asynchronous particle swarm optimization. Int. J. Numer. Meth. Eng. **67**(4), 578–595 (2006)
9. Tu, K.-Y., Liang, Z.-C.: Parallel computation models of particle swarm optimization implemented by multiple threads. Expert Syst. Appl. **38**(5), 5858–5866 (2011)
10. Schutte, J.F., Reinbolt, J.A., Fregly, B.J., Haftka, R.T., George, A.D.: Parallel global optimization with the particle swarm algorithm. Int. J. Numer. Meth. Eng. **61**(13), 2296–2315 (2004)
11. Laguna-Sánchez, G.A., Olguín-Carbajal, M., Cruz-Cortés, N., Barrón-Fernández, R., Álvarez-Cedillo, J.A.: Comparative study of parallel variants for a particle swarm optimization algorithm implemented on a multithreading GPU. J. Appl. Res. Technol. **7**(3), 292–307 (2009)
12. Roberge, V., Tarbouchi, M.: Comparison of parallel particle swarm optimizers for graphical processing units and multicore processors. Int. J. Comput. Intell. Appl. **12**(1), 20 (2013)
13. Zhou, Y., Tan, Y.: GPU-based parallel particle swarm optimization. In: IEEE Congress on Evolutionary Computation, 2009, CEC 2009, pp. 1493–1500. IEEE (2009)
14. Ouyang, A., Tang, Z., Zhou, X., Xu, Y., Pan, G., Li, K.: Parallel hybrid PSO with CUDA for lD heat conduction equation. Comput. Fluids **110**, 198–210 (2014)
15. James, K., Russell, E.: Particle swarm optimization. In: Proceedings of 1995 IEEE International Conference on Neural Networks, pp. 1942–1948 (1995)
16. Shi, Y., Eberhart, R.: A modified particle swarm optimizer. In: Evolutionary Computation Proceedings, 1998. IEEE World Congress on Computational Intelligence., The 1998 IEEE International Conference on, pp. 69–73. IEEE (1998)
17. Romanyukha, A.A., Yashin, A.I.: Age related changes in population of peripheral T cells: towards a model of immunosenescence. Mech. Ageing Dev. **124**(4), 433–443 (2003)
18. Kennedy, J., Clerc, M (2006). http://www.particleswarm.info/standard_pso_2006.c. Accessed 10 July 2015
19. Angeline, P.J.: Evolutionary optimization versus particle swarm optimization: philosophy and performance differences. In: Porto, V.W., Saravanan, N., Waagen, D., Eiben, A.E. (eds.) Evolutionary Programming VII. LNCS, pp. 601–610. Springer, Heidelberg (1998)

20. Shi, Y., Eberhart, R.C.: Empirical study of particle swarm optimization. In: Proceedings of the 1999 Congress on Evolutionary Computation, 1999, CEC 1999, vol. 3. IEEE (1999)
21. Pacheco, P.: An Introduction to Parallel Programming. Elsevier, San Francisco (2011)

ACFUEGOS: An Unstructured Triangular Cellular Automata for Modelling Forest Fire Propagation

Gerardo M. Ortigoza[1]([⊠]), Alberto Lorandi[2], and Iris Neri[1]

[1] Facultad de Ingeniería, Universidad Veracruzana, Boca del Río, Veracruz, Mexico
gortigoza@uv.mx
[2] Instituto de Ingeniería, Universidad Veracruzana, Boca del Río, Veracruz, Mexico

Abstract. In this work we propose the use of a cellular automata defined on unstructured triangular grids to simulate forest fire propagation. This approach allow us to model computational domains with complex geometries (polygonal boundaries). It still retains the easy implementation of cellular automata and it does not present the anisotropy induced by regular grids. The forest fire spread is modeled by using ignition and stop burning probabilities. The computational domain is discretized by an unstructured triangular grid; each cell (triangle) assumes four states: non flamable, unburned fuel, burning and burned. Ignition probabilities for grass, shrubs and timber are estimated assuming Anderson's 13 fuel models and a maximum rate of spread. These probabilities are modified by the effects of different variables such as: slope, wind (direction/intensity), relative humidity and ambient temperature. The cellular automata code was implemented in C++, the serial runnigs of the code were performed in an Intel Core CPU 2.90 GHz 8 processors workstation. The numerical simulations reproduce the qualitative behavior of forest fires under the effect of type of fuel, slope and wind (direction/intensity).

Keywords: Cellular automata · Unstructured triangular grids · Forest fire · Spotting

1 Introduction

Every year forest fires around the world devastate enormous areas of land and cause extensive damage, both to property and human life. These fires spread rapidly and without adequate models to forecast their growth, firefighters are unable to contain them as efficiently as they would otherwise be able to. In a forest fire management system, computer models of fire are used to understand how fast would fire move and to predict what area would it combust. The main fire spread models can be grouped into: empirical (or statistical), semi-empirical and physical. Empirical models predict the most probable fire behavior from average conditions and accumulated information obtained from laboratory, outdoor experimental fire and historical fires. Semi-empirical models are based on

© Springer International Publishing Switzerland 2016
I. Gitler and J. Klapp (Eds.): ISUM 2015, CCIS 595, pp. 132–143, 2016.
DOI: 10.1007/978-3-319-32243-8_9

a global energy balance and on the assumption that the energy transfered to the unburned fuel is proportional to the energy released by the combustion of the fuel. A popular semi-empirical model is the Rothermel model [21] which is the basis for many systems in the USA, including BEHAVE, FARSITE, NFDRS, RERAP among others. Because of their discrete nature and their suitability for implementation on digital computers, cellular automata seem to be appropriate for modeling forest fire spreading and they are considered as semi-empirical models.

The work is organized as follows: in Sect. 2 we present a cellular automata model for fire propagation using a unstructured triangular grid; it also includes some modeling of the ignition and burning probabilities and how they are affected by different variables such as: type of fuel, slope, wind, relative humidity and temperature; Sect. 3 shows some numerical simulations for a case study. Finally in Sect. 4 we include some conclusions of this work.

2 An Unstructured Triangular Cellular Automata Model for Fire Propagation

A cellular automaton A is a tuple (d, S, N, f) where d is the dimension of space, S is a finite set of states, N a finite subset of $\mathbb{Z}^d$ is the neighborhood and f: $S^N \to S$ is the *local rule, or transition function*, of the automaton. A configuration of a cellular automaton is a coloring of the space by S, an element of $S^{\mathbb{Z}^d}$. The global rule $G : S^{\mathbb{Z}^d} \to S^{\mathbb{Z}^d}$ of a cellular automaton maps a configuration $c \in S^{\mathbb{Z}^d}$ to the configuration $G(c)$ obtained by applying f uniformly in each cell: for all position $z \in S^{\mathbb{Z}^d}, G(c)(z) = f(c(z + v_1), ..., c(z + v_k))$, where $N = \{v_1, ..., v_k\}$. CA methods have been used for fire propagation simulations using regular grids [11,20]. Holland [12] and Dunn [9] recommend the use of irregular grids to model virtual landscape in order to reduce the bias induced by rectangular grids; in [17] the presented numerical experiments on unstructured triangular grids show agreement with these observations. Thus, in this work we define a forest fire spread model on an unstructured triangular grid. Besides reducing bias in the movement of information and the representation of real-world geometries (bounded straight-line polygonal domains), its finite element mesh structure provides flexibility to identify neighborhoods, visualization and boundary conditions implementations. In our numerical implementation the region of interest is discretized by using a unstructured triangular mesh. Each triangle is considered as a cell and Neumann neighborhoods are assumed. Let us consider a simplified model of cellular automata which evolves according the following assumptions:

1. The spatial domain is discretized using an unstructured triangular grid, each cell is a triangle.
2. Neumann neighborhoods are assumed (a cell and its three neighbors).

3. At each time, each cell can assume one of the following four values:
   (0) representing a non fuel cell (not flammable).
   (1) representing a fuel cell.
   (2) representing a burning cell.
   (3) representing a burned cell.
4. Two probabilities are assigned to each cell: p_i ignition probability and p_q stop burning probability. The first one characterizes the ability of a fuel to catch fire and the second one the ability to maintain the combustion.
5. Fire spreads from a burning cell to a fuel neighboring cell with probability p_i
6. The transitions rules are defined by
   $$\begin{cases} (1) \to (2) \text{ with probability } p_i. \\ (0) \to (0) \text{ a not flammable cell will not catch fire.} \\ (2) \to (3) \text{ a burning cell evolves into a burned cell with probability } p_q. \\ (3) \to (3) \text{ burned cells remain burned.} \end{cases}$$

The probability of ignition depends on each type of fuel and also it can be related to another variables such as: ambient temperature, relative humidity, wind (speed/direction) and land slope.

2.1 Modeling Ignition and Burning Probabilities

To estimate the ignition probability we use the 13 fuel models defined by Anderson [1]. Table 1 shows fire rates of spread for some of the 13 fuels of

Table 1. Fuel types and its rates of spread m/s

Fuel types	ROS (ch/hr)	Mean ROS (m/s)
Group Grass and grass-dominated		
1 Short grass (1 foot)	78	72.33 ch/hr = 0.4042 m/s
2 Timber (grass and understory)	35	
3 Tall grass (2.5 feet)	104	
Chaparral and shrub fields		
4 Chaparral (6 feet)	75	36.25 ch/hr = 0.2026 m/s
5 Brush (2 feet)	18	
6 Dormant brush, hardwood slash	32	
7 Southern rough	20	
Timber litter		
8 Closed timber litter	1.6	5.6667 ch/hr = 0.0317 m/s
9 Hardwood litter	7.5	
10 Timber (litter and understory)	7.9	
Slash		
11 Light logging slash	6	
12 Medium logging slash	13	
13 Heavy logging slash	13.5	

Andersons. Assuming a maximun rate of spread **MROS = 4.02 m/s** we divide each rate of spread from the third column of Table 1 by this MRS to obtain the ignition probabilities p_i: 0.1005473, 0.0503980, 0.0078856 for grass, shrubs and timber, respectively.

Now let us estimate the stop burning probability. The upper size limit for fine fuels is set to 6 mm for McArthur Forest Fire Danger Meter and 10 mm for the Forest Fire Behaviour Tables for Western Australia [5], so we assumed these diameter's values: 6 mm for grass, 10 mm for shrubs and 16 cm for timber. According to Burrows [5] flame residence time for individual particles (1–16 mm in diameter) increases with particle size according to the equation $t_r = 0.871d^{1.875}$, here t_r is the flame residence time in seconds, d= round wood diameter mm. We use this equation for grass and shrubs. On the other hand for the case of timber, Cheney et al. [8] developed an equation to predict flame residence time of silvertop ash logs from experiments conducted in a hearth using pilot ignition. Log diameters ranged from 0.6 cm to 25 cm, each log was 70 cm in length. $t_r = 1.7d^{1.686}$ t_r residence time of flames in minutes and d is the diameter of log in cm, so for timber we use this equation. Table 2 summarizes the residence time for the three fuels.

Table 2. Residence time in seconds for three types of fuels

Fuel type	Residence time in seconds
Grass	25.0641 s
Shrubs	65.3158 s
Timber	7077.1 s

In a 2 h period time the stop burning probability p_q can be estimated as: 0.9965,0.9909,0.0171 for grass, shrubs and timber respectively. To estime the stop burning probability at each time step, we take $\Delta t M = 2$ h period time, where $\Delta t = radius/MROS$, here M is the number of steps and $radius$ is the average radius of the mesh. For a radius of 11.99 m and a MROS of 4.02 m/s we have $\Delta t = 2.9826$ s, M=2414. In this case at each time step the burning probability is $\frac{p_q}{M}$, that gives 0.0004128, 0.0004104 and 0.00000707 for grass, shrub and timber, respectively. Note that we need to keep a record of the time that each cell has been burning. While the cell is still burning p_q accumulates at each time step until the cell burns out.

2.2   Modeling Slope Probability

Slope significantly influences the forward rate of spread of surface fires by modifying the degree of preheating of the unburned fuel immediately in front of the flames. The effect of slope (ground elevation) can be modeled by equation [6]

$$R_s = R_0 exp(\beta\theta_s);$$

here R_0 is the spread rate at zero slope, θ_s is the slope angle in degrees between the center of the burning cell and the center of the neighboring fuel cell

$$\theta_s = \frac{180}{\pi} atan \left(\frac{h_2 - h_1}{r} \right),$$

with $h_2 - h_1$ been the height difference, r the distance between centers (the burning and the neigboring fuel cell) and β a constant that can be adjusted from experimental data. We adjusted $\beta = 0.0693$ from the data experiments of Butler et al. [6]. The ignition probability p_i is modified by the slope effects as:

$$p_i * exp(0.0693\theta_s).$$

2.3   Modeling Wind Probability

The combustion rate of a fire is positively influenced by the rate of oxygen supply to the fire, thus the effect of wind speed is a very important factor in the fire behaviour and rate of spread. Exponential functions have been found to provide an adequate representation of the relationship between wind speed and rate of the spread. An observable effect of the high wind speeds upon the flame front is that at some threshold wind speeds local flame extinction has been theorised to occur. Empirical evidence from February 1967 Hobart fires in Tasmania, Australia, indicated that at very high winds speeds (40–45 Km/h), the rate of spread in grassfires decreased with increasing wind speed. A possible explanation put forward by McArthur was that as the wind increases above a critical threshold, the flame front in light fuels becomes progressively narrower and fragmented, inducing a decrease in the average rate of fire spread. He noticed this decrease as wind velocity increase above 26–28 miles per hour (12.07 m/s) and from the McArthurt [14] figure as redrafted for Rothermel [21] the maximum rate of spread is 8 mi/h (3.57 m/s). Let us defined a maximum rate of spread for a forest fire. Noble [16] presents wind and rate of spread data for three grassfires in Australia winds between 47 and 53 Km/h result in spread rates between 280 and 380 m/min. The 2005 Wangary fire in the Eyre Peninsula of South Australia had grasfire runs of 215 and 245 m/min driven by average wind speeds between 46 and 61 Km/h [10].

Table 3. Maximum rates of spread at wind speeds

Author reported	Mean wind speed at the interval	Mean ROS at the interval
McArthurt/Rothermel	12.07 m/s	3.57 m/s
Noble	13.88 m/s	5.5 m/s
Gould	14.861 m/s	3.83 m/s
Mean	13.6 m/s	4.02 m/s

Table 3 shows reported maximum fire rates of spread and a mean of these values. Now using the rates of spread for differente wind speeds data obtained by Mendes et al. [15] and including mean values obtained above (last row) we proceed to fit a exponential curve $f(w) = 0.009313 * exp(0.4611 * w)$. Assuming that the ignition probability is modified by the effects of the wind, we take the component of the wind in the direction of the propagation (from the center of the burning cell to the center of a neighboring cell), this increases or decreases the ignition probability. Let (x, y) be the components of the direction vector from the center cell to the neighboring cell, let $W = (w_1, w_2)$ be the wind vector, we compute w_t, the component of the wind in the direction of the neighboring cell:

$$w_t = \frac{w_1 x + w_2 y}{\sqrt{x^2 + y^2}}.$$

Thus the combined effect of slope, wind and fuel type results in the spread probability

$$p_i * exp(0.4611 w_t) * exp(0.6930 \theta_s).$$

2.4 Modelling the Effects of Weather Variables on Ignition and Burning Probabilities

Effects on The Ignition Probability. Ambient temperature and relative humidity affect the ignition probability of fuel; Chau-Chin [7] experiments reported that low relative humidity resulted in a higher ignition probability but when higher temperatures ocurred, moderate relative humidity also resulted in a higher ignition ocurrence. The twelve data points obtained by Chau-Chin are quadratic-cubic (quadratic relative humidity/cubic in temperature) extrapolated. We assumed that the change in the ignition probability p_i is proportional to the difference between p_i and the given value $p_{(RH,T)}$ of the graph, thus our modified ignition probability is

$$p_i + p_i * (p_{(RH,T)} - p_i). \tag{1}$$

We calculate the variations of the ignition probabilities for grass, shrubs and timber due to the variations in relative humidity and ambient temperature, Table 4 shows the interval (minimum and maximum) values that these ignition probabilities can take. Fine fuels as grass and shrubs are more sensitive to changes in relative humidity and ambient temperature.

Table 4. Minimum and maximum values that ignition p_i probability can take by the effects of temperature and relative humidity

Fuel type	p_i	Interval	Interval's length
Grass	0.1	[0.0914,0.19]	0.0986
Shrubs	0.05	[0.0482,0.0975]	0.0493
Timber	0.0078	[0.0079,0.0155]	0.0076

Fuel moisture content (FMC) is recognised as the variable with the greatest influence on the fuel ignitability. Ignition probability as a function of moisture content has been estimated by using logistic regression [3,4,19]. Bianchi [3] obtained the equation

$$p_{i_{FM}} = \frac{1}{1 + e^{-(6.64 - 0.28FM)}}$$

for Ñire and cypress fuels. We assume that the change in p_i is proportional to the difference between p_i and $p_{i_{FM}}$:

$$p_i + p_i * (p_{i_{FM}} - p_i). \tag{2}$$

Effects on the Stop Burning Probability. To estimate the effects of relative humidity and fuel moisture on the stop burning probability for our model, we use some research results reported by Beverly and Wotton [2]. They obtained the following exponential expressions for the probability of sustained burning P_s as functions of relative humidity (RH) and moisture content (MC)

$$P_s = \frac{1}{1 + e^{-(7.3703 - 0.1725*RH)}}, \quad P_s = \frac{1}{1 + e^{-(2.8566 - 0.2456*MC)}}$$

Thus, the stop burning probability p_q is given by $p_q = 1 - P_s$. The stop burning probability is modified by relative humidity and moisture content in a similar way as the ignition probability was modified by the effects of temperature, relative humidity and fuel moisture content in Eqs. 1 and 2.

2.5   Modelling Spotting

Spotting is the phenomenon by which burning material, called firebrands, are loafted by the plume, transported via the fire-influenced wind field and deposited to ignite new fires ahead of the contiguous fire front. Our model includes the spotfire probability as a function of relative humidity reported by Weir [22]. His data were used to adjust an exponential curve

$$P_{spotting} = 20.14 * e^{-0.1383*HR} + 0.02981.$$

Spotting is a very complex phenomenon, so by assuming some simplifications our spotting model states:

1. Firebrands start to propagate downwind after the flame/plume structure collapses, so a burning cell that changes to burned-out is considered as a source of spotting fire.
2. The probability of spotting depends on the relative humidity.
3. Intensity of the fire in the source cell is estimated by the number of burning neighboring cells.
4. A cell is considered as a source of spotting depending on the type of fuel that encloses, we assumed spotting is only presented in trees.
5. Wind intensity is related to the spotting distance by using extended neighborhoods.

6. Wind direction drives the transport of firebrand material, we assumed that they are dispersed in a 28 degrees arc from the starting fire cell.
7. A new fire starts depending on the ignition probability of the type of fuel at landing.

3   A Case Study

We considered a case study for the Cofre de Perote National Park, a natural protected area situated (long,lat) 19.57,-97.23. From the INEGI [13] data files

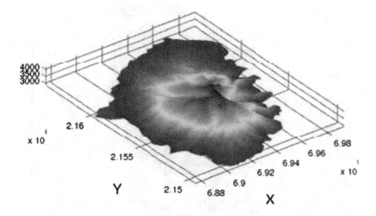

Fig. 1. Elevation map for the Cofre de Perote area.

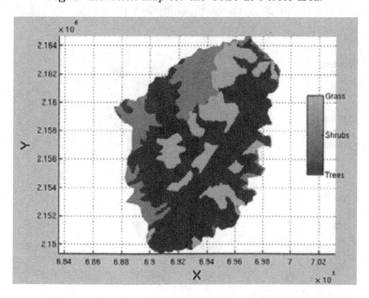

Fig. 2. Initial condition of a fire (red spot), three fuels are assumed: grass, shrubs and trees (Color figure online).

such as: boundary polygon, elevations and type of vegetation are obtained. A triangular mesh consisting of 90006 nodes and 178909 triangles was built with an unstructured grid generator.

Figure 1 shows the elevation map of the study area. In [18] some numerical experiments/simulations were presented to show the good performance of the model to simulate fire spread in three fuels, under the action of slope, and wind direction/intensity.

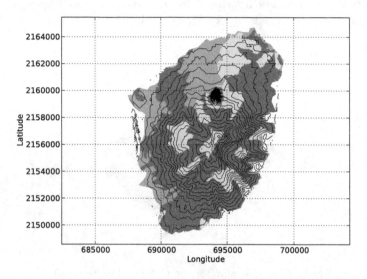

Fig. 3. Fire spread no wind, 20 % relative humidity and 40^0 C temperature, 20 % FMC.

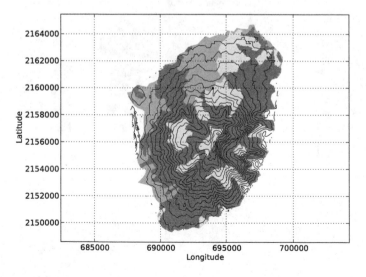

Fig. 4. Fire spread no wind, 50 % relative humidity and 10^0 C temperature, 50 % FMC.

Figure 2 shows the initial condition of a fire (red spot) in the area of study, three fuels are assumed: grass, shrubs and trees.

Figures 3 and 4 show fire spread at no wind conditions with different ambient variables: relative humidity, temperature and fuel moisture content. After 100 time iterations, we notice that the fire at Fig. 3 is more aggressive (bigger area) that fire at Fig. 4.

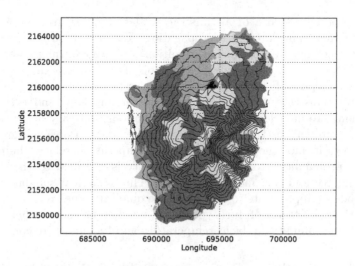

Fig. 5. Fire spread with a 21.21 km/h Northeastern directed wind, 20 % relative humidity and 40⁰ C temperature, 20 % FMC.

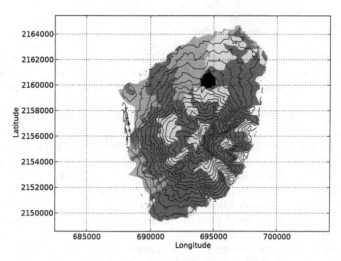

Fig. 6. Fire spread with a 21.21 km/h Northeastern directed wind, 20 % relative humidity and 40⁰ C temperature, 20 % FMC with spotting.

Figures 5 and 6 show fire spread with a 21.21 Km/h Northeastern directed wind 20 % relative humidity and 40^0 C temperature, 20 % FMC with non spotting and spotting effects, only 50 iterations. We note that spotting makes the fire at Fig. 6 more aggressive that fire at Fig. 5.

4   Conclusions

We have proposed the use of an unstructured triangular grid for a cellular automata for modeling forest fire propagation. The fire spread is modeled by a four states cellular automata, here ignition and stop burning probabilities are defined at each cell depending of the type of fuel that each cell encloses. Three different types of fuels were considered: grass, shrubs and trees. Important factors in the forest fire spreading phenomena such as slope and wind (intensity/direction) are modeled by exponential functions and they are included in the model by modifying the ignition probability. Data from experiments are extrapolated to include the effects of ambient temperature/relative humidity in the ignition probability; stop burning probability is modified by the effects of relative humidity and fuel moisture content. The numerical simulations show that the model is appropriate to reproduce the qualitative behavior of forest fire spread for the main factor of: fuel type, slope, wind and some weather variables such as relative humidity, ambient temperature and fuel moisture content.

Acknowledgments. This work has been supported by the National Council of Sciences and Technology CONACYT. Proyect 151437, Ciencias Básicas.

References

1. Anderson, H.E.: Aids to Determining Fuel Models For Estimating Fire Behavior, United States Department of Agriculture, Forest Servicei Intermountain, Forest and Range Experiment Station Ogden, UT 84401 General Technical Report INT-122 (1982)
2. Beverly, J.L., Wotton, B.M.: Modelling the probability of sustained flaming: predictive value of fire weather index components compared with observations of site weather and fuel moisture conditions. Int. J. Wildland Fire **16**(2), 161–173 (2007)
3. Bianchi, L.O., Defosse, G.E.: Ignition probability of fine dead surface fuels of native Patagonian forests or Argentina. Forest Syst. [S.l.] **23**(1), 129–138 (2014). http://revistas.inia.es/index.php/fs/article/view/4632
4. Blackmarr, W.H.: Moisture Content Influences Ignitability of Slash Pine Litter, Res. Note SE-173. Asheville, NC: U.S. Department of Agriculture, Forest Service, Southeastern Forest Experiment Station, p. 7 (1972)
5. Burrows, N.D.: Flame residence times and rates of weight loss of eucalypt forest fuel particles. Int. J. Wildland Fire **190**, 137–143 (2002)
6. Butler, B.W., Anderson, W.R., Catchpole, E.A.: Influence of slope on fire spread rate. In: The Fire Environment Innovations, Management and Policy Conference Proceedings (2007)

7. Lin, C.-C.: Influences of temperature, relative humidity, and heat sources on ignition: a laboratory test. Taiwan J. Sci. **20**(1), 89–93 (2005)
8. Cheney, N.P., Wilson, A.G., McCaw, L.: Deveploment of a Australian fire danger rating system, Rural Industries Resaerch and Development Corporation RIRDC final report No. CSF-35A (1990)
9. Dunn, A.: Simulating complex systems by cellular automata understanding complex systems. In: Kroc, J., Sloot, P.M.A., Hoekstra, A.G. (eds.) Hierarchical Cellular Automata Methods, pp. 59–80. Springer, Heidelberg (2010)
10. Guld, J.S.: Development of bushfire spread of the Wangary fire 10th and 11th January 2005, Lower Eyre peninsula, South Australia, preliminary report CSIRO (2005)
11. Hernández Encinas, L., Hoya White, S., Martín del Rey, A., Rodríguez Sánchez, G.: Modelling forest fire spread using hexagonal cellular automata. Appl. Math. Model. **31**(6), 1213–1227 (2007)
12. Holland, E.P., Aegerter, J.N., Dytham, C., Smith, G.C.: Landscape as a model: the importance of geometry. PLoS Comput. Biol. **3**(10), e200 (2007)
13. Instituto National de Estadística y Geografía (2015). www.inegi.org.mx
14. McArthur, A.G.: The tasmanian bushfire of 7th February and associated behavior characteristics. In: Mass Fire Symposium: The Technical Cooperation Programme, vol. 1, paper A7 (1969)
15. Mendes-Lopez, J., Ventura, J., Amaral, J.: Flame characteristics, temperatures-time curves, and rate of spread in fires propagating in a bed of Pinus pinaster needles. Int. J. Wildland Fire **12**, 67–84 (2003)
16. Noble, J.C.: Behavior of a very fast grassland wildfire on the Riverine Plain of southeastern Australia. Int. J. Wildland Fire **1**, 189–196 (1991)
17. Ortigoza, G.: Unstructured triangular cellular automata for modeling geographic spread. Appl. Math. Comput. Elsevier **258**, 520–536 (2015)
18. Ortigoza, G.: An Unstructured Triangular Cellular Automata for Modeling Fire Propagation, Forest Ecology and Management Elsevier (2015, Submitted to)
19. Plucinski, M.P., Catchpole, W.R.: Predicting ignition thresholds in litter layers. In: Ghassemi, F., Post, D.A., Sivapalan, M., Vertessy, R. (eds.) MODSIM 2001 International Congress on Modelling and Simulation, vol. 1, pp. 967–971. Modelling and Simulation Society of Australia and New Zealand (2001)
20. Quartieri, J., Mastorakis, N.E., Iannone, G., Guarnaccia, C.: A Cellular Automata Model for Fire spreading prediction, Latest Trends on Urban Planning and transportation (2010)
21. Rothermel, R.C.: A mathematical model for predicting fire spread in wildland fuels, Res. Pap. INT-115. Ogden, UT: U.S. Department of Agriculture, Intermountain Forest and Range Experiment Station, p. 40 (1972)
22. Weir, J.R.: Using Relative Humidity to Predict Spotfire Probability on Prescribed Burns, USDA Forest Service RMRS-P-47 (2007)

An Open MPI Extension for Supporting Task Based Parallelism in Heterogeneous CPU-GPU Clusters

Uriel Cabello$^{(\boxtimes)}$, José Rodríguez, and Amilcar Meneses-Viveros

Department of Computer Science, Center of Research and Advanced Studies
(Cinvestav), Mexico City, Mexico
jcabello@computacion.cs.cinvestav.mx,
{jrodriguez,ameneses}@cs.cinvestav.mx

Abstract. In this work we identify and analyze some of the patterns appearing in the development and deployment of scientific applications over clusters equipped with heterogeneous computing resources.

The main contributions of this work are the identification of the patterns aforementioned, as well as the design and implementation of an Open MPI extension that supports the development and deployment of applications programmed using a task approach.

In order to illustrate how to use our extension, we provide the implementation and performance evaluation of two sample applications: the N-Body problem and the general matrix multiplication.

1 Introduction

One of the most remarkable advances in the cluster computing paradigm is the ability to employ multiple computing units optimized for the execution of repetitive operations. Nowadays each node in a cluster computer is equipped not only with traditional CPUs, but also, with graphical processing units (GPUs), accelerated processing units (APUs), and other kind of accelerators like the Intel Xeon Phi co-processor, having hundreds of cores, designed to speed up the execution of applications based on the single instruction multiple data (SIMD) programming model.

In order to keep all those resources working in a coordinated and cooperative way, two basic elements must be provided: (1) A communication layer between nodes and (2) a framework for writing and executing programs in heterogeneous platforms. The communications layer known as middleware is the responsible for performing data distribution, communication, synchronization, and other services required for the execution of the application. In this field the open message passing interface (Open MPI) is one of the most used and well documented implementations of the MPI middleware specification. On the other hand a framework for programming heterogeneous resources can be fulfilled by using the OpenCL specification, a vendor independent framework for developing SIMD applications employing a standard API.

© Springer International Publishing Switzerland 2016
I. Gitler and J. Klapp (Eds.): ISUM 2015, CCIS 595, pp. 144–155, 2016.
DOI: 10.1007/978-3-319-32243-8_10

Inspite of the existence of the tools aforementioned, the development and deployment of applications that can take advantage of heterogeneous computing resources remains as a handcrafted and error prone activity where programmers must be aware of many overwhelming hard o time consuming tasks that can be automated by frameworks. Another issue arising when programming in heterogeneous environments is the problem of under-utilization of resources, because several applications using the SIMD model, keeps the CPU idle while the GPU performs the parallel work.

Some related works deal with the problem of programming applications for heterogeneous clusters. However, many of them, focus on solving communication issues [1,2] but, few focus on harnessing multiple accelerators. On the other hand some works solve the problem of programming for multiple GPUs but focus on NVIDIA devices [3]. Some others deal with heterogeneous accelerators but underestimate the problems related to communication in large scale systems [4–7]. Finally, some other works solve the problem of communication by using nonstandard communication systems [8].

Our proposal consists of a set of tools implemented on top of Open MPI, designed to ease the development and deployment of applications using a task programming model. Task decomposition allows the programmer to focus on the workload distribution to multiple worker devices dedicated to execute procedures over fixed blocks of data. The overwhelming work of finding and initializing devices, is delegated to the Open MPI run time system which becomes responsible for handling the devices available in the cluster, as well as, to performing data transfers among them using the appropriated memory hierarchy such as: inter device copy, intra-node copy or inter-node copy.

The rest of this paper is organized as follows: in Sect. 2 we introduce some definitions and basic concepts required to use our extensions. In Sect. 3 we present the architecture of our extension and present the functions forming our API. In Sect. 4 we present some study cases in order to demonstrate how to use our extensions and we present some graphs to show the performance achieved when porting applications to the task based programming model. Finally in Sect. 5 we present the conclusions obtained on the development of this proposal and the future directions of this work.

2   Background

In this section we describe the architecture of a heterogeneous computing system, then we present the key concept of this work: the concept of task, and finally we do a brief review of the architecture of Open MPI.

2.1   Task Based Programming in Heterogeneous Systems

A heterogeneous computing system consists of the integration of multiple independent computing units with different capabilities, interconnected by fast and

slow communication channels. Figure 1 depicts a typical heterogeneous computing system. In this environment multiple programming models are required to
harness the capabilities of the system, this scenario is commonly referred to
as the *"MPI+X"* programming model where MPI provides the infrastructure
required to handle the distributed memory model while *"X"* is the complementary tool exploiting the advantages of shared memory. Typical examples of *"X"*
includes CUDA, OpenCL, OpenMP, and Pthreads.

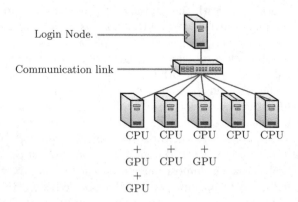

Login Node.

Communication link

CPU CPU CPU CPU CPU
+   +   +
GPU CPU GPU
+
GPU

Fig. 1. Heterogeneous computing environment.

In spite of the existence of OpenCL as a tool for heterogeneous parallel
programming one of the main disadvantages and criticism of OpenCL is the
fact that too many steps are required to achieve the execution of kernels on the
device. When OpenCL is compared against the CUDA runtime API, we find
that several steps like device handler initialization, device context initialization,
memory buffer setup, kernel building, and parameter setup are some of the
tasks that CUDA executes transparently for the user. This problem becomes
more relevant when the goal is to setup the execution of kernels in clusters with
heterogeneous components as is the case shown in Fig. 1.

Another issue that arises when working with clusters is the problem of
data distribution, even though the MPI specification provides multiple functions designed to perform collective data distribution, the chunks of data cannot
be copied directly into the device memory where they will be used. Therefore
the programmer must be aware of finding the appropriate rank, context, and,
device to perform coherent data transfers.

In order to deal with the issues aforementioned in this work we employ a programming model based on tasks. In the scope of this work, tasks are structures
composed by a set of related instructions known as *"procedures"* and independent blocks of data hereinafter referred to as *"entities"* that must be processed
by a *"worker"* device.

Unlike the traditional single program multiple data (SPMD) programming
model of MPI, where the applications are designed in such a way that each

process gets a chunk of data based on its rank and then executes the procedure using that data, in the task based programming model, users must design their applications in such a way that the data must be stored in indivisible blocks called entities and then, each device can execute the *procedure* using a set of entities regardless of its location. This approach has the advantage of divide the data in chunks, coherent for the logic of the application regardless of the number of processing units. Even though this can be seen as an important restriction many applications can specify its data in terms of entities.

2.2   Architecture of Open MPI

Open MPI (OMPI) is an open source implementation of the MPI specification that has a component-based design, which means that multiple independent components can be developed separately, plugged or removed from the MPI core at run time. This architecture is known as the modular component architecture (MCA) and is the key for flexibility and reuse in Open MPI.

The MCA is organized in several blocks called frameworks, which are public interfaces between service requests and specific service implementations. Those frameworks are organized in three layers: the Open Portable Access Layer (OPAL), the Open MPI Run-Time Environment (ORTE), and the Open MPI (OMPI) layer. Each one of these layers provides utility functions for the upper layers as shown in Fig. 2, and user applications are allowed to interact only with the upper OMPI layer using the MPI API.

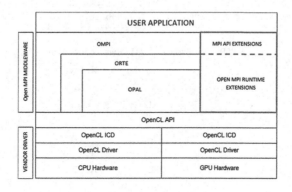

Fig. 2. Open MPI internal architecture.

The architecture of OpenMPI has been designed to enable the addition of extensions to the system in order to provide new services. In Fig. 2 we show an Open MPI extension composed of two main blocks: the API extension and the run time extension. The former is an interface between the user application and the new set of functions, and the latter is a set of functions that can interact with the Open MPI run time system and with the OpenCL API.

3   Design of the Open MPI Extension

In this section we describe our approach to address the issues pointed out before. The proposal consists of the design of an Open MPI extension that automates many of the steps required for the execution of applications in heterogeneous clusters. To achieve this goal we have identified the following set of steps required to complete the execution of a kernel: device exploration, device setup, kernel distribution, kernel compilation, data distribution, host to device data copy, kernel execution request, and device to host data copy.

Our system provides automatic detection and initialization of the computing devices available on each host in the cluster. Our proposal also eases the distribution of data among the devices, and finally, it makes all the requests for the execution of the kernel program on each device.

3.1   Architecture of the Extension

In this section we introduce the architecture of our proposal. We present the main components and the set of functions of our API.

According to the Open MPI architecture rules, our extension has a modular design composed by the API extension, the run-time extension and a binding layer. An overview of the architecture is depicted in Fig. 3.

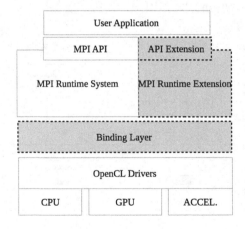

Fig. 3. Architecture of the Open MPI extension.

On the top of this schema we find the user application interacting with the Open MPI runtime system through an API that extends the standard MPI specification [9]. The functions in our OMPI extension are designed to ease the process of creation and execution of kernels on each device, but also, provides tools for transparent and efficient data distribution. The functions in our API extension are summarized in the Table 1.

Table 1. The MPI API extension

int OMPI_XclCommitEntityType(int blockcount, int* blocklen, MPI_Aint* displacements, MPI_Datatype* basictypes, MPI_Datatype * newDatatype)
int OMPI_XclCollectDevicesInfo(int DEVICE_SELECTION, MPI_Comm comm)
int OMPI_XclCreateKernel(MPI_Comm comm, char* srcPath, char* kernelName)
int OMPI_XclExecKernel(MPI_Comm comm, int taskIdx, int workDims, size_t * globalThreads, size_t * localThreads, const char * fmt, ...)
int OMPI_XclScatter(const char* datafileName, int* count, MPI_Datatype entityType, void *hostbuffer, int trayIdx, MPI_Comm comm)
int OMPI_XclGather(int trayIdx, int* count, MPI_Datatype entityType, void *hostbuffer, const char* datafileName, MPI_Comm comm)
int OMPI_XclSend(int trayIdx, int count, MPI_Datatype entityType, int src_task, int dest_task, int TAG, MPI_Comm comm)
int OMPI_XclRecv(int trayIdx, int count, MPI_Datatype entityType, int src_task, int dest_task, int TAG, MPI_Comm comm)
int OMPI_XclSendRecv(int src_task, int src_trayIdx, int dest_task, int dest_trayIdx, int count, MPI_Datatype entityType, MPI_Comm comm)
int OMPI_XclReadTaskBuffer(int taskIdx, int trayIdx, int bufferSize, void * hostBuffer, MPI_Comm comm)
int OMPI_XclWriteTaskBuffer(int taskIdx, int trayIdx, int bufferSize, void * hostBuffer, MPI_Comm comm)
int OMPI_XclFreeTaskTray(int taskIdx, int trayIdx, MPI_Comm comm)
int OMPI_XclFreeAllTrays(int taskIdx, MPI_Comm comm)
int OMPI_XclFreeTask(int taskIdx, MPI_Comm comm)
int OMPI_XclFreeAllTasks(MPI_Comm comm)
int OMPI_XclWaitAllTasks(MPI_Comm comm)

In the run time layer we find the set of functions used to handle the computing devices and to provide a unique global image of the tasks running in the system. This set of functions is composed by OpenCL instructions called by the run time system and data structures designed to provide a consistent system image, the user has no access to that function set, and no user interaction is required at all.

The next layer in Fig. 3 is the binding layer. This layer has two main functions:

1. Works as an interface that connects the MPI run-time system with the OpenCL device driver while keeps the code for each module isolated.
2. Makes our system more dynamic by enabling to modify and even to connect multiple implementations of the multi-device management library without the necessity of any modification or recompilation of the MPI system already installed in the cluster.

Finally at the end of Fig. 3 we can find vendor device drivers, in this layer we have the multiple implementations of OpenCL found on each host and the ICD loader brings the mechanism to work with all of them.

4 Analysis and Results

To demonstrate the advantages of our extensions we present the implementation of two benchmark applications: the N-body simulation problem, and the general matrix multiplication (GEMM). We analyze the performance of those applications under different scenarios.

4.1 N-Body Simulation Problem

The N-Body simulation problem is implemented by defining an entity for each particle in the system. The entity is composed by the position, the weight, and the velocity of the particle and three spatial dimensions are used for defining position and velocity. This definition is reflected in line 2 of Listing 1. The next step consists of query the number of tasks defined for the execution as shown on line 4. This instruction returns the global amount of tasks in the system using the kind of device specified, if ALL_DEVICES is specified, a configuration file must be provided to specify the task scheduling scheme otherwise round robin scheduling is employed. Using this approach is possible to perform load balancing based on the knowledge that the user has over its environment, in lines 5–12 we perform data distribution, line 14 creates and distributes the kernel.

Listing 1. N-Body Initialization

```
1   #define mymod(n,m) ((n % m) + m) % m;
2   OMPI_commit_EntityType(blockcount, blocklen, displacements,
3                          basictypes, &MPIentityType);
4   numTasks=OMPI_collectDevicesInfo(ALL_DEVICES, MPI_COMM_WORLD);
5   err = OMPI_XclScatter("dataFile.dat", &ePerRank,
6           MPIentityType, NULL, 0, MPI_COMM_WORLD );
7           /*First allocate a host buffer.*/
8   bodyArr = (entityType*) malloc(ePerRank * sizeof(entityType));
9
10          /*Then perform data splitting.*/
11  err|= OMPI_XclScatter("dataFile.dat", NULL,
12          MPIentityType, bodyArr, 0, MPI_COMM_WORLD );
13          /*Create the kernel.*/
14  err|=OMPI_XclCreateKernel(MPI_COMM_WORLD,"NBodyExt.cl","computeForces");
```

In lines 17 to 23 of Listing 2 we execute the computation of forces between all pairs of particles stored on each task and in line 25 we set a synchronization point before to execute an exchange of entities between different tasks.

Listing 2. N-Body execution

```
15          /*Finally perfom the execution.*/
16  for (step = 0; step < numTasks; step++) {
17   for (taskIdx = 0; taskIdx < numTasks; taskIdx++) {
18    int srcTask = mymod((step+taskIdx-numTasks),numTasks);
19    err |= OMPI_XclSendRecv(srcTask, 0, taskIdx, 1,
20          ePerTask, MPIentityType, MPI_COMM_WORLD );
```

```
21    err |= OMPI_XclExecKernel(MPI_COMM_SELF, taskIdx, Dims,
22         globalDims, localDims, "%T, %T, %d ,%f ,%f, %d",0 ,
23         1, numBodies,0.0005, 0.01, numTasks);
24    }
25    err |= OMPI_XclWaitAllTasks(MPI_COMM_WORLD);
26  }
```

In Fig. 4 we depict the results of the execution of the n-body simulation problem using different sizes. In this figure is possible appreciate the increase in performance by using both devices. To achieve an increase in performance when using both the CPU and the GPU a scheduling file is provided assigning 75 % of the workload to the GPU and 25 % to the CPU.

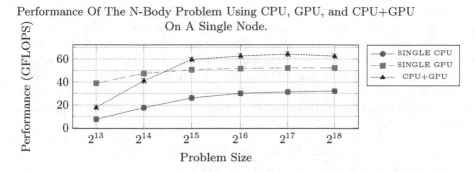

Fig. 4. Performance of the N-Body problem using the CPU and the GPU to accelerate the execution. The host is equipped with an Intel core i7 processor and a Nvidia 640m SE GPU card.

In Fig. 5 we show the result of the execution of this application using a single node with multiple heterogeneous GPUs.

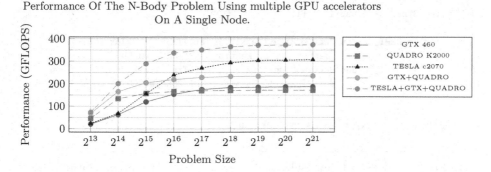

Fig. 5. Performance of the N-Body problem using multiple GPU accelerators. The host is equipped with one GTX 460, one QUADRO K2000, and, one TESLA c2070 GPU cards.

4.2 SGEMM

We now present a task based implementation of the general matrix multiplication problem. The major restriction to achieve scalability in this application is the problem of data dependencies to perform the inner product between rows of A and columns of B. In order to address this restriction our entities are defined as sub-matrices of the matrix A and B respectively. Therefore the first step consist on store the matrices in blocks instead of the row major or column major forms. Once the matrix is stored in the appropriate format we can proceed to perform matrix multiplication by blocks, where each block is mapped to one task, this approach has the advantage to transport small chunks of data using different memory hierarchies avoiding the saturation of inter-host communication channel.

Similarly as we did in the case of N-Body the tasks and kernel initialization must be done, after that we can proceed to the execution of blocked matrix multiplication. In line 3 of the code shown in Listing 3, we request the multiplication of two block matrices, this multiplication can be executed in parallel on each device. After that, lines 13 and 15 perform the transference of a block of matrix A and B to the corresponding task, and finally line 19 performs a synchronization among all tasks before to proceed with the next multiplication step.

Listing 3. GEMM execution

```
1   for(step = 0; step < sqrt(numTasks); step++) {
2     for (taskIdx = 0; taskIdx < numTasks; taskIdx++) {
3      err |= OMPI_XclExecKernel(MPI_COMM_SELF, taskIdx, Dims,
4                            globalDims, localDims,"%T %T %T %d %d",
5                            3*(step%2), 3*(step%2)+1,
6                            2, rPBlock_A, cPBlock_A);
7       srcATray =3*(step%2);
8       destATray=3*((step+1)%2);
9
10      srcBTray =3*(step%2)+1;
11      destBTray=3*((step+1)%2)+1;
12
13      err |= OMPI_XclSendRecv(myRight[taskIdx], srcATray ,taskIdx ,
14                          destATray, 1, Aentity, MPI_COMM_WORLD );
15      err |= OMPI_XclSendRecv(myDown[taskIdx], srcBTray ,taskIdx ,
16                          destBTray, 1, Bentity, MPI_COMM_WORLD );
17
18    }
19    err |= OMPI_XclWaitAllTasks(MPI_COMM_WORLD );
20  }
```

In Fig. 6 are depicted the results of the execution of the matrix multiplication under different scenarios, different matrix sizes, and using several hosts. In this case as we increase the size of the problem, a single GPU device becomes unable to perform the multiplication due to the lack of memory space, however using the task based approach the application is able to use more resources to sparse the data without require any modification to the source code.

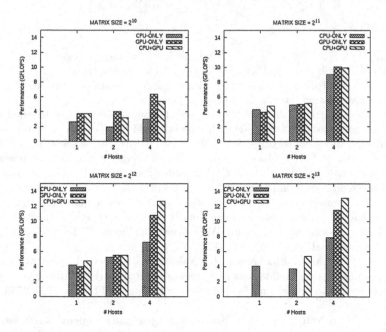

Fig. 6. Performance in the execution of SGEMM using multiple sizes and multiple accelerators. Each host is equipped with an Intel core i7 processor and an Nvidia 8000GS GPU card.

5   Conclusions and Future Work

Even though MPI remains as one of the most used middleware for high performance computing, the quick progress and evolution of computing technologies reinforces the need to keep developing programming tools moving as fast as hardware changes. In this sense, the idea of this work is to present a mechanism through which, the programmers that use MPI for parallel programming can also harness the advantages of several heterogeneous computing devices, without dealing with the complexities associated with the use of several programming tools.

In this work we did a review of the steps required to setup multiple devices commonly found in heterogeneous clusters to execute scientific applications. We have taken advantage of the facilities given by Open MPI to aggregate new functionality to its runtime system but also to create new functions callable through API extensions. Using this platform we designed an extension able to automate many of the steps required to schedule task in heterogeneous computing devices like CPUs or GPUs.

In the future, we propose the development and inclusion of a mechanism to detect failures in the execution of tasks and move them through the remaining nodes, in order to make our system fault tolerant. Another line of work consists on the implementation of a mechanism to support dynamic task parallelism.

References

1. Huang, C., Lawlor, O., Kalé, L.V.: Adaptive MPI. In: Rauchwerger, L. (ed.) LCPC 2003. LNCS, vol. 2958, pp. 306–322. Springer, Heidelberg (2004)
2. Karonis, N.T., Toonen, B., Foster, I.: Mpich-g2: A grid-enabled implementation of the message passing interface (2002)
3. Song, F., Dongarra, J.: A scalable framework for heterogeneous gpu-based clusters. In: Proceedings of the Twenty-Fourth Annual ACM Symposium on Parallelism in Algorithms and Architectures, SPAA 2012, pp. 91–100. ACM, New York (2012)
4. Kim, J., Seo, S., Lee, J., Nah, J., Jo, G., Lee, J.: Snucl: an opencl framework for heterogeneous cpu/gpu clusters. In: Proceedings of the 26th ACM International Conference on Supercomputing, ICS 2012, pp. 341–352. ACM, New York (2012)
5. Kegel, P., Steuwer, M., Gorlatch, S.: dopencl: towards a uniform programming approach for distributed heterogeneous multi-/many-core systems. In: Parallel and Distributed Processing Symposium Workshops PhD Forum (IPDPSW), 2012 IEEE 26th International, pp. 174–186 (2012)
6. Aoki, R., Oikawa, S., Tsuchiyama, R., Nakamura, T.: Hybrid opencl: connecting different opencl implementations over network. In: 2010 IEEE 10th International Conference on Computer and Information Technology (CIT), pp. 2729–2735, June 2010
7. Barak, A., Ben-Nun, T., Levy, E., Shiloh, A.: A package for opencl based heterogeneous computing on clusters with many gpu devices. In: 2010 IEEE International Conference on Cluster Computing Workshops and Posters (CLUSTER WORK-SHOPS), pp. 1–7, September 2010
8. Alves, A., Rufino, J., Pina, A., Santos, L.P.: clOpenCL - supporting distributed heterogeneous computing in HPC clusters. In: Caragiannis, I., et al. (eds.) Euro-Par Workshops 2012. LNCS, vol. 7640, pp. 112–122. Springer, Heidelberg (2013)
9. The MPI Forum. MPI: A Message-Passing Interface Standard, 10 2012. Ver. 3.0
10. Sun, E., Schaa, D., Bagley, R., Rubin, N., Kaeli, D.: Enabling task-level scheduling on heterogeneous platforms. In: Proceedings of the 5th Annual Workshop on General Purpose Processing with Graphics Processing Units, GPGPU-5, pp. 84–93. ACM, New York (2012)
11. Denis, A., Pérez, C., Priol, T.: Towards high performance CORBA and MPI middlewares for grid computing. In: Lee, C.A. (ed.) GRID 2001. LNCS, vol. 2242, pp. 14–25. Springer, Heidelberg (2001)
12. Seymour, K., Nakada, H., Matsuoka, S., Dongarra, J., Lee, C., Casanova, H.: Gridrpc: A remote procedure call api for grid computing (2002)
13. Foster, I.: Globus toolkit version 4: software for service-oriented systems. In: Jin, H., Reed, D., Jiang, W. (eds.) NPC 2005. LNCS, vol. 3779, pp. 2–13. Springer, Heidelberg (2005)
14. Vadhiyar, S.S., Dongarra, J.J.: Gradsolvea grid-based RPC system for parallel computing with application-level scheduling. J. Parallel Distrib. Comput. **64**(6), 774–783 (2004). YJPDC Special Issue on Middleware
15. Cybenko, G.: Dynamic load balancing for distributed memory multiprocessors. J. Parallel Distrib Comput. **7**(2), 279–301 (1989)
16. Barak, A., Margolin, A., Shiloh, A.: Automatic resource-centric process migration for MPI. In: Träff, J.L., Benkner, S., Dongarra, J.J. (eds.) EuroMPI 2012. LNCS, vol. 7490, pp. 163–172. Springer, Heidelberg (2012)

17. Bhatelé, A., Kalé, L.V., Kumar, S.: Dynamic topology aware load balancing algorithms for molecular dynamics applications. In: Proceedings of the 23rd International Conference on Supercomputing, ICS 2009, pp. 110–116. ACM, New York (2009)
18. Hu, Y.F., Blake, R.J., Emerson, D.R.: An optimal migration algorithm for dynamic load balancing. Concurrency Pract. Experience 10(6), 467–483 (1998)
19. Li, Y., Yang, Y., Ma, M., Zhou, L.: A hybrid load balancing strategy of sequential tasks for grid computing environments. Future Gener. Comput. Syst. 25(8), 819–828 (2009)
20. Li, Y., Lan, Z.: A survey of load balancing in grid computing. In: Zhang, J., He, J.-H., Fu, Y. (eds.) CIS 2004. LNCS, vol. 3314, pp. 280–285. Springer, Heidelberg (2004)
21. Ravi, V.T., Ma, W., Chiu, D., Agrawal, G.: Compiler and runtime support for enabling generalized reduction computations on heterogeneous parallel configurations. In: Proceedings of the 24th ACM International Conference on Supercomputing, ICS 2010, pp. 137–146. ACM, New York (2010)
22. Beltrn, M., Guzmn, A.: How to balance the load on heterogeneous clusters. Int. J. High Perform. Comput. Appl. 23(1), 99–118 (2009)
23. Boveiri, H.R.: Aco-mts: a new approach for multiprocessor task scheduling based on ant colony optimization. In: 2010 International Conference on Intelligent and Advanced Systems (ICIAS), pp. 1–5 (2010)
24. Willebeek-LeMair, M.H., Reeves, A.P.: Strategies for dynamic load balancing on highly parallel computers. IEEE Trans. Parallel Distrib. Syst. 4(9), 979–993 (1993)
25. Romdhanne, B.B., Nikaein, N., Bonnet, C.: Coordinator-master-worker model for efficient large scale network simulation. In: Proceedings of the 6th International ICST Conference on Simulation Tools and Techniques, SimuTools 2013, ICST, Brussels, Belgium, Belgium, ICST (Institute for Computer Sciences, Social-Informatics and Telecommunications Engineering), pp. 119–128 (2013)
26. Brown, J.A., Porter, L., Tullsen, D.M.: Fast thread migration via cache working set prediction. In: 2011 IEEE 17th International Symposium on High Performance Computer Architecture (HPCA), pp. 193–204 (2011)
27. Shirahata, K., Sato, H., Matsuoka, S.: Hybrid map task scheduling for gpu-based heterogeneous clusters. In: 2010 IEEE Second International Conference on Cloud Computing Technology and Science (CloudCom), pp. 733–740 (2010)
28. Acosta, A., Blanco, V., Almeida, F.: Towards the dynamic load balancing on heterogeneous multi-gpu systems. In: 2012 IEEE 10th International Symposium on Parallel and Distributed Processing with Applications (ISPA), pp. 646–653 (2012)
29. Milojičić, D.S., Douglis, F., Paindaveine, Y., Wheeler, R., Zhou, S.: Process migration. ACM Comput. Surv. 32(3), 241–299 (2000)
30. The Khronos Group. The OpenCL specification, 11 2012. Ver. 1.2

Parallel Meshing for Finite Element Analysis

Víctor E. Cardoso[✉] and Salvador Botello

Centro de Investigación en Matemáticas A. C. (CIMAT), Jalisco S/N, Valenciana,
36240 Guanajuato, Mexico
{victorc,botello}@cimat.mx

Abstract. Finite Element (FE) analysis is a well-established method to solve engineering problems, some of them require fine grained precision and, by consequence, huge meshes. A common bottle-neck in FE calculations is domain meshing. In this paper we discuss our implementation of a parallel-meshing tool. Firstly, we create a rough mesh with a serial procedure based on a Constrained Delaunay Triangulation; secondly, such a mesh is divided into N parts via spectral-bisection, where N is the number of available threads; and finally, the N parts are refined simultaneously by independent threads using Delaunay-refinement. Other proposals that use a thread to refine each part, need a user-defined subdivision. This approach calculates such a subdivision automatically while reducing the thread-communication overhead. Some researchers propose similar schemes using orthogonal-trees to create regular meshes in parallel, without any guaranty about element quality, while the Delaunay techniques have nice quality properties already proven [1–3]. Although this implementation uses a shared-memory scheme, it could be adapted in a distributed-memory strategy.

1 Introduction

Most physical phenomena are modelled with Partial Differential Equations (PDEs), including structural mechanics, fluid dynamics, electromagnetic dynamics and several diffusive process, such as heat transfer. Engineers, scientist and mathematicians developed the Finite Element (FE) analysis during the last 60 years in order to solve this PDEs in elaborated domains, where the analytical solution can not be calculated. These domains must be discretised into FEs in order to interpolate the solution.

A mesh is a subdivision of the domain into FEs used to approximate the solution. The meshing routines are becoming the bottle neck of important industrial processes and the parallel meshing has emerged as a new research field in three big areas: Computational Geometry, Numerical Methods and Parallel Computing. For this reason we present a parallel meshing implementation using a shared memory scheme.

FE simulations require a mesh of the domain which is used to assembly a system of equations to approximate the solution upon the nodes of the mesh, using this values to interpolate the function inside the elements. A mesh is a subdivision of a geometry into FEs, the simplest finite elements are triangles

© Springer International Publishing Switzerland 2016
I. Gitler and J. Klapp (Eds.): ISUM 2015, CCIS 595, pp. 156–168, 2016.
DOI: 10.1007/978-3-319-32243-8_11

in 2D and tetrahedra in 3D, which can be used to build quadrilaterals in 2D and hexahedra of triangular faces in 3D, as proposed in [4]. These elements are enough to obtain accurate estimations of the solution for any problem. From here, we are going to refer to triangular and tetrahedra meshes as simplex-meshes in order to simplify the discussion.

The first simplex-mesh generators, and still used until today, are the most naive solution of the meshing problem. They create a regular pattern of simplices over an enveloping box of the domain, keeping the interior simplices, removing the exterior ones and modifying the simplices intersected by the boundary, forcing their nodes to lie over the contour of the geometry, as illustrated in Fig. 1.

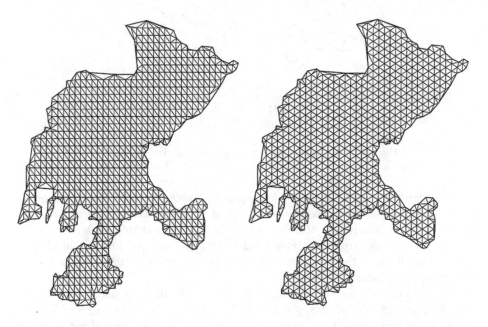

Fig. 1. Simplex-meshes based on a regular pattern of simplices. The geometry corresponds to the state of Zacatecas, Mexico.

As one could expect, this simplex-meshing procedure generates a huge number of simplices when the geometry has small local features, which are formally defined by Ruppert [1]. The local features determinate the maximum size of a simplex at any point of the domain, as illustrated in Fig. 2.

Roughly speaking, larger number of FEs enhance the accuracy of the solution, unfortunately, this imply expensive computations and most of the time with a little diminution of the numerical error. This is an insane cost-benefit relation and one should not allow such an abuse. A proposed solution to this undesirable side-effect is the use of balanced orthogonal-trees (oct-trees in 3D and quad-trees in 2D) to create size-adapted regular simplices, see [5]. The balanced trees create simplices with the maximum possible size following a predefined pattern, as shown in Fig. 3.

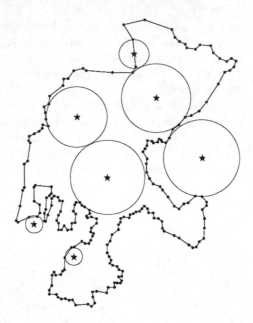

Fig. 2. Local feature of several points, marked as stars.

Although these techniques are highly parallelisable, the mathematicians were unsatisfied because the meshes were not optimal in any sense, furthermore, the meshes were not unique for the same geometry (what a shame for a scientist!), because with a simple rotation of the model, the algorithm produces a completely different mesh, since the simplices are taken from regular patterns aligned with the orthogonal planes X, Y and Z.

The prescripted cure for this pain were the advancing-front algorithms which start by meshing. The recipe is simple, take a face of the front as basis for the new simplex and complete it by inserting a new vertex, which will get as large as needed to maximize the quality of the simplex, repeat the simplex generation until the front disappears. In mesh surfaces, the initial front is the mesh of the segments bounding such surfaces, and in mesh volumes, the initial front is the mesh of the surfaces bounding such volumes. The advancing-front technique is illustrated in Fig. 4.

At that point, the engineers started to propose quality measures to design optimal-meshes. The most-common quality measures compare any simplex against an equilateral simplex, assuming that this is the most perfect simplex. From this point of view, a mesh should have the maximum number of simplices close to be equilateral.

In the mid of the 80's, the researchers establish that the optimal mesh, without any constraint, is the mesh that maximises the minimum angle of the simplices between all the possible triangulations (in the n-dimensional Euclidean space). Fortunately, it can be demonstrated that the Delaunay Triangulation

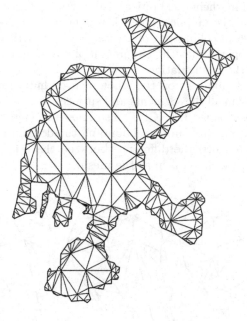

Fig. 3. Mesh produced using a quad-tree algorithm.

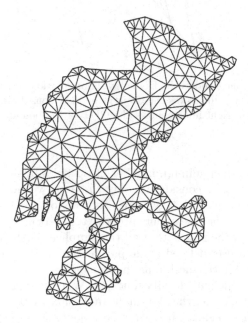

Fig. 4. The advancing front technique starts by meshing the boundary, such a mesh is used as initial front to start the interior meshing.

(DT), a well studied mathematical object, is the triangulation which maximises the minimum angle of the simplices and it is unique if there are not degeneracies, such as cocircularities or collinearity of the whole set of vertices, see [6]. Further, the DT have the property that the circumball of any simplex does not contain any other vertex of the triangulation.

The DT produces simplices on the whole convex hull of the domain but it does not always contain all the segments and surfaces bounding the domain. The definition of the Constrained DT (CDT, also known as General DT) forces the inclusion of all segments and surfaces bounding the domain into the triangulation, see [7]. Figure 5 shows the difference between the DT, the CDT and the CDT of the domain, which is taken as the mesh.

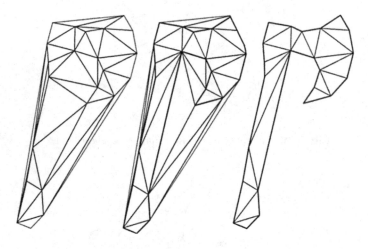

Fig. 5. The most left image shows the Delaunay Triangulation (DT) of the set of input vertices, the middle image illustrates the Constrained DT considering (CDT) the input segments, and the most right image shows the CDT of the bounded domain, which is taken as the mesh.

The DT produces the minimum number of triangles by maximising the minimum angle of its simplices considering only the input vertices, but most of the times it contains simplices with tiny angles that distort the interpolation of the FE analysis. Therefore, the researchers propose to insert new vertices in order to satisfy two constrains, the first is that all the simplices in the mesh should have as minimum angle, a user-defined angle parameter, and the second is that the length of all the edges in the mesh must be as close as possible to some edge-size calculated from a user-defined density function. When designing this algorithms, the scientists should consider that an input angle smaller than 20.7 degrees produces at least another angle smaller than 20.7 degrees, as demonstrated by [3]. In the literature, the new inserted vertices are known as Steiner vertices, and the choice of their location has been studied intensively in [1–3,8].

The pioneering works of Chew [8] and Ruppert [1] propose to insert the Steiner points in the circumcenters of the poor-quality and big simplices, because by the Delaunay definition (no simplex can contain a vertex inside its circumball) these simplices are "broken" into smaller and quality-enhanced elements. The differences between the approaches of Chew and Ruppert are in how they handle the boundaries and how they process the circumcenters that lie outside the domain. These algorithms are commonly known as Delaunay-refinement techniques.

The Delaunay-refinement algorithms are unique meshing techniques with a solid theoretical support, which guarantees bounds in the minimum angle of the simplices. Furthermore, the insertion of Steiner points are local operations that can be implemented in an efficient manner to speed-up the mesh generation, the algorithm of Bowyer has a complexity of $O(N)$ in the worst case (see [9]), where N is the number of Steiner points. These algorithms uses as quality measure the *circumradius to shortest-edge ratio*, which have been accepted by the meshing community as a good quality indicator.

2   Algorithm

We follow the algorithm proposed by Shewchuk [3], also known as the Terminator because its ability to avoid infinite loops, with the modifications presented by Miller [2], which guarantee a minimum angle of 26.45 degrees in bidimensional domains for inputs with angles larger than 36.53, and the least quantity of minimum angles when the input contain angles smaller than this bound.

In summary, the Terminator has three main steps, the first step is to generate a CDT of the input vertices, which can be calculated by computing the DT and forcing the input faces and segments, a posteriori, to be into the mesh. The Delaunay Wall algorithm, abbreviated as DeWall, can build the Delaunay simplices with a worst case complexity of $O(NlogN)$, where N is the number of input vertices, see [6]. The second step consist in removing the simplices upon concavities and holes, by indicating to the algorithm which simplex lies in a concavity or inside a hole, then such a simplex is deleted and their neighbouring simplices are checked, creating an advancing deletion front until finish. The final step is the Delaunay-refinement procedure. Figure 6 illustrates the three main steps of the algorithm.

2.1   Delaunay-Refinement

The Delaunay-refinement is an iterative procedure which inserts the circumcenter of poor-quality simplices as new vertices in the mesh. Most of the time the final mesh, after removing the poor-quality simplices, is not fine enough to fit our accuracy necessities and we must mark as poor-quality simplices all the simplices that are bigger that some value indicated by a user-defined density function.

When splitting a simplex, non of the new simplices may have a *circumradius to shortest-edge ratio* smaller than one in order to guarantee the termination

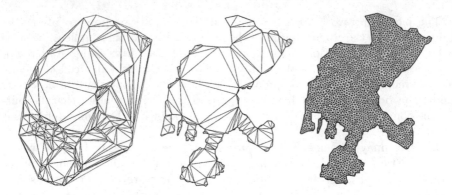

Fig. 6. From left to right the illustration shows the CDT, the triangulation after removing concavities, and the mesh after the Delaunay-refinement.

of the algorithm. A *circumradius to shortest-edge ratio* greater that one means that no edge in the new simplices will be smaller than the smallest edge of the removed simplex.

Observe that, in the case of a bidimensional triangulation, the *circumradius to shortest-edge ratio* is directly related with the minimum angle of a triangle by the following equation

$$\frac{r}{\beta} = \frac{1}{2\sin(\theta)}, \tag{1}$$

where r is the circumradius, β is the shortest edge and θ is the minimum angle of a triangle. Assuming that the minimum angle admissible is 26.45 degrees, then the *circumradius to shortest-edge ratio* should be greater or equal than 1.123 approximately.

2.2   Subsegment Splitting

An edge of the mesh is a generic edge produced during the tessellation, while a subsegment is an edge that is forming part of an input segment. A subsegment is conformed by the points p_1 and p_2, and it is encroached if its diametral circle contains at least one vertex inside, the diametral circle is centered at the midpoint of the segment, denoted m_p, and its radius is the distance from m_p to p_1 (or p_2).

If some subsegment in the mesh is encroached, then the circumcenter of some simplex in the mesh lies outside the domain and it can not be inserted during the Delaunay-refinement procedure, as is shown in Fig. 7. Therefore, all the encroached subsegments must be subdivided before refining the simplices of the mesh. The subdivision of a segment is achieved by inserting its midpoint, m_p.

2.3   Small Inputs Treatment Using Concentric Shells

If the input geometry contains angles smaller than 36.53 degrees, termination can not be proven. Therefore, Ruppert proposed to split the subsegments using

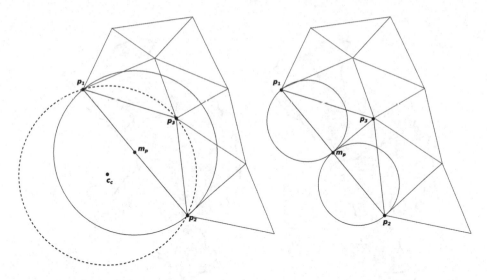

Fig. 7. In the left we can see how the segment formed by the vertices p_1 and p_2 is encroached by p_3, and the circumcenter, c_c, can not be inserted because it lies outside the domain. In the right we see how the subsegments created after inserting the midpoint, m_p, are not encroached by any vertex.

concentric shells instead of the midpoints if the subsegments contain only one input vertex, see [1,3].

The concentric shell splitting point, denoted s_p, is the nearest point to the midpoint of the segment that is a power of two and it is calculated as follows

$$k = \log_2 \left(\|m_p - p_1\| / u \right), \tag{2}$$

$$d = u2^{R(k)} / \|p_2 - p_1\|, \tag{3}$$

$$s_p = (1 - d)p_1 + dp_2, \tag{4}$$

where u is the unit length utilised, $R(k)$ is the integer closest to the real power of two, denoted k, and d is the distance from the concentric shell splitting point to p_1. The value of u affects considerably the performance of the algorithm, we recommend $u = 1 \times 10^{-3}$.

2.4   Parallelisation

Since the vertex insertion is a local operation, the parallelisation relies on the subdivision of the domain into balanced subdomains (same load), which are going to be exhaustively refined by a single thread. Due to the overhead produced by the threads management and the domain segmentation, the parallelisation is worth only if the final mesh will contain more than a few dozens of thousands of vertices.

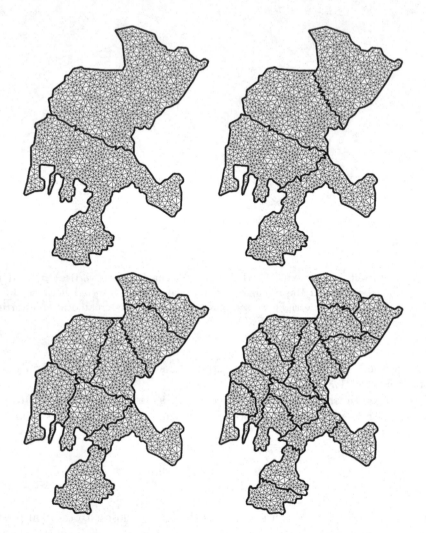

Fig. 8. Domain segmentation of a rough mesh (3000 simplices) using spectral-bisection for 2, 4, 8 and 16 partitions.

Algorithm 1. Parallel-meshing

    Serial-meshing using thousands of simplices.

    Spectral-bisection using N partitions.

    Parallel for i ... N, executes simultaneously in separated threads.

        Delaunay-refinement of the ith partition.

    End parallel for

Algorithm 2. Serial-meshing

Build the Delaunay Triangulation (DT) using the DeWall algorithm.
Build the Constrained DT by modifying the current DT.
Remove simplices into holes and concavities.
Delaunay-refinement until reach N simplices.

Algorithm 3. Delaunay-refinement

Insert in L_s all the encroached subsegments.
Split all subsegments in L_s.
Insert in L_z all the simplices with bad quality or too big.
While L_z is not empty:
    Extract the worst simplex, w, in L_z.
    Calculate the circumcenter, c, of w.
    Insert into L_E the set of subsegments encroached by c.
    If L_E is empty
        Insert c into the mesh.
        Insert in L_z the set of new simplices with bad quality or too big.
    Else
        For each s_e in L_E
            If the concentric-shell allows s_e to be splitted:
                Insert s_e into L_s
        Insert w in L_z again (for another try).
        Split all subsegments in L_s.
    End if
End while

At first we refine the mesh until obtaining at least 1000 vertices in a serial procedure, which can be calculated in milliseconds, then we use spectral bisection to segment the domain, see [10]. The spectral bisection algorithm produces subdomains of similar volume and reduces the size of the frontiers between subdomains, both features are advantages to the parallelisation. In one hand because if the volume distribution is uniform, then the work-load of the processors is almost the same, reducing the computing time. In the other hand, because if the frontier size between subdomains is small, then the collisions between processes decrease; a collision occurs when two threads try to delete the same simplex. Figure 8 illustrates the domain segmentation calculated by the spectral bisection algorithm.

The spectral-bisection algorithm is based on spectral graph theory, where the eigenvectors of the Laplacian matrix, denoted $\mathbf{B}$, are used to make the partitions. Let $\mathbf{D}$ be the diagonal matrix containing the degree of the vertices (number of connections), and let $\mathbf{A}$ be the adjacency matrix, which has one in $\mathbf{A}_{ij}$ if the vertices i and j are connected, and zero otherwise. The Laplacian matrix is constructed as $\mathbf{B} = \mathbf{D} - \mathbf{A}$, note that the sum of the rows in $\mathbf{B}$ is always zero. It can be demonstrated that: (a) $\mathbf{B}$ is positive semidefinite, and (b) if the graph is connected (which is the case of a FE mesh), **B** has only one eigenvalue zero. The eigenvector corresponding to the second smallest eigenvalue is used to divide the graph, by ranking the vertices according to the entries of this eigenvector. In [10] is explained how to perform bisections, quadrisections, octasections and higher order partitionings.

Finally, the team of threads will refine the whole mesh simultaneously in a shared memory scheme, since this memory scheme facilitates the management of collisions, by locking the simplices (in the subdomain boundaries) if they are being processed. Each simplex has a binary locking variable (one single byte could store eight locking variables), which is enabled when some thread is operating on a neighbouring simplex, to prevent that several threads write the data of the same simplex. The boundary between partitions is going to evolve due to the refinement process, and the new simplices are assigned to the same partition of the parent simplex, which is the simplex that must be removed in order to create the new ones.

The Algorithm 1 (Parallel-meshing), the Algorithm 2 (Serial-meshing) and the Algorithm 3 (Delaunay-refinement) summarise the discussion by listing the main tasks of the procedure.

3   Results

Figure 9 displays the speed-up, denoted S_{up}, as a function of the number of threads, denoted N_{th}. The speed-up is calculated as follows:

$$S_{up} = t_s/t_p, \tag{5}$$

where t_s is the time consumed by the Terminator algorithm in [3], and t_p is the time used by our parallel implementation.

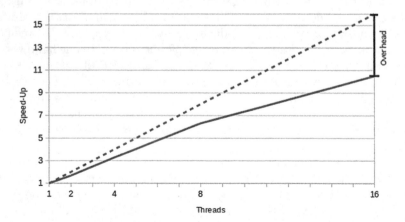

Fig. 9. The increasing solid-curve of the speed-up exhibits the scaling of the algorithm, for one, two, four, eight and sixteen threads. The dashed-line shows the ideal speed-up, without any over-head. Five million of vertices were used to create this graph

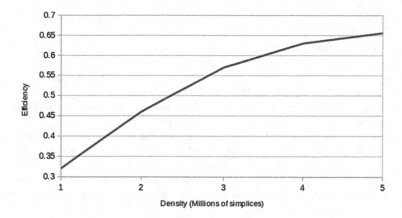

Fig. 10. The efficiency goes to one asymptotically as the density of simplices increases. Sixteen threads were used to create this graph.

Figure 10 shows the efficiency, denoted E_{ff}, as a function of the density of vertices in the mesh, where the efficiency is calculated as

$$E_{ff} = S_{up}/N_{th}, \tag{6}$$

The Zacatecas map, illustrated in the previous sections, was utilised to test the performance of the algorithm.

4   Conclusions

Most of the meshing tools in the academy and in the industry calculate a simplex-mesh in serial procedures, which is becoming the bottle-neck of the whole FE computations. By this reason our parallel implementation exploits the local property of vertex insertion in Delaunay-refinement techniques. The simplices can be taken as basis to build polygonal, quadrilateral, polyhedra and hexahedral meshes.

Spectral-bisection is used to subdivide a gross mesh into several partitions, the same number as the available threads, which will refine simultaneously the whole mesh, a single thread per partition. The efficiency of the parallelisation goes to one asymptotically for high density meshes, but is not worthy for small meshes. As can be seen in Fig. 10, the parallelisation is worthy only if the final mesh will contain at least dozens of thousands of vertices.

The future work aims to reduce the collisions between threads, trying to process the same simplices on the partition boundaries, to enhance the performance in shared memory schemes and simplify the implementation in distributed memory strategies.

References

1. Ruppert, J.: A delaunay refinement algorithm for quality 2-dimensional mesh generation. J. Algorithms **18**, 548–585 (1995)
2. Miller, G.L., Pav, S.E., Walkington, N.J.: When and why ruppert's algorithm works. In: IMR, pp. 91–102 (2003)
3. Shewchuk, J.R.: Reprint of: Delaunay refinement algorithms for triangular mesh generations. Comput. Geom. **47**, 741–778 (2014)
4. Remacle, J.F., Lambrechts, J., Seny, B., Marchandise, E., Johnen, A., Geuzaine, C.: Blossom-quad: a non-uniform quadrilateral mesh generator using a minimum-cost perfect-matching algorithm. Int. J. Numer. Methods Eng. **89**, 1102–1119 (2012)
5. Mitchell, S.A., Vavasis, S.A.: Quality mesh generation in three dimensions. In: Proceedings of the Eight Annual Symposium on Computational Geometry, pp. 212–221 (1992)
6. Cignoni, P., Montani, C., Scopigno, R.: Dewall: A fast divide and conquer Delaunay triangulation algorithm in e^d. Comput. Aided Des. **30**, 333–341 (1998)
7. Chew, L.P.: Constrained Delaunay triangulations. Algorithmica **4**, 97–108 (1989)
8. Chew, L.P.: Guaranteed-quality mesh generation for curved surfaces. In: Proceedings of the Ninth Annual ACM Symposium on Computational Geometry, pp. 274–280 (1993)
9. Bowyer, A.: Computing Dirichlet tessellations. Comput. J. **24**, 384–409 (1981)
10. Hendrickson, B., Leland, R.: An improved spectral graph partitioning algorithm for mapping parallel computations. J. Sci. Comput. **16**, 452–469 (1995)

Dynamic Communication-Aware Scheduling with Uncertainty of Workflow Applications in Clouds

Vanessa Miranda[1], Andrei Tchernykh[1(✉)], and Dzmitry Kliazovich[2]

[1] CICESE Research Center, Ensenada, B.C., Mexico
vanessa.vsphinx@gmail.com, chernykh@cicese.mx
[2] University of Luxembourg, Luxembourg, Luxembourg
Dzmitry.Kliazovich@uni.lu

Abstract. Cloud computing has emerged as a new approach to bring computing as a service, in both academia and industry. One of the challenging issues is scientific workflow execution, where the job scheduling problem becomes more complex, especially when communication processes are taken into account. To provide good performance, many algorithms have been designed for distributed environments. However, these algorithms are not adapted to the uncertain and dynamic nature of cloud computing. In this paper, we present a general view on scheduling problems in cloud computing with communication, and compare existed solutions based on three models of cloud applications named CU-DAG, EB-DAG and CA-DAG. We formulate the problem and review several workflow scheduling algorithms. We discuss the main difficulties of using existed application models in the domain of computations on clouds. Finally, we show that our CA-DAG approach, based on separate vertices for computing and communications, and introducing communication awareness, allows us to mitigate uncertainty in a more efficient way.

Keywords: Cloud computing · Scheduling · Workflow · Communication awareness · Uncertainty · DAG

1 Introduction

Nowadays, there is a need for new technologies that allow rapid access to services, applications and information. The high cost of these technologies has hindered progress in science and business over the years. Cloud computing is a new approach that brings users closer to computer capabilities without licensing software, investing in hardware, repairing and updating issues.

Shane Robinson [1] defined cloud computing as "Everything as a Service", a new approach to deliver services in a pay per use basis. Computer Sciences Corporation [2] shows that 3645 users reported that improved data center efficiency and lower operational costs are the main reasons for the adoption of cloud solutions.

On the other hand, cloud computing still has many issues that need to be addressed including efficient service provisioning, virtual machine migration, energy efficiency,

© Springer International Publishing Switzerland 2016
I. Gitler and J. Klapp (Eds.): ISUM 2015, CCIS 595, pp. 169–187, 2016.
DOI: 10.1007/978-3-319-32243-8_12

server consolidation, traffic management, data security, software frameworks, and many other [3, 25, 26].

According to the National Institute of Standards and Technology (NIST) cloud computing is defined as "a model for enabling ubiquitous, convenient, on-demand network access to a shared pool of configurable computing resources (e.g., networks, servers, storage, applications and services) that can be rapidly provisioned and released with minimal management effort or service provider interaction" [4]. In general, cloud computing provides the hardware and platform level resources as services on an on-demand basis.

A key dimension of scheduling policies concerns with how to map a set of tasks to a set of resources. Typically, there are two ways: static scheduling and dynamic scheduling. With the static approach, we know the detailed information about job characteristics and network topology characteristics in advance making it possible to achieve a near optimal schedule even for complex workflows. The static approach produces schedules only when all tasks are ready. Unfortunately, the availability and performance of cloud resources is difficult to predict. These resources are not dedicated to one particular user, and, besides, there is no knowledge of network's topology.

Though service-oriented architecture assumes everything as a service, most popular offers of cloud providers are Software (SaaS), Platform (PaaS), and Infrastructure (IaaS) as a service.

In SaaS, there are extensive and complex workflows which cover interaction between clients (users), service providers and data bases. For example, to access to a bank account it is necessary to check the user identity, access database, verify balance, decide if it is sufficient, and, finally, return the result to the user.

With the adoption of the Cloud computing and development of corresponding technologies, scientists and engineers can build more and more complex applications and workflows to manage and process large data sets, and execute scientific experiments on distributed resources, etc. [5]. Pandey et al. [6] defines a workflow as a process consisting of a series of steps that simplifies the complexity of execution and management of applications. Workflow implies complex communications between tasks. However, communication-aware scheduling problems that require availability of communication resources are rarely addressed. The communication properties are captured weakly by current application models and scheduling solutions. Unfortunately, it may result in inefficient utilization of cloud infrastructure and communication media.

Cloud applications and services can be represented by workflows modeled by DAGs [23, 24, 27, 29]. The vertices of a DAG represent the amount of computing that has to be processed for successful execution of the application, while the edges define precedence constraints. Such a workflow model works well for HPC applications, but fails in clouds where communication processes often become a bottleneck.

There are three main approaches to adapt the standard DAG model to the increased complexity: communication-unaware (CU-DAG), edges-based (EB-DAG), and CA-DAG introduced in [11].

In EB-DAG, vertices represent both computing and communication requirements of a job. In CU-DAG, edges are associated with the communications performed by the tasks. However, both models appeared to have shortcomings. The first model fails to make distinction between the computing and communication tasks of a job preventing their efficient scheduling on processors and communication network. The latter approach does not allow a single communication process to precede two computing tasks, as a single edge cannot lead to two different vertices in a DAG. In CA-DAG, two types of vertices are considered: one for computing and one for communications. Details are discussed in Sect. 5.

1.1 Uncertainty

Current approaches for cloud scheduling are not very efficient. Most of them focus on deterministic environments and assume having complete knowledge about user tasks and the system. However, in real clouds, there is a considerable level of uncertainty, being the main problem of cloud computing bringing additional challenges to end-users, resource providers, and brokering [9].

Providers might not know the quantity of data that can be managed, or the amount of computation required for a group of tasks. For example, every time a user inquires about the status of a bank account, the reply time may differ. Furthermore, the use of virtualization techniques almost completely prevents obtaining exact knowledge about the system. Parameters like an effective processor speed, number of available processors, and actual bandwidth constantly change over time. Therefore, providers are always searching how to improve the management of resources to ensure Quality of Service (QoS). Uncertainty may be presented in different components of the computational and communication process.

Tchernykh et al. [9] discuss various types and sources of uncertainty: variety of data types and their values, dynamic elasticity, dynamic performance changing, virtualization with loose coupling of applications to the infrastructure, resource provisioning time variation, migration, consolidation, inaccuracy of application runtime estimation, variation of processing times and data transmission, workload uncertainty, cost (dynamic pricing), processing time constraints, effective bandwidth variation, resource availability, and other phenomena. The authors describe their impact on service provisioning, effective performance, effective bandwidth, processing time, available memory, number of available processors, available storage, data transfer time, resource capacity, network capacity, etc.

Uncertainty can be viewed as a lack of precise knowledge for future needs and parameters, or the lack of complete vision for the possible outcomes [10]. It can be classified in several different ways according to their nature as: (1) The long-term uncertainty is due to the object being poorly understood and inadvertent factors that can influence its behavior; (2) Retrospective uncertainty is due to the lack of information about the behavior of the object in the past; (3) Technical uncertainty is a consequence of the impossibility of predicting the exact results of decisions; (4) Stochastic uncertainty is a result of the probabilistic (stochastic) nature of the studied processes and phenomena, where the following cases can be distinguished: there is reliable statistical information; the situation is known to be stochastic, but the necessary statistical information to assess its probability characteristics is not available; a hypothesis on the stochastic nature requires verification; (5) Constraint uncertainty is due to partial or complete ignorance of the conditions under which the solutions have to be taken; (6) Participant uncertainty occurs in a situation of conflict of main stakeholders: cloud providers, users and administrators, where each side has own preferences, incomplete, inaccurate information about the motives and behavior of opposing sides; (7) Goal uncertainty is associated with conflicts and inability to select one goal in the decision or building multi objective optimization model. It addresses the problem of competing interests and multi-criteria choice of optimal decisions under uncertainty; (8) Condition uncertainty occurs when a failure or a complete lack of information about the conditions under which decisions are made; (9) Objective uncertainty occurs when there is no ambiguity when choosing solutions, there is more than one objective function to be optimized simultaneously, and there exists a possibly infinite number of Pareto optimal solutions.

As already discussed, cloud scheduling algorithms are generally split into an allocation part and a local execution part. At the first part, a suitable machine for each job is allocated using a given selection criterion.

To mitigate uncertainty of such a scheme, prediction of job execution time and queue waiting times is important to increase resource allocation efficiency. However, accurate job runtime prediction is a challenging problem. It is difficult to improve prediction by historical data, prediction correction, prediction fallback, machine learning techniques including linear, quadratic and nonparametric regression, decision trees, support vector machine and k-nearest neighborhood, statistical prediction, self-similarity and heavy-tails characteristics, etc. [13, 27, 30–32].

1.2   Quality of Service

Low levels of QoS can be caused by poor scheduling decisions, leading to unacceptably long task execution times and low throughput. Accordingly, the scheduling algorithms for cloud computing must be able to adapt to dynamic changes of the system that are not adequately provided by traditional approaches to resource optimization. Moreover, most of these algorithms do not take into account an important aspect of variation in communication delays.

The need for data transfer among tasks, which is often heavy, can slow down task execution significantly. Therefore, accounting for these communications is essential to attain efficient hardware and software utilization. Given its importance, several heuristic methods have been developed for considering communications in the scheduling problems. The most widely used are list scheduling, task clustering and genetic algorithms.

Most cloud computing applications require availability of communication resources for their operations. All of the surveyed cloud applications impose communication requirements in terms of the network bandwidth, delay or both. Applications, such as video streaming, cloud storage, and cloud backup require high bandwidth to transfer large amounts of data to or from the end users, while performing almost no computations.

The availability of the communication resources becomes crucial and determines how cloud applications interact with the end users. Indeed, most of the cloud applications process requests from and deliver results to many parts of the Internet. In addition to these external communications, cloud applications interact among themselves produce internal datacenter traffic, which may account for as much as 75 % of the total traffic [7].

Current models of cloud applications rely mostly on the HPC concepts [8, 27, 28]. These models are based on DAGs. Such models perfectly fit to the computationally intensive HPC applications, but fail for most part of cloud applications, where communications must be taken into account as well.

2 Communication Awareness

In this section, we discuss general properties of the communication-aware model of cloud applications. As we already mentioned most scheduling algorithms employ an idealized model where the problem is represented as a DAG.

Most of these algorithms are based on a very simple model, which does not accurately reflect real parallel systems. They imply several simplified assumptions: inter-processor communications are supported by dedicated sub-systems, communications are completely concurrent, and communication networks are fully connected. Last two assumptions avoid the consideration of contention for communication resources in task scheduling.

In order to solve these drawbacks, several models have been proposed to adapt the standard DAG model by either allowing vertices to represent both computing and communication requirements of a task (Communication-unaware models, see Sect. 5) and associating edges with the communications performed tasks (Edges-based models, see Sect. 5).

Nevertheless, these approaches are not quite adequate either. In the first model, if a resource is occupied by one communication, any other communication requiring the same resource has to wait until it becomes available. In turn, the task depending on the delayed communication is also forced to wait. Thus, conflicts among communications result in significantly higher overall execution time. The second model, called edge scheduling, achieved contention awareness by scheduling the edges of the DAG onto the links of the topology graph, though, this approach has a drawback. With the purpose of mapping edges onto the links, the topology graph is assumed to contain all the necessary information about nodes, edges and their connectivity information, at any time.

The above mentioned models provide a dedicated bandwidth along a predefined network path for the whole duration of the communication. On the other hand, most of current communication networks are packet-switched and packet routing decisions are taken at every hop, independently. Moreover, most of the data-center network topologies introduce multipath connections as a mean to provide resilience and load balancing. All these create excellent possibility to parallelize data center communications allowing us to divide a single communication task into n different independent communication tasks.

We use the communication-aware model of cloud applications, called CA-DAG [11]. It allows making separate resource allocation decisions, assigning processors to handle computing jobs and network resources for information transmissions, such as application database requests. It is based on DAGs that in addition to computing vertices include separate vertices to represent communications. This communication-aware model creates space for the optimization of many existing solutions to resource allocation, as well as developing completely new scheduling schemes of improved efficiency.

3 Related Work

In this section, we give a brief overview of the distributed computing scheduling techniques that take into account communication costs.

Table 1 shows the summary of algorithm domains. Table 2 presents the main characteristics of described algorithms, and Table 3 summarizes the criteria used to study quality of the algorithms.

Table 1. Environments and models of related work's algorithms

Algorithms		Data centers	Clusters	Grid computing	Distributed computing	Cloud	Three-level (tier)	Two level (tier)
mGACA	Genetic Acyclic Clustering Algorithm			•				
CCTS	Communication Contention in Task Scheduling				•			
PSO	Particle Swarm Optimization-based Heuristic					•		
BAR	Balance-Reduce					•		
SHEFT	Scalable Heterogeneous-Earliest-Finish-Time					•		
DBA	Distributing Bartering Algorithm					•		
DENS	Data center energy-efficient network-aware scheduling	•					•	
NS2	Network simulator 2					•		
NAMC	Network-aware Migration control	•						•
CA-DAG	Communication-Aware Directed Acyclic Graph					•		

mGACA – Genetic Acyclic Clustering Algorithm [19]. It combines task clustering with a meta-heuristic for efficient scheduling of applications with communication costs, especially for large communications. The major feature of the algorithm is that it takes advantage of the effectiveness of task clustering for reducing communication delays combined with the ability of the genetic algorithms for exploring and exploiting information of the search space of the scheduling problem.

CCTS – Communication Contention in Task Scheduling [21]. The authors study the theoretical background of edge scheduling including aspects like heterogeneity, routing and causality. They propose a new system model for task scheduling that abandons the assumptions of a fully connected network and concurrent communication, capturing both end-points and network contention.

PSO – Particle Swarm Optimization-based Heuristic [6]. This paper presents a particle swarm optimization (PSO) based heuristic to schedule applications to cloud resources that takes into account both computation cost and data transmission cost. The optimization process uses two components: the scheduling heuristic that assign all the "ready" tasks, and the PSO steps for task-resource mapping optimization. The algorithm updates the communication costs, based on average communication time between resources, in every scheduling loop. It also re-computes the task-resource mapping so that it optimizes the cost of computation, based on the current network and resource conditions.

BAR – Balance Reduce [17]. The authors focus on data locality of systems where workflows are split into many small blocks, and all blocks are replicated over several servers. To process workflow efficiently, each job is divided into many tasks, and each task is allocated to a server to deal with a workflow block. They propose heuristic task scheduling algorithm called BAlance-Reduce (BAR), in which, firstly, an initial task allocation is produced, then, the job completion time is reduced by tuning the initial task allocation. They define the cost of a task as the sum of the execution time and the input data transferring time. The authors conclude that it is hard to obtain a near-optimal solution when the remote cost changes frequently. So, in this context, in a poor network environment, BAR tries its best to enhance data locality.

SHEFT - Scalable-Heterogeneous-Earliest-Finish-Time algorithm [16]. The authors propose SHEFT algorithm that used a priority list to address the scheduling problem where the number of resources cannot be automatically determined on demand by the size of a workflow, and the resources assigned to a workflow usually are not released until the workflow completes an execution. They assume that resources within one cluster usually share the same network communication and have the same data transfer rate. The model accommodates both heterogeneous and homogeneous computing environments in terms of computing capability and data communication.

DBA – Distributing Bartering Algorithm [18]. The authors proposed a decentralized affinity-aware migration technique that incorporates heterogeneity and dynamism in network topology and job communication patterns to allocate virtual machines on the available physical resources. Their technique monitors network affinity between pairs of virtual machines and uses a distributed bartering algorithm coupled with migration to dynamically adjust virtual machine placement such that communication overhead is minimized.

DENS – Data center Energy-efficient Network-aware Scheduling [15]. The authors present a scheduling methodology that combines energy efficiency and network awareness. Their approach is to receive and analyze a runtime feedback from the data center switches and links as well as take decisions and actions based on the network feedback. The goal is to achieve the balance between individual job performances, QoS requirements, traffic demands and energy consumed by the data center. They select the computing resource for job execution based on the load level and communication potential of data center components. Their methodology is relevant in data centers running data-intensive jobs which require low computational load, but produce heavy data streams.

NS2 - Network Simulator 2 [22]. The authors use a Grid model as a set of inter-connected geographically dispersed Grid sites. At each site, one or more resources are presented. The status and properties of these resources are stored in an information service repository. Based on this information and the network management, they calculate job execution speed and end time.

Table 2. Main characteristics of related work's algorithms

Algorithm	Centralized	Decentralized	Hierarchical	On line	Off line	Clairvoyant	Nonclairvoyant	QoS	Migration cost	Network delay	Static	Dynamic	Communication cost	Migration
mCAGA	•				•				•	•				
CCTS	•				•					•	•	•		
PSO				•	•							•	•	
BAR	•		•	•	•						•		•	
SHEFT			•	•			•			•		•	•	
DBA	•		•	•			•		•	•		•		
DENS	•		•	•			•	•		•		•		
NS2	•				•	•			•	•	•			
NAMC		•	•	•		•				•		•		•
CA-DAG	•			•						•		•		

Table 3. Criteria for evaluation of algorithms

Algorithm	Utilization	Performance	Overhead	Response time	Scalability	Throughput	Energy	Makespan
mCAGA			•					•
CCTS								•
PSO	•					•		
BAR								•
SHEFT								•
DBA		•	•					
DENS		•	•					
NS2			•	•		•		
NAMC			•		•	•		
CA-DAG								•

NAMC - Network-Aware Migration Control [22]. The authors introduced a network topology aware scheduling model for VM live migrations. They take network bandwidth requirements of migrations and network topologies into account. They execute migrations over a dedicated bandwidth limited network link, and try to minimize the maximum bandwidth usage at each point in time while holding migrations deadlines. During a migration, the bandwidth usage is increased up to a user defined maximum limit.

To achieve this, the communication network is presented by a new topology graph for the representation static and dynamic networks of arbitrary, possibly heterogeneous structure.

4 Problem Definition

4.1 Job

We consider n independent jobs $J_1, J_2, \ldots, J_n$ that must be scheduled on federation of clouds. The job J_j is described by a tuple $\{r_j, G_j\}$ that consists of job release time $r_j \geq 0$, and the program represented by a directed acyclic graph $G = (V, E, \omega, \varphi)$. We use CA-DAG model of applications, where the set of vertices $V = \{V_c, V_{comm}\}$ is composed of two non-overlapping subsets V_c and V_{comm}. The set $V_c \subseteq V$ represents computing tasks, and the set $V_{comm} \subset V$ represents communication tasks of the program.

The set of edges E consists of directed edges e_{ij} representing dependence between node $v_i \in V$, and node $v_j \in V$, meaning that a task v_j relies on the input from the task v_i, and v_j cannot be started until this input is received. A particular case is when the size of this input is zero. It helps to define the execution order of tasks, which exchange no data.

The main difference between communication vertices V_{comm} and edges E is that V_{comm} represents communication tasks occurred in the network, making them a subject to communication contention, significant delay, and link errors. Edges E represent the results of exchange between tasks considered to be executed on the same physical server. Such communications often involve processor caches. They are fast and the associated delay is multiple orders of magnitude lower than the delay in a network and can be neglected. Consequently, the edge set E corresponds to the dependences between computing and communication tasks defining the order of their execution.

The release time of a job is not available before the job is submitted, and its processing time is unknown until the job has completed its execution.

4.2 Cloud Infrastructure

We address scheduling problem in the hierarchical federated cloud environment, with k independent clouds $C_1, C_2, \ldots, C_k$ and local provider cloud C.

Cloud C consists of m nodes (data centers) $D_1, D_2, \ldots, D_m$. Each node D_i consists of b_i servers (blades, boards) and p_i processors for all $i = 1..m$. We assume that processors are identical and have the same number of cores. Let m_i be the number of identical cores of one processor in D_i.

We denote the total number of cores belonging to the data center D_i by $\bar{m}_i = b_i \cdot p_i \cdot m_i$, and belonging to all data centers in the cloud C by $\bar{m} = \sum_{i=1}^{m} \bar{m}_i$.

The processor of data center D_i is described by a tuple $\{m_i, s_i, mem_i, band_i, eff_i\}$, where s_i is a measure of instruction execution speed (MIPS), mem_i is the amount of memory (MB), $band_i$ is the available bandwidth (Mbps), and eff_i is energy efficiency (MIPS per watt). We assume that data center processors have enough resources to execute any job, but these resources are not infinite. Due to virtualization and resource sharing the amount of available resources are constantly changes, which causes uncertainty in job assignment.

A job can be allocated to one cloud only, while replication of jobs is not considered. Jobs submitted to one cloud can be migrated to another one. The admissible set of data centers for a job J_j is defined as a set of indexes $\{a_1^j, \ldots, a_l^j\}$ of data centers that can be used for migration of the job J_i. A data center contains a set of routers and switches that transport traffic between computing servers and to the outside world. They are characterized by the amount of traffic flowing through them (Mbps). A switch connects to other switches or computational nodes. The interconnection of processors is static, but their utilization changes. An overload can occur due to a large amount of I/O being pushed through them. The interconnection network architecture is three-tier fat tree, the most common nowadays. It consists of the access, aggregation, and core layers. The interconnection between clouds is done through public Internet.

5 Communication Models

We distinguish three models based on the standard DAG model: communication-unaware (CU-DAG), edges-based (EB-DAG), and communication-aware model (CA-DAG). As mentioned before, the vertices of the EB-DAG represent both computing and communication requirements of a task. In the CU-DAG, edges are associated with the communications performed by tasks. In CA-DAG, two types of vertices are considered: one for computing and one for communications. Edges define dependences between tasks and order of execution.

Let us briefly discuss their main properties. For more details, see [11].

Communication-Unaware Model (CU-DAG). The representation of computing and communication demands of a task as a single vertex (see Fig. 1) makes it almost impossible to produce an efficient schedule. Let us consider a computing task that requires information from a database as an input. The delay of sending and handling a database query as well as receiving a reply can be significant. During this time the computing work, being scheduled for execution, stays on hold waiting for input data, even if a part of it does not depend on waited data. For the example presented in Fig. 1, we are able to schedule T2 and T3 in parallel or share a single core in time, i.e., perform computing for the T2, while T3 waits for the input, and process T3, while T2 is sending its output.

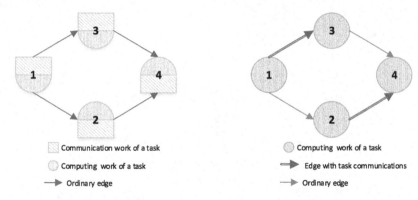

Fig. 1. CU-DAG model   **Fig. 2.** EB-DAG model

However, a precise knowledge of the communication patterns of both tasks should be available. There is another shortcoming of the reviewed model. Suppose T2 computes data, and (a) sends them to the network for the database update (represented by a grey segment of the vertex), and (b) feeds them as an input to T4. With CU-DAG, T4 will wait for the successful completion of T2 including database update. On the other hand, T4 could be started in parallel to the database update. It would be logical to separate these two fundamentally different activities and schedule them separately for an efficient execution.

Edge-Based Model (EB-DAG). In this model, the DAG is defined as a directed acyclic graph $G = (V, E, w, c)$, where vertices V represent computing tasks, and a set of edges E describes communications between tasks. $w(n)$ is a computation cost of a node $n \in V$, and $c(e_{ij})$ is the communication cost of the link $e_{ij} \in E$. Task scheduling implies mapping tasks V on a set of processors specifying starting time, and duration for each task.

One significant drawback is that it prevents two different computing tasks from using the same data transfer to receive an input. Let us consider T2 and T3, Fig. 2. Suppose that the tasks require the same data from the database to start their execution. In practice, it can be done with a single database query, which implies a single edge of the graph. However, a single edge cannot lead to two different vertices. As a result, either two different edges trigger two different queries, or an empty vertex needs to be added as a mean to branch a DAG edge.

Another shortcoming of this model is in edge scheduling. To schedule communications, the DAG edges are mapped to the network links represented by the topology graph of the network. The topology graph is assumed to contain accurate information on network nodes, connections between them, and data transfer rates of all of the links. Accurate knowledge of the actual bandwidth is mainly inaccessible. This is due to the diverse nature of the network traffic that is produced at different layers of the protocol stack and mixed in the communication links and network routers.

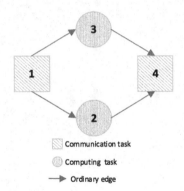

Fig. 3. CA-DAG communication model

Communication-Aware Model (CA-DAG). CA-DAG could solve some shortcomings of previous models, see Fig. 3. The main advantage of this model is that it allows separate resource allocation decisions, assigning processors to handle computing jobs and network resources for information transmissions.

5.1 Scheduling Example

Let us consider a typical cloud webmail application. On a highly abstract level its operation can be represented with the following four steps [11]:

```
Step 1: Receive user request and process it.
Step 2: Generate personalized advertisement.
Step 3: Request list of email messages from database.
Step 4: Generate HTML page and send it to the user.
```

In Fig. 4, the DAG vertices related to the computing tasks are represented by circles, while the communication related vertices are shown using square shapes.

Let us consider scheduling of nine tasks T0–T8 on identical computers to optimize total execution time:

```
T0: processes the arrival of user request
T1: identifies a user, and prepares a database query
T2: analyses user profile to determine targeted advertisement
T3: retrieves personalized advertisement from the database
T4: queries database for the list of user email messages
T5: prepares a list of email messages
T6: groups messages into conversations
T7: combines outputs of T3, T5, T6, and generates HTML page
T8: sends output to user
```

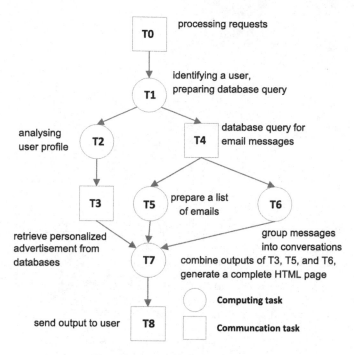

Fig. 4. Example of CA-DAG [11]

Computing resources are represented by two processors of a data center p_1 and p_2. The communication resources are represented with network links l_1 and l_2 interconnecting computing resources and database DB.

Figure 5 shows several possible schedules using these representations for processors and communication links: (a) CA-DAG, p_1, l_1; (b) CU-DAG, p_1, l_1; (c) CU-DAG, p_1, p_2, l_1; (d) EB-DAG, p_1, p_2, l_1; (e) EB-DAG, p_1, l_1, l_2.

Figure 5(a) shows a Gantt chart schedule for the CA-DAG. Computing tasks T1, T2, T5, T6, and T7 are scheduled on the processor p_1, while communication-related tasks T0, T3, T4, and T8 are scheduled at the network link l_1.

Representing communication tasks T0, T3, T4, T8 by vertices allows us to allocate them to the network resources independently from the processor unit. The processor time is not wasted by waiting for communications to be completed.

T4 is executed simultaneously with the analysis of a user profile T2, the list of email messages T5 can be generated, while database is being queried for a personalized advertisement T3. Such a scheduling flexibility is unavailable when communication work is seen as a part of a task description.

Figure 5(b) presents a schedule for CU-DAG. The inability to control allocation of network resources and distinguish the size of task communications, results in a larger makespan. The processor has to wait for finishing communications before it can start the computational portion of the task. To match the makespan of the CA-DAG, an additional processing unit would be required (see Fig. 5(c)).

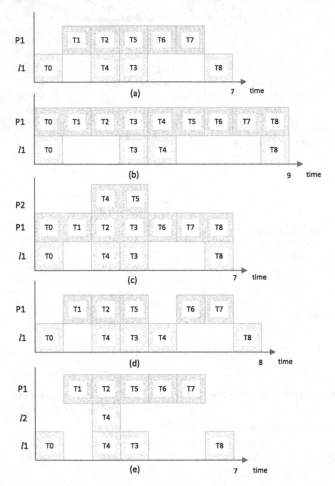

Fig. 5. Gant charts: (a) communication-aware CA-DAG model, (b) communication-unaware CU-DAG model and one processor, (c) communication-unaware CU-DAG model and two processors, (d) edges-based communication EB-DAG model and network link, (e) edges-based communication EB-DAG model and two network links

The EB-DAG with edges to model communication processes cannot model certain required communication types. In our example, for instance, T4 is the edge that represents the database request. It is impossible that this single edge leads to two different computing tasks T5 and T6. An additional edge has to duplicate the communication effort.

Figure 5(d) shows other EB-DAG scheduling. It requires scheduling two copies of the edge T4 leading from T1 to T5 and T6. To produce a schedule with makespan equals to the CA-DAG schedule, an additional network link is needed, so that both copies of the edge T4 can be scheduled in parallel (Fig. 5(e)).

5.2   Scheduling Approach

We use a two-level scheduling approach as shown in Fig. 6.

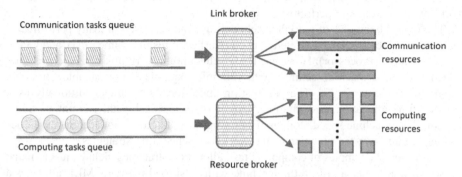

Fig. 6. General diagram of the scheduling approach

At the upper level, two lists of tasks that are ready to be started are maintained. Independent computing tasks with no predecessors, with predecessors that completed their execution, and all available data are entered into the computing tasks queue. Upon completion of the computing task its immediate successors may become available and enter into the computing list, and communication tasks enter into communication task queue. Communication tasks can also start their execution only after all their dependencies have been satisfied.

5.3   Lower Level Allocation Strategies

On the second level, allocation policies of the brokers are responsible for selecting suitable computing servers, also called machines in the rest of the paper, and communication link (path) for a task allocation. These computing- and communication-aware resource allocation policies can be characterized by the type and amount of information used for allocation decision, and optimization criteria.

Schedulers can target several different objectives, including response time, Quality of Service (QoS), energy and cooling efficiency, and a combination of them. To this end, schedulers should use multi-criteria decision support. Especially, it is important in scenarios that contain aspects which are multi-objective by nature, for instance, system performance related issues and user QoS demands.

One set of criteria may correspond to the optimization of the load of computing servers. Another one could be oriented on data traffic and/or network optimization. They are interdependent and may have conflicting goals due to computing resource allocation, that has a big impact on data traffic, and data traffic on the computing resource optimization.

Important criteria are related with energy, heat, and cooling optimization. Cloud resource providers and users also have conflicting performance goals: from minimizing response time to optimizing user and provider cost optimization.

Workflow scheduling has diversified into many research directions: analysis of workflow structure properties in order to identify tasks clusters; minimization of critical path execution time; selection of admissible resources; allocation of suitable resources for data intensive workflows; scheduling subject to QoS constraints, fine tuning workflow execution and performance analysis, etc.

The typical examples of workflow scheduling strategies used in many performance evaluation studies are: HEFT (Heterogeneous Earliest Finishing Time First), and CPOP (Critical Path on Processor). However, DAG scheduling algorithms designed for static DAGs and static machine settings with full information are not suitable for cloud scheduling contexts [9, 27]. The information about local schedules traditionally used for workflow allocation, task runtime, length of the critical path, amount of transmission data, machine speed, communication bandwidth, etc. is not accurate and does not help to improve the outcome of the workflow scheduling strategies.

Other typical examples of computing task allocation strategies include, just to name a few: MLp allocates a task to the machine with least load per core, MLB allocates a task to the machine with least computational work per core, MST allocates a task to the machine with earliest start time, MCT allocates task to the machine with earliest task completion time, etc. [13, 29].

MTT allocates communication task to the link with earliest transmission time, MaxB allocates communication task to the link with highest bandwidth, LL allocates communication task to the link to balance transmission load, etc.

They can be categorized as: knowledge-free, with no information about tasks and resources; energy-aware, with power consumption information; speed-aware with speed of machines information; bandwidth-aware, with actual bandwidth information, etc.

CA-DAG is based on separate vertices for computing and communications. Such a dual computing-communication task representation allows making separate resource allocation decisions to handle computing jobs and network resources for information transmissions. It mitigates uncertainty in more efficient way, making decisions based on the current or predicted information, and dynamically adapt them to cope with different objective preferences, workloads, and cloud properties.

The proposed communication-aware model creates space for optimization of many existing solutions to resource allocation as well as developing completely new scheduling schemes of improved efficiency.

6   Conclusions

In this paper, we discuss a problem of scheduling workflow applications in clouds under uncertainty. We present an overview of the job scheduling under a dynamic context of cloud computing using three models of cloud applications with communication CU-DAG, EB-DAG and CA-DAG. We show that communication-aware model CA-DAG has advantages under certain conditions.

However, further study is required to assess its actual efficiency and effectiveness. This will be subject of future work requiring a better understanding of workflow scheduling on real data with presence of uncertainty. We design and implement data intensive workflow scheduling strategies considering a cloud model. We study CA-DAG and scheduling strategies addressing optimization of response time and energy consumption. We will conduct a comprehensive performance evaluation study using real logs to demonstrate that CA-DAG performs well with respect to several metrics that reflect both user- and system-centric goals.

Acknowledgment. This work is partially supported by CONACYT (Consejo Nacional de Ciencia y Tecnología, México), grant no. 178415. The work of D. Dzmitry Kliazovich is partly funded by National Research Fund, Luxembourg in the framework of ECO-CLOUD (C12/IS/3977641) project.

References

1. Robison, S.: HP Shane Robison Executive Viewpoint: The Next Wave: Everything as a Service. http://www.hp.com/hpinfo/execteam/articles/robison. Accessed 30 January 2014
2. CSC: CSC cloud usage index latest report, Computer Sciences Corporation. http://www.csc.com/au/ds/39454/75790-csc_cloud_usage_index_latest_report. Accessed 20 January 2014
3. Zhang, Q., Cheng, L., Boutaba, R.: Cloud computing: state-of-the-art and research challenges. J. Internet Serv. Appl. **1**(1), 7–18 (2010)
4. N. US Department of Commerce, Final Version of NIST Cloud Computing Definition Published. http://www.nist.gov/itl/csd/cloud-102511.cfm. Accessed 20 January 2014
5. Hollinsworth, D.: The workflow reference model. In: Workflow Management Coalition, vol. TC00–1003 (1995)
6. Pandey, S., Wu, L., Guru, S.M., Buyya, R.: A particle swarm optimization-based heuristic for scheduling workflow applications in cloud computing environments. In: 2010 24th IEEE International Conference on Advanced Information Networking and Applications (AINA), pp. 400–407 (2010)
7. Kandula, S., Sengupta, S., Greenberg, A., Patel, P., Chaiken, R.: The nature of data center traffic: measurements & analysis. In: Proceedings of the 9th ACM SIGCOMM Conference on Internet Measurement Conference, New York, NY, USA, pp. 202–208 (2009)
8. AbdelBaky, M., Parashar, M., Kim, H., Jordan, K.E., Sachdeva, V., Sexton, J., Jamjoom, H., Shae, Z.Y., Pencheva, G., Tavakoli, T., Wheeler, M.F.: Enabling high-performance computing as a service. Computer **45**(10), 72–80 (2012)
9. Tchernykh, A., Schwiegelsohn, U., Alexandrov, V., Talbi, E.: Towards understanding uncertainty in cloud computing resource provisioning. SPU 2015 - solving problems with uncertainties (3rd Workshop). In: Conjunction with the 15th International Conference on Computational Science (ICCS 2015), Reykjavík, Iceland, 1–3 June 2015. Procedia Computer Science, Elsevier, vol. 51, pp. 1772–1781 (2015)
10. Tychinsky A.: Innovation Management of Companies: Modern Approaches, Algorithms, Experience. Taganrog Institute of Technology, Taganrog (2006). http://www.aup.ru/books/m87/
11. Kliazovich, D., Pecero, J., Tchernykh, A., Bouvry, P., Khan, S., Zomaya, A.: CA-DAG: modeling communication-aware applications for scheduling in cloud computing. J. Grid Comput., 1–17 (2015). Springer, Netherlands
12. Tsafrir, D., Etsion, Y., Feitelson, D.G.: Backfilling using system-generated predictions rather than user runtime estimates. IEEE Trans. Parallel Distrib. Syst. **18**(6), 789–803 (2007)

13. Ramírez-Alcaraz, J.M., Tchernykh, A., Yahyapour, R., Schwiegelshohn, U., Quezada-Pina, A., González-García, J.L., Hirales-Carbajal, A.: Job allocation strategies with user run time estimates for online scheduling in hierarchical Grids. J. Grid Comput. 9(1), 95–116 (2011)
14. Zitzler, E.: Evolutionary Algorithms for Multiobjective Optimization: Methods and Applications, vol. 63. Shaker, Ithaca (1999)
15. Kliazovich, D., Bouvry, P., Khan, S.U.: DENS: data center energy-efficient network-aware scheduling. Cluster Comput. 16(1), 65–75 (2013)
16. Liu, K., Jin, H., Chen, J., Liu, X., Yuan, D., Yang, Y.: A compromised-time-cost scheduling algorithm in swindew-c for instance-intensive cost-constrained workflows on a cloud computing platform. Int. J. High Perform. Comput. Appl. 24(4), 445–456 (2010)
17. Jin, J., Luo, J., Song, A., Dong, F., Xiong, R.: BAR: an efficient data locality driven task scheduling algorithm for cloud computing. In: 11th IEEE/ACM International Symposium on Cluster, Cloud and Grid Computing (CCGrid 2011), pp. 295–304 (2011)
18. Sonnek, J., Greensky, J., Reutiman, R., Chandra, A.: Starling: minimizing communication overhead in virtualized computing platforms using decentralized affinity-aware migration. In: 39th International Conference on Parallel Processing (ICPP 2010), pp. 228–237 (2010)
19. Pecero, J.E., Trystram, D., Zomaya, A.Y.: A new genetic algorithm for scheduling for large communication delays. In: Sips, H., Epema, D., Lin, H.-X. (eds.) Euro-Par 2009. LNCS, vol. 5704, pp. 241–252. Springer, Heidelberg (2009)
20. Stage, A., Setzer, T.: Network-aware migration control and scheduling of differentiated virtual machine workloads. In: Proceedings of the 2009 ICSE Workshop on Software Engineering Challenges of Cloud Computing, pp. 9–14. IEEE Computer Society (2009)
21. Sinnen, O., Sousa, L.A.: Communication contention in task scheduling. IEEE Trans. Parallel Distrib. Syst. 16(6), 503–515 (2005)
22. Volckaert, B., Thysebaert, P., De Leenheer, M., De Turck, F., Dhoedt, B., Demeester, P.: Network aware scheduling in grids. In: Proceedings of the 9th European Conference on Networks and Optical Communications, p. 9 (2004)
23. Malawski, M., Juve, G., Deelman, E., Nabrzyski, J.: Cost-and deadline-constrained provisioning for scientific workflow ensembles in IaaS clouds. In: Proceedings of the International Conference on High Performance Computing, Networking, Storage and Analysis, p. 22 (2012)
24. Yu, J., Buyya, R.: A taxonomy of workflow management systems for grid computing. J. Grid Comput. 3(3–4), 171–200 (2005)
25. Tchernykh, A., Pecero, J., Barrondo, A., Schaeffer, E.: Adaptive energy efficient scheduling in peer-to-peer desktop grids. Future Gener. Comput. Systems 36, 209–220 (2014)
26. Tchernykh, A., Lozano, L., Schwiegelshohn, U., Bouvry, P., Pecero, J.E., Nesmachnow, S., Drozdov, A.Y.: Online bi-objective scheduling for IaaS clouds with ensuring quality of service. J. Grid Comput., 1–18 (2015). Springer
27. Carbajal, A.H., Tchernykh, A., Yahyapour, R., Röblitz, T., Ramírez-Alcaraz, J.M., González-García, J.L.: Multiple workflow scheduling strategies with user run time estimates on a grid. J. Grid Comput. 10(2), 325–346 (2012). Springer-Verlag, New York, USA
28. Quezada, A., Tchernykh, A., González, J., Hirales, A., Ramírez, J.-M., Schwiegelshohn, U., Yahyapour, R., Miranda, V.: Adaptive parallel job scheduling with resource admissible allocation on two level hierarchical grids. Future Gener. Comput. Syst. 28(7), 965–976 (2012)
29. Rodriguez, A., Tchernykh, A., Ecker, K.: Algorithms for dynamic scheduling of unit execution time tasks. Eur. J. Oper. Res. 146(2), 403–416 (2003). Elsevier Science, North-Holland

30. Kianpisheh, S., Jalili, S., Charkari, N.M.: Predicting job wait time in grid environment by applying machine learning methods on historical information. Int. J. Grid Distrib. Comput. 5(3) (2012)

31. Iverson, M.A., Ozguner, F.; Follen, G.J.: Run-time statistical estimation of task execution times for heterogeneous distributed computing. In: Proceedings of 5th IEEE International Symposium on High Performance Distributed Computing, 1996, pp. 263–270 (1996)

32. Ramirez-Velarde, R.V., Rodriguez-Dagnino, R.M.: From commodity computers to high-performance environments: scalability analysis using self-similarity, large deviations and heavy-tails. Concurrency Comput. Pract. Exp. **22**, 1494–1515 (2010)

Structure Optimization
with a Bio-inspired Method

J. Miguel Vargas-Felix[✉] and Salvador Botello-Rionda

Centro de Investigación en Matemáticas,
Callejón Jalisco s/n, Col. Valenciana, 36240 Guanajuato, GTO, Mexico
{miguelvargas,botello}@cimat.mx

Abstract. We explore a structure optimization strategy that is analogous to how bones are formed in embryos, where shape and strength are mostly defined. The strategy starts with a rectangular grid of elements of uniform thickness with boundary displacements and force conditions. The thickness of each element can grow or shrink depending on the internal strain, this process is done iteratively. The internal strain is found using the finite element method solving a solid mechanics problem. The final shape depends only on five parameters (von Mises threshold, thickness grow and shrink factors, maximum and minimum thickness). An evolutionary algorithm is used to search an optimal combination of these five parameters that gives a shape that uses the minimal amount of material but also keeps the strain under a maximum threshold. This algorithm requires to test thousands of shapes, thus super-computing is needed. Evaluation of shapes are done in a computer cluster. We will describe algorithms, software implementation and some results.

Keywords: Shape optimization · Evolutionary algorithms · Finite element

1 Introduction

Our goal is to create solid structures (see Fig. 1) that work under certain conditions (forces or imposed displacements), while weight, displacement, and strains are minimized.

To do such, we will apply meta-heuristics with a minimum of assumptions about the problem and its geometry. The evaluation of the structure is done using solid analysis with Finite Element Method [1].

1.1 Topological Optimization

When a topological optimization is applied, a domain can be divided in a grid of elements, each element is a degree of freedom (DOG), Fig. 1 shows an example. A problem with a 2D domain can have thousands of DOG, for a 3D problem the number raises to millions. A strategy to reduce the complexity of the search space is to use binary elements (Fig. 2).

The aim of the method described below is to work with just a few degrees of freedom, following the idea of how bone shape is defined in mammals.

© Springer International Publishing Switzerland 2016
I. Gitler and J. Klapp (Eds.): ISUM 2015, CCIS 595, pp. 188–200, 2016.
DOI: 10.1007/978-3-319-32243-8_13

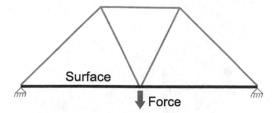

Fig. 1. Bridge structure that support a load using a minimum of material.

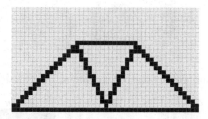

Fig. 2. Example of a grid used for topological optimization.

1.2 Bone Shape

The shape of a bone is mostly defined during embryonic development. A study [2] explains that at first the bone has a very basic shape, then it grows and adapts itself to have an almost optimal shape to support loads.

In [2] it is demonstrated that the bone reacts to the force created by the growing muscles. Because of external load forces inside the bone strains are generated. In the bone cells where the strain is bigger the osteoblasts make the concentration of calcium increase, otherwise it is reduced. This procedure makes bones attain a more resistant shape, with a tendency towards an optimal (Fig. 3).

If the muscles, attached to a bone, are paralyzed no strain is generated and a bone will not develop an optimal shape (Fig. 4).

2   Structure Optimization Using Internal Strain

The Finite element method is used to model the structure, it starts with an empty rectangular domain. The measurement used for internal strain is the von Mises stress or equivalent tensile stress.

Some research has been done on creating a simple method that uses internal strains to optimize structures [3].

- This method does not use binary elements, instead the thickness of elements variates in a continuous way.
- How thickness will grow or shrink will depend on the von Mises stress inside each element.
- Optimization is done iteratively.

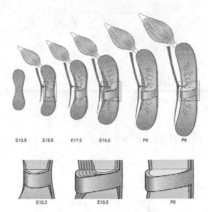

Fig. 3. Model of mouse embryonic bone development, image from [2] (with permission).

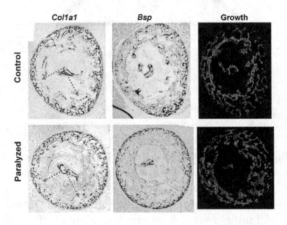

Fig. 4. Osteoblast distribution is controlled by mechanical load, image from [2] (with permission).

- There is not a fitness function.
- The method works as a cellular automaton.
- There are only five degrees of freedom to control the optimization process.

2.1 Cellular Automaton

The rules to control the thickness t_e of the element (cell) are simple: The thickness can grow by a factor f_{up} or be reduced by a factor f_{down}.

Let σ_{vM} the von Mises strain inside the element and σ_{vM}^* a threshold criteria.

$$
\begin{array}{l}
\text{if } \sigma_{vM} > \sigma_{vM}^* \text{ then} \\
\quad t_e \leftarrow f_{up} t_e, \text{ with } 1 < f_{up} \\
\text{else} \\
\quad t_e \leftarrow f_{down} t_e, \text{ with } f_{down} < 1
\end{array}
$$

There are top t_{top} and bottom t_{bottom} limits for the thickness:

$$\boxed{\begin{array}{l} \text{if } t_e > t_{\text{top}} \text{ then } t_e \leftarrow t_{\text{top}} \\ \text{if } t_e < t_{\text{bottom}} \text{ then } t_e \leftarrow t_{\text{off}}, \text{ where } t_{\text{off}} \approx 0.0001 \end{array}}$$

The evolution process of the cellular automaton depends on five parameters:

- von Mises threshold σ_{vM}^{*}.
- Increase thickness factor f_{up}.
- Reduction of thickness factor f_{down}.
- Top thickness value t_{top}.
- Bottom thickness value t_{bottom}.

3   Example: Arc

This is piece of steel with two fixed corners that has to support a force applied on a point, see Fig. 5.

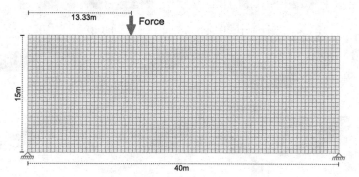

Fig. 5. Geometry of the arc problem.

Table 1. Parameters used to obtain a valid structure.

Parameter	Value
von Mises threshold σ_{vM}^{*}	2.00
Increase factor f_{up}	1.02
Reduction factor f_{down}	0.91
Top limit f_{top}	8.00
Bottom limit f_{bottom}	0.25

3.1   Successful Arc Structure

For the parameters in Table 1, a successful structure is generated.

The evolution of the cellular automaton is shown in the sequence of images, warmer colors indicate more thickness, cooler colors less thickness. If thickness falls below f_{bottom} the element is not shown.

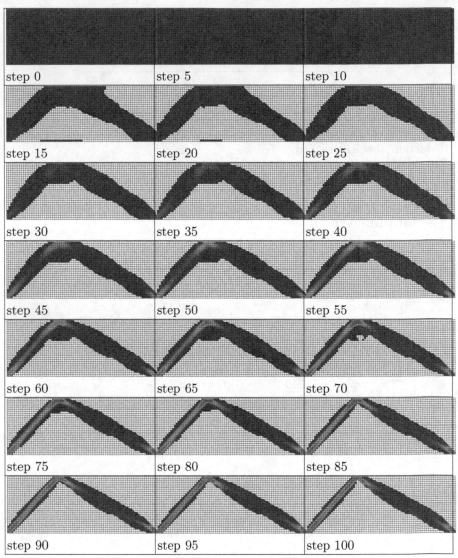

The final result is shown in Fig. 6.

Table 2. Parameters used to obtain an invalid structure.

Parameter	Value
von Mises threshold σ_{vM}^*	2.00
Increase factor f_{up}	1.01
Reduction factor f_{down}	0.92
Top limit f_{top}	7.38
Bottom limit f_{bottom}	0.50

3.2   Invalid Arc Structure

The parameters used are in Table 2. In this case the top and bottom limits have been changed. In particular the bottom limit has been increased, with this changes, structure development fails.

Looking at the evolution of the cellular automaton, in both cases success and failure, at early iterations the thickness of the right part of the structure is reduced. In the successful case thickness of this side is increased in the following iterations, until it creates the right part of the structure. If the bottom limit is raised too much the evolution of the right side will be cut too soon, producing an invalid arc structure.

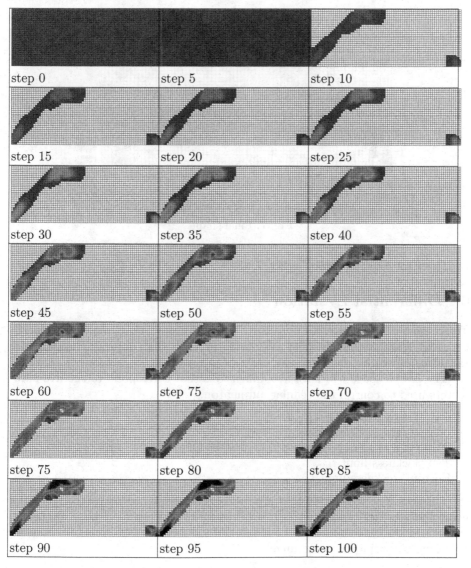

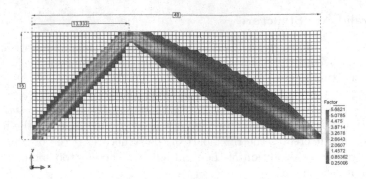

Fig. 6. Final shape.

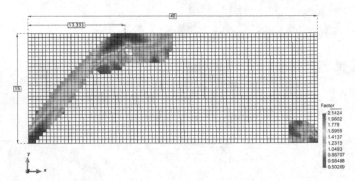

Fig. 7. Final shape.

The final result is shown in Fig. 7.

4   Differential Evolution

To search for structures that tend to an optimal shape, a meta-heuristics has to be used. What we have to find are the parameters that improve the structure (in terms of weight, displacement, and internal strain).

The search space will have five dimensions that correspond to the five parameters used to control the cellular automaton.

– von Mises threshold σ^*_{vM}.
– Increase thickness factor f_{up}.
– Reduction of thickness factor f_{down}.
– Top thickness limit t_{top}.
– Bottom thickness limit t_{bottom}.

The search of parameters that produce a good shape is done using differential evolution [4]. The fitness function will measure the weight of the structure w, maximum displacement d and the maximum von Mises in the structure σ_{vM}, we propose a very simple fitness function

$$F := w \cdot d \cdot \sigma_{\mathrm{vM}}.$$

The number of steps of the cellular automaton will be determined heuristically based on some test cases. For our experiments, 100 is the number of steps chosen. Each evaluation of the fitness function will have to complete this amount of steps.

Parameters of the differential evolution will be: population size $N \sim 64$, crossover probability $Cr = 0.8$, and differential weight $D = 0.5$.

The algorithm of differential evolution is:

Let $\mathbf{x}_i \in \mathbb{R}^5$ the i-th individual of the population $\mathbf{x} \in \mathbb{R}^{5 \times N}$
for each $\mathbf{x}_i \in \mathbf{x}$
$\quad \mathbf{x}_i^d \leftarrow U\left(v_{\min}^d, v_{\max}^d\right), d \leftarrow 1, 2, \ldots, 5$
for $g \leftarrow 1, 2, \ldots, g_{\max}$
$\quad$ for $i \leftarrow 1, 2, \ldots, N$
$\quad\quad a \leftarrow U(1, N), b \leftarrow U(1, N), c \leftarrow U(1, N)$ with $i \neq a \neq b \neq c, b \neq a, c \neq a, c \neq b$
$\quad\quad k \leftarrow U(1, 5)$
$\quad\quad$ for $d \leftarrow 1, 2, \ldots, 5$
$\quad\quad\quad$ if $U(0, 1) < Cr \ \vee \ d = k$
$\quad\quad\quad\quad \mathbf{y}_i^d \leftarrow \mathbf{x}_a^d + D \cdot \left(\mathbf{x}_b^d - \mathbf{x}_c^d\right)$
$\quad\quad\quad$ else
$\quad\quad\quad\quad \mathbf{y}_i^d \leftarrow \mathbf{x}_i^d$
$\quad\quad$ if $F(\mathbf{x}_i) > F(\mathbf{y}_i)$ then $\mathbf{x}_i \leftarrow \mathbf{y}_i$
$\quad\quad$ if $F(\mathbf{best}) > F(\mathbf{x}_i)$ then $\mathbf{best} \leftarrow \mathbf{x}_i$

4.1   Implementation

The program to run this method was programed in C++ using the MPI (Message Passing Interface) library for communication between computers in a cluster. The finite element library used to solve each iteration of the cellular automaton was FEMT[1].

The cluster used to test this method has 64 cores (Fig. 8), to maximize the usage, the population size was chosen to be 64. Solution speed was increased

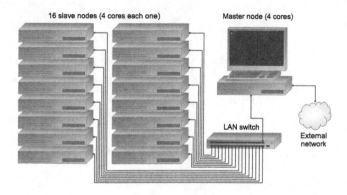

Fig. 8. Diagram of the cluster used to run the optimizer.

---
[1] http://www.cimat.mx/~miguelvargas/FEMT.

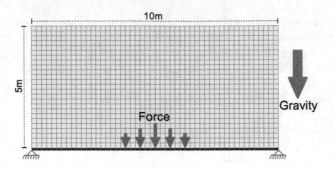

Fig. 9. Geometry of the problem.

by loading all data for the structure on each core, only the elemental matrix is assembled for each step of the cellular automaton.

The solver used was Cholesky factorization for sparse matrices. Reordering of the matrix is done once and only the Cholesky factors are updated, this calculus is done in parallel using OpenMP [5].

For the examples shown the solution of the finite element problem takes approximately 200 ms.

The cellular automaton uses 100 iterations, so the calculation of each generation of the differential evolution algorithm takes approx 20 s.

5   Global Optimization Example: Bridge

A steel bar that has two supports on opposite sides, it has to support its own weight and also a force concentrated in the middle (Fig. 9).

The next table shows some the best individual after n evaluations, an its fitness function.

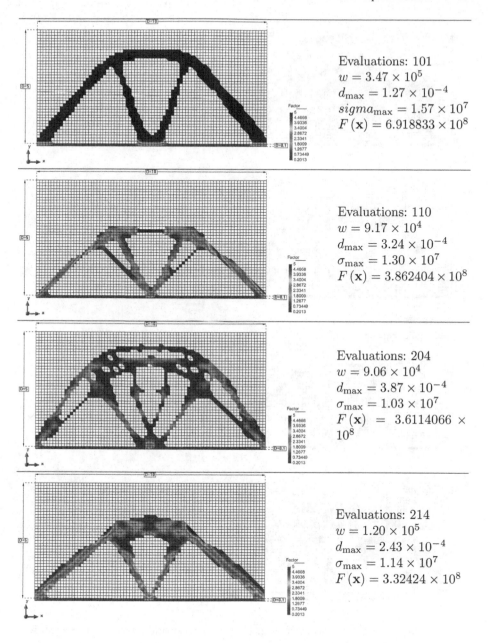

Evaluations: 101
$w = 3.47 \times 10^5$
$d_{\max} = 1.27 \times 10^{-4}$
$sigma_{\max} = 1.57 \times 10^7$
$F(\mathbf{x}) = 6.918833 \times 10^8$

Evaluations: 110
$w = 9.17 \times 10^4$
$d_{\max} = 3.24 \times 10^{-4}$
$\sigma_{\max} = 1.30 \times 10^7$
$F(\mathbf{x}) = 3.862404 \times 10^8$

Evaluations: 204
$w = 9.06 \times 10^4$
$d_{\max} = 3.87 \times 10^{-4}$
$\sigma_{\max} = 1.03 \times 10^7$
$F(\mathbf{x}) = 3.6114066 \times 10^8$

Evaluations: 214
$w = 1.20 \times 10^5$
$d_{\max} = 2.43 \times 10^{-4}$
$\sigma_{\max} = 1.14 \times 10^7$
$F(\mathbf{x}) = 3.32424 \times 10^8$

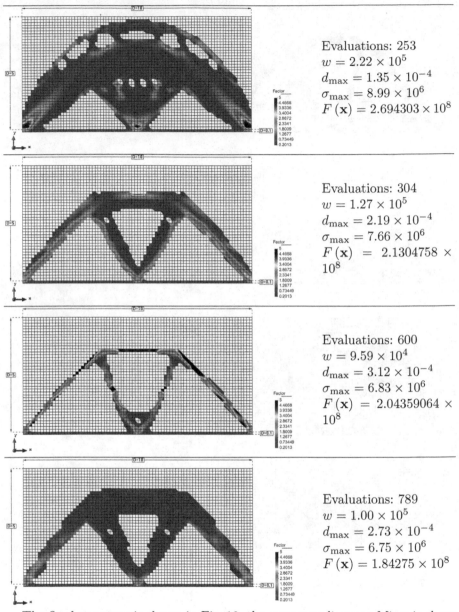

Evaluations: 253
$w = 2.22 \times 10^5$
$d_{\max} = 1.35 \times 10^{-4}$
$\sigma_{\max} = 8.99 \times 10^6$
$F(\mathbf{x}) = 2.694303 \times 10^8$

Evaluations: 304
$w = 1.27 \times 10^5$
$d_{\max} = 2.19 \times 10^{-4}$
$\sigma_{\max} = 7.66 \times 10^6$
$F(\mathbf{x}) = 2.1304758 \times 10^8$

Evaluations: 600
$w = 9.59 \times 10^4$
$d_{\max} = 3.12 \times 10^{-4}$
$\sigma_{\max} = 6.83 \times 10^6$
$F(\mathbf{x}) = 2.04359064 \times 10^8$

Evaluations: 789
$w = 1.00 \times 10^5$
$d_{\max} = 2.73 \times 10^{-4}$
$\sigma_{\max} = 6.75 \times 10^6$
$F(\mathbf{x}) = 1.84275 \times 10^8$

The final structure is shown in Fig. 10, the corresponding von Mises is shown in Fig. 11.

The parameters for the final structure are:

$$\mathbf{x} = \left(\sigma_{\mathrm{vM}}^* = 4.55 \times 10^6, f_{\mathrm{up}} = 1.03, f_{\mathrm{down}} = 0.96, f_{\mathrm{top}} = 5, f_{\mathrm{bottom}} = 0.2 \right)$$

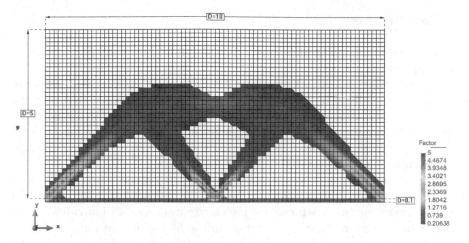

Fig. 10. Geometry of the problem.

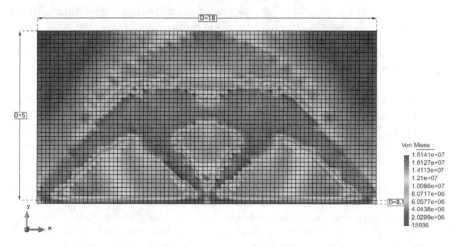

Fig. 11. Final von Mises.

The resulting fitness function:

$$w = 1.03 \times 10^5, d_{\max} = 2.79 \times 10^{-4}, \sigma_{\max} = 1.06 \times 10^7$$

$$F(\mathbf{x}) = 3.046122 \times 10^8.$$

6 Conclusions

We have presented a bio-inspired method to search for optimal structures under load conditions.

It is interesting to see that in mammals the shape and internal structure of the bone is not codified in the genes. Only some thresholds associated with the behavior of bone cells are codified. With this idea we can reduce an optimization problem with thousands or millions of degrees of freedom (the state of each element in the geometry) to an optimization with just a few degrees of freedom (the parameters used for the cellular automaton).

The evaluation of the fitness functions is expensive because we have to leave the cellular automaton to operate for many steps, we used parallelization in a cluster to overcome this, each core on the cluster evaluates an individual.

Some interesting research can be done in the future, for instance we used a very simple fitness function, a more intelligent selection of this function could be useful to get better and faster results. Also, more complex methods can be used for the optimization, like Estimation of Distribution Algorithms. In the near future we will test this method on 3D structures.

References

1. Zienkiewicz, O.C., Taylor, R.L., Zhu, J.Z.: The Finite Element Method: Its Basis and Fundamentals, 6th edn. Elsevier Butterworth-Heinemann, Oxford (2005)
2. Sharir, A., Stern, T., Rot, C., Shahar, R., Zelzer, E.: Muscle force regulates bone shaping for optimal load-bearing capacity during embryo-genesis. Development **138**, 3247–3259 (2011). Department of Molecular Genetics, Weizmann Institute of Science
3. Torres-Molina, R.: Un Nuevo Enfoque de Optimización de Estructuras por el Método de los Elementos Finitos Universitat Politècnica de Catalunya. Escola d'Enginyeria de Telecomunicació i Aeroespacial de Castelldefels (2011)
4. Storn, R., Price, K.: Differential evolution. A simple and efficient heuristic for global optimization over continuous. J. Glob. Optim. **11**, 341–359 (1997)
5. Vargas-Felix, J.M., Botello-Rionda, S.: Parallel direct solvers for finite element problems. Comunicaciones del CIMAT, I-10-08 (CC) (2010)

An Agglomeration Strategy for the Parallel Processes Mapping onto a Distributed Computing Architecture

Juan C. Catana-Salazar[1(✉)] and Jorge L. Ortega-Arjona[2]

[1] Posgrado en Ciencia e Ingeniería de la Computación,
Universidad Nacional Autónoma de México, Mexico City, Mexico
j.catanas@uxmcc2.iimas.unam.mx
[2] Departamento de Matemáticas, Facultad de Ciencias,
Universidad Nacional Autónoma de México, Mexico City, Mexico
jloa@ciencias.unam.mx

Abstract. Parallel processes, by nature, tend to interchange a high amount of data between them to maintain a highly cohesive system. Nevertheless, when a parallel system is executed on a distributed computing architecture, communications over the network and the time spent by them become very important.

This paper introduces a strategy, based on the Max-flow min-cut theorem, to agglomerate and allocate parallel processes onto a distributed computing architecture. The main goal of the strategy is to decrease the amount of remote communications and increase the amount of local communications. The strategy allocates the processes "carefully" over the distributed nodes, and that causes the communication time of the parallel system to be minimized.

Keywords: Parallel process · Mapping problem · Networks flows

1 Introduction

A parallel system is a set of processes that communicate with each other and collaborate to accomplish a common goal. Parallel systems not only have multiple instruction flows executing at the same time, but also multiple data flows between processes [7].

A parallel system can be classified depending on its communication or synchronization needs. The granularity $g(p_i)$ is a qualitative measure obtained by dividing the processing time $t_{proc}(p_i)$ and communication time $t_{com}(p_i)$ of a process p_i [5], see Eq. 1.

$$g(p_i) = \frac{t_{proc}(p_i)}{t_{com}(p_i)} \tag{1}$$

Three types of granularity derived from the relation between processing and communication times are shown next:

© Springer International Publishing Switzerland 2016
I. Gitler and J. Klapp (Eds.): ISUM 2015, CCIS 595, pp. 201–212, 2016.
DOI: 10.1007/978-3-319-32243-8_14

1. **Fine granularity:** Says a process is fine grained if $t_{com} > t_{proc}$.
2. **Medium granularity:** A process is medium grained when $t_{com} \simeq t_{proc}$.
3. **Coarse granularity:** Says a process is coarse grained when $t_{com} < t_{proc}$.

Any parallel machine or multiprocessor system must implement communications via one or more memory blocks. There is a broad variety of memory architectures, which mainly differ on the memory access method [9]. Two widely used memory architectures are the following:

1. **Shared memory:** Memory is directly accessed, commonly through a bus, by every processor in the system. Every processor has a common "snapshot" of the shared memory [7].
2. **Distributed memory:** There are many memory blocks housing many processes. The processes hosted in a memory block can only "see" the local data. The processes, hosted in different memory blocks, needs a network channel to interchange data [7,9].

The main difference between memory architectures is the communication time, in the shared memory architecture communication time is fast and uniform in access time, due to the "closeness" between memory and processors. On the other hand in a distributed memory architecture, communication time is variable and depends on external characteristics related with the network channel, network protocols etc. [7].

The execution time $ET(P)$ of a parallel system P can be defined (in a very simplified way) as, the processing time $PT(P)$ plus the communication time of the system $CT(P)$.

For each communication $c(p_i, p_j)$ between two processes p_i and p_j, such that both are hosted at the same memory block. A constant communication time, t_{cons} is added to the execution time $ET(P)$. Additionally, for each communication $c(p_k, p_l)$ between two processes p_k and p_l, such that both are hosted on different memory blocks. A variable communication time t_{var} is added to the execution time $ET(P)$, where:

$$t_{cons} \ll t_{var} \tag{2}$$

Let $c_l(P)$ be the amount of local communications and $c_r(P)$ the amount of remote communications of P. Then $CT(P)$ is equal to $c_l(P)$ constant time communications plus $c_r(P)$ variable time communications. See Eq. 3.

$$ET(P) = PT(P) + c_l(P) * t_{cons} + c_r(P) * t_{var} \tag{3}$$

This paper introduces a strategy, based on the Max-flow min-cut theorem, to agglomerate and allocate the processes of a parallel system onto a distributed computing architecture with k processing nodes. The main goal of the strategy is to minimize the communication time $CT(P)$ of P, by increasing $c_l(P)$ the amount of local communications and decreasing $c_r(P)$ the amount of remote communications among processes. The mapping of the parallel processes is determined in a statical off-line manner. The balanced workload on the processing nodes, is not considered by this strategy.

In Sect. 2 a set of definitions are introduced to help establish a few tools needed by the strategy proposed in this work. Section 3 describes the agglomeration problem and presents additional considerations. Section 4 shows the strategy in a detailed way. Section 5 shows a case study where the proposed strategy is applied in a real life case. Finally Sect. 6 shows the conclusions of this work.

2   Background

In this section are presented two main themes, parallel software methodology and network flows.

2.1   Parallel Software Methodology

There are many parallel software methodologies proposed in the literature. The common goal of every methodology is to have an easy way to translate a sequential problem into a parallel system. It is also desirable to consider factors such as performance and efficiency.

The following four steps, can be found in every parallel software methodology:

1. **Partitioning or Decomposition.** The partitioning stage involves the division of a general problem into a set of independent modules that can be executed in parallel. That does not imply having the same number of processes as the number of processors. This stage is concerned with finding parallelism in every opportunity, regardless of the resources available to the system [4,5].
2. **Communication.** The parallel modules, generated by the previous stage, can be executed concurrently but not independently. Every parallel process is linked to data provided by other tasks, so that data is propagated along the parallel system [1]. Local communications implies two geographically close communicating processes. In contrast, remote communication implies two processes that communicate through a network medium [1].
3. **Agglomeration and Granularity Adjustment.** The agglomeration stage is responsible of controlling the granularity, either to increase the parallel processing or decrease the communication costs. The main idea is to use the locality, i.e., to group some tasks in a way that reduces communication over the network [4].
4. **Mapping.** The parallel processes must be mapped or allocated into a set of processors to be executed, this is called the mapping problem. Also it is defined as the problem of maximize the number of communicating processes pairs allocated in two directly connected processors [2,4]. The allocation can be specified statically or can be determined in execution time [3].

2.2 Network Flows

A network flow $G_{nf} = (V, E)$ is a strictly directed graph, where each edge $a = (u, v) \in E$ has a capacity $c(a) \geq 0$. If E has an edge $a = (u, v)$, then there is not an edge $a_r = (v, u)$ in the opposite direction [6].

A network flow has two special vertices, a source vertex s, and a target vertex t. The source vertex is responsible of generating the flow to be routed through the edges of the network [3,6].

Assume that, for all $v \in V$ there is a *path* $s \to v \to t$, i.e. the graph is connected. Note that $v \in V - \{s\}$ has at least one incident edge, then $|E| \geq |V| - 1$ [6].

There are two interesting problems in this type of graphs, which are presented below:

1. **Min Cut Problem:** An $s - t$ cut, where $s \in A$ and $t \in B$, is a partition of the set V into two groups $V = \{A, B\}$.

   The capacity of a cut is defined as $c(A, B)$, which is equal to the sum of capacities of each edge $e \in E$ that goes out from A [3].

$$cap(A, B) = \sum_{e \ goes \ out \ A} c(e) \tag{4}$$

   The minimum cut problem refers to find an $s - t$ cut of minimum capacity [3].

2. **Max Flow Problem:** An $s - t$ flow is defined as a function that satisfies two properties [3]:

   (a) **Capacity:** All flow assigned to an edge e should be less or equal than its capacity $c(e)$.

$$0 \leq f(e) \leq c(e), \quad \forall e \in E \tag{5}$$

   (b) **Preservation:** The total flow entering to a vertex $v \in V - \{s, t\}$, should be equal to the total flow coming out from it.

$$\sum_{e \ goes \ to \ v} f(e) = \sum_{e' \ goes \ out \ v} f(e'), \quad \forall v \in V(G) - \{s, t\} \tag{6}$$

The *maximum flow problem* refers to finding an $s - t$ flow of maximum value, with no infringement of the capacity and preservation properties [3,6].

Every edge $e = (u, v)$ in a network flow G_{nf} has a residual edge $e_r = (v, u)$ associated to it, such that $c(e_r) = f(e)$. The residual edge is allowed to transfer flow directed to the target vertex t, so that when a flow g pass through a residual edge e_r then $f(e) = f(e) - g$.

It turns out that the *min cut problem* and the *max flow problem* are closely related, and it is shown by the next lemma.

The *net flow* across a cut (A, B), is the sum of the flow on the edges that goes from A to B, minus the sum of the flow on the edges that goes from B to A.

Lemma 1 (Flow Value). *Let f be any flow assigned to edges of E. Let (A, B) any $s - t$ cut from the network flow. Then, the net flow sent across the cut is equal to the value of f [3].*

$$val(f) = net(f) = \sum_{e \text{ goes out } A} f_{out}(e) - \sum_{e \text{ enters to } A} f_{in}(e) \qquad (7)$$

By the previous lemma is easy to see the duality of this two problems, such that the maximum value of a flow f, across a $s - t$ cut, should be less or equal than the minimum cut's capacity on the network.

$$val(f) = net(f) \; across \; (A, B) \leq c(A, B) \qquad (8)$$

There exists an algorithm to find the max flow and the min cut over a network flow called Ford-Fulkerson algorithm. The algorithm is based in one important concept called *augmenting path*. An augmenting path is a simple directed path, from s to t, with positive capacities edges, such that, the flow over the network can be increased [6].

Theorem 1 Augmenting Path Theorem. *A flow f, which is obtained by the Ford-Fulkerson algorithm, is maximum if, there is no more augmenting paths in the network flow [6].*

As a corollary by previous theorem and lemmas:

Theorem 2 Maximum Flow Minimum Cut Theorem. *Let f be a $s - t$ flow such that there is no an augmented path in the graph G. Let (A, B) be an $s - t$ cut in G such that $net(f) = c(A, B)$. f is the maximum flow value in G, and $c(A, B)$ is the minimum capacity for every $s - t$ cut in G [6].*

3 The Agglomeration Problem

As mentioned in the *Agglomeration and Granularity Adjustment* stage of the methodology presented in Sect. 2.1, is in this step where the problem of minimizing the communication costs of a parallel system can be addressed.

In order to agglomerate a set of parallel processes, it is necessary to group some of them in accordance to a given criterion, for the purposes of this work the main criterion is the minimization of communication costs.

The agglomeration problem can be seen as a more general problem called graph partitioning. Most partitioning problems are known to be *NP-Hard*, meaning that there is no efficient way to solve them. Instead, the use of heuristics and approximation algorithms has been proposed as a solution [12].

The partitioning problem is defined as follows: Let $G = (V, E)$ be a graph with weighted edges, where $|V| = n$. The (k, v)-balanced partitioning problem, for some $k \geq 2$, aims to decompose G into subsets at most size $v\frac{n}{k}$. Where the aggregated weight of the k edges connecting two vertices from different components is minimal [12].

In particular, the k-balanced partitioning problem is shown as a *NP-Complete* problem in [12]. Even the $(2, 1)$-balanced partitioning problem, which seems to be more easy, is also an *NP-Complete* problem [8, 10].

There are two main approaches of the approximation algorithms for graph partitioning. The local algorithms, which make decisions based on local search strategies, such as the Kernighan-Lin algorithm [13] and the Fiduccia-Mattheyses algorithm [14], and the global algorithms that rely on properties of the entire graph, the best known is the spectral partitioning algorithm [15].

The agglomeration problem, as here is defined with no load balance considerations, can be directly addressed by the minimum k-cut problem. The minimum k-cut problem asks for a minimum set of weighted edges whose removal leaves k connected components [11].

The minimum set of weighted edges, to disconnect a graph into two components, can be found in polynomial time by the Ford-Fulkerson algorithm [3]. For a k decomposition of the graph, compute the minimum cut of each subgraph and take the lightest one, repeat until there are k connected components. The previous algorithm guarantees a $2 - \frac{2}{k}$ approximation [11].

3.1   The Minimum Communication Cut Algorithm

Consider the network flow shown in Fig. 1. Such graph has a minimum cut shaped by edges $(s, 2)$ and $(3, 5)$ of value 19.

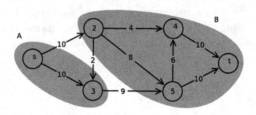

Fig. 1. Network Flow. Grey shapes represent the two partitions (A, B) computed by the Ford-Fulkerson algorithm.

Note that edge $(2, 3)$ is incident to the partition A, and its weight is not considered for the value of the flow.

Remark 1. By definition, the capacity of a cut does not consider any edge incident to the partition A, but in the context of parallel processes such edges are communications among processes of the system, such that, the flow transmitted across those edges must be considered by the agglomeration step.

Therefore it can be said that:

Definition 1. *A minimum communication cut, for the parallel processes agglomeration problem, is the sum of capacities of edges directed to the partition A plus the sum of capacities of edges directed to the partition B.*

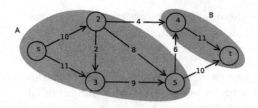

Fig. 2. Minimum communication cut from the network flow shown in Fig. 1.

Taking Remark 1 into account, the communication cut shown in Fig. 1 is of value 21. And the minimum communication cut, of the same graph, is given by the edges $(2, 4)$, $(5, 4)$ y $(5, t)$ of value 20 (see Fig. 2).

Algorithm 1, takes as input parameters a network flow G, a source vertex s, and a target vertex t. It gives as a result the minimum communication cut of the graph G.

The Algorithm 1 first compute the minimum cut of G by using the Ford-Fulkerson algorithm. Then is replaced every edge e in $mincut(G)$, such that e is incident to the partition A, by its inverse edge. Finally, is repeated the computation of the minimum cut over the new G until get a minimum cut with no incident edges to the partition A.

Algorithm 1. Minimum Communication Cut(G, s, t)

$mincut(G) \leftarrow$ Ford-Fulkerson(G, s, t)
while $\exists\, e \in mincut(G)$ incident to A **do**
  for all $e \in mincut(G)$ incident to A **do**
    $G \leftarrow G - e$
    $G \leftarrow G + e_{inverse}$
  end for
  $mincut(G) \leftarrow$ Ford-Fulkerson(G, s, t)
end while

Note that reversing an edge whose flow is greater than zero may cause the violation of conservation and capacity properties. Because of that, is important to prove the next lemma.

Let $G = (V, E)$ be a network flow, and $mincut(G) = \{e_1, e_2, ..., e_k\}$ the set of edges in the minimum cut of G.

Lemma 2. *For all edge $e = (y, x) \in mincut(G)$, where $y \in B$ y $x \in A$, has an assigned flow $f(e) = 0$.*

Proof. By contradiction suppose that $f(e) > 0$.

Note that for all edge $e' \in mincut(G)$, that goes from the partition A to the partition B, has a flow $f(e') = c(e')$, otherwise it would not be a minimum cut.

W. l. g. suppose there is at least one edge e that goes from the partition B to partition the A, which by assumption has a flow $f(e) > 0$. Therefor, there is a residual edge e_r assigned to e with $c(e_r) > 0$, there are two cases:

1. There is at least one path P_{s-t} that uses e_r to transfer flow from the vertex s to the vertex t, thus $mincut(G)$ is not a minimum cut of G.
2. There is no path P_{s-t} that uses e_r to transfer flow from the vertex s to vertex t, meaning that there is one $mincut(G)'$ such that $c(mincut(G)') < c(mincut(G))$.

Any case contradicts the assumptions $\Rightarrow\Leftarrow$.   □

4   The Agglomeration Strategy

In this section the agglomeration strategy for parallel processes mapping is introduced.

4.1   Building the Software Graph

Consider the parallel processes defined in the *decomposition* stage of the methodology presented in Sect. 2.1, such processes can be represented as a set of vertices V_{sw}.

Let E_{sw} be the set of edges that represent the relations between two processes established in the *communication* stage, such that, for all $p_i, p_j \in V_{sw}$ there is an edge $e_{p_i-p_j}$ if this processes interchange $d > 0$ units of data. For all $e_{p_i-p_j} \in E_{sw}$ there is an associated capacity $c(e_{p_i-p_j}) = d$

An edge capacity is equal to the sum of data units interchanged by two processes during execution time. The number of data units is totally dependent on the nature of the parallel system. The amount of communications must be well defined and be representable as a positive integer, otherwise there is no sense in agglomerating by using this strategy.

Let $G_{sw} = \{V_{sw}, E_{sw}\}$ be the software graph that represents a parallel system P.

4.2   Transformation to a Network Flow

In order to transform the software graph into a network flow, is necessary to classify the vertices of G_{sw} considering the following criterion:

– **Initial Vertices or Flow Generators:** Most of them are main processes which generate and send data to other processes in the system. Sometimes they communicate with each other or do some processing.
– **Dealers or Flow Distributors:** They receive data from flow generator vertices. Usually they do some processing but their main function is to distribute data across end vertices.

- **End Vertices or Processing Vertices:** They represent slave processes, and their main purpose is to do processing tasks with data received from initial or dealer vertices. Sometimes they communicate with each other.

Let $G_{nf} = \{V_{nf}, E_{nf}\}$ be a network flow, such that G_{nf} is directed and has no parallel edges. Then:

1. Let s, t be two vertices, such that s is a source vertex and t is target vertex, then:

$$V_{nf} = V_{sw} \cup \{s, t\} \tag{9}$$

2. The vertex s should have a directed edge e_g for every generator vertex v_{gen} in the software graph, such that:

$$E_{nf} = E_{sw} \cup \{e_g\} \mid e_g = (s, v_{gen}) \ \forall \ v_{gen} \in V_{sw} \tag{10}$$

The capacity $c(e_g)$ of every edge $e_g = (s, v_{gen})$ should be equal or greater than the sum of capacities of every edge that goes out from v_{gen}.

$$c(e_g) \geq \sum c(e_{out}) \mid e_{out} = (v_{gen}, u), \ \forall \ e_{out} \in v_{gen} \tag{11}$$

3. For every end vertex v_f, there is a directed edge e_f ending at t:

$$E_{nf} = E_{sw} \cup \{e_f\} \mid e_f = (v_{end}, t), \ \forall \ v_{end} \in V_{sw} \tag{12}$$

The capacity $c(e_f)$ of every edge $e_f = (v_{fin}, t)$ should be equal o greater than the sum of capacities of every edge that ends at v_{end}.

$$c(e_f) \geq \sum c(e_{in}) \mid e_{in} = (u, v_{gen}), \ \forall \ e_{in} \in v_{end}. \tag{13}$$

4.3   Applying the Algorithm

Given a network flow G_{nf}, the agglomeration problem can be addressed by using the greedy algorithm to solve the minimum k-cut problem, as described in Sect. 3, and using the Algorithm 1 instead of the traditional Ford-Fulkerson algorithm.

As a result a k agglomeration of the parallel system P, which can be directly allocated into the k processing nodes of the computer architecture is obtained.

5   Case Study

In this section a case study applying the agglomeration strategy presented in Sect. 4 it is described.

Symmetric and positive defined matrices are very special and they appear very frequent in some scientific applications. A special factorization method called Cholesky decomposition, which is two times faster than other alternatives to solve linear system equations, can be used with this kind of matrices [16].

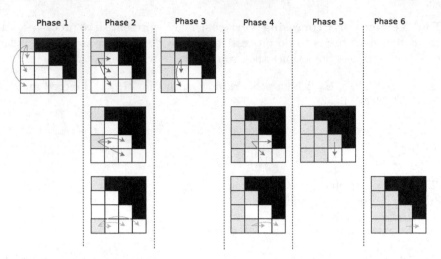

Fig. 3. Data dependency for the Cholesky decomposition on a 4×4 matrix. Gray cells denote an element already computed. The arrows denote a data transmission.

Figure 3 shows the data dependency to compute the Cholesky decomposition on a 4×4 matrix. Due to the symmetry of this matrix, it is enough to work only with the inferior side of the matrix.

Particularly, in this instance the problem is decomposed by cells, meaning that every cell of the matrix represents a parallel process. The arrows between cells become communications between processes needed to transfer data units.

Let Ch be the parallel system that computes the Cholesky decomposition. The software graph depicted in Fig. 4 represents the structure of Ch. The amount of data transferred over each edge is one unit, while the total amount of communications of the parallel system is 20 units.

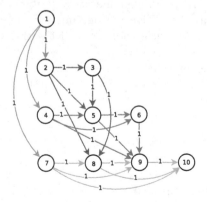

Fig. 4. Software graph for a cell decomposition on a 4×4 matrix.

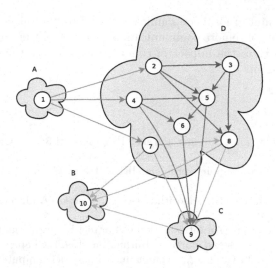

Fig. 5. Agglomeration of the network flow of the Cholesky decomposition problem.

Based on the vertex classification presented in Sect. 4.2, is easy to see that vertex 1 is the only flow generator vertex, while the vertex 10 is the only end vertex. So that, for this example it is not necessary to add the special vertices s and t.

For the agglomeration stage, consider the execution of the parallel system on a *cluster* of $k = 4$ distributed nodes. The resulting agglomeration, obtained by the Algorithm 1, is shown in Fig. 5.

The local and remote communication costs of the agglomeration are:

Partition A: $c_l = 0$, $c_r = 3$.
Partition B: $c_l = 0$, $c_r = 0$.
Partition C: $c_l = 0$, $c_r = 1$.
Partition D: $c_l = 9$, $c_r = 7$.

Such that, the communication time, induced by the agglomeration, of the parallel system Ch is:

$$CT(Ch) = 9 * t_{constant} + 11 * t_{variable}. \tag{14}$$

6   Conclusions

The performance of a parallel system is inherently affected by communication between processes. The communication time added to the execution time of a system is proportional to the amount of data exchanged by the parallel system and the type of communication that it implements.

In general, communication cost through shared memory is less expensive than communication cost via a network medium. Therefore, it is necessary to maximize the amount of local communications and to minimize (to the possible extent) the amount of remote communications, to control the total communication time and mitigate the impact of communications over the execution time of the parallel system.

References

1. Foster, I.: Design and Building Parallel Programs v1.3: An Online Publishing Project (1995)
2. Bokhar, S.: On the mapping problem. IEEE Trans. Comput. **c–30**(3), 207–214 (1981)
3. Kleinberg, J., Tardos, E.: Algorithm Design. Pearson-Addison Wesley, Boston (2005)
4. Chandy, M., Taylor, S.: An Introduction to Parallel Programming: Part II Parallel Program Design. Jones and Bartlett, Burlington (1992). Chap. 7
5. Culler, D., Singh, J., Gupta, A., Kaufmann, K.: parallel computer arquitecture, a hardware / software approach. In: Parallel Programs (1997). Chap. 2
6. Cormen, T., Leiserson, C., Rivest, R., Stein, C.: Introduction to Algorithms, 2nd edn. MIT Press and McGraw-Hill, Cambridge (2001). Sect. 26.2: The Ford-Fulkerson method
7. Blaise, B.: Introduction to Parallel Computing. Lawrence Livermore National Laboratory (2012). Accessed 11 Sept. 2007
8. Steven, S.: Sorting and Searching. The Algorithm Design Manual, 2nd edn. Springer, London (2008)
9. Bondy, J., Murty, U.S.R.: Graph Theory. Springer, London (2008)
10. Garey, M., Johnson, D.: Computers and Intractability. Bell Telephone Laboratories, A Guide of the Theory of NP-Completeness (1979)
11. Vazirani, V.V.: Approximation Algorithms. Springer, New York (2001)
12. Andreev, K., Racke, H.: Balanced graph partitioning. Theor. Comput. Syst. **39**(6), 929–939 (2006)
13. Kernighan, B.W., Lin, S.: An efficient heuristic procedure for partitioning graphs. Bell Syst. Tech. J. **49**, 291–307 (1970). doi:10.1002/j.1538-7305.1970.tb01770.x
14. Fiduccia, M.: A linear-time heuristic for improving network partitions. In: 19th Design Automation Conference (1982)
15. Chung, F.R.K.: Spectral Graph Theory, vol. 92. Am. Math. Soc. (1997)
16. Press, W.H., Teukolsky, S.A., Vetterling, W.T., Flannery, B.P.: Numerical Recipes in C, The art of Scientific Computing, 2nd edn. Cambridge University Press, Cambridge (1992)

Parallel Implementation of an Evolutionary Algorithm for Function Minimization on a GPGPU

Betrand J. Almeida Arrieta, Oscar Alvarado-Nava, Hilda M. Chablé Martínez, Eduardo Rodríguez-Martínez, and Francisco Javier Zaragoza Martínez[✉]

Universidad Autónoma Metropolitana, Unidad Azcapotzalco, Mexico, Mexico
al208200282@alumnos.azc.uam.mx, {oan,hmcm,erm,franz}@correo.azc.uam.mx
http://www.azc.uam.mx

Abstract. We describe the parallel implementation of an evolutionary programming algorithm for minimization of nonlinear, continuous, real-valued functions of n variables. The parallel implementation was carried using the GPGPU (General-Purpose Computing on Graphics Processing Units) technique. Evolutionary programming (EP) was selected from the available evolutionary algorithm paradigms because it presents low dependency between its genetic operators. This feature provided a particular advantage to parallelize the mutation and evaluation stages in EP using a master-slave model. The obtained results report a linear speed up with respect to the number of cores in the test platform.

Keywords: Evolutionary algorithms · GPU · GPGPU · Optimization · Parallel computing

1 Introduction

Evolutionary algorithms (EAs) have drawn the attention of the scientific community as fast and reliable heuristic optimization methods based on the principles of biological evolution and natural selection. Their biggest advantage is their ability to find a good approximation to the global optimum by means of a directed search, escaping from local optima through mechanisms that mimic biological evolution and reproduction. There are four popular paradigms in EAs: genetic algorithms (GAs), evolutionary programming (EP), genetic programming (GP), and evolutionary strategies (ESs). Among them, EP benefits the most from the chosen representation structure for a given problem. The first representation employed for EP was a finite state machine [1]. It was used to simulate evolution as a learning process, and was abandoned in the mid-80's in favor of a structure capable of representing continuous parameters in combinatorial optimization problems [2]. Since then, EP has been successfully applied in the optimization of real and continuous functions [3]. EP differs from GP in that the structure of the program to be optimized is fixed, while its numerical parameters are allowed

© Springer International Publishing Switzerland 2016
I. Gitler and J. Klapp (Eds.): ISUM 2015, CCIS 595, pp. 213–224, 2016.
DOI: 10.1007/978-3-319-32243-8_15

to evolve. In contrast to GA, which highlights crossover, the only genetic operator in EP is mutation. Additionally, the mutation process in EP is a unitary operation, i.e. it only depends on the individual currently being mutated. The characteristics previously mentioned make EP algorithms specially suitable for their implementation on parallel architectures.

As in most EAs, parallelization in EP can be defined as the distribution of the main task on different processors. The definition of the algorithm main task leads to different parallelization models. When it is taken as the underlying search process, the paralization scheme will boost the algorithm exploratory skills. Tongchim and Yao [4] proposed a multipopulation EP, where the search space is divided into multiple copies of the same EP, also called islands. Each copy runs on a different processor, maintaining a different population. Communication among the different islands is governed by migration policies which define the individuals to be exchanged, as well as the direction and time in which interchange will occur. A well designed set of migration policies increases the diversity and promotes species formation, which leads into a reduction in running time and function evaluations. However, designing an optimal set of migration policies is not an easy task. Although several approaches have been employed in order to discover the best migration rates and frequencies [5–9], the results are often inconclusive, since sometimes the best policy is to exchange the best individual among islands connected in a ring fashion, and in others is enough to swap a random individual among a grid.

This work presents an alternative parallelization, where we are interested in increasing throughput and keeping the exploratory skills of panmictic EP [10]. Specifically, we implemented a global parallelization model [11] using an architecture consisting of a multi-core processor (CPU) interacting with a graphic processing unit (GPU). The proposed implementation is the same as the sequential one, although it is faster, especially for time consuming objective functions. Additional features of the proposed implementation are its low cost when comparing to an implementation in a cluster of computers, and better scalability compared to an implementation using multi-threading.

2   Evolutionary Programming

Figure 1 shows the pseudocode describing the basic operations of a sequential EP (SEP) algorithm. The algorithm starts assigning a fitness value to each individual in the initial population P_0 by calling the **Evaluate**() routine, then it iterates on a sequence of mutation (line 04), evaluation (line 05), selection and population update (line 06). The **Mutate**() routine produces a new set of potential solutions P_t' from mutated versions of each individual in the current population P_t. Then, the algorithm assigns a fitness value to each individual in P_t by calling the **Evaluate**() routine. Finally, a new population P_{t+1} is generated with the winners of a random tournament between individuals from P_t and P_t'. This model is known as centralized *pancmitic model* because the main cycle is executed in a single process and all individuals can potentially mate with

---

Algorithm. SEP

Require: Initial population P_0 with K individuals, where the j-th individual is represented as $\text{Ind}_j = [\mathbf{X}_j, \boldsymbol{\sigma}_j]$

Output: P_{MinGen}

---

01. $t \leftarrow 0$
02.   **Evaluate** (P_t)
03.   **REPEAT**
04. $P'_t \leftarrow$ **Mutate**(P_t)
05.   **Evaluate**(P'_t)
06. $P_{t+1} \leftarrow$ **Selection**$(P'_t \cup P_t)$
07. $t \leftarrow t + 1$
08.   **UNTIL** $t = MinGen$

Fig. 1. Sequential evolutionary programming (SEP) algorithm.

each other. In the following subsections we describe in detail each mentioned operation for the proposed SEP algorithm.

2.1   Chromosome Structure

In this paper, each individual in the population encodes a potential solution to the problem $\min_{\mathbf{X} \in \mathbb{R}^n} f(\mathbf{X})$, thus, it was decided to describe the j-th individual in the population as $\text{Ind}_j = [\mathbf{X}_j, \boldsymbol{\sigma}_j]$, where $\mathbf{X}_j = [X_{j,1}, ..., X_{j,n}]$ is a real number vector representing the solution associated with the j-th individual, and $\boldsymbol{\sigma}_j = [\sigma_{j,1}, ..., \sigma_{j,n}]$ is a real number vector showing the exploratory range of the mutation operator.

2.2   Mutation

The selected mutation method was Gaussian mutation with self-adjusting variances, which takes advantage of the previously described chromosome structure and gradually modifies the exploratory range of the mutation operator. The mutation operator transforms each chromosome following the equations

$$\sigma'_{j,i} = \sigma_{j,i} \left(1 + \psi \, N(0,1)\right)$$
$$X'_{j,i} = X_{j,i} + \sigma'_{j,i} \, N_i(0,1), \; i = 1, \dots, n \tag{1}$$

where $\text{Ind}'_j = [\mathbf{X}'_j, \boldsymbol{\sigma}'_j]$ is the offspring of the j-th individual, $N_i(0,1)$ is the i-th element in a vector $\mathbf{N}(0,1)$ of random numbers with normal distribution (zero mean and standard deviation of one), $N(0,1)$ is a single random number from a normal distribution, and ψ is a coefficient controlling the distribution of σ.

2.3   Fitness Function

The selected fitness function is

$$E_j = -f(\mathbf{X}_j) \tag{2}$$

Algorithm. Mutation

Requiere: Population P with K individuals, where the j-th individual is encoded as $\text{Ind}_j = [\mathbf{X}_j, \boldsymbol{\sigma}_j]$

Output: Offspring P', where the j-th individual is encoded as $\text{Ind}'_j = [\mathbf{X}'_j, \boldsymbol{\sigma}'_j]$

```
01.   FOR j = 1, K
02.      FOR i = 1, n
03.         σ'_{j,i} = σ_{j,i} (1 + ψ N(0,1))
04.         X'_{j,i} = X_{j,i} + σ'_{j,i} N_i(0,1)
05.      END FOR
06.      P'(j) = Ind'_j
07.   END FOR
```

Fig. 2. Mutation subroutine for a SEP algorithm.

where $f(\mathbf{X}_j)$ is the value of the function $f(\cdot)$ at the coordinates given by the point $\mathbf{X}_j$. The above fitness function is not normalized and its upper and lower bounds depends entirely on $f(\cdot)$. Additionally, given two individuals Ind_k and Ind_l, the inequality $E_k > E_l$ is true if and only if Ind_k encodes a better solution than Ind_l.

Algorithm. Evaluation

Requiere: Population P of K individuals

Output: Fitness values in vector E

```
01.   FOR j = 1, K
02.      E_j = -f(X_j)
03.   END FOR
```

Fig. 3. Evaluation subroutine for SEP algorithm.

2.4   Competition and Selection

After assigning a fitness value to each member in P_t and P'_t, a new population P_{t+1} is built from the top $\tau_E \%$ individuals in P_t (named P_E), and the top $(100 - \tau_E) \%$ from the sorted union $P_t - P_E \cup P'_t$. This elitist strategy keeps good solutions while maintaining diversity in the population. In a preliminary study to find the optimal value for τ_E, we run SEP with constant parameters $MinGen = 900$, $K = 100$, $n = 100$, and four different elitism factors $\tau_E = \{20, 30, 40, 50\}$. This experiment was run four times, recording the fitness value of the best individual in the last population at each run. The mean values over the four runs, corresponding with the values of τ_E, are $\mu = \{16.95, 2.14, 0.93, 1.94\}$. Clearly, fixing $\tau_E = 40$ gives an individual that is closer to the global optimum for Eq. (3) than any other tested value.

3   GPGPU

The fast growth of the video-game industry, the development of high-definition 3D graphics, and the market demand of graphic applications with low execution time, have led to the development of highly parallel architectures capable of high image processing throughput, namely graphics processing units (GPUs). The operation of a GPU allows us to visualize it as a set of core arrays sharing memory resources and working on independently data-flows. This generalization has allowed the use of GPUs in applications that were traditionally executed on CPUs, giving rise to the term GPGPU (General-Purpose Computing on Graphics Processing Units) which recently has become an alternative to fully or partially parallelized applications, where higher performance is sought regarding execution time [12]. Another important characteristic of GPGPU is its significantly lower cost when compared to that of an implementation using a cluster of computers. Additionally, the programming model offered by CUDA (short from Compute Unified Device Architecture) grants direct access to the different levels of shared memory on a GPU through a set of high-level instructions appended directly to C/C++. This feature facilitates the development and acceleration of applications [13].

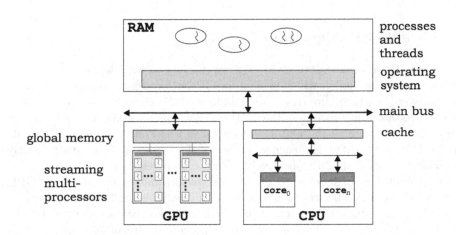

Fig. 4. Computing system with one multi-core CPU and one GPU.

Currently, it is common to find computing systems like the one shown on Fig. 4. This system consists of a multi-core CPU interacting with a GPU with several streaming-multiprocessors (SM), each one with 2^3 cores. An application implemented in the aforementioned system could benefit from the large number of available computing units, however it would be necessary to consider an additional design step to account for the architectural difference between a CPU and a GPU regarding memory access. In configurations like the one shown in Fig. 4, both CPU and GPU form a shared memory system, where the communication between execution threads is carried out by means of memory access instructions. Every core in both CPU and GPU has several memory levels, some of them are shared and others private. Communication between threads inside the GPU is implemented with low latency instructions and memory access restrictions. These restrictions are the main bottleneck a programmer has to deal with when designing applications for a GPU. The differences between GPUs and a multi-core CPUs are not only regarding memory access for execution threads. A multi-core CPU is optimized for sequential execution of a large instruction set, making use of a sophisticated control unit. Because each core in a CPU is superscalar, instructions on a single thread are segmented and executed out of their original order, but keeping their sequential appearance. Furthermore, the existence of cache memory on a CPU is of utmost importance to reduce data access and instruction latency. On the other hand, GPUs were originally designed to simultaneously perform a large number of floating-point operations for image and video processing. Causing most of the chip area to be used for the implementation of a floating-point unit operations (FPU) and optimization for a massive number of threads. A GPU can be modeled as a set of FPU arrays, each one associated to a small memory block that helps to reduce shared memory access by execution threads, and increases memory bandwidth by a factor of approximately ten times when compared to a CPU [14].

4   Parallel EP Algorithm

Following the recommendations in [11], we decided to parallelize SEP using a global parallelism model, which is ideal for GPGPU systems because it is based on a master-slave structure [10]. The main loop of the algorithm is executed in a master process, which resides in the CPU and controls the slave processes. When the main loop executes the mutation (line 04 in Fig. 1) and evaluation (line 05 in Fig. 1) subroutines, it launches a number of slave processes that concurrently evaluate Eqs. (1) and (2), respectively. The slave processes are organized in an array of multi-thread blocks (16 threads per block) and executed on the GPU cores. Each block can be scheduled on any of the available multiprocessors within a GPU, in any order, concurrently or sequentially, so that a compiled CUDA program can execute on any number of multiprocessors. In the remaining of this section we present the implementation details of the parallelized modules in the proposed parallel evolutionary programming (PEP) algorithm.

4.1   Parallel Evaluation Subroutine

In general, the most expensive part in an evolutionary algorithm is computation of the fitness values [15]. As can be observed in Fig. 3, assuming a single evaluation of the objective function takes at least t_E s, the total time invested by the algorithm in Fig. 1 to compute the fitness values would be of at least $(MinGen + 1) \cdot K \cdot t_E$ s. Such time can be reduced to $(MinGen + 1) \cdot t_E$ with the proposed master-slave model because the K slave processes concurrently evaluate the objective function for each individual in the population. The implementation strategy consists in assigning one thread per iteration of the loop shown in Fig. 3. Each thread executes a copy of the *kernel* function called `evaluation`, which computes the fitness value of one individual as shown in line 06 of Fig. 5. The pointer `float *eval` indicates the array location where the computed fitness value will be stored. Such fitness value corresponds to the individual indexed by the variable `int tid`, which is dynamically computed at running time using CUDA's built-in variables `threadIdx`, `blockIdx` and `blockDim`, which uniquely identify a single thread. The current population P_t is encoded into the one-dimensional array pointed by the variable `float *x_prime` thus, an offset must be added to the thread ID to find the starting index of the matching individual. This offset is given by the constant `CHROM_SIZE`. It must be noted that the array holding the current population is transferred to the GPU global memory before launching the slave processes.

```
1  __global__ void evaluation(float *x_prime,
2                              float *eval){
3      // handle the data at this index
4      int tid = blockIdx.x * blockDim.x + threadIdx.x;
5
6      eval[tid] = eval_individual(x_prime[tid*CHROM_SIZE]);
7  }
```

Fig. 5. CUDA/C++ snippet of the evaluation kernel.

4.2 Parallel Mutation Subroutine

The parallel mutation subroutine also follows the master-slave model and aims to reduce its execution time. Figure 6 shows a graphic representation of the proposed parallel mutation subroutine. If we assume that evaluating the pair of equations in (1) takes at least t_M s, the total time spent in mutation operations over $MinGen$ generations would be at least $MinGen \cdot K \cdot n \cdot t_M$ s. Because the mutation process of the j-th individual is independent of the other $K-1$ population members, the two **FOR** loops shown in Fig. 2 can be simplified by launching $K \cdot n$ threads. The job of each thread consists of evaluating the pair of equations in (1) for chromosome i of the j-th individual. Each thread executes a copy of the *kernel function* shown in Fig. 7, where the two-dimensional index (i, j), that uniquely identifies a chromosome in a given individual, is transformed into a one-dimensional index $d = i \times j$ represented by the variable `int tid`. The mutated version of the chromosome d, represented by $(X'_{j,i}, \sigma'_{j,i})$, is computed as shown in lines 09 and 10 of Fig. 7, where `float *x`, `float *sig`, `float *x_prime`, `float *sig_prime` are pointers indicating the location of $X_{j,i}$, $\sigma_{j,i}$, $X'_{j,i}$, and $\sigma'_{j,i}$, respectively, inside one-dimensional arrays indexed by `int tid`.

GPU global memory

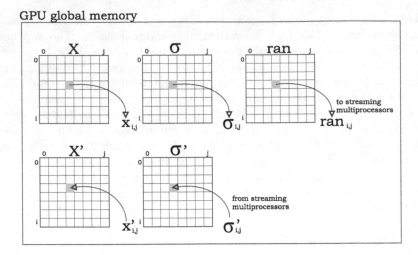

Fig. 6. Global memory access scheme of the data.

In addition to the aforementioned variables, a set of $n + 1$ random numbers are needed to compute Ind'_j. These arrays, of size $K \times n$ and K respectively, are indexed by the pointers `float *ran` and `float *ran_i`. Each thread, running inside the GPU, maps its corresponding elements `ran[tid]` and `ran_i[(int) (tid/POP_SIZE)]` into a Gaussian function with zero mean and unity variance, by calling the subroutine `float normal(float n)`. With the previously described architecture, the total time spent in mutation operations is reduced to $MinGen \cdot t_M$, if and only if $K \times n < N_t$, where N_t is the maximum number of threads running in parallel in the GPU. Note that, unlike the parallel evaluation module, where a thread calculates the fitness value of one individual, the mutation module requires n parallel threads to produce the mutated version of one individual, so that the i-th individual will be assigned to n threads.

5   Experiments and Results

5.1   Test Platform

A test system capable of running GPGPU applications must consist of a general purpose CPU and an nVidia GPU because CUDA's programming model is only available for nVidia GPUs. The selected test platform consisted of a DELL PowerEdge C610x running Windows Multipoint Server, with a 6-core Intel Xeon processor and an nVidia Tesla M2090. The Tesla M2090 has a total of 2^6 streaming-multiprocessors, each one supporting a maximum of 2^{10} concurrent threads, which give a total of $N_t = 2^{16}$ threads running in parallel at any given time.

```
1  __global__ void mutation( float *x,        float *sig,
2                            float *ran ,     float * ran_i
3                            float *x_prime,  float *sig_prime ) {
4      // handle the data at this index
5      int tid = threadIdx.x + blockIdx.x * blockDim.x;
6
7      N               = normal(ran[tid]);
8      Ni              = normal(ran_i[(int)(tid/POP_SIZE)]);
9      x_prime[tid]    = x[tid] + sig[tid] * N ;
10     sig_prime[tid]  = sig[tid] * (1 +  Ni );
11 }
```

Fig. 7. CUDA/C++ snippet of the mutation kernel.

5.2 Experiments

For all performed experiments, two different unconstrained minimization problems of the form $\min_{\mathbf{X} \in \mathbb{R}^n} f_i(\mathbf{X})$, $i = 1, 2$ were considered, where

$$f_1(\mathbf{X_1}, \mathbf{X_2}, \mathbf{X_3}, \dots, \mathbf{X_n}) = \sum_{i=1}^{n/2}(100(X_{2i-1}^2 - X_{2i})^2 + (X_{2i-1} - 1)^2) \quad (3)$$

$$f_2(\mathbf{X_1}, \mathbf{X_2}, \mathbf{X_3}, \dots, \mathbf{X_n}) = A\,n + \sum_{i=1}^{n}(X_i^2 - A\,cos(2\pi X_i)) \quad (4)$$

are two non-convex, multidimensional, well-known testing functions for optimization problems. Equation (3) consists of $n/2$ uncoupled 2D Rosenbrock problems with a global minimum at $(X_1, X_2, X_3, \dots, X_n) = (1, 1, 1, \dots, 1)$. Equation (4) is known as the Rastringin function, it features several local minima and a global minimum at $(X_1, X_2, X_3, \dots, X_n) = (0, 0, 0, \dots, 0)$, for all experiments we set $A = 10$ for in Eq. (4). These kind of minimization problems are specially suited to global search methods, however their computational complexity increases with the dimensionality of $\mathbf{X}$. We selected $n = 1000$ in all considered scenarios to intentionally enhance this weakness.

We decided to measure PEP performance by comparing the time needed by both versions, PEP and SEP, to reach *MinGen* generations. SEP was run in a single core CPU, and PEP in the mentioned GPGPU system. Such comparison was performed using four different population sizes K : 5000, 10000,

Table 1. Single iteration times (sec.) and acceleration factors (α) for different population size (K).

K	f_1			f_2		
	SEP	PEP	α	SEP	PEP	α
5,000	665.3699	48.3108	13.7726	1,189.1700	45.9462	25.8175
10,000	1,422.4299	142.2810	9.9973	3,167.9100	84.1845	37.6305
20,000	3,995.82	202.2842	19.7534	7,091.91	232.6177	30.4873
30,000	6,075	309.7995	19.6094	8,909.82	354.8277	25.1102

20000 and 30000. The parameters kept constant in both implementations were $MinGen = 900$, $n = 1000$, $\tau_E = 40$, and $\psi = 0.2$. The results of this experiment are reported on Table 1. The reported times not only consider execution time but also the additional overhead incurred by memory transfers between CPU and GPU, and the time needed by the GPU to create, manage and launch threads. Often, the mentioned time overheads can be neglected as the GPGPU architecture is designed to reduce them as much as possible, making the time reduction formulas presented in Sects. 4.1 and 4.2 a plausible approximation to the times reported in Table 1. However, when $K \times n > N_t$, the remaining $(K \times n) - N_t$ threads will be held in a queue until there is an available SM to process them. Note that threads can only be assigned to a single SM in batches of maximum 2^{10} threads for the Tesla M2090, this may vary for other architectures. This queuing policy increases the time needed for threads managing when $K \times n >> N_t$, and in the worst case would dominate execution time. Nevertheless, this analysis is strongly dependent on the selected architecture and goes beyond the propose of the present work. Figure 8 shows PEP's convergence rate for a population size of 100 and a chromosome size of 10, reaching the global minimum for function (3) at generation 71488, with a tolerance of 1E-6. While the algorithm approaches the minimum at a high speed during the first generations, the convergence rate slows down near the end, as it is expeceted when the population is dominated by the characteristics of the best individual.

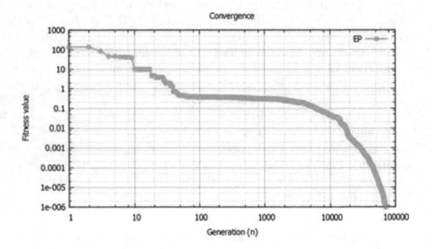

Fig. 8. PEP's convergence rate in the minimization of Eq. (3).

5.3   Acceleration Factor

With the results shown previously, we got a qualitative measure of how good is PEP when comparing it with SEP. However, the potential benefit of a parallel implementation is properly measured by its acceleration factor [12], defined as

$\alpha = \frac{t_1}{t_N}$, where t_1 is the execution time of a given application in a single processor, and t_N is the execution time of the same application running on N processors. The columns labeled as α, on Table 1, show the acceleration factor computed using the times provided for SEP and PEP. As expected, the largest acceleration gain is obtained in the more complex problem (lower-right corner of Table 1), which correspond to the minimization of f_2 using $K = 30,000$ individuals.

6   Conclusions and Future Work

In this work we measured the eciency of an evolutionary algorithm applied to the minimization of real-valued functions. The algorithm was parallelized using a master-slave model and was executed in a GPGPU system. Two different, non-convex, continuous, nonlinear, real-valued functions were used as objective functions of the minimization problem. The results report a drastic improvement in execution time for the parallel implementation of an evolutionary programming algorithm. The reported improvement can be attributed to two factors. First, the parallel implementation using a GPU benefited from the many threads executed concurrently. Second, when compared to a parallel implementation using multithreading or a cluster of computers, the GPU implementation benefited from the low-creating cost and low latency. It is natural that the highest acceleration factor was obtained for the biggest problem because as population size increases, and the evaluation time of a single individual remains constant, the acceleration factor will increase as long as we do not reach the constraint imposed by N_t in a GPU. Even if we exceeded N_t the cost induced by allocating the extra threads will be negligible, and the acceleration gain will remain significant. Another aspect that can be highlighted in the parallel implementation is that the number of execution threads dynamically increases with the size of the problem, but the execution time remains almost constant, keeping in mind the constraint imposed by N_t. Future work may consist on comparing the performance of cellular models of parallelism in EAs, implemented in different parallel architectures such as multi-core CPU using OpenMP and PThreads. Additionally, the effects of parallel implementations on multi-objective optimization problems, using GPGPU systems, can be explored.

References

1. Fogel, L.J., Owens, A.J., Walsh, M.J.: Artificial Intelligence Through Simulated Evolution. Wiley, New York (1966)
2. Fogel, D.B.: Evolutionary Computation: Towards a New Philosophy of Machine Intelligence. IEEE Press, New York (1995)
3. Fogel, D.B., Stayton, L.C.: On the effectiveness of crossover in simulated evolutionary optimization. Bio. Syst. **32**(3), 171–182 (1994)
4. Tongchim, S., Yao, X.: Parallel evolutionary programming. In: Proceedings of the IEEE Congress on Evolutionary Computing, Portland, OR, pp. 1362–1367 (2004)

5. Fernández, F., Tomassini, M., Vanneschi, L.: Studying the influence of communication topology and migration on distributed genetic programming. In: Miller, J., Tomassini, M., Lanzi, P.L., Ryan, C., Tetamanzi, A.G.B., Langdon, W.B. (eds.) EuroGP 2001. LNCS, vol. 2038, p. 51. Springer, Heidelberg (2001)

6. Fernández, F., Tomassini, M., Punch, W.F., Sánchez, J.M.: Experimental study of multipopulation parallel genetic programming. In: Poli, R., Banzhaf, W., Langdon, W.B., Miller, J., Nordin, P., Fogarty, T.C. (eds.) EuroGP 2000. LNCS, vol. 1802, pp. 283–293. Springer, Heidelberg (2000)

7. Tanese, R.: Distributed genetic algorithms. In: Schaffer, J.D., (ed.) ICGA-3, pp. 434–439(1989)

8. Alba, E., Troya, J.M.: Influence of the migration policy in parallel distributed gas with structured and panmictic populations. Appl. Intell. **12**(3), 163–181 (2000)

9. Cantu-Paz, E., Goldberg, D.E.: Predicting speedups of idealized bounding cases of parallel genetic algorithms. In: Bäck, T., (ed.) Proceedings of the 7th International Conference on Genetic Algorithms, pp. 113–120 (1997)

10. Alba, E., Tomassini, M.: Parallelism and evolutionary algorithms. IEEE Trans. Evol. Comput. **6**(5), 443–462 (2002)

11. Levine, D.: Users guide to the PGAPack parallel genetic algorithm library. Argonne Nat. Lab., Math. Comput. Sci. Div., Tech. Rep. ANL-95/18, January 1995

12. Gebali, F.: Algorithms and Parallel Computing. Wiley, Hoboken (2011)

13. Sanders, J., Kandrot, E.: CUDA by Example: An Introduction to General-Purpose GPU Programming. Addison Wesley, Upper Saddle River (2011)

14. Kirk, D.B., Huw, W.M.W.: Programming Massively Parallel Processors: A Hands-On Approach. Morgan Kaufmann, San Francisco (2010)

15. Aziz, N.I.A., Sulaiman, S.I., Musikin, I., Shaari, S.: Assessment of evolutionary programming models for single-objective optimization. In: Musirin, I., Salimin, R.H. (eds.) Proceedings of the 7th IEEE International PEOCO, Langkawi, Malaysia, pp. 304–308 (2013)

Calculation of the Stability Zones of Hill's Equation with a GPU on Matlab

Miguel Ramírez[✉] and Joaquín Collado

Automatic Control Department, Cinvestav, IPN 2508 Avenue,
07360 Mexico, D.F., Mexico
{mramirez,jcollado}@ctrl.cinvestav.mx

Abstract. A method to calculate the stability zones for linear periodic systems is presented. The calculation often requires the solution of a large number of ordinary differential equations (ODE) therefore the computation time is huge. The goal of this contribution is to speed-up the computation time using the parallel architecture of the GPU (Graphics Processing Unit). The linear periodic differential equation is discretized to obtain a discrete system in which the stability is determined. We emphasize the advantages of the presented method for systems of two or more degrees of freedom.

1 Introduction

The equation

$$\ddot{y} + (\alpha + \beta p(t))y = 0 \qquad p(t+T) = p(t) \tag{1}$$

known as Hill's equation (with $\dot{y} = \frac{dy}{dt}$), has been studied in detail in [20, 27], and generically can not be solved analytically[1]. Hence for a general $p(t)$, to find a solution of (1) it is necessary to use a numerical method. For this reason the analysis of the periodic systems focus on describing the behavior of the solution i.e. if the solutions are asymptotically stable, stable, unstable or if there are periodic solutions.

It is important to know for which pair (α, β) of parameters the system is stable/unstable. If the stability of Eq. (1) is analyzed for a each of its parameters and making a plot of α versus β as in Fig. 1, the stable (white) and unstable (gray) zones are obtained which are named Arnold's tongues [2], since unstable zones looks like tongues. The goal of this contribution is to calculate the Arnold's tongues with a GPU in order to speed-up the computation time. In control theory parallel computing is not a new tool [3, 21]. The stability of several million time varying differential equations, are analyzed and the Arnold's tongues are plotted in a few minutes, with help of GPU (Graphics Processing Unit) Nvidia Tesla 2075.

---

[1] Some exceptions are: (a) Meissner equation $\ddot{y} + (\alpha + \beta sign\,(\cos(t)))y = 0$ [24], (b) when $p(t)$ is a periodic train of impulses [23], (c) when $p(t)$ is a periodic linear piece-wise function [23], and (d) for Lamé equation [15].

© Springer International Publishing Switzerland 2016
I. Gitler and J. Klapp (Eds.): ISUM 2015, CCIS 595, pp. 225–239, 2016.
DOI: 10.1007/978-3-319-32243-8_16

There are many methods to compute the Arnold's tongues, the easiest is to integrate the differential equation for each parameter (α, β) and analyze the stability (with the Floquet-Lyapunov theorem); then to make a plot with 1000×1000 points of resolution it is required integrate one million differential equations, thus the technique has a slow performance in regard to computation time, nevertheless, the performance can be speed up using GPUs.

For systems of one degree of freedom (DOF) the spectral methods [26] provide stability plots in seconds, but it is not viable for equations with two or more DOF. In [14,17] the "infinite determinants" are exposed, where the periodic solutions of (1) are approximated by Fourier series in order to evaluate the boundaries between stable and unstable zones. It is possible to apply the truncated infinite determinants to equations with two DOF [14] but some cumbersome modifications are required (because in two dimensions not all boundaries are periodic [14,27]), and if the periodic function has frequencies 1 and 1000, at least a determinant of 1000×1000 should be analyzed. Thus this paper focuses on how to compute the Arnold's tongues for systems with two or more (DOF) that is to say when $y \in \mathbb{R}^n$ for $n \geq 2$ in Eq. (1).

In Sect. 2, a review of linear time periodic systems and the Floquet-Lyapunov theory which describe the stability conditions of this kind of systems are exposed. In Sect. 3 "the integration" method to plot the Arnold's tongues and the algorithm to implement the method on a GPU are exposed. In Sect. 4 the secondary contribution of the paper is developed, a technique to discretize Hill's equation and new test of stability with its algorithms is fixed. It should be noted that, we choose to use Matlab to reduce the required programming effort. If it is necessary to minimize further the execution time of the algorithm, an implementation of the algorithm in C++ should be developed.

2 Mathematical Background

2.1 Parametric Resonance

Given the equation $\ddot{x} + \omega_0^2 x = f(t)$, $f(t) = A \cos \omega t$, when ω is equal to ω_0, there is a "Linear Resonance"[2] that causes the solution to grow linearly [19] namely, the system becomes unstable. On the other hand it can be observed in (2) that $p(t)$ is a function of the Eq. (2) called parametric excitation, unlike $f(t)$ that is an external signal.

$$\ddot{y} + (\alpha + \beta p(t))y = 0 \qquad p(t + T) = p(t) \tag{2}$$

The parametric resonance is an instability point that is caused by a rational relationship between the frequency of parametric excitation and the natural frequency of free oscillation in the absence of the excitation [8]. If $\omega = 1$ (or $T = 2\pi$) is the frequency excitation of $p(t)$, and $\sqrt{\alpha}$ the natural frequency

---

[2] We introduce the non-standard norm of "Linear Resonance", in order to compare with "Parametric Resonance".

in (2) when $\beta = 0$, then parametric resonance occurs when $\alpha = n^2/4$ for all $n \in \mathbb{N}$. The parametric resonance instability appears in intervals for each $\beta = \beta_0$, opposed to the linear resonance in which instability appears only in a single point. Another difference is that linear resonance grows polynomially while the parametric resonance grows exponentially. For this reason the study and the plotting of the stability zones is important [12].

2.2   Periodic Linear Systems

Consider the linear periodic differential equation

$$\dot{x} = A(t)x \quad x(t_0) = x_0 \tag{3}$$

with $x(t) \in \mathbb{R}^n$, $A(t) = A(t+T) \in \mathbb{R}^{n \times n}$, where T is the fundamental period. Let $N(t) \in \mathbb{R}^{n \times n}$ be a fundamental matrix [7,10] which has n linearly independent solutions of (3) in each of its columns, hence $N(t)$ is not singular. The state transition matrix [5,10,11] is defined as $\Phi(t, t_0) \triangleq N(t)N^{-1}(t_0)$,[3] the solution of (3) can be written as $x(t) = \Phi(t, t_0)x_0$. The state transition matrix evaluated in one period $M_{t_0} = \Phi(t_0 + T, t_0)$ is called the monodromy matrix of (3). M_{t_0} is similar to M_t, $\forall\, t_0, t \in [0, T]$ [1], therefore without loss of generality $M_0 = M \triangleq \Phi(T, 0)$.

Theorem 1. *[Lyapunov-Floquet] Let M be the monodromy matrix associated to Eq. (3), and its spectrum $\sigma(M) = \{\lambda_1, ..., \lambda_n\}$ the eigenvalues of M, then system (3) is:*

  (i) *Asymptotically Stable if and only if, all the eigenvalues of M have module less than one, namely $|\lambda_i| < 1$ for all $i = 1, ...n$*
 (ii) *Stable if and only if, the eigenvalues of M have module less or equal than one, $|\lambda_i| \leq 1$, and the eigenvalues which has module one are roots simple of the minimal polynomial of M*
(iii) *Unstable if and only if, M has one eigenvalue of module greater than one, or all eigenvalues $|\lambda_j| \leq 1$ and there exist λ_j with module equal to one which are multiple root of the minimal polynomial of M.*

Proof. For any $t \geqslant 0$ we can express $t = kT + \tau$ for $k \in \mathbb{N}$ with $\tau \in [0, T)$. Then writing the solution of (3) and using the transition state matrix properties [5]

$$
\begin{aligned}
x(t) &= \Phi(t, 0)x_0 \\
&= \Phi(kT + \tau, 0)x_0 \\
&= \Phi(kT + \tau, kT)\Phi(kT, (k-1)\,T)\Phi((k-1)\,T, (k-2)\,T)...\Phi(T, 0)x_0 \\
&= \Phi(\tau, 0)\underbrace{\Phi(T, 0)\Phi(T, 0)...\Phi(T, 0)}_{k-times}x_0 \\
&= \Phi(\tau, 0)\left[\Phi(T, 0)\right]^k x_0 = \Phi(\tau, 0)\left[M\right]^k x_0
\end{aligned}
$$

---

[3] It may proved that $\Phi(t, t_0)$ does not depend on the particular fundamental matrix $N(t)$ chosen [5].

Then the state grows to infinity $x(t) \to \infty$ if and only if $t \to \infty$ for all linear systems [7] therefore, since τ is a finite number $\Phi(\tau, 0)$ is bounded, the initial conditions x_0 are bounded, hence the only term which could be not bounded is M^k, thus (3) is stable if and only if M^k is bounded: (i) then $M^k \to 0_{n \times n}$ as $k \to \infty$ if all eigenvalues have module less than one (ii) M^k is bounded if $|\lambda_i| \le 1$ & $\exists |\lambda_j| = 1$: λ_j is a simple root of minimal polynomial of M and (iii) $M^k \to \infty$ if (a) $\exists \lambda_j : |\lambda_i| > 1$ or (b) $|\lambda_i| \le 1$ & $\exists |\lambda_j| = 1$: λ_j is a multiple root of minimal polynomail of M. $\square$

When the Hill's equation is a Hamiltonian system [24, 27], the monodromy matrix M is symplectic [27]. The symplectic matrices have a property that if $\lambda \in \sigma(M)$ then $\lambda^{-1} \in \sigma(M)$, namely the eigenvalues of M are symmetric with respect to the unit circle.

As example, let be the Hill's equation for two degrees of freedom

$$\ddot{y} + P(t)y = 0$$

with $y \in \mathbb{R}^2$, $P(t) = P(t + T) \in \mathbb{R}^{2 \times 2}$ if

$$x = \begin{bmatrix} x_1 \\ x_2 \end{bmatrix} = \begin{bmatrix} y \\ \dot{y} \end{bmatrix} \rightarrow \begin{bmatrix} \dot{x}_1 \\ \dot{x}_2 \end{bmatrix} = \begin{bmatrix} \dot{y} \\ \ddot{y} \end{bmatrix}$$

can be written as (3)

$$\dot{x} = A(t)x \quad \text{where} \quad A = \begin{bmatrix} 0 & I_2 \\ -P(t) & 0 \end{bmatrix} \tag{4}$$

Given the definition of linear Hamiltonian systems [24], the system (4) is a Hamiltonian system if the matrix A can be written as $A = JA^T J$ where $J = \begin{bmatrix} 0_{n \times n} & I_{n \times n} \\ -I_{n \times n} & 0_{n \times n} \end{bmatrix}$ hence, (4) is a Hamiltonian system if $P(t) = P(t)^T$. Thus, the monodromy matrix M associated to (4) has four eigenvalues therefore, if (4) is stable all eigenvalues of M must be on the unit circle, if there is one eigenvalue inside of the unit circle then (4) is unstable because $|\lambda_1| < 1 \to |\lambda_2| = \frac{1}{|\lambda_1|} > 1$.

2.3   Stability Zones (Arnold's Tongues)

An especial case of Hill's equations is the Mathieu equation

$$x'' + \left(\tilde{\alpha} + \tilde{\beta} \cos \left(\omega + \tilde{t} \right) \right) x = 0 \tag{5}$$

(where derivative x' is respect to $\tilde{t}$) If the time is rescaled $t = \omega \tilde{t}$ then

$$\omega^2 \left[\ddot{x} + \left(\frac{\tilde{\alpha}}{\omega^2} + \frac{\tilde{\beta}}{\omega^2} \cos \left(\tilde{t} \right) \right) x \right] = 0$$

$$\ddot{x} + (\alpha + \beta \cos(t)) x = 0 \tag{6}$$

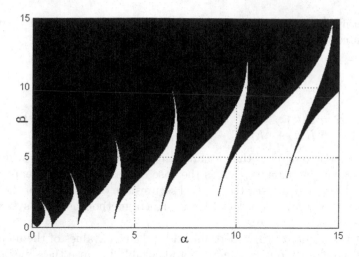

Fig. 1. Arnold's tongues of Mathieu's equation (6)

(5) and (6) are equivalent, hence it should be noted that plot α versus β is similar to plot ω versus β. In the Fig. 1 the Arnold's tongues for (6) are shown. In this case it's plotted α versus β, namely for each pair (α, β) we computed (with Runge-Kutta method) the monodromy matrix of (6) and applied the Floquet-Lyapunov theorem in order to know the stability of each point therefore the stability of (6) depends on their parameters (α, β).

3   Integration of Hill's Equation Using a GPU

The monodromy matrix is a fundamental matrix evaluated on T with normalized initial conditions i.e. $M = \Phi(T, 0) = N(T)N^{-1}(0)$ with $N(0) = I_n$, thus computing with Runge-Kutta methods [6] $N(T) = [\eta_1(T)\ \eta_2(T)\ \eta_3(T)\ \eta_4(T)]$ where $\eta_i(t)$ are linearly independent solutions of (4), and using the Floquet-Lyapunov theorem we know the stability of the system (4). The next algorithm shows how to plot the Arnold's tongues for the equation:

$$\ddot{y} + D\dot{y} + [\alpha A + \beta(B sign(\cos rt) + C sign(\sin mt))]\, y = 0 \qquad (7)$$

(a matrix generalization of Meissner's equation) with $A, B \in \mathbb{R}^{n\times n}$, $D \in \mathbb{R}^{n\times n}$ diagonal, $y \in \mathbb{R}^n$, the study of these equation is useful for many mechanics problems see [22]. Making the change of variables $x = \left[x_1^T\ x_2^T\right]^T = \left[y^T\ \dot{y}^T\right]^T$ (7) can be put into the form (3)

$$\dot{x} = R(t)x \qquad (8)$$

where

$$R(t) = \begin{bmatrix} 0_{n\times n} & I_{n\times n} \\ -\alpha A - \beta(B sign(\cos t) + C sign(\sin t)) & -D \end{bmatrix}$$

Remembering the Runge Kutta of fourth order method [6] the first derivative is approximated by

$$x_{i+1} = x_i + \frac{1}{6}h\left(k_1 + 2k_2 + 2k_3 + k_4\right) \tag{9}$$

where

$$k_1 = R(t_i)x_i \qquad\qquad k_2 = R\left(t_i + \tfrac{1}{2}h\right)\left(x_i + \tfrac{1}{2}k_1\right)$$
$$k_3 = R\left(t_i + \tfrac{1}{2}h\right)\left(x_i + \tfrac{1}{2}k_2\right) \ k_4 = R\left(t_i + h\right)\left(x_i + k_3\right)$$

An important remark is that we are going to integrate systems which might have eigenvalues on $j\omega$ axis, that is the case of Hamiltonian systems. The use of the fourth order Runge-Kutta method secures the convergence of the integration. In fact the minimum order of Runge-Kutta method used for systems with eigenvalues on $j\omega$ is four [6].

Then the stability of (8) is determined by the eigenvalues of the monodromy matrix M. Obviously our problem is parallelizable because the solution of one pair (α_1, β_1) does not depend of the solution of another pair (α_0, β_0). Hence:

1. First define all parameters of equation A, D, B, C, r, m and the interval for axes, i.e. β, α minimum and maximum and the number of points in each axes. Usually we work with six thousand points on the α axis and one thousand on the β axis that is to say we have 6 millions of points on the plot to analyze. To do this use the command "alfa= parallel.gpu.GPUArray.linspace(alfa_min, alfa_max, alfa_size)".
2. Make the code of Runge Kutta method on the GPU file which returns the vector of solution evaluate on T that is $\eta_i(T)$, remember we only are interested in the $N(T) = [\eta_1(T)\ \eta_2(T)\ \eta_3(T)\ \eta_4(T)]$ and save on the file "ode.m".
3. Define the initial conditions $x_0 = \begin{bmatrix}1\,0\,0\,0\end{bmatrix}^T$ and Call the GPU with the comamd "arrayfun(@ode,alfa,beta,x0)", keep $\eta_1(T)$
4. Repeat the step two to $x_0 = \begin{bmatrix}0\,1\,0\,0\end{bmatrix}^T$ to obtain $\eta_2(T)$, do this to $x_0 = \begin{bmatrix}0\,0\,1\,0\end{bmatrix}^T \rightarrow \eta_3(T)$ and $x_0 = \begin{bmatrix}0\,0\,0\,1\end{bmatrix}^T \rightarrow \eta_4(T)$.
5. Construct $M = [\eta_1(T)\ \eta_2(T)\ \eta_3(T)\ \eta_4(T)]$ the monodromy matrix.
6. Compute the eigenvalues to use the test of stability if $|\lambda| \leq 1$ stable where $\lambda \in \sigma(M)$ (since the numerical inaccuracy in the code line is written $|\lambda| \leq 1.0001$).
7. Plot the Arnold's tongues.

Note. Instead of step six it can use the modified power method (explained in the next section) as test of stability.

The Fig. 2 shows the Arnold's tongues for

$$\ddot{y} + D\dot{y} + \left[\alpha A + \beta\left(B sign(\cos rt) + C sign(\sin mt)\right)\right]y = 0 \tag{10}$$

$$A = \begin{bmatrix}1 & 0\\0 & 2\end{bmatrix},\ B = \begin{bmatrix}3 & 3\\3 & 3\end{bmatrix},\ C = \begin{bmatrix}0 & -1\\-1 & 0\end{bmatrix},\ D = \begin{bmatrix}0.01 & 0\\0 & 0.01\end{bmatrix} \tag{11}$$

and below are shown the pseudo-code of algorithm for this example.

MATLAB

```
%Define Parameters
alfa=parallel.gpu.GPUArray.linspace(a_min,a_max,a_size);
```

Calling to GPU

```
for beta=beta_min:inc_beta:beta_max
  [X1] =arrayfun(@ode,alfa,beta,x0,'Matrices');m1(n,:)=gather(X1);
  [X2] =arrayfun(@ode,alfa,beta,x0,'Matrices');m2(n,:)=gather(X2);
  [X3] =arrayfun(@ode,alfa,beta,x0,'Matrices');m3(n,:)=gather(X3);
  [X4] =arrayfun(@ode,alfa,beta,x0,'Matrices');m4(n,:)=gather(X4);
  n=n+1;
end
```

Plot the Arnold's Tongues

```
for b=1:beta_size
   for a=a_min:a_size
      M=[m1 m2 m3 m4]; % monodromy matrix for each (alfa,beta)
         if abs (max(eig(M)))<1.0001  %STABLE
         else    %UNSTABLE
            x(i)=alfa;
            y(i)=beta;
            i=i+1;
         end
   end
end
plot(x,y)
```

GPU Function 'ode.m'

```
%ode function
-Runge Kutta Algorithm
return X\newline{}
```

4   Discretization

The second method to calculate the Arnold's tongues consists in the discretization of Hill's equation. Since (1) is linear has a unique and continuous solution, then we can approximate $\dot{y}$ as:

$$\dot{y} \approx \frac{y\left(t + \frac{h}{2}\right) - y\left(t - \frac{h}{2}\right)}{h}$$

$$\ddot{y}(t) \approx \frac{y\left(t + h\right) - 2y\left(t\right) + y\left(t - h\right)}{h^2} \tag{12}$$

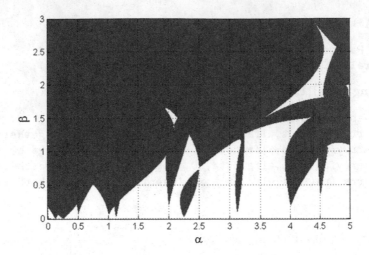

Fig. 2. Arnold's tongues for Meissner's equation (10) with (11) made by integration technique

where h is small, this approximations is known as *central differences*. Substituting (12) in (1) we have

$$\ddot{y}(t_k) \approx \frac{y(t+h) - 2y(t) + y(t-h)}{h^2} = \frac{y_{k+1} - 2y_k + y_{k-1}}{h^2}$$

$$\frac{y_{k+1} - 2y_k + y_{k-1}}{h^2} + p(t_k)y_k = 0$$

$$y_{k+1} = (2 - h^2 p(t_k))y_k - y_{k-1}$$
$$y_{k+2} = (2 - h^2 p(t_k))y_{k+1} - y_k$$

hence we obtain a periodic time varying equation where $p(t_k) = p(t_k + T_k)$. Using the Lifting technique [4] it is possible obtain a discrete shift invariant system. Let be

$$z_{k+1} = A_k y_k \tag{13}$$

a linear periodic (with $A_k \in \mathbb{R}^{2n \times 2n}$ $A_k = A_{k+N}$) discrete system, where N is the minimum period obtained from the discretization for $k = 0, 1, 2...N - 1$, if T is the minimum period in continuous time ($h = \frac{T}{N}$). Then for the first period

$$z_1 = A_0 z_0$$
$$z_2 = A_1 z_1 = A_1 A_0 z_0$$
$$z_3 = A_2 z_2 = A_2 A_1 A_0 z_0$$
$$\vdots$$
$$z_k = A_{k-1} z_{k-1} = A_{k-1} A_{k-2} \cdots A_1 A_0 z_0$$

for the next period

$$z_{k+1} = (A_0 A_{k-1} A_{k-2} \cdots A_2 A_1) z_0$$
$$z_{k+2} = (A_1 A_0 A_{k-1} A_{k-2} \cdots A_2) z_1$$
$$\vdots$$
$$z_{k+N} = (A_{k-1} A_{k-2} A_{k-3}..A_0) z_{N-1}$$

making the change of variables $x_k = \begin{bmatrix} z_{Nk+1} & z_{Nk+2} & \cdots & z_{Nk+N} \end{bmatrix}^T$ we have the discrete shift invariant system

$$x_{k+1} = \mathcal{A} z_k \tag{14}$$

where

$$\mathcal{A} = \begin{bmatrix} A_0 A_{k-1} A_{k-2} \cdots A_1 & 0 & \cdots & 0 \\ 0 & A_1 A_0 A_{k-1} \cdots A_2 & \vdots & 0 \\ \vdots & \vdots & \ddots & \vdots \\ 0 & 0 & \cdots & A_{k-1} A_{k-2}..A_0 \end{bmatrix}$$

As it is known Eq. (14) is asymptotically stable if and only if $\sigma(\mathcal{A}) \subset D = \{\rho \in \mathbb{C} \mid |\rho| < 1\}$. Since $\mathcal{A}$ is block diagonal

$$\sigma(\mathcal{A}) = \sigma(A_0 A_{k-1} \cdots A_2 A_1) + \sigma(A_1 A_0 A_{k-1} \cdots A_2) + \ldots + \sigma(A_{k-1} A_{k-2}..A_0)$$

if A_i, A_j are not singular then $\sigma(A_i A_j) = \sigma(A_j A_i)$ [18], thus

$$\sigma(\mathcal{A}) = \sigma(A_0 A_{k-1} \cdots A_2 A_1) = \sigma(A_1 A_0 A_{k-1} \cdots A_2) = \ldots = \sigma(A_{k-1} A_{k-2}..A_0)$$

therefore it is sufficient to compute $\sigma(A_0 A_{k-1} A_{k-2} \cdots A_2 A_1)$ to analyze the stability of (14). Hence the algorithm to plot the Arnold's tongues is reduced to analyze the eigenvalues of $A_0 A_{k-1} A_{k-2} \cdots A_2 A_1$ from the discrete system [16]. In order to improve the discretization it can use the formula

$$x_{i+1} = x_i + \frac{1}{6} h (k_1 + 2k_2 + 2k_3 + k_4) \tag{15}$$

instead of (12) where k_i are the same of the Runge Kutta method [6] and is equivalent to the Taylor's series

$$x_{k+1} = I_k + h A_k + \frac{h^2}{2} A_k^2 + \frac{h^3}{6} A_k^3 + \frac{h^4}{24} A_k^4 \tag{16}$$

the programmer needs choose between to use (16) or (15) to discretize (3). We are increasing from 2 to 4 the order of the discretization, therefore for the same h, we have less error in the higher order method. Summarizing the technique:

1. Put the differential equation into the form of (3).
2. Apply (16) with $h = (T/N)$ where N is the number of points by period of the discretization.
3. Compute $L = A_{k-1} A_{k-2} A_{k-3}..A_0$ to know the stability of (3) which depends of the eigenvalues of $L = A_{k-1} A_{k-2} A_{k-3}..A_0$.

4.1   The Modified Power Method

Let $A \in \mathbb{R}^{n \times n}$ be a matrix with eigenvalues λ_i for $i = 1, ..n$, such that $|\lambda_1| > |\lambda_j|$ for $j = 2, ...n$ namely there exists one eigenvalue larger than the rest. For sake of simplicity assume that eigenvalues of A are different. Let $x_0 = \alpha_1 x_1 + ... + \alpha_n x_n$ be an initial vector where x_i are eigenvectors of A $(Ax_i = \lambda_i x_i)$ and $\alpha_1 \neq 0$. Then

$$Ax_0 = A(\alpha_1 x_1 + ... + \alpha_n x_n) = \alpha_1 Ax_1 + ... + \alpha_n Ax_n$$
$$= \alpha_1 \lambda_i x_1 + ... + \alpha_n \lambda_n x_n$$

premultiplying by A

$$AAx_0 = A(\alpha_1 \lambda_1 x_1 + ... + \alpha_n \lambda_n x_n) = \alpha_1 \lambda_1 Ax_1 + ... + \alpha_n \lambda_n Ax_n$$
$$= \alpha_1 \lambda_1^2 x_1 + ... + \alpha_n \lambda_n^2 x_n$$

repeat k times, then

$$A^k x_0 = \alpha_1 \lambda_1^k x_1 + ... + \alpha_n \lambda_n^k x_n$$

$$A^k x_0 = \lambda_1^k \left(\alpha_1 x_1 + ... + \alpha_n \left(\frac{\lambda_n^k}{\lambda_1} \right) x_n \right) \tag{17}$$

since $|\lambda_1| > |\lambda_j|$

$$\lim_{k \to \infty} \left(\frac{\lambda_j^k}{\lambda_1} \right) = 0 \qquad j = 2, ..n$$

therefore for large k

$$A^k x_0 \approx \alpha_1 \lambda_1^k x_1 = \alpha_1 A^k x_1 \tag{18}$$

Remark 1. $A^k x_0$ aligns with x_1 for large k, then we know x_1, is the eigenvector associated to λ_1, the largest eigenvalue, then

$$\left\| A^k x_0 \right\| \approx \alpha_1 \left| \lambda_1^k \right| \|x_1\|$$

$$\left\| A^{k+1} x_0 \right\| \approx \alpha_1 \left| \lambda_1^{k+1} \right| \|x_1\|$$

thus

$$|\lambda_1| \approx \frac{\left\| A^{k+1} x_0 \right\|}{\left\| A^k x_0 \right\|}$$

Hence when $k \to \infty$, x_0 has the same direction as the eigenvector associated to λ_1 so we can estimate an eigenvector or an eigenvalue. The main idea is to compute eigenvalues or eigenvectors by using power methods [9,13] and QR-Methods see [9,25], therefore obtaining a test to check instability.

Remembering the system (8) is stable if and only if its monodromy matrix has all eigenvalues with module less or equal than one, from Eq. (17) and selecting a normalized initial vector $x_0 = \alpha_1 x_1 + ... + \alpha_n x_n$, $\|x_0\|_2 = 1$ we have

$$\left\| M^k x_0 \right\| \leq \left| \lambda_1^k \right| \left\| \left(\alpha_1 x_1 + ... + \alpha_n \left(\frac{\lambda_n^k}{\lambda_1} \right) x_n \right) \right\| \tag{19}$$

if the system (8) is stable then $|\lambda_1| = |\lambda_2| = ... = |\lambda_n| = 1$ then $\left|\frac{\lambda_n^k}{\lambda_1}\right| = 1$ and (19) becomes

$$\left\|M^k x_0\right\| \leq |\lambda_1^k| \left\|(\alpha_1 x_1 + ... + \alpha_n x_n)\right\| \tag{20}$$

but $\|x_0\|_2 = 1$ hence, (8) is stable

$$\left\|M^k x_0\right\| \leq 1 \tag{21}$$

if the inequality (21) is true. This method speed-up the computation time because the eigenvalues computation is not necessary. In the code line the condition is written as $\left|M^k x_0\right| \leq P = 1.0001$. Due to numerical errors, if the absolute value $|\lambda|$ is close to one as $|\lambda| \approx 1.000001$ later iterations for K large this value is $(|\lambda| = 1.000001)^K$ hence it is convenient to use

$$\bar{P} = P^K \tag{22}$$

as test of stability [9].

4.2   Algorithm for the Discretization Method

The next algorithm explain step by step how to plot the Arnold's tongues for the n-dimensional Hill's equation:

$$\ddot{x} + D\dot{x} + [\alpha A + \beta (B \cos mt + C \sin rt)] x = 0 \tag{23}$$

$A, B \in \mathbb{R}^{n \times n}, D \in \mathbb{R}^{n \times n}$ diagonal matrix, $x \in \mathbb{R}^n$ again we use the change of variable $y = \begin{bmatrix} y_1 & y_2 \end{bmatrix}^T = \begin{bmatrix} x & \dot{x} \end{bmatrix}^T$ then

$$\dot{y} = R(t)y \tag{24}$$

$$R(t) = \begin{bmatrix} 0_{n \times n} & I_{n \times n} \\ -\alpha A - \beta (B \cos t + C \sin t) & -D \end{bmatrix}$$

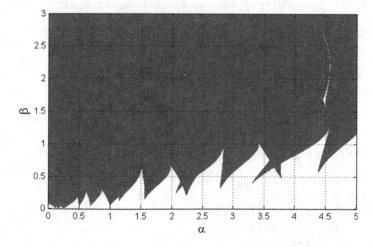

Fig. 3. Arnold's tongues of (23) wiht (26) by Discretization Method Algorithm

1. First define all parameters of equation A, D, B, C, r, m and the interval for axes, i.e. β, α minimum and maximum and the number of points in each axes. Usually we work with five or six thousand points on the α axis and one thousand on the β axis. Therefore, we have 6 millions of points on the plot to analyze. To do this use the comand "alfa= parallel.gpu.GPUArray.linspace(alfa_min, alfa_max, alfa_size)".
2. Make the code to discretize with Eq. (16) and perform

$$L = A_{k-1}A_{k-2}A_{k-3}..A_0 \tag{25}$$

matrix, where $h = (T/N)$, we usually choose N on multiples of 360 because $T = 2\pi$ (in the example use $N = 3(360)$).
3. In the same GPU file discretization.m use the power method to test stability, fix a random initial vector x_0 and normalize. Choose the number of iteration K keep in mind that K must be large for the convergence of method, for the example we use $K = 10000$, apply the test (22). The function program returns a flag which indicates if the pair (α, β) is unstable.
4. Call the GPU function "arrayfun(@discretization,alfa,beta,x0)".
5. Plot the Arnold's tongues.

In the Fig. 3 is shown the Arnold's tongues when

$$A = \begin{bmatrix} 1 & 0 \\ 0 & 2 \end{bmatrix}, \ B = \begin{bmatrix} 1 & 3 \\ 0 & 1 \end{bmatrix}, \ C = \begin{bmatrix} 0 & 0 \\ 0 & 0 \end{bmatrix}, \ D = \begin{bmatrix} 0.01 & 0 \\ 0 & 0.01 \end{bmatrix} \tag{26}$$

a particular case for two dimensions of (23), and below is shown the pseudo-code of algorithm to this example

MATLAB

```
%Define Parameters
alfa=parallel.gpu.GPUArray.linspace(a_min,a_max,a_size);
```

Calling to GPU

```
for beta=beta_min:inc_beta:beta_max
    [u] =arrayfun(@discretization,alfa,beta,Matrices);
    flag(n,:)=gather(u);
    n=n+1;
end
```

Plot the Arnold's Tongues

```
for b=1:beta_size
    for a=a_min:a_size
        if flag(b,a)==1 %stable
            else %unstable
                x(i)=alfa;
                y(i)=beta;
```

```
                i=i+1;
            end
        end
    end
plot(x,y)
```

GPU Function 'discretization.m'

```
%gpu function
Discretization
Power method
u=1; %stable
u=0; %unstable
```

5   GPU Performance

In Table 1, the speed-up factor to calculate the Arnold's tongues between using or not the GPU for a particular case of 1 million of points on the grid is shown. We reduce 521 times the computation time for the integration technique, and 109 times the discretization time using parallel computing on GPU. It is worth to compare the speed-up between these two techniques, in Fig. 4 is shown the computation time versus the number of analyzed points. Figure 4 can be useful to choose which technique to use. It is better to use the integration method when working with 0.5 to 5 million of points. However, discretization method is more suitable when working with 3 to 7 million of points.

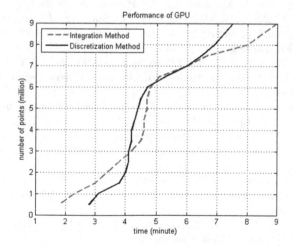

Fig. 4. Performance of GPU

Table 1. Faster factor for 1 million points

Method	Time without GPU	Time with GPU	Speed-up factor
Integration	20 h	2.3 min	521
Discretization	6 h	3.3 min	109

6   Conclusions

The computation of the Arnold's tongues has been accelerated using a GPU more than one hundred times. A method to discretize and analyze the stability of Hill's equation of n- DOF was exposed, the same method can be used with any time periodic linear system. On the other hand a parallel algorithm for the integration with GPU on Matlab was developed. We hope the methods presented in this work can help in the analysis of periodic differential equations. As future work, it would be worthwhile to develop the code for CUDA and compare the performance obtained, with that of Matlab.

References

1. Adrianova, L.Y.: Introduction to Linear Systems of Differential Equations, vol. 146. American Mathematical Soc., Providence (1995)
2. Arnold, V.I.: Remarks on the perturbation theory for problems of mathieu type. Russ. Math. Surv. **38**(4), 215–233 (1983)
3. Benner, P., Ezzatti, P., Quintana-Ortí, E.S., Remón, A.: Using hybrid CPU-GPU platforms to accelerate the computation of the matrix sign function. In: Lin, H.-X., Alexander, M., Forsell, M., Knüpfer, A., Prodan, R., Sousa, L., Streit, A. (eds.) Euro-Par 2009. LNCS, vol. 6043, pp. 132–139. Springer, Heidelberg (2010)
4. Bittanti, S., Colaneri, P.: Periodic Systems: Filtering and Control. Communications and Control Engineering. Springer, London (2008)
5. Brockett, R.: Finite Dimensional Linear Systems. Wiley, New York (1970)
6. Butcher, J.: The Numerical Analysis of Ordinary Differential Equations. Wiley, Chichester (1987)
7. Cesari, L.: Asymptotic Behavior and Stability Problems in Ordinary Differential Equations, 2nd edn. Springer, Heidelberg (1963)
8. Champneys, A.: Dynamics of parametric excitation. In: Meyers, R.A. (ed.) Encyclopedia of Complexity and Systems Science, pp. 2323–2345. Springer, New York (2009)
9. Chatelin, F.: Eigenvalues of Matrices. SIAM, Philadelphia (2012)
10. Chen, C.T.: Linear System Theory and Design. Oxford University Press, Inc., New York (1995)
11. Coddington, E.A., Levinson, N.: Theory of Ordinary Differential Equations. Tata McGraw-Hill Education, New York (1955)
12. Fossen, T.I., Nijmeijer, H.: Parametric Resonance in Dynamical Systems. Springer, New York (2012)
13. Golub, G.H., Van Loan, C.F.: Matrix Computations. John Hopkins University Press, Baltimore (1989)

14. Hansen, J.: Stability diagrams for coupled Mathieu-equations. Ing.-Archiv. **55**(6), 463–473 (1985)
15. Hermite, C.: Sur quelques Applications des Fonctions Elliptiques. Gauthier Villars, Paris (1885)
16. Jardón, H.: Control de sistemas modelados por la ecuación de Hill basado en discretización. Master's thesis, Departamento de Control Automático Cinvestav (2010)
17. Jordan, D.W., Smith, P.: Nonlinear Ordinary Differential Equations: An Introduction for Scientists and Engineers. Oxford University Press, New York (2007)
18. Lancaster, P.: The Theory of Matrices: With Applications. Academic Press, New York (1985)
19. Landau, L.: Mechanics. Course of Theoretical Physics, vol. 1. Butterworth-Heinemann, Oxford (1976)
20. Magnus, W., Winkler, S.: Hill's Equation. Wiley, New York (1966)
21. Quintana-Ort, E.S., Van De Geijn, R.: Parallel solution of selected problems in control theory. In: Proceedings of the Ninth SIAM Conference on Parallel Processing for Scientific Computing. Citeseer (1999)
22. Ramírez, M.: Zonas de Estabilidad- Inestabilidad para la Ecuación de Hill en Dimensión. Master's thesis, Departamento de Control Automático Cinvestav (2012)
23. Richards, J.A.: Analysis of Periodically Time-Varying Systems. Communications and Control Engineering Series. Springer, Heidelberg (1983)
24. Seyranian, A.P., Mailybaev, A.A.: Multiparameter Stability Theory with Mechanical Applications, vol. 13. World Scientific, Singapore (2003)
25. Stewart, G.W.: Introduction to Matrix Computations. Academic Press, New York (1973)
26. Trefethen, L.N.: Spectral Methods in MATLAB, vol. 10. SIAM, Philadelphia (2000)
27. Yakubovich, V., Starzhinskii, V.: Linear Differential Equations with Periodic Coefficients, vol. 2. Wiley, New York (1975)

Improving Performance of DAOPHOT-FIND by Using GPU Architecture

Rubén Hernández Pérez$^{(\boxtimes)}$, Ruslan Gabbasov, and Joel Suárez Cansíno

Centro de Investigación en Tecnologías de Información y Sistemas,
Instituto de Ciencias Básicas e Ingeniería, Universidad Autónoma del Estado
de Hidalgo, Carretera Pachuca–Tulancingo Km. 4.5, Cd. Universitaria,
42090 Mineral de la Reforma, HGO, Mexico
rub3n.hernandez.perez@gmail.com

Abstract. In astronomy there have been big changes in the availability
of data, much of it provided freely and publicly via internet, allowing
people to access the same data as used by professional astronomers for
their own investigations. The data obtained from different telescopes
have increased in size too, forcing the community to boost the performance of algorithms for image processing, pattern recognition, and, in
particular, tasks for finding and characterizing astronomical objects. One
of such packages is DAOPHOT designed to deal with crowded astronomical fields. However, the tasks are computationally intensive because
they require the execution of many floating point operations. In order
to face such computational challenge, we propose an implementation of
DAOPHOT's particular task FIND, using massive parallel computation
architecture supported by GPUs, which allows us to process large images
at least two times faster. This work presents the analysis and comparison
of time complexity between the implementations of the FIND algorithm
both in CPU and GPU.

1 Introduction

Automatic source extraction from astronomical images started in the middle
of the 60's, with the first automatic machines GALAXY in Edinburg [6] and
APMS in Minneapolis [7] that allowed simple flux and position measurements
better than what could be done by hand. Since then, software for detection and
classification has evolved at a relatively slow pace, mainly because simple techniques meet most scientific specifications. Over the years the popularity of the
difficult art of stellar photometry in crowded fields has derived in many computer
programs which extract information from two-dimensional digital images. One of
those computer programs is DAOPHOT [1], which continues being developed at
the Dominion Astrophysical Observatory and allows performing tasks like finding objects by measuring the signal intensity enhancement over the background
and Point Spread Function (PSF) fitting [5]. The program shows good accuracy
and robustness but is relatively slow [2].

The increasing use of internet and massive databases allows anyone to have
access to raw data for astronomy research. Web sites like SkyView [12] provide

© Springer International Publishing Switzerland 2016
I. Gitler and J. Klapp (Eds.): ISUM 2015, CCIS 595, pp. 240–249, 2016.
DOI: 10.1007/978-3-319-32243-8_17

images of any part of the observed sky at wavelengths ranging from Radio to Gamma-Ray. Through its simple web interface, it is possible to acquire images and to perform investigation by our own, but it is still necessary to support those investigations with packages and software to process and extract information from images. As mentioned before, DAOPHOT helps to perform such tasks and with the access to modern computer technology this process becomes increasingly easier and it is possible to analyse large amounts of data in a short period of time. However, it is necessary to make an effort to implement algorithms and routines in a way that exploits all capabilities of such technology.

The necessary operations for finding objects in astronomical images are computationally intensive, mainly because of the size of the images which increase due to the advance of technology of detectors. For example, the Large Synoptic Survey Telescope (LSST) is expected to produce several terabytes of data every night using its 3200 megapixel camera [3]. In addition, many automatic telescopes acquire raw data in real time and the matter of speed is crucial for image processing. Rapid processor development allowed the execution of a continuously increasing number of operations, and the processors became faster every year until 2005, when a physical limit was reached by the fact that energy consumption varies as the cube of clock rate [8], not only because of the operations of the processors themselves, but the energy needed to cool down the chip too. To overcome this obstacle, multi-core technology emerged as a new direction to improve performance without increasing the clock rate of processors. The implications of this new direction are found in the development of new software. The vast majority of the software written for astronomy before 2005 is designed to run sequentially, and for this reason it is necessary to make an effort to rewrite the algorithms to take full advantage of the capabilities of this new hardware.

Along with the development of multi-core CPUs, the powerful gaming industry had devised its own processors called Graphics Processing Units or GPUs, which are based on different principles than those of CPUs [8]. A GPU is an specialized processor that is equipped with a large number of special hardware units for mathematical and fast floating point operations. The primary goal of GPUs is to provide high-performance for gaming and rich 3D experience [9], but the demand for high performance computation has caused this processors to have a more general purpose, having recently burst onto the scientific computing scene as an innovative technology that has demonstrated substantial performance and energy efficiency improvements [10].

In this paper we present a modification of a popular stellar photometry package DAOPHOT that makes use of GPU hardware. In particular, the task FIND devoted to finding the stars in the images was optimized. We show that substantial time reduction can be obtained, although there is still space for improvement.

2 FIND Algorithm

DAOPHOT package deals with the difficult problem of performing accurate photometry in crowded fields. It consists of several routines and algorithms to perform tasks that include finding objects, aperture photometry, obtaining the point spread function among others. The focus of this work is on the first task mentioned, and we briefly describe the FIND algorithm. More details can be found in the documentation made by Stetson [1], the reference guide by Davis [4], and in the original code itself which is well commented. We use the latest version of Daophot II package (v1.3-6) included as a part of Starlink software available at [13].

The FIND algorithm attempts to find stars in a two-dimensional image by going through the image pixel by pixel asking the question, "If there is a star centred in this pixel, how bright is it?". The answer for this question is estimated numerically by fitting a truncated Gaussian profile to the values in a surrounding sub-array of pixels (sub-picture). To explain the operations performed, let the brightness in the $(i, j) - pixel$ represented by $D_{i,j}$ and let G represent the unit-height, circular, bivariate Gaussian function:

$$G(\Delta i, \Delta j; \sigma) = e^{-(\Delta i^2 + \Delta j^2)/2\sigma^2}, \tag{1}$$

where σ is the standard deviation. Then the central brightness which best fits the pixels around the point (i_0, j_0) in the sub-picture $H_{i_0 j_0}$ is given by:

$$D_{ij} \doteq H_{i_0 j_0} G(i - i_0, j - j_0; \sigma) + b \qquad (i, j) \text{ near } (i_0, j_0) \tag{2}$$

Where b is the estimated value of the background of the image which can be obtained from the images in several ways, DAOPHOT's implementation uses a function $mode$ to calculate this value. The symbol "$\doteq$" denotes a least-squares fit to the data for some set of pixels (i, j) in a defined region around and including (i_0, j_0). Then the numerical value of $H_{i_0 j_0}$ can be obtained by a simple linear least squares using the number of pixels, n, involved in the fit as:

$$H_{i_0 j_0} = \frac{\Sigma(GD) - (\Sigma G)(\Sigma D)/n}{\Sigma(G^2) - (\Sigma G)^2/n} \tag{3}$$

Equation 3 is the arithmetic equivalent of convolving the original image with the kernel function. Having calculated the H array of the same size of the original data D the routine runs through H looking for positions of local maxima, producing a list of positive brightness enhancements. There are two other criteria for detecting objects performed by the routine, the first one is a sharpness criterion that compares H_{i_0, j_0} to the height of a two-dimensional delta-function, d, defined by taking the observed intensity difference between the central pixel of the presumed star and the mean of the remaining pixels used in the fits of Eq. 3:

$$d_{i_0, j_0} \equiv D_{i_0, j_0}/\langle D_{i,j}\rangle, \quad (i, j) \neq (i_0, j_0), \quad sharp \equiv d_{i_0, j_0}/H_{i_0, j_0} \tag{4}$$

The second one is a roundness criterion; images of stars are strongly peaked functions of both x and y so that for round, well-guided images $h_x \approx h_y$. The roundness criterion readily distinguishes stars ($round \approx 0$) from bad rows and columns ($round \approx \pm 2$):

$$round \equiv 2\left(\frac{h_y - h_x}{h_y + h_x}\right) \tag{5}$$

3   Implementation

The FIND algorithm was implemented both in GPU and CPU in order to compare the response time between implementations and to identify reduction on time complexity. For the CPU implementation, the source code of DAOPHOT-FIND was translated from the original Fortran language to C language and compiled with GCC version 4.9.2 by adding the flag $-O3$ in order to turn on all optimizations provided by the compiler, and ran on a Intel Core i7 of 2.5 GHz. In the same way, GPU implementation was made by translating the original code to CUDA C language. The NVCC compiler provided with the NVIDIA Toolkit 7.0 was used including flags sm_50 and fast math library $-use\_fast\_math$. This new code was executed in a GeForce GTX 860M with 5 streaming multiprocessors and 640 CUDA Cores.

The difference between CPU and GPU code can be easily illustrated through the following snippet of code, representing the construction of the kernel for the profile fitting according to Eq. 1.

```
void constructKernel(
        float *kernel, int nbox, int nhalf, float sigsq) {

    int i, j, id;
    float rsq;

    for(i=0; i<nbox; i++) {
        for(j=0; j<nbox; j++) {
            id = i *  nbox + j;
            rsq = (j-nhalf)*(j-nhalf) + (i-nhalf)*(i-nhalf);
            kernel[id] = expf(-0.5*rsq/sigsq);
        }
    }
}
```

The GPU code looks almost the same, the main difference is the absence of loop instructions for; instead there is an index composed by the variables $blockIdx.x$ and $threadIdx.x$ provided by CUDA to identify each process as unique. By mapping this index to the position of the kernel, it is possible to calculate all their values in parallel. For this part of the FIND algorithm, the process for GPU was launched with as many blocks and threads as the dimensions of the kernel, <<<nbox, nbox>>>. The rest of the tasks, including convolution and criteria for roundness and sharpness were transformed in a similar way.

```
__global__ void constructKernel(
        float *kernel, int nhalf, float hsigsq) {

    int id = blockIdx.x * blockDim.x + threadIdx.x;
    float rsq;
```

```
    rsq = (blockIdx.x-nhalf)*(blockIdx.x-nhalf);
    rsq += (threadIdx.x-nhalf)*(threadIdx.x-nhalf);
    kernel[id] = __expf(rsq*hsigsq);
}
```

There are two details that can improve the performance of calculation for the Gaussian function. First, the arguments of __expf(rsq*hsigsq) differ since the value of $hsigsq = -1/(2*sigsq)$ can be calculated on the CPU before passing it as the argument. The second detail is the use of the function __expf(), which is optimized for GPU execution in combination with the flag $-use\_fast\_math$ mentioned before.

Another way to use indexes provided by CUDA, is by launching the GPU kernel with threads distributed in two dimensions as shown in the next snippet of code. In this case the kernel should be called with just one block and as many threads as pixels of the kernel for profile fitting <<<1, dim3(nbox, nbox)>>> or <<<1, nbox*nbox>>>. Since this part of the process is made only once, and the space of the kernel is really small (7×7 pixels used for the tests), no important difference was detected in the response time between the different forms for launching this GPU kernel.

```
Launching <<<1, dim3(nbox, nbox)>>>
    id = threadIdx.x * nbox + threadIdx.y;
    rsq = (threadIdx.x-nhalf)*(threadIdx.x-nhalf);
    rsq += (threadIdx.y-nhalf)*(threadIdx.y-nhalf);
    kernel[id] = __expf(rsq*hsigsq);

Launching <<<1, nbox*nbox>>>
    id = threadIdx.x;
    rsq = (id/nbox-nhalf)*(id/nbox-nhalf);
    rsq += (id%nbox-nhalf)*(id%nbox-nhalf);
    kernel[id] = __expf(rsq*hsigsq);
```

According to Eq. (3), the image convolution is the next step in the image analysis of FIND algorithm. In this process another important aspect of GPUs can be considered which is memory management. Since Shared memory resides on chip it's i/o operations are much faster than operations in Global memory. One of the implementations proposed basically splits the image in tiles, each of them launched as blocks of threads. With this approach, each thread is responsible for loading data from Global to Shared memory and perform mathematical operations for the convolution. One limitation of this approach, is the size of the tile, where the threads of one block are used for mapping the data needed for a single tile. A GPU such as GM107 having a limit of 1024 threads per block, could manage tiles of 32×32 pixels maximum (1024 elements).

The approach we use for this work is a little bit different. By analysing FIND algorithm in the part of convolution, there are many conditional statements in the convolution process to ensure the correct values for each pixel. A GPU executes threads in groups of 32 (*warp*), which are efficiently used if all 32 threads follow the same execution path, but conditional branches diverge the threads, since the warp serially executes each branch path leading to poor performance. The other important thing about the operations of FIND, is data access which is made just once for each pixel of the image and once for the values of the kernel. This means that improving performance by using shared memory to load data (as splitting the image in tiles) may not be a good idea, because FIND does not perform a simple convolution and the operations are made over variables, rather than data stored in Global memory.

For these reasons, the approach used for testing executes as many threads as pixels in the image, while fixes the number of threads per block, and changes the number of blocks according to the image size `<<<ImageSize/128, 128>>>`, and each thread performing all operations needs to convolve a single pixel. We found that in the testing process the use of 128 threads per block produces better results than other configurations. Within the code, the index of each thread is mapped to each pixel of the image as given by the following sequence of instructions

```
id = blockIdx.x * blockDim.x + threadIdx.x;
jx = id / ncol;
jy = id % ncol;
```

Furthermore, in order to improve performance based on the same concept of using different segments of GPU memory, a modification of this last approach was made. This new implementation takes advantage of Constant Memory by copying the values of the kernel for profile fitting, reducing operations on Global Memory. However, the implementation does not show much improvement, and in fact, we found that the complexity of FIND resides in the calculations and decision making rather than on the data access.

The testing procedure uses seven square images with different resolutions taken from the SkyView database [12] and centered on the galaxy Malin 1. Figure 1 shows an example of the image with a resolution of 512 pixels per side. We chose a rather uncrowded field since here we are more interested in the measurement of the performance than in the accuracy of the method. The range of the resolution of each image goes from 64 to 4096 pixels per side. Over this set of images, both CPU and GPU implementations of FIND use the same size of kernel in order to compare the execution time between them. The size of the kernel is calculated according to description of DAOPHOT [1] by applying the formula $2 * max(2.0, 0.637 * FWHM) + 1$, where the value of $FWHM$ is set to 5, resulting in a kernel size of 7 pixels. Table 1 shows the obtained results. In order to ensure that the results are not influenced by operating system processes or other operations of CPU or GPU, each test is executed five times and the averaged results are displayed.

Fig. 1. DSS Blue image of sky $2 \times 2\,°$ centred at Malin 1, a giant low surface brightness (LSB) spiral galaxy (Color figure online).

4   Results

Table 1 shows the difference between time consumed among the implementations in CPU, GPU without splitting the images in tiles and GPU by splitting the images in tiles. This difference is directly proportional to the size of the image. For large source images such as 2048 or 4096 pixels the CPU time starts to increase faster than GPU time. One would expect that by splitting the image in tiles and using the Shared and Constant Memory of a GPU, the performance should increase against GPU without splitting, but very surprisingly this is not the case. The analysis of the FIND algorithm shows that there are many more operations than in traditional convolution, including many branch statements and few memory access operations. In this case, the number of launched threads is the main cause for the low response time of the GPU that uses splitting of the image, when comparing with the GPU implementation without splitting.

Every time the image is processed using the splitting in tiles approach, blocks with a number of $(tileSize+kernelSize)^2$ threads each are launched to load data and perform operations, but actually only $tileSize^2$ threads perform operations, the rest of threads just load data. This means that for an image of 4096 pixels by side, using a kernel of 7 pixels by side and split in tiles of 16 pixels, there are $4096^2/23^2 = 65,536$ blocks each of them with 23^2 threads, but only 16^2 threads

Table 1. Results of the experiments over the 7 uncrowded images. The kernel size was fixed to require the same number of calculations in both implementations. Size of images and kernel are in pixels by side and the execution time is in seconds.

Input data		Average time/second		
Image Size	Kernel size	CPU	GPU	GPU (Tiles)
64	7	0.00038	0.00239	0.00048
128	7	0.00198	0.00413	0.00133
256	7	0.00562	0.00769	0.00502
512	7	0.02627	0.01524	0.01741
1024	7	0.09047	0.04563	0.06869
2048	7	0.33287	0.16260	0.25277
4096	7	1.32711	0.63014	1.01233

are really working, implying that less than 50 % of the threads of the block, perform the operations of FIND.

In a formal way, time complexity for the above implementations is analysed by fitting the following polynomial function with three parameters a, b and c

$$t = ax^b + c \tag{6}$$

In Eq. (6), t is the time consumption of the implementation as a function of the pixels per side of the image, x. Since the variable x represents the resolution per side of the image and the real input of the implementations is the complete image, then one should expect that a nonlinear regression will produce an approximated value of 2 and 0 for the parameters b and c, respectively. Table 2 shows the coefficients of the best fitted function for the obtained data through the conducted experiment.

Table 2. Results of the best fitted function in the experiment over the 7 images, the kernel size was fixed to have same number of calculations needed in all the implementations.

Implementation	a	b	c
CPU	8.58E-8	1.989	0.0021
GPU	4.63E-8	1.974	0.0040
GPU (Tiles)	6.22E-8	1.996	0.0010

The reduction in time is mainly obtained through the parameter a and Table 2 shows that the implementation on GPU consumes a smaller time, which is represented by the value of the parameter a. The parameter b, which is of major interest, was reduced too, but not in such a large amount. Figure 2 illustrates the behaviour of the equation using the parameters calculated in the CPU case and the two approaches in GPU.

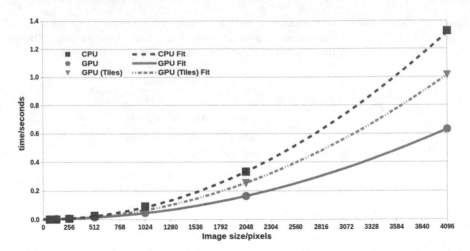

Fig. 2. Time consumption for CPU and GPU implementations of FIND task for different sizes of the images. The symbols represent the experimental data, while the lines correspond to the respective fitted functions.

5   Conclusions

This work presents advances in the implementation of DAOPHOT package on parallel GPU architecture using CUDA programming platform. As a first step we implemented the FIND algorithm and compared its performance against the sequential CPU version. The performed test shows that it is possible to reduce the time consumption of the FIND algorithm, through the implementation on a GPU architecture that is commonly found in modern computers. The time consumption reduction gives an advantage to perform the task of finding objects, specially when dealing with large image resolutions and image sequences. However, our results do not show a reduction in time complexity of GPU as large as expected. Our simple implementation of FIND is a demonstration of how easy is to exploit GPU architecture, but some additional programming changes are needed in order to get their full capabilities. It is possible to improve the performance of this parallel implementation by using nearly all the blocks and thread dimensions available to calculate all independent operations, and subsequently reducing the results [11]. On the other hand, the effort to do these improvements must analyse which of the operations can be calculated independently, and how they can be classified in order to perform the required reductions. This is a point that needs special attention because, as we have shown, reductions cannot be implemented as a trivial program on a GPU, and it is necessary to keep the way in which data are arranged along the whole task execution. Finally, it is necessary to consider that using the Shared Memory of a GPU, does not better performance in all cases. The identification of the kind of operations performed by the algorithm and the detection of memory interactions, rather than calculations with variables in a thread, are necessary conditions to further improve the performance of the algorithm.

References

1. Stetson, P.B.: DAOPHOT - a computer program for crowded-field stellar photometry. Publ. Astron. Soc. Pac. **99**, 191–222 (1987). ISSN 0004–6280
2. Becker, A.C., et al.: In pursuit of LSST science requirements: a comparison of photometry algorithms. Publ. Astron. Soc. Pac. **119**, 1462–1482 (2007)
3. http://www.lsst.org/
4. Davis, L.E.: A Reference Guide to the IRAF/DAOPHOT Package. NOAO, Tucson (1994)
5. Sterken, C., Manfroid, J.: A Guide. Astrophysics and Space Science Library, vol. 175. Springer, The Netherlands (1992)
6. Stoy R.H.: In: Proper Motions. International Astronomical Union colloquium, vol. 7, p. 48. University of Minnesota, Minneapolis (1970)
7. La Bonte A.E.: In: Proper Motions. International Astronomical Union colloquium, vol. 7, p. 26. University of Minnesota, Minneapolis (1970)
8. Tsutsui, S., Collet, P. (eds.): Massively Parallel Evolutionary Computation on GPGPUs. Natural Computing Series. Springer, Heidelberg (2013). doi:10.1007/978-3-642-37959-8-1
9. Kyrkou, C.: Architectures for high performance computing. In: Survey on Stream Processor and Graphics Processing Units (2010). http://sokryk.tripod.com/Stream_Processors_and_GPUs_-_Architectures_for_High_Performance_Computing.pdf
10. Farber, R.: CUDA Application Desing and Development. Morgan Kaufmann, USA (2011)
11. Kirk, D.B., Hwu, W.W.: Programming Massively Parallel Processors A Hands-on Approach. Elsevier, USA (2010)
12. http://skyview.gsfc.nasa.gov/
13. http://starlink.eao.hawaii.edu/starlink

A VHDL-Based Modeling of Network Interface Card Buffers: Design and Teaching Methodology

Godofredo R. Garay[1], Andrei Tchernykh[2(✉)],
Alexander Yu. Drozdov[3], Sergey V. Novikov[3],
and Victor E. Vladislavlev[3]

[1] Camagüey University, Camagüey, Cuba
godofredo.garay@reduc.edu.cu
[2] CICESE Research Center, Ensenada, Baja California, Mexico
chernykh@cicese.mx
[3] Moscow Institute of Physics and Technology, Moscow, Russia
alexander.y.drozdov@gmail.com,
serg.v.novikov@gmail.com,
victor.vladislavlev@gmail.com

Abstract. The design of High Performance Computing (HPC) relies to a large extent on simulations to optimize components of such complex systems. A key hardware component of the interconnection network in HPC environments is the Network Interface Card (NIC). In spite of the popularity of simulation-based approaches in the computer architecture domain, few authors have focused on simulators design methodologies. In this paper, we describe the stages of implementing a simulation model to solve a real problem—modeling NIC buffer. We present a general methodology for helping users to build Hardware Description Language (HDL)/SystemC models targeted to fulfil features such as performance evaluation of compute nodes. The developed VHDL model allows reproducibility and can be used as a tool in the area of HPC education.

Keywords: Simulation · Design methodology · VHDL · NIC · Real-Time Calculus

1 Introduction

The design of High Performance Computing (HPC) relies to a large extent on simulations to optimize the various components of such a complex system. Among the key hardware components that determine system performance is the interconnection network. At this level, performance evaluation studies include assessing network interface bandwidth, link bandwidth, network topology, network technology, routing algorithm, deadlock prevention techniques, etc. [1–3]. In particular, NICs play a key role in the performance of HPC applications [4].

Traditionally, multi-drop buses (as considered in this paper) have found many applications in computer systems, particularly in the I/O and memory systems, but signal integrity constraints of high-speed electronics have made multi-drop electrical

© Springer International Publishing Switzerland 2016
I. Gitler and J. Klapp (Eds.): ISUM 2015, CCIS 595, pp. 250–273, 2016.
DOI: 10.1007/978-3-319-32243-8_18

buses infeasible. For this reason, point-to-point links are displacing multi-drop buses, for example, in the migration of PCI/PCI-X to PCI Express. Nevertheless, it should be taken into consideration that the difficulty of creating a multi-drop bus electrically can be avoided using optics; see [5]. Furthermore, the current trend toward virtualized compute platforms has motivated the analysis of I/O resources contention (e.g., at PCI Express level). Conceptually, this problem is similar to the one happening in the former I/O parallel bus generations. For this reason, we consider that our approach can be extended to model such virtualized platforms.

Modeling and simulation techniques have made successful contributions to different areas in industry and academia. However, there are certain key issues that are preventing these approaches from addressing larger domains and from achieving wide-scale impact. One of them is reproducibility. This concept is related to replicability, i.e., the ability to reproduce and, if needed, independently recreate computational models associated with published work [6].

Using a higher level of abstraction for modeling the interconnection network of an HPC system allows the modeling of all important networking aspects, including buffering, without having to resort to even lower abstraction levels that would significantly increase the simulator complexity and simulation runtimes, without resulting in deeper insights. Hardware description languages (HDLs) such as VHDL and Verilog, as well as System-Level Description Languages (e.g., SystemC and SpeC [7]) can be used for this purpose. Using these languages, simulation models can be implemented at different abstraction levels.

A step forward of their design is to find a set of sequential steps that sufficiently governs the development of simulation models of complex compute nodes in HPC environments. Various authors have focused on modeling and design methodologies to support the design process of complex systems. For example, in the field of manufacturing machinery [8], mechatronic systems [9], multiprocessor system-on-chip (MPSoC) [10].

The objective of this paper is to discuss a design methodology, aiming to have an HDL-based simulation model of the network-to-memory data path in a compute node. This model allows us to validate a Real-Time Calculus-based (RTC) model of the data path [11]. RTC is a high-level analysis technique previously proposed for stream-processing hard real time systems. It is frequently used to evaluate trade-offs in packet processing architectures. We focus on computing the backlog bound provided by RTC. In addition, our model determines the impact of specific features of the hardware components of the data path on the FIFO-buffer requirements in a network interface card.

The main contribution of this paper is to illustrate the stages computer architects may follow in implementing a simulation model to solve a real problem—modeling NIC buffer. We present a general methodology for helping users to build Hardware Description Language (HDL) such as VHDL or Verilog, as well as SystemC models targeted to fulfil features such as performance evaluation of compute nodes. The developed VHDL-based simulation model allows reproducibility and can be used as a teaching tool in the area of HPC education, also.

The paper illustrates how we can design a simulation model using hardware description languages to analyze the performance of network interfaces in comparison with alternative ways such as general purpose programming languages, simulation frameworks, and full-system simulators. Also, we give some details about the elements of the VHDL model of the communication data path to be evaluated.

The paper has been organized as follows. Section 2 describes the design phases of the proposed methodology. Section 3 presents our case of study describing NIC buffers simulation model. Section 4 describes the design principals. Section 5 discusses the proposed conceptual model. Section 6 describes inputs parameters, modeling assumptions, and the process definition. Section 7 validates the conceptual model. Section 8 describes our simulation model and presents examples of its applicability. Finally, Sect. 9 presents the conclusion and future work.

2 Design Phases

In this section, we describe eight major phases for the proper simulation model design and implementation [12]. Although these phases are generally applied in sequence, one may need to return to the previous phases due to changes in scope and objectives of the study. In particular, phases 3 through 6 of the process may be repeated for each major alternative studied as part of the project (Fig. 1). We discuss each phase in detail by identifying the steps to follow for its successful execution.

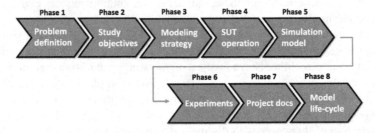

Fig. 1. Flowchart of design phases from problem definition to model implementation (Phases 1–5), and from experimentation to life cycle support (Phases 6–8)

The phase 1 of the simulation process is the problem definition. It has the most effect on the total simulation study since a wrong problem definition can waste a lot of time and money on the project. This phase may include the following steps: (1) define the objectives of the study; (2) list the specific issues to be addressed; (3) determine the boundary or domain of the study; (4) determine the level of detail or proper abstraction level; (5) determine if a simulation model is actually needed and an analytical method work; (6) estimate the required resources needed to do the study; (7) perform a cost-benefit analysis; and (8) create a planning chart of the proposed project; and (9) write a formal proposal.

The objectives of the design study of the phase 2 must be clearly specified by its clients. Once the objectives of the simulation study are finalized, it is important to determine if one model can satisfy all the objectives of the study. This phase may include the following steps: (1) estimate the life cycle of the model; (2) list broad assumptions; (3) estimate the number of models required; (4) determine the animation requirements; (5) select the tool; (6) determine the level of data available and what data is needed; (7) determine the human requirements and skill levels; (8) determine the audience (usually more than one level of management); (9) identify the deliverables; (10) determine the priority of this study in relationship to other studies; (11) set milestone dates; and (12) write the Project Functional Specifications.

The modeling strategy to be used in the study is the phase 3 of the simulation process. Modeling strategy involves making decisions regarding how a system should be represented in terms of the capabilities and elements provided by the chosen simulation tool. The overall strategy should focus on finding a model concept that minimizes the simulation effort while ensuring that all objectives of the project are met and all specific issues are investigated. This phase may contain the following steps: (1) decide on continuous, discrete, or combined modeling; (2) determine the elements that drive the system; (3) determine the entities that should represent the system elements; (4) determine the level of detail needed to describe the system components; (5) determine the graphics requirements of the model; (6) identify the areas that utilize special control logic; and (7) determine how to collect statistics in the model and communicate results to the customer.

The formulation of the model inputs, assumptions, and the process definition is the phase 4 of the process. At this phase, the modeler describes in detail the operating logic of the system and performs data collection and analysis tasks. This phase may include the following steps: (1) specify to operating philosophy of the system; (2) describe the physical constraints of the system; (3) describe the creation and termination of dynamic elements; (4) describe the process in detail; (5) obtain the operation specifications; (6) obtain the material handling specifications; (7) list all the assumptions; (8) analyze the input data; (9) specify the runtime parameters; (10) write the detailed Project Functional Specifications; and (11) validate the conceptual model.

The building of the model, its verification, and operational validation constitute the phase 5 of the simulation process. At this phase, the modeler uses well-known software techniques for model building, verification and validation. This phase may include the following guidelines: beware of the tool limitations; construct flow diagrams as needed; use modular techniques of model building, verification, and validation; reuse existing code as much as possible; make verification runs using deterministic data and trace as needed; use proper naming conventions; use macros as much as possible; use structured programming techniques; document the model code as model is built; walk through the logic or code with the client; set up official model validation meetings; perform input-output validation; calibrate the model, if necessary.

Experimentation with the model and applying the design of experiments techniques constitute the phase 6 of the simulation process. At this phase, the project team may decide to investigate other Alternative Models and go back to the previous phases of the process for each major model change. During this phase, rather than building a design of experiments for the whole study, the modeler generally identifies the major variables and eliminates the insignificant variables one step at a time. Once a few major variables are identified, a design of experiments study may be conducted in detail, especially if the study has a long-life cycle. One of the objectives of this phase is to involve the client as much as possible in the evaluation of the output under different conditions so that the behavioral characteristics of the system as modeled are well understood by the client. The steps of this phase are as follows: (1) make a pilot run to determine warm-up and steady-state periods; (2) identify the major variables by changing one variable at a time for several scenarios; (3) perform design of experiments if needed; (4) build confidence intervals for output data; (5) apply variance reduction techniques whenever possible; (6) build confidence intervals when comparing alternatives; and (7) analyze the results and identify cause and effect relations among input and output variables.

Project documentation and presentation is the phase 7 of the simulation process. Good documentation and presentation play a key role in the success of a simulation study. The tasks of this phase are performed in parallel to the tasks of other phases of the process. The important factors that should be considered at this phase are that (a) different levels of documentation and presentation are generally required for project, (b) long-term use of models requires better model documentation, (c) selling simulation to others require bottom-line measures (e.g., cost savings) to be highlighted as part of the project presentation, and (d) output values from the simulation should be supported with the factors causing those results. This phase may include the following elements of documentation: project Book; documentation of model input, code, and output; project Functional Specifications; user Manual; Maintenance Manual; discussion and explanation of model results; recommendations for further areas of study; and final Project Report and presentation.

The model life-cycle tasks constitute the final phase 8 of the simulation process. This phase applies to long-term simulation life-cycle studies where the simulation models are maintained throughout the life of the real system. On the other hand, short-term simulation studies are those where once the simulation results are used in the decision-making, the model is not used any more by the client. Currently, about sixty to seventy percent of the simulation studies can be categorized as short-term studies while the rest are longer term in the way that they will be reused after the initial simulation study has been completed.

In many cases, long-term life-cycle models are used for multiple purposes including all four categories. The long-term life-cycle models require additional tasks as given in the following steps of this phase: (1) construct user-friendly model input and output interfaces; (2) determine model and training responsibility; (3) establish data integrity and collection procedures; and (4) perform field data validation tests.

3   Case Study: NIC Buffers Simulation Model

For the purposes of demonstrating the design methodology, a case study is presented below. We combine the phases/steps described in the previous section into an explicit and holistic model development approach, which demonstrate the applicability of the methodology from concept to realization.

3.1   The Problem Definition

The objectives of our study are four fold: to find the proper NIC buffer capacities to avoid overflows at card level when considering back-to-back packet reception; to measure various NIC performance indicators such as maximum buffer-fill level, and dropped packets count; to provide the required parameters for calibrating a RTC-based model of the NIC; and to identify the bottleneck operations of the system.

Before specification of all issues, let us give some basic definitions.

NIC is a constituent element of system network interface. A network interface allows a computer system to send and receive packets over a network [13]. It consists of two components:

(1) A network adapter (also known as host interface, Network Interface Card, or NIC), the hardware that connects the network medium with the host I/O bus, moves data, generates communication events, provide protection;

(2) the network software (often, we refer to as the software) on the host that handles application communication requests, implements communication protocols and manages the adapter.

For providing a comprehensive glimpse of network interface functions, Fig. 2 illustrates the components of a network interface in terms of a "Five-layer Internet model" or "TCP/IP protocol suite" as proposed in [14].

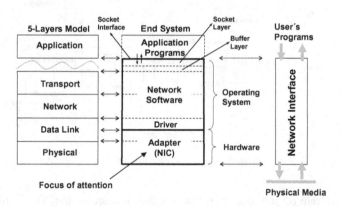

Fig. 2. Focus of attention: NIC functionality and operation.

As you can see, the adapter (hardware component) operates at Data Link layer whereas the software operates at data link, network and transport layer. A part of the data-link layer functions are performed in software by the data-link driver (NIC driver).

Commonly, for packet buffering, a NIC controller incorporates two independent FIFOs for transferring data to/from the system interface and from/to the network. These FIFOs provides temporary storage of data. Also, at this step, the client should specify the minimum and maximum values of the variables to be considered.

We address the following issues: computer organization; PCI bus specifications; Bus arbitration process; Bus access latency; PCI transactions; Latency Timer; Direct Memory Access (DMA) burst size; characteristics of PCI/PCI-X compatible devices; NIC functionality and operation; network workload; network interface; and NIC functionality and operation.

Here, we answer the question: What are the maximum buffer requirements we need to avoid dropping packets at the NIC due to FIFO overflow?

The objectives of the study together with the specific issues to be addressed by the study identify the information required by the simulation model as well as the inputs and components needed by the model in order to generate the required output information. The task of determining which components of the real system to include and exclude from the simulation model requires both insight on how the real system operates and experience in simulation modeling. A good method is to make a list of all components in the real system and identify those needed for the simulation model.

The influence of each component on the other components of the system should be discussed before finalizing the list of components to be included in the model. At this step we keep model boundary at a minimum. It should be extended later in the study only if crucial system behavior cannot be exhibited by the model.

The main components are workload, compute node, NIC, and simulation statistics and control (Fig. 3).

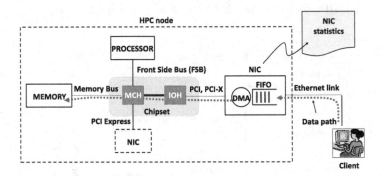

Fig. 3. System under test (SUT).

We concentrate on the following features that impact on the NIC buffer requirements: (1) the network workload, (2) NIC operation, (3) NIC-System interconnect characteristics (e.g., a parallel I/O bus), and (4) memory subsystem operation (e.g., memory controller, memory bus, and memory modules).

3.2   Abstraction Level

The model should include enough information to get confident answers for the specific questions asked from the study. In many cases, the availability of data and time, experience of the modeler, animation requirements, and expectations of the client are more dominant factors in determining the level of detail than the specific issues to be addressed by the study. The objective of the modeler should be to build the highest-level macro model that will satisfy the objectives of the study. Regarding the network workload, we model the worst-case Ethernet traffic, i.e., corner cases consisting of a constant traffic of raw fixed-size frames[1], as well as Jumbo frames (Fig. 4). Here, an accurate packet time and interarrival time should be generated.

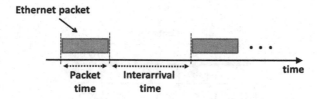

Fig. 4. Network workload parameters.

With respect to the internal NIC operation, we model a store-and-forward network card. The overhead due to NIC-side processing at the received end-system is modeled by using a configurable latency. Commonly, the hardware of the NIC maintains a circular descriptor ring structure for buffer management. The overhead due to NIC-side processing tasks such as packet identification, layer 2/3/4 processing, i.e., CRC Calculation, IP/TCP/UDP checksum calculation, or TCP offloading is modeled by using a configurable latency. Once processing stage has elapsed, a communication task (DMA transfer) of packet payload and the corresponding buffer descriptor (BD) across the I/O bus is performed (Fig. 5).

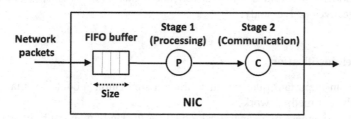

Fig. 5. Modeling NIC operation as a two-stage processing resource.

From the simulation viewpoint, it should be considered some general requirements such as the implementation of the FIFO buffer as a circular ring, the parallelism/concurrency that typically exhibits hardware systems (Fig. 6).

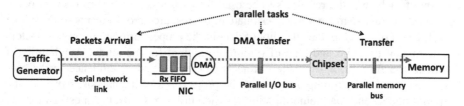

Fig. 6. Example of the existing hardware level parallelism in a compute node.

---

[1] It should be noted that in this work the terms "Ethernet frame", and "Ethernet packet", i.e., data units exchanged at the data-link level, are used interchangeably.

Regarding the next component in the network-to-memory data paths, i.e., NIC-System parallel interconnect, its access latency and operation will be considered. Here, bus contention should be taken into consideration (Fig. 7).

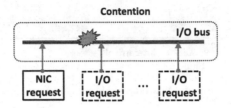

Fig. 7. I/O bus contention due to concurrent I/O devices access requests.

Finally, the last component in the data path is the memory subsystem. In our studied case, this component is modelled at very high level as we consider that the I/O-bus bandwidth in the SUT lags the memory subsystem bandwidth.

The broad or macro-level assumptions of the model decided at this step of the process are influenced equally by the objectives of the study and by the availability of resources (time, personnel, and funds) for the project. In some cases, lack of time may force the modeler to build a macro level model that satisfies only a subset of the original objectives of the study.

3.3   Model Justification

In this step, an important question may arise: a simulation model is actually needed; will an analytical method work?

The appropriateness of an analytical model for the study may not be easy to identify at the first phase of the study but may become evident as late as at the fifth phase of the study while the simulation model is being developed. In many cases, the availability of analytical models for the simplified version of the system can be useful in validating the simulation model later in the study.

Estimating how long a project will take and which resources will be used for the study is an important step. The detailed list of tasks to be performed in the study, the duration of each task, the resources to be used for each task and cost of each resource are needed in order to make a sound estimate of the resource requirements of the whole project. Level of detail and availability of data in the proper form are important factors in determining the time and type of resources required for the study. Availability of historical data from prior simulation projects can increase the confidence in the estimated resource levels, timing and cost of the project. A PERT analysis that gives the minimum, mode, and maximum duration for each task can be useful in estimating the total project time at different levels of confidence.

The cost-benefit analysis should be performed as a check-point in any study. A simple cost-benefit calculation for the study may also aid the modeler in determining the proper level of detail to include in the model.

It is common to observe a cost-benefit ratio of one to one hundred to one to one thousand from a typical simulation study when one looks at the total benefits gained throughout the life of the system.

Simulation projects can easily get out of hand, especially if the rate of change in the scope of the project exceeds the rate at which the results are available to the clients of the project. A Gantt chart showing the tasks with milestone points can help control the project.

The information gathered at the previous steps of this phase should be summarized in a formal proposal format to the client. If the proposal is for an outside client, it may also include sections on background of the simulation company, itemized cost and duration of the phases of the project, payment terms, and warranty.

4 Design

The simulation model can be used just to gather the necessary information to solve a problem, both as a training tool and for solving a problem, or as an on-going scheduling tool, etc. Each of these uses will affect how the model should be created.

The broad or macro level assumptions are finalized at this step. Which components of the real system will be excluded, included as a black box, included in moderate detail, or included in fine detail is decided at this step.

It is important to keep a formal list of broad assumptions throughout the study, starting at the design phase, since the scope of work and the micro level assumptions to be made in model building will depend on them. These assumptions should be kept in mind all through the process and included in the Final Report. A trap which many modelers may fall into is waiting until the end of the study to record their assumptions: by then, they may have forgotten many of them and wasted a lot of time in inadvertently changing the scope of work throughout the process.

In Ethernet, packets cannot be transmitted back-to-back. That is, there must be a gap between each packet. The IEEE specification calls this parameter the Inter Frame Gap. So, to accurately generate the worst-case network traffic, the start-to-start packet time should be computed. To this end, the packet time on the wire (PT) and Inter Frame Gap (IFG) should be considered (Table 1).

Table 1. Ethernet parameters (in bit times) for full-duplex trasnmission (worst case).

Parameter	Minimum-size packets (Ethernet)	Maximum-size packets (Ethernet)	Jumbo packets (Alteon)
Packet time	576	12208	72208
Inter Frame Gap	96	96	96
Packet start-to-start	672	12304	72304

Notice Table 1, the actual value of bit time (time per bit) depends of the Ethernet standard being modeled. Values of 0.1 µs, 0.01 µs, 1 ns, and 0.1 ns should be considered for modeling the standards, Ethernet, Fast Ethernet, Gigabit Ethernet, and 10 Gigabit Ethernet, respectively [15].

To implement the model of a generic network interface card, the module NIC is used. This module is the most important one and complex of NICSim-vhd. It interfaces with the network and the PCI-like parallel bus considered in this work. Structurally, the module, NIC, is composed of three submodules (BuffMngr, NICCtrl and DMACtrl).

The models in a study are developed in stages, each model representing an alternate solution for the problem. The first model developed is generally labeled as the Base Model, followed by Alternate Model 1, Alternate Model 2, etc. Each model may be tested under different variations of its parameters.

In some studies the number of models may be well-defined at the beginning of the study including the number of variations of their parameters to be tested while in others the alternate models are considered only if the previous models do perform unsatisfactorily. If the latter, the project team should assume a certain number of models for the project and proceed with the process.

Animation is an important tool in the simulation process and is utilized during model verification and validation, in selling of the simulation results to management, in generating new ideas for the design and operation of a system, and for training. Different detail levels of animation may be required for different purposes. 3-D detailed animation may be required in a detailed engineering verification simulation study. On the other hand, a simple (or no) animation may suffice in a computer architecture simulation studies.

A key issue in the analytical model validation and calibration is to monitor the FIFO-buffer fill-level, and provide parameters required to construct RTC descriptions of network workload and hardware components (e.g., NIC, I/O bus, memory subsystem) involved in the data path via arrival curves and service curves.

Because of none of the reviewed alternative ways fits well our requirements, implementation details of our VHDL-based simulation model (called NICSim-vhd) are also briefly described. In NICSim-vhd, we simulate both the scenarios under which a FIFO overflow occurs and the scenarios under which the buffer is bounded. To this end, various configuration parameters such as transmission line speed, DMA burst size, NIC latency, I/O-bus frequency and width are provided.

Selecting the best simulation tool for the study depends on many factors including the life-cycle of the project, tools the client currently owns, tools the simulation group has experience with, the animation requirements of the study, the detail level of the study, and the system considered in the study. Sometimes trying to force a simulation tool to perform beyond its designed intentions may add more time and cost to the process and slow down the execution of the model considerably. The project team should weigh all these factors before selecting the simulation tool for the study.

The main software tools used in the simulation model development process are GHDL and GTKWave. Specifically, GHDL [16] is an open-source command-line VHDL simulator that it is available for GNU/Linux systems and for Windows. This simulator implements VHDL standard as defined by IEEE 1076 and supports most of the 1987 standard and most features added by the 1993 standard. In addition, GHDL simulator can produce Value Change Dump (VCD) files which can be viewed with a wave viewer such as GTKWave [17].

Data collection activities may take a lot of time in a study and it is important that the modeler get involved early in setting up the data collection plans for the study. The modeler should examine all the data available and learn how and when it was collected. The modeler should check if macro or summary level data is available on all stochastic processes in the system. Before deciding whether to collect any more data, the modeler should assess how crucial the missing data may be for the study. Based on experience, if it is decided to collect data on some process, the actual data collection should be started only if there is no macro data available or experts disagree on estimates for the process. Even in such a case, the data collection should be at a macro level initially. Detailed data collection should be made only after the simulation model has been used to verify that the data is crucial for the study (Phase 6).

The human requirements in a simulation study are due to (1) interaction with people familiar in management of the system, (2) interaction with people familiar with the engineering details of the system, (3) modeler(s) familiar with the simulation tool to be used as well as experience with modeling similar type of systems, and (4) data collection required by the study. It is best to have an engineer and an engineering manager from the client's company be part of the simulation project team. In some studies, due to time limitations of the project, one may need to divide the modeling tasks among several modelers. It is important for a simulation manager to understand the limitations and strengths of the modelers in the project team. Data collection for a study may be done directly by the modeler(s), engineers familiar with the system, or by a third party. It is important that the modeler and data collection people meet and plan for the procedure to use for data collection. The modeler should visit the site of data collection and observe the data collection process if he or she is not involved in collecting the data directly.

It is very important to include the highest level of management possible from the client company in the modeling process. Many times each level of management has a different agenda and will require different types of information from the model. A good method is to informally record the information needed by each level of management from the client's organization and address this somewhere in the final report. If the study addresses as many issues as possible for these managers even though these managers may not be the direct customers of the project, the credibility and success rate of the project will increase.

Deliverables of a simulation study may include deliverables in report and file form as well as deliverables such as model-specific or generic simulation training, and customized user interfaces for model input and output.

5 Conceptual Model

Step 1. Modeling approach: continuous, discrete, or combined. Some of the elements (parts, people) in a system are dynamic in nature, in the sense that they move through the system causing other entities to react to them in response to some signal. Other elements are static in nature in a sense that they wait for the dynamic entities or resources to act upon them and pull or push them through the system. The modeler, considering the complexity, size, and detail level of the model, decides which elements should drive the system. One may classify models as part(entity)-driven or resource (machine)-driven models. In part-driven models, the parts are dynamic and they move from one resource to another as resources become available. On the other hand, in resource-driven models, resources pick the parts that they want to serve and send them to their next resource after completion. It is generally easier to build part-driven models. Resource-driven models are generally recommended if there are too many parts in the system or the resource allocation logic is very complex. It is possible to have models with both part and resource-driven characteristics.

Step 2. Determine the elements that drive the system. Some of the elements (parts, people) in a system are dynamic in nature, in the sense that they move through the system causing other entities to react to them in response to some signal. Other elements are static in nature in a sense that they wait for the dynamic entities or resources to act upon them and pull or push them through the system. The modeler, considering the complexity, size, and detail level of the model, decides which elements should drive the system. One may classify models as part/entity-driven or resource(machine)-driven models. In part-driven models, the parts are dynamic and they move from one resource to another as resources become available. On the other hand, in resource-driven models, resources pick the parts that they want to serve and send them to their next resource after completion. It is generally easier to build part-driven models. Resource-driven models are generally recommended if there are too many parts in the system or the resource allocation logic is very complex. It is possible to have models with both part and resource-driven characteristics.

Step 3. Determine the entities that should represent the system elements. Each simulation tool makes its own finite types of entities available to the modeler to be used to represent the real system components.

Our simulation model consists of six VHDL modules (Traffgen, Clkgen, NIC, IOsub, Memsub, and Statsgen). According to the VHDL terminology, every module is a design entity, and the inputs and outputs are called ports (input and/or output). The ports of the instances are connected using signals.

Step 4. Determine the level of detail needed to describe the system components. The model detail is further discussed at this step by identifying the simulation tool constructs to be used to represent each real system component. The level of detail put into a model should depend mainly on the objectives of the study. It is not always easy to eliminate the unnecessary detail since the customer may question the validity of the model if the components are not modeled in detail. It is recommended that the detail should be added to a model in stages starting with a simple macro level model of the system. For each black box that will be used to represent a system component, the modeler should list the reasons why a black box is going to be used in the model. The reasons may include lack of time, perceived indifference of the output measures to the component, the objectives of the study, lack of data, and cost of modeling.

In the following, we describe our design entities.

- `Clkgen`: The clock generator (`Clkgen`) allows us to generate the different clock signals required in our model (Fig. 8a).
- `Traffgen`: The traffic generator (`Traffgen`) allows us to model the worst-case traffic for different Ethernet standards (e.g., 10, 100, 1000 Mbit/s, and 10 Gbit/s). In all cases, the arrival of fixed-size Ethernet packets (e.g., minimum, maximum, and jumbo) can be simulated with it (Fig. 8b).
- `NIC`: The module is the most important component in our simulation model. Internally, it is composed of three submodules (`BuffMngr`, `NICCtrl` and `DMACtrl`). Basically, the function of the buffer manager (`BuffMngr`) is to monitor the level of filling in the buffer. The DMA controller (`DMACtrl`) deals with DMA transfers. On the other hand, the NIC controller (`NICCtrl`) is responsible for overall packet transfer flow. Thus, it controls the sequence of actions required during packet and descriptor transfers. Note that the NIC-side processing is simulated through a configurable delay (Fig. 8c).

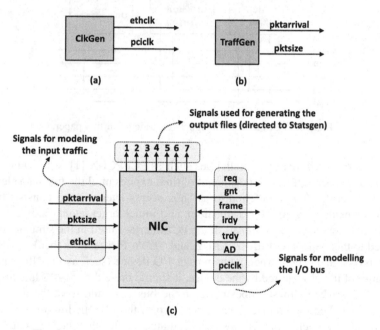

Fig. 8. Model entities: ClockGen and TraffGen and NIC entity.

- `IOsub`: In our case study, the I/O subsystem (`IOsub`) models a multi-drop parallel I/O-bus such as PCI/PCI-X. Structurally, the `IOSub` module consists of two sub-modules: `Arbiter` and `Othermaster`. The `Arbiter` deals with the arbitration process and `Othermaster` simulates the workload generated by other I/O units connected to the bus (Fig. 9).
- `Memsub`: The memory-subsystem module (`MemSub`) is the target of transactions across the I/O bus. It just simulates the initial target latency (Fig. 10).

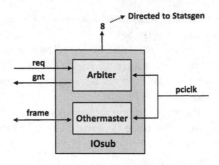

Fig. 9. IOSub entity.

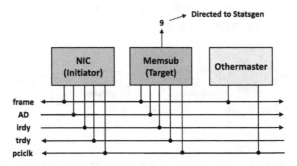

Fig. 10. PCI-bus control signals considered in this paper.

It should be noted that in a parallel bus such as PCI/PCI-X [1], when a bus master (e.g., the NIC) asserts REQ, a finite amount of time expires until the first data element is actually transferred. This is referred to as "bus access latency" and consists of three components, namely, arbitration, acquisition, and initial target latencies. For modeling bus access latency, the control signals of the PCI interface used in the simulation model developed in this paper are: FRAME, IRDY, and TRDY. Please, note that FRAME is like a "bus busy" signal. Thus, when a bus-master I/O device (such as the NIC) owns the bus because of it was acquired by the device, it should drive the FRAME line to '0'. On the other hand, when a master does not own the bus, it should have the line released (driving a 'Z'). The module Othermaster drives the FRAME line to low during a random number of cycles. In this way, it is simulated the fact that the bus is busy due to a transaction in progress performed by any other I/O device connected to it (Fig. 10). In our model, AD line is used for transaction target identification. Because of both the NIC and Othermaster can drive FRAME line to low, 1bit AD line is used in order to the Memsub (i.e., the target of the NIC-to-memory transfers) can determine if it is the target of the current transaction (when FRAME = '0' and AD = '0'), otherwise, the target of the current simulated transaction is any other device connected to the bus (when FRAME = '0' and AD = '1').

- `Statsgen`: The main functions of the statistics generator (`Statsgen`) are: (i) keeping track of buffer fill-level and (ii) providing the required parameters values to analytical model calibration. In addition, this module provides other buffer statistics such as the count of dropped, received, and transferred packets. All this information can be obtained from various trace files.

Step 5. Determine the graphics requirements of the model. The animation requirements of the model are discussed in detail at this step by considering factors such as animation expectations of the client, execution speed of the animated simulation model, use of animation as a verification tool, use of animation as a selling tool, ease of building the static and dynamic animation components, and the availability of built-in icons in the animation library.

Step 6. Identify the areas that utilize special control logic. Systems with multiple machines or servers may require complex decision-making and control logic. During this step, the modeler discusses the best way of modeling the complex decision-making processes in the system.

Step 7. Determine how to collect statistics in the model and communicate results to the Customer. All the simulation tools produce standard output reports that may or may not readily translate into useful information for the customer. The modeler may need to define variables, counters, histograms, time series, pie charts, etc. to collect the appropriate data in a form that communicates the results effectively to the client. In many cases, the modeler may need to write user interfaces in a spreadsheet program to summarize the output data.

6 Inputs, Assumptions, and Process Definition

Operating philosophy describes the way that the management runs or intends to run the system. The issues considered include the number of shifts per day, the length of each shift, shift-end policies, scheduled breaks for workers and machines, strip logic for some machines, setup time, tool change, repair policies, off-line storage policies, production batch sizes and sequence, etc.

Physical constraints refer to those studies where layout options exist for the placement of material handling equipment, machines, and storages. In "green field" systems, one may have more options in number, type and placement of equipment, machines and storages. For existing systems, options may be limited on the placement of the new equipment in the system.

Once the dynamic elements of the model have been identified in the previous phase of the process, in this phase, the detailed logic of entry and exit of the dynamic elements is considered. Issues to be finalized include existence of infinite buffers before the first and after the last processors in the system and the logic to be used in arrival of entities to the system. For multiple dynamic elements case, arrival rates of each entity type, batch size, changeover time on processors and scrap and repair rates of each entity type have to be specified.

The process flow and the logic describing that flow as entities move through the system have to be specified in detail. The priority assignments for the entities as they compete for the resources and vice versa have to be described. Repair entity logic and priorities should be identified.

Operation specifications include data for each operation in the model including processing time, downtime distribution, percentage down, scrap and reject rate, setup time, capacity, etc. "Operation" in this case may refer to machining or service operations but excludes the material handling and storage activities in the system.

Material handling specifications include data for each type of material handling equipment in the model including transfer times in terms of acceleration, deceleration, minimum and maximum speeds, downtime distribution, percentage down, capacity, pickup and drop times, etc.

All the macro and micro level assumptions of the model are summarized at this step. This includes assumptions regarding the behavior of model components, input data, model detail level, startup conditions of the model, etc.

Input data should be analyzed and tested for reasonableness by the project team and line engineers and operators. Patterns in data should be identified, if any, and incorporated as part of input data generation. Theoretical distributions should be fitted to actual data and used in the model whenever possible (Law).

Runtime parameters are the variables whose values are to be changed from one simulation run to another in the study.

The detailed information gathered at the previous and current phases of the project should be used to update the Project Functional Specifications. This information should further be incorporated into the Maintenance Manual, model code, and the Final Project Report. By default, the information should be in the Project Book too. The detailed version of the Project Functional Specifications should be read carefully by the client engineers familiar with the system and corrected, if necessary.

7   Validation of the Conceptual Model

In this section, we analyze the network-to-memory data path from the perspective of RTC in order to show the requirements for the analytical model calibration and validation. According to our needs, various alternative ways that can be employed to validate the RTC model are reviewed and compared.

Acceptance of the model assumptions, operating philosophy, process flow, operation specifications, input data analysis, and runtime parameters by the client implies that the client validates the conceptual model of the modeler(s). A rigorous validation procedure for the conceptual model as discussed here is as important as the verification and ope-rational validation of the model because, being earlier than the others, it saves time and redirects the project team in the right direction before a lot of time is wasted in the study.

7.1 Analytical Model Calibration and Validation

In RTC, the basic model consists of a resource that receives incoming processing and communication requests and executes them using available processing and communication capacity. To this end, some non-decreasing functions such as the arrival and service functions as well as the arrival and services curves (upper and lower) are introduced. Similar to the arrival curves describing packet flows, the processing or communication capability of a resource is described by using service curves [18–20].

The task model represents the different packet processing and communication functions that occur within a network node, for example, NIC-side processing, bus access latency, and DMA transfer over the I/O bus to the chipset [11].

For model calibration and validation purposes (see [11] for details), a RTC-based data path model of the SUT is derived (Step 1 in Fig. 11). A simulator (or simulation model) of the SUT (Step 2) is required for calibrating the RTC model (Step 3). The accumulated buffer space in the RTC-based data path model, i.e., b1 + b2 + b3 + b4, allows us to derive the NIC buffer-size requirements by analytical methods. To compute such buffer space, the features provided by RTC are used. To this end, a resultant RTC component for the tandem of logical components, NIC, ARB, ACQ, and MEMSUB, is obtained. Then, by computing the backlog b of such component, the maximum buffer-size requirements are obtained (Step 4). To validate the analytically-obtained results, experimental studies using the VHDL model are performed. The buffer-size requirements obtained by analytical methods are compared versus maximum buffer requirements provided by the simulation model (Step 5).

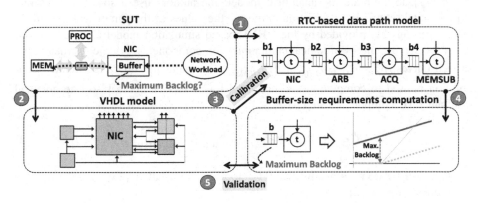

Fig. 11. Relationship between the conceptual validation, verification, and operational validation of the model.

Notice in Fig. 11 that the logical RTC components, NIC, ARB, ACQ, and MEMSUB, are connected by a bus, which is able to transfer one data block per I/O-bus cycle.

Since we are interested in modeling a PCI-like parallel bus, the objective of the components, ARB and ACQ, is to model the overhead due to arbitration and acquisition latencies. Finally, the function of the component MEMSUB is to model the overhead due to the initial target latency also known as target response. In addition to the overhead cycles, all these logical components also model the transmission cycles that are needed to transfer packet payloads and descriptors. Note that in our model no wait cycles are inserted during the data phase of the I/O transactions because we consider that the initiator of transactions, i.e., the NIC, is fast enough and is able to completely consume the bandwidth offered by the I/O bus; that is, the NIC is always ready to transfer a data block per bus cycle. Therefore, no additional buffer is required to model the overhead of wait cycles.

In our case, if α_f^u describe the arrival curves of the flow f in terms communication requests (e.g., data blocks) demanded from r, and, on the other hand, the bounding-curve β_r^l describes the communication capability of r in terms of the same units (i.e., "data blocks per I/O-bus cycles" that are transferred by r), then, the maximum backlog required by packets of flow f at the resource r can be given by the following inequality [18, 21].

$$backlog \leq sup_{t \geq 0}\left\{\alpha_f^u(t) - \beta_r^l\right\} \tag{1}$$

The backlog is defined as the amount of data units held inside the system (e.g., bits, bytes, packets, data blocks, etc.) (see Boudec and Thiran [22]). If the system has a single buffer, the backlog is related to the queue length. If the system is more complex, then, the backlog is the number of data units in transit, assuming that we can observe input and output simultaneously. Figure 2 shows the overall scheme for comparing the results obtained using the analytical method with those obtained from simulations used in our reference paper.

In [11], to calibrate the analytical model, the authors use a so-called "baseline experimental setup". For calibration purposes, the values of the parameters L_β and R_β (Step 3 in Fig. 11) provided by the VHDL-based simulation model are used to construct the service curves of logical communication components. After constructing the service curves, $\beta_{NIC}^l, \beta_{ARB}^l, \beta_{ACQ}^l$, and β_{MEMSUB}^l, by using the Eq. 2, an iterated convolution is used to compute the accumulated lower service curve β^l of the obtained resultant RTC component (Step 4):

$$\beta^l = \left(\left(\left(\beta_{NIC}^l \otimes \beta_{ARB}^l\right) \otimes \beta_{ACQ}^l\right) \otimes \beta_{MEMSUB}^l\right) \tag{2}$$

This can be done either by the RTC toolbox for Matlab [23], or by symbolic techniques [18, 21, 22].

Once, the bounding-curves β^l and α^u for the baseline configuration are constructed, the maximum backlog (i.e., the maximum NIC buffer-size requirements are computed by using the function rtcplotv(f,g) provided by the Matlab toolbox (Step 4 in Fig. 11).

To validate the RTC model, the simulator should fulfill two main goals. The first one concerns the monitoring of the FIFO fill-level. The second one relies on providing RTC descriptions of the logical communication component in which the network-to-memory data path has been decomposed. In the data-path model considered in this work, the basic data unit entering the system in order to be transfer consists of two components: packet and descriptor.

As illustrated in Fig. 11, during the trip of an incoming data unit from the network to the system memory, it should cross a tandem of logical communication components, whose operation is characterized by means of service curve. The procedure to compute the value of the parameters required for building the segments of the bounding curves of the network workload, and the operation of the logical communication resources has been shown in Fig. 12. Thus, in order to build the upper arrival curve, the parameters, PS (Packet Size), DS (Descriptor Size), and R_α, are required.

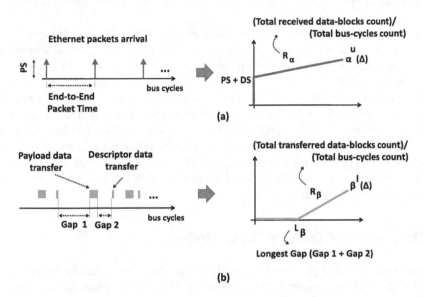

Fig. 12. (a) Building the arrival curve that characterizes the network workload from a trace that represents the instant of time when a whole packet is received by the NIC. (b) building the service curve that characterizes the communication capabilities of a resource with non-deterministic behavior from a trace in terms of both transmission and non-transmission cycles, as seen at the output of component.

On the other hand, to build the lower services curves, the parameters, L_β and R_β are required. Note that PS and DS are expressed in data blocks, and L_β are expressed in I/O-bus cycles. Finally, R_β are expressed in terms of received data blocks per bus cycles, and R_β in transferred data blocks per bus cycles (i.e., in the same unit). To clarify how bounding-curves are constructed, Fig. 12a shows the way of calculating the parameters required for building the upper arrival curve. Similarly, the way of calculating the parameters required for building the lower service curves is shown in Fig. 12b.

In the next section, the major simulation-based approaches known in literature for the performance evaluations of computer systems are classified. Moreover, a comparison of them according our needs is presented.

7.2 Alternative Ways to Validate the RTC Model

To a proper tool selection, a survey of nine alternatives ways that can be used to validate the RTC model was carried out. Survey results were compared and contrasted according a set of criteria [24].

Surveyed tools include hardware description languages (e.g., VHDL and Verilog), and system-level description languages (e.g., SystemC and SpeC). Also, different categories of simulators are considered; for example, component-oriented simulators (DRAMSim, ScriptSim, Moses, Spinach, NepSim), and full-system simulators (Simics, and M5).

In [24], the alternatives described above are compared. The capabilities of the simulation model to generate the parameters required to build the arrival and service curves as well as the general simulation-model requirements shown in Figs. 11 and 12, are taken into account.

We want to note that none of the reviewed alternative ways provides neither the parameters required for building the upper arrival curve (i.e., M and R_{WL}) nor the parameters required for building the lower service curves (i.e., L_{NIC} and R_{NIC}, L_{ARB} and R_{ARB}, L_{ACQ} and R_{ACQ}, L_{MEM} and R_{MEM}) used in our analytical model. Similarly, none of the alternative ways is intended to monitor the FIFO fill-level; consequently. Hence, we decide to implement a new VHDL-based simulation model to cover our needs; for a more in-depth look, see [24].

8   Description of the Simulation Model

To constitute the global program (executable model) that corresponds to the simulation model of data path, we assemble those modules (VHDL files) previously implemented. Thus, once composed the global program, all those modules cooperate to realize both the functions and the characteristics of the hardware components that are being modeled (Fig. 13).

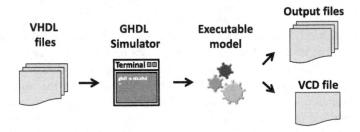

Fig. 13. Converting the VHDL model (NICSim-vhd) into an executable model and obtaining simulation outputs.

After running the executable model, six output files are created (input.out, nic.out, arb.out, acq.out, memsub.out, and buffer.out). All these files are generated by the Statsgen module (recall Figs. 8, 9 and 10).

More details of the structural and behavioral descriptions of all the modules/ submodules of NICSim-vhd can be found at https://github.com/ggaray/nicsim-vhd.

9 Conclusions

To validate the RTC-based analytical model of the network-to-memory data path, we have proposed the main features of a VHDL-based simulation model. We show how it can analyze the performance of FIFO-buffers in network interface cards, and provide the required parameters for building RTC descriptions of the logical communication components of the data path. The main details of the HDL model have been presented in the paper. We note that although the VHDL language was chosen for modeling purposes due to software availability and standardization issues, the implementation of the simulation model in SystemC can be considered as another interesting approach.

Our simulation model can incorporate some improvements that we will develop in future work. For example, modeling variable input-packet sizes that follows a given probabilistic distribution (Poisson, etc.), or generates input packets from a real Ethernet trace. In addition, NIC latency will be modelled as a function of input-packets size due to per-byte data-touching operations within the NIC such as CRC and checksum calculation. Also, a PCI Express multi-drop parallel bus topology as well as more detailed model of the memory subsystem that considers the memory bus contention will be modelled. Finally, others performance metrics such as throughput will be provided by the individual model components (e.g., the NIC, I/O subsystems) and by the whole system.

This paper serves to increase the successful use of simulation techniques in the computer systems performance analysis by highlighting the importance of conceptual design and its validation.

Acknowledgments. This work is supported by the Ministry of Education and Science of Russian Federation under contract No02.G25.31.0061 12/02/2013 (Government Regulation No 218 from 09/04/2010).

References

1. Minkenberg, C., Denzel, W., Rodriguez, G., Birke, R.: End-to-end modeling and simulation of high- performance computing systems. In: Bangsow, S. (ed.) Use Cases of Discrete Event Simulation, pp. 201–240. Springer, Heidelberg (2012)
2. Liao, X.-K., Pang, Z.-B., Wang, K.-F., Lu, Y.-T., Xie, M., Xia, J., Dong, D.-Z., Suo, G.: High performance interconnect network for Tianhe system. J. Comput. Sci. Technol. **30**, 259–272 (2015)
3. Nüssle, M., Fröning, H., Kapferer, S., Brüning, U.: Accelerate communication, not computation! In: Vanderbauwhede, W., Benkrid, K. (eds.) High-Performance Computing Using FPGAs, pp. 507–542. Springer, New York (2013)

4. Rodriguez, G., Minkenberg, C., Luijten, R.P., Beivide, R., Geoffray, P., Labarta, J., Valero, M., Poole, S.: The network adapter: the missing link between MPI applications and network performance. In: 2012 IEEE 24th International Symposium on Computer Architecture and High Performance Computing (SBAC-PAD), pp. 1–8 (2012)

5. Tan, M., Rosenberg, P., Yeo, J.S., McLaren, M., Mathai, S., Morris, T., Kuo, H.P., Straznicky, J., Jouppi, N.P., Wang, S.-Y.: A high-speed optical multi-drop bus for computer interconnections. Appl. Phys. A **95**, 945–953 (2009)

6. Taylor, S.J.E., Khan, A., Morse, K.L., Tolk, A., Yilmaz, L., Zander, J., Mosterman, P.J.: Grand challenges for modeling and simulation: simulation everywhere—from cyberinfrastructure to clouds to citizens. SIMULATION, 0037549715590594 (2015)

7. Abdulhameed, A., Hammad, A., Mountassir, H., Tatibouet, B.: An approach based on SysML and SystemC to simulate complex systems. In: 2014 2nd International Conference on Model-Driven Engineering and Software Development (MODELSWARD), pp. 555–560 (2014)

8. Bassi, L., Secchi, C., Bonfe, M., Fantuzzi, C.: A SysML-based methodology for manufacturing machinery modeling and design. IEEEASME Trans. Mechatron. **16**, 1049–1062 (2011)

9. Wang, Y., Yu, Y., Xie, C., Zhang, X., Jiang, W.: A proposed approach to mechatronics design education: Integrating design methodology, simulation with projects. Mechatronics **23**, 942–948 (2013)

10. Shafik, R.A., Al-Hashimi, B.M., Chakrabarty, K.: System-level design methodology. In: Mathew, J., Shafik, R.A., Pradhan, D.K. (eds.) Energy-Efficient Fault-Tolerant Systems, pp. 169–210. Springer, New York (2014)

11. Garay, G.R., Ortega, J., Díaz, A.F., Corrales, L., Alarcón-Aquino, V.: System performance evaluation by combining RTC and VHDL simulation: a case study on NICs. J. Syst. Archit. **59**, 1277–1298 (2013)

12. Ülgen, O.: Simulation Methodology: A Practitioner's Perspective. Dearborn MI University, Michigan (2006)

13. Alvarez, G.R.G.: A survey of analytical modeling of network interfaces in the era of the 10 Gigabit Ethernet. Presented at the 2009 6th International Conference on Electrical Engineering, Computing Science and Automatic Control, CCE, January 2009 (2009)

14. Kurose, J.F., Ross, K.W.: Computer Networking: A Top-Down Approach: International Edition. Pearson Higher Ed., New York (2013)

15. Karlin, S.C., Peterson, L.: Maximum packet rates for full-duplex ethernet. Department of Computer Science (2002)

16. Gingold, T.: Ghdl-where vhdl meets gcc. http://ghdl.free.fr

17. Bybell, T.: Gtkwave. http://gtkwave.sourceforge.net

18. Chakraborty, S., Künzli, S., Thiele, L., Herkersdorf, A., Sagmeister, P.: Performance evaluation of network processor architectures: combining simulation with analytical estimation. Comput. Netw. **41**, 641–665 (2003)

19. Chakraborty, S., Kunzli, S., Thiele, L.: A general framework for analysing system properties in platform-based embedded system designs. Presented at the Design, Automation and Test in Europe Conference and Exhibition (2003)

20. Garay, G.R., Ortega, J., Alarcon-Aquino, V.: Comparing Real-Time Calculus with the existing analytical approaches for the performance evaluation of network interfaces. In: 21st International Conference on Electrical Communications and Computers (CONIELECOMP), Los Alamitos, CA, USA, pp. 119– 124 (2011)

21. Thiele, L., Chakraborty, S., Gries, M., Kunzli, S.: A framework for evaluating design tradeoffs in packet processing architectures. Presented at the Proceedings of the 39th Design Automation Conference (2002)

22. Boudec, J.-Y.L., Thiran, P.: Network Calculus: A Theory of Deterministic Queuing Systems for the Internet. LNCS, vol. 2050. Springer, Heidelberg (2001)
23. Wandeler, E., Thiele, L.: Real-Time Calculus (RTC) Toolbox (2006)
24. Garay, G.R., León, M., Aguilar, R., Alarcon, V.: Comparing simulation alternatives for high-level abstraction modeling of NIC's buffer requirements in a network node. In: Electronics, Robotics and Automotive Mechanics Conference (CERMA), September 2010 (2010)

HPC Applications and Simulations

Elastic Full Waveform Inversion (FWI) of Reflection Data with a Phase Misfit Function

Jean Kormann$^{(\boxtimes)}$, Juan Esteban Rodríguez, Miguel Ferrer, Natalia Gutiérrez, Josep de la Puente, Mauricio Hanzich, and José María Cela

Computer Applications in Science and Engineering,
Barcelona Supercomputing Center, Jordi Girona 29, 08034 Barcelona, Spain
jean.kormann@bsc.es

Abstract. Full Waveform Inversion of elastic dataset is challenging due to the complexity introduced by free-surface effects or P-S wave conversions among others. In this context, large offsets are preferred for inversion because they favor transmission modes which are more linearly related to P-wave velocity. In this paper, we present an original approach which allows to dynamically select the near offset at each frequency. We illustrate this approach with the inversion of a dataset without density. In order to deal with a more realistic scenario, we next present the inversion with density effects included into the modeling. As inverting density is known to be a hard task, we choose to not invert it. This approach leads to the use of a phase misfit function, which is more connected to the kinematics of the problem than the classic L^2 norm.

Keywords: Full waveform inversion · Elastic waves · High-performance computing

1 Introduction

Full-waveform inversion (FWI) of seismic datasets allows to retrieve physical properties directly from the seismic traces, once sufficient conditions on the initial guess, data quality and frequency bandwidth are provided. Its high-resolving capacity with respect to other imaging methods makes FWI an attractive tool for both academy and industry. Nevertheless, the non-uniqueness of the solution and its high computational cost make performing FWI a challenging task even with modern High Performance Computing architectures.

Typically, due to the non-linearity of the problem, inversion strategies are used which increase the success ratio of FWI. One of the most widely used strategies is starting with large offsets and selecting (windowing) early arrivals of the P-wave. This strategy favors transmission modes over reflection modes, being the former more linearly related to P-wave velocity [2,3,7,9]. This strategy also facilitates retrieving the lowest possible wavelengths of the model, as the data typically is limited in the low-frequency end. Nevertheless, not always are long offsets available. Analogously, for a fixed offset length, the deepest regions

© Springer International Publishing Switzerland 2016
I. Gitler and J. Klapp (Eds.): ISUM 2015, CCIS 595, pp. 277–284, 2016.
DOI: 10.1007/978-3-319-32243-8_19

are not well covered with refracting waves. Hence it is of great interest to be able to extract as much information as possible from reflection modes in FWI.

In former studies, using reflection modes for FWI has been considered a challenging task [6]. The incapacity for retrieving the longest wavelengths in the model has stirred the interest in modifying the typical FWI workflows by employing image-domain misfit functions [11] or intertwined FWI/migration algorithms [8,10].

We show how, with a careful choice of offsets and a phase-based misfit function [4], reflection datasets can be successfully inverted. Furthermore, we exemplify our strategy with elastic FWI instead of acoustic FWI, which is much more challenging in terms of complexity and cost.

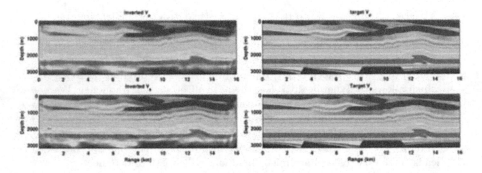

Fig. 1. Models and results for the constant-density dataset: V_p (top, right) and V_s (bottom, right) are the target model; V_p (top, left) and V_s (bottom, left) are the FWI results obtained using the DOC strategy and modified L^2 norm.

2   Theory

Regarding the elastic modeling needed for FWI, we use the time-domain elastic isotropic approach for solving the elastic wave equation:

$$\rho(\mathbf{x})\dot{\mathbf{v}}(\mathbf{x}, t) = \nabla \cdot \sigma(\mathbf{x}, t) + \mathbf{f}_s(\mathbf{x}_s, t),$$
$$\dot{\sigma}(\mathbf{x}, t) = \mathbf{C}(\mathbf{x}) : \nabla \mathbf{v}(\mathbf{x}, t) \tag{1}$$

where f_s is the source function at position $\mathbf{x}_s$, $\mathbf{v}$ the particle velocity, ρ the density, and σ the stress field.

With respect to the misfit function, instead of the classic L^2 norm we prefer a locally normalized version L^2_{mod} which has shown to be more robust in our testing. This function is defined as:

$$L^2_{\text{mod}} = \frac{1}{2} \sum_{i=1}^{N} \sum_{j=1}^{n} \left[\frac{u_j^i(\mathbf{m})}{\max_j(|u^i(\mathbf{m})|)} - \frac{u_j^i(\mathbf{m}_{\text{real}})}{\max_j(|u^i(\mathbf{m}_{\text{real}})|)} \right) \right]^2, \tag{2}$$

where N is the number of receivers, n the number of samples of each trace, u the measurement obtained from the current model $\mathbf{m}$ or the real model $\mathbf{m}_{real}$, in which case we call the measurement data. The search direction $\mathbf{p}_k$ at the kth iteration is obtained by means of a non-linear conjugate gradient method, it is given by

$$\mathbf{p}_k = \nabla \epsilon_k + \beta_k \mathbf{p}_{k-1}. \tag{3}$$

For obtaining β_k the Polak-Ribière criterion is used. Finally, a line search algorithm finds the optimum α_k and then updates the models according to

$$\mathbf{m}_k = \mathbf{m}_{k-1} + \alpha_k \mathbf{p}_k. \tag{4}$$

We apply a two-step preconditioning: At a first stage, we apply a change of variable, and choose to work with $\tilde{m} = \log_e(\mathbf{m})$ instead of $\mathbf{m}$. This is equivalent to multiplying the gradients of λ and μ, the Lamé parameters, by the parameters themselves. The last step compensates for geometrical spreading by using the preconditioner proposed by [5].

3   Results

In the following we present the inversion of a model based upon the 3D SEG/EAGE Overthrust model [1]. We chose a 2D slice of the model and devised an acquisition geometry involving sources located at 50 m deep, and with a spacing of 200 m starting from the inline location x = 1050 m, resulting in a total of 71 shots. We have simulated 10 s of traces using a Ricker wavelet with central frequency at 10 Hz. Furthermore, we used a heterogeneous density model for the data and included a free-surface condition. The V_s and ρ models were set proportional to V_p by a factor of 0.5 and 0.41, respectively. A dataset with constant density was also generated. For checking purposes with a dataset. No preprocessing of the data has been done to remove ground roll or window seismic phases. The data has been used in the FWI as it is.

The FWI starting models were obtained by applying a Gaussian smoothing to the target models (see Fig. 1, right panels) with a correlation length of 500 m. Our FWI uses a multi-grid and multi-scale strategy, sweeping with low-pass filters from low to high frequencies. We want to stress that the computational grid does not match the receiver and source grids, as the grid is regenerated, and the model consequently interpolated, at each frequency band. Last but not least, we did not fix any part of the model during the inversion and we have not used any kind of regularization in our inversions.

3.1   Dynamic Offset Control

In order to validate our FWI against other approaches [2], we first used the dataset obtained with a constant density model, with a value set to 1000 kg/m^3. Our approach for FWI consists in constraining the maximum offset to the longest wavelength of the compressional wave at the present frequency maximum. We call this approach Dynamic Offset Control (DOC). In this way, the maximum receiver offset is 3530 m for the lowest frequency of 1.7 Hz. This strategy has the side effect of reducing the computational domain as we move to the higher frequencies while minimizing the effect of the surface wave on the gradients. Finally, by selecting only near-offset traces, we are able to avoid cycle skipping between synthetic data and can use the whole trace length in our FWI. This leads to a fast and reliable inversion scheme. For this test we can rely on our modified L^2 norm defined in Eq. 2. Table 1 summarizes the multi-scale, multi-grid strategy used for this case.

Table 1. Multi-grid and multi-scale parameters for 2D FWI in the constant density case; from top to bottom: cut-off frequency, mesh size, spatial discretization, and number of iterations.

FWI strategy				
1.7 Hz	2.5 Hz	3.4 Hz	5.2 Hz	7.3 Hz
72×352	96×483	124×606	160×800	196×975
45.0 m	33.0 m	25.8 m	20.0 m	16.3 m
0	10	10	10	10

Figure 1 shows the inverted models after 50 iterations divided among 5 frequencies. We observe that the inversion is successful, with a good resolution of all the features, even for the deepest layers. Reflectors show a good continuity and the fracture zone is clearly delineated. We remark, once again, the very small dataset and the straightforward FWI scheme used.

3.2   Including Density into the Dataset

In a more challenging test, we used the dataset generated with a heterogeneous density model. The inversion, however, will only invert the P- and S-wave velocities. As our density model in FWI is homogenous and constant throughout the inversion, we cannot expect to explain completely the data with our FWI. We remark that density is rarely well known and is very challenging to invert with FWI. Our goal here is to concentrate on the wave kinematics which can be explained in terms of P- and S-wave velocity while ignoring the dynamic part which has a strong impact on the amplitude of each phase. To that goal we must use a misfit function which focuses on correcting phases instead of amplitudes. The classic L^2 would behave poorly in this case. Our modified L^2_{mod} norm in Eq. 2 is better suited as the normalizations will help focusing on phase changes. Nevertheless, a proper phase-focused misfit function was presented by [5] and has been applied in the present FWI exercise. This phase misfit function relies on time-frequency analysis, and is obtained by the cross-correlation of the Gabor transform between the synthetics and the data.

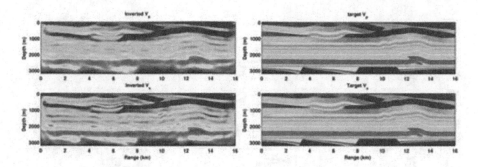

Fig. 2. Models and results for the heterogeneous density elastic datase: V_p (top, right) and V_s (bottom, right) are the target model; V_p (top, left) and V_s (bottom, left) are the FWI results obtained using the DOC strategy and phase misfit.

The combination of DOC and phase misfit in FWI results in better phase correspondence between synthetic and data. This allowed us to use larger frequency jumps in our FWI strategy without suffering from cycle-skipping. Assuming that the starting frequency is the same as the one used in the previous section, we can perform FWI by doubling the frequency at each frequency iteration; a strategy which is summarized in Table 2.

Table 2. Multi-grid and multi-scale parameters for 2D FWI in the heterogeneous density case; from top to bottom: cut-off frequency, mesh size, spatial discretization, and number of iterations.

FWI strategy		
1.7 Hz	3.4 Hz	6.8 Hz
48×238	92×457	160×800
67.5 m	34.9 m	20.0 m
15	20	20

Figure 2 presents the FWI results for this heterogeneous-density dataset after 55 iterations and for 3 different frequencies. We observe that the inversion results are very good, even at larger depth. The upper part is very well recovered, with no clear footprint of the acquisition geometry. Nevertheless, the effects of density are visible, especially when comparing Figs. 1 and 2. We loose the continuity of some reflectors, especially for the finest structures. We also observe some overestimation of the velocities, especially for the reflector lying at depth 1000 m and range 6 km. Nevertheless, we observe a smooth convergence and stability during the inversion: misfit reduction at 6.8 Hz reaches 26 per cent after 20 iterations (as can be seen in Fig. 4).

In Fig. 3 we pick three velocity profiles for both V_p (top) and V_s (bottom) at ranges 6, 10, and 14 km. We observe a very good agreement between target

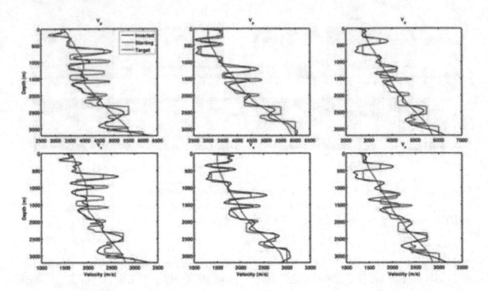

Fig. 3. Top (from left to right): P-wave velocity profiles at range 6, 10 and 14 Km respectively; Bottom (from left to right): S-wave velocity profiles at range 6, 10 and 14 Km respectively;

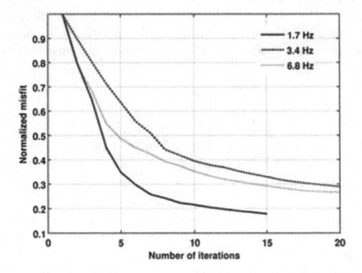

Fig. 4. Normalized misfit for the 3 inverted frequencies.

and inverted profiles, especially for V_s velocities, as expected due to the S-wave having a higher resolving power. There is also a good correlation of the low-frequency content, and the velocity amplitudes are almost correctly recovered by the method. We remark that this result has been obtained from data that included density effects while ignoring density in our elastic FWI scheme, and using only very short offsets.

4   Summary and Discussion

We have shown an elastic FWI successfully working on data dominated by reflections, using only near-source offsets. For this purpose, we have introduced an offset selection method called Dynamic Offset Control (DOC). We have applied DOC to 2D elastic datasets and demonstrated that we can recover accurately the elastic models even when we include density in the data. Furthermore, DOC allows us to reduce the maximum aperture of each shot in FWI, hence mitigating the increase in computational cost when moving into higher frequencies, which hints at making 3D elastic inversion more feasible. A key ingredient to our FWI results is using a phase misfit function [5], that is more naturally connected to the kinematic behavior of the waves. We believe that density is a proxy for amplitude-dominant phenomena which we do not include in our FWI scheme, and postulate that DOC with phase misfits might work well also in case of having attenuation in the data. Finally, we want to stress that we used a rather conventional FWI workflow, with no data windowing, phase selections or ground roll removal. Neither we used regularization or layer freezing.

Acknowledgments. The authors want to thank Repsol for the permission to publish the present research, carried out at the Repsol-BSC Research Center. This project has received funding from the European Union's Horizon 2020 research and innovation programme under the Marie Skłodowska-Curie grant agreement No 644602.

References

1. Aminzadeh, F., Brac, J., Kunz, T.: 3-D salt and overthrust models: SEG/EAGE 3-D modeling series 1: SEG (1997)
2. Brossier, R., Operto, S., Virieux, J.: Seismic imaging of complex onshore structures by 2D elastic frequency-domain full-waveform inversion. Geophysics **74**, WCC105–WCC118 (2009)
3. Canales, J.: Small-scale structure of the Kane oceanic core complex, Mid-Atlantic Ridge 23°30′N, from waveform tomography of multichannel seismic data. Geophys. Res. Lett. **37**, L21305 (2010)
4. Fichtner, A., Kennet, B.-N.-L., Bunge, H.-P., Igel, H.: Theoretical background for continental- and global-scale full-waveform inversion in the time-frequency domain. Geophys. J. Int. **175**, 665–685 (2008)
5. Fichtner, A., Kennet, B.-N.-L., Igel, H., Bunge, H.-P.: Full seismic waveform tomography for upper-mantle structure in the Australasian region. Geophys. J. Int. **179**, 1703–1725 (2009)
6. Plessix, R.-E., Rynja, H., et al.: VTI full waveform inversion: a parameterization study with a narrow azimuth streamer data example (2010)
7. Sears, T., Singh, S., Barton, P.: Elastic full waveform inversion of multi-component OBC seismic data. Geophys. Prospect. **56**, 843–862 (2008)

8. Wang, S., Chen, F., Zhang, H., Shen, Y.: Reflection-based full waveform inversion (RFWI) in the frequency domain. SEG Technical Program Expanded Abstracts 2013, pp. 877–881 (2013)
9. Warner, M., Ratcliffe, A., Nangoo, T., Morgan, J., Umpleby, A., Shah, N., Vinje, V., Stekl, I., Guasch, L., Win, C., Conroy, G., Bertrand, A.: Anisotropic 3D full-waveform inversion. Geophysics **78**, R59–R80 (2013)
10. Xu, S., Wang, D., Chen, F., Lambaré, G., Zhang, Y.: Inversion on reflected seismic wave. SEG Technical Program Expanded Abstracts 2012, pp. 1–7 (2012)
11. Zhang, S., Schuster, G., Abdullah, K.: Image-domain full waveform inversion: SEG Technical Program Expanded Abstracts **2013**, 861–865 (2013)

Numerical Simulations of a Dam Overflowing. Case Study: "La Esperanza" Dam in Hidalgo, Mexico. Implications for Risk Evaluation

Omar S. Areu-Rangel[1], Dante Tolentino[1], Itza Mendoza-Sanchez[1], Carlos E. Alvarado-Rodríguez[2,4], Jaime Klapp[3,4], and Rosanna Bonasia[5(✉)]

[1] Instituto Politécnico Nacional, ESIA, UZ, Miguel Bernard S/N, Edificio de Posgrado, 07738 Mexico, D.F., Mexico
[2] Universidad of Guanajuato, División de Ciencias Naturales y Exactas, Noria Alta, Guanajuato, Mexico
[3] Departamento de Física, Instituto Nacional de Investigaciones Nucleares, La Marquesa Ocoyoacac S/N, Ocoyoacac, Edo. de México, Mexico
[4] "ABACUS" Centro de Matemáticas Aplicadas y Cómputo de Alto Rendimiento, Departamento de Matemáticas, Centro de Investigación y de Estudios Avanzados (CINVESTAV-IPN), Carretera México-Toluca Km 38.5, La Marquesa, 52740 Ocoyoacac, Estado de México, Mexico
[5] CONACyT Research Fellow at Instituto Politécnico Nacional, ESIA, UZ, Miguel Bernard S/N, Edificio de Posgrado, 07738 Mexico, D.F., Mexico
rosannabonasia017@gmail.com

Abstract. Dam safety is an issue that affects directly or indirectly all society sectors. Up to now, Mexico does not have a proper federal or state legislation to evaluate dam safety, thus it is difficult to assign liability when total or partial dam failure occurs or to prevent failure by programming cost-effective dam supervision. Dam safety risk analysis by means of numerical simulations has the objective of evaluating the occurrence probability of a phenomenon, or group of phenomena, that affects dam safety. This work is focused on obtaining the overflow probability of the dam "La Esperanza" located in Hidalgo, Mexico. With this purpose, first, a statistical hydrologic analysis using daily maximum rains was conducted to obtain dam inflow as a function of rainfall duration and return periods. Second, different inflow scenarios were simulated to obtain their associated maximum hydraulic head values using the Smoothed Particle Hydrodynamics (SPH) numerical method. Finally, simulation results of maximum hydraulic head reached by water particles were used to calculate the overflow probability. We have obtained a high overflow probability for the "La Esperanza" dam warranting more studies, for this and other dams with similar conditions, given that the hazard potential to populated downstream areas is high.

Keywords: Winds · Turbulence · Collapse · Hydrodynamics · Simulations

© Springer International Publishing Switzerland 2016
I. Gitler and J. Klapp (Eds.): ISUM 2015, CCIS 595, pp. 285–295, 2016.
DOI: 10.1007/978-3-319-32243-8_20

1   Introduction

Mexico has about 8000 unregistered dams, small embankments and a total of 5166 registered, from which 16 % are large and 84 % small dams [2]. Most of the unregistered dams were designed and built between the 1940's and 1970's (with municipal or state funding) without following regulatory guidelines nor design standards. At the present time these dams have a high risk of collapse or damage because they are at the end of their designed life and have severe problems of sediments accumulation. The damage is generally reflected in loss of human life, livestock, agricultural fields, property, infrastructure, public services and propagation of diseases. In this context risk analysis that take into account spatial and temporal variations of the phenomena involved in dam failure and the condition in which hydraulic structures exist are of vital importance.

Risk analysis should undertake inspections of dams and embarkments. The inspection has to be a planned process, starting with background information of the structure (previous studies, blueprints design, pictures), in order to compare actual and historical conditions. It should also include detailed records of dam performance, such as instrumentation and operation, as well as flood and earthquake frequency, among others. In the case of old dams, as described in the previous paragraph, there is no information on their initial hydraulic or structural design. Furthermore, the Mexican Monitoring Dam System that registers daily inflow and observable faults, is only available for 0.64 % of the registered large dams and does not include old dams. Therefore an alternative efficient methodology is needed to determine the actual hazard potential, including structural and hydrologic failure, of old and small dams for which there is a general lack of historical and performance records.

During dam design, reservoir flood volume as well as spillway and embankment capacity are determined with the objective of avoiding overflowing and overtopping failure. Flood design obeys a relationship between inflow and discharge flows to store a fraction of the probable maximum flood and release the exceedance downstream. However when a flooding design occurs the probability of simultaneous downstream flooding is high thus exceedance discharges will generate a higher impact downstream [9]. In this sense it is important to assess the probability of dam overflow occurrence (over and around the dam face), to manage risk of flooding downstream.

In this work we present an evaluation of the probability of dam overflow as a function of precipitation intensity for the dam "La Esperanza" located in Hidalgo, Mexico. The work is organized as follow: first we present a brief description of the site; second, we apply a statistical process to obtain probable maximum daily precipitation, precipitation intensity for different return periods, and dam inflow as a function of precipitation intensity; third we simulate different inflow scenarios, by means of the SPH-based code DualSPhysics [3] and we obtain associated hydraulic head values. Finally we calculate the probability of overflowing by defining an overflowing index and a security threshold that relates the storage capacity and the amount of water received in the dam due to different precipitation events.

2   Site Description

The dam "La Esperanza" was constructed to store irrigation water. It is located in the municipality of Cuautepéc in the state of Hidalgo, at about 5 Km southeast from the town Tulancingo (Fig. 1), which has 151,584 inhabitants (INEGI2011). The dam is built in the Tulancingo River Basin, which is fed by El Chico river, a branch of the Grande river, which has a drainage area of 170 km^2.

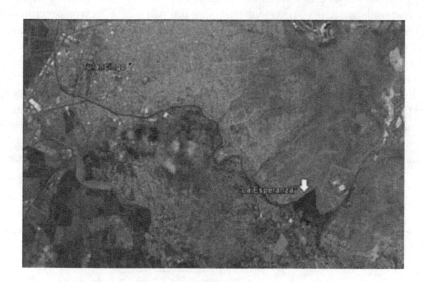

Fig. 1. Location of the dam "La Esperanza".

The dam has a total volume of 4.2 million cubic meters, from which 3.8 Mm^3 is the actual water storage volume, 0.4 Mm^3 is designed to receive sediments, and 0.6 Mm^3 is the over storage volume. At present 2.7 Mm^3 of the dam is filled with sediments surpassing the designed value and thereby the designed force on the embarkment.

The construction encompasses a rock-fill embankment with an impervious concrete layer on the upstream side. It has an uncontrolled side channel spillway, that releases water whenever the reservoir elevation exceeds the spillway crest level. The length of the spillway is 75 m with an elevation of 2,208.40 m.a.s.l., a flood capacity of 2,209.6 m.a.s.l., and 1 m of additional freeboard.

The mean annual discharge in normal conditions is 9.4 Mm^3 for irrigation of 15 km^2. Its average working discharge is 200 m^3/s, the maximum discharge recorded from construction (1943) to 1982 was on September 29th 1955 with 375 m^3/s.

The downstream land from the dam that could potentially be affected if overflowing occurs is as follow in km^2: urban area 7.57, rural area 1.85, agriculture 8.73 and vegetation 4.33.

3 Hydrologic Study

Design storm associated to regional precipitation conditions and return periods, give information on the probability that an extraordinary event occurs. For choosing the different scenarios for inflow we used the unit hydrograph theory, (UH theory, [10]), that is defined as the flow resulting from an exceeding precipitation unitary occurring uniformly all over the basin and over a defined unitary duration. The fundamental assumptions of the UH theory are: (i) the basin responds as a linear system; (ii) the intensity of effective precipitation is distributed uniformly over the whole basin; (iii) the excess of the precipitation is of constant intensity all along the duration of the precipitation; (iv) the duration of the hydrograph of direct runoff, is independent of effective precipitation and only depends on effective duration of precipitation. The scenarios of peak flow in this work were selected based on the triangular unit hydrograph (TUH), a simplification to the synthetic UHs proposed by [7]. The parameters that characterize a TUH and the final prediction (peak flow) are the basin area, concentration time and the number that defines the excess in rainfall.

The peak flow related to different return periods was calculated as follows:

$$Q_p = \frac{0.208 A P_e}{t_p},$$ (1)

being A the area of the basin, t_p peak time, and P_e effective precipitation is given by:

$$P_e = \frac{[P - \frac{508}{n} + 5.08]^2}{P - \frac{2032}{n} - 20.32},$$ (2)

being P the precipitation associated to a given return period calculated as the intensity times duration ($P = Id$).

For the calculation of the intensity we used the formula of [4] for estimating intervals of 5 min to 24 h and return periods longer than 1 year:

$$I_t^T = \frac{a P_t^{10} log(10^{2-F} T t^{F-1})}{(t+b)^2},$$ (3)

where I is the intensity in mm/h, P_t^{10} is the precipitation duration with t return period of 10 years and T the duration of excess in minutes.

Table 1 shows the values calculated for intensity, effective precipitation and peak flow for different return periods. The parameters of Table 1 were used to construct the TUH associated to each return period from where the scenarios of peak flow were obtained for each numerical simulation (Fig. 2).

4 Numerical Simulations

Numerical simulations of different inflow scenarios were performed using the DualSHPhysics model, an open-source code that implements the SPH method

Table 1. Values calculated for intensity, effective precipitation and peak flow.

Return period (y)	Intensities[a] (mm)	Effective precipitation (mm)	Peak flow (m³/s)
5	12.22	3.71	98.31
10	14.46	4.72	139.71
50	19.66	7.14	248.46
100	21.90	8.21	299.22
500	27.11	10.72	423.47
1000	29.35	11.81	478.93
5000	34.55	14.34	611.14
10000	36.79	15.44	669.28
50000	42.00	18.01	1042.61

[a]Intensities refer to a 300 min duration.

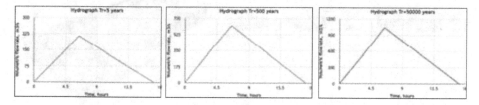

Fig. 2. Triangular unit hydrographs associated to three of the nine considered return periods.

in graphic processing units (GPUs). SPH is a mesh-free Lagrangian model developed in the 1970's to model astrophysical systems [8] and nowadays applied to a wide range of fluid dynamics systems. The basic principle of SPH is that a given function $A(r)$ may be approximated with an integral interpolation:

$$A(r) = \int A(r')W(r - r', h)dr', \tag{4}$$

where h is the smoothed length and $W(r - r', h)$ is the weight function known as kernel.

Applying a Lagrangian approximation to Eq. 4, a discrete notation of the interpolation in a given point is obtained:

$$A(r) = \sum_b m_b \frac{A_b}{\rho_b} W(r - r_b, h), \tag{5}$$

with the b index of the summation that executes all the particles inside a function defined by the kernel. m_b and ρ_b are the mass and density of the particle b, r_b is the position vector and $W(r_a - r_b, h)$ is the weighting function that refers to particles a and b.

In the present work we simulated different scenarios of inflow related to variable precipitation durations for each return period. Results from Sect. 3 were used to select peak flows for each return period. Additionally we used the TUH (Fig. 2) to randomly select four scenarios of inflow that correspond to different rain durations. We performed a total of 45 simulations.

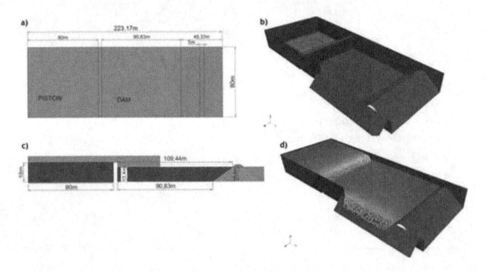

Fig. 3. (a) Plan of the geometrical configuration used in the simulations, including the geometry of the dam "La Esperanza" and the water tank piston used to generate a constant inflow; (b) three-dimensional view of the configuration; (c) transversal section of the geometrical configuration filled with water; and (d) three-dimensional view with water that comes out from the spillway.

The geometrical configuration used in the simulations is shown in Fig. 3. In order to generate a constant inflow into the dam, a rectangular tank (80 m by 25 m) located next to the dam was added to the simulations (Fig. 3a and c). At the bottom of the tank a piston was also simulated so that it induced a constant inflow into the dam. The volume of water inside the tank was defined as a function of the constant inflow simulating conditions (Fig. 3b and d). The rectangular tank that represents the dam was defined considering the real dimensions of the dam "La Esperanza" (Fig. 3a and c). The volume of water contained in the dam accounts for the volume reduction due to sediments contained in the dam, which are approximately $100\,000\,\mathrm{m^3}$. Parameters and principal characteristics of the simulations are shown in Table 2.

Simulation results are mainly the hydraulic head along the spillway and embankment. These results were obtained for each scenario of inflow value corresponding to different return periods. Figure 4 shows the distance traveled by a water particle for a simulation when the first overflow occurs with a return period of $T_r = 500$ yrs and a constant inflow of $Q = 4956.5\,\mathrm{m^3/s}$. The plot in

Table 2. Parameters and principal characteristics of the simulations

Parameter	Value
Kernel function	Wendland
Time-step algorithm	Verlet
Viscosity treatment	Artificial with $\alpha = 0.1$
Interparticle distance	1 m
Mean total number of particles[a]	272412
Mean physical time[a]	200 s
Computation time	1800 s

[a]Total number of particles and Physical time vary according to the different simulated inflow scenarios. Values in the table refers to means between all scenarios.

Fig. 4 follows a surface particle from the reservoir entrance until the particle exits through the embankment, e.g. each particle corresponds to sequential time steps that start with an initial time $t = 30$ s and ends with a final time $t = 180$ s when the particle exits the reservoir. In the simulations it is assumed that overflow occurs when the hydraulic head of particles arriving to the embankment exceeds the embankment height of 15.6 m. It can be seen in Fig. 4 that at the beginning of the simulation, when the inflow arrives to the reservoir the hydraulic head decreases ($y = 15.55$ m). Tracking the water particle along the reservoir (x axis), the hydraulic head (y axis) increases and thus the water storage temporarily increases in the reservoir. This corresponds to the wedge storage of the dam (red line in Fig. 4).

5   Probability of Overflowing

The security level of a system (e.g. dam, transmission tower, bridge, marine platform, among others) associated to a limit state of service or failure could be estimated by knowing both the capacity of the system and the solicitation to which it is subjected [1,11]. In the particular case of dams, overflowing occurs when the storage capacity is exceeded and the water flows through the spillway or the embankment. In this case a solicitation is defined as the amount of water received by the dam due to precipitation events. To estimate the relationship between storage capacity and solicitation due to precipitation events for a given dam we used an overflow index (I_d) that relates the design hydraulic head with the one generated by the solicitation. The I_d is expressed as:

$$I_d = \frac{T_D(T_R)}{T_C}, \tag{6}$$

where $T_D(T_R)$ is the hydraulic head associated to a return period, T_R and T_C is the design hydraulic head of the embankment.

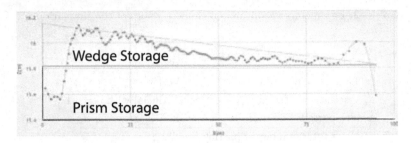

Fig. 4. Position of a particle of water in the x-y plane. The simulation corresponds to a return period of $T_r = 500$ y, when the first overflow occurs (Color figure online).

According to Eq. 6, values of $I_d < 1$ means that the water particles do not reach the designed hydraulic head, no overflowing occurs, and values of $I_d \geq 1$ indicates overflowing. If the logarithm of I_d is taken it would be possible to define a security threshold $W = \ln(I_d)$. Therefore, overflowing occurs when $W \geq 0$. In this study the dam security is obtained as follows [5]:

$$\beta(T_R) = \frac{-E[W])}{\gamma[W]}, \tag{7}$$

where E is the expected value of W and γ its standard deviation calculated as follow:

$$E[W] = a + b\ln(T_R), \tag{8}$$

$$\gamma[W] = c + d\ln(T_R). \tag{9}$$

The parameters of Eqs. 8 and 9 can be determined by a regression analysis (minimum square).

Given the security of the system β it is possible to calculate the overflow probability as:

$$p_d = \phi[\beta(T_R)], \tag{10}$$

where ϕ is the normal standard probability function.

Based on the simulations performed in Sect. 4, the security level $\beta(T_R)$ and the likelihood of overflow p_d associated with different return periods, were obtained. In Fig. 5 we show the overflow index expressed in terms of the safety margin W.

It is worth noting that the overflow of water particles occurs starting from a return period $T_R \leq 0$, which means that an overflow risk due to a heavy rain event exists.

The values of variances associated to different return periods are shown in Fig. 6.

It is important to note that the standard deviation values for the return period of interest were obtained based on the adjustment values of the variance as $\sqrt{W - h(T_R)}$. In Fig. 7 security levels associated to different return periods are shown and Table 3 presents overflow probability values.

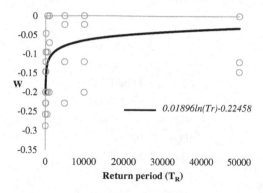

Fig. 5. Overflow index expressed in terms of the safety margin.

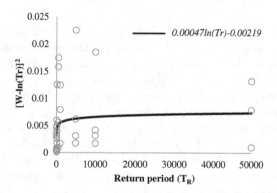

Fig. 6. Variance values associated with the studied case.

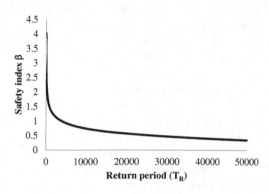

Fig. 7. Security index related to different return periods.

Table 3. Overflow probability values.

T_R	p_d
5	2.92333E-05
10	2.06993E-04
50	4.29298E-03
100	1.04927E-02
500	4.71824E-02
1000	7.56924E-01
5000	1.72943E-01
10000	2.26014E-01
50000	3.63739E-01

6 Summary and Discussion

The dam "La Esperanza" located in Hidalgo, Mexico, was built in the 1940's. At present the dam is near the end of its designed life and contains high volumes of sediment deposited. These conditions generate a high overflow risk.

To reveal the risk level of the hydraulic structure, in this study we first conducted a hydrologic analysis of parameters involved in the overflowing phenomenon: intensity and effective precipitation of annual daily maximum rainfall and associated values of inflow corresponding to different return periods.

We selected 45 scenarios of constant inflow corresponding to different rainfall duration and simulated with a SPH model (DualSPHysics), where the boundary conditions considered the real geometry of the studied dam. From the numerical simulations we obtained the position in the vertical axis of water particles (hydraulic head) at non overflowing and overflowing conditions, where overflowing was assumed as the moment where the water level of the particles exceeded the height of the embankment.

Simulation results were statistically analyzed using a defined relation between the storage capacity of the dam and the amount of water received by the dam due to precipitation events. This allowed us to define an overflow index that relates the designed hydraulic head with the hydraulic head resulting from the inflow scenarios simulated. The security of the dam was obtained through a first order approximation of second order moments.

In general, structural systems are designed to comply with security values of $\beta \geq 3.5$ [6,12]. However security values of the dam obtained in this study are low compared to values for other structural systems (bridge or marine platform). Therefore non desirable security levels occurred approximately 30 years after the construction of the dam. Specifically in this study non desired security levels are strictly related to high probabilities of overflowing of the dam. Considering the potential hazards of flooding populated areas downstream of a dam, as the case of the inhabited area located downstream of "La Esperanza", results from this study justifies the importance of conducting more studies on the probability of overflowing of this dam and other dams with similar conditions, in order to prevent damages by designing adequate containment projects.

Acknowledgments. Financial support has been provided to Rosanna Bonasia, Dante Tolentino and Omar S. Areu-Rangel through: Consejo Nacional de Ciencia y Tecnología (CONACYT), México; from the following programs: Cátedras, Retención and National Fellowship respectively. Any opinions, findings, conclusions, or recommendations expressed in this article are those of the authors and do not necessarily reflect the views of CONACYT. This work was partially supported by ABACUS, CONACyT grant EDOMEX-2011-C01-165873.

References

1. Alamilla, J., Esteva, L.: Seismic reliability functions for multistory frame and well-frame systems. Earthq. Eng. Struct. Dyn. **35**, 1899–1924 (2006)
2. Arreguin, F., Murillo, R., Marengo, H.: Inventario nacional de presas. Tecnología y Ciencias del Agua **4**(4), 179–185 (2013)
3. Barreiro, A., Crespo, A.J.C., Dominguez, J.M., Gómez-Gesteira, M.: Smoothed particle hydrodynamics for coastal engineering problems. Comput. Struct. **120**, 96 (2013)
4. Chen, C.I.: Rainfall intensity-duration-frequency formulas. J. Hydraul. Eng. **109**, 1603 (1983)
5. Cornell, C.A.: A probability-based structural code. J. Am. Concr. Inst. **66**(12), 974–985 (1969)
6. Esteva, L., Diaz, O.J., García, J., Sierra, J., Ismael, E.: Life-cycle optimization in the establishment of performance-acceptance parameters for seismic design. Struct. Saf. **24**(2–4), 187–204 (2002)
7. Mockus, V.: Use of storm and watershed characteristics in synthetic unit hydrograph analysis and application. U.S. Soil Conservation Service, vol. NA (1957)
8. Monaghan, J.J., Gingold, R.A.: Smoothed particle hydrodynamics: theory and application to non-spherical stars. Mon. Not. R. Astron. Soc. **81**, 375 (1977)
9. Ramírez, A.I.: La seguridad de presas desde la prespectiva hidrológica. Tecnología y Ciencias del Agua **II**(2), 157–173 (2010)
10. Sherman, L.K.: Streamflow from rainfall by the unit graph method. Eng. News Rec. **108**, 501 (1932)
11. Tolentino, D., Ruiz, S.E., Torres, M.A.: Simplified closed-form expressions for the mean failure rate of structures considering structural deterioration. Struct. Infrastruct. Eng. **8**(1), 483–496 (2012)
12. Tolentino, D., Ruiz, S.E.: Time-dependent confidence factor for structures with cumulative damage. Earthq. Spectra **31**(1), 441–461 (2015)

Recovering Historical Climate Records Using Parallel Artificial Neural Networks in GPU

Juan Pablo Balarini[✉] and Sergio Nesmachnow

Facultad de Ingeniería, Centro de Cálculo, Universidad de la República, Montevideo, Uruguay
{jpbalarini,sergion}@fing.edu.uy

Abstract. This article presents a parallel implementation of Artificial Neural Networks over Graphic Processing Units, and its application for recovering historical climate records from the Digi-Clima project. Several strategies are introduced to handle large volumes of historical pluviometer records, and the parallel deployment is described. The experimental evaluation demonstrates that the proposed approach is useful for recovering the climate information, achieving classification rates up to 76 % for a set of real images from the Digi-Clima project. The parallel algorithm allows reducing the execution times, with an acceleration factor of up to 2.15 ×.

Keywords: Artificial Neural Networks · Image processing · Climate records · GPU

1 Introduction

Studying the behavior of climate variables through time is crucial for science, industry, disaster prediction, and many other applications. Climate prediction is very important in short-term decision making, e.g. in agriculture, but also for long-term situations, e.g. to know sea levels in the next hundred years. Specific applications, such as pump control on sewer systems, or water level prediction in a flood warning system can benefit of knowing long-term series (30+ years) of climate variables.

The scientific community is interested on recovering climate data stored through the years. When the search looks back in time, climate records are very scarce and difficult to recover. Furthermore, the preservation of records gathered in the pre-digital era is in danger of destruction. In Uruguay, we keep a systematic recording of climate variables from the early 1900s, most of them stored in paper. This data is of great value for science, but it has limited utilization in nowadays computerized systems, mainly due to the paper storage, and of course its preservation is in danger.

A transcription is needed for the historical information to be properly used on nowadays systems. In some cases, just like for pluviometer records, the transcription can be automatized by using digitalization and data recovering. The Digi-Clima project [1] proposes developing an efficient application for digitalizing the scanned output of pluviometers, originally collected in graphic paper bands, recovering the climate data, and storing it in a database of historical climate records.

© Springer International Publishing Switzerland 2016
I. Gitler and J. Klapp (Eds.): ISUM 2015, CCIS 595, pp. 296–310, 2016.
DOI: 10.1007/978-3-319-32243-8_21

Previous articles have presented the application of parallel scientific computing techniques to solve the problem tackled in the Digi-Clima project. In [2, 3] the solutions developed by applying parallel computing techniques in cluster and grid computing platforms were described. Both approaches were appropriate to solve the problem, achieving accurate speedup values when executing in dedicated computing infrastructures. The approach described in [4] is based on using volunteer-computing platforms. All the previous works were based on using specific image-processing techniques for recovering the information, which use several features of advanced MATLAB routines, including interpolation, counting, noise reduction, and others. In this article, we introduce a novel approach to tackle the problem using soft computing techniques: we apply Artificial Neural Networks (ANN) trained on Graphic Processing Units (GPU), to recover the rain information stored in paper data bands.

The main contributions of this article are: (i) introducing an ANN approach for recovering historical climate information; (ii) a deployment over GPUs that allows reducing the execution times significantly; and (iii) the experimental analysis performed using a set of representative images from the Digi-Clima project, which demonstrates the efficacy of the proposed approach, achieving classification rates up to 76 %.

The rest of the article is organized as follows. Section 2 describes the Digi-Clima project and reviews related works about historical climate data processing. Section 3 introduces the main concepts about ANNs and GPUs for parallel computing. After that, the strategies for climate data classification using ANN are described in Sect. 4. Section 5 reports the experimental evaluation of the proposed approach, studying the solution quality and computational efficiency. Finally, Sect. 6 summarizes the conclusions and formulates the main lines for future work.

2   Digi-Clima: Recovering Historical Climate Records

This section describes the Digi-Clima project and related works about recovering historical climate data.

2.1   The Digi-Clima Project

In Uruguay, the National Direction of Meteorology systematically stored climate data (manuscript reports, graphic records of pluviometers and other devices) from the early 1900s. They are very useful for studying climate phenomena and for weather forecasting using numerical models. However, analyzing and using the historical climate data is very difficult due to the paper-format in which they are stored, and their preservation is in danger, because of the paper deterioration when the records are handled.

The Digi-Clima project proposes developing a semi-automatic method for digitalizing the rain intensity records from weather stations across the country, in order to guarantee their preservation. The resulting data is stored in a database of historical climate records, making possible the utilization of the data in numerical models.

The rain records are stored in millimeter paper bands, where a pluviometer recorded the amount of rain accumulated in a certain period for a given zone of the country.

Each band contains the pluviometer records and manuscript annotations: the begin/end of the register, and the rain records scale for the band, among other information. The pluviometer draws a continuous line, reasonably smooth and (piecewise) monotonically increasing, indicating the amount of rain accumulated on the device. The value grows until the pluviometer capacity is reached. Then, a vertical fall to zero indicates that the device is emptied, and the measuring process starts again.

Figure 1 describes the recording process using pluviometers and presents an example of the historical rain records. The sample band shows several of the troubles that make the recovering problem difficult: a discontinuous ink line, ink stains, different intensity levels, and other defects due to measuring using an analogic device. Furthermore, manuscript annotations are also present in the band to account for additional data, usually written by operators when removing the band from the pluviometer.

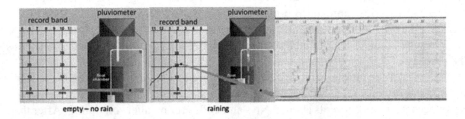

Fig. 1. Recording process and historical record band.

2.2   Related Work

Some previous works have tackled similar problems, but using different approaches than the semi-automatic recovering proposed by Digi-Clima. A number previous works were focused on analyzing specific short-time climate phenomena, thus they analyzed significantly fewer volumes of data than the ones handled by Digi-Clima.

One of the first initiatives for systematic recovering historical climate data was the CLIWOC project [5], which built a database of climate observations based on thousands records (date, location, weather, wind speed/direction, sea, ice, air temperature and pressure) stored manually and in natural language from vessels logbooks between 1750 and 1850. CLIWOC also developed a dictionary that allowed unifying several criteria and terminology used in the logbooks in more than 100 years.

The RECLAIM project [6] continues the work started in CLIWOC, by processing data that were not included in the original process. At the long-term, RECLAIM proposes processing records from the instrumental era (from 1853 to nowadays).

The Old Weather Project [7] focuses on extracting data from digital images by using volunteer human operators. In order to make more attractive the task and gathering more collaborators, the project developed an online game: a player subscribes and chooses a real ship with climate data logbooks to digitalize, earning experience and points by transcribing data, which allows him to be promoted to higher ranks.

The previous projects are related to Digi-Clima and demonstrate that the research community is interested in the problem of recovering historical climate data stored in non-digital format. Other works [2–4] applied parallel computing in cluster, grid, and cloud computing platforms to speed up the digitalization process in Digi-Clima.

The review of the related work allowed our research group to understand the state-of-the-art about recovering historical data. However, none the similar projects have developed efficient methods for automatic transcription of data, because all of them are based on human operators. Furthermore, there are no antecedents of applying soft computing/parallel computing techniques to the recovering process. Thus, the approach applied in this article is a contribution in this line of research, by proposing using an efficient ANN approach to efficiently solve the digitalization problem.

3   Artificial Neural Networks and GPU Computing

This section presents a brief theoretical background on ANN and parallel computing in GPU.

3.1   Artificial Neural Networks

ANNs provide a practical method for learning real, discrete, and/or vector-valued functions from examples, by fitting a training set of input-output pairs. ANNs are robust to errors in the training data and has been successfully applied to problems such as image and speech recognition, and learning robot control strategies [8, 12].

Figure 2(a) presents the general schema of an ANN. There is a set of *neurons* connected with each other. Each neuron receives several input data, perform a linear combination and produces a result, which evaluates some function $f(x)$ for the value x.

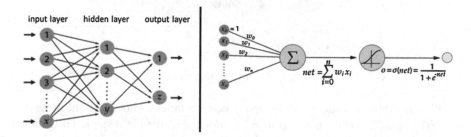

Fig. 2. (a) Schema of an ANN and (b) A single neuron.

The neurons are grouped in several layers: (i) *input layer*: receives the problem input; (ii) *hidden layer(s)*: receives data from the input layer or from another hidden layer, and forwards the processed data to the next layer; (iii) *output layer*: determines the output of the processing for a certain problem instance.

Figure 2(b) shows a schema for a neuron: first, a linear combination of the neuron input data x_i, weights w_i, and an independent coefficient w_0 is made; then, the output is evaluated at some well-known *activation function*, to produce the neuron output.

We use *backpropagation* [9] to train the ANN to recover historical climate data. Backpropagation learns the weights for a multilayer ANN with a fixed set of units and interconnections, by applying the gradient descent method to minimize the squared error between the output values and the target values. The learning problem implies searching in a large space defined by all possible weight values for all neurons. The proposed ANN sigmoid-type neurons with activation function $F(x) = 1/(1 + e^{-x})$.

3.2 GPU Computing

GPUs provide a large computing power by using hundreds of processing units with reasonable clock frequencies. In the last ten years, GPUs have been used as powerful parallel hardware to execute applications efficiently. High-level languages were developed to exploit the GPU capabilities. NVIDIA CUDA [10] extends the C language, providing three software layers: a low-level driver for CPU-GPU data transfers, a high-level API, and a set of libraries for scientific computing. Three software layers are used in CUDA to communicate with the GPU (see Fig. 3): a low-level hardware driver that performs the CPU-GPU data communications, a high-level API, and a set of libraries such as CUBLAS for linear algebra and CUFFT for Fourier transforms.

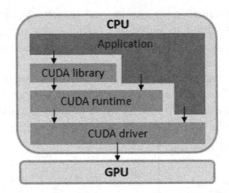

Fig. 3. CUDA *Architecture*

GPUs are able to create, manage, and execute a large number of light processes (*threads*) in parallel. Threads are grouped in *blocks* executed in a single GPU multiprocessor. Three memory spaces are available: the *local memory* of each thread, a *shared memory* for threads in a block; and the *global memory* of the GPU. Two important features to achieve efficiency are avoid thread creation (reducing the creation overhead), and minimize the access to slow global memory, preferably using the shared memory, placed within the GPU chip and providing a faster way to store data.

In this work, we implemented a specific version of the backpropagation algorithm in GPU, taking into account the communication between the GPU processing units. GPU threads are assigned to execute over certain neurons on the ANN. Before executing a on the GPU, a function-dependent domain decomposition is applied to maximize the parallel execution (each GPU thread works independently from each other), and to avoid serializations in the memory access.

4   Historical Climate Record Classification Using ANN

This section describes the proposed strategies for recovering climate records using ANNs. All approaches are based on using the data of a *training set* of images to train the ANN to be used later to process other images in the Digi-Clima database.

4.1   Proposed Strategies

We studied three strategies for solving the problem, which are described next.

Full Image, One Neuron Per Pixel. Our first idea was applying a common approach for image processing with ANNs, using all the image data (one neuron per pixel) as input. This approach has been previously used for face recognition [10, 11], and we adapted it for pluviometer image processing by including a second hidden layer and the parallel GPU version. The output of the ANN is the time series of rain records.

After performing validation experiments, this approach was discarded mainly because the ANN gave much importance to noise (background, annotations), failing to learn the correct information. Furthermore, for Digi-Clima images, we also detected other drawbacks: (i) both ANN/GPU did not properly handle full information from large uncompressed images; (ii) the GPU memory limit is easily reached; and (iii) the processing times increase significantly, making more difficult to validate the solution.

Swapping Strategies. They are based on reducing the input information for the ANN. Initially, we divided the image in zones, taking into account the relative position of each zone for the classification (Fig. 4(a)). This approach was unable to get a good learning behavior, as zones that do not provide useful information confuse the ANN.

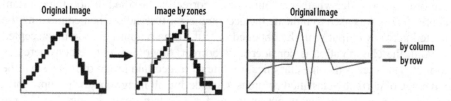

Fig. 4. Swapping strategies: (a) by zones and (b) by rows/columns.

After that, we proposed swapping horizontally/vertically, using rows/columns as the ANN input (Fig. 4(b)). After initial validation experiments performed on random black and white images with size 32×30 pixels, we concluded that using columns is a more useful approach, due to the continuity of the rain records and the reduced influence of noise. Swapping by rows confuses the ANN, mainly due to large discontinuities on row values and due to existing more than one rain value per row.

An improved technique was then included in the column swapping approach, using information from nearby columns for the classification. This information is useful to process regions with discontinuities and breaks in the ink line. We followed an incremental strategy, by studying the ANN architecture and learning behavior for small images (32 × 30 pixels) and then increasing the size and complexity of the images, until finding a correct method for classifying representative Digi-Clima images.

4.2 ANN Architecture and Implementation Details

Input and Output. In order to reduce the information handled, the ANN input is encoded as real numbers. For the swapping strategies approach, when dividing the image in zones, every pixel in a zone is an input to the network (i.e., if the zone size is M × N pixels, the ANN has M × N input neurons). When swapping by rows, the ANN has as many inputs as columns the row has. When swapping by columns, the ANN has as many inputs as rows the column has. The ANN always uses as neuron input the gray-level value of the input image.

Three approaches were studied for the ANN output: (i) using one (real) output neuron for the functional value for each column; (ii) encoding the value for a given column, having as many outputs as rows in the image: the ANN output for a certain column is the index of the activated output, or the one with the largest value if multiple neurons are active; and (iii) encoding the value for a given column in binary: for example if the target output for certain column is 20 (meaning that the most active pixel for that column is on the 20th row), the ANN encodes that value as 10100, meaning that only the 5th and the 3rd neuron are active and the others are not. In this case only $\log_2 n$ outputs are needed for encoding an image with n rows. Preliminary experiments demonstrated that the first and the second approach obtained the best results.

Learning Process. Each column from each image on the training set is used to feed the ANN for training. The inputs for each iteration are the processed column and a given number (*total_neighbours*) of neighboring columns.

In order to consider whether a column was correctly classified or not, the constant *accepted_error* was used to indicate the accepted error threshold when contrasting the expected network output with the obtained output. If the output is inside the accepted threshold, the classification is considered as correct, otherwise will be considered as incorrect. This means that the classification rate over a certain group of images will be the average of correctly classified columns, considering all images on the group. Moreover, the error on the hidden an output layers for a certain image is computed as the accumulated error on every image column, meaning that the error over a certain group of images is computed as the sum of the error on every image of the group.

4.3 Parallel Implementation on GPU

The ANN training phase is a key component of the proposed algorithm for recovering historical climate data. The training applies the *backpropagtion* method entirely on the GPU, applying a functional decomposition approach. Figure 5 shows the conceptual diagram of the steps performed to train the ANN, for the entire training data set.

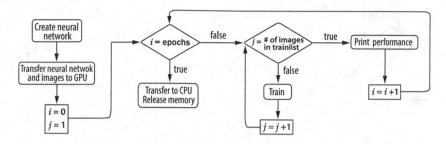

Fig. 5. Conceptual diagram of parallel ANN training in GPU.

Figure 6 presents a schema of the ANN training using backpropagation. This process is a concatenation of functions that execute in parallel, as described in Fig. 7.

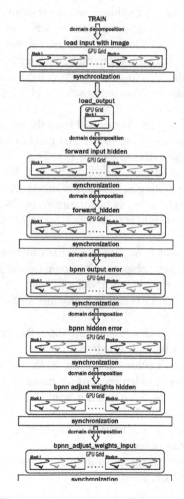

Fig. 6. ANN training: parallel approach.

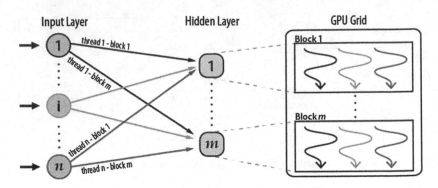

Fig. 7. Parallel ANN in GPU: forward from input layer to hidden layer.

The GPU architecture is mostly exploited when performing training and classification. First, the *load_input_with_image* function, which is responsible for loading the ANN input, is called with as many blocks as *total_neighbours* (neighbouring columns) and as many threads per block as rows the image has; each block will load a column from the image. After that, the *load_output-* function loads the expected output for the ANN for a certain image. This function only uses one block and one thread because of its simplicity.

Then, the *forward_input_hidden* function obtains the output for the neurons on the hidden layer, using data from the input layer. The parallel algorithm creates as many blocks as hidden neurons exist in the ANN (see Fig. 7). Each block will work with one neuron from the hidden layer and each thread in a block will compute the linear combination of the weights corresponding to the neuron, using the data that comes from the input layer (the algorithm works using as many threads per block as input neurons are). The *forward hidden* function is similar to *forward_input_hidden*, but for computing the output for the output layer.

The *bpnn_output_error* and *bpnn_hidden_error* functions are used to obtain the error on output and hidden layers, respectively. *bpnn_output_error* uses one block and as many threads as output neurons in the ANN, and *bpnn-_hidden_error* uses as many blocks as hidden neurons in the ANN and as many threads per block as output neurons in the ANN.

The *bpnn_adjust_weights_hidden* function modifies the weights that propagate from the hidden layer to the output layer. It is called with as many blocks as output neurons and as many threads as hidden neurons are in the ANN. For each block, this function adjusts the weights that go from hidden neurons (as many as threads) to output neurons. Finally, the *bpnn_adjust_weights_input* function adjusts the weights that propagate from the input layer to the hidden layer. It works in a similar way to the previous function, with the difference that the number of threads is larger because of the larger number of neurons in the input layer considered for the problem.

Similar ideas were applied to the remaining functions, changing the role of each block and each thread on a block.

4.4 Other GPU Considerations

Throughout the provided implementation, all constants have their type defined. This implementation decision was made because a precision loss was detected when performing conversions (e.g. `double` to `float`), affecting the numerical efficacy of the proposed algorithm. Since all GPU memory must be contiguous, static structures are used, because when transferring data from CPU to GPU the *cudaMemcpy* function copies only contiguous memory directions. Moreover, the CPU stack size had to be enlarged to 512 MB in order to allow storing big images.

In addition, certain implementation decisions were taken to improve the final performance of the proposed algorithm. First, it was decided to use shared memory in certain GPU kernels, to hide the latency of global memory access. Another element to take into account is that most threads running on GPU performed several calculations, in order to avoid the limit for the number of threads per block in the execution platform (1024 in CUDA compute capabilities 2.0).

A weakness of the proposed implementation is that it heavily relies on the hardware used. This fact impacts on the number of threads per block that can be created and in the use of certain CUDA functions (i.e. use of the *atomicAdd* function with data of float type).

5 Experimental Analysis

This section reports the experimental evaluation of the proposed ANN approach for recovering historical climate records, studying the classification rate and computational efficiency of the proposed GPU implementation.

5.1 Evaluation Platform and Problem Instances

Evaluation Platform. The parallel algorithm was developed in C ++, using CUDA, Python (for auxiliary programs), and Fedora 15 (64 bits) OS. The experimental evaluation was performed on an Intel Core i7-2600 3.4 GHz processor with 16 GB RAM DDR3 and Fedora 15 (64 bits), using a GeForce GTX 480 GPU, with 1.5 GB RAM.

Problem Instances. Three image sets were used in the experimental analysis: (i) 30 small images (32 × 30 pixels) randomly generated for debug and validation: 10 images (320 training samples) in the *training list*, and 10 images (320 samples) in both validation sets (named *test1* and *test2*); (ii) 30 medium-size images (2096 × 456 pixels), without noise and one active row for each column: 10 images (20960 training samples) in the *training list* and 5 images (10480 validation samples) in both test1 and test2; and (iii) 58 pre-processed Digi-Clima images, built by applying filters to eliminate irrelevant data on the original images (size 7086 × 1496 pixels, JPEG, 400 DPI, 3 color channels, 24 bits) and scaled down to 2096 × 456 pixels: 28 images (58688 training samples) in the *training list*, and 15 images (31440 validation samples) in both test1 and test2.

5.2   Results and Discussion

For the algorithm validation, we considered that the rate of correctly classified records for instances never seen by the ANN should be greater than 75 %, meaning that we can rebuild the pluviometer graph without losing relevant information, according to our empirical experience from the Digi-Clima project.

The ANN training is performed using all the images on the training set, and then the performance is evaluated using the images from sets test1 and test2 (concluding a cycle). Depending on image size (due to execution times), training and evaluation over all images is performed n times (n epochs) to conclude an execution cycle. The reported values are the average of 5 execution cycles.

Solution Quality. In the classification experiments, we first studied the classification rates for small images, in order to later scale the solution. We report the results using the swapping by column strategy, as it computed the best results overall.

The results for 32 × 30 images are presented in Table 1, using one hidden layer with 5 and 20 neurons, and using two hidden layers, with 50 and 10 hidden neurons each. The results correspond to 100 epochs and using 30 outputs, one for each row in the image. The considered accepted error rate was 0 %, meaning that the classification for some column is correct if it exactly matches its expected value.

Table 1.   Classification rates, small images (32 × 30 pixels)

Neurons			Classification rate	Learning parameters	
Input	Hidden	Output		Learning rate	Momentum
Sequential					
90	5	30	74.93 %	0.90	0.30
90	**20**	**30**	**93.92 %**	**0.80**	**0.30**
90	50 + 10	30	83.34 %	0.90	0.30
Parallel					
90	5	30	68.62 %	0.90	0.30
90	**20**	**30**	**93.90 %**	**0.80**	**0.30**
90	50 + 10	30	78.27 %	0.70	0.30

It is observed that classification rates up to 93.90 % are obtained when using 20 neurons in the hidden layer. However, increasing the number of hidden neurons does not allow achieving better results; despite of representing a more complex function, it is more difficult to learn the correct information. The differences on the classification rates between the parallel and the sequential algorithm is due to the different representation for floating point numbers in CPU and GPU.

We studied different architectures using several numbers of neighboring columns (0, 2, 4, 6, 8). The best classification results (93.43 % for the sequential and 92.49 % for the parallel implementation) were obtained when using two neighbours, learning rate 0.3, 90 neurons in the input layer, 20 in the hidden layer, and 30 output neurons.

Table 2 reports the results for 2096 × 456 images (raw and pre-processed) using: one hidden layer with 30 and 90 neurons; two hidden layers, with 90 and 30 neurons each; and 456 (one output per row) and one neuron. The results correspond to 100 and 500 epochs (for the best network architecture). The accepted error rate is 5 %.

Table 2. Classification rates, medium-size images (2096 × 456 pixels)

Neurons			Epochs	Image type	Classification rate	Learning parameters	
Input	Hidden	Output				Learning rate	Neighbours
Sequential							
1368	30	456	100	raw	36.68 %	0.04	3
1368	30	1	100	raw	49.90 %	0.05	3
1368	90	456	100	pre-processed	52.91 %	0.10	3
1368	90 + 30	1	100	pre-processed	59.63 %	0.20	3
1368	**90 + 30**	**1**	**500**	**pre-processed**	**74.26 %**	**0.20**	**3**
Parallel							
1368	30	456	100	raw	34.98 %	0.50	3
1368	30	1	100	raw	50.01 %	0.05	3
1368	90	456	100	pre-processed	52.78 %	0.10	3
1368	90 + 30	1	100	pre-processed	61.05 %	0.20	3
1368	**90 + 30**	**1**	**500**	**pre-processed**	**76.23 %**	**0.20**	**3**

The results in Table 2 indicate that the best classification rates are obtained when using two hidden layers, with 90 and 30 neurons. When increasing the number of epochs, the classification rate for the algorithm improves. Using a *learning_rate* 0.20, classification rates of 76.23 % are achieved using 500 epochs.

We conclude that the proposed approach is valid to address the historical records recovering problem. We found an ANN architecture that uses a single output neuron and obtains classification rates greater than 75 % for new instances.

Execution Times. Table 3 reports the execution times of the proposed ANN on GPU when using different architectures and parameters (neighboring columns and neurons in each layer). The execution times are average and standard deviation computed in 10 independent executions performed for each scenario. The *speedup* indicates the acceleration when using the parallel ANN with respect to the sequential one.

Table 3 shows that the proposed parallel implementation in GPU reduces the training times significantly when compared against a sequential implementation. The best speedup is obtained for 60 neurons in the hidden layer: 1.67 when using one output neuron per row, and 2.15, the best overall, when using only one output neuron. For the architecture that obtained the best classification values (one output neuron, 90 + 30 hidden neurons), the speedup value is 1.78. These results suggest that the proposed parallel ANN implementation in GPU is an efficient option to speed up the resolution of the historical climate records classification problem.

Table 3. Performance evaluation of the proposed ANN on GPU

Image size	Input	Hidden	Output	Time sequential(s)	Time parallel(s)	Speedup
2096 × 456	1368	30	456	4933.01 ± 12.91	4613.69 ± 7.29	1.06
2096 × 456	1368	60	456	10523.91 ± 28.95	6285.34 ± 11.14	1.67
2096 × 456	1368	90	456	12037.62 ± 74.37	7856.80 ± 7.49	1.53
2096 × 456	1368	90 + 30	456	16907.92 ± 27.90	11455.66 ± 14.77	1.47
2096 × 456	1368	30	1	3330.55 ± 7.09	2998.31 ± 9.29	1.11
2096 × 456	1368	60	1	9081.93 ± 11.46	4214.83 ± 20.72	2.15
2096 × 456	1368	90	1	10358.51 ± 22.38	5545.01 ± 18.86	1.86
2096 × 456	1368	90 + 30	1	10598.11 ± 27.37	5928.30 ± 21.83	1.78

In order to further analyze the speedup behavior of the proposed parallel ANN implementation, we studied how each function involved on the training process contributes to the overall training time, by performing a profiling for both the sequential and the parallel ANN implementation in GPU. The results are summarized in Fig. 8.

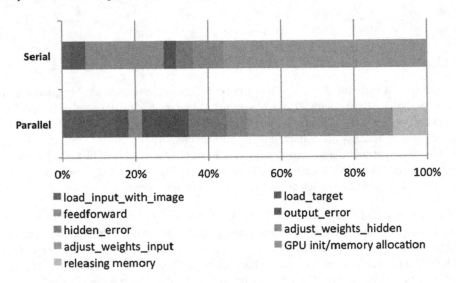

Fig. 8. Profiling (execution times) for the sequential and parallel ANN implementations

On the sequential implementation, the most computationally intensive functions are *bpnn_feedforward* and *bpnn_adjust_weights_input*, demanding more than 80 % of the total training time. The *bpnn_feedforward* function is a set of parallelizable functions (*bpnn_forward_input_hidden* and *bpnn_forward_hidden*) that compute the output for every neuron on the network (a simple linear combination), using only data from connected neurons. In this case, we create a block per neuron (or for a group of neurons) and create as many threads as the number of connected neurons (each thread will compute a simple multiplication and the block will sum the results of all threads).

The *bpnn_adjust_weights* is a highly parallelizable function: it iterates over all neurons and adjusts its corresponding weights using only data from that neuron; it does not need data from other neighboring or connected neurons. This reduces considerably the memory access serialization and allows creating threads that are independent from each other. According to the profiling times, the described parallelization allows obtaining a relative gain of almost 3 when contrasted with the sequential algorithm. This value can be considered a maximum for speedup for this particular problem and network architecture, mainly because the primary source of speedup here is due to decomposing the problem in smaller parts, so every thread on the GPU performs small operations that are executed in parallel. In the case of the presented ANN, the decomposition consists of computing data related to a neuron or a group of them. The main bottlenecks on this implementation are the data serialization on memory access on the GPU and the over-head times that are not present on the serial implementation (initializing the GPU, allo-cating memory on the GPU, copying memory from CPU to GPU, etc.).

6   Conclusions and Future Work

ANNs have proved to be effective for solving many real-world problems, but due to the large execution times required for the training phase, they are not especially popular to handle large data sets and/or complex problems. However, the current paradigm of parallel GPU computing allows achieving significant performance improvements. In this line of work, this article presented a parallel GPU implementation of an ANN approach for the historical climate records classification problem. The proposed approach also provides a general method for solving classification/recognition/image processing problems.

The main contribution of our work is the design and implementation of an ANN-based algorithm that obtains accurate classification rates (over 75 %) on reasonable execution times, providing a new alternative for recovering historical climate data in the context of the Digi-Clima project. The proposed parallel strategy is based on executing multiple threads on a GPU, each one working with multiple neurons, trying to keep threads independent from each other. Each kernel function was designed to take advantage of the GPU architecture (i.e., each kernel process multiple neurons to avoid the thread creation overhead) and the shared memory was used to avoid latency on the global memory access.

The experimental analysis shows that reasonable accurate classification results are obtained, and that the GPU implementation allows reducing the execution times when compared to a sequential implementation. A speedup of 2.15 is obtained when using an ANN with 1368 inputs, 60 hidden neurons and a single output. As presented on the experimental analysis, the obtained speedup is near the best value achievable for a GPU implementation considering the network architecture and the particular image processing problem solved.

The main lines for future work are focused on improving the efficacy and efficiency of the algorithm. Better execution times could be achieved by adjusting kernel param-eters to avoid thread divergence, or by improving the GPU resource management (e.g. shared memory) for problem instances of considerable size. Certain constants in the ANN (e.g. momentum/learning_rate) could be auto-tuned by the algorithm to obtain the best classification rates. The proposed approach can also be used for classification/processing similar types of images produced by other electronic devices, such as electrocardiograms, seismometers, etc.

References

1. Nesmachnow, S., Usera, G., Brasileiro, F.: Digi-Clima Grid: procesamiento de imágenes y computación distribuida para la recuperación de datos del acervo climático. IEEE Computing Latin America (2014)
2. Usera, G., Nesmachnow, S., Brasileiro, F., Da Silva, M., García S.: Recovering historical climate records through grid computing. In: Latin American eScience Workshop 2013, São Paulo, Brazil (2013)
3. Nesmachnow, S., García, S., Usera, G., Brasileiro, F.: Grid computing para la recuperación de datos climáticos. In: VI Conferencia Latinoamericana de Computación de Alto Rendimiento, San José, Costa Rica (2013)
4. Nesmachnow, S., Da Silva, M.: Semi-automatic historical climate data recovering using a distributed volunteer grid infrastructure. In: 5th ISUM Conference, Ensenada, México (2014)
5. García, R., Können, G., Wheeler, D., Prieto, M., Jones, P., Koek, F.: CLIWOC: a climatological database for the World's oceans 1750–1854. Clim. Change **73**, 1–12 (2005)
6. Wilkinson, C., Woodruff, S., Brohan, P., Claesson, S., Freeman, E., Lubker, S., Marzin, C., Wheeler, D.: Recovery of logbooks and international marine data: the RECLAIM Project. Int. J. Climatology **31**(7), 968–979 (2011)
7. Old weather project. http://www.oldweather.org. (Accessed July 2014)
8. Mitchell, T.: Machine Learning. McGraw Hill, New York (1997)
9. Glorot, X., Bengio, Y.: Understanding the difficulty of training deep feedforward neural networks. J. Mach. Learn. Res. **9**, 249–256 (2010)
10. Wilt, N.: The CUDA Handbook: A Comprehensive Guide to GPU Programming. Addison-Wesley Professional, Boston (2013)
11. Balarini, J., Rodríguez, M., Nesmachnow, S.: Facial recognition using neural networks over GPGPU. CLEI Electr. J. **15**(3), 1–12 (2012)
12. Bishop, C.: Neural Networks for Pattern Recognition. Clarendon Press, Oxford (1995)

A Parallel Multithreading Algorithm
for Self-gravity Calculation on Agglomerates

Sergio Nesmachnow$^{(\boxtimes)}$, Daniel Frascarelli, and Gonzalo Tancredi

Universidad de la República, Montevideo, Uruguay
sergion@fing.edu.uy

Abstract. This article presents the application of parallel multithreading strategies for the calculation of the self-gravity force field in astronomical small bodies. Efficient and accurate algorithms are needed to simulate the dynamic of asteroids and comets, which are formed by the agglomeration of many (i.e. in the order of million) small objects. Parallel high performance computing comes to help researchers to perform the required simulations of large systems in reasonable execution times. In this article, we describe several strategies for the computation on shared-memory high performance computing infrastructures and a experimental analysis studying the execution time, speedup and computational efficiency are reported. Promising results are reported for the strategy that applies a smart isolation lineal approach for dividing the calculation work to be performed by each computing element. The experimental results demonstrate that this strategy achieves almost-linear speedup, allowing researchers to perform accurate simulations in reduced execution times, even for those cases where very large systems are studied.

1 Introduction

Self gravity is the main force that maintain together several astronomical objects, including comets and asteroids that are agglomerates of small particles [2]. Small particles in the agglomeration, which are called grains, are subjected to a self-gravity field and also to mechanical interactions (elastic or inelastic collisions, frictional interactions).

For studying the evolution of those systems, researchers must numerically solve the equations of motion of the particles. When dealing with realistic large systems (e.g. in the order of few million particles in the agglomeration) computing the all-to-all interactions between particles has a significantly large computational cost, making very difficult to study the object movement during periods of time. Traditional numerical techniques such as the Discrete Element Method (DEM) are usually applied in the analysis of granular bodies. By assuming that only short-range mechanical interactions exists among particles, it is possible to drastically reduce the computational costs of the all-to-all calculations [11]. However, this kind of techniques are not useful for computing the self-gravity field, because the gravitational influences among particles are long-range interactions. A different strategy must be used to allow researchers to simulate realistic objects in reasonable execution times in this case.

© Springer International Publishing Switzerland 2016
I. Gitler and J. Klapp (Eds.): ISUM 2015, CCIS 595, pp. 311–325, 2016.
DOI: 10.1007/978-3-319-32243-8_22

High performance computing comes to help scientists to perform large simulations and solve complex problems that demand very large computing power, while meeting the time constraints imposed by nowadays scientific standards [4]. Instead of using a single computing resource, high performance computing propose using several computing resources simultaneously (in parallel). This way, a cooperative strategy is implemented, based on dividing the workload into several processes, in order to efficiently solve complex problems in reasonable execution times. A common approach for parallel programming consists in dividing the data handled by the application into several disjoint pieces to be processed in parallel by different processes executing on different computing resources. This technique is called *domain decomposition* or *data parallel*. The different processes communicate and synchronize with each other, via a shared resource (usually a shared memory) or explicit message passing, in order to implement the cooperation that allow solving the subproblems and integrate the partial results to build a solution of the original problem.

In this line of work, this article describes several strategies for designing an efficient and accurate parallel multithreading algorithm for self-gravity computation for granular bodies. We extend the analysis reported in our previous work on the topic [5], where the main details of the computational approach were presented. Our algorithms apply a shared-memory paradigm using a pool of light processes (*threads*) executing on different computing units (*cores*), while sharing a single memory space. The proposed multithreading algorithm allows dealing with realistic million-particle systems in efficient times, and the experimental analysis demonstrate that it scales efficiently regarding both the number of particles and the number of threads.

The article is organized as follows. The problem formulation and a review of the related work is presented in Sect. 2. The simulation approach and the proposed strategies for parallel calculation of the self-gravity in small astronomical bodies are described in Sect. 3. The experimental evaluation is reported in Sect. 4, studying the execution time, speedup and computational efficiency for the simulation of realistic bodies accounting for the agglomeration of up to more than one million particles. Finally, Sect. 5 presents the main conclusions of the research and formulates the main lines for future work.

2   The Self-gravity Calculation Problem

This section introduces the problem of self-gravity calculation and a review of the related work published on the literature about the topic.

2.1   Self-gravity Calculation

The self-gravity calculation problem considers an astronomical body formed by an agglomerate of N particles. Each particle in the body has a mass M_i (different from each other) and its center is located in the position $\vec{r_i}$. The self-gravitational potential on the particle j (V_j) due to the action of the rest of the particles in the body is given by the expression in Eq. 1, where G is the gravitational constant and $\| \overrightarrow{r} \|$ is the norm of the vector $\overrightarrow{r}$,

$$V_j = -\sum_{i \neq j} \frac{GM_i}{\| \overrightarrow{r_j} - \overrightarrow{r_i} \|} \tag{1}$$

When performing a numerical simulations of the evolution for a given astronomical body, the self-gravitational potential on all particles that form the object must be known at each time step in the simulation. However, applying a straight-forward approach for the exact calculation of the self-gravitational potential on all the particles is computationally inefficient, especially when objects formed by a large number of particles are studied, as it demands $O(N^2)$ operations. For example, the direct method is computationally too expensive when N is on the order of million objects, as it is the case for medium-size asteroids in the Solar System. Different strategies have been proposed to reduce the computational cost of the self-gravity calculation, thus allowing to perform realistic simulations in reasonable execution times.

A classical approach is to substitute the exact value of the gravitational potential by a smooth function of the position. Spherical an bi-spherical harmonics have been used as fitting functions [6]. Each particle is propagated in this background field for a short time before the correspondent fitting is computed again. This is a fast method that only requires $O(N \log N)$ operations for the self-gravity calculation. However, the main disadvantage of this approach is the loss of accuracy, because the proposed substitution does not represent a realistic situation.

From the point of view of the gravity force, the mass of distant bodies can be condensed to the center of mass, without introducing significant errors. Another approach proposes to use a hierarchical grouping method. Using a tree structure to represent N-body systems was proposed by Appel [1]. The tree structure stores the particles in the leaves of the tree and groups close particles (i.e., those particles included in groups according to a given distance function) as leaves of nearby branches. A well-known efficient implementation of a full hierarchical tree approach was presented by Barnes and Hut [3], and later incorporated into an integration algorithm by Richardson [8] to simulate the dynamical evolution of planetesimals and the rotational and collisional evolution of asteroids. This kind of hierarchical approaches also requires $O(N \log N)$ operations and provides significantly more accurate results than approximations using smooth functions of the position.

High performance computing techniques has been applied to the hierarchical grouping approach. The implementation by Richardson, Michel, and Walsh [9] uses parallel data structures to simulate up to millions of interacting particles. However, the time step used in the experimental analysis (5 s) is too large to properly simulate the mechanical interactions of soft particles. Traditional DEM simulations usually require time steps of around 10^{-4} s [11]. Therefore, in case the time step is reduced to the value required by DEM simulations, the calculation of the self-gravity is still a too expensive process.

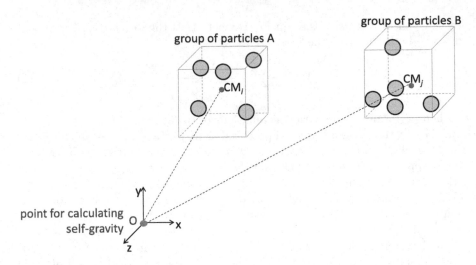

Fig. 1. Conceptual diagram of MADA technique introduced in our previous work [5]: computing the contribution of particles in groups A and B to the self-gravity potential in point O (red) (Color figure online).

Following the hierarchical grouping approach [10], we have proposed a methodology for approximating the influence of distant masses, the Mass Approximation Distance Algorithm (MADA) [5]. MADA applies this approach in order to handle object formed by a large number of particles. Figure 1 present the main concepts behind the MADA approximation: when computing the self-gravity on a given point O, the mass of distant particles such as the ones on groups A and B are substituted by a single mass located in the center of mass for each group (CM_i and CM_j). In the implementation our parallel multithreading algorithm, we use a suitable data structure that groups distant particles and substitutes them by a combined mass at the center of mass.

The MADA strategy allows designing a scalable algorithm able to deal with a very large number of particles by applying parallel high performance computing techniques, such as the multithreading algorithms described in this article. The approach combining MADA and parallel computing helps to perform realistic simulations for small astronomical bodies.

In this work, we focus on efficient and accurate computation of the self-gravity interactions between a large number of particles (i.e. more than a million particles) in an agglomerated object, by designing and implementing different parallel multithreading techniques.

3   The Proposed Parallel Multithreading Strategies for Self-gravity Calculation

3.1   General Scheme of the Parallel Multithreading Algorithm

The parallel multithreading algorithm follows a general scheme that applies a domain decomposition approach. Using the information about the domain and the set of particles to simulate, a tri-dimensional grid that overlaps with the particles is generated. Cells within the grid define the minimum processing unit for the calculation. The algorithm considers each cell in the grid and iterates over all the other cells, computing the gravity influence over (a virtual point in the center of) the first cell. The MADA technique is used to compute the center of mass for distant cells, thus reducing the number of interactions in the calculation. A dynamic grid cell subdivision is applied considering different "levels", according to the distance to the point where the calculation is performed (see [5]).

The parallel computation is performed for both the self-gravity calculation in the points defined by the grid and the interpolation for points that are not defined in the grid.

The diagram in Fig. 2 graphically shows the different sections of the parallel multithreading algorithm. The main stages are the domain decomposition, the self-gravity calculation, and the interpolation for values that are not in the grid. Control routines such as thread barriers and synchronization are also shown to describe how the parallel algorithm works.

Specifically, five major stages are defined in the algorithm:

1. *initialization*: the relevant parameters for the simulation (e.g. size of the simulation domain, number of particles, etc.) are read from a configuration file, and the shared memory space used for communication and synchronization is initialized;
2. *creation of threads*: the pool of threads, its associated data structures, and all other necessary objects are created;
3. *self-gravity calculation*: the self-gravity computation itself is performed in a parallel section by the pool of *worker* threads;
4. *interpolation*: applies an interpolation technique to compute the self-gravity potential in those points that are not in the grid; this task is performed in a parallel section by the same pool of threads used to compute the self-gravity;
5. *output*: write results of the self-gravity calculation for the entire domain (grid+interpolation points).

The most time-consuming stages in the algorithm are the self-gravity calculation and the interpolation. Thus, the algorithm uses a pool of threads to perform these tasks in parallel. By using the pool of threads and a dynamic workload assignment, we apply a reutilization approach that greatly improves the computational efficiency by avoiding to perform superfluous thread creation/destroying operations, which will have a negative impact on performance. In addition, a repository of calculated data is used to avoid recomputing the same value more than once and a specific fast access data structure is used to store information about particles and cells.

3.2   Strategies for Self-gravity Calculation

We studied several strategies for self-gravity calculation, which apply different approaches for dividing the work to be performed by each thread in the parallel

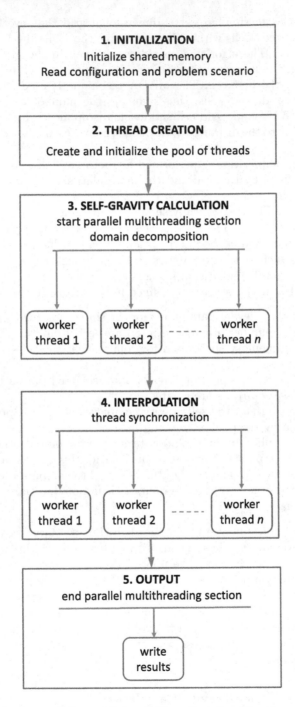

Fig. 2. General scheme of the parallel multithreading algorithm for self-gravity calculation.

implementation of the proposed multithreading algorithm. All strategies are used to implement the iteration in the group of cells (and sub-cells) proposed by the MADA technique in order to compute the self-gravity for the group of particles according to the expression in Eq. 1. The strategies differ in the way they process the data, i.e. how they iterate over the calculation points, and in the assignment of cells to each thread. The strategies are described next:

– *Interlocking linear strategy* (single starting point): this strategy implements a simple linear assignment of cells to threads. Threads are ordered lexicographically from 0 to n, and all threads start from the same initial point. The first free cell (cell #0) is assigned to the first thread, the second free cell (cell #1) is assigned to the second thread, and so on, until all threads have a cell to perform the computation. When the first round of assignments is computed, a second one is started, taking into account the unprocessed cells in the computing domain (i.e. a *dynamic* workload assignment is applied). Figure 3 represents the interlocking linear strategy, where each color is used to represent the cells assigned to a different thread (colors represent cells already processed and light colors represent unprocessed cells). An array of semaphores is used to avoid a single cell to be processed by more than one thread, thus avoiding repeating the calculations. Each semaphore is used to synchronize the access to the shared memory region that stores the status of each cell (unprocessed, processing, processed).
– *Circular concentric strategy* (dual starting points): this strategy is conceived to improve the previous one, taking into account the calculations performed,

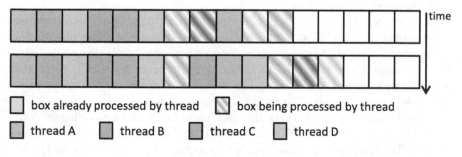

Fig. 3. Diagram of the *interlocking linear* strategy (Color figure online).

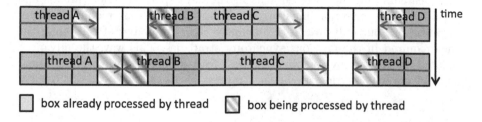

Fig. 4. Diagram of the *circular* concentric strategy.

the order of the calculations, and the values already stored in the process. Half of the threads start from the grid center, and the other half of threads start from the grid border. Each time that a thread starts execution, it computes the center of mass for the corresponding cell. This value does not change during the computation, because it only depends on the particles in the cell. Thus, it can be stored (*cached*) as a data associated to the cell, to be used by other threads during the calculation. The strategy relies on re-using the computed center of mass in the procedure: threads starting from the center of the grid compute and cache values for cells near the center of the grid, to be used by threads starting from the border, and vice versa. Figure 4 represents the computations in the circular concentric strategy. Semaphores are still needed to synchronize the access to shared memory and to avoid processing the same data more than once.

- *Basic isolated linear strategy* (multiple starting points): this strategy propose the utilization of threads that start from different (non-consecutive) cells. Threads are uniformly distributed in order to minimize collisions in the access to shared memory, and the cells are processed linearly. Considering a set of cells c_i, i from 0 to n, and the set of threads t_j, j from 0 to $h-1$, the set of cells is divided such that thread t_j is assigned to compute from cell $j \times \frac{n}{h}$. Each thread executes in a separated set of cells and no explicit synchronization (using semaphores) is needed. Figure 5 represents the computations in the basic isolated linear strategy. The dynamic workload assignment is not applied in this strategy, trying to improve the computational efficiency by avoiding the synchronization and the use of semaphores. As a consequence, the strategy is prone to load balancing issues when a given threads requires a larger execution time than the others.

- *Advanced isolated linear strategy* (multiple starting points): this strategy tries to overcome the load balancing problems detected in the previous one. Instead of working on isolated sets of cells, this method gives each thread the capability of start processing cells from the data space of another thread, after finishing processing its own cells. The main ideas of the computations in the advanced isolated linear strategy are represented in Fig. 6.

This strategy comprises two different stages: the initial processing is identical to the basic isolated linear strategy, assigning a different set of cells to each thread. However, once a thread finishes processing the initial data, in the second stage each thread works like in the interlocking linear strategy. Threads start searching for unprocessed cells in the data space of other threads and performing the corresponding computation. Semaphores are required for synchronization, but only over a significantly shorter number of cells than the ones required in the previous synchrony strategies. This way, the advanced isolated linear strategy combines the best features of the basic isolated linear strategy and the interlocking linear strategy.

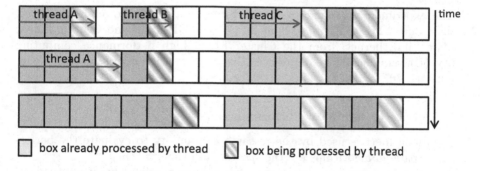

Fig. 5. Diagram of the *basic isolated linear* strategy.

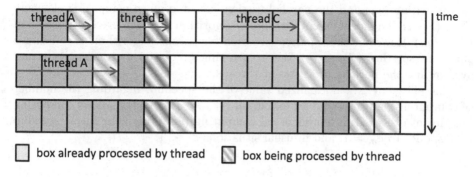

Fig. 6. Diagram of the *advanced* isolated linear strategy.

4   Experimental Analysis

This section reports the experimental analysis of the proposed multithreading algorithm for self-gravity calculation.

4.1   Problem Instances

The proposed multithreading algorithm for self-gravity calculation was evaluated over different scenarios that model realistic agglomerates. Particles are assumed to be of different size, and they are enclosed in a sphere. Three scenarios were defined by varying the number of particles and the radii of the sphere:

- *Scenario A – small:* contains 17621 particles in a sphere of radius 10 m.
- *Scenario B – medium:* contains 148435 particles in a sphere of radius 20 m.
- *Scenario C – large:* contains 1218024 particles in a sphere of radius 40 m.

4.2   Development and Execution Platform

The proposed multithreading algorithm for self-gravity calculation was implemented in the C programming language, using the `pthread` library and the GNU gcc compiler.

The experimental evaluation was performed on a Dell Power Edge server, Magny-Cours AMD Opteron 6172 at 2.1 GHz, 24 GB RAM and CentOS Linux, and Gigabit Ethernet, from the Cluster FING high performance computing facility (Universidad de la República, Uruguay, website http://www.fing.edu. uy/cluster) [7].

4.3   Metrics to Evaluate Performance

The common metrics used by the research community to evaluate the performance of parallel algorithms are the *speedup* and the *efficiency*.

The speedup evaluates how much faster is a parallel algorithm than its sequential version. It is defined as the ratio of the execution times of the sequential algorithm (T_1) and the parallel version executed on m computing elements (T_m) (Eq. 2). The ideal case for a parallel algorithm is to achieve linear speedup $(S_m = m)$. However, the common situation for parallel algorithms is to achieve sublinear speedup $(S_m < m)$, due to the times required to communicate and synchronize the parallel processes or threads.

The efficiency is a normalized value of the speedup, regarding the number of computing elements used for execution (Eq. 3). This metric allows comparing algorithms executed in non-identical computing platforms. The linear speedup corresponds to $e_m = 1$, and in usual situations $e_m < 1$.

$$S_m = \frac{T_1}{T_m}. \tag{2}$$

$$e_m = \frac{S_m}{m}. \tag{3}$$

4.4   Analysis of Workload Distribution Strategies

In order to analyze the computational efficiency of the different workload distribution strategies, we performed an experimental evaluation using scenario C (the largest one, considering 1218024 particles in a sphere of radius 40 m.) and 12 threads to execute the parallel algorithm.

Table 1 reports the average and standard deviation (σ) on the execution times for each one of the proposed strategies for workload distribution, obtained in five independent executions performed for each strategy.

From the results reported in Table 1 we conclude that the *advanced isolated linear* strategy allows achieving the best performance for the problem instances solved. It is also the most robust strategy, as suggested by the lowest value of standard deviation among the compared methods. The interlocking linear strategy is the second-best option. The circular concentric strategy does not takes advantage of the precomputed values; on the contrary, the complex logic included to handle the threads synchronization and the circular distributions makes the strategy less efficient than the interlocking method.

The basic isolated linear strategy perform the worst, mainly due to the imbalance in the workload performed by each thread. In this strategy, the performance

Table 1. Execution time analysis of the proposed strategies for workload distribution in the parallel algorithm.

Strategy	Execution time (s)	
	Average	σ
Interlocking linear	186.2	4.6
Circular concentric	198.3	10.6
Basic isolated linear	254.0	19.2
Advanced isolated linear	180.1	2.7

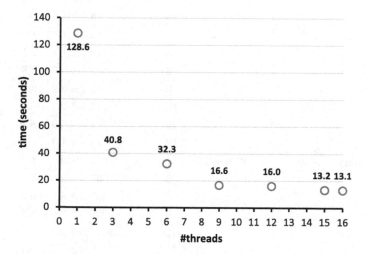

Fig. 7. Execution time results (scenario A, radius 10 m, 17621 particles).

of the algorithm is constrained by the execution time of the slowest thread. However, when including the two-stages operation, the advanced isolated linear strategy allows reducing the execution time significantly.

All results reported in the following subsection were computed using the advanced isolated linear strategy for workload distribution in the parallel multithreading algorithm.

4.5   Results and Discussion

Numerical Efficacy. In order to test the numerical errors of the proposed multithreading method for self-gravity calculation, we solved a problem with 1022208 particles of the same size (0.34 m each) enclosed in a sphere of radius 40 m, and using a single thread. This problem has spherical symmetry, and the analytical expression for the gravitational potential as a function of the distance to the center of mass is known, allowing to compare the results of our mass approximation method against the exact theoretical value. The absolute error respect to the theoretical gravitational potential estimate was always less than

Table 2. Experimental results: execution time and speedup of the multithreading algorithm using different number of threads, for the three studied problem scenarios.

Scenario	Radius (m)	#Particles	#Threads	Time (s)	Speedup
A – small	10	17621	1	128.6 ± 2.8	1.0
			3	40.8 ± 6.0	3.2
			6	32.3 ± 1.2	4.0
			9	16.6 ± 1.0	7.7
			12	16.0 ± 0.4	8.0
			15	13.2 ± 1.0	9.7
			16	13.1 ± 1.6	**9.8**
B – medium	20	148435	1	206.1 ± 1.3	1.0
			3	98.7 ± 1.7	2.1
			6	53.8 ± 0.7	3.8
			9	33.1 ± 0.9	6.2
			12	28.5 ± 0.7	7.2
			15	24.5 ± 0.9	**8.4**
			16	24.8 ± 1.4	8.3
C – large	40	1218024	1	1911.3 ± 9	1.0
			3	537.3 ± 0.8	3.6
			6	302.2 ± 3.9	6.3
			9	225.3 ± 3.4	8.5
			12	180.3 ± 3.1	10.6
			15	146 ± 1.6	13.1
			16	142.5 ± 3.8	**13.4**

10^{-4} J/kg. The relative error respect to the theoretical gravitational potential estimate in all computations was below 0.1 %.

Computational Efficiency. Table 2 reports the computational efficiency results (execution time and speedup) of the multithreading algorithm using different number of threads, for the three studied problem scenarios. The average and standard deviation results for the execution time are computed over six different (independent) executions performed for each scenario and each number of threads. Figures 7, 8 and 9 graphically reports the execution time for each problem scenario when varying the number of threads.

The results reported in Table 2 and Figs. 7, 8 and 9 demonstrate that the proposed algorithm is able to significantly improve the time required for the self-gravity calculation.

When using 16 threads, the multithreading algorithm achieves a speedup factor of 13.4 for the largest scenario, which correspond to a computational efficiency of 0.85. The speedup behavior of the proposed multithreading algorithm

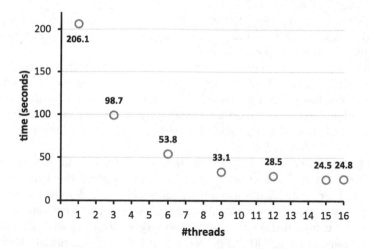

Fig. 8. Execution time results (scenario B, radius 20 m, 148435 particles).

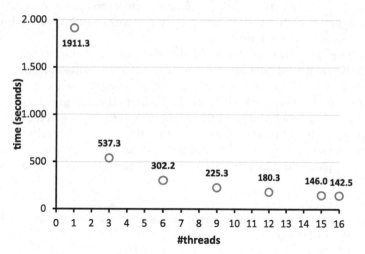

Fig. 9. Execution time results (scenario C, radius 40 m, 1218024 particles).

is close to linear. Furthermore, the best speedup/efficiency results are obtained for the simulation that handles the largest number of particles, demonstrating a good scalability behavior. Simulations of more than one million particles, which demand 1920 s (more than half an hour) can be performed in less than two and a half minutes by using 16 threads.

5   Conclusions and Future Work

This article has presented a parallel multithreading algorithm for computing the self-gravity interactions in astronomical objects formed by the agglomeration of many particles. Several strategies for workload distribution have been proposed in order to design an efficient, fully-scalable method that allows performing realistic simulations in reduced execution times.

We perform an experimental evaluation of the proposed multithreading algorithm, comparing different strategies for workload assignment. The advanced isolated linear strategy, using multiple starting points was the most efficient strategy among the studied variants, applying a two-stages processes that allows reducing the number of synchronization between threads while also avoiding delays due to non-balanced workloads.

The experimental results demonstrate that the proposed multithreading algorithm for self-gravity calculation is able to significantly reduce the execution times required for simulation, especially when solving problem instances involving a large (i.e. more than a million) particles. Efficient speedup values are obtained when using 16 threads to solve the largest scenario with 1218024 particles in a sphere of radius 40 m The correspondent computational efficiency in 0.85, demonstrating a very good scalability behavior.

The main lines for future work are focused on improving the parallel algorithm by further studying the influence of synchronization and shared memory access when using a large number of threads.

We are currently working on including the proposed multithreading algorithm for self-gravity calculation into the ESyS Particle software, following our previous work [11]. When combined with mechanical interactions (e.g. collisions) the computed gravitational potential will be computed in the grid nodes, approximated using the interpolation, and then substituted by a smooth function of the position for a number of time steps, before computing the self-gravity field again. This approach can also benefit of distributed memory parallel computing, which is currently implemented in ESyS particle using the Message Passing Interface library.

Acknowledgment. The research reported in this article is partly supported by ANII and PEDECIBA, Uruguay.

References

1. Appel, A.W.: An efficient program for many-body simulation. SIAM J. Sci. Stat. Comp. **6**(1), 85–103 (1985)
2. Asphaug, E.: The shifting sands of asteroids. Science **316**, 993–994 (2007)
3. Barnes, J., Hut, P.: A hierarchical $\mathcal{O}$ ($N \log N$) force-calculation algorithm. Nature **324**(6096), 446–449 (1986)
4. Foster, I.: Designing and Building Parallel Programs: Concepts and Tools for Parallel Software Engineering. Addison-Wesley Longman Publishing Co., Inc., Boston (1995)
5. Frascarelli, D., Nesmachnow, S., Tancredi, G.: High-performance computing of self-gravity for small solar system bodies. IEEE Comput. **47**(9), 34–39 (2014)
6. Hockney, R., Eastwood, J.: Computer Simulation Using Particles. McGraw-Hill, New York (1981)

7. Nesmachnow, S.: Computación científica de alto desempeño en la Facultad de Ingeniería, Universidad de la República. Rev. Asoc. Ing. Uruguay **61**, 12–15 (2010). (text in Spanish)
8. Richardson, D.: Tree code simulations of planetary rings. Mon. Not. Roy. Astron. Soc. **269**, 493 (1994)
9. Richardson, D., Michel, P., Walsh, K., Flynn, K.: Numerical simulations of asteroids modelled as gravitational aggregates with cohesion. Planet. Space Sci. **57**, 183–192 (2009)
10. Sánchez, D., Scheeres, D.: DEM simulation of rotation-induced reshaping and disruption of rubble-pile asteroids. Icarus **218**, 876–894 (2012)
11. Tancredi, G., Maciel, A., Heredia, L., Richeri, P., Nesmachnow, S.: Granular physics in low-gravity environments using discrete element method. Mon. Not. R. Astron. Soc. **420**, 3368–3380 (2012)

Simulating Radially Outward Winds Within a Turbulent Gas Clump

Guillermo Arreaga-García[1](✉) and Silvio Oreste Topa[2]

[1] Departamento de Investigación en Física,
Universidad de Sonora Hermosillo, Sonora, Mexico
garreaga@cifus.uson.mx
[2] EESA Num. 1, Tornquist, Pcia. de Buenos Aires, Argentina

Abstract. By using the particle-based code Gadget2, we follow the evolution of a gas clump, in which a gravitational collapse is initially induced. The particles representing the gas clump have initially a velocity according to a turbulent spectrum built in a Fourier space of 64^3 grid elements. In a very early stage of evolution of the clump, a set of gas particles representing the wind, suddenly move outwards from the clump's center. We consider only two kinds of winds, namely: one with spherical symmetry and a second one being a bipolar collimated jet. In order to assess the dynamical change in the clump due to interaction with the winds, we show iso-velocity and iso-density plots for all our simulations.

Keywords: Winds · Turbulence · Collapse · Hydrodynamics · Simulations

1   Introduction

Stars are born in large gas structures made of molecular hydrogen. These gas structures are named clumps; see Ref. [1]. These clumps have typical sizes and masses of a few pc (parsecs) and a few hundred or even thousands of $M_\odot$ (solar masses), respectively[1].

The physical process by which the molecular gas is transformed from a gas structure into some stars is mainly gravitational collapse, whose main effects on the gas clump are that the gas density is increased while its size is reduced. At some point during this transformation process from gas to star, the densest gas structures settled down in more or less dynamically stable gas objects called protostars[2]. For instance, the number density of a typical large clump structure ranges around 10^3 molecules per cm^{-3} whilst that of a typical protostar ranges

---

[1] A parsec (pc) is equivalent to 3.08×10^{18} cm and a solar mass $M_\odot$ is equivalent to 1.99×10^{33} g.

[2] Any star does radiate its own energy produced by thermonuclear reactions in its interior, but a protostar does not. This is the main difference between a star and a protostar; but they can share some dynamical properties as they are stable structures of different stages of the same formation process.

© Springer International Publishing Switzerland 2016
I. Gitler and J. Klapp (Eds.): ISUM 2015, CCIS 595, pp. 326–342, 2016.
DOI: 10.1007/978-3-319-32243-8_23

around 10^{14} molecules per cm^{-3}. To achieve a better understanding of the huge change in scales, we mention that the number density of a typical star is around 10^{24} molecules per cm^{-3}.

The process of gravitational collapse is not the only process acting upon the gas structures in the interstellar medium, as many other phenomena can have a great influence on the evolution of the clump, among others: (i) the highly ionized gas ejected by the explosion of supernovas; (ii) the bipolar collimated winds ejected by a massive protostar; (iii) rapidly expanding H_{II} regions which hit the slower and less dense gas structures.

Recently, in Ref. [2], a set of SPH simulations were conducted to study star formation triggered by an expanding H_{II} region within a spherical gas structure with uniform density that was not globally collapsing. The expanding shock plays the role of a snowplow, which sweeps out the gas of the surrounding medium. The density of the swept out gas increases as a consequence of this agglomeration process, and a gravitational collapse may then be locally initiated. Small gas over-densities can be formed in this way, which may achieve the protostar stage. Because these two processes are complementary in forming proto-stars, this star formation scenario was named the collect and collapse model.

Furthermore, in order to study the effects of proto-stellar outflows on the turbulence of a star forming region, in Refs. [3,4], magneto-hydrodynamics simulations (MHD) were conducted with a mesh based code which implements the Adaptive Mesh Refinement technique (AMR).

In this paper, we investigate the change in the dynamical configuration of a typical turbulent clump when a wind of particles is outwardly ejected from the central region of the clump. The most important difference between the present paper and Ref. [2] is the turbulent nature of our clump. Turbulence makes a big change in the spatial distribution as the clump becomes filamentary and flocculent.

2   The Physical System

In this section we briefly describe the physics of the clump and the winds, which will be considered in the following sections.

2.1   The Initial Clump

We here consider a typical spherical clump with a radius $R_0 = 2$ pc and mass $M_0 = 1219\,M_\odot$. Initially, it has a radially uniform density distribution with an average density given by $\rho_0 = 2.4 \times 10^{-21}\,\mathrm{g\,cm^{-3}}$, which is equivalent to a number density $n_0 \approx 600$ molecules cm^{-3} for molecular hydrogen with molecular mass $\mu = 4.0 \times 10^{-24}\,\mathrm{g/mol}$. The size and mass of this clump are chosen here to be typical in the statistical sense, in accordance with Ref. [1].

The free fall time t_{ff} is defined as the time needed for an external particle to reach the center of the clump when gravity is the only force pulling the particle.

In this idealized gravitational collapse, we have

$$t_{ff} \approx \sqrt{\frac{3\,\pi}{32\,G\,\rho_0}} \tag{1}$$

where G is Newton's universal gravitational constant. For our clump, we have $t_{ff} = 1.3 \times 10^6$ years.

Following Ref. [5], the dynamical properties of the initial distribution of the gas are usually characterized by α, the ratio of the thermal energy to the gravitational energy, and β, that of the rotational energy to the gravitational energy. For a spherical clump, the approximate total gravitational potential energy is $< E_{grav} > \approx -\frac{3}{5}\frac{G\,M_0^2}{R_0}$. The average total thermal energy (kinetic plus potential interaction terms of the molecules) is $< E_{therm} > \approx \frac{3}{2}\mathcal{N}\,k\,T = \frac{3}{2}M_0\,c_0^2$, where k is the Boltzmann constant, T is the equilibrium temperature, $\mathcal{N}$ is the total number of molecules in the gas and c_0 is the speed of sound, see Sect. 3.4 for a more precise definition.

The kinetic energy $< E_{kin} >$ can be estimated by $M_0\,v_{av}^2/2$, where v_{av} is the average translational velocity of the clump. In order to have both energies of the same order of magnitude, $< E_{kin} > \approx < E_{grav} >$, the gas elements of the clump must attain average velocities within the range

$$v_{av}/c_0 \approx 3 - 3.5 \tag{2}$$

or $v_{av} \approx 1.6\,\text{km/s}$, for a speed of sound given by

$$c_0 = 0.54\,\text{km/s} = 54862.91 \text{ cm/s} \tag{3}$$

so that the corresponding temperature associated with the clump is $T \approx 25\,\text{K}$.

It is possible to define the crossing time by means of

$$t_{cr} \approx \frac{R_0}{c_0} = 3.56 \times 10^6\,\text{yr} \tag{4}$$

which sets a time scale for a sound wave to travel across the clump. To make the crossing time comparable in magnitude to the free fall time of Eq. 1, the front wave must have velocities around $v_{req}/c_0 \approx 2.6$ or $v_{req} \approx 1.45$ km/s, which are velocities a little bit slower than the ones estimated above, see Eq. 2. Anyway, in this paper we will treat propagation velocities of gas particles ranging around $2 - 3$ Mach.

2.2   The Wind

In this paper we consider two kinds of winds: the first kind has a fully spherical symmetry and the second kind is a bipolar collimated jet.

The dynamical characteristics of the wind strongly depends on its type of source. All stars eject winds of the first kind, which are driven by the stellar radiation. For instance, in cool stars, like the ones observed in the AGB (Asymtotic Giant Branch) of the Galaxy, the winds cause a mass loss in the range

$10^{-8} - 10^{-4} \, M_\odot/\mathrm{yr}$ whereas the terminal wind velocities are around $10-45 \, \mathrm{km/s}$. In OB stars, the mass loss ranges over $10^{-6} - 10^{-4} \, M_\odot/\mathrm{yr}$ and the terminal wind velocities can go up to thousands of km/s.

Supernovas dump around 10^4 joules of thermal and kinetic energy into the interstellar medium. But there are many types of supernovae, so that the mass losses and terminal velocities are very different, see Ref. [6]. For example, for a supernova whose progenitor was a He star, the mass loss and terminal velocities are within the ranges $10^{-7} - 10^{-4} \, M_\odot/\mathrm{yr}$ and $100 - 1000 \, \mathrm{km/s}$, respectively. When the progenitor was a RSG star, then their values range over $10^{-5} - 10^{-4} \, M_\odot/\mathrm{yr}$ and $10 - 40 \, \mathrm{km/s}$, respectively.

It seems that all protostars eject highly collimated jets of gas during their formation process by gravitational collapse. The origin of these jets is still unclear but it may be that the accretion disk and magnetic field around the protostars play a crucial role in determining the velocities and the degree of collimation of the jets. For the molecular winds associated with protostarts of Class 0 and Class 1, the characteristic velocities are around $20 \, \mathrm{km/s}$. However, for optical jets of highly ionized gas, the typical jet velocities are a few hundred km/s; see Ref. [7] and the references therein.

3 The Computational Method

In this section we briefly describe the way we set up the physical system outlined above in computational terms.

3.1 The Initial Configuration of Particles

We set $N = 10$ million SPH particles for representing the gas clump. By means of a rectangular mesh we make the partition of the simulation volume in small elements each with a volume $\Delta x \, \Delta y \, \Delta z$; at the center of each volume we place a particle (the ith, say), with a mass determined by its location according to the density profile being considered, that is: $m_i = \rho(x_i, y_i, z_i) \times \Delta x \, \Delta y \, \Delta z$ with $i = 1, \ldots, N$. Next, we displace each particle from its location by a distance on the order of $\Delta x/4.0$ in a random spatial direction.

As was stated earlier, in this paper we only consider a uniform density clump, for which $\rho(x_i, y_i, z_i) \equiv \rho_0$, for all the simulations (see Sect. 2.1). Therefore, all the particles have the same mass irrespective of whether a wind or clump particle.

3.2 The Initial Turbulent Velocity of Particles

To generate the turbulent velocity spectrum for the clump particles, we follow a procedure based on the papers [8,9]. We set a second mesh N_x, N_y, N_z with the size of each element given by $\delta x = R_0/N_x$, $\delta y = R_0/N_y$ and $\delta z = R_0/N_z$. In Fourier space, the partition is $\delta K_x = 1.0/\left(N_x \times \delta x\right)$, $\delta K_y = 1.0/\left(N_y \times \delta y\right)$ and $\delta K_z = 1.0/\left(N_z \times \delta z\right)$. Each Fourier mode has the components $K_x = i_{K_x} \delta K_x$, $K_y = i_{K_y} \delta K_y$ and $K_z = i_{K_z} \delta K_z$, where the indices i_{K_x}, i_{K_y} and i_{K_z} take values in the intervals $[-N_x/2, N_x/2]$, $[-N_y/2, N_y/2]$ and $[-N_z/2, N_z/2]$, respectively. The wave number magnitude is $K = \sqrt{K_x^2 + K_y^2 + K_z^2}$, and so $K_{min} = 0$ and $K_{max} = \frac{\sqrt{3}\,N_x}{2\,R_0}$. The Fourier wave can equally be described by a wave length $\lambda = 2\,\pi/K$, then we see that $K \approx \frac{1}{R_0}$ and $\lambda \approx R_0$.

Following [9], the components of the particle velocity are

$$v = \Sigma_{-K_{max}}^{K_{max}} \left| K^{\frac{-n-2}{2}} \right| \times$$

$$\begin{cases} \left[K_z\, C_{K_y} \sin\left(\boldsymbol{K} \cdot \boldsymbol{r} + \varPhi_{K_y} \right) - K_y\, C_{K_z} \sin\left(\boldsymbol{K} \cdot \boldsymbol{r} + \varPhi_{K_z} \right) \right] \text{for } v_x \\ \left[-K_x\, C_{K_z} \sin\left(\boldsymbol{K} \cdot \boldsymbol{r} + \varPhi_{K_z} \right) + K_z\, C_{K_x} \sin\left(\boldsymbol{K} \cdot \boldsymbol{r} + \varPhi_{K_x} \right) \right] \text{for } v_y \\ \left[-K_x\, C_{K_y} \sin\left(\boldsymbol{K} \cdot \boldsymbol{r} + \varPhi_{K_y} \right) + K_y\, C_{K_x} \sin\left(\boldsymbol{K} \cdot \boldsymbol{r} + \varPhi_{K_x} \right) \right] \text{for } v_z \end{cases} \quad (5)$$

where the spectral index n was fixed at $n = -1$ and thus we have $v^2 \approx K^{-3}$. The vector $\boldsymbol{C}_K$ whose components are denoted by $\left(C_{K_x}, C_{K_y}, C_{K_z} \right)$, take values obeying a Rayleigh distribution. The wave phase vector, $\varPhi_K$, given by $\left(\varPhi_{K_x}, \varPhi_{K_y}, \varPhi_{K_z} \right)$ takes random values on the interval $[0, 2\,\pi]$. The components of the vector $\boldsymbol{C}$ are calculated by means of $C = \sigma \times \sqrt{-2.0 \times \log\left(1.0 - u\right)}$, where u is a random number in the interval $(0, 1)$. σ is a fixed parameter with value $\sigma = 1.0$.

3.3 The Set up of the Particle Wind

Let us consider the equation of mass conservation for a set of particles moving radially outwards, that is

$$\dot{M} = 4\,\pi\,r^2\,\rho(r) \times v(r) \quad (6)$$

We fix the mass loss $\dot{M}$ as a parameter of the simulation and also fix the wind density to have the uniform value ρ_0. We then determine the wind velocities according to Eq. 6. As the velocity magnitude diverges for particles around $r \approx 0$, we set a cut velocity value such that the maximum velocity allowed in our simulations is v_{max}.

Of course, there are other possibilities, which will be considered elsewhere: one is to fix the radial density $\rho(r)$ and/or the velocity profile $v(r)$ in order to obtain the mass loss $\dot{M}$ as a result. Besides, for modeling an expanding H_{II} region, the authors of Ref. [2] proposed another and more complicated velocity function, but anyway it gives a constant expansion velocity at the last stages of time evolution, so that the average velocity of the shocked shell considered by [2] is $v_{cc}/c_0 \approx 5.6$ or $v_{cc} \approx 3.7\,\text{km/s}$.

3.4 Initial Energies

In a particle based code, we approximate the thermal energy of the clump by calculating the sum over all the N particles described in Sect. 3.1, that is

$$E_{therm} = \sum_{i=1}^{N} \frac{3}{2} \frac{P_i(\rho)\, m_i}{\rho_i}, \quad (7)$$

where P_i is the pressure associated with particle i with density ρ_i by means of the equation of state given in Eq. 12. In a similar way, the approximate potential energy is

$$E_{pot} = \sum_{i=1}^{N} \frac{1}{2} m_i \, \Phi_i. \tag{8}$$

where Φ_i is the gravitational potential of particle i. For the clump considered in this paper, the values of the speed of sound c_0 (see Eq. 3) and the level of turbulence are chosen so that the energy ratios have the numerical values

$$\alpha \equiv \frac{E_{therm}}{|E_{grav}|} = 0.3$$
$$\beta \equiv \frac{E_{kin}}{|E_{grav}|} = 1.0. \tag{9}$$

3.5   Resolution and Thermodynamical Considerations

Following Refs. [10,11], in order to avoid artificial fragmentation, the SPH code must fulfil certain resolution criteria, imposed on the Jeans wavelength λ_J, which is given by

$$\lambda_J = \sqrt{\frac{\pi c^2}{G \rho}}, \tag{10}$$

where c is the instantaneous speed of sound and ρ is the local density. To obtain a more useful form for a particle based code, the Jeans wavelength λ_J is transformed into the Jeans mass given by

$$M_J \equiv \frac{4}{3} \pi \rho \left(\frac{\lambda_J}{2} \right)^3 = \frac{\pi^{\frac{5}{2}}}{6} \frac{c^3}{\sqrt{G^3 \rho}}. \tag{11}$$

In this paper, the values of the density and speed of sound are updated according to the following equation of state

$$p = c_0^2 \rho \left[1 + \left(\frac{\rho}{\rho_{crit}} \right)^{\gamma - 1} \right], \tag{12}$$

as proposed by [12], where $\gamma \equiv 5/3$ and for the critical density we assume the value $\rho_{crit} = 5.0 \times 10^{-14} \, \mathrm{g \, cm^{-3}}$.

For the turbulent clump under consideration, we have $m_r \approx M_J/(2N_{neigh}) \approx 7.47 \times 10^{33}$ g, where we take $N_{neigh} = 40$.

In this paper, the mass of an SPH particle is $m_p = 1.98 \times 10^{29}$ g, so that $m_p/m_r = 2.5 \times 10^{-4}$ and therefore the Jeans resolution requirement is satisfied very easily.

In a previous paper of collapse reported in Ref. [13], by means of a convergence study, we demonstrated the correctness of a regular cartesian grid to make collapse calculation, as is used here to make the partition of the simulation domain in small volume elements, each of which has a SPH particle located not necessarily in its center, see Sect. 3.1.

4   The Evolution Code

We carry out the time evolution of the initial distribution of particles with the fully parallel Gadget2 code, which is described in detail by Ref. [14]. Gadget2 is based on the $tree - PM$ method for computing the gravitational forces and on the standard SPH method for solving the Euler equations of hydrodynamics. *Gadget2* incorporates the following standard features: (i) each particle i has its own smoothing length h_i; (ii) the particles are also allowed to have individual gravitational softening lengths ϵ_i, whose values are adjusted such that for every time step ϵ_i, h_i is of order unity. Gadget2 fixes the value of ϵ_i for each time-step using the minimum value of the smoothing length of all particles, that is, if $h_{min} = min(h_i)$ for $i = 1, 2 \ldots N$, then $\epsilon_i = h_{min}$.

The *Gadget2* code has an implementation of a Monaghan-Balsara form for the artificial viscosity, see Ref. [15] and Ref. [16]. The strength of the viscosity is regulated by setting the parameter $\alpha_\nu = 0.75$ and $\beta_\nu = \frac{3}{2} \times \alpha_\nu$, see Eq. (14) in Ref. [14]. We here fix the Courant factor to 0.1.

We now mention here that the public Gadget2 code used in this paper, presents some potential technical problems when wind particles are simultaneously evolved with clump particles; these problems are caused by the different mass scales involved, as the discretized version of the Navier-Stokes hydrodynamical equations are written in the so called density-entropy formulation, see Ref. [17]: mainly that the particle time-step becomes prohibitively small to achieve the overall evolution of the system.

We finally mention that the initial condition code was written in ANSI-C and it makes use of a Fourier mesh of 643 grid elements in order to obtain the turbulent velocity field of 10 million SPH particles. It takes 300 CPU hours running on one INTEL-Xeon processor at 3.2 GHz. All the simulations presented in this work were conducted on a high performance Linux cluster with 46 dual cores located at the University of Sonora (ACARUS). The simulations were calculated over 300 CPU hours on a fully parallelized scheme using 12 cores per each run. The proprietary program pvwave-8.0 was used as the main the visualization tool for showing the results of this paper.

5   Results

To present the results of our simulations, we consider a slice of particles around the equatorial plane of the clump; with these particles (around 10,000) we make plots containing two complementary panels: one to show colored regions of iso-density and the other one to show the velocity field of the particles. We also make $3D$ plots built with the 500,000 densest particles of each simulation. Later, we present plots with the velocity distributions and radial velocity profile, for which we use all the simulation particles.

In Table 1 we show the values we use to define the simulations and also we give some results described below. In this Table and in all the subsequent figures, we use the following labels: "Tur" to indicate the gas clump; when the

Table 1. The models.

Label	t_{start}/t_{ff}	$\dot{M}\ [M_\odot/\mathrm{yr}]$	$\frac{R_s}{R_0}$	$M_g\ [M_\odot]$	$M_\infty\ [M_\odot]$	v_{max}/c_s	v_∞/c_s
Tur	0.0	—	—	1219	333	100	10
Tur+Wind	0.05	1.0×10^{-4}	0.1	6.84	359	100	11
Tur+Wind+Col	0.05	1.0×10^{-3}	0.05	4.51	422	100	72

winds appear within the clump, we use the label "Tur+Wind" to refer to the spherically symmetric case and the label "Tur+Wind+Col" for the bipolar jet.

5.1   The Evolution of the Turbulent Clump

One of the characteristics of turbulence is the appearance of a filamentary and flocculent structure across the clump, a structure which can already be seen in the first two panels of Fig. 1. Because of the initial conditions chosen for the clump, there is a clear tendency to a global collapse towards its central region, as can be seen in the last panels of Fig. 1.

We emphasize now a very important fact occurring at the outer regions of the turbulent clump. The turbulent clump is not in hydrodynamic equilibrium and there is no external pressure acting upon the clump, then the outermost particles have a non equilibrated thermal pressure. Therefore, the outer clump particles expand outwards. So, we have to keep in mind this expansion effect for the problem at hand, as we shall quantify the mass of the clump swept out by the winds.

5.2   The Effects of Winds in the Evolution of the Turbulent Clump

As one can see in the two first panels of Fig. 2, a very small fraction of gas particles can attain velocities much higher than those velocities provided from the turbulence alone, which are around 2 Mach. Eighty per cent of the simulation particles have velocities less than $v/c_s < 4$.

The winds are suddenly activated at the time $t/t_{ff} = 0.05$, when the clump has already acquired a fully flocculent aspect, which is a consequence of the huge number of gas collisions produced randomly across the clump. This time also marks the occurrence of the highest peak in the clump's density curve, shown in the third panel of Fig. 2

Besides, we notice by looking at the third panel Fig. 2, that the global collapse of the clump does not change even when the winds are introduced, as the peak density curve of each run goes to higher values. However, the wind of the first kind makes the collapse take place slower as its density peak curve shows less steepness in the middle stages of its evolution.

The iso-density plots for the simulation $Tur + Wind$ are shown in Fig. 3. By the time $t/t_{ff} = 0.36$, we see a void created in the central region of the clump because both the wind particles and those particles which are swept out move towards the outer parts of the clump. However, gravity and viscosity act together in such a way that the particles quickly fill the void, as can be seen in the last panel of Fig. 3.

When we consider the model "$Tur + Wind + Col$", so that a collimated gas of particles is ejected, we see that the effects on the clump are more significant, but essentially the same phenomena as seen in the model "$Tur + Wind$" take place, as can be seen in Fig. 4.

In Fig. 5 we present $3D$ plots of the densest particles for both models. In Figs. 6 and 7 we present $3D$ plots at two different times in which one can distinguish the wind and the gas particles.

We emphasize that the fraction of gas swept out by the winds is really significant: hundreds of solar masses move even far beyond the clump radius R_0. In the fourth column of Table 1, we show that the initial mass contained within the radius R_s (which defines the outer boundary of the initial wind configuration) is around 7 and 5 $M_\odot$, respectively. It is then surprising to notice that the total mass dragged outside R_0 by the end of the simulation time is around 359 and 422 $M_\odot$, respectively, as is shown in the fifth column of Table 1.

Lastly, in columns 6 and 7 of Table 1, we show the velocities attained by those particles located far outside the initial clump. Furthermore, we mention that these velocities are not terminal, but are only the velocities during the time we follow these simulations.

6   Discussion

We mentioned in Sect. 3.4 that the clump under consideration here is initially given a ratios of thermal (α) and kinetic energies (β) to the gravitational energy, respectively, such that the clump collapse is greatly favored. In fact, as we see in Sect. 5.1, the clump presents a strong collapse towards the central region, in which no fragmentation is observed. This behavior can be seen in other turbulent simulations, when the turbulent Jeans mass (in analogy to the thermal Jeans mass) is large, so that only one turbulent Jeans mass is "contained" in the total clump mass, see Ref. [20].

The winds are activated in a very early stage of the clump evolution, when turbulence is still ongoing. Soon after, turbulence quickly decays, so that a purely gravity driven collapse will take place in the clump. As we see in Sect. 5.2, the winds act firstly as a disruptive perturbation on the clump's near environment. Despite of this, the clump particles quickly reform this evacuated central region. Now, in Ref. [21] we found that the wind models show a strong tendency to form accretion centers in the central region of the clump. It was noticed there that great differences appeared when we compared the number and location of the accretion centers obtained for the turbulent clump and for the clump in the presence of wind. Unfortunately, these results are not included in this paper for a lack of space. Although we try to indicate them by means of the first panel of Fig. 5.

Thus, in view of these results, we consider that the expected fate of the turbulent clump is really affected by the wind-clump interaction, as compared

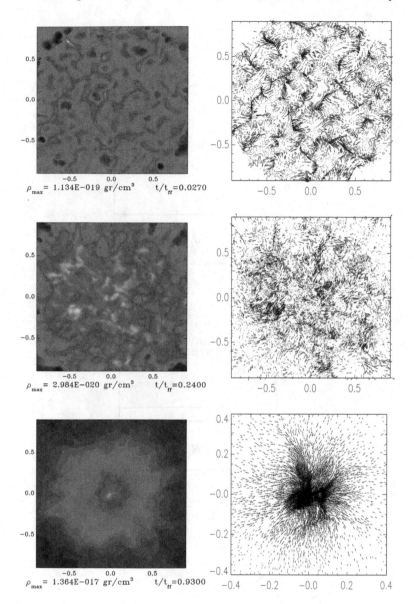

Fig. 1. Iso-density plots for the turbulent clump.

with the purely gravity driven collapse, despite that it seems to be the dominant physics in determining the time evolution of the clump. This behavior appears to be the case in general, at least for observed gas structures around 0.1 pc in size, as is discussed in Ref. [20].

It must be noted that in this paper, as a first approximation, the wind emission is a unique event, as it is emitted just for only one time. It would be

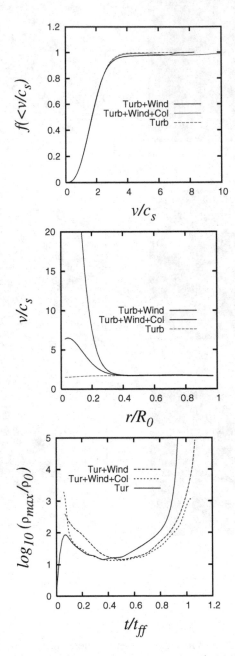

Fig. 2. (top) The velocity distribution of the particles; (middle) the velocity radial profile; and (bottom) the peak density time evolution.

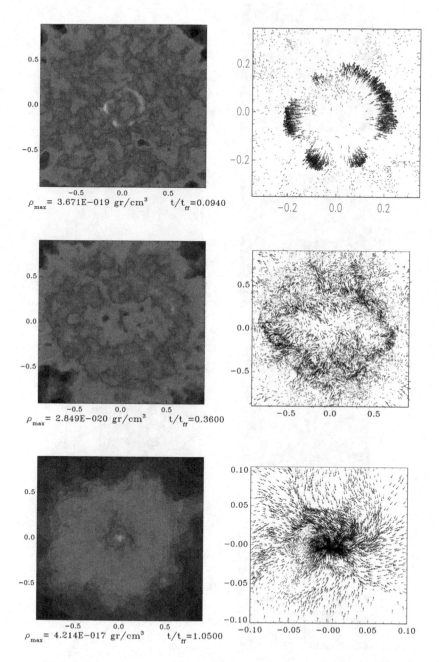

Fig. 3. Iso-density and velocity plots for the model "Tur+Wind".

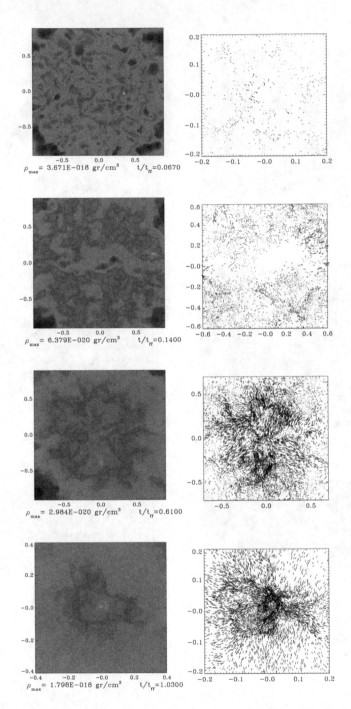

Fig. 4. Iso-density and velocity plots for the model "Tur+Wind+Col".

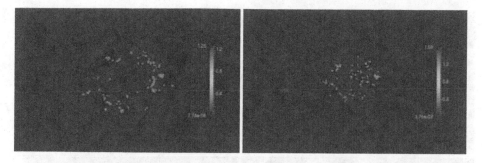

Fig. 5. $3D$ plot of the densest particles for models (left) $Tur + Win$ and (right) $Tur + Win + Col$ at the corresponding snapshots shown in the second lines of Figs. 3 and 4, respectively.

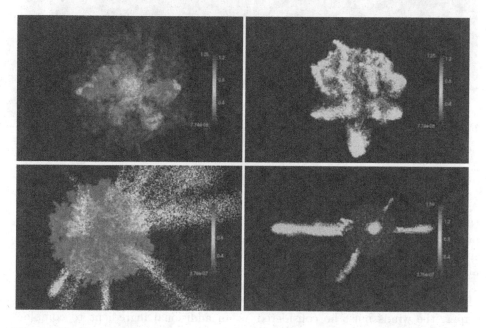

Fig. 6. $3D$ plot of the turbulent clump (in blue) with winds (in yellow) and formed accretion centers (in red) for models (top) $Tur + Win$, and (bottom) $Tur + Win + Col$, corresponding to the plots shown in the second line of Figs. 3 and 4, respectively.

interesting to make that the winds be created and emitted in each time step, so that a continuous emission rate can be simulated. In this case, one would expect that the collapse delay be larger and that the disruption wind effects be more important too.

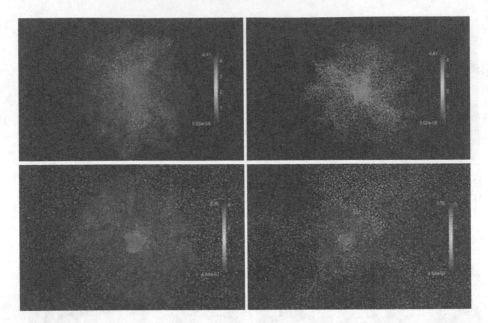

Fig. 7. $3D$ plot of the turbulent clump (in blue) with winds (in yellow) for models (top) $Tur + Win$ and (bottom) $Tur + Win + Col$, corresponding to last snapshot available.

7   Concluding Remarks

A star formation scenario based only on the collapse of turbulence gas structures gives a very highly efficient transformation of the gas into protostars. This points is in contradiction with observations. Besides, a physical system showing simultaneously in-fall and outflow motions are observed in cluster like NGC 1333 and NGC 2264, see Refs. [18,19].

Because of this, another scenario must be considered, or at least a theoretical complement to the turbulent model is needed. As we have shown in this paper, the winds must be considered as an additional ingredient to complement the turbulent model with the hope that this new model can alleviate some of the problems mentioned above as they make a delay in the runaway collapse of the clump, see Fig. 2.

We have shown here that all the wind models show a strong tendency to form accretion centers in the central region of the clump. It must be noted that some differences appear when we compare the accretion centers obtained for the wind models, as can be seen in Figs. 5, 6 and 7.

Acknowledgments. We would like to thank ACARUS-UNISON for the use of their computing facilities in the making of this paper.

References

1. Bergin, E.A., Tafalla, M.: Cold dark clouds: the initial conditions for star formation. Ann. Rev. Astron. Astrophys. **45**(1), 339–396 (2007)
2. Dale, J.E., Bonnell, I.A., Whitworth, A.P.: Ionization induced star formation— I. The collect-and-collapse model. Mon. Not. R. Astron. Soc. **375**(4), 1291–1298 (2007)
3. Li, Z.-Y., Nakamura, F.: Cluster formation in protostellar outflow-driven turbulence. Astrophys. J. Lett. **640**(2), L187–L190 (2006)
4. Nakamura, F., Li, Z.-Y.: Protostellar turbulence driven by collimated outflows. Astrophys. J. **662**(1), 395–412 (2007)
5. Bodenheimer, P., Burkert, A., Klein, R.I., Boss, A.P.: Multiple fragmentation of protostars. In: Mannings, V.G., Boss, A.P., Russell, S.S. (eds.) Protostars and Planets, 4th edn, p. 675. University of Arizona Press, Tucson (2000)
6. Smith, N.: Wondering about things. Ann. Rev. Astron. Astrophys. **52**, 1–45 (2014)
7. Gueth, F., Guilloteau, S.: The jet-driven molecular outflow of HH 211. Astron. Astrophys. **343**(2), 571–584 (1999)
8. Dubinski, J., Narayan, R., Phillips, T.G.: Turbulence in molecular clouds. Astrophys. J. **448**(1), 226–231 (1995)
9. Dobbs, C.L., Bonnell, I.A., Clark, P.C.: Centrally condensed turbulent cores: massive stars or fragmentation? Mon. Not. R. Astron. Soc. Lett. **360**(1), 2–8 (2005)
10. Truelove, J.K., Klein, R.I., Mckee, C.F., Holliman II, J.H., Howell, L.H., Greenough, J.A.: The jeans condition: a new constraint on spatial resolution in simulations of isothermal self-gravitational hydrodynamics. Astrophys. J. Lett. **489**(2), L179 (1997)
11. Bate, M.R., Burkert, A.: Resolution requirements for smoothed particle hydrodynamics calculations with selfgravity. Mon. Not. R. Astron. Soc. **288**(4), 1060–1072 (1997)
12. Boss, A.P., Fisher, R.T., Klein, R.I., McKee, C.F.: The jeans condition and collapsing molecular cloud cores: filaments or binaries? Astrophys. J. **528**(1), 325–335 (2000)
13. Arreaga, G., Klapp, J., Sigalotti, L., Gabbasov, R.: Gravitational collapse and fragmentation of molecular cloud cors with GADGET2. Astrophys. J. **666**, 290–308 (2007)
14. Springel, V.: The cosmological simulation code GADGET-2. Mon. Not. R. Astron. Soc. **364**(4), 1105–1134 (2005)
15. Monaghan, J.J., Gingold, R.A.: On the fragmentation of differentially rotating clouds. Mon. Not. R. Astron. Soc. **204**(3), 715–733 (1983)
16. Balsara, D.S.: Von Neumann stability analysis of smoothed particle hydrodynamics—suggestions for optimal algorithms. J. Comput. Phys. **121**(2), 357–372 (1995)
17. Hopkins, P.F.: A general class of Lagrangian smoothed particle hydrodynamics methods and implications for fluid mixing problems. Mon. Not. R. Astron. Soc. **428**(4), 2840–2856 (2013)
18. Walsh, A.J., Bourke, T.L., Myers, P.C.: Observations of global and local infall in NGC 1333. Astrophys. J. **637**(2), 860–868 (2006)
19. Peretto, N., André, P., Belloche, A.: Probing the formation of intermediate- to high-mass stars in protoclusters: a detailed millimeter study of the NGC 2264 clumps. Astron. Astrophys. **445**(3), 979–998 (2006)

20. Palau, A., Ballesteros-Paredes, J., Vazquez-Semanedi, E., Sanchez-Monge, A., Estalella, R., Fall, M., Zapata, L.A., Camacho, V., Gomez, L., Naranjo-Romero, R., Busquet, G., Fontani, F.: Gravity or turbulence? - III. Evidence of pure thermal Jeans fragmentation at $\sim$ 0.1 pc scale. Mon. Not. R. Astron. Soc. **453**(4), 3785–3797 (2015)
21. Arreaga-Garcia, G., Saucedo-Morales, J.C.: Hydrodynamic modeling of the interaction of winds within a collapsing turbulent gas cloud. Adv. Astron. **2015** (2015). Article ID 0196304

Using a Parallel Genetic Algorithm to Fit a Pulsed Townsend Discharge Simulation to Experiments

Eduardo Basurto[1]($\boxtimes$), Carlos A. Vargas[1], Catalina Haro-Pérez[1],
Gerardo Odriozola[1], Braulio Rojas[2], Jaime de Urquijo[2],
and Alexandre Bekstein[2]

[1] Departamento de Ciencias Básicas, Universidad Autónoma
Metropolitana-Azcapotzalco, Av. San Pablo 180, 02200 Mexico, D.F., Mexico
ebasurto@correo.azc.uam.mx
[2] Instituto de Ciencias Físicas, Universidad Nacional Autónoma de México,
PO Box 48-3, 62251 Cuernavaca, Morelos, Mexico

Abstract. A genetic algorithm has been used to obtain the transport/reaction coefficients which describe the experimental ionic avalanches as obtained in a pulsed discharge operated in the Townsend regime. The calculation of the avalanche currents involves solving the continuity equations for the charged species present in the discharge by means of an explicit finite difference method. This is done by taking into account the drift and reactions of ions and electrons. In this work we apply this procedure to study the discharge of two pure gases, namely, SF_6 and N_2. In both cases the algorithm deals with a large number of transport/reaction coefficients (fitting parameters) and produces a solution in a small number of steps. For this purpose the algorithm generates a population of 480 individuals each one defined by a large number of genes (transport/reaction coefficients). Each individual determines a solution of the ionic avalanches which is compared to the experiment and a fitness function is defined to sort the individuals. This sorted population is then employed to obtained a new generation of individuals by using five evolution rules. The algorithm can be easily parallelized and produces an excellent agreement with the experimental data.

1 Introduction

The number of applications involving low temperature plasmas has been increasing in recent years; such is the case, for instance, of semiconductor manufacturing, high voltage isolation and power transmission systems, sterilization of medical equipment, control of air pollutants, and characterization of chemical reactions involving ions or electrons in the Earth's atmosphere [1–3]. These new applications demand reliable models describing the dynamics of the particular plasma under study and provide a proper understanding of the phenomena without the need of building expensive prototypes. An important requirement of these models consists on a reliable determination of the set of transport/reaction

I. Gitler and J. Klapp (Eds.): ISUM 2015, CCIS 595, pp. 343–355, 2016.
DOI: 10.1007/978-3-319-32243-8_24

coefficients (also known as swarm parameters) such as electron and ion drift and diffusion, ionization, electron attachment/detachment, and ion conversion coefficients. A well-established experimental method of proven capacity for the production of reliable electron/ion swarm parameters is the Pulsed Townsend Method (PTM) [4–10].

In order to determine the swarm coefficients, the theoretical transient current is fitted to the experimental data obtained from the PTM. In turn, the theoretical transient current was obtained by solving the system of continuity equations with the aid of the SIMAV-4 [11–13] code. SIMAV-4 is a very powerful tool to study systems of multiple ions and electrons according to their respective reaction schemes.

The number of parameters to be fitted, that is the transport/reaction coefficients, are 16 and 8 for the SF_6 and N_2 systems, respectively. These numbers are dictated by the set of species and reactions involved in each particular process. Note that this large number of parameters may lead to local minima, and hence the search for the absolute minimum is not trivial. This makes necessary the implementation of a optimization algorithm. In this work we choose the Genetic Algorithm (GA) due to its excellent performance and robustness, as compared to other optimization algorithms [14,15]. Moreover, its implementation and parallelization is straightforward.

2   The Pulsed Townsend Method

This section is dedicated to provide the essentials of the experimental technique, including the experimental setup, the reaction scheme, and the continuity equations that are solved to obtain solutions for the transient current.

2.1   Experimental Setup

The experimental setup is explained in detail by de Urquijo et al. [7]. Basically, the apparatus consists of a vacuum chamber filled with the gas under study at a fixed pressure, with a pair of parallel electrodes inside, connected to a constant potential difference, using a high voltage DC power supply. A photon pulse (2–6 ns FWHM) emitted by a UV laser strikes the cathode. The photoelectrons produced by this action drift towards the anode by the action of an electric field, and can react with the neutral species producing, for instance, electrons, positive and negative ions, and metastable components. The amount and resulting products of the reaction, in turn, depend on the pressure, the external applied voltage, and the gap distance between electrodes. The species produced by the electrons may also react with the neutral components, with the negative species moving towards the anode, and the positive ones moving to the cathode. The total current is detected by a transimpedance amplifier, the output signal of which is captured by a digital oscilloscope and transferred to a database in a computer for later analysis. A scheme of the experimental arrangement is shown in Fig. 1.

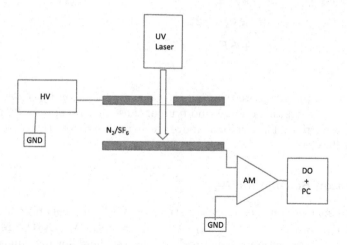

Fig. 1. Schematic layout of the Townsend Chamber, HV: high voltage power supply; AM: transimpedance amplifier; DO: digital oscilloscope; and PC: computer with communications interface.

The total current between the electrodes is the sum of the individual currents due to each charged species moving between the electrodes. It is given by

$$I_T(t) = \sum_{i=1}^{N_c} \frac{q_i N_i(t) v_i}{d}, \tag{1}$$

where N_c, i, q_i, $N_i(t)$, d, v_i, are the charged species number, the index of the charged species, the charge of species i, the number of particles of species i moving between the electrodes at time t, the electrode spacing, and the drift velocity of species i, respectively.

2.2   Reaction Scheme for SF_6

The charged species appearing in the case of the SF_6 avalanches are [13]: e^-, SF_6^-, SF_5^-, F^-, $(SF_6 \cdot SF_6)^-$, and SF_x^+. The corresponding reaction scheme is given by the following equations:

$$e^- + SF_6 \xrightarrow{\alpha} 2e^- + SF_x^+ \tag{2}$$

$$SF_6^- + 2SF_6 \xrightarrow{\beta} (SF_6 \cdot SF_6)^- + SF_6 \tag{3}$$

$$e^- + SF_6 \xrightarrow{\eta_1} SF_6^- \tag{4}$$

$$e^- + SF_6 \xrightarrow{\eta_2} SF_5^- + F \tag{5}$$

$$e^- + SF_6 \xrightarrow{\eta_3} F^- + SF_5 \tag{6}$$

$$F^- + SF_6 \xrightarrow{\delta} e^- + SF_6 + F \tag{7}$$

$$SF_6^- + SF_6 \xrightarrow{\mu_1} SF_5^- + SF_6 + F \tag{8}$$

$$SF_6^- + SF_6 \xrightarrow{\mu_2} F^- + SF_5 + SF_6 \tag{9}$$

$$SF_5^- + SF_6 \xrightarrow{\mu_3} F^- + SF_4 + SF_6 \tag{10}$$

$$F^- + SF_6 \xrightarrow{\mu_4} SF_6^- + F. \tag{11}$$

Here the neutral products are required for mass conservation but could be more complex; nevertheless the amount and type of these neutral species do not affect the discharge current. The symbols above the arrows indicate the corresponding reaction coefficients.

2.3   Reaction Scheme for N_2

The charged species considered for the study of N_2 discharges are: e^-, N_2^+, N_4^+, N_6^+, where the ions $N_4^+ = (N_2 \cdot N_2)^+$ and $N_6^+ = (N_2 \cdot N2 \cdot N_2)^+$ are clusters. The corresponding reaction scheme is described by the following equations:

$$e^- + N_2 \xrightarrow{\alpha} N_2^+ + e^- \tag{12}$$

$$N_2^+ + 2N_2 \xrightarrow{\beta_{24}} N_4^+ N_2 \tag{13}$$

$$N_4^+ + N_2 \xrightarrow{\mu_d} N_2^+ + 2N_2 \tag{14}$$

$$N_4^+ + 2N_2 \xrightarrow{\beta_{46}} N_6^+ + N_2, \tag{15}$$

where, again, the neutral products are needed to fulfill mass conservation, and could be more complex. Nevertheless the amount and type of these neutral components do not affect the discharge outcome. As for the previous case, the symbols above the arrows indicate the corresponding reaction coefficients.

2.4   Continuity Equations

To study the dynamics of the charge carrier densities during a pulsed Townsend discharge, or avalanche, the charge carriers are considered as a fluid. The continuity equation for the charge carrier of species i is given by

$$\frac{\partial n_i(z,t)}{\partial t} + \frac{\partial j_i(z,t)}{\partial z} = \sum_{k=1}^{N_c} a_{i,k} v_k n_k(z,t), \tag{16}$$

where

$$j_i(z,t) = v_i n_i(z,t) - D_i \frac{\partial n_i(z,t)}{\partial z} \tag{17}$$

is the current density of species i, n_i is its density, N_c is the number of charged species; $a_{i,k}$ is the coefficient of the reaction of species k producing species i, and v_i and D_i are the drift velocity and longitudinal diffusion coefficient for species i, respectively.

The system of partial differential equations resulting from applying the reaction scheme to the continuity equation is solved by the explicit finite difference method, where the spatial variable z, is divided into steps of width $h = d/1000$, and the integration time is given by $\tau = h/(2v_e)$.

Continuity Equations for SF_6. For the case of SF_6 gas, the continuity equations to be solved are:

$$\frac{\partial n_e(z,t)}{\partial t} = -v_e \frac{\partial n_e(z,t)}{\partial z} + (\alpha - \eta_1 - \eta_2 - \eta_3)v_e n_e(z,t) + \delta v_F n_F(z,t) \quad (18)$$

$$\frac{\partial n_{6m}(z,t)}{\partial t} = -v_{6m}\frac{\partial n_{6m}(z,t)}{\partial z} + (\beta + \mu_1 + \mu_2)v_{6m}n_{6m}(z,t) + \eta_1 v_e n_e(z,t)$$
$$+ \mu_4 v_F n_{6m}(z,t) \quad (19)$$

$$\frac{\partial n_{5m}(z,t)}{\partial t} = -v_{5m}\frac{\partial n_{5m}(z,t)}{\partial z} + \eta_2 v_e n_e(z,t) - \mu_3 v_{5m}n_{5m}(z,t) \quad (20)$$

$$\frac{\partial n_F(z,t)}{\partial t} = -v_F\frac{\partial n_F(z,t)}{\partial z} + (\delta + \mu_4)v_F n_F(z,t) + \eta_3 v_e n_e(z,t)$$
$$+ \mu_2 v_{6m}n_{6m}(z,t) + \mu_3 v_{5m}n_{5m}(z,t) \quad (21)$$

$$\frac{\partial n_c(z,t)}{\partial t} = -v_c\frac{\partial n_c(z,t)}{\partial z} + \beta v_{6m}n_{6m}(z,t) \quad (22)$$

$$\frac{\partial n_p(z,t)}{\partial t} = v_p\frac{\partial n_p(z,t)}{\partial z} + \alpha v_e n_e(z,t), \quad (23)$$

where n_e, n_{6m}, n_{5m}, n_F, n_c, and n_p are the densities of species e^-, SF_6^-, SF_5^-, F^-, $(SF_6 \cdot SF_6)^-$, and SF_x^+, respectively.

Continuity Equations for N_2. For the N_2 gas, the continuity equations to be solved are:

$$\frac{\partial n_e(z,t)}{\partial t} = -v_e\frac{\partial n_e(z,t)}{\partial z} + \alpha v_e n_e(z,t) \quad (24)$$

$$\frac{\partial n_{2p}(z,t)}{\partial t} = v_{2p}\frac{\partial n_{2p}(z,t)}{\partial z} + \alpha v_e n_e(z,t) - \beta_{24}v_{2p}n_{2p}(z,t)$$
$$+ \mu_d v_{4p}n_{4p}(z,t) \quad (25)$$

$$\frac{\partial n_{4p}(z,t)}{\partial t} = v_{4p}\frac{\partial n_{4p}(z,t)}{\partial z} + +\beta_{24}v_{2p}n_{2p}(z,t)$$
$$- \mu_d v_{4p}n_{4p}(z,t) \quad (26)$$

$$\frac{\partial n_{6p}(z,t)}{\partial t} = v_{6p}\frac{\partial n_p(z,t)}{\partial z} + \beta_{46}v_{4p}n_{4p}(z,t), \quad (27)$$

where n_e, n_{2p}, n_{4p}, and n_{6p}, are the densities of species e^-, N_2^+, N_4^+, and N_6^+, respectively.

3   Genetic Algorithm

The Little Genetic Algorithm, written by Coley [15], is used in this work. The genes of an individual are set as the transport/reaction parameters employed for solving the corresponding system of continuity equations. The list of genes for

Table 1. List of genes for each individual for SF_6 and N_2 cases

SF_6 genes				N_2 genes	
i	gen[i]	i	gen[i]	i	gen[i]
1	α	9	μ_3	1	α
2	β	10	μ_4	2	β_{24}
3	η_1	11	v_e	3	β_{46}
4	η_2	12	$v_{SF_6^-}$	4	μ_d
5	η_3	13	$v_{SF_5^-}$	5	v_e
6	δ	14	v_{F^-}	6	$v_{N_2^+}$
7	μ_1	15	$v_{(SF_6 \cdot SF_6)-}$	7	$v_{N_4^+}$
8	μ_2	16	$v_{SF_x^+}$	8	$v_{N_6^+}$

each individual for the SF_6 and N_2 systems are shown in Table 1. The parameters for the GA, such as the number of individuals inside a generation, crossover rate, and composition of the new population are chosen to minimize the number of steps, and to achieve an error below 5 % of the swarm parameters. The set of operations used to create the individuals belonging to the new generation are described in the following sections. These are Elite Crossover, Mutation of the Elite, Democratic Crossover, Spontaneous Creation, and Elitism Survival.

3.1   Elite Crossover

For the Elite Crossover (EC) process, we define pairs of individuals where one of them is taken from the top 10 % of the sorted population, and the couple from the second best 10 % percent. The couples are randomly matched. In order to preserve genes and the population number, each pair produces two new individuals or offsprings. In order to select which genes are inherited to the next generation, an R vector of random numbers homogeneously distributed between 0 and 1 is created. Thus, if one offspring has the gene of parent 1, the other offspring will have this gene from parent 2. In this way we guaranty that all genes from the parents are present in the next generation. This operation reads as follows for each gene i

$$Child_1[gen_i] = \begin{cases} Parent_1[gen_i] & \text{if } R[i] \geq 0.5 \\ Parent_2[gen_i] & \text{if } R[i] < 0.5 \end{cases} \qquad (28)$$

$$Child_2[gen_i] = \begin{cases} Parent_1[gen_i] & \text{if } R[i] < 0.5 \\ Parent_2[gen_i] & \text{if } R[i] \geq 0.5 \end{cases} \qquad (29)$$

where N_g is the number of genes and $[gen_i]$ stands for gene i, and i runs from 1 to N_g. This operation creates the 20 % of the individuals of the new population.

3.2   Mutation of the Elite

For the Mutation of the Elite (ME) process consists on changing the current value of a gene at most in $\pm 10\%$. This process is only applied to the top 20% of the sorted population. For this operation a vector R_m of random numbers homogeneously distributed between -0.1 and 0.1 is generated. In this case the i-th gene for the mutated individual is given by

$$Mutating\ Individual[gen_i] = Individual[gen_i] * (1 + R_m[i]). \qquad (30)$$

3.3   Democratic Crossover

This process is similar to the Elite Crossover. The difference relies on the fact that the couple of the individual corresponding to the top 10% is selected from the worst 80%. Again, this operation produces 20% of the individuals for the new population. The equations governing this process are identical to the EC process (see Eqs. (28) and (29)).

3.4   Spontaneous Creation

The Spontaneous Creation (SC) process is used to prevent the algorithm to get arrested into a local minimum. A new group of individuals is created with their gene values randomly chosen within the search space. The number of individuals created by using the SC process represents the 20% of the new generation.

3.5   Elitism Survival

The Elitism Survival (ES) process consists on keeping the best individuals; in this case the top 20% of the population survive for the next generation. Note that this process saves computer time since it is not necessary to recalculate the solution of the set of continuity equations.

3.6   Fitness

The Fitness function of an individual, $F[i]$, is defined as

$$F[i] = \sqrt{\frac{1}{n_d} \sum_{j=0}^{n_d-1} (I_{si}(t_j) - I_e(t_j))^2}, \qquad (31)$$

where I_{si} and I_e are the theoretical and experimental transient currents for the i-th individual, respectively. t_j is the time at point j and n_d is the number of experimental points. In our case the perfect individual is the one fulfilling $F[i] = 0$. The individuals are sorted according to their value $F[i]$, in ascending order. Due to the noise in the experimental data, in general it is not possible to obtain $F[i] = 0$. In this work we stop the population evolution once a value of $F[i] \leq 0.173$ is reached.

3.7   The Genetic Algorithm Program

The GA program was coded in Fortran 95 and OpenMP [16] to use multiple processors simultaneously. In order to have a wide range of system applications, the GA subroutines were grouped into one module, and the system-specific routines were grouped in a separated module. The use of modules allows us to easily modify the program to study other gases. In this paper we present two systems, namely SF_6 and N_2. The SIMAV-4 code [11–13] is used to solve the continuity equations for SF_6 and N_2, from which the theoretical transient current was obtained. This last version of the program takes into account the velocity of electrons and ions as fitting parameters improving the previous one [17]. The GA algorithm can be sketched as follows

1. The initial population (G0) is generated with random individuals.
2. Fitness is calculated for all individuals of G0.
3. The individuals of G0 are sorted according to their fitness.
4. Operations EC, ME, DC and SC are performed on G0.
5. The ES operation is performed on G0.
6. New generation (G1) is constructed with individuals obtained in the steps 4 and 5.
7. Fitness is calculated for individuals created in step 4.
8. The individuals of G1 are sorted.
9. A new G0 = G1 is built
10. Whenever the condition $F[i] \leq 0.173$ is not fulfilled, go to step 4.
11. The evolution ends and the best individual is the first one in the list of G0.

In our case steps 2 and 7 are the most computing demanding parts of the GA algorithm since the Fitness evaluation implies the calculation of the theoretical transient current which is done by solving the whole system of continuity equations. This is performed by calling the SIMAV-4 program (command CALL SYSTEM (SIMAV-4)) for each individual of the population. The parallelization of the program is focused on these two steps and the number of threads depends on the hardware. The multi-threaded part of the program was written using the "$OMP PARALLEL DO" OpenMP directive.

We have optimized the parameters of the GA program, such as the number of individuals in the population, the percentages used in every evolution rule, to minimize the number of generations for fulfilling $F[i] \leq 0.173$. This condition assures differences between the genes of the best individuals of the two last generations to be less than 5%.

The fast convergence of the GA for 3 different tests is shown in Fig. 2. Note that the $F[i] \leq 0.173$ criterion is fulfilled before producing 20 generations. The GA parameters chosen for this test are: number of individual in population $NI = 480$, stop searching when $Fitness < 1.73$, and a 20% for the evolution processes as defined in the previous sections. The values of these particular parameters are chosen to get the best convergence.

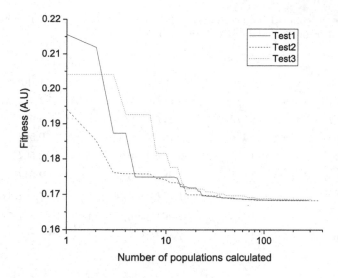

Fig. 2. Fitness of the best individual for the GA program for the system SF_6 as a function of the generation number, showing a fast convergence of the GA for 3 different tests.

4   Results and Discussion

4.1   GA Results

The GA produced excellent results and a fast convergence to obtain the swarm parameters with a maximum difference of 5 % between the genes of the best individuals of the two last generations. The GA succeeded before reaching the generation number 20. During this optimization of the swarm parameters the program solves the continuity equation for only 9600 individuals. This is much less than the number required in an exhaustive search. For instance, by considering a gross search with 10 possible values for each variable it would be necessary to evaluate 10^{16} and 10^8 individuals for the SF_6 and N_2 systems, respectively. The most time consuming part of the optimization is the SIMAV-4 solving process, which uses more than 99 % of the computer power. Hence, the parallelization of this process directly impacts on the execution time. This is straightforward to implement since all SIMAV-4 processes work with different individuals.

4.2 SF_6 Results

The comparison between the experimental and theoretical transient currents calculated for the best individual of the GA is shown in Fig. 3. The experimental transient current corresponds to pure SF_6, for a density-normalized electric field $E/N = 360Td$ (1 $Townsend = 10^{-17}$ V cm^2), and a gas pressure of 10 Torr. We can observe an excellent agreement between the theoretical transient current

Table 2. The outcome of the GA algorithm, i.e., the fitted swarm parameters for the best individual in both studied cases, SF_6 and N_2.

SF_6 genes				N_2 genes	
Gene	Values	Gene	Values	Gene	Values
α/N	$2.66E-17\,\mathrm{cm}^2$	μ_3/N	$3.21E-18\,\mathrm{cm}^2$	α/N	$3.80E-18\,\mathrm{cm}^2$
β/N^2	$5.64E-33\,\mathrm{cm}^5$	μ_4/N	$1.21E-18\,\mathrm{cm}^2$	β_{24}/N^2	$0.05E-31\,\mathrm{cm}^5$
η_1/N	$1.06E-17\,\mathrm{cm}^2$	V_e	$2.13E7\,\mathrm{cm/s}$	β_{46}/N^2	$0.50E-34\,\mathrm{cm}^5$
η_2/N	$1.46E-17\,\mathrm{cm}^2$	$V_{SF_6^-}$	$6.16E4\,\mathrm{cm/s}$	μ_d	$0.50E-17\,\mathrm{cm}^2$
η_3/N	$5.70E-19\,\mathrm{cm}^2$	$V_{SF_5^-}$	$6.98E4\,\mathrm{cm/s}$	v_e	$2.01E7\,\mathrm{cm/s}$
ND	$1.00E-18\,\mathrm{cm}^1\mathrm{s}^1$	V_{F^-}	$1.75E5\,\mathrm{cm/s}$	$V_{N_2^+}$	$7.00E4\,\mathrm{cm/s}$
μ_1/N	$1.08E-16\,\mathrm{cm}^2$	$V_{(SF6\cdot SF_6)^-}$	$2.96E4\,\mathrm{cm/s}$	$V_{N_4^+}$	$1.35E5\,\mathrm{cm/s}$
μ_2/N	$2.86E-18\,\mathrm{cm}^2$	$V_{SF_x^+}$	$7.48E4\,\mathrm{cm/s}$	$V_{N_6^+}$	$5.50E4\,\mathrm{cm/s}$

(I_{total}) and the experimental one ($I_{Exp.}$). It is noted that the current of positive ions SF_x^+ dominates the overall current, while the species SF_6^- reacts quickly to become SF_5^-, F^-, or cluster species of the shape $(SF_6\cdot SF_6)^-$. The latter cluster appears at the start of the discharge and its corresponding current remains almost constant up to $10\,\mu\mathrm{s}$. Thereafter, it continuously decreases until the end of the discharge, being the only species left at this stage. The current produced by the F^- ion has a maximum close to $5\,\mu\mathrm{s}$ and decreases rapidly to almost disappear after $20\,\mu\mathrm{s}$. The corresponding values of the genes (the outcome of the GA algorithm, i.e., the fitted swarm parameters) for the simulation are presented in Table 2.

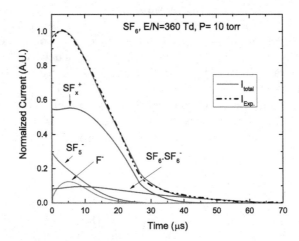

Fig. 3. Comparison between the experimental and theoretical transient currents, the latter calculated for the best individual of the GA for SF_6.

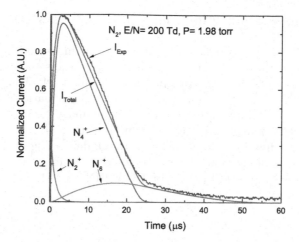

Fig. 4. Comparison between the experimental and theoretical transient current, the latter calculated for the best individual of the GA for N_2

4.3 N_2 Results

The comparison between the experimental and theoretical transient currents, the latter calculated for the best individual of the GA is shown in Fig. 4. The experimental transient current corresponds to pure N_2, with a value of the electric field normalized by the gas density $E/N = 200 Td$, and a gas pressure of 1.98 Torr. It is observed that the predominant ion is N_4^+, having its peak near $t = 3\ \mu s$, whereas the population of N_2^+ drastically reduces to its disappearance to form N_4^+. Hence, the disappearance of N_2^+ coincides with the observed maximum of N_4^+. On the other hand, the N_6^+ species increases slowly and reaches its maximum at $17\ \mu s$, thereafter it decreases slowly reaching its zero value at about $t = 50\ \mu s$. In this case the difference between the theoretical and experimental transient current is noticeable in the time interval that goes from 7 to 10 μs, and for $t \geq 25\ \mu s$. The values of the genes or transport/reaction parameters of the simulation are presented in Table 2.

5   Conclusions

The Genetic Algorithm presented in this paper produces excellent results and its convergence is fast, since it is reached before 20 generations. In the case of SF_6 an excellent agreement between simulation and experiment is achieved, whereas for the N_2 case, only a good agreement can be claimed. One possible reason for this small discrepancy may stem on the Photon Feedback process, which was recently observed [18]. For taking into account this process it would be necessary its inclusion in the proposed reaction scheme. Photon feedback arises from electron collisions that produce metastable states which, upon decay, emit a photon in the UV range, mostly at 337.1 nm. This leads to a new electron emitted by photoelectric effect from the cathode, and this is why it is known as Photon Feedback.

Typically, a single gas or gas mixture requires the measurement of 300 transient currents to be fully characterized. This requires the same number of optimization procedures as the single one presented in this work. Thus, more efforts are necessary to optimize the solution of the continuity equations (SIMAV-4) in order to reduce the Fitness evaluation time. Preliminary results from the optimization to SIMAV-4 using an adaptive time step method, shows a reduction in the calculation time by a factor from 10 to 30, depending on the respective presence or absence of electrons during the ion drift regime.

This work was supported by PAPIIT-UNAM IN 111104.

References

1. Roth, J.R.: Industrial Plasma Engineering, Volume 2: Applications to Nonthermal Plasma Processing. Institute of Physics Publishing, Bristol and Philadelphia (2001)
2. Mizuno, A.: Industrial applications of atmospheric non-thermal plasma in environmental remediation. Plasma Phys. Control. Fusion **49**, A1–A15 (2007)
3. Bárdos, L., Baránková, H.: Cold atmospheric plasma: sources, processes, and applications. Thin Solid Films **518**, 6705–6713 (2010)
4. Basurto, E., de Urquijo, J., Cisneros, C., Alvarez, I.: Mobility of the He^+, Ne^+, Ar^+, N_2^+, O_2^+, and CO_2^+ ions in their parent gas. Phys. Rev. E **61**, 3053–3057 (2000)
5. Basurto, E., de Urquijo, J., Cisneros, C., Alvarez, I.: N^+ charge transfer and N_2^+ dissociation in N_2 at swarm energies. Phys. Rev. E **63**, 016407 (2001)
6. de Urquijo, J., Basurto, E.: Electron attachment, ionization and drift in $c - C_4F_8$. J. Phys. D: Appl. Phys. **34**, 1352–1354 (2001)
7. de Urquijo, J., Basurto, E., Hernández-Ávila, J.L.: Effective ionization, electron and ion transport in $SF_6 - He$ mixtures. J. Phys. D: Appl. Phys. **34**, 2151–2159 (2001)
8. Basurto, E., de Urquijo, J.: Mobility of CF_3^+ in CF_4, CHF_2^+ in CHF_3, and C^+ in Ar. J. Appl. Phys. **91**, 36–39 (2002)
9. Hernández-Ávila, J.L., Basurto, E., de Urquijo, J.: Electron transport and swarm parameters in CO_2 and its mixtures with SF_6. J. Phys. D: Appl. Phys. **35**, 2264–2269 (2002)
10. de Urquijo, J., Juárez, A.M.: The mobility of negative ions in CF_3I, CF_3IN_2, CF_3IAr, CF_3IXe, C_2F_6, and CHF_3, and of positive ions in C_2F_4 and $c - C_4F_8$. IEEE Trans. Plasma Sci. **37**, 1665–1669 (2009)
11. de Urquijo, J., Juárez, A.M., Rodríguez-Luna, J.C., Ramos-Salas, J.S.: A numerical simulation code for electronic and ionic transients from a time-resolved pulsed Townsend experiment. IEEE Trans. Plasma Sci. **35**, 1204–1209 (2007)
12. Rodríguez Luna, J.C.: Estudio de los efectos del desprendimiento electrónico y las reacciones en negativo-molécula en la avalancha de hexafluoruro de azufre, tesis de Maestria (2011)
13. Bekstein, A., de Urquijo, J., Ducasse, O., Rodríguez-Luna, J.C., Juárez, A.M.: Determination of transport and reaction swarm coefficients from the analysis of complex transient pulses from the pulsed Townsend experiment. J. Phys.: Conf. Ser. **370**, 012006 (2012)

14. El-Beltagy, M.A., Keane, A.J.: Optimisation for multilevel problems: a comparison of various algorithms. In: Parmee, I.C. (ed.) Adaptive Computing in Design and Manufacture, pp. 111–120. Springer, London (1998)
15. Coley, D.A.: An Introduction to Genetic Algorithms for Scientists and Engineers. World Scientific, Singapore (1999)
16. Hermanns, M.: Parallel Programming in Fortran 95 using OpenMP, Universidad Politécnica de Madrid. OpenMP documentation. http://www.openmp.org/presentations/miguel/F95_OpenMPv1_v2.pdf
17. Rojas, B., Bekstein, A., de Urquijo, J.: A genetic algorithm to optimize the fitting of avalanches observed from a pulsed Townsend experiment. In: ESCAMPIG XXI, Viana do Castelo, Portugal, 10–14 July 2012
18. Basurto, E., Serkovic, L.N., de Urquijo, J.: Observation of secondary ionization by photon feedback in a Townsend discharge. In: 32nd ICPIG. IAI, Romania, 26–31 July 2015

Parallelizing the Bayesian Analysis of Blinking and Bleaching for Super-Resolution Microscopy

Haydee O. Hernández[1,2], Paloma Hidalgo[2,3], Christopher D. Wood[1,2], Ramón González[3], and Adán Guerrero[1,2(✉)]

[1] Laboratorio Nacional de Microscopía Avanzada, Universidad Nacional Autónoma de México, 62210 Cuernavaca, Morelos, Mexico
[2] Instituto de Biotecnología, Universidad Nacional Autónoma de México, 62210 Cuernavaca, Morelos, Mexico
{hoha,hopr,chris,adanog}@ibt.unam.mx
[3] Centro de Investigación en Dinámica Celular. Instituto de Investigación en Ciencias Básicas y Aplicadas, Universidad Autónoma del Estado de Morelos, 62209 Cuernavaca, Morelos, Mexico
rgonzalez@uaem.mx

Abstract. Super-resolution microscopy techniques overcome the diffraction limit of optical microscopy. The bayesian analysis of blinking and bleaching (3B analysis) is a super-resolution microscopy method that resolves biological structures with a lateral spatial resolution in the range of 50 nm. This method requires an extensive processing time to generate each super-resolution image. We present the parallelization of the 3B analysis for a personal computer and for a cluster which reduces the time for 3B analysis, and provide Parallel 3B an ImageJ plugin that extends the current implementation of the algorithm to parallel computing.

Keywords: Super-resolution microscopy · 3B · Cluster · Parallel processing · Image processing

1 Introduction

In optical microscopes the diffraction barrier, also called Abbe's limit, restricts the spatial discrimination of neighboring objects that are closer than approximately half the wavelength of the light used to image the specimen [1]. To overcome Abbe's limit, super-resolution (SR) techniques exploit the fluorescence properties of molecules and proteins (fluorophores) by promoting the switching between dark and emitting states [2].

Localization SR techniques are based on the single-molecule principle. This principle depends on the localization of single emitters from a temporal sequence of images collected with a highly sensitive electron-multiplying CCD (EMCCD) camera coupled to an optical microscope [2, 3]. Localization SR techniques resolve structures separated by as little as 20 nm, however they can only be applied if the density of molecules in the sample is below approximately 10 mol/μm^2 [4]. An alternative approach is to apply the 3B technique which analyzes the entire time series globally [5]. The algorithm generates a probability map of fluorophore localization by deriving a weighted average over all possible models; the set of models includes varying numbers of emitters, emitter

© Springer International Publishing Switzerland 2016
I. Gitler and J. Klapp (Eds.): ISUM 2015, CCIS 595, pp. 356–366, 2016.
DOI: 10.1007/978-3-319-32243-8_25

localizations and temporal dynamics of the states of the fluorophores [5]. The information stored in the image sequence is iteratively compared with the models using Bayesian inference [5].

The 3B software is currently supplied as a standalone program that must be compiled and installed before use, thus limiting its usage to those reasonably familiar with programming [5]. The imaging community has greatly benefited from the existence of standard open source software packages; ImageJ in particular has become a standard tool in laboratories that work with microscopy images [6]. The authors of 3B also provide an ImageJ plugin for the 3B software, which includes both a 3B analysis suite, and software for performing the final SR reconstruction [7].

The current implementation of this method has the disadvantage that the analysis is laborious (hours to days), compared with other localization methods as PALM [8], STORM [9] or SOFI [10], which create super-resolution images in a few minutes as adequate sampling from the set of all possible models generated by 3B is a demanding computational task [5].

In 2013, the 3B analysis was parallelized with the use of Amazon EC2 cloud computing servers [11]. This implementation splits the analysis of the image sequence into spatial mosaics covering a minor part of the entire imaging field, usually of 1 μm^2. However, using the Amazon EC2 cloud would be prohibitively expensive for laboratories with scarce resources and/or large numbers of samples to analyze.

Parallelization requires the reduction of the area to be analyzed in the sequence of images. A mosaic of subregions covering the dataset is generated such that the individual mosaic sections are amenable to analysis in parallel on multiple processors.

Frequently, microscopy images include regions that do not provide information, only representing the background. We can improve the processing by detecting and removing these "empty" regions from the analysis pipeline, thus ensuring that only fluorophore-containing sections are sent for processing and analysis.

With this idea in mind and the supplementary codes provided in [11], we implement the parallelization of 3B on both a cluster and a personal computer. Furthermore, we present an analysis of the relationship between the size of the mosaic and both processing time and image quality.

Considering the parallelization and the plugin made for 3B, both were combined both into an ImageJ plugin (Parallel 3B) to parallelize 3B analysis on a personal computer. A graphic user interface is provided to improve user-friendliness.

2   Methods

2.1   Preparation of Biological Samples. Microtubules

Human foreskin fibroblasts (HFF) cells were grown on coverslips to approximately 90% confluence. Cells were processed for immunofluorescence following the description in [12]. Briefly, cells were fixed using 3.7% formaldehyde, permeabilized with PBS/Triton X-100 (137 mM NaCl, 2.7 mM Kcl, 10 mM Na_2HPO_4 and 1.8 mM KH_2PO_4/0.5% Triton X-100), and incubated with the primary mouse monoclonal antibody against alpha-tubulin (1:500) (eBioscience). After application of the primary antibody, cells were incubated with the secondary antibody mouse anti-IgG Alexa Fluor 488 (Invitrogen). The coverslips were mounted on glass slides in 1.5% glucose oxidase + 100 mM β-mercaptoethanol to induce the blinking of the fluorophores [13, 14]. All samples were examined using an Olympus IX-81 inverted microscope.

2.2 Set up of the Optical Microscope

All super-resolution imaging measurements were performed on an Olympus IX-81 inverted microscope configured for total internal reflection fluorescence (TIRF) excitation (Olympus, cell^TIRF™ Illuminator). The critical angle was set up such that the evanescence field had a penetration depth of ~200 nm (Xcellence software v1.2, Olympus soft imaging solution GMBH). The samples were continuously illuminated using excitation sources depending on the fluorophore in use. Alexa Fluor 488 dyes were excited with a 488 nm diode-pumped solid-state laser. Beam selection and modulation of laser intensities were controlled via xcellence software v.1.2. A full multiband laser cube set was used to discriminate the selected light sources (LF 405/488/561/635 A-OMF, Bright Line; Semrock). Fluorescence was collected using an Olympus UApo N 100x/1.49 numerical aperture, oil-immersion objective lens, with an extra 1.6x intermediate magnification lens. All movies were recorded onto a 65 × 65 pixel region of an electron-multiplying charge couple device (EMCCD) camera (iXon 897, Model No: DU-897E-CS0-#BV; Andor) at 100 nm per pixel, and within a 50 ms interval (300 images).

2.3 Bayesian Analysis of the Blinking and Bleaching

Sub-diffraction images were derived from the Bayesian analysis of the stochastic Blinking and Bleaching of the Alexa Fluor 488 dye [5]. For each super-resolution reconstruction, 300 images were acquired at 20 frames per second with an exposure time of 50 ms at full laser power, spreading the bleaching of the sample over the length of the entire acquisition time. The maximum laser power coming out of the optical fiber measured at the back focal plane of the objective lens, for the 488 nm laser line, was 23.1 mW. The image sequences were analyzed with the 3B algorithm considering a pixel size of 100 nm and a full width half maximum of the point spread function of 270 nm (for Alexa Fluor 488), measured experimentally with 0.17 μm fluorescent beads (PS-Speck™ Microscope Point Source Kit, Molecular Probes, Inc.). All other parameters were set up using default values. The 3B analysis was run over 200 iterations, as recommended by the authors in [5], and the final super-resolution reconstruction was created at a pixel size of 10 nm with the ImageJ plugin for 3B analysis [7]. The resolution increase observed in our imaging set up by 3B analysis was up to 5 times below the Abbe's limit (~50 nm).

2.4 Parallelization of 3B

Due to the excessive computational time for 3B analysis and the cost of parallelizing in Amazon EC2, we implemented the parallelization on a personal computer and a cluster.

The authors of 3B suggest that 200 iterations are sufficient to ensure the convergence of the ensemble model that provides the best probability map estimation of fluorophore localization, hence the code was modified to finalize the analysis at this iteration point [5].

Parallelization on a Personal Computer. We parallelize the analysis of the sequence of images taken over time using subregions, as devised for use on the Amazon EC2 cloud computing environment. Each subregion was analyzed with the 3B algorithm on a personal computer (PC) with an IntelTM-Corei7-2700 CPU@3.4 GHz processor. For comparative purposes, a sequence of images of podosomes was taken from the original 3B article and used as sample data [5, 7]. This image sequence (300 images) was cropped to end up with a dataset of 52×52 pxs.

For the parallelization test we decided to apply the 3B analysis over the 52×52 pxs podosome dataset with four protocols with the following subregion sizes: 10×10 pxs, 15×15 pxs, 20×20 pxs, and 25×25 pxs. The overlap between the subregions for all the protocols was 5 pxs. (Fig. 1).

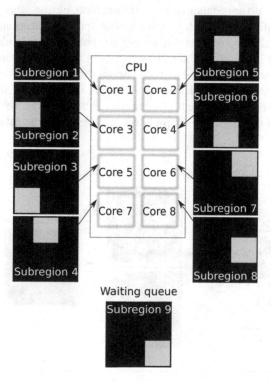

Fig. 1. Parallelization scheme of the protocol with 20×20 pxs subregions with 5 pxs overlapping on a PC with an IntelTM-Corei7-2700 CPU@3.4 GHz processor for a sequence of images of 52×52 pxs. Each subregion was sent to a core with sequence of images to be analyzed with the 3B software. Notice the waiting queue of subregions to be analyzed when all the cores are busy.

All the subregions were defined prior to the 3B analysis. A script was executed to send each subregion to be analyzed by the 3B algorithm to a different core on the PC

(Fig. 1). When all the cores were busy, the next subregion remained in the queue until a core was released, which repeated until all subregions of the protocol were analyzed. Finally, we interleaved all of the resultant analyzed subregions to generate the SR image.

Index of Dispersion. Localization SR techniques require optical microscopes with one or several digital cameras acquiring images of the samples; these cameras most commonly have a CCD image sensor (although sCMOS image sensor cameras are sometimes employed). Photon shot noise results from the inherent statistical variation of the number of incident photons on the CCD [15]. Photoelectrons generated within the semiconductor device constitute the signal, the magnitude of which is perturbed by fluctuations that follow the Poisson statistical distribution of the number of photons incident on the CCD at a given location. The Poisson distribution implies that the variance (σ^2) and the mean (μ) are equal. The shot noise is limited by $\sqrt{N}$, where N is the number of detected photons [15].

Parallelization reduces the computational time of 3B analysis. However if the subregions to be analyzed do not contain relevant information, i.e. the subregion just contains shot noise, calculations are wasted in analyzing spurious information. In order to discriminate the analysis of regions containing just shot noise, we made use of the index of dispersion. This index gives the relation between the variance and the mean, and hence identifies which regions contain only photon shot noise.

Specifically, if the index of dispersion is less or equal to one, it implies that the subregion does not contain relevant information and hence, it can be discarded. Otherwise, it is assumed that emitting fluorophores are present in the subregion (Fig. 2.d).

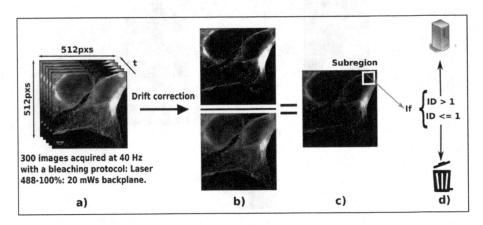

Fig. 2. Parallelization scheme of the 3B analysis on a cluster. (a) Sequence of images of the microtubules limited by diffraction. The scale bar represents 5 µm. (b) Index of dispersion of the entire image sequence, defined as the variance of the sequence divided by the mean (image below). (c) The resulting image of the index of dispersion. The white square is a subregion of 20 × 20 pxs. (d) Selection of the regions with relevant information. If the subregion generated in (c) has a pixel with a dispersion value greater than one, the subregion is sent to the cluster, otherwise, it is rejected.

This ensures a reduction in the subregions to be analyzed and reduces the computing time to produce the SR image.

Parallelization on a Cluster. In this implementation, we divided the analysis of the data in subregions of 20 × 20 pxs with an overlap of 5 pxs between the subregions. We used a sequence of images of microtubules (300 images of 512 × 512 pxs) as samples.

First, we corrected the drift between the images in the sequence because this can affect the analysis [16]. Then, we generated the subregions using the index of dispersion to reduce the number of subregions to be analyzed; thereby reducing the computing time of 3B analysis and the transfer time of the data to the cluster.

Our results are found using the cluster of the Biotechnology Institute of the National Autonomous University of Mexico (UNAM) (cluster.ibt.unam.mx/wordpress).

All parallelization scripts and the Parallel3D plugin for ImageJ are available on the internet at (https://bitbucket.org/hoha441/parallel-3b/src), the Parallel3B plugin for ImageJ is also provided.

3 Results

3.1 Parallelization on a PC

The 3B analysis of the podosomes allowed comparison of our results with those obtained in the article entitled "Accelerating 3B single-molecule super-resolution microscopy with cloud computing" [11]. Podosomes are cylindrical actin based cytoskeletal structures found on the outer surface of the plasma membrane of animal cells that participate in cell adhesion, migration and degradation of the extracellular matrix [17, 18]. We present below the SR images of the podosomes and the computational time for each protocol.

The parallelization of the 3B analysis of the 300 images of the podosomes (52 × 52 pxs) with the different protocols (10 × 10 pxs, 15 × 15 pxs, 20 × 20 pxs, and 25 × 25 pxs) generated 81, 16, 9, and 4 subregions, respectively.

The first graph (Fig. 3.a) shows the cumulative distribution function for each of the protocols used in the analysis of the podosome data, which shows the computational time for every subregion of the protocol. The extremes of the distribution are the minimum and the maximum time for each protocol. The computational time for the complete image is not displayed because it took more than 24 h. This indicates that the protocol for the smallest subregion (10 × 10 pxs) gave the best time for parallelization for a large number of cores, i.e. when we have access at least to the same number of cores at 3.4 GHz as the number of subregions generated.

The following chart (Fig. 3.b) displays the same information as above but in a box plot, which shows the distribution of computational time the parallelization for each of the protocols for analysis of the podosomes data. The computational time of the analysis for the complete image is approximately 125 h, and compared to the other protocols it is clear that parallelization significantly reduces it.

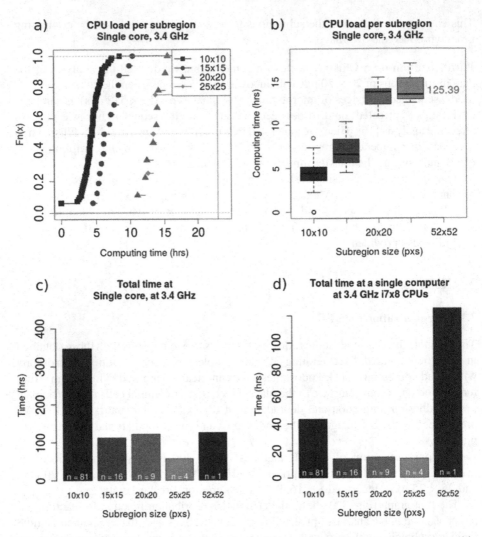

Fig. 3. Total computational times for the analysis of the sequence of images of podosomes with 3B. (a) Cumulative distribution function of the computational time for each parallelization protocol. The vertical line denotes 24 h (b) Distribution of the computational time for each protocol. The optimal computational time was found using the protocol with the smallest subregions. (c) Computational time in a single core, i.e. if the analysis was performed sequential. The best computational time was found using the protocol with subregions of 25 × 25 pxs. (d) Computational time for the data analysis parallelization with 3B on a PC with eight cores. The protocol for subregions of 15 × 15 pxs was optimal for a CPU with eight cores.

The third graph (Fig. 3.c) shows the total computational time for the complete analysis of the sequence of images of the podosomes with 3B, if the analysis were sequential, i.e. with only one processor at 3.4 GHz for all the subregions of the different protocols.

This shows given the number of subregions generated and the total computational time of each of these, the optimal protocol is 25 × 25 pxs.

Finally the last chart (Fig. 3.d.) shows the total time for computing all the subregions of the different protocols on a PC with an IntelTM-Corei7-2700 CPU@3.4 GHz processor with eight cores. In this case, the best time for the complete reconstruction was found using the protocols of 15 × 15 pxs and 25 × 25 pxs.

Although the improvement in overall duration of the analysis is considerable, image quality is affected as a consequence of segregating the analysis of the original image in a mosaic of subregions. This artifact manifests as a lack of continuity in the structures of the sample; it appears as a mesh structure, due to the incorrect estimation of the background of the region analyzed [5].

Figure 4 shows the SR images of the podosomes resulting from different parallelization protocols. The SR images of the protocols of 10 × 10 pxs (Fig. 4.b) and 15 × 15 pxs (Fig. 4. c), do not have enough information to correctly process the noise data, and therefore show mesh structures. In contrast, the SR images of the protocols at larger mosaic subregions sizes show continuity in the biological structures and have an

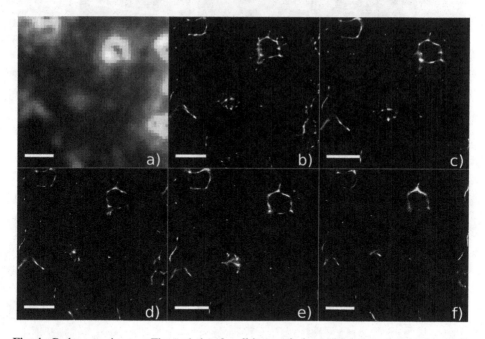

Fig. 4. Podosomes images. The scale bar for all images is 1 μm. (a) Average projection of the 300 diffraction-limited images of the podosomes. (b) Super-resolution image generated with the parallelization protocol for subregions of 10 × 10 pxs with an overlap of 5 pxs. (c) Super-resolution image generated using the parallelization protocol with subregions of 15 × 15 pxs and an overlap of 5 pxs. (d) Super-resolution image generated with the parallelization protocol with subregions of 20 × 20 pxs and an overlap of 5 pxs. (e) Super-resolution image generated using the parallelization protocol with subregions of 25 × 25 pxs and an overlap of 5 pxs. (f) Super-resolution image generated with 3B analysis of the complete image (52 × 52 pxs).

improved spatial resolution compared to the reference to the original sequence of images obtained under diffraction–limited conditions (Fig. 4.a).

3.2 Parallelization on a Cluster

Our test on a computer cluster is performed using a biological sample stained against micro-tubules. These are well known cytoskeletal structures, widely used to test the proficiency of SR algorithms [19]. The width of a single microtubule is approximately 25 nm.

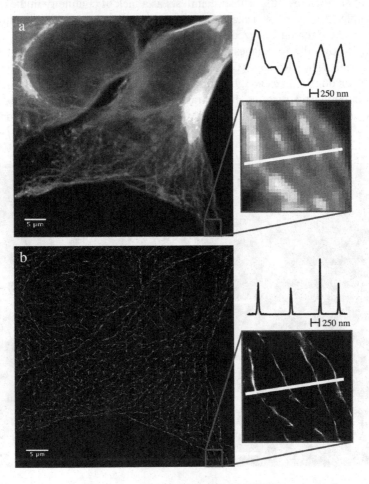

Fig. 5. Microtubules images. (a) Average projection of the 300 images in the sequence limited by diffraction of the microtubules. (b) Super-resolution image generated with the parallelization protocol for a cluster using subregions of 20 × 20 pxs with an overlap of 5 pxs and discarding the subregions without relevant information.

The first step was to correct the sample drift between the 300 images sequence of 512 × 512 pxs of the microtubules. After that, we generate subregions of 20 × 20 pxs with an overlap of 5 pxs between them, followed by application of the index of dispersion filter to discard fluorophore-free subregions. The remaining regions were then sent to the cluster for 3B analysis.

With this protocol, 1023 subregions were generated instead of the expected 1089; reducing the computation expense for data manipulation and analysis. The image (Fig. 5.a) is the average projection of the sequence of images of the microtubules limited by diffraction. The image below (Fig. 5.b) is the resulting SR image of the parallelization of the analysis of the sequence of the microtubules.

4 Conclusions

The parallelization of data analysis for the 3B SR technique on a 8-core PC processor showed that the optimal size for the subregions is 25×25 pxs, as it generates fewer subregions for analysis and the SR image contains fewer notorious artifacts. These artifacts in the SR images are most problematic for subregions smaller than 20×20 pxs.

The results presented in [11] reduced the computation time to a similar degree to that demonstrated here. However the SR image of the podosomes shown there, present similar in Hu Y et al. (2013) show similar mesh-type artifact to those obtained by us with the protocols using subregions of 10×10 pxs and 15×15 pxs. [11]. We conclude that important care must be taken when parallelizing 3B analysis to avoid the generation of image artifacts, and that the presence of such errors will depend on the size and continuity of the structures to be resolved.

As a result of this study we developed "Parallel 3B", an ImageJ plugin to run 3B in parallel given a size of subregions and overlaps for a sequence of images. We expect that this tool will contribute to the wide adoption of 3B analysis on parallel computing platforms.

Acknowledgments. We are thankful with the Biotechnology Institute of UNAM for providing access to the computer cluster and to M. Sc. Jerome Verleyen for his support while using it. We are also thankful to Arturo Pimentel, Andrés Saralegui and Xochitl Alvarado from the National Advanced Microscopy Laboratory (UNAM) for their helpful discussions. This research was funded by UNAM-DGAPA-PAPIIT IN202312, in collaboration with Dr. Alberto Darszon.

References

1. Abbe, E.: Beiträge zur theorie des mikroskops und der mikroskopischen wahrnehmung. Arch. Mikroskop. Anat. **9**, 413 (1873)
2. Small, A., Stahlheber, S.: Fluorophore localization algorithms for super-resolution microscopy. Nat. Methods **11**(3), 267–279 (2014)
3. Deschout, H., Cella Zanacchi, F., Mlodzianoski, M., Diaspro, A., Bewersdorf, J., Hess, S.T., Braeckmans, K.: Precisely and accurately localizing single emitters in fluorescence microscopy. Nat. Methods **11**(3), 253–266 (2014)
4. Holden, S.J., Uphoff, S., Kapanidis, A.N.: DAOSTORM: an algorithm for high- density super-resolution microscopy. Nat. Methods **8**(4), 279–280 (2011)

5. Cox, S., Rosten, E., Monypenny, J., Jovanovic-Talisman, T., Burnette, D.T., Lippincott-Schwartz, J., Jones, G.E., Heintzmann, R.: Bayesian localization microscopy reveals nanoscale podosome dynamics. Nat. Methods **9**(2), 195–200 (2012)
6. Schneider, C.A., Rasband, W.S., Eliceiri, K.W.: NIH Image to ImageJ: 25 years of image analysis. Nat. Methods **9**(7), 671–675 (2012)
7. Rosten, E., Jones, G.E., Cox, S.: ImageJ plug-in for Bayesian analysis of blinking and bleaching. Nat. Methods **10**(2), 97–98 (2013)
8. Betzig, E., Patterson, G.H., Sougrat, R., Lindwasser, O.W., Olenych, S., Bonifacino, J.S., Davidson, M.W., Lippincott-Schwartz, J., Hess, H.F.: Imaging intracellular fluorescent proteins at nanometer resolution. Science **313**(5793), 1642–1645 (2006)
9. Rust, M.J., Bates, M., Zhuang, X.: Sub-diffraction-limit imaging by stochastic optical reconstruction microscopy (STORM). Nat. Methods **3**(10), 793–795 (2006)
10. Dertinger, T., Colyer, R., Iyer, G., Weiss, S., Enderlein, J.: Fast, background-free, 3D super-resolution optical fluctuation imaging (SOFI). Proc. Natl. Acad. Sci. U.S.A **106**(52), 22287–22292 (2009)
11. Hu, Y.S., Nan, X., Sengupta, P., Lippincott-Schwartz, J., Cang, H.: Accelerating 3B single-molecule super-resolution microscopy with cloud computing. Nat. Methods **10**(2), 96–97 (2013)
12. Gonzalez, R., Huang, W., Finnen, R., Bragg, C., Flint, S.J.: Adenovirus E1B 55-kilodalton protein is required for both regulation of mRNA export and efficient entry into the late phase of infection in normal human fibroblasts. J. Virol. **80**(2), 964–974 (2006)
13. Dempsey, G.T., Vaughan, J.C., Chen, K.H., Bates, M., Zhuang, X.: Evaluation of fluorophores for optimal performance in localization-based super-resolution imaging. Nat. Methods **8**(12), 1027–1036 (2011)
14. Heilemann, M., van de Linde, S., Mukherjee, A., Sauer, M.: Super-resolution imaging with small organic fluorophores. Angew. Chem. **48**(37), 6903–6908 (2009)
15. Cheezum, M.K., Walker, W.F., Guilford, W.H.: Quantitative comparison of algorithms for tracking single fluorescent particles. Biophys. J. **81**(4), 2378–2388 (2001)
16. Wang, Y., Schnitzbauer, J., Hu, Z., Li, X., Cheng, Y., Huang, Z.L., Huang, B.: Localization events-based sample drift correction for localization microscopy with redundant cross-correlation algorithm. Opt. Express **22**(13), 15982–15991 (2014)
17. Linder, S., Aepfelbacher, M.: Podosomes: adhesion hot-spots of invasive cells. Trends Cell Biol. **13**(7), 376–385 (2003)
18. Linder, S., Kopp, P.: Podosomes at a glance. J. Cell Sci. **118**(Pt 10), 2079–2082 (2005)
19. Endesfelder, U., Heilemann, M.: Art and artifacts in single-molecule localization microscopy: beyond attractive images. Nat. Methods **11**(3), 235–238 (2014)

Double Diffusion Numerical Simulation for an Aired Room with Inner Pollutant Sources

J. Serrano-Arellano[1](✉), J. Félix[2], and J.M. Riesco-Ávila[3]

[1] División de Arquitectura e Ingeniería en Energías Renovables,
Instituto Tecnológico Superior de Huichapan-ITESHU-DGEST-SEP. Dom. Conocido S/N,
El Saucillo, 42411 Huichapan, Hidalgo, Mexico
`jserrano@iteshu.edu.mx`
[2] Laboratorio de Partículas elementales, Departamento de Física,
Universidad de Guanajuato, León, Guanajuato, Mexico
`felix@fisica.ugto.mx`
[3] Departamento de Ingeniería Mecánica, Universidad de Guanajuato,
Carretera Salamanca-Valle de Santiago Km 3.5 + 1.8 Km. Comunidad de Palo Blanco,
36885 Salamanca, Guanajuato, Mexico
`riesco@ugto.mx`

Abstract. Numerical simulations are fundamental in the development of scientific knowledge due to their capability to quantitatively predict the behavior of key variables. However, the main obstacle is computational power, bounding the total computational times, which vary from a few minutes to impractical times of several years, implying the necessity to develop parallel computing. In this study, we present the results of the numerical simulation of thermal and mass transfer inside an aired-conditioned room, physically represented by a cavity with different boundary conditions. The finite volume technique is used to solve the key equations, including a k-ε turbulence model to improve the flux calculations. The results are presented in flux, mass, heat, temperature and contaminant concentration diagrams; they show that sources located at the top of the cavity provide improved thermal comfort and air quality conditions in the room.

Keywords: Double diffusion · Turbulence · Aired cavity · Thermal comfort

1 Introduction

Nowadays it is common the construction of buildings that consume large energy budgets for the provision of internal conditions of thermal comfort and air quality. The architects still lack the protocols and methodologies to take into account the thermal properties of the materials, the spatial orientations, the size of doors and windows, the air temperature, the solar heat transfer, etc., given that these variables are interconnected. When these variables are ignored, the result is a building with an expensive microclimate and high maintenance costs.

One alternative is to change the construction plans, taking into account the elements to improve the conditions of thermal comfort and air quality inside the building.

© Springer International Publishing Switzerland 2016
I. Gitler and J. Klapp (Eds.): ISUM 2015, CCIS 595, pp. 367–379, 2016.
DOI: 10.1007/978-3-319-32243-8_26

For example, the use of appropriate ventilation -defined as the flux of air from the outside, resulting from pressure and temperature gradients-. The effectiveness of the ventilation (natural ventilation) is a function of doors and windows sizes, and dominant air directions. However, mechanical ventilation can be achieved using fans, diffusers, extractors, and other tools. One way to improve ventilation in buildings is calculating the convective coefficients necessary to achieve improved conditions of temperature and air quality. To calculate those coefficients, we require to measure the air flow regime, the velocity field, the temperature and the concentration of pollutants in the air inside the room. Consult [1] for a tridimensional numerical study for the calculation of the recirculation patterns of air in ventilated rooms using turbulence models. The air was introduced from the roof and exhausted at a vertical wall. Velocity distributions are shown for two different models, which do not agree with each other. However, from the engineering point of view, as pointed out by the authors, the models are useful to obtain the airflow patterns inside the building. In [2], the authors used an experimental model of a ventilated cavity with turbulent flow, with a description of the geometry and boundary conditions. The main goal was to test the ability to predict the airflow by some CFD codes from the International Energy Agency. They use an adiabatic twofold cavity with air intake and outtake in opposite walls of the room. Two studies were performed, with the Reynolds number based on the length of the cavity. The main goal was to predict the flow generated by flotation forces. The results suggest that for an Archimedes number greater or equal to 0.02, when cool air gets in, the flow deviates from the ceiling before reaching the vertical wall. In [3] there is a numerical study of heat transfer in a twofold rectangular cavity with ventilation, where all the walls are adiabatic, except the left vertical wall, which gets a constant heat flux. The flow intake is localized at the middle of the left vertical wall and the outtake at the middle of the right vertical wall, with a 0.25 h ratio between the size of the apertures and the height. The convection of the mixture was analyzed when the forced and natural flows assist each other and vice versa. The results are shown using stream lines and isotherms, providing out correlations between the heat flux and the Reynolds number. A strong correlation is obtained between the flow pattern and the natural convection. We refer the reader to a set of publications related to ventilated cavities [4–10]. The numerical studies are an alternative when experimentation is not possible. The main goal of the numerical computation of the flow patterns is to reproduce experimental results and predict changes as a function of the flexible parameters. We present a numerical study showing ventilation, providing thermal gains at the interior of the cavity as a function of heat transfer and mass flow; the results are shown in graphs, using temperature and concentration fields, and isolines for mass flow and heat flux.

2   Physical Model of a Ventilated Cavity

The numerical model assumes that the room is like a ventilated cavity, where we study the relevant physical parameters. This model is represented in Fig. 1. This consists of two dimensional rectangular geometry with air outputs and inputs. It is considered that the right vertical wall is solid and opaque and gets some solar radiation, with loses by convection and radiation in the exterior, and gains in the interior in the form of a heat flux, producing temperature variations.

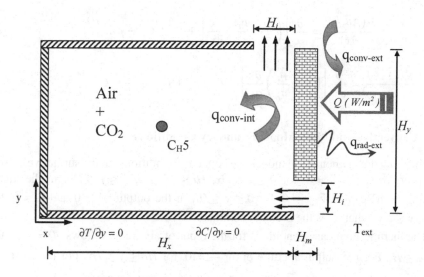

Fig. 1. Physical model of a ventilated cavity.

The mixture of air and pollutants in the interior is turbulent, therefore, the model will be performed by the RANS technique, this is, the Navier-Stokes equations of energy and mass will be averaged in time. The time average process of the variables *(T, v, u, P y C)* is known as *Reynolds average*, [11]. It is necessary to provide additional equations for the closure of the problem, given that the averaged Navier-Stokes introduces the Reynolds stress tensor $\rho\tau_{ij}$, the heat flux vector $\rho Cp\,\overline{u_j'T'}$ and mass transference vector $\rho\overline{u_j'C'}$. To this aim, we use a turbulent viscosity relating turbulent stresses with velocity gradients

$$\overline{\rho u_i' u_j'} = -\mu_t \left[\frac{\partial \overline{u}_i}{\partial x_j} + \frac{\partial \overline{u}_j}{\partial x_i} \right] + \frac{2}{3}\rho\,\kappa\,\delta_{ij}. \tag{1}$$

The heat turbulent flux is modeled using the Fourier law for heat conduction

$$\rho Cp\overline{u_j'T} = -\frac{\mu_t}{\sigma_T}\frac{\partial \overline{T'}}{\partial x_i}. \tag{2}$$

The turbulent mass flux is modeled using Fick's law for the molecular diffusion

$$\rho\overline{u_j'C'} = -\frac{\mu_t}{Sc_t}\frac{\partial \overline{C}}{\partial x_i}. \tag{3}$$

The Eqs. (1), (2) and (3) are related using a turbulent eddy viscosity $\mu_t = C_\mu \frac{\rho k^2}{\varepsilon}$, where the equations for the turbulent kinetic energy (k) and the turbulent kinetic energy dissipation (ε) are given as follows

$$\frac{\partial(\rho \bar{u}_i k)}{\partial x_i} = \frac{\partial}{\partial x_i}\left[\left(\mu + \frac{\mu_t}{\sigma_\kappa}\right)\frac{\partial k}{\partial x_i}\right] + P_\kappa + G_\kappa - \rho\varepsilon, \tag{4}$$

$$\frac{\partial(\rho \bar{u}_i \varepsilon)}{\partial x_i} = \frac{\partial}{\partial x_i}\left[\left(\mu + \frac{\mu_t}{\sigma_\varepsilon}\right)\frac{\partial \varepsilon}{\partial x_i}\right] + C_{\varepsilon 1}\left[P_\kappa + C_{\varepsilon_3}G_\kappa\right]\frac{\varepsilon}{k} - C_{\varepsilon 2}\frac{\rho\varepsilon^2}{k}. \tag{5}$$

2.1 Convective and Mass Model Boundary Conditions

Starting with the mathematical model, the boundary conditions for the surface velocities are as follows: $\bar{u} = \bar{v} = 0$, for $0 \leq x \leq Hx$, $Hi \leq y \leq Hy$, $0 \leq y \leq Ho$, in the input. $\bar{u} = \bar{u}_{inlet} = f(Re)$ and $\bar{v}_{inlet} = 0$, for $0 \leq y \leq Hi$, in the output. $\frac{\partial \bar{u}}{\partial n} = 0$ and $\frac{\partial \bar{v}}{\partial n} = 0$, for $Ho \leq y \leq Hy$, where n is the normal coordinate.

The thermal boundary conditions for the input of air are as follows: $\bar{T} = T_{inlet}$, for $0 \leq y \leq Hi$. For the output aperture of air $\frac{\partial \bar{T}}{\partial n} = 0$, for $Ho \leq y \leq Hy$. For the adiabatic walls $\frac{\partial \bar{T}}{\partial n} = 0$, for $0 \leq x \leq Hx$ and $0 \leq y \leq Ho$, where n is the normal coordinate.

The boundary conditions at the interface of the opaque wall with the flux in the cavity is $q_{cond-wall} = q_{conv-int}$ for $Hi \leq y \leq Hy$. The boundary conditions for the carbon dioxide are as follows: $\bar{C} = C_{inlet}$, for $0 \leq y \leq Hi$. For the output aperture of air $\frac{\partial \bar{C}}{\partial n} = 0$, for $Ho \leq y \leq Hy$. For all walls $\frac{\partial \bar{C}}{\partial n} = 0$, for $0 \leq x \leq Hx$ and $0 \leq y \leq Ho$, where n in the normal coordinate. For the pollutant source, the boundary conditions are as follows: $\bar{C} = C_H$, for $Hi \leq y \leq Hy$.

The boundary conditions of the conductive model are as follows: In the bottom adiabatic boundary $\frac{\partial T_m}{\partial y} = 0$, for $0 \leq x \leq Hm$. In the upper adiabatic boundary $\frac{\partial T_m}{\partial y} = 0$, for $0 \leq x \leq Hm$.

The boundary at the right side of the opaque wall gets a constant heat flux, losing convective and radiative towards exterior side at T_{ext}, where $q_{total} = q_{cond-wall} + q_{rad-ext} + q_{conv-ext}$. With these boundary conditions, the next step is to apply the numerical method.

3 Numerical Procedure

The discretized equations were solved via a FORTRAN program, written to workout different problems [12–14]. The code was run in a PC with a Pentium Intel core I7 processor, needing one hour for each run.

The numerical procedure is based on the finite volume technique [15] with a generalized transport equation, which integrated over a finite control volume and transformed into an algebraic equation.

The general procedure to analyze the model is the following: (1) assume initial values for all variables $(u, v, T, \ldots \varepsilon)$; (2) calculate the mixture velocity distributions and pressure (u, v, p), applying the SIMPLEC algorithm [16]; (3) with the new calculated values of velocity distributions, calculate the field of temperatures (T), the turbulent kinetic energy (k) and the turbulent dissipative kinetic energy (ε); (4) apply the convergence criterion, and repeat the process until it is satisfied with a residual criterion.

We study the independence of the solution with the mesh resolution starting with a mesh of 91×61 control units, following with increments of 10 computational nodes on each of the three coordinate axis. It was found that the mesh of 191×81 units provides enough resolution, for there were no significant changes in the results with respect to the 201×91 cell mesh. In general, the differences were less than 1 % in average values for the velocities and temperature.

3.1 Verification of the Theoretical and Numerical Procedure

The verification of our code has been shown in different problems [12–14]. For the verification and validation of the turbulent flow theory and code, see [17]. It consists of a ventilated cavity with isothermal and turbulent flow. The vertical walls show opposite inputs and outputs. The height of the cavity is $H = 3.0$ m; its length, $L = 9.0$ m. The air is pushed to get into in the upper aperture of the left vertical wall and get out in the inferior aperture of the right vertical wall. All the walls are considered adiabatic. The length of the input aperture is $0.056 \times H$ and that of the output aperture is $0.16 \times H$. The compared results were the horizontal components of the dimensionless velocity at different sections of the cavity. The comparison of numerical and experimental results shows enough agreement for our purposes.

4   Results

The dimensions of the cavity remain fixed (4 m × 3 m). The height of the apertures, 0.3 m, is the average size of air diffusors in systems of controlled air temperature. The properties of the right vertical wall are those of a light concrete wall [18]. The exterior temperature is 35° C. The temperature of the fluid at the input is 24° C with a CO_2 concentration of 360 ppm. The flux of heat on the light concrete wall was 750 W/m^2.

We have changed the location of the pollutant source and observed its effects on the concentration field. We considered nine positions of the pollutant source inside the cavity and identify them by the names: $C_H1, C_H2, \ldots, C_H9$. The first location of the pollutant source is near the left-top corner of the computational domain, at 1 m from the left wall and 2.25 m from the bottom. The second and third positions of the sources are 1 and 2 m to the right of the first. Two more rows of positions for the source are located at 0.75 and 1.5 m downwards from the first row, respectively. Figure 2 shows the location of the pollutant source for the nine cases.

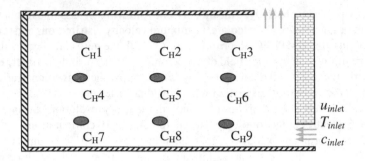

Fig. 2. Localization of pollutant sources.

We show the streamlines of the flow, and the iso-lines of heat, temperature, mass density, and concentration, in Figs. 3, 4, 5, 6 and 7, respectively.

Figure 3 shows the streamlines for the nine locations of the pollutant source. The source has a mass flow of 3000 ppm and a Reynolds number of 10000.

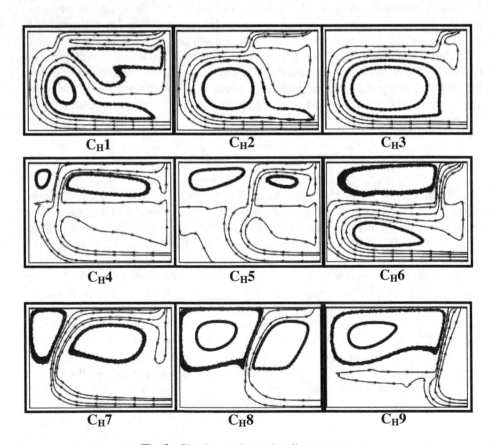

Fig. 3. Flux layout for each pollutant source.

In all cases, the flow starts at the bottom-right corner and exits at the top-right corner, producing a series of vortices. A buoyancy force is produced at the pollutant source. See Fig. 3.

In the C_H1 case, we find a small recirculation zone, a small vortex. This vortex grows subsequently for the C_H2 and C_H3 cases. When the sources are located in the second row, that is for C_H4, C_H5 and C_H6, we find two recirculation zones, one below the pollutant source, with a low level of pollutant concentration, and another above the source.

When the pollutant source is located in the middle-center (C_H5), we find four zones with their respective recirculation. If the pollutant zone is located in the middle-right (C_H6), again we find two zones -upper and lower- with their respective recirculation. When the pollutant source is located in the bottom-right (C_H7), the flow entirely passes the cavity; the pollutant source indicates its direction; it changes direction after the flow reaches the pollutant source. When the pollutant source is located in the bottom-center (C_H8), we observe that the flow gets in from the bottom-right and reaches the middle of the cavity; there, at the pollutant source, changes its direction, generating two zones of recirculation in the bottom of the cavity. When the pollutant source is located in the

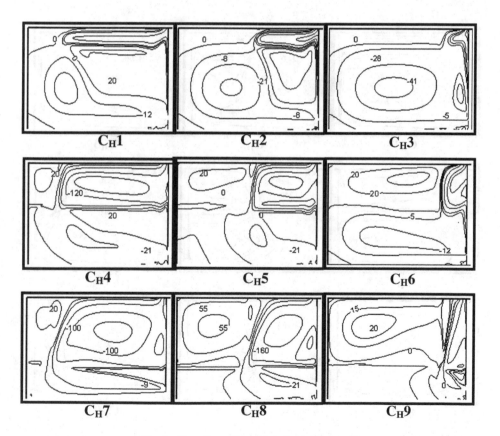

Fig. 4. Heat lines for each pollutant sources.

bottom-right (C_H9), the flow stops, displaces, distorts, and pushes toward the top; a large circulation appears at the bottom.

Figure 4 shows the heat lines as function of the pollutant sources ($C_H1, C_H2,...C_H9$); their function is conditioned by the streamlines.

When the pollutant source is located in the top-left (C_H1), the heat lines accumulate at the top. If the pollutant source is located in the top-center (C_H2), the low-density heat lines accumulate at the middle top-center; two re-circulation zones appear. For the case when the pollutant source is located in the top-right (C_H3), the heat is transported near the conductive heat wall. If the pollutant source is located in the middle-left (C_H4), the heat transport is increased and re-circulations zones appear at the top. If the pollutant source is located in the middle-center (C_H5), the heat transport is performed at the top-right. If the pollutant source is located in the middle-right (C_H6), the heat transport is performed at the right vertical wall. For the case when the pollutant source is located in the bottom-left (C_H7), the heat transport is performed at almost the entire cavity; a recirculation zone appears at the top. If the pollutant source is located in the bottom-center (C_H8), the heat transport is performed at almost the entire cavity; two re-circulations zones appear at the top. And finally, if the pollutant source is located in the bottom-right

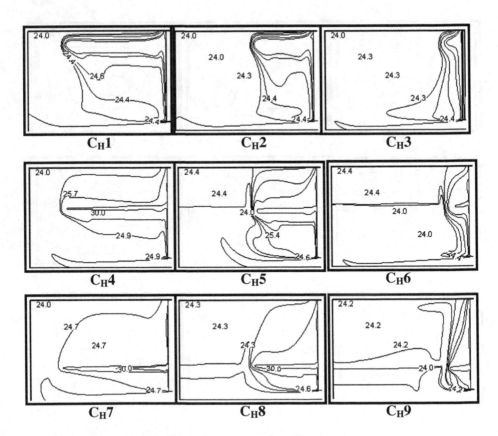

Fig. 5. Isotherms for each pollutant source.

(C_H9), the low heat transport is performed at the top; a big re-circulation zone appears at the top.

The Fig. 5 shows the isothermal curves as function of the pollutant sources (C_H1, C_H2,...C_H9).

If the pollutant source is located in the top-left (C_H1), the isothermal curves concentrate at the top, near the heat conductor wall, where high temperatures are concentrated. For the case when the pollutant source is located in the top-center (C_H2), the isothermal curves concentrate at the top-right, near the heat conductor wall, with uniform temperatures. If the pollutant source is located in the top-right (C_H3), the isothermal curves concentrate at the bottom-right, near the heat conductor wall, with uniform temperatures. For the case when the pollutant source is located in the middle-left (C_H4), the isothermal curves concentrate at the bottom-center and at the top-center, with low and high temperatures, respectively. If the pollutant source is located in the middle-center (C_H5), the isothermal curves concentrated at the bottom-center and at the top-center go to the right and the temperatures go down. If the pollutant source is located in the middle-right (C_H6), the isothermal curves concentrated at the bottom-center and at the top-center grow up

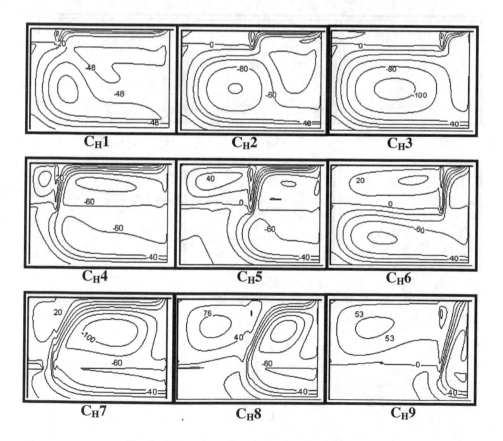

Fig. 6. Mass streamlines for each pollutant source.

and the temperatures remain uniform. When the pollutant source is located in the bottom-left (C_H7), the isothermal curves concentrate at the top, and the temperatures remain uniform. And finally, for the case when the pollutant source is located in the bottom-center and bottom-right (C_H8, C_H9), the isothermal curves concentrate at the right side, and the temperatures remain uniform at the left side.

The Fig. 6 shows the mass density iso-lines as function of the pollutant sources (C_H1, C_H2,...C_H9).

When the pollutant source is located in the top-left (C_H1), the mass streamlines are created at the bottom, starting at the incoming flow aperture. If the pollutant source is located in the top-center (C_H2), the mass streamlines are generated at the center. When the pollutant source is located in the top-right (C_H3), the mass streamlines generated are elongated, high concentrated, and extended. If the pollutant source is located in the middle-left (C_H4), two high mass streamlines are generated, at the pollutant source up to the outgoing aperture, one at the top and another one at the bottom. For the case when the pollutant source is located in the middle-center (C_H5), four non-symmetrical mass streamlines are generated, one at each quadrant. When the pollutant source is located in the middle-right (C_H6), non-symmetrical mass streamlines are generated, starting at the

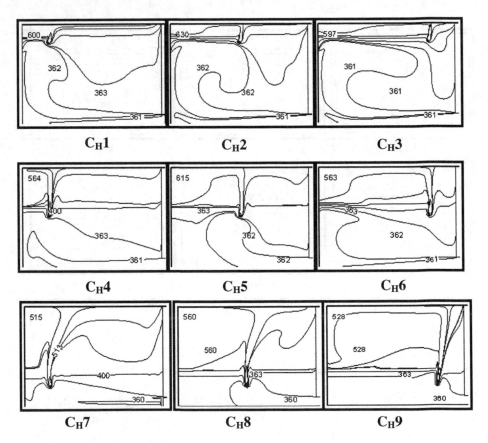

Fig. 7. Iso-concentrations for each pollutant source.

input entrance, moving all along the cavity and getting back at the middle toward the pollutant source. If the pollutant source is located in the bottom-left (C_H7), high non-symmetrical mass streamlines are generated, right in the middle. When the pollutant source is located in the bottom-center (C_H8), two non-symmetrical mass streamlines are generated at the top. Finally, if the pollutant source is located in the bottom-right (C_H9), two non-symmetrical and very low mass streamlines are generated at the top.

The Fig. 7 shows the iso-concentrations as function of the pollutant sources (C_H1, C_H2,...C_H9).

When the pollutant source is located in the top (C_H1, C_H2, C_H3), non-uniform low concentration lines are formed at the top, near the pollutant source, with higher concentrations there. When the pollutant source is located in the middle (C_H4, C_H5, C_H6), two non-uniform low concentration lines are formed, one at the top and another one at the bottom, with higher concentrations at the pollutant source. When the pollutant source is located at the bottom (C_H7, C_H8, C_H9), almost-uniform low concentration lines are formed, with higher concentrations at the pollutant source, all the way up almost uniformly.

The average concentration lines for the pollutant source are 464 ppm, 493 ppm, and 470 ppm, respectively. In contrast with the lowest average concentration of 382 ppm for the C_H1 case.

Table 1 shows a resume of the results, temperature and average concentration, for each of the pollutant source places (C_H1, C_H2, ..., C_H9). The lowest average temperature, the best temperature distribution, the lowest average concentration lines, and cutoff of heat are obtained when the pollutant source is located in the top-right (C_H3), and the input flow is at the bottom. The flow goes from the bottom to the top, hitting the pollutant source and generating large re-circulations. These results are counter commonsense.

Table 1. Average values of temperature and concentrations.

Place	T Aver. (°C)	C Aver. (ppm)
C_H1	297.7	382
C_H2	297.5	390
C_H3	297.3	391
C_H4	298.2	435
C_H5	297.9	460
C_H6	297.5	440
C_H7	298.0	463
C_H8	298.0	493
C_H9	297.4	470

5   Conclusions

From the analysis of the different localizations of the pollutant sources, we conclude that the pollutant source close to the output aperture top-right (C_H3) gives a better temperature distribution: Minimum $T_{average}$ equals to 24.3°C.

From the analysis of the concentration lines, we found the pollutant source at C_H1 gives the most adequate best concentration lines and the lowest average concentration, $C_{average} = 382$ ppm. The heat flow and mass flow are functions of the pollutant source position. To improve the thermal ambient, the heat source must be located at the top and to improve the quality of the air, the pollutant source must be located close to the flow output.

Acknowledgements. We are thankful to CONACyT for their financial support, project I0017, Fondo SEP-CONACyT 000000000223179.

References

1. Sakamoto, Y., Matsuo, Y.: Numerical predictions of three-dimensional flow in a ventilated room using turbulence models. Appl. Math. Model. **4**, 67–72 (1980)
2. Nielsen, P.: Specification of a Two Dimensional Test Case. Energy conservation in buildings and community system. Annex 20. Denmark, November 1990
3. Raji, A., Hasnaoui, M., Bahlaoui, A.: Numerical study of natural convection dominated heat transfer in a ventilated cavity: Case of forced flow playing simultaneous assisting and opposing roles. Int. J. Heat Fluid Flow **29**, 1174–1181 (2008)
4. Béghein, C., Haghighat, F., Allard, F.: Numerical study of double-diffusive natural convection in a square cavity. Int. J. Heat Mass Transf. **45**, 846–883 (1992)
5. Deng, H.-Q., Tang, F.-G.: Numerical visualization of mass and heat transport for mixed convective heat transfer by streamline and heatline. Int. J. Heat Mass Transf. **45**, 2387–2396 (2002)
6. Henkes, R.A., Hoogendoorn, C.J.: Comparison exercise for computations of turbulent natural convection in inclosures. Numer. Heat Transfer, Part B **28**, 59–78 (1995)
7. Liu, D., Zhao, Y.-F., Tang, F.-G.: Numerical analysis of two contaminants removal from a three-dimensional cavity. Int. J. Heat Mass Transf. **51**, 378–382 (2008)
8. Rahman, M.M., Alim, M.A., Mamun, M.A.H., Chowdhury, M.K., Islam, A.K.M.S.: Numerical study of opposing mixed convection in a vented enclosure. ARPN J. Eng. Appl. Sci. **2**, 25–36 (2007)
9. Saha, S., Mamun, H.A., Hossain, Z.M., Islam, S.A.: Mixed convection in a enclosure with different inlet and exit configurations. J. Fluid Mech. **1**, 78–93 (2008)
10. Liu, D., Zhao, F.-Y., Wang, H.-Q., Rank, E.: History source identification of airborne pollutant dispersions in a slot ventilated building enclosure. Int. J. Therm. Sci. **64**, 81–92 (2013)
11. Wilcox, D.: Turbulence Modeling for CFD. DCW Industries, La Canada (2000)
12. Serrano-Arellano, J., Xamán, J., Álvarez, G.: Optimum ventilation based on the ventilation effectiveness for temperature and CO_2 distribution in ventilated cavities. Int. J. Heat Mass Transf. **62**, 9–21 (2013)
13. Serrano-Arellano, J., Xamán, J., Álvarez, G., Gijón-Rivera, M.: Heat and mass transfer by natural convection in a square cavity filled with a mixture of Air–CO_2. Int. J. Heat Mass Transf. **64**, 725–734 (2013)
14. Serrano-Arellano, J., Gijón-Rivera, M.: Conjugate heat and mass transfer by natural convection in a square cavity filled with a mixture of Air–CO_2. Int. J. Heat Mass Transf. **70**, 103–113 (2014)

15. Patankar, S.: Numerical Heat Transfer and Fluid Flow. Hemisphere Publishing Co., Mc. Graw Hill Co., New York (1980)
16. Van Doormaal, J., Raithby, G.: Enhancements of the SIMPLE method for predicting incompressible fluid flow. Numer. Heat Transf. **7**, 147–163 (1984)
17. Nielsen, P.: Computational fluid dynamics. Indoor Air **14**(Suppl 7), 134–143 (2004)
18. Tun, C.M.: Análisis de la Transferencia de Calor Conjugada en Cavidades Ventiladas con Flujo Turbulento. Tesis de Maestría, CENIDET, México (2007)

Implementation of the Macro and Micro Mechanical Cochlea Model in a GPU

José Luis Oropeza Rodríguez[✉], José Francisco Reyes Saldaña, and Sergio Suárez Guerra

Computing Research Center, National Polytechnic Institute, Juan de Dios Batiz s/n, P.O. 07038 Mexico, Mexico
{joropeza,ssuarez}@cic.ipn.mx, jfreyes0114@gmail.com

Abstract. For a long time, cochlea models have been an interesting area of study for scientists in different fields such as medicine, especially in otorhinolaryngology, physics and acoustic engineering, among others. That is because, in mammals, this organ is the most important element in the transduction of the sound pressure that is received by the outer and middle ear.

In this paper we present a method to simulate the macro and micro mechanical model developed by Neely [3], using a Graphics Processing Unit (GPU). We use a linear model for the cochlea that has produced results close to those obtained by Von Bèkesy. The principal characteristic of this cochlea model is that is a linear representation of the cochlea, being one of the most important models found in the literature, producing results close to those of Von Bèkesy, pioneer in the analysis and study of the human cochlea.

We use the finite difference method to discretize the ordinary differential equations (ODEs) that represents the properties of the mass, stiffness and damping of the cochlea, specifically of the Corti Organ, also named the micro mechanical model of the cochlea. We use Thomas' algorithm to invert the matrix obtained from the discretization, and we implement both, a serial and a parallel algorithm for the numerical solution. We obtain a speedup of 284.09 and an efficiency of 0.568.

Keyword: Cochlea models

1 Introduction

The development of cochlear mechanics analysis and modeling started during the 20th century. The first steps appeared around 1925, but the field expanded strongly after 1950. The mathematical—biophysical approach remained mostly linear until the late 1970 s, even though several nonlinear auditory phenomena were well known [8].

The initial study of the linear cochlea is relevant because

- It gives a proper introduction to the mathematical and biophysical concepts that are in use in the field.
- Current insight in analysis of complex systems is largely based on tools from linear signal analysis.
- Major developments started with the analysis of a linear cochlea [8, 9].

© Springer International Publishing Switzerland 2016
I. Gitler and J. Klapp (Eds.): ISUM 2015, CCIS 595, pp. 380–391, 2016.
DOI: 10.1007/978-3-319-32243-8_27

The first mechanical theory of the cochlea was proposed by Peterson and Bogert in 1950 [10]. It was based on hydrodynamics, considering the cochlea as a system of two channels that vary in shape, similar in cross section, and separated by an elastic membrane with constant dynamic variables. The model makes use of the parameters reported in the experimental work of Bèkèsy [7, 9]. In the following years, theories about the mechanics of the cochlea were developed, but in 1971 Rhode reported physical measurements of its physiology, and the theories that were proposed previously were found inadequate [11, 12].

Later in 1972, Lesser and Berkley developed a model that matches all the previously reported observations, modeling the cochlea as a system with fluid flow, and the basilar membrane as a system of concatenated, forced, harmonic oscilators [15]. In 1976, Allen [13] used the Lesser and Berkley model to obtain the parameters of the basilar membrane using the Green's function, obtaining an approximate set of parameters of its behavior. Later in 1981, Neely [14] proposed a two-dimensional mathematical model of the cochlea and their numerical solution using finite differences approximations of the Laplace's equation, obtaining, so far and to the best of our knowledge, the best parameters of the mechanical response of the cochlea.

The solution to the model of the basilar membrane as a system of forced harmonic oscillators has been proposed by Lesser and Berkeley in 1972 [15], using potential flow theory and Fourier series. Later in 1974 [16], Siebert generalized the solution of Lesser and Berkley considering a mechanical force at the two ends of the basilar membrane. A similar solution was found in 1981 by Peskin [17]. The following studies considered the physical structure of the basilar membrane to solve the model, emphasizing studies in 1984 by Rhode [18], in 1985 by Hudspeth [19] and 1996 by Boer [20]. In recent years, authors have developed solutions considering state space models: in 2007 by Elliott et al. [21] and 2008 by Ku et al. [21]. Recently, these studies have been used for Automatic Speech Recognition Systems [5, 6].

In the works mentioned above, the simulation of the behavior of the cochlea was computed using a serial code. Nevertheless, the main function of the cochlea is to analyze the signals in parallel. That is, when a composite signal reaches the cochlea, it is distributed along this organ, delivering it to the auditory nerves. This decomposition follows the principle of parallelism. We propose the use of GPU to analyze and simulate this physiological behavior.

2 Characteristics and Generalities

The cochlea is a long, narrow, fluid-filled tunnel which spirals through the temporal bone. This tunnel is divided along its length by a cochlear partition into an upper compartment called scala vestibuli (SV) and a lower compartment called scala timpani (ST). At the apex of the cochlea, the SV and ST are connected by the helicotrema [1]. A set of models to represent the operation of the cochlea has been proposed [2, 3, 21, 22]; among others. In mammals, vibrations of the stapes set up a wave with a particular shape on the basilar membrane. The amplitude envelope of the wave first increases along the channel and then decreases after a maximum. The position at the peak of the envelope is dependent on the frequency of the stimulus [4]. The amplitude of the envelope is a two-dimensional function of space and frequency of stimulation. The curve shown in Fig. 1 is a cross-section of the function for fixed frequency. If low frequencies excite the cochlea, the envelope is closer to the apex, but if high frequencies excite it, the envelope is closer to the base.

The micromechanical anatomical structure is illustrated in Fig. 2 showing a radial cross-section (RCS) of the cochlear partition (CP). In the model, the basilar membrane (BM) and tectorial membrane (TM) are each represented as a lumped mass with both stiffness and damping in their attachment to the surrounding bone. When the cochlea determines the frequency of the incoming signal from the location of the maximum amplitude on the basilar membrane, the organ of Corti is excited, in conjunction with the movement of the tectorial membrane; the inner and outer hair cells are excited obtaining an electrical pulse that travels along the by auditory nerve.

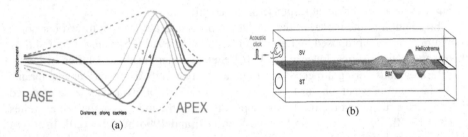

Fig. 1. (a) Envelope wave displacement inside the cochlea (b) 2-dimensional box of the two compartments inside of the cochlea

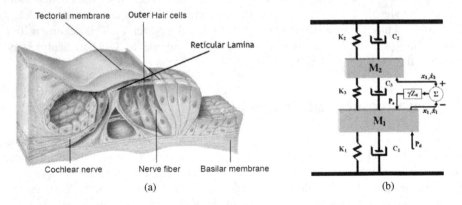

Fig. 2. (a) Anatomical structure of the cochlear partition. (b) The outer hair cells, micro mechanical representation.

The study of the cochlear model will be divided in two ways. First, the study of the hydrodynamic motion, with the pressure exciting the basilar membrane. And second, the study of the motion of the outer hair cells. It is known as the model of Macro and Micro Mechanical Cochlear [3], which is represented in Fig. 2. The equations that describe the Macro Mechanical Cochlear are [3]:

$$\frac{d^2}{dx^2}P_d(x) = \frac{2\rho}{H}\ddot{\varepsilon}(x) \tag{1}$$

$$\frac{d^2}{dx^2}P_d(0) = 2\rho\,\ddot{\varepsilon}_s \tag{2}$$

$$\frac{d^2}{dx^2}P_d(L) = 2\rho\,\ddot{\varepsilon}(h) \tag{3}$$

The Eqs. (1), (2) and (3) were solved by finite differences, using central differences for (1), forward differences for (2) and backward difference for (3), gene-rating a tridiagonal matrix system [16] which we solved using Thomas' algorithm. It represents the micro mechanical, because it uses the organ of Corti values, as can be seen in Fig. 2.

The matrix has the following structure:

$$
\begin{bmatrix}
\left(\frac{2\rho i\omega}{Z_m}\right) & \left(\frac{1}{\Delta}\right) & & & & (0) \\
& & & & & \\
0 & 0 & \frac{1}{\Delta^2} & -\left(\frac{2}{\Delta^2}+\frac{2\rho i\omega}{HZ_p(X_n)}\right) & \frac{1}{\Delta^2} & \\
& & & & & \\
0 & 0 & & & \left(\frac{1}{\Delta}\right) & -\left(\frac{1}{\Delta}-\frac{2\rho i\omega}{C_h}\right)
\end{bmatrix}
\begin{bmatrix}
P_d(X_1) \\
P_d(X_2) \\
\vdots \\
P_d(X_{n-1}) \\
P_d(X_n) \\
P_d(X_{n+1}) \\
\vdots \\
P_d(X_{N-1}) \\
P_d(X_N)
\end{bmatrix}
=
\begin{bmatrix}
\left(\frac{2\rho i\omega\,A_m}{Z_m\,G_m\,A_s}\right) \\
0 \\
\vdots \\
0 \\
0 \\
0 \\
0 \\
\vdots \\
0
\end{bmatrix}. \tag{4}
$$

Solving for P_d we obtain the maximum amplitude on the basilar membrane, as shown in Fig. 3. A set of variables related to the physiology of the cochlea are needed to solve Eq. (4), some of them described in Table 1. These values are substituted into Zp and Z_m, following [3]. The rest of the parameters were taken from the same paper.

Table 1. Values used in equation

Parámetro	Neely and Kim 1986 (cgs)	Ku (coclea humana, 2008)	Elliot (2007)
$k_1(x)$	$1.1 * 10^9 e^{-4x}$	$1.65 * 10^8 e^{-2.79(x+0.00373)}$	$4.95 * 10^8 e^{-3.2(x+0.00375)}$
$c_1(x)$	$20 + 1500 e^{-2x}$	$0.9 + 999 e^{-1.53(x+0.00373)}$	$0.1 + 1970 e^{-1.79(x+0.00375)}$
$m_1(x)$	$3 * 10^{-3}$	$4.5 * 10^{-4}$	$1.35 * 10^{-3}$
$k_2(x)$	$7 * 10^6 e^{-4.4x}$	$1.05 * 10^6 e^{-3.07(x+0.00373)}$	$3.15 * 10^6 e^{-3.52(x+0.00375)}$
$c_2(x)$	$10 e^{-2.2x}$	$3 e^{-1.71(x+0.00373)}$	$11.3 e^{-1.76(x+0.00375)}$

(*Continued*)

Table 1. (*Continued*)

Parámetro	Neely and Kim 1986 (cgs)	Ku (coclea humana, 2008)	Elliot (2007)
$m_2(x)$	$0.5 * 10^{-3}$	$0.72 * 10^{-4} + 0.28710^{-2}x$	$2.3 * 10^{-4}$
$k_3(x)$	$1 * 10^7 e^{-4x}$	$1.5 * 10^6 e^{-2.79(x+0.00373)}$	$4.5 * 10^6 e^{-3.2(x+0.00375)}$
$c_3(x)$	$2e^{-0.8x}$	$0.66e^{-0.593(x+0.00373)}$	$2.25e^{-0.64(x+0.00375)}$
$k_4(x)$	$6.15 * 10^8 e^{-4x}$	$9.23 * 10^7 e^{-2.79(x+0.00373)}$	$2.84 * 10^8 e^{-3.2(x+0.00375)}$
$c_4(x)$	$1040e^{-2x}$	$330e^{-1.44(x+0.00373)}$	$965e^{-1.64(x+0.00375)}$
gamma	1	1	1
g	1	1	1
b	0.4	0.4	0.4
L	2.5	3.5	3.5
H	0.1	0.1	0.1
K_m	$2.1 * 10^6$	$2.63 * 10^7$	$2.63 * 10^7$
C_m	400	$2.8 * 10^3$	$2.8 * 10^3$
M_m	$45 * 10^3$	$2.96 * 10^{-3}$	$2.96 * 10^{-3}$
C_h	0.1	35	21
A_s	0.01	$3.2 * 10^{-2}$	$3.2 * 10^{-2}$
Rho	0.35	1	1
N	250	500	500
Gm	0.5	0.5	0.5

Figure 3 shows the behavior of the basilar membrane using the values shown in Table 1. Before 300 Hz the behavior of the micro and macro mechanical model is not adequate, independently of the parameters used. This result is a consequence of the characteristics of the model proposed in [3].

Figure 3 shows the solution of Eq. (4) for a set of values of P_d. It's important to mention that the model is linear and active elements are essential for simulating the high sensitivity and sharp tuning characteristics of the mammalian cochlea. The active elements represent the motile action of outer hair cells; they are postulated to be mechanical force generators that are powered by the electrochemical energy of the cochlear endolymph, controlled by the bending of the outer hair cells stereocilia, bidirectionally coupled to cochlear partition mechanics. The active elements are spatially distributed and perform collectively as a cochlear amplifier. Excessive gain in the cochlear amplifier causes spontaneous oscillations and thereby generates spontaneous otoacoustic emissions. As we mentioned above, Neely's model [3] and later works have considered that we can put a number of these micromechanisms equidistant along the cochlea. We used this principle to establish the following relation between a minimal and maximal distance.

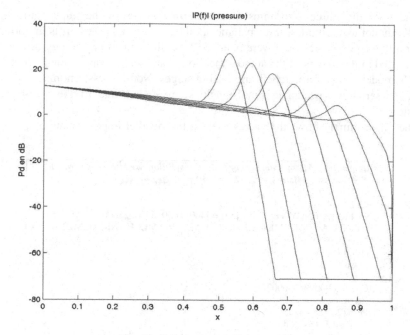

Fig. 3. Solution to Neely's model.

3 Experiments and Results

For our implementation in CUDA C++; a GPU was used with the features shown in Table 2. The following three experiments have the same number of operations, this is because only the hearing constant was changed in the cochlea for the parameters set by Neely [3] to those used by Elliot and Ku respectively [21, 22].

Threads per Warp	32
Warps per Multiprocessor	64
Threads per Multiprocessor	2048
Thread Blocks per Multiprocessor	16
Total No. of 32-bit registers per Multiprocessor	65536
Register allocation unit size	256
Register allocation granularity warp Registers per Thread	63
Shared Memory per Multiprocessor (bytes)	49152
Shared Memory Allocation unit size	256
Warp allocation granularity	4
Maximum Thread Block Size	1024

The following three algorithms illustrate some stages of the implementation of Neely's model using the last three parameters mentioned in Table 1. It is important to mention that some values used were obtained from the human physiology aspects and not reported in the papers of the authors mentioned above. The operational structure of Neely's model allows for parallelization using stages. Nonetheless, Thomas' algorithm was kept serial. Considerable time penalties are found due to the serial matrix inversion.

The Algorithm 1 shows the values used in the parallel implementation.

Algorithm 1. First parameters of the serial solution used in the Macro and Micro Mechanical Model proposed by Neely

```
set N = 500
set Nf = 4
set FREQUENCY VECTOR f[Nf] = [400; 1600; 6400; 25600]
set INITIAL PARAMETERS OF THE MACRO MECHANICAL MODEL
rho = 1
H = 0.1
B = 0.4
L = 2.5
Ch = 0.00000000000001
Δx=L/N
Pe = (2.848e - 4)
for i = 0 TO i < N do
  x[i] = i
end for
for i = 0 TO i < N do
 for j = 0 TO j < NF do
 s,k1,k2,k3,k4,c1,c2,c3,c4,m1,m2,gama,g,b As Complex
 s[j] = complex(0, (2 * pi * f[j]))
 k1[i + (j * N)] = complex(1.1e9 * exp(-4 * x[i]), 0)
 k2[i + (j * N)] = complex(7e6 * exp(-4.4 * x[i]), 0)
 k3[i + (j * N)] = complex(1e7 * exp(-4 * x[i]), 0)
 k4[i + (j * N)] = complex(6.15e8 *exp(-4 * x[i]), 0)
 c1[i + (j * N)] = complex(20 + 1500 * exp(-2 * x[i]), 0)
 c2[i + (j * N)] = complex(10 * exp(-2.2 * x[i]), 0)
 c3[i + (j * N)] = complex(2 * exp(-0.8 * x[i]), 0)
 c4[i + (j * N)] = complex(1040 * exp(-2 * x[i]), 0)
 m1 = complex(3e – 3, 0)
 m2 = complex(0.5e – 3, 0)
 gama = complex(1.0)
 g = complex(1.0)
 b = complex(0.4, 0)
 end for
 end for
```

Above we show the pseudocode of the algorithms implemented for the most important stages of our implementation.

Algorithm 2 is Thomas' method for the inversion of the matrix. This is the only serial part of our implementation.

```
a,b,c,d As Complex
tid=threadIdx.x + blockIdx.x*blockDim.x
formar los vectores a,b,c y d de Thomas
a[tid] = (1/Δx)
b[tid] = (-2/Δx) - (rho * s[blockIdx.x] * Y cp[tid])
c[tid] = (1/Δx)
d[tid] = complex(0, 0)
Set values to the initial conditions
if tid == 0 then
   a[tid] = 0
   b[tid] = ((rho * s)=Zm[blockIdx.x]) - (1/Δx)
num[blockIdx.x] = rho * s[blockIdx.x] * Am * Pe
den[blockIdx.x] = Zm * Gm * As
d[tid] = num[blockIdx.x]/den[blockIdx.x]
 end if
Set values to the last conditions
if tid == N - 1 then
   b[tid] = ((rho * s[blockIdx.x])/Ch) - (1/Δx)
   c[tid] = 0
end if
```

Finally, we show the implementation of the Cochlear impedance partition that represents the coupling join between the macro and micro mechanical model, used to solve the matrix in Eq. (4).

Algorithm 3. Calculus of the Cochlear Impedances Partition used in Parallel implementation of the Macro and Micro Mechanical Model proposed by Neely

```
invs,Z1,Z2,Z3,Z4,HC,aux,Ha,Hb,Zp,Ycp As Complex
tid=threadIdx.x + blockIdx.x*blockDim.x
invs[blockIdx.x] = 1/s[blockIdx.x]
Z1[tid] = invs[blockIdx.x] * k1[tid] + c1[tid] + m1 * s[blockIdx.x]
Z2[tid] = invs[blockIdx.x] * k2[tid] + c2[tid] + m2 * s[blockIdx.x]
Z3[tid] = invs[blockIdx.x] * k3[tid] + c3[tid]
Z4[tid] = invs[blockIdx.x] * k4[tid] + c4[tid]
Hc[tid] = Z2[tid]/(Z2[tid] + Z3[tid])
aux[tid] = gama * Z4[tid]
Ha[tid)] = (Z3[tid] * aux[tid])
Hb[tid] = (Z1[tid] + Hc[tid] * Ha[tid])
Zp[tid] = (g/b) * Hb[tid]
Y cp[tid] = Δx * (1/H) * (1/Zp[tid])
```

As a first experiment, the solution obtained with the GPU was compared with that found with a serial C++ code. We used the four frequencies mentioned by Neely [3] in his experiments to study the response of the model. For the solution that generates pressure differences on the basilar membrane, along the cochlear partition, the following frequencies were used: 400 Hz, 1600 Hz, 6400 Hz and 25600 Hz. Figure 4 shows the results of these pressures calculated with the GPU and the CPU.

As a second experiment, the solution in CUDA C++ and posteriorly in C++ were compared, the four frequencies mentioned by Neely [3] were used with the parameters set by Emery Ku [22]. To obtain the solution of the pressure generated along the

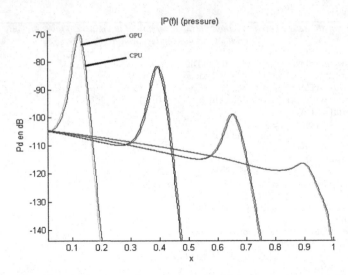

Fig. 4. Pressure difference in dB vs distance along cochlea using values proposed by Neely

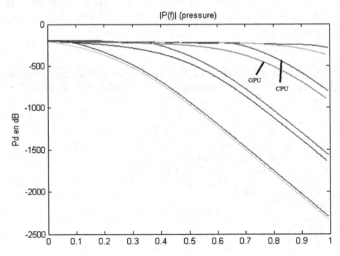

Fig. 5. Pressure difference in dB vs distance along cochlea using values proposed by Emery Ku

cochlear partition on the basilar membrane, we use the frequencies: 400 Hz, 1600 Hz, 6400 Hz and 25600 Hz. Figure 5 shows results of the pressure calculated with the GPU and CPU. The difference between the response of the CPU and GPU showed in Fig. 5 illustrate the response for different frequencies for both implementations, pointing to errors and limits of the specific GPU implementation.

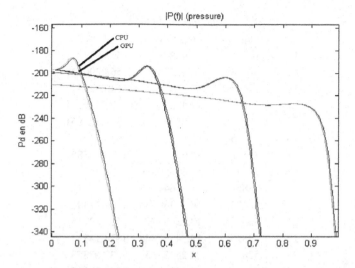

Fig. 6. Pressure difference in dB vs distance along cochlea using the values proposed by Elliot

As a third experiment, solutions in CUDA C ++ and C ++ were computed. Both implementations use the four frequencies mentioned by Neely [3]. In this case, the parameters presented by S. Elliot [21] were used to compute the solution of the pressure generated along the cochlear partition on the basilar membrane, for the following frequencies: 400 Hz, 1600 Hz, 6400 Hz and 25600 Hz. Figure 6 shows the results of these pressures calculated with the GPU and CPU. The timing of the serial implementation was T_{sec} = 3.9660 s and the time measured in the parallel implementation was T_{par} = 0.01396032 s, for a speed up of $S = T_{sec}/T_{par}$ = 284.09. While the performance of this implementation is evaluated as $E = T_{sec}/nT_{par}$, with $n = 500$ threads in execution, for an efficiency then $E = 0.568$.

The following table shows the results obtained from the parallel implementation of Neely's model on the GPU. The values show the distance given the frequency used to excite the model.

Table 2. Frequency vs. distance proposed

Item	Distance (x)	Presion in dB	Frequency
1	2.6495	4E-10	78.825638
2	2.5995	0.000007	116.197052
3	2.5495	0.0004	150.462677
4	2.4995	0.01	184.646286
5	2.4495	0.02	220.126266
6	2.3995	0.03	257.798676
7	2.3495	0.04	298.382843
8	2.2995	0.105	342.535828
9	2.2495	0.2994	390.906982
10	2.1945	1.467	444.168732

(Continued)

Table 2. (*Continued*)

Item	Distance (x)	Presion in dB	Frequency
11	2.14425	2.948	503.037781
12	2.09425	4.417	568.290527
13	2.044	5.914	640.777527
14	1.994	7.428	721.436951
15	1.939	8.957	811.307861
16	1.88875	10.5	911.545593
17	1.83875	12.05	1023.43585
18	1.7885	13.60354819	1148.4126
19	1.7385	15.14644558	1288.07617
20	1.68325	16.69369339	1444.21497
21	1.63325	18.2303772	1618.82715
22	1.58325	19.74352844	1814.1471
23	1.528	21.2573763	2032.67358
24	1.478	22.74038167	2277.20313
25	1.42275	24.21123255	2550.86353
26	1.37275	25.64727042	2857.15649
27	1.31775	27.07376244	3200

4   Conclusions and Future Works

This paper describes serial and parallel implementations of the micro and macro cochlear model of Neely. Neely's model has been successful in reproducing the experimental results of Bèkèsy. We have used the parameters of Elliot and Emery Ku, that followed the work of Neely. The model was implemented in parallel on the GPU given that, in principle, the response of the cochlea to a signal is a physiological parallel process. Our computational parallel model tries to closely imitate some of the features of the actual organ. The parallel implementation reaches a speed up of 284.09.

Acknowledgment. We are thankful to the Center for Computing Research of the National Polytechnic Institute (IPN). This research was funded by the SIP project 2015104.

References

1. Keener, J., Sneyd, J.: Mathematical Physiology. Springer, New York (2008)
2. Elliott, S.J., Lineton, B., Ni, G.: Fluid coupling in a discrete model of cochlear mechanics. J. Acoust. Soc. Am. **130**, 1441–1451 (2011)
3. Neely, S.T.: A model for active elements in cochlear biomechanics. J. Acoust. Soc. Am. **79**, 1472–1480 (1986)
4. Békésy, G.: Concerning the pleasures of observing, and the mechanics of the inner ear. Nobel Lecture, December 11, 1961

5. Mario, J.H., Rodríguez, J.L.O., Guerra, S.S., Fernández, R.B.: Computational model of the cochlea using resonance analysis. Journal Revista Mexicana Ingeniería Biomédica 33(2), 77–86 (2012)
6. Mario, J.H.: Modelo mecánico acústico del oído interno en reconocimiento de voz, Ph. D. Thesis, Center for Computing Research-IPN, Junio, 2013
7. von Bèkèsy, G.: Experiments in hearing. Mc Graw Hill, New York (1960)
8. Hendrikus, D.: Cochlear Mechanics Introduction to a Time Domain Analysis of the Nonlinear Cochlea. Springer, New York (2012). ISBN 978-1-4419-6116-7
9. Divya, S., Olga, S., Patricia, L.: A frequency-position function for the human cochlear spiral ganglion. Audiol. Neurotol. 11(1), 16–20 (2006)
10. Peterson, L.C., Bogert, B.P.: A dynamical theory of the cochlea. J. Acoust. Soc. Am. 22, 175–184 (1952)
11. Rhode, W.S.: Observations of the vibration of the basilar membrane in squirrel monkeys using the mössbauer technique. J. Acoust. Soc. Am. 49, 1218–1231 (1971)
12. Rhode, W.S., Robles, L.: Evidence of Mossbauer experiments for nonlinear vibration in the cochlea. J. Acoust. Soc. Am. 55, 558–596 (1974)
13. Allen, J.B., Hirano, M.: Two-Dimensional cochlear fluid model: new results. J. Acoust. Soc. Am. 61, 110–119 (1971)
14. Neely, S.T.: Finite difference solution of a two-dimensional mathematical model of the cochlea. J. Acoust. Soc. Am. 69, 1386–1396 (1981)
15. Lesser, M.B., Berkeley, D.A.: Fluid Mechanics of the cochlea. Part 1. J. Fluid Mech. 51, 497–512 (1972)
16. Siebert, W.M.: Ranke revisited-a simple short-wave cochlear model. J. Acoust. Soc. Am. 56, 594–600 (1974)
17. Peskin, C.S.: Lectures on mathematical aspects of physiology. AMS Lect. Appl. Math. 19, 38–69 (1981)
18. Rhode, W.S.: Cochlear Mechanics. Ann. Rev. Physiol. 46, 231–246 (1984)
19. Hudspeth, A.J.: The cellular basis of hearing: the biophysics of hair cells. Science 230, 745–752 (1985)
20. Boer, S.E.: Mechanics of the cochlea: modeling effects. In: Dallos, P., Fay, R.R. (eds.) the cochlea. Springer, New York (1996)
21. Elliot, S.J., Ku, E.M., Lineton, B.A.: A state space model for cochlear mechanics. J. Acoust. Soc. Amer. 122, 2759–2771 (2007)
22. Ku, E.M., Elliot, S.J., Lineton, B.A.: Statistics of instabilities in a state space model of the human cochlea. J. Acoust. Soc. Amer. 124, 1068–1079 (2008)

Parallel Replica Exchange Monte Carlo Applied to Hard Systems

Gustavo Bautista-Carbajal[1], Carlos A. Vargas[2], Eduardo Basurto[2], and Gerardo Odriozola[2(✉)]

[1] Academia de Matemáticas,
Universidad Autónoma de la Ciudad de México, 07160 México, D.F., Mexico
[2] Departamento de Ciencias Básicas, Universidad Autónoma
Metropolitana-Azcapotzalco, Av. San Pablo 180, 02200 México D.F., Mexico
godriozo@azc.uam.mx

Abstract. In this chapter we show how the replica exchange Monte Carlo algorithm can be used to study hard systems, i.e. systems composed by hard particles such as spheres, ellipsoids, disks, and ellipses, among others. The method is based on the definition of an extended ensemble which usually uses temperature as the expansion variable. This way, the low temperature replicas perform local sampling on the configuration space while high temperature replicas produce large jumps. The replica swap moves allow for a low temperature replica to heat, reach another region of configuration space, and cool back, enhancing the sampling of low-temperature, uneven free energy landscapes. Each replica is handled by a single thread making the parallelization straightforward. On the other hand, hard particles cannot overlap and do not contribute to the potential energy. In this case we carry out a pressure expansion of the isothermal-isobaric ensemble. Here we show how this expansion is able to resolve the phase diagrams of hard systems in two and three dimensions.

1 Introduction

With the purpose of improving the usually poor sampling of systems at low temperatures or high pressures, it was proposed to replicate the system simulation cell, setting each replica at different thermodynamic conditions, and to study the set of replicas as a whole, while allowing them to swap conditions by pairs [1,2]. The method is known as Replica Exchange Monte Carlo (REMC) [1,2], or parallel tempering [3], and allows to implement an ergodic walk through free energy barriers connecting disjoint configuration subspaces by defining a set of close enough thermodynamic states. In other words, it is possible to keep all replicas at equilibrium, while they travel along the set of thermodynamic states. The method is clear and simple, can be implemented by means of Monte Carlo (MC) or molecular dynamics to produce new configurations from old ones, has broad applicability, and its parallelization is extremely simple since each replica is independent of the others until the swap stage. All these features have lead to a very

I. Gitler and J. Klapp (Eds.): ISUM 2015, CCIS 595, pp. 392–418, 2016.
DOI: 10.1007/978-3-319-32243-8_28

large acceptance and has been included in several well established molecular packages, such as Gromacs [4,5]. Its wide applicability covers from the proposal of different zeolite structures [6], to the study of transitions between protein conformations [7], passing through the access to the phase equilibrium of many single and multicomponent systems [8–10], and the study of glasses [11].

The REMC method is most frequently employed to sample an extended canonical ensemble in temperature. This way, high temperature replicas can escape from local free energy minima, allowing the whole set of replicas to reach equilibrium. That is, a replica at the lowest temperature can eventually swap to higher temperatures, produce large jumps on configuration space, and return by swapping to the lowest temperature to sample a different local free energy minimum. A pair of local minima may correspond, for instance, to a couple of proteins conformations. In such a case, the average number of configurations sampled by each replica at each conformation is linked to the free energy depth of each local minimum. In this example, the relation between the pair potential attraction of the constituting atoms and the temperature plays a key role. In other words, the enthalpic contribution to the free energy is important. When the free energy landscape is mainly dictated by the entropic term, i.e. by the excluded volume repulsive interactions [12–14], setting the temperature as the expansion variable has a small effect on sampling. This situation occurs at high temperatures or when the potential well depths are shallow. That is, the sampling gain of applying the algorithm diminishes. In particular, the gain is null when dealing with hard body systems such as hard spheres, rods, plates, dumbbells, ellipsoids, and their mixtures, since these models are limiting cases where all allowed pair contributions to the potential energy are zero. An alternative to apply the REMC method to this kind of systems is to perform an expansion in pressure of the isothermal-isobaric ensemble instead of a temperature expansion of the canonical ensemble. In such a case, the high pressure replicas would carry out the sampling at local free energy minima whereas the replicas at low pressures would produce large jumps on configuration space. In this chapter we present some applications of this method. These are the determination of the equations of state of hard spheres and discs (in three and two dimensions, respectively), and the resolution of the phase diagrams of ellipsoids of revolution and ellipses (again, in three and two dimensions, respectively). We are also including the resulting equation of state of a glass former binary mixture of hard spheres.

Transitions represent a challenge for computer simulations [15,16]. This is especially true for transitions involving solid phases. Many techniques which work well for studying liquid-gas transitions do not work properly for solids or dense fluids [17]. Consequently, freezing and melting points are hard to determine [15]. For instance, it was in this century that an accurate determination of the freezing and melting points of hard spheres was given by simulations [15,16]. This contrasts with the theoretical values which were available approximately forty years before. This is despite the intense study of the hard sphere system through the past decades, and the fact that the hard sphere model was one of the first ones ever studied by computer simulations [18–20]. Hence, it should

not come as a surprise that the phase diagrams of other more complicated hard
body systems are still unrevealed. On the other hand, the hard sphere fluid
branch persists above the fluid solid transition turning metastable, and its fate
at large volume fraction remains under debate [21]. Since the fluid branch cannot extend surpassing the closed packed density, it may either go unstable, or it
may exhibit a singularity with a diverging pressure and a vanishing isothermal
compressibility. In addition, a thermodynamic glass transition may occur along
the way [21–25], given by a diverging timescale for structural relaxation [26–29],
a change of slope in the equation of state, and a jump in the compressibility.
This is known as the thermodynamic signature of the dynamical glass transition
in hard spheres and its search by computer simulations has given both possible
results, its existence [30] and its absence [11]. The REMC method combined with
the sampling of an extended isothermal-isobaric ensemble in pressure may help
in this direction.

The aim of this chapter is to show how the replica exchange Monte Carlo can
be successfully applied to study several aspects of hard body systems. For this
purpose, the method is implemented by defining an isothermal-isobaric ensemble
extension in pressure. The chapter is structured as follows. Section 2 describes the
replica exchange method. We have separated this section into two: temperature
expansion of the canonical ensemble and pressure expansion of the isothermal-
isobaric ensemble. Results are given in two sections. These are: applications
in three dimensions (Sect. 3) and applications in two dimensions (Sect. 4). 3D
applications include resolving the equations of state for monodisperse and a
particular non-crystallizing binary mixture of hard spheres, and the resolution
of the phase diagram of spheroids. 2D applications are focused on the fluid-
solid transition of hard disks and the phase diagram of ellipses. Finally, Sect. 5
summarizes the most relevant conclusions.

2   Replica Exchange Monte Carlo

As mentioned above, we have split this section into two. We first present the
method by performing a temperature expansion of the canonical ensemble since
this is the most frequent approach. In the next subsection we show the pressure
expansion of the isobaric-isothermal ensemble, which is then used to produce
the results shown in the following section.

2.1   Temperature Expansion of the Canonical Ensemble

The most frequent replica exchange implementation considers n_r identical replicas each following a simulation sampling from canonical ensembles with different
temperatures [2, 31, 32] (see the top panel of Fig. 1). In line with this implementation, an extended ensemble can be defined so that its partition function is
given by

$$Q_{extended} = \prod_{i=1}^{n_r} Q_{NVT_i},$$ (1)

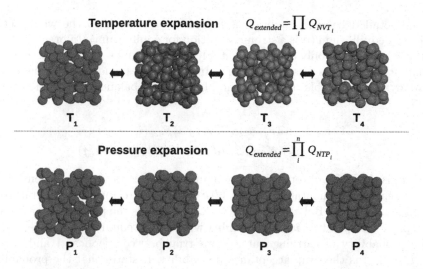

Temperature expansion $Q_{extended} = \prod_i Q_{NVT_i}$

T_1 T_2 T_3 T_4

Pressure expansion $Q_{extended} = \prod_i^n Q_{NTP_i}$

P_1 P_2 P_3 P_4

Fig. 1. Sketch for the canonical ensemble expansion in temperature (top) and for the isothermal-isobaric ensemble expansion in pressure (bottom). Temperature and pressure increase with the corresponding index. Pressures P_1, P_2, P_3, and P_4 correspond to the labels at the top panel of Fig. 3.

being Q_{NVT_i} the partition function of ensemble i at temperature T_i, N the number of particles at each replica, and V the volume of each replica. N and V are the same for all replicas. Hence, there are n_r replicas sampling from n_r ensembles, a replica for each ensemble. In principle, it would be possible to work with an overpopulation of replicas (more replicas than ensembles) or with an underpopulated system, defining less replicas than ensembles. However, we cannot see any clear advantage of doing so. The sampling of each replica at each ensemble is performed following, in our case, a standard MC procedure. Producing new configurations from old ones can also be implemented by the integration of the equations of motion using a standard molecular dynamics algorithm or by more sophisticated MC schemes. The standard MC scheme involves carrying out a large number of particle displacements and rotations (when dealing with anisotropic particles) on each replica. Since replicas are independent, this step, which consumes most of the computer power, is easily parallelized. The existence of the extended ensemble justifies the implementation of swap trial moves between any two replicas, whenever the detailed balance condition is satisfied. This step is accomplished when the replicas produce new have produced new uncorrelated configurations from the old ones (by performing a large number of MC moves). Hence, swap trials should not be frequently done. In addition, this step involves some knowledge of all the replicas, what implies data transference among threads. Additionally, it is usually anticipated by a barrier, which leads to idle processes until the last replica ends its standard MC cycle (see reference [33] for an algorithm to minimize the efficiency loss due to barriers).

The detailed balance condition is forced in order to keep the whole set of replicas at equilibrium (it is a strong condition for equilibrium). In practice, swap trials are carried out only on replicas at adjacent ensembles since the acceptance probability steeply decreases with increasing differences among the values of the thermodynamic variable of expansion. The detailed balance condition is given by [17]

$$\mathcal{N}(\boldsymbol{r}_i, \beta_i)\mathcal{N}(\boldsymbol{r}_j, \beta_j)\alpha(i, j \rightarrow j, i)P_{acc}(i, j \rightarrow j, i) = \\ \mathcal{N}(\boldsymbol{r}_j, \beta_i)\mathcal{N}(\boldsymbol{r}_i, \beta_j)\alpha(j, i \rightarrow i, j)P_{acc}(j, i \rightarrow i, j) \tag{2}$$

where $\boldsymbol{r}_i$ is the point of replica i in configuration space (a set of positions defining the replica i configuration), $\beta_i = 1/(k_B T_i)$ is the reciprocal temperature of ensemble i, k_B is the Boltzmann constant, $\mathcal{N}(\boldsymbol{r}_i, \beta_i)$ is the probability of finding the replica i at point $\boldsymbol{r}_i$ in the ensemble with β_i (at equilibrium), $\alpha(i, j \rightarrow j, i)$ is the probability of carrying out a swap trial between replicas i and j, and $P_{acc}(i, j \rightarrow j, i)$ is the swap acceptance probability. It states that the probability of swapping replicas i and j times the probability of having the replicas with configurations $\boldsymbol{r}_i$ and $\boldsymbol{r}_j$ at ensembles with β_i and β_j, respectively, must equal the probability of performing the reverse swap move times the probability of having the replicas with configurations $\boldsymbol{r}_i$ and $\boldsymbol{r}_j$ at ensembles with β_j and β_i, respectively. In other words, the probability of generating a new configuration from an old one is decomposed into two terms, $\alpha(i, j \rightarrow j, i)$ and $P_{acc}(i, j \rightarrow j, i)$. The simplest implementation sets $\alpha(i, j \rightarrow j, i) = \alpha(j, i \rightarrow i, j)$, i.e. all swap trials are given the same a priori probability of being accomplished. Hence, Eq. 2 turns

$$\frac{P_{acc}(i, j \rightarrow j, i)}{P_{acc}(j, i \rightarrow i, j)} = \frac{\mathcal{N}(\boldsymbol{r}_j, \beta_i)\mathcal{N}(\boldsymbol{r}_i, \beta_j)}{\mathcal{N}(\boldsymbol{r}_i, \beta_i)\mathcal{N}(\boldsymbol{r}_j, \beta_j)} = \frac{e^{-\beta_i U_j} e^{-\beta_j U_i}}{e^{-\beta_i U_i} e^{-\beta_j U_j}} \tag{3}$$

where U_i is the potential energy of replica i. Note that for the second equality we have employed the canonical expression for $\mathcal{N}(\boldsymbol{r}_i, \beta_i)$ which is proportional to the corresponding Boltzmann factor. One way of fulfilling Eq. 3 is by implementing the following swap acceptance probability,

$$P_{acc}(i, j \rightarrow j, i) = \min(1, \exp[(\beta_j - \beta_i)(U_i - U_j)]). \tag{4}$$

By introducing these swap trials, the replicas can travel through all ensembles. It is good custom to observe the trajectories of the replicas in the thermodynamic space to check this last statement (it is a necessary condition for the method to work properly). Since high temperature ensembles produce large jumps on configuration space, the sampling of the extended ensemble evolves and the whole set of replicas does not get jammed. This allows overcoming free-energy barriers at low temperatures.

2.2   Pressure Expansion of the Isothermal-Isobaric Ensemble

As mentioned in the introduction, the expansion of the canonical ensemble in temperature is not appropriate for the study of hard systems. To take advantage of the method, we must carry out the expansion of the isothermal-isobaric ensemble in pressure instead [34]. In this case, the partition function of the extended ensemble is given by [34, 35]

$$Q_{\text{extended}} = \prod_{i=1}^{n_r} Q_{NTP_i}, \tag{5}$$

where Q_{NTP_i} is the partition function of the isothermal-isobaric ensemble at pressure P_i, temperature T, and N particles. Here, all replicas have the same temperature T and number of particles N. The sampling performed on each replica is done by standard NTP_i simulations, which involves trial displacements, particle rotations (for anisotropic particles), volume changes, and trial cell deformations. Once a large number of trials has been computed, threads reach a barrier to enter the swap stage. Again, the detailed balance condition must be satisfied. Since we are considering the isothermal-isobaric ensemble, the probabilities in the configuration (defined by coordinates and volume in this case) are proportional to $\exp[-\beta(U(\boldsymbol{r}_i, V_i) + PV_i - N\beta^{-1}\ln(V_i))]$. Thus, the detailed balance condition leads to

$$\frac{P_{acc}(i, j \rightarrow j, i)}{P_{acc}(j, i \rightarrow i, j)} = \frac{\mathscr{N}(\boldsymbol{r}_j, P_i)\mathscr{N}(\boldsymbol{r}_i, P_j)}{\mathscr{N}(\boldsymbol{r}_i, P_i)\mathscr{N}(\boldsymbol{r}_j, P_j)} =$$

$$\frac{\exp\left[-\beta(U(\boldsymbol{r}_j, V_j) + P_iV_j - N\beta^{-1}\ln(V_j) + U(\boldsymbol{r}_i, V_i) + P_jV_i - N\beta^{-1}\ln(V_i))\right]}{\exp\left[-\beta(U(\boldsymbol{r}_i, V_i) + P_iV_i - N\beta^{-1}\ln(V_i) + U(\boldsymbol{r}_j, V_j) + P_jV_j - N\beta^{-1}\ln(V_j))\right]}$$

from which

$$\frac{P_{acc}(i, j \rightarrow j, i)}{P_{acc}(j, i \rightarrow i, j)} = \exp\left[-\beta(P_iV_j + P_jV_i - P_iV_i - P_jV_j)\right] \tag{6}$$

and

$$P_{\text{acc}}(i, j \rightarrow j, i) = \min(1, \exp[\beta(P_i - P_j)(V_i - V_j)]), \tag{7}$$

whenever the algorithm forces $\alpha(i, j \rightarrow j, i) = \alpha(j, i \rightarrow i, j)$ by construction. In this case $V_i - V_j$ is the volume difference between replicas i and j. Note that the algorithm always accepts a swap having $P_i > P_j$ and $V_i > V_j$, i.e. denser configurations are set at larger pressures. When $P_i > P_j$ and $V_j < V_i$, there is, however, some finite probability of accepting the swap trial. This probability is a decreasing function of the pressure difference between adjacent ensembles and thus, adjacent pressures should be close enough to provide reasonable exchange acceptance rates. Also, the ensemble at the smallest pressure must ensure large jumps in configuration space, so that the high pressure ensembles can be efficiently sampled.

To strictly fulfill the detailed balance condition, the probability of accomplishing the reverse move for all trials should not be zero. This condition is broken when implementing serial cycles. Hence, different trials should be picked at random [17]. The probability for selecting a particle displacement trial, P_d, a rotation, P_r, a volume change trial, P_v, a cell deformation (at constant volume), P_c, and a swap trial, P_s, are fixed to

$$P_d = P_r = n_r N/(n_r(2N+2)+w),$$
$$P_v = n_r/(n_r(2N+2)+w),$$
$$P_c = n_r/(n_r(2N+2)+w),$$
$$P_s = w/(n_r(2N+2)+w),$$
(8)

where $w \ll 1$ is (practically) proportional to the probability of performing a swap trial. Note that $P_d + P_r + P_v + P_c + P_s = 1$, as it should. The probability density function to have the next swap trial move at n_t is given by

$$P(n_t) = P_s \exp(-P_s n_t).$$
(9)

Therefore, we compute the number of trial moves to be carried out before the next swap as $n_t = -\ln(\xi)/P_s - 1$, being ξ a random number uniformly distributed in the interval $(0, 1)$ [36]. This number of trials is then evenly distributed on all replicas for the parallel stage. All particles of a given replica have the same a priori probability of being selected to accomplish a displacement or a rotational trial. The same is true for selecting a replica to perform a volume change or a cell deformation trial.

As mentioned in the previous paragraph, trials $[1, n_t - 1]$ are displacements, rotations, volume changes, and cell deformations, which can be independently carried out on the replicas. We have implemented the parallelization by using the message passing interface (MPI) in n_r threads, though parallelization on graphic devices should be possible (and recommendable nowadays). In our implementation, the swap stage is accomplished in a single thread and so the efficiency of the parallelization increases with decreasing w. We are employing $w < 1/100$ in all cases. Verlet neighbor lists are used for improving performance (in case of anisotropic particles we follow the method given elsewhere [37,38]).

Simulations are started from random loose configurations or by setting a particular crystal structure. In both cases we avoid overlapping configurations. We first carry out a large enough number of trial moves at the desired state points, until observing the replicas to reach a stationary state. This is done in order to yield equilibrated configurations. During this stage, the maximum particle displacements and rotations, maximum volume changes, and maximum cell deformations, are adjusted independently at each ensemble to yield acceptance rates close to 0.3. Hence, high pressure replicas have smaller maximum displacements (for all kinds of displacements) than low pressure replicas. Note that adjusting maximum displacements also breaks the detailed balance condition (when a maximum displacement is diminished after a maximum accepted trial, the reverse move cannot be performed). Hence, these adjustments are done only at this stage. Next, we carry out a sufficiently large run from which we sample to compute ensemble averages. As in a typical Monte Carlo simulation, several structural and thermodynamic properties can be accessed.

Pressures should be allocated in such a way to yield approximately the same swap acceptance rate for all pairs of adjacent ensembles. In the absence of transitions, this is usually done by setting a geometrical increasing pressure with the ensemble index. In the vicinity of transitions, however, ensembles should be closely allocated in pressure. In line with this, we have implemented an algorithm to smoothly adjust the ensemble pressures to yield an approximately constant swap acceptance rate while keeping constant the maximum and minimum pressures. The initial pressures follow the geometric progression with the ensemble index to match the highest and smallest values and the number of replicas to be considered. Note that the shift of the ensemble pressures also violates the balance condition. Thus, this adjustment is carried out only during equilibration. Since for a temperature expansion the efficiency of the method peaks at swap acceptance rates close to 20 % [39], we assume a similar behavior for a pressure expansion. For a given pressure range to be covered, this swap acceptance rate is matched by increasing/decreasing the number of replicas (ensembles).

3   Applications in Three Dimensions

In this section we summarize the main results obtained for monodisperse hard spheres, a binary mixture of hard spheres, and hard ellipsoids of revolution. All these systems are studied in bulk. The presence of walls or any type of confinement (an external field, for instance) strongly affects these results and are out of the scope of this section.

3.1   Monodisperse Hard Spheres

As mentioned in the introduction, the hard sphere model was one of the first ones ever studied by computer simulations [18–20]. Furthermore, under certain conditions, it is a good model for monodisperse spherical colloids. Its equation of state [24,40], freezing and melting points are well established [15,16], and so, it can be used as a reference system to validate the implementation and correctness of new algorithms. For this purpose we have run a set of 70 (n_r) small replicas (with $N = 32$ and another with $N = 108$) to compare our results with those previously reported in the literature.

The outcome of the algorithm is shown in Fig. 2 for the $N = 32$ system (panel (a)) and for the $N = 108$ system (panel (b)). These are the probability density functions (PDFs) to find a replica at a given volume fraction $\varphi = v_{sp}\rho$ for all ensembles. Here, $v_{sp} = \pi\sigma^3/6$ is the volume of a hard sphere of diameter σ and $\rho = N/V$ is the number density. There are 70 curves, each one corresponding to each ensemble, i.e. we are considering 70 different pressures. Pressure increases from left to right in both panels and produce the expected shift of the PDFs to the right (the higher the pressure the larger the density). The leftmost curve corresponds to $\beta P = 2.16\sigma^{-3}$ and the rightmost to $\beta P = 100\sigma^{-3}$. In general, PDFs are Gaussian in shape and are centered at the ensemble average density. The width of the bell-shaped curves is related to the dimensionless compressibility by means of the fluctuation-dissipation theorem as follows

$$\chi = \frac{\delta\rho}{\delta(\beta P)} = N\left(\frac{\langle\rho^2\rangle - \langle\rho\rangle^2}{\langle\rho\rangle^2}\right). \tag{10}$$

Since χ is an intensive property, N in Eq. 10 compensates the fact that fluctuations are smaller for larger systems. Note that the Gaussian curves are wider in

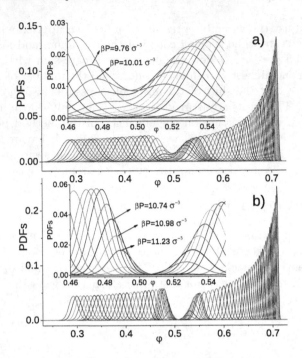

Fig. 2. The 70 probability density functions, PDFs, to find the replicas at a given volume density, φ, for the monodisperse hard sphere system. Curves shift to the right with increasing pressure (density). Panel (a) corresponds to $N = 32$ and panel (b) to $N = 108$. Insets zoom in the corresponding data at the fluid-solid transition. The closest curves to the transition are highlighted. The figure is taken from reference [34].

the top panel than in the bottom one. Since swap acceptance rates depend on how overlapped are the probability density functions, more replicas are needed in order to increase the system size and keep a constant swap acceptance rate.

As pressure increases, the curves shift to the right and narrow, decreasing χ. Close to $\varphi = 0.5$, however, the Gaussian shape of the curves breaks, turning into bimodals. There appears a clear behavior of the system to avoid configurations with $\varphi \simeq 0.5$. This behavior is more marked for increasing N. In the thermodynamic limit, the probability of finding configurations with $\varphi \simeq 0.5$ vanishes. In this region, the bimodals yield two peaks, one below $\varphi = 0.49$ and another above $\varphi = 0.51$. This occurs for $\beta P \sim 10\sigma^{-3}$ (for $N = 32$), pointing out the hard sphere fluid-solid transition. The insets of Fig. 2 zoom in the volume fraction region close to 0.5, showing the details of the PDFs clearer. There we have highlighted the curves close to the transition. Note that increasing N leads to a slight widen and shift of the transition region.

From the sampling of the replicas one can easily compute average thermodynamic quantities and structural properties to characterize the system behavior. As an example we are showing in the topmost panel of Fig. 3 the pressure as

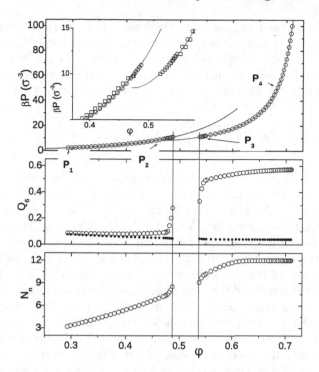

Fig. 3. Hard spheres equation of state (top) for $N = 108$ (circles). The red line corresponds to the hard sphere fluid equation of state given by Speedy [24] and the blue one to the hard spheres cubic centered equation of state [40]. The inset zooms in the same panel and squares are added for the $N = 32$ data. The labels P_1, P_2, P_3, and P_4 are pressures in correspondence with the snapshots of the bottom panel of Fig. 1. The panel at the middle shows the order parameter, Q_6, as a function of φ (circles), and its value for a completely uncorrelated set of points $1/\sqrt{N N_n/2}$ (bullets). The panel at the bottom shows the number of first neighbors, N_n, as a function of the volume fraction, φ. The figure is taken from reference [34]

a function of the ensemble average volume fraction for $N = 108$ (circles), and a couple of structural properties in the other two panels. The corresponding inset zooms in the transition region, where square symbols are added from the $N = 32$ data. As can be seen, the pressure-volume fraction relationship (equation of state) is not very sensitive to the system size, leaving aside the transition region. In fact, our data practically coincide with the Padé approximation to simulation data obtained from the hard sphere fluid branch [24] (red line), and the fit to the hard sphere face cubic centered branch of the equation of state [40] (blue line), both data series considered as a well established reference in the literature. For a precise determination of the phase boundaries one should employ the histogram re-weighting technique as a function of $1/N$, followed by an extrapolation towards the thermodynamic limit, $N \to 0$. The histogram re-weighting method is given elsewhere [41, 42].

The middle and bottom panels of Fig. 3 show (for the $N = 108$ system) the order parameter, Q_6, and the number of first shell neighbors, N_n, as a function of φ, respectively. N_n is computed by accounting for all pairs of particles with a center to center distance smaller than 1.2σ. This procedure define vectors (bonds) joining the centers of these pairs. Then, Q_6 is given by [43, 44]

$$Q_6 = \left(\frac{4\pi}{13} \sum_{m=-6}^{m=6} | <Y_{6m}(\theta, \phi)> |^2 \right)^{1/2} \tag{11}$$

where $< Y_{6m}(\theta, \phi) >$ is the ensemble average over all bonds of the spherical harmonics of the polar angles θ and ϕ (measured with respect to any fixed coordinate system). Q_6 goes to zero for increasing N for a completely uncorrelated set of points, following $1/\sqrt{NN_n/2} \pm 1/\sqrt{13NN_n}$ [44]. The middle panel includes this function. Q_6 is small for the fluid region, pointing out the absence of bond ordering, and reaches 0.5732 for $\beta P = 100\sigma^{-3}$, which is slightly lower than the Q_6 value of the face cubic centered arrangement, 0.5745. In addition, it is well above the value of the hexagonal close packed structure, $Q_6 = 0.4848$. This is, however, a consequence of working with cubic shaped simulation cells (only a face cubic centered arrange can be fitted in a cubic cell with $N = 108$). Unfortunately, in this case we did not include the cell deformations trials, which would add important degrees of freedom to our small systems and could confirm the hard sphere preference of producing face cubic centered arrangements over hexagonal close packed ones. It is worth mentioning the sharply increase of Q_6 at the fluid-solid transition. Also N_n monotonically increases with φ, showing a much modest jump at the transition. N_n goes to 12 for increasing pressure, which is the largest possible hard sphere coordination number. This is, of course, a consequence of the Kepler conjecture stating that the hard sphere maximally achievable density in three dimensional Euclidean space corresponds to a face cubic centered or a hexagonal close packed structure, being $\varphi = \pi/\sqrt{18}$. A prove by exhaustion of the conjecture was recently given [45].

3.2   Polydisperse Hard Spheres

A certain degree of polydispersity hinders the natural tendency of equally sized hard spheres to crystallize [46]. In addition, by increasing the polydispersity the smaller spheres can either layer against larger spheres or fill voids between neighboring larger particles. Hence, polydisperse hard spheres may pack to higher volume fractions than the monodisperse system [47]. Indeed, some particular binary mixtures can crystallize to produce very large packing fractions [48]. In real nano, micro, and milli-structured materials the particle size distribution is never strictly monodisperse, so it should not come as a surprise that polydisperse hard sphere models have found many applications such as storage in silos, metallic alloys, and colloidal dispersions, among others [49]. Quite recently, it has been proposed a simple relationship involving the first, second, and third moments of the size distribution to produce an excellent collapse of the equations of state of several non-crystallizing, polydisperse systems up to the glass transition volume fraction and a significant narrowing of the different out-of-equilibrium glass branches [49]. This allows to easily predict the equation of state of any given polydisperse system from a particular non-crystallizing mixture. Thus, in this chapter we restrict ourselves to present results only for a 50:50 binary mixture of hard spheres with a diameter ratio of 1.4. This particular mixture does not crystallize even at very large densities [22,50,51]. The aim of this chapter is to show how the REMC method can lead to reliable thermodynamic information at large densities, where sampling from equilibrium becomes a severe issue for standard algorithms.

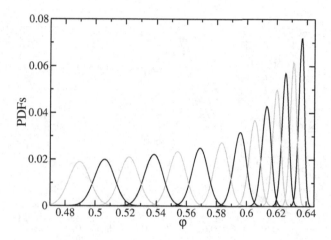

Fig. 4. Probability density functions, PDFs, to find the replicas at a given volume density, φ, for the 50:50 binary hard sphere system. $N = 100$ particles and n_r replicas are considered. The figure is taken from reference [11].

One can think of several tests to establish whether the produced results are indeed representative of thermal equilibrium. However, although these tests are capable of detecting an out of equilibrium trajectory, the fact of not detecting the absence of equilibrium is not a strong enough condition to guarantee sampling from equilibrium. One of these tests could be checking that all replicas reach all ensembles. This was done in reference [11] for this particular binary mixture. In the same work we have also checked that the pressure set on each ensemble coincides with that measured from the ensemble average of the sampled configurations. For hard sphere mixtures, the system structure and the pressure are related by [52]

$$\frac{\beta P}{\rho} = 1 + \frac{2\pi\rho}{3} \sum_\alpha \sum_\gamma x_\alpha x_\gamma \sigma_{\alpha\gamma}^3 g_{\alpha\gamma}(\sigma_{\alpha\gamma}) \tag{12}$$

where α and γ run over all species (two in our case), and x_α, $\sigma_{\alpha\gamma}$, and $g_{\alpha\gamma}(\sigma_{\alpha\gamma})$ are the number fraction of particles of species α, the contact distance between the species, and the radial distribution functions evaluated at $\sigma_{\alpha\gamma}$, respectively. The test should produce consistent pressures whenever all $g_{\alpha\gamma}(\sigma_{\alpha\gamma})$ are evaluated by means of a careful extrapolation of $g_{\alpha\gamma}(r)$ towards contact.

The PDFs can also show signs of an out of equilibrium system. When some replicas remain trapped in long-lived metastable states the PDFs get distorted and evolve with sampling. Usually we observe that the PDFs change in the first simulation steps until reaching a stationary state. In the absence of a phase transition, the PDFs of an equilibrated system should be all Gaussian in shape. They should look like shown in Fig. 4. This figure is obtained by considering $N = 100$ and $n_r = 14$. As for the monodisperse case, the PDFs turn higher and narrower as pressure is increased, pointing out a decrease of the compressibility.

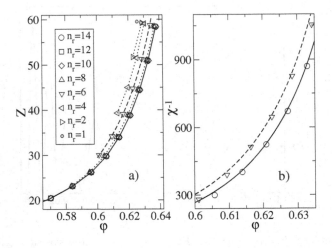

Fig. 5. (a) Equation of state, $Z = \beta P/\rho = Z(\varphi)$, for $N = 60$ and for an increasing number of replicas (from $n_r = 1$ to $n_r = 14$). (b) Checking relationship 10). The lines show $1/\chi$ as obtained from the first equality of Eq. 10 and symbols correspond to a direct evaluation from fluctuations. The figure is taken from reference [11].

Another test to detect an out of equilibrium condition could be checking the results obtained by starting from different initial conditions. Ergodicity implies that the same results should be obtained. We have produced results for $n_r = 1, 2, 4, 6, 8, 10, 12,$ and 14 and from different initial conditions, by setting always $N = 60$, $\beta P = 38\sigma_s^{-3}$ (being σ_s the diameter of the smallest species) for the highest pressure, and a geometrical factor of 0.865 for allocating the pressures of the other ensembles. We have also performed three independent runs for the $n_r = 1$ case. The same number of trial moves was considered for all runs, in order to make the comparison more reliable. The obtained state points, $Z(\varphi) = \beta P/\rho$ are shown in panel (a) of Fig. 5. In this test it is observed how results become reproducible only for $n_r \geq 8$, whenever the lowest volume density reaches values below $\varphi = 0.58$. When a smaller number of replicas is set, Z is always larger than that obtained for $n_r \geq 8$. This points out that thermalization is not reached for $n_r \geq 8$. It is worth mentioning that the three independent runs with $n_r = 1$ produce clearly different results. Hence, for the number of trials set in this test, a standard MC algorithm ($n_r = 1$) is not able to yield equilibrium results at large densities.

Santen and Krauth [53] suggested another test. It is known that an equilibrated system fulfills Eq. 10. Hence, one can check whether this relation is satisfied or not. In other words, there should be a well defined relationship between the location of PDFs averages and their broadness. The first equality of Eq. 10 links χ with the PDFs averages and allows χ to be calculated from the derivative with respect to the density of a polynomial fit to the pressure. The second equality can be directly computed from the PDFs. Figure 5(b) shows χ^{-1} as a function of density as obtained from the first equality (lines) and the second (symbols). This figure shows that not only for $n_r = 14$ lines and symbols agree but also for the case with $n_r = 6$, case for which equilibrium has not been established. In this case, all replicas are trapped in a glassy state and are basically frozen in free energy local minima where they sample quasi-equilibrium short-lived fluctuations. This suggests that the consistency of both χ determinations only guarantees that a stationary state has been reached, making no difference with the other test. Fulfilling all of them is a necessary but not sufficient condition for equilibrium.

In this study we have found that thermalized results could be obtained up to $\varphi \approx 0.63$ by employing the replica exchange method with small system sizes, $N \leq 100$. This volume fraction is beyond two important 'critical' packing fractions defined dynamically, the mode-coupling transition $\varphi_{\mathrm{mct}} = 0.592$ and the divergence extrapolated using a Vogel-Fulcher-Tamman expression, $\varphi_{\mathrm{vft}} = 0.615$. From the equation of state $Z(\varphi)$ and the dimensionless isothermal compressibility $\chi(\varphi)$, we have found no signature of a thermodynamic glass transition for this particular system. This is however in contrast with some findings for different polydisperse hard sphere systems [30].

3.3   Hard Ellipsoids

An ellipsoid can be handled to match the shape of several grains, micro and nano-structured materials, and even to match certain molecular shapes. Ellipsoids are, indeed, a generalization of the sphere. In general they have three different axes, but here we focus on those with two equal axes. These are known as spheroids and can be split into two families, oblates and prolates. Oblates are plate-shaped (those having the axis of revolution shorter than the other two equal axes), whereas prolates are needle shaped (those having the axis of revolution larger than the other two). For each fixed shape, we can build a monodisperse (in size and shape) system of particles to produce the equation of state. For small anisotropies the equation of state is expected to be similar to that found for spheres. For large anisotropies there must be a nematic ordering of the liquid phase before reaching the fluid-solid transition. A nematic fluid has no ordering of the vectors joining the particles centers (small Q_6) but the particles orientations are long-ranged correlated. Note that a spheroid orientation is completely defined by a single vector and in a nematic fluid these vectors turn (almost) parallel (or anti-parallel, making no difference due to symmetry). Hence, a change of the particle anisotropy leads to a different equation of state, and to the appearance and disappearance of phases and transitions. The chart containing the different phases at equilibrium as a function of the particle anisotropy is known as the phase diagram. The first phase diagram for spheroids was given in the 1980s [54,55]. In this chapter we are showing a revisited version [56,57].

The contact distance for a couple of ellipsoids (and for anisotropic particles in general) is a function of their relative position and orientation. This distance can be numerically solved by following the algorithm given elsewhere [58–60]. A similar algorithm can be employed to solve the contact distance of spheroellipsoids [61]. Here, we employed an analytical approximation based on the Berne and Pechukas first approach [62]. It reads [63]

$$\sigma_{RBP} = \frac{\sigma_\perp}{\sqrt{1 - \frac{1}{2}\chi[A^+ + A^-] + (1-\chi)\chi'[A^+A^-]^\gamma}}, \tag{13}$$

with

$$A^\pm = \frac{(\hat{\mathbf{r}} \cdot \hat{\mathbf{u}}_i \pm \hat{\mathbf{r}} \cdot \hat{\mathbf{u}}_j)^2}{1 \pm \chi \hat{\mathbf{u}}_i \cdot \hat{\mathbf{u}}_j}, \tag{14}$$

$$\chi = \frac{\sigma_\parallel^2 - \sigma_\perp^2}{\sigma_\parallel^2 + \sigma_\perp^2} \quad , \quad \chi' = \left(\frac{\sigma_\parallel - \sigma_\perp}{\sigma_\parallel + \sigma_\perp}\right)^2. \tag{15}$$

In this expression, $\sigma_\parallel$ and $\sigma_\perp$ are the parallel and perpendicular diameters with respect to the ellipsoid axis of revolution, respectively. $\hat{\mathbf{u}}_i$ and $\hat{\mathbf{u}}_j$ are unit vectors along the axis of revolution of each particle, and as mentioned they define the orientations of particles i and j. $\hat{\mathbf{r}}$ is the unit vector along the direction joining the particle centers. Finally, γ was introduced [64] to further approach to the exact Perram and Wertheim numerical solution. Its values are given in [64]. The average difference between the analytical approach and the exact numerical solution is always below 0.8 % for $0.2 \leq \alpha \leq 5$. The aspect ratio of the ellipsoids is defined as $\alpha = \sigma_\parallel/\sigma_\perp$, such that $\alpha < 1$ corresponds to oblates, and $\alpha > 1$ to prolates. Similarly, we define the maximum aspect ratio as $\delta = \sigma_{max}/\sigma_{min}$, where σ_{max} and σ_{min} are the maximum and minimum diameters, respectively. The volume of the ellipsoid is given by $v_e = \pi\sigma_\perp^2\sigma_\parallel/6$ and the volume fraction $\varphi = v_e\rho$.

An example of the equation of state, $Z(\varphi)$, the isothermal dimensionless compressibility, $\chi(\varphi)$, and the order parameter, $Q_6(\varphi)$, is shown in Fig. 6 for oblates with $\delta = 1.2$. Then, this case corresponds to quasi-spherical particles, as shown in panels (d), (e), and (f). Panels (a), (b), and (c) also include arrows pointing to the phase transitions. From low to high pressure, these are a fluid-solid phase transition, where an isotropic fluid and a plastic crystal coexist [55], a solid-solid transition involving a plastic crystal and a sfcc crystal, and a very high pressure solid-solid transition, between the sfcc structure and the sm2 crystal. The solid structures, i.e. the plastic, the sfcc (standing for stretched face cubic centered) and the sm2 are shown in panels (d), (e), and (f), respectively. All solids

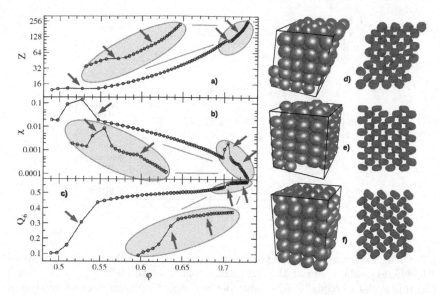

Fig. 6. (a) Equation of state, $Z(\varphi)$, for oblates with $\delta = 1.2$. (b) Isothermal dimensionless compressibility, $\chi(\varphi)$. (c) Order parameter, $Q_6(\varphi)$. The insets zoom in the highlighted regions. Arrows point out the transitions. For increasing density (pressure), these are: fluid-plastic, plastic-sfcc, and sfcc-sm2. The plastic, sfcc, and sm2 equilibrium structures are shown in panels (d), (e) and (f), respectively. Right panels show front views where spheroids are represented by plate-like particles to highlight their positions and orientations. Data are taken from reference [57].

show strong correlations among the bonds of neighboring particles, that is, large Q_6 values. The plastic results when no long range correlation appears between particle orientations. In this case it corresponds to the equilibrium structure in the density range $0.55 < \varphi < 0.7$. Larger pressures lead to the orientational arrangement of the structure. It first appears a sfcc, and then, at very large pressures, a sm2. The sfcc is the resulting structure of stretching (shrinking) a face cubic centered arrangement of spheres to obtain prolates (oblates). Note that stretching (or shrinking) preserves both, occupied and void space, so that the volume fraction is invariant. The structure appearing at the highest pressures, and presumably the structure leading to the maximum volume fraction when close packed [65], is known as sm2 (simple monoclinic with two orientations) [66,67]. As can be seen, the equation of state and the phase behavior turn extremely rich when dealing with anisotropic particles. The first two transitions are first order, as pointed out by the $Z(\varphi)$ discontinuity (see panel a) of Fig. 6). Conversely, the sfcc-sm2 transition is of higher order, according to the continuous $Z(\varphi)$ (Fig. 6(a)), and the very small kink of $\chi(\varphi)$ (Fig. 6(b)). The order parameter $Q_6(\varphi)$ also presents signatures at the transitions, as shown by the arrows in panel (c). In particular, it shows a very tiny increase for the subtle sfcc-sm2 transition.

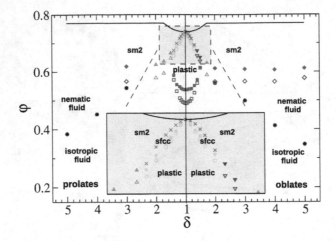

Fig. 7. Phase diagram of hard ellipsoids of revolution. The spherical case is given for $\delta = 1$, whereas oblates are at the right and prolates at the left. The dark solid line at the top is the maximally achievable density [65]. Configurations above this line are forbidden. There are several transitions: isotropic-nematic fluid-fluid (asterisks), isotropic-plastic fluid-solid (squares), nematic-sm2 fluid-solid (diamonds), isotropic-sm2 fluid-solid (upward triangles), plastic-sm2 solid-solid (downward triangles), plastic-sfcc solid-solid (circles), and sfcc-sm2 solid-solid (crosses). Pairs of open and solid symbols point to coexistence regions. Single symbols correspond to higher order transitions. The inset zooms in the sfcc stable region. Data are taken from reference [57].

By considering several anisotropies (for prolates and oblates) and by carrying out a similar analysis, it is possible to build a phase diagram. The result is shown in Fig. 7. The chart is split in half by the hard sphere case ($\delta = 1$). This vertical, middle line corresponds to the data presented in Subsect. 3.1. Oblate cases are at the right and prolate cases are at the left. The particles asymmetry increases by moving away from this central line. The maximally achievable density [65] is given as a black solid line at the top of the phase diagram. Above this line one cannot produce configurations without overlaps. The transitions detected by the replica exchange method are given in this chart. Asterisks correspond to isotropic-nematic fluid-fluid transitions, squares to isotropic-plastic fluid-solid transitions, diamonds to nematic-sm2 fluid-solid transitions, upward triangles to isotropic-sm2 fluid-solid transitions, downward triangles to plastic-sm2 solid-solid transitions, circles to plastic-sfcc solid-solid transitions, and crosses to sfcc-sm2 solid-solid transitions. We have found that the isotropic-nematic fluid-fluid and the sfcc-sm2 solid-solid transitions are not first order. Single symbols are employed to show their locations, and a couple of symbols are used to point out first order transitions and their corresponding coexistence regions. We are also including a zoom in of the high density area above the plastic region as an inset in the same figure. We do this in order to show the narrow density region where the sfcc solid spontaneously forms. Its existence as a stable structure above the plastic solid region is in agreement with the analysis of Radu et al. [67]. The sm2 appearance at extremely high pressures supports the conjecture of being the structure leading to the maximum volume fraction when close packed.

4 Applications in Two Dimensions

Results from two dimensional computational studies are useful to understand the nature of real three dimensional arrangements confined at interfaces [68–70], between parallel solid walls [71], and into a lamellar matrix of surfactants [72]. These are, indeed, quasi-two dimensional systems but the two dimensional approach is able to capture most of their physical behavior. For instance, experiments and two dimensional simulations agree to show that needles, squares, octapods, and ellipsoidal anisotropic particles show a rich phase diagram when confined to a quasi-2D plane [73–79]. In turn, these quasi-2D mesophases and nanocrystals can be employed as basic units for the synthesis of superlattice structures [80], multilayer arrangements by layer-by-layer assembly [81,82], and for template assisted assembly processes [83]. Here we present results of the replica exchange method applied to hard discs and ellipses in a two dimensional plane.

4.1 Hard Discs

Hard discs are probably the most simple 2D-system model. However, the type of phase transition this model shows was recently elucidated. Although the study of 2D systems by means of simulations is in principle more easily implemented and requires a smaller amount of computer resources, its phase behavior is not simpler at all. On the one hand, the solid phase of 2D-systems is characterized by a quasi-long-range but not a true-long-range positional order. In other words, positional correlations decay to zero following a power-law. Nonetheless, bond orientational correlations are indeed, long-ranged. Thus, a 2D-solid is not considered a crystal, since true crystals should preserve both bond orientational order and positional order for all distances. On the other hand, Kosterlitz, Thouless, Halperin, Nelson, and Young (KTHNY) [84,85], have proposed the existence of a hexatic phase between the solid and the liquid phases. This phase would be characterized by quasi-long-range bond orientational correlations instead of the full long-range of the solid [73,86–89]. Hence, this phase would be something halfway between the liquid and the solid. In their original scenario, the solid would melt into a hexatic phase before turning into a liquid, for decreasing pressure. The theory predicts the two transitions to be continuous. The KTHNY two-step continuous transition and a single first order transition have been the two of several scenarios which have received larger support [90]. The technical difficulty for the confirmation or refusal of this theory by means of computer simulations, is that it requires extremely large system sizes to capture and clearly determine these different very long-ranged decays. Quite recent long-scale computer simulations (with 1024^2 particles) settle the issue revealing a liquid-hexatic first order transition, followed by a continuous hexatic-solid one [91]. So, the hypothetical hexatic

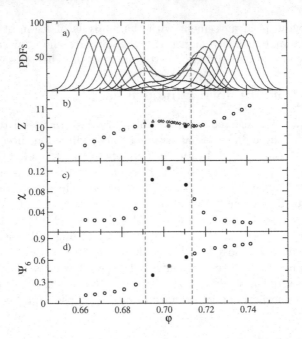

Fig. 8. (a) Probability density functions, PDFs. The thick red line (bimodal) corresponds to the pressure at which the transition takes place. Thick black lines correspond to the adjacent pressures. (b) Equation of state, $Z(\varphi)$. (c) Dimensionless isothermal compressibility, $\chi(\varphi)$. (d) Overall bond order parameter, Ψ_6. Filled symbols of panels (b)–(d) correspond to the thicker lines of panel (a). Dashed vertical lines are located at the peaks of the red line PDF. In panel (b), small triangles and diamonds are taken from the large scale simulations of Jaster ($N = 128^2$) and Bernard and Krauth ($N = 1024^2$), respectively [90,91]. Figure taken from reference [92].

phase really exists, but the way the solid melts yielding the liquid as decreasing pressure is somewhat different from the two-step continuous transition. In this subsection we compare the results of the replica exchange method to those given in references [90,91].

The equation of state for disks in a plane is shown in panel (b) of Fig. 8, that is, $Z(\varphi)$ where $\varphi = a_e\rho$, $a_e = \pi\sigma^2/4$, $\rho = N/A$, $N = 400$, $n_r = 16$, and A is the area of the simulation cell. We are including in this plot the results of the large scale NVT MC simulations with $N = 128^2$ carried out by Jaster [90] as solid triangles, and those of Bernard and Krauth [91] with $N = 1024^2$ as diamonds. These results are located along the liquid-hexatic and hexatic-solid coexistence regions where size effects are expected to be important. Differences between our results and theirs are not very large, though. Outside this region differences practically disappear. Nonetheless, even very large systems show small differences for increasing the system size [91]. We are also including in panel (a) the probability density functions from where the averages are taken, the dimensionless isothermal compressibility $\chi(\varphi)$ as obtained from density fluctuations in panel (c), and the global order parameter $\Psi_6 = 1/N|\sum_i^N \varphi_{6,i}|$ in panel (d), being $\varphi_{6,i} = 1/N_i^b \sum_j^{N_i^b} \exp(6\theta_{ij}\sqrt{-1})$, N_i^b the number of bonding particles to particle i, and θ_{ij} the angle between the ij-bond and an arbitrary fixed reference axis. All these features support a first order transition. However, the $Z(\varphi)$-plateau, the $\chi(\varphi)$ peak, and the development of an overall bond order are well known facts for this system which do not constitute enough evidence to establish the nature of the liquid-hexatic and hexatic-solid transitions. As mentioned, their nature has been recently elucidated [91]. For the liquid-hexatic transition a bubble formation (hexatic in fluid) was detected, which is a hallmark of a first-order transition. The same work reports a coexistence interval of $0.700 < \varphi < 0.716$ for the fluid-hexatic transition and a second continuous transition at $\varphi \gtrsim 0.720$. Hence, the hexatic phase takes place in the density range $0.716 < \varphi < 0.720$. From our results we would conclude that there exists a wide first order transition in the region $0.691 \lesssim \varphi \lesssim 0.713$. The vertical dashed lines of Fig. 8 point out the coexistence interval. Taking into account Bernard and Krauth conclusions, this coexistence should be fluid-hexatic. The hexatic-solid would be relatively close to $\varphi_s \approx 0.717$ and it is hidden by the first order transition. We are not capturing this subtle continuous transition. Bernard and Krauth capture it from the shift of positional order decay from exponential to power-law, on a length scale of $\sim 100\sigma$ (explaining the necessity of large system sizes). It should also be noted that our coexistence region is wider and shifted to the left as compared to the fluid-hexatic coexistence given in reference [91]. This not so large mismatch is a consequence of finite size effects.

4.2   Hard Ellipses

Analogous to the sphere-ellipsoid three dimensional case, ellipses can be seen as the generalization of disks. We recover the disk case for $\delta = 1$ and the equation of state changes with increasing particle anisotropy. Again, a phase diagram can be build. A δ value approaching unity would produce an equation of state very close to the one presented in the previous subsection, whereas needle like 2D particles would yield an isotropic-nematic transition before the solid phase, by increasing pressure. Although similar to the three dimensional case, one must study the decay of the radial orientational functions to clearly determine the isotropic-nematic transition, and the decay of the six-fold, bond orientational radial function for capturing a solid phase. This implies larger system sizes than for the 3D case. We are using $N = 400$, which, according to Xu et al. [89], it is sufficient to minimize size effects (leaving aside the fluid-hexatic and hexatic-solid transitions).

The left panel of Fig. 9 shows the obtained phase diagram. At the right panel we show the compressibility factor, $Z(\varphi)$, at which the transitions take place. Here, φ is given by $\varphi = a_e\rho$, with $a_e = \pi\sigma_{max}\sigma_{min}/4 = \pi\sigma_{min}^2\delta/4$, and $\delta = \sigma_{max}/\sigma_{min}$ as defined for the ellipsoids. In addition, we are including snapshots corresponding to the different phases, as labeled. These are the plastic, isotropic, nematic, and solid phases. In panel (a), volume fractions between a

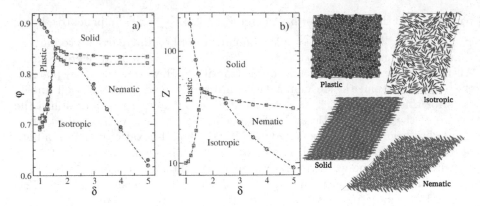

Fig. 9. (a) Phase diagram of hard ellipses. $\delta = 1$ corresponds to the disks' system. The obtained transitions are: isotropic-plastic, isotropic-solid, isotropic-nematic, nematic-solid, and plastic-solid. First order transitions are shown by a couple of square symbols whereas continuous transitions are shown as single circles. Red circles correspond to data from Xu et al. [89]. (b) The corresponding compressibility factor at the transitions. Dashed lines are guides to the eye. The snapshots correspond to the different phases appearing in the phase diagram. We are using red for particles aligned to the nematic director and blue for those perpendicular to it, and a linear combination of these colors for intermediate cases. Figure taken from reference [92].

couple of square symbols correspond to a coexistence region, whereas continuous transitions are depicted by single circles. We are employing circles for the plastic-solid transition, although a tiny coexistence is found for $\delta = 1.4$ and 1.5. This transition takes place at very large pressures and it is hard to capture. All dashed lines are guides to the eye. Red circles of panel (a) show the data of Xu et al. [89]. Our results agree with their predictions for both the isotropic-plastic and the isotropic-nematic transitions. A comparison with the early results of Cuesta and Frenkel [74], and Vieillard-Baron [93] is provided in reference [89].

We may split the phase diagram into three regions. The first would be a low anisotropy region, $1 < \delta \lesssim 1.6$, where two transitions are found. These are a low-pressure isotropic-plastic and a high-pressure plastic-solid transitions. According to Bernard and Krauth conclusions [91], for $\delta = 1$ the low-pressure transition is in fact an isotropic-hexatic first order transition closely followed by a subtle hexatic-solid transition. Consequently, for $1 < \delta \lesssim 1.6$ we are obtaining an isotropic-hexatic first order transition, which would be the one we are capturing, followed by a mild and hidden hexatic-plastic continuous transition. Similar conclusions are drawn by the $g_6(r)$ analysis of Xu et al. [89]. Since the hexatic region is small, we are not pointing it out in the phase diagram. The high pressure transition is also first order with a small coexistence density region. The second region of the phase diagram corresponds to intermediate anisotropies, i. e. for $1.6 \lesssim \delta \lesssim 2.4$, where we observe only a single isotropic-solid transition. In this case bond-orientational and orientational order appear together. Finally, the third region corresponds to $2.4 \lesssim \delta$, where an isotropic-nematic transition preempts the fluid-solid transition as increasing pressure. Note that all fluid-solid transitions should follow the two-step fluid-hexatic, hexatic-solid route.

5 Conclusions

We have shown how the replica exchange Monte Carlo method is a powerful and easy to implement alternative for the study of hard systems. For this purpose we have defined a pressure expansion of the isothermal-isobaric ensemble, instead of the much broadly employed temperature expansion of the canonical ensemble. This way, high pressure replicas perform local sampling of the configurational space whereas low pressure replicas produce large jumps in configurational space. This is completely analogous to the low temperature- high temperature sampling of the temperature expansion.

The method is able to capture all kinds of transitions involving positional ordering/disordering and orientational ordering/disordering. Examples are the fluid-crystal transition of hard spheres, the isotropic-nematic fluid-fluid transition of anisotropic particles such as spheroids and ellipses (in three and two dimensions), and even solid-solid transitions such as the plastic-crystal transitions appearing for spheroids of small anisotropy. Indeed, the method allowed for a full and consistent resolution of the phase diagram of spheroids (which turned out to be richer than expected).

We have also explored the possibility of employing the method to access dense equilibrated configurations of a non-crystallizing, binary hard-sphere mixture. This was done in order to search for a possible thermodynamic signature of the dynamic glass transition. In this regard our results show that no such a signature exists for a 50:50 binary mixture of hard spheres with a diameter ratio of 1.4, up to volume fractions of 0.63. This is, at least, for the small system size we have considered.

The acceptance rate of the swap trials (swaps are the central part of the method) increases with decreasing the system size. That is, the method takes advantage of density (potential energy) fluctuations for a pressure (temperature) expansion. Hence, as the system size is decreased the ensembles can be further separated in pressure (temperature) space. This, together with our limited computational resources (four desktops were used), explains why we have kept our system sizes to a minimum. Nonetheless, our results are very precise inside a single phase region and locate first order transitions a little bit shifted to smaller densities. To our knowledge, higher order transitions are also very precisely captured. Hence, letting aside very special cases such as the complex fluid-hexatic-solid transition in two dimensions, where the subtle hexatic-solid transition is somehow hidden by the fluid-hexatic first order transition, small system sizes should be preferred to study size-insensitive properties and maximize knowledge for a given finite computer power.

It is worth mentioning that this method can be implemented independently of the method chosen to update configurations. This is Monte Carlo and molecular dynamics simulations can be implemented employing the replica exchange method. For hard bodies, there are several algorithms which vary on complexity and efficiency. A nice example is the event driven Monte Carlo algorithm employed for elucidating the complex melting of hard disks [91].

Traditional methods for elucidating the stable solid at certain thermodynamic conditions require comparing the free energies of different candidate structures. Unfortunately, free energies, and other properties which are directly linked to the accessible volume of the phase space, cannot be computed from simulations (they are not ensemble averages) [54]. The usual method to go around the issue is by means of thermodynamic integration, which requires knowledge of the free energy value of a reference state (for instance the ideal gas or harmonic crystal). For anisotropic particles, the proposal of candidate structures, and the calculation of the free energy of the reference states, can be tricky. Replica exchange avoids these steps. This makes this method more robust, in the sense that is it less human dependent.

References

1. Lyubartsev, A.P., Martsinovski, A.A., Shevkunov, S.V., Vorontsov-Velyaminov, P.N.: New approach to Monte Carlo calculation of the free energy: method of expanded ensembles. J. Chem. Phys. **96**, 1776 (1991)
2. Marinari, E., Parisi, G.: Simulated tempering: a new Monte Carlo scheme. Europhys. Lett. **19**, 451 (1992)
3. Yan, Q.L., de Pablo, J.J.: Hyper parallel tempering Monte Carlo: application to the lennard-jones fluid and the restricted primitive model. J. Chem. Phys. **111**, 9509 (1999)
4. van der Spoel, D., Lindahl, E., Hess, B., Groenhof, G., Mark, A.E., Berendsen, H.J.C.: Gromacs: fast, flexible and free. J. Comput. Chem. **26**, 1701 (2005)
5. Hess, B., Kutzner, C., van der Spoel, D., Lindahl, E.: Gromacs 4: algorithms for highly efficient, load-balanced, and scalable molecular simulation. **4**, 435 (2008)
6. Falcioni, M., Deem, M.W.: A biased Monte Carlo scheme for zeolite structure solution. J. Chem. Phys. **110**, 1754 (1999)
7. Hernández-Rojas, J., Llorente, J.M.G.: Microcanonical versus canonical analysis of protein folding. Phys. Rev. Lett. **100**, 258104 (2008)
8. Fiore, C.E.: First-order phase transitions: a study through the parallel tempering method. Phys. Rev. E. **78**, 041109 (2008)
9. Imperio, A., Reatto, L.: Microphase separation in two-dimensional systems with competing interactions. J. Chem. Phys. **124**, 164712 (2006)
10. Arnold, A., Holm, C.: Interactions of like-charged rods at low temperatures: analytical theory vs. simulations. Eur. Phys. J. E **27**, 21 (2008)
11. Odriozola, G., Berthier, L.: Equilibrium equation of state of a hard sphere binary mixture at very large densities using replica exchange Monte Carlo simulations. J. Chem. Phys. **134**, 054504 (2011)
12. Fortini, A., Dijkstra, M.: Phase behaviour of hard spheres confined between parallel hard plates: manipulation of colloidal crystal structures by confinement. J. Phys. Condens. Matter **18**, L371 (2006)
13. Damasceno, P.F., Engel, M., Glotzer, S.C.: Crystalline assemblies and densest packings of a family of truncated tetrahedra and the role of directional entropic forces. ACS Nano **6**, 609 (2012)

14. van Anders, G., Ahmed, N.K., Smith, R., Engel, M., Glotzer, S.C.: Entropically patchy particles: engineering valence through shape entropy. ACS Nano **8**, 931 (2014)
15. Wilding, N.B., Bruce, A.D.: Freezing by Monte Carlo phase switch. Phys. Rev. Lett. **85**, 5138 (2000)
16. Noya, E.G., Vega, C., de Miguel, E.: Determination of the melting point of hard spheres from direct coexistence simulation methods. J. Chem. Phys. **128**, 154507 (2008)
17. Frenkel, D., Smit, B.: Understanding Molecular Simulation. Academic, New York (1996)
18. Rosenbluth, M.N., Rosenbluth, A.W.: Further results on Monte Carlo equations of state. J. Chem. Phys. **22**, 881 (1954)
19. Wood, W.W., Jacobson, J.D.: Preliminary results from a recalculation of the Monte Carlo equation of state of hard spheres. J. Chem. Phys. **27**, 1207 (1957)
20. Alder, B.J., Wainwright, T.E.: Phase transition for a hard sphere system. J. Chem. Phys. **27**, 1208 (1957)
21. Parisi, G., Zamponi, F.: Mean-field theory of hard sphere glasses and jamming. Rev. Mod. Phys. **82**, 789 (2010)
22. Speedy, R.J.: On the reproducibility of glasses. J. Chem. Phys. **100**, 6684 (1994)
23. van Blaaderen, A., Wiltzius, P.: Real-space structure of colloidal hard-sphere glasses. Science **270**, 1177 (1995)
24. Speedy, R.J.: Pressure of the metastable hard-sphere fluid. J. Phys. Condens. Matter **9**, 8591 (1997)
25. Angelani, L., Foffi, G.: Configurational entropy of hard spheres. J. Phys. Condens. Matter **19**, 256207 (2007)
26. Pusey, P.N., van Megen, W.: Observation of a glass transition in suspensions of spherical colloidal particles. Phys. Rev. Lett. **59**, 2083 (1987)
27. van Megen, W., Mortensen, T.C., Williams, S.R., Müller, J.: Measurement of the self-intermediate scattering function of suspensions of hard spherical particles near the glass transition. Phys. Rev. E **58**, 6073 (1998)
28. Cheng, Z., Zhu, J., Chaikin, P.M., Phan, S.-E., Russel, W.B.: Nature of the divergence in low shear viscosity of colloidal hard-sphere dispersions. Phys. Rev. E **65**, 041405 (2002)
29. Brambilla, G., El Masri, D., Pierno, M., Berthier, L., Cipelletti, L., Petekidis, G., Schofield, A.B.: Probing the equilibrium dynamics of colloidal hard spheres above the mode-coupling glass transition. Phys. Rev. Lett. **102**, 085703 (2009)
30. Hermes, M., Dijkstra, M.: Thermodynamic signature of the dynamic glass transition in hard spheres. J. Phys. Condens. Matter **22**, 104114 (2010)
31. Lyubartsev, A.P., Martinovski, A.A., Shevkunov, S.V., Vorontsov-Velyaminov, P.N.: New approach to Monte Carlo calculation of the free energy: method of expanded ensembles. J. Chem. Phys. **96**, 1776 (1992)
32. Hukushima, K., Nemoto, K.: Exchange Monte Carlo method and application to spin glass simulations. J. Phys. Soc. Jpn. **65**, 1604 (1996)
33. Gallicchio, E., Xia, J., Flynn, W.F., Zhang, B., Samlalsingh, S., Mentes, A., Levy, R.M.: Asynchronous replica exchange software for grid and heterogeneous computing. Comput. Phys. Commun. (2015). doi:10.1016/j.cpc.2015.06.010
34. Odriozola, G.: Replica exchange Monte Carlo applied to hard spheres. J. Chem. Phys. **131**, 144107 (2009)
35. Okabe, T., Kawata, M., Okamoto, Y., Mikami, M.: Replica-exchange Monte Carlo method for the isobaric-isothermal ensemble. Chem. Phys. Lett. **335**, 435 (2001)

36. Gillespie, D.T.: Exact stochastic simulation of coupled chemical reactions. J. Chem. Phys. **81**, 2340 (1994)
37. Donev, A., Torquato, S., Stillinger, F.H.: Neighbor list collision-driven molecular dynamics simulation for nonspherical hard particles. I. Algorithmic details. J. Comput. Phys. **202**, 737 (2005)
38. Donev, A., Torquato, S., Stillinger, F.H.: Neighbor list collision-driven molecular dynamics simulation for nonspherical hard particles. II. Applications to ellipses and ellipsoids. J. Comput. Phys. **202**, 765 (2005)
39. Rathore, N., Chopra, M., de Pablo, J.J.: Optimal allocation of replicas in parallel tempering simulations. J. Chem. Phys. **122**, 024111 (2005)
40. Speedy, R.J.: Pressure and entropy of hard-sphere crystals. J. Phys. Condens. Matter **10**, 4387 (1998)
41. Ferrenberg, A.M., Swendsen, R.H.: New Monte Carlo technique for studying phase transitions. Phys. Rev. Lett. **61**, 2635 (1988)
42. Ferrenberg, A.M., Swendsen, R.H.: Optimized Monte Carlo data analysis. Phys. Rev. Lett. **63**, 1195 (1989)
43. Steinhardt, P.J., Nelson, D.R., Ronchetti, M.: Bond-orientational order in liquids and glasses. Phys. Rev. B **28**, 784 (1983)
44. Rintoul, M.D., Torquato, S.: Computer simulations of dense hard sphere systems. J. Chem. Phys. **105**, 9258 (1996)
45. Hales, T.C., Ferguson, S.P.: The Kepler Conjecture: The Hales-Ferguson Proof. Springer, New York (2011)
46. Pusey, P.N.: The effect of polydispersity on the crystallization of hard spherical colloids. J. Phys. France **48**, 709 (1987)
47. Ogarko, V., Luding, S.: Prediction of polydisperse hard-sphere mixture behavior using tridisperse systems. Soft Matter **9**, 9530 (2013)
48. O'Toole, P.I., Hudson, T.S.: New high-density packings of similarly sized binary spheres. J. Phys. Chem. C **115**, 19037 (2011)
49. Santos, A., Yuste, S.B., López de Haro, M., Odriozola, G., Ogarko, V.: Simple effective rule to estimate the jamming packing fraction of polydisperse hard spheres. Phys. Rev. E **89**, 040302(R) (2014)
50. Berthier, L., Witten, T.A.: Glass transition of dense fluids of hard and compressible spheres. Phys. Rev. E **80**, 021502 (2009)
51. Perera, D.N., Harrowell, P.: Stability and structure of a supercooled liquid mixture in two dimensions. Phys. Rev. E **59**, 5721 (1999)
52. Biben, T., Hansen, J.P.: Phase separation of asymmetric binary hard-sphere fluids. Phys. Rev. Lett. **66**, 2215 (1991)
53. Santen, L., Krauth, W.: Absence of thermodynamic phase transition in a model glass former. Nature **405**, 550 (2000)
54. Frenkel, D., Mulder, B.M., McTague, J.P.: Phase diagram of a system of hard ellipsoids. Phys. Rev. Lett. **52**, 287 (1984)
55. Frenkel, D., Mulder, B.M.: The hard ellipsoid-of-revolution fluid. I. Monte Carlo simulations. Mol. Phys. **55**, 1171 (1985)
56. Odriozola, G.: Revisiting the phase diagram of hard ellipsoids. J. Chem. Phys. **136**, 134505 (2012)
57. Bautista-Carbajal, G., Moncho-Jordá, A., Odriozola, G.: Further details on the phase diagram of hard ellipsoids of revolution. J. Chem. Phys. **138**, 064501 (2013)
58. Perram, J.W., Wertheim, M.S., Lebowitz, J.L., Williams, G.O.: Monte Carlo simulation of hard spheroids. Chem. Phys. Lett. **105**, 277 (1984)
59. Perram, J.W., Wertheim, M.S.: Statistical mechanics of hard ellipsoids. I. Overlap algorithm and the contact function. J. Comput. Phys. **58**, 409 (1985)

60. Paramonov, L., Yaliraki, S.N.: The directional contact distance of two ellipsoids: coarse-grained potentials for anisotropic interactions. J. Chem. Phys. **123**, 194111 (2005)
61. Vesely, F.J.: Nematic-smectic transition of parallel hard spheroellipsoids. J. Chem. Phys. **141**, 064109 (2014)
62. Berne, B.J., Pechukas, P.: Gaussian model potentials for molecular interactions. J. Chem. Phys. **56**, 4213 (1972)
63. Rickayzen, G.: A model for the study of the structure of hard molecular fluids. Mol. Phys. **95**, 393 (1998)
64. de Guevara-Rodríguez, F.J., Odriozola, G.: Hard ellipsoids: analytically approaching the exact overlap distance. J. Chem. Phys. **135**, 084508 (2011)
65. Donev, A., Stillinger, F.H., Chaikin, P.M., Torquato, S.: Unusually dense crystal packings of ellipsoids. Phys. Rev. Lett. **92**, 255506 (2004)
66. Pfleiderer, P., Schilling, T.: Simple monoclinic crystal phase in suspensions of hard ellipsoids. Phys. Rev. E **75**, 020402 (2007)
67. Radu, M., Pfleiderer, P., Schilling, T.: Solid-solid phase transition in hard ellipsoids. J. Chem. Phys. **131**, 164513 (2009)
68. Herod, T.E., Duran, R.S.: Two and three-dimensional nanoparticles of liquid-crystals prepared at the air liquid interface. Langmuir **14**, 6606 (1998)
69. Kim, F., Kwan, S., Akana, J., Yang, P.D.: Langmuir-Blodgett nanorod assembly. J. Amm. Chem. Soc. **123**, 4360 (2001)
70. Davies, G.B., Krüger, T., Coveney, P.V., Harting, J., Bremse, F.: Interface deformations affect the orientation transition of magnetic ellipsoidal particles adsorbed at fluid-fluid interfaces. Soft Matter **10**, 6742 (2014)
71. Zheng, Z., Wang, F., Han, Y.: Glass transitions in quasi-two-dimensional suspensions of colloidal ellipsoids. Phys. Rev. Lett. **107**, 065702 (2011)
72. Constantin, D., Davidson, P., Chanéac, C.: Lyotropic lamellar phase doped with a nematic phase of magnetic nanorods. Langmuir **26**, 4586 (2010)
73. Frenkel, D., Eppenga, R.: Evidence for algebraic orientational order in a two-dimensional hard-core nematic. Phys. Rev. A **31**, 1776 (1985)
74. Cuesta, J.A., Frenkel, D.: Monte Carlo simulation of two-dimensional hard ellipses. Phys. Rev. A **42**, 2126 (1990)
75. Donev, A., Burton, J., Stillinger, F.H., Torquato, S.: Tetratic order in the phase behavior of a hard-rectangle system. Phys. Rev. B **73**, 054109 (2006)
76. Avendaño, C., Escobedo, F.A.: Phase behavior of rounded hard-squares. Soft Matter **8**, 4675 (2012)
77. Shah, A.A., Kang, H., Kohlstedt, K.L., Ahn, K.H., Glotzer, S.C., Monroe, C.W., Solomon, M.J.: Liquid crystal order in colloidal suspensions of spheroidal particles by direct current electric field assembly. Small **8**, 1551 (2012)
78. Qi, W., de Graaf, J., Qiao, F., Marras, S., Manna, L., Dijkstra, M.: Ordered two-dimensional superstructures of colloidal octapod-shaped nanocrystals on flat substrates. Nano Lett. **12**, 5299 (2012)
79. Qi, W., de Graaf, J., Qiao, F., Marras, S., Manna, L., Dijkstra, M.: Phase diagram of octapod-shaped nanocrystals in a quasi-two-dimensional planar geometry. J. Chem. Phys. **138**, 154504 (2013)
80. Quan, Z., Fang, J.: Superlattices with non-spherical building blocks. Nano Today **5**, 390 (2010)
81. Schmitt, J., Gruenewald, T., Decher, G., Pershan, P., Kjaer, K., Losche, M.: Internal structure of layer by layer adsorbed polyelectrolyte films - a neutron and x-ray reflectivity study. Macromolecules **26**, 7058 (1993)

82. Decher, G.: Fuzzy nanoassemblies: toward layered polymeric multicomposites. Science **277**, 1232 (1997)

83. Rycenga, M., Camargo, P.H.C., Xia, Y.: Template-assisted self-assembly: a versatile approach to complex micro- and nanostructures. Soft Matter **5**, 1129 (2009)

84. Kosterlitz, J.M., Thouless, D.J.: Ordering, metastability and phase transitions in two-dimensional systems. J. Phys. C **6**, 1181 (1973)

85. Halperin, B.I., Nelson, D.R.: Theory of two-dimensional melting. Phys. Rev. Lett. **41**, 121 (1978)

86. Straley, J.P.: Liquid crystals in two dimensions. Phys. Rev. A **4**, 675 (1971)

87. Bates, M.A., Frenkel, D.: Phase behavior of two-dimensional hard rod fluids. J. Chem. Phys. **112**, 10034 (2000)

88. Zheng, Z., Han, Y.: Self-diffusion in two-dimensional hard ellipsoid suspensions. J. Chem. Phys. **133**, 124509 (2010)

89. Xu, W.S., Li, Y.W., Sun, Z.Y., An, L.J.: Hard ellipses: Equation of state, structure, and self-diffusion. J. Chem. Phys. **139**, 024501 (2013)

90. Jaster, A.: Computer simulations of the two-dimensional melting transition using hard disks. Phys. Rev. E **59**, 2594 (1999)

91. Bernard, E.P., Krauth, W.: Two-step melting in two dimensions: first-order liquid-hexatic transition. Phys. Rev. Lett. **107**, 155704 (2011)

92. Bautista-Carbajal, G., Odriozola, G.: Phase diagram of two-dimensional hard ellipses. J. Chem. Phys. **140**, 204502 (2014)

93. Vieillard-Baron, J.: Phase transitions of the classical hard-ellipse system. J. Chem. Phys. **56**, 4729 (1972)

Accelerating AZKIND Simulations of Light Water Nuclear Reactor Cores Using PARALUTION on GPU

Andrés Rodríguez-Hernandez[1(✉)], Armando M. Gómez-Torres[1],
Edmundo del Valle-Gallegos[2], Javier Jimenez-Escalante[3],
Nico Trost[3], and Victor H. Sanchez-Espinoza[3]

[1] Instituto Nacional de Investigaciones Nucleares,
Ocoyoacac, Estado de México, Mexico
andres.rodriguez@inin.gob.mx

[2] ESFM – Departamento de Física, Instituto Politécnico Nacional,
Zacatenco, Mexico, D.F., Mexico

[3] Institute for Neutron Physics and Reactor Technology,
Karlsruhe Institute of Technology, Karlsruhe, Germany

Abstract. This paper presents the results of the accelerated solution of the linear algebraic system $Av = b$ arising from a nodal finite element method implemented in the neutron diffusion code AZKIND to solve 3D problems. The numerical solution of full nuclear reactor cores with AZKIND implies the generation of large sparse algebraic systems that produce bottle-necks in the iterative solution. Aiming to alleviate the overload of the algorithm, an acceleration technique has to be implemented. Consequently, a Fortran plug-in of the open source linear algebra PARALUTION library (C ++) was integrated into the AZKIND source code (Fortran 95). This implementation allows AZKIND to use GPUs as well as CPUs, threading into the GPU thousands of arithmetic operations for parallel processing. Selected examples of preliminary investigations performed for a cluster of nuclear fuel assemblies are presented and the obtained results are discussed in this paper.

1 Introduction

Parallel computing is the computer science discipline that deals with the system architecture and software issues related to the concurrent execution of applications. The interest in parallel computing dates back to the late 1950's, with advancements surfacing in the form of supercomputers throughout the 60's and 70's. These were shared memory multiprocessors, with multiple processors working side-by-side on shared data. In the mid 1980's, a new kind of parallel computing was launched when a supercomputer for scientific applications from 64 Intel 8086/8087 processors was built. This system showed that extreme performance could be achieved and these massively parallel processors came to dominate the top end of computing.

Starting in the late 80's, clusters came to compete and eventually displace multiple parallel processors (MPP) for many applications. Today, clusters are the workhorse of

© Springer International Publishing Switzerland 2016
I. Gitler and J. Klapp (Eds.): ISUM 2015, CCIS 595, pp. 419–431, 2016.
DOI: 10.1007/978-3-319-32243-8_29

scientific computing and are the dominant architecture in the data centers. Parallel computing is becoming mainstream based on multi-core processors.

The software has been very active part of the evolution of parallel computing. Some standards have emerged. For MPPs and clusters, a number of application programming interfaces converged to a single standard called MPI by the mid 1990's. For shared memory multiprocessor computing, a similar process unfolded with convergence around two standards by the mid to late 1990's: pthreads and OpenMP. As multi-core processors bring parallel computing to mainstream customers, the key challenge in computing today is to transition the software industry to parallel programming.

In the particular case of the nuclear industry, since the late 1950's, the need to perform nuclear safety analyses was essential in the licensing process, mainly for commercial nuclear power plants. In this sense, the application of scientific computer calculations has made possible these safety analyses, but always struggling with computer capabilities. In the former efforts, for the operational and safety analysis, the main goal was to get a static or dynamic solution to a set of differential equations for neutron diffusion and neutron transport with technology and methods present in those years. In this huge task, numerical techniques were used by applying finite differences, finite elements, and nowadays, nodal finite elements. No matter which numerical method is used, with any of these methods the analyst always ends facing the problem of solving an extremely large algebraic system that challenges computer capabilities. It is desirable for the nuclear safety analyst to obtain the results of each reactor simulation in a relatively short time.

In the last few years, the technological developments of supercomputers or high performance computer equipment have made possible the use of supercomputing in many science areas, where the nuclear field is not the exception.

A proper combination of parallel computing software, like already developed linear algebra libraries, and a specific project can give as a result a computational platform to simulate nuclear reactor states in very short time periods. The work presented here describes the implementation of the linear algebra library PARALUTION into the neutron kinetics code AZKIND.

2 Description of AZKIND

2.1 AZKIND Background

The computer code "**AZ**tlan **KI**netics in **N**eutron **D**iffusion", AZKIND, is part of a set of neutron codes selected for implementation in the AZTLAN Platform [1]. The original development NRKin3D was a master degree project [2] written in Fortran 77. The first task to convert this academic code into a real reactor simulator code was to migrate it to Fortran 90/95 language, chiefly for dynamic management of memory allocation. The next step to follow was the parallel processing algorithms implementation to generate results in short acceptable times. AZKIND comprises the computer subprograms PRTN0 [3] and NRKin3D to calculate reactor steady states and reactor kinetics, respectively.

2.2 AZKIND Theory Description

This computer code is based on multi-group neutron diffusion theory. For G neutron energy groups and I_p delayed neutron precursor concentrations, the neutron diffusion kinetics equations are given by [4]:

$$
\frac{1}{v^g}\frac{\partial}{\partial t}\phi^g(\vec{r},t) = \nabla \cdot D^g \nabla \phi^g(\vec{r},t) - \Sigma_R^g \phi^g(\vec{r},t) + \sum_{\substack{g'=1 \\ g' \neq g}}^{G} \Sigma_s^{g' \to g} \phi^{g'}(\vec{r},t)
$$

$$
+ (1-\beta)\chi^g \sum_{g'=1}^{G} v^{g'}(\vec{r},t)\Sigma_f^{g'}\phi^{g'}(\vec{r},t) + \sum_{i=1}^{I_p} \chi_i^g \lambda_i C_i(\vec{r},t); \tag{1a}
$$

$$
g=1,\ldots,G; i=1,\ldots,I_p; \ \forall(\vec{r},t) \in \Omega \times (0,T];
$$

$$
\frac{\partial}{\partial t} C_i(\vec{r},t) = \beta_i \sum_{g=1}^{G} v^g(\vec{r},t)\Sigma_f^g(\vec{r},t)\phi^g(\vec{r},t) - \lambda_i C_i(\vec{r},t); \tag{1b}
$$

$$
g=1,\ldots,G; i=1,\ldots,I_p; \forall(\vec{r},t) \in \Omega \times (0,T];
$$

In addition, initial conditions and boundary conditions must be satisfied by neutron fluxes and neutron precursor's functions. The parameters involved in the above equations are described in [2].

The spatial discretization ($\vec{r}$) of these equations is strongly connected with the discretization of a nuclear reactor of volume Ω. Representing the neutron flux and the precursors concentration in terms of base functions defined over Ω, it is possible to write:

$$
\phi^g(\vec{r},t) \equiv \sum_{k=1}^{N_f} u_k(\vec{r})\phi_k^g(t); C_i(\vec{r},t) \equiv \sum_{m=1}^{N_p} v_m(\vec{r})C_i^m(t); \tag{2}
$$

where Nf and Np are the number of unknowns to be determined for neutron flux and delayed neutron precursors, respectively. Substituting expressions (2) into Eqs. (1a) and (1b), and applying the Galerkin process for space discretization, as described in [2], the resulting algebraic system of equations can be expressed in matrix notation as follows,

$$
\frac{1}{v^g}M_f \frac{\partial}{\partial t}\phi^g(t) = -K^g\phi^g(t) - \sum_{g'=1}^{G} S^{g' \to g}\phi^{g'}(t)
$$

$$
+ (1-\beta)\chi^g \sum_{g'=1}^{G} F^{gg'}(t)\phi^{g'}(t) + \sum_{i=1}^{I_p} F^{gi}C_i(t); \tag{3a}
$$

$$M_p \frac{\partial}{\partial t} C_i(t) = \sum_{g'=1}^{G} P^{ig'}(t) \phi^{g'}(t) - \lambda_i M_p C_i(t);$$

(3b)

$$g = 1, \ldots, G; i = 1, \ldots, I_p; \forall (\vec{r}, t) \in \Omega(0, T];$$

where $\phi^g(t) = \left[\phi_1^g(t), \ldots, \phi_{N_f}^g(t) \right]^T$ and $C_i(t) = \left[C_i^1(t), \ldots, C_i^{N_p}(t) \right]^T$, and the matrix elements are shown, only for three main matrices, in the following table:

After simplification of the expressions (3a) and (3b), an algebraic system is obtained, including only the flux vector as the array values to be determined for each energy group.

The general process is to solve the resulting linear algebraic system using an initial flux vector to find the neutron flux solution vector, and use this neutron flux to calculate the new delayed neutron precursor concentrations vector. This process is carried out for each time step over the total interval $(0, T]$.

Section 2.2.1 explains the calculus of the matrix elements with the use of nodal functions to evaluate the integral expressions in Table 1 over each node Ω_h in the full domain Ω.

Table 1. Matrix elements from the spatial discretization.

Matrix	Type	Dimension	Elements
M_f	Mass	$N_f \times N_f$	$m_{f,jk} \equiv \int_\Omega u_j u_k d\vec{r}$
M_p	Mass	$N_p \times N_p$	$m_{p,lm} \equiv \int_\Omega v_l v_m d\vec{r}$
K^g	Stiffness	$N_f \times N_f$	$k_{jk}^g \equiv \int_\Omega D^g \nabla u_j \nabla u_k d\vec{r}$

2.2.1 Nodal Finite Element Method in Spatial Discretization

A particular Nodal Finite Element (NFE) is characterized by the fact that for each cell (node) the function unknowns to be determined are the (00) Legendre moment (average) of the unknown function over each face of the node and the (000) Legendre moment over the cell volume.

Figure 1 shows (left) a physical domain Ω represented graphically after generating an xyz mesh. The right hand side shows a cuboid-type cell with directions through the faces: (x) Right, Left; (y) Near, Far; (z) Top, Bottom; and C for the average of the function over the cell volume.

Taking into consideration the general form to build up nodal schemes [5], the moments of a function (at edges and cell) over a node like the one shown in Fig. 1 can be written for the nodal finite element method RTN-0 (Raviart-Thomas-Nédélec).

In the NFE method RTN-0, the normalized zero order Legendre polynomials, defined over the unit cell $\Omega_{ijk} = [-1,1] \times [-1,1] \times [-1,1]$ and correlated to each physical cell $\Omega_{ijk} = [x_i, x_{i+1}] \times [y_i, y_{i+1}] \times [z_i, z_{i+1}]$, are used to calculate the elements of the matrices in Eqs. (3a) and (3b).

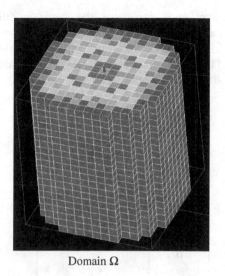

Domain Ω

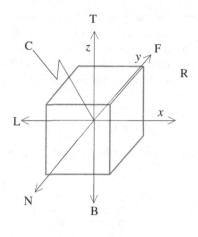

Physical local node Ω_h

Fig. 1. Discretization of domain Ω and representation of a node or cell.

2.2.2 Discretization of the Time Variable

Once the spatial discretization is done, the θ-method [2] is applied for discretization of the time variable appearing in the set of ordinary differential equations given by (1a) and (1b) or the Eqs. (3a) and (3b). For the time integration over the interval $(0,T]$, this interval is divided in n time-steps $\Delta tl = [t_l, t_{l+1}]$ and the following approach is assumed:

$$\int_{t_l}^{t_{l+1}} f(t)dt \cong h_l[\theta f_{l+1} + (1 - \theta)f_l]$$

where $hl = \Delta tl$, $fl \equiv f(tl)$, $fl + 1 \equiv f(tl + 1)$, and θ is the integration parameter.

In this way, when carrying out the time integration, both parameters θf and θp for neutron flux and delayed neutron precursors are considered. Depending on the values assigned to these parameters, different time integration schemes are generated [2].

3   AZKIND Algebraic System

As a result from the application of the RTN-0 nodal finite element method and the use of the θ-method approach, the resulting algebraic system is represented as a typical arrange of matrix-vector multiplication $A\underline{v} = \underline{b}$, where A and $\underline{b}$ are known and the unknown vector $\underline{v}$ is computed for each time step Δtl.

The algebraic system to be solved in AZKIND turns out to be a complex problem when it is used to compute the solution for real nuclear reactor cases. It is complex in the sense that the non-symmetric matrix A becomes a very large sparse matrix changing for each time step. The matrix generated by AZKIND has nnz non-zero elements. Even if some generated matrix element eventually takes up a zero value, the matrix is still considered to have *nnz* elements as these are all used to solve the algebraic system.

Searching for an iterative algorithm for non-symmetric linear systems, the method of bi-conjugate gradients stable (BiCGStab) [13] was used because it has been proven to be an efficient and fast converging method for Krylov subspaces.

3.1   Simple Didactic Example

This section describes a small array with a domain partition shown in Fig. 2.

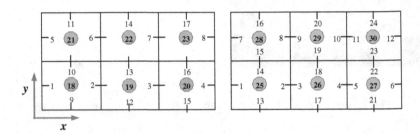

Fig. 2. Simple example consisting of 6 cells in the *xy* plane and 2 *z* layers.

In the plane *xy* there is a domain with an *x*-mesh with 3 cuts, and both, *y*-mesh and *z*-mesh with 2 cuts. The total number of cells is 12. In Fig. 2(a) the mesh points for neutron flux appear showing continuity conditions. Precursor concentrations not necessarily meet this condition. Only 2 neutron energy groups are considered ($G = 2$).

Figure 3 shows the schematic matrix representation for this simple example. The number of matrix blocks numbered in brackets [*,*] is given by $G^2 = 4$. Each block is built up with matrix elements corresponding to the directions *x*, *y*, *z*, and *c*.

All the "marks" in the matrix *A* are the *nnz* elements, and the empty zones are zeros not existing in AZKIND. The matrix is considered well-structured with diagonal elements and sparse elements coming from the coupling of each node with the node edges for each direction *x*, *y*, and *z*.

For the simple example shown in Fig. 2 the number of matrix rows and columns is *nrow* = 128 and *ncol* = 128 respectively, and the number of non-zero elements is *nnz* = 1120. In Sect. 6 we shall describe a study case for the nodalization of a hypothetical nuclear reactor for which *nnz* is extremely large in comparison to the case we have exposed in this section. The problem grows greatly with an increase in the number of energy groups.

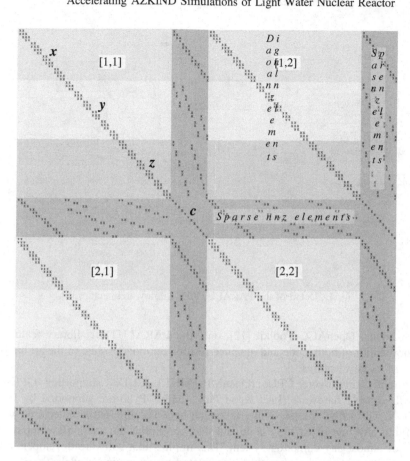

Fig. 3. Schematic A matrix generated by AZKIND for 2 energy groups.

4 PARALUTION Library

PARALUTION [6] is an open source C ++ library to solve sparse systems of linear equations with parallel processing. It offers a variety of iterative solvers such as the CG, BiCGStab and GMRES Krylov methods, and preconditioners based on additive (Jacobi, Gauss–Seidel) and multiplicative (ILUp, ILUT, power(q)-pattern enhanced multi-colored ILU(p) method) splitting schemes as well as approximate inverse preconditioning approaches, see Fig. 4.

PARALUTION also features different matrix formats which are crucial for GPU (Graphics Processing Unit) internal bandwidth exploitation. Furthermore, it offers several hardware backends for execution on multi/manycore CPU and GPU devices. Due to its generic and flexible design, it allows seamless integration within any scientific software package, such as COBAYA3 [7] and the present AZKIND project [1].

While there are several scientific libraries for our purpose to speed up the computation time of the sparse linear systems solution procedure, such as ViennaCL [8], Intel MKL [9], AMD Core Math Library [10], Nvidia cuSPARSE [11], or the new

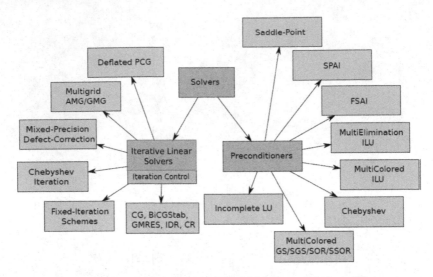

Fig. 4. Detail of the PARALUTION Library architecture [6].

release Nvidia OpenACC Toolkit [12], only the PARALUTION library features the high portability of both, code and obtained results, on modern state of the art hardware as one of its key features.

Currently, multi-core CPUs (OpenMP, MKL), CUDA supporting GPUs and OpenCL capable hardware (Intel Xeon Phi, AMD GPUs) are supported by PARA-LUTION. This offers the possibility to switch between different architectures without modifying any line of existing code and thus to exploit the available computational power of almost any computer system. This implies that software developers do not necessarily have to deal with architecture-related programming models.

PARALUTION comes with a plugin support for FORTRAN, OpenFOAM and Deal.II packages. The Fortran plug-in makes possible to communicate Fortran- compiled libraries with the C ++-compiled library with the use of an appropriate interface module. The Fortran plug-in was integrated in the specific project AZKIND to be run in different architectures.

5   AZKIND Parallel Processing Implementation

Given a particular reactor core configuration, the AZKIND code has the option of simulating only a steady state (SS) reactor condition, only a dynamic case using previously generated initial steady state data as input, or simulating a steady state plus a reactor dynamics calculation. The diagram in Fig. 5 shows how AZKIND has been constructed including the implementation of the PARALUTION Fortran plug-in.

In the left side of Fig. 5, dynamic calculation is performed using the PARALU-TION solver called in AZKIND with the use of the module interface, as it is shown in more detail in the right side.

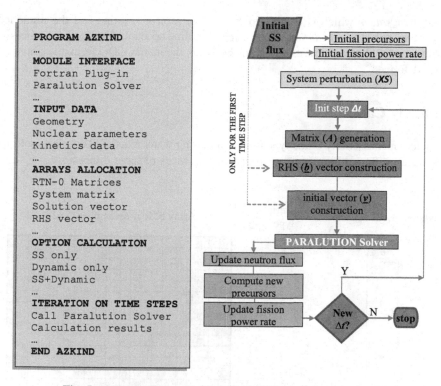

Fig. 5. AZKIND flow with PARALUTION parallel processing.

The dynamic calculation is performed sequentially for each time step, until the total interval (0,T] is completed. Here it is important to point out that in the original AZKIND code, the Bi-CGStab solver was implemented using reference [13], working in serial computer processing. The preconditioning matrix was constructed with the inverse of the square root of each diagonal matrix element, $\left(\sqrt{a_{ii}}\right)^{-1}$.

AZKIND works with vector arrays for each x, y, z, and c direction (see Fig. 1) and PARALUTION receives full arrays only. Then, first of all, it was necessary to create a subroutine to write AZKIND matrix A in a Matrix Market format [14] to be read by the PARALUTION solver. Also, the "searched" solution vector $\underline{v}$ and the right-hand-side vector $\underline{b}$ were constructed by concatenating the respective AZKIND directed-arrays, for each time step before calling the PARALUTION solver.

For the solver converging on each time step, it was necessary to create a subroutine to de-concatenate the reached solution vector $\underline{v}$ to have directed-arrays in order to continue the AZKIND procedure for each x, y, z, and c direction to update the neutron flux, recalculate the new delayed neutron precursors concentration, and to compute the new fission power rate; continuing this cycle until the whole time interval (0,T] is completed.

The process with PARALUTION solver implemented is as follows: AZKIND reads the input data and generates A, $\underline{v}$ and $\underline{b}$. PARALUTION Fortran *plug-in* reads the matrix in COO format [14] and assigns the vector arrays. The *plug-in* calls the *paralution_solver* which is comprised of the *ConvertTo()* routine and the numerical solver *bicgstab*. The *paralution_solver* execution time accounts for these two processes running on GPU. Before the execution of *bicgstab*, the matrix COO format is converted to CSR format.

6   Study Case

A nuclear fuel assembly of the type used in a boiling water reactor (BWR) was selected to simulate different arrangements to produce matrices of large dimensions.

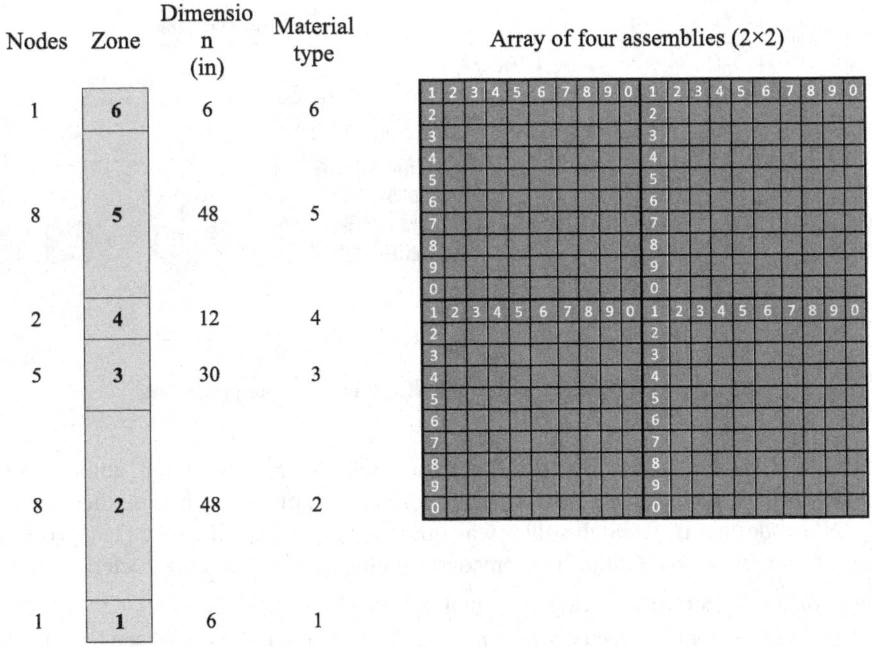

Fig. 6. Typical fuel assembly for a BWR and assembly cross section.

6.1   Fuel Assembly Description

Figure 6 shows schematically a typical nuclear fuel assembly. Full details of this fuel, were provided to the SERPENT [15] code on another task of AZTLAN project [1]. Nuclear data obtained for the fuel assembly with SERPENT correspond to homogeneous zones or fuel cells, i.e., pin by pin information is not needed. Nuclear data for this homogenization is the information required by AZKIND. Comparing the multiplication factor for assembly and for cells, generated with both codes AZKIND and SERPENT, the results are acceptable; but it is not necessary to present them here.

6.2   Generation of Matrices

The fuel assembly described in Fig. 6 was used to generate matrices with different dimensions. The most simple case was to consider only one assembly (array 1×1) where the xyz-mesh was 10 intervals in x-direction, 10 intervals in y-direction and 150 intervals in z-direction or axial direction. Table 2 shows matrix dimensions for different arrays of fuel assemblies, where the largest case corresponds to the 10×10 array (100 assemblies), which can be considered as a one-quarter part of a small BWR reactor core.

Table 2. Parallel processing time (seconds) in different architectures.

Assemblies array	1×1	2×2	4×4	6×6	10×10
Matrix dimension	n	n	n	n	n
Non-zero elements	126,200	492,800	1,947,200	4,363,200	12,080,000
	nnz	nnz	nnz	nnz	nnz
	1,332,400	5,305,600	21,174,400	47,606,400	132,160,000
Serial[a]	36	179	820	1812	4721
Elite 800G1	5.67	28.12	138.50	225.99	744.81
Lenovo 50–70	7.37	16.65	61.12	*No memory*	*No memory*
WS Z620	4.23	8.22	29.24	38.60	*No memory*

[a] *Serial processing (one core Intel Core i7) with the algorithm Bi-CGStab implemented in AZKIND from the original NRKin3D* [2].

In particular, for the one-quarter reactor core, a smaller matrix could be used for a real reactor simulation if the z-mesh is changed from 150 to 25 axial nodes, as it is customary used in current BWR reactor core simulations. With this change the matrix dimension (n) is 2,030,000 with 22,060,000 nnz elements; comparable to the 4×4 array dimension. Nevertheless, the fine z-mesh of 150 axial nodes was used in order to challenge the computer equipment capabilities and the performance of the AZKIND code.

7   Numerical Results

The equipment employed to run AZKIND with parallel processing was: a desktop computer HP ELITE 800G1 with a processor Intel Core i7 of 8 cores; a workstation HP Z620 with card GPU Tesla K20c with 2,496 processor cores; and a notebook Lenovo 50–70 with card GPU GeForce GTX 860 M with 640 processor cores.

Table 2 presents *paralution_solver* execution times of simulations with only one time-step and using a zero perturbation scheme in each case:

As already expected, the serial executions have very large times compared to the execution times of the parallel processing using the described equipment. The execution times in parallel processing also increase considerably when matrix dimension increases, but these times are reduced when more processor cores are used.

In the case of the Lenovo 50–70 and the WS Z620, the matrix format conversion could not be executed in this first trial in the device (GPU), instead, the conversion was performed on the host (CPU). The numerical solver *bicgstab* was indeed performed in the device, but the time spent in the conversion process contributed negatively as can it be seen in Table 2, at least more remarkable for the simplest array (1 × 1), when compared to Elite result using only 8 cores.

In Table 2, *"No memory"* means not enough memory in CPU to convert these large matrices. The text *"No memory"* in WS Z620 also means not enough memory in the GPU card to load the 10 × 10 array's matrix.

For the analysis of the acceleration or "speedup", a definition of the logarithmic speedup is used [16], also known as relative speedup:

$$S = T_1/T_n$$

Where T_1 is the computing time using a single processor (serial calculation) and T_n is the computing time using n processor cores. The speedup results are as follows,

Tables 2 and 3 show an excellent computing acceleration, even though the speedup for small matrices is similar for the three computer architectures used. It also can be seen that the speedup values scaling is not linear.

Table 3. Speedup comparison (S).

Array Equipment	1 × 1	2 × 2	4 × 4	6 × 6	10 × 10
Elite 800G1	6.35	6.37	5.92	8.02	6.34
Lenovo 50–70	4.88	10.75	13.42	–	–
WS Z620	8.51	21.78	28.08	46.94	–

8   Conclusions and Outlook

Parallel computing times are very small compared to those obtained in sequential computing. Speedup is highly noticeable when using a good number of processor cores, even for large algebraic systems.

The AZKIND neutronics code is envisaged to be further developed to become a useful and powerful tool for the analysis of light water reactor cores given its strong capability to perform parallel computations.

In this work it was also shown the key features of the C ++ PARALUTION library, such as portability and scalability for its integration in specific Fortran projects as AZKIND.

Experience gained from this work will be applied to implement parallel processing in other AZTLAN Platform codes: the neutron transport code AZTRAN, and the neutron diffusion code in hexagonal geometry AZNHEX.

As a final remark, it will be necessary to run this coupled specific project with a PARALUTION licensed version as it already allows the use of high computing hardware full capabilities, together with MPI for distributed tasks.

Acknowledgement. The authors acknowledge the financial support from the National Strategic Project No. 212602 (AZTLAN Platform) as part of the Sectorial Fund for Energetic Sustainability CONACYT – SENER.

References

1. A. Gómez, et al.: Project ININ-CONACYT No. CO-072. Development of a Mexican Platform for Analysis and Design of Nuclear Reactors (2014)
2. Rodríguez, A.: Solution of the nuclear reactor kinetics equations in 3D using the nodal method RTN-0. MSc Thesis. National Polytechnic Institute. ESFM, Department of Nuclear Engineering, México (2002)
3. Salas C.A.: numerical solution of the neutrons diffusion equations, in XYZ using the nodal method RTN-0. MSc Thesis. National Polytechnic Institute, ESFM, Department of Nuclear Engineering (1995)
4. Duderstadt, J.J., Hamilton, L.J.: Nuclear Reactor Analysis. John Wiley & Sons, New York (1976)
5. Hennart, J.P.: A general family of nodal schemes. SIAM J. Sci. Stat. Comput. 7(1), 264–287 (1986)
6. Lukarski, D.: PARALUTION project, version 0.8.0 (2014). http://www.paralution.com/
7. Trost, N., et al.: Accelerating COBAYA3 on multi-core CPU and GPU systems using PARALUTION. Annals of Nuclear energy (in Press, 2014)
8. Rupp, K., Rudolf, F., Weinbub, J.: ViennaCL – A high level linear algebra library for GPUs and multi-core CPUs. In: International Workshop on GPUs and Scientific Applications, pp. 51–56 (2010)
9. Intel: Intel Math Kernel Library (MKL), version 11.0 (2011). http://software.intel.com/en-us/intel-mkl
10. AMD-2013: Core Math Library (ACML), version 5.3.1 (2003). http://developer.amd.com/tools-and-sdks/cpu-development/amd-core-math-library-acml/
11. NVIDIA-2014: cuSPARSE. https://developer.nvidia.com/cusparse
12. NVIDIA-2015: OpenACC. https://developer.nvidia.com/openacc
13. Van der Vorst, H.A.: BI-CGSTAB: A fast and smoothly converging variant of BI-CG for the solution of nonlinear systems. SIAM J. Sci. Stat. Comput. 13(2), 631–644 (1992)
14. Matrix Market internet site. http://math.nist.gov/MatrixMarket/
15. Lepänen, J.: Development of a dynamic simulation mode in the SERPENT Monte Carlo code. In: Proceedings of the M&C 2013, Sun Valley, ID, 5–9 May 2013
16. Nesmachnow, S.: Workshop 4: Scientific computing on distributed memory systems. In: International Supercomputing Conference ISUM 2015, México (2015)

Rheological Properties of Brushes on Cancerous Epithelial Cells Under the Influence of an External Oscillatory Force

J.D. Hernández Velázquez[1], S. Mejía-Rosales[1], and Armando Gama Goicochea[2(✉)]

[1] CICFIM, UANL, San Nicolás de los Garza, Nuevo León, Mexico
[2] TESE, Ecatepec de Morelos, Estado de México, Mexico
agama@alumni.stanford.edu

Abstract. The rheological properties of brushes of different length on the surface of human epithelial cancerous cells are studied here by means of coarse – grained numerical simulations, where the surface of the cell is subjected to an external oscillatory force acting on the plane of the cell's surface. We model explicitly the tip of an atomic force microscope and the cancerous cell as a surface covered by brushes of different length, and take into account the interactions of the brush chains with the tip and with each other, leading to complex rheological behavior as displayed by the profiles of viscosity and the friction coefficient of this complex system. We comment briefly on how these findings can help in the experimental effort to understand the nature of the cancer growth in human epithelial cells.

Keywords: Rheology · Cancerous cells · Oscillatory force · DPD

1 Introduction

It is known that cervical cancer is one of the leading types of cancer in women over 35 years of age [1]. In an effort to understand the characteristics of this and other types of cancer, several physical approaches have been applied recently to gain new insights about how metastasis occurs, development of non – invasive detection methods, and perhaps even help in the design of new treatment [2–5]. One of those approaches consists in the characterization of cancerous cells using atomic force microscopy (AFM) [6]. Using AFM, several groups have determined that cancerous cells from different types of tissue are softer than their normal counterparts [2–5, 7, 8], while others claim that the mechanical response of malignant cells depends on the type of cancer [9, 10]. Most of the research on this topic has focused on the response of the cells' surface as a whole. One notable exception is the work of Iyer and collaborators [11], who measured the force exerted by the tip of an AFM on the brushes that covered cancerous cervical epithelial cells, finding a force profile qualitatively different from the one measured on healthy cells. The difference was attributed to the inhomogeneous composition of the brushes that cover the cancer cells, while normal cells are covered by brushes of approximately the same length. These experiments are important, not only because they help establish the role played by the brushes that typically cover most types of epithelial cells, which may be different from the role played by the surface of the cell, but also because they can be used to design improved detection methods.

© Springer International Publishing Switzerland 2016
I. Gitler and J. Klapp (Eds.): ISUM 2015, CCIS 595, pp. 432–446, 2016.
DOI: 10.1007/978-3-319-32243-8_30

On the modeling side, it has been shown [12] that the softness or stiffness of the individual "structures" that make up the brushes is responsible of the apparent softness or stiffness of the brush as a whole. These "structures" or "molecules" can be of different nature; they can be microridges, microtubules or microvilli [13], whose purpose is to provide motility to the cell and increase nutrient absorption. They can move on the surface of the cells, although it has been shown [12] that the mechanical response of epithelial cells to the force exerted by an AFM is considerably more dependent on the softness/stiffness of the brushes than on their ability to move or not on the surface of the cells. Since it can be envisaged that a correlation exists between the stiffness of brushes on cancerous cells, and cancer stadia, it is befitting to study this issue further.

In this contribution we report results of non – equilibrium numerical simulations at the mesoscopic level of brushes on a surface under oscillatory flow on the plane of the surface. The motivation for performing simulations of this type stems from recent experiments with AFM on cancer cells under non – equilibrium conditions [11]. Two key aspects are novel in this work: firstly, the curvature of the tip of the AFM is incorporated explicitly, which makes our predictions useful for those workers who use nano-meter – size tips in their AFM. Secondly, we have included a three – body interaction between neighboring bonds along the chains that make up the "molecules" of the brushes, so that their softness or stiffness can be controlled directly. By subjecting this system to a sinusoidal external force along the plane of the cell's surface one can obtain rheological properties such as the viscosity and friction between the brush and the AFM, which can be useful for an improved characterization of this illness. The rest of this chapter is organized as follows: in Sect. 2 we presented the model, methods and systems studied; the results and their discussion are reported in Sect. 3. Finally, our conclusions are laid out in Sect. 4.

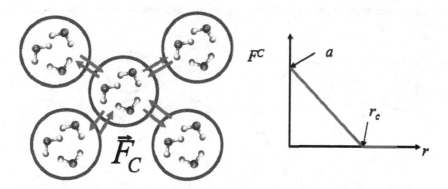

Fig. 1. A schematic representation of the coarse – graining involved in DPD, where in this particular example each DPD particle (blue circles) groups three water molecules. The conservative force (F^C) acts as a local pressure between pairs of particles and it has a simple, linearly decaying and repulsive character – see the red line in the right panel of the figure. The conservative force becomes zero at relative distances larger than a cutoff radius, r_c, and it is equal to an interaction constant a when $r = 0$, which is determined by the chemical nature of the pair of DPD interacting particles. Adapted from [17] (Color figure online).

2   Models and Methods

The simulations whose results are the purpose of this contribution use the interaction model known as dissipative particle dynamics (DPD) [14], which consists of the simultaneous integration of the equation of motion of all particles that make up the system, to obtain their positions and momenta. In this regard, DPD is identical to standard simulations of molecular dynamics [15]. The difference stems from the introduction of a natural thermostat into the algorithm, which arises from the balancing of the dissipative and random forces [16]; this is the major advantage of DPD over other simulation algorithms. The conservative force that acts between particles is simple (repulsive, linearly decaying) and, like the random and dissipative forces, of short range, which is the reason why DPD is useful to model systems at the mesoscopic level. Figure 1 illustrates the coarse – graining degree and the nature of the conservative force in the DPD model. However, it must be kept in mind that one is free to choose other types of forces, such as the Lennard – Jones model, with the DPD algorithm.

As stated above, one of the major advantages of the DPD model is its naturally emerging thermostat, which has been shown to compete very favorably with other thermostats, especially under non – equilibrium circumstances [18], which are precisely the central focus of this work. Figure 2 is meant to show what the forces that make up the thermostat represent, namely, the dissipative force (F_D) and the random force (F_R), coupled through the fluctuation – dissipation theorem to lead to constant global temperature [16].

This model is now well known and there are recent reviews available [18, 20], therefore we shall skip details for the sake of brevity. We solve the forces for the system of particles using the algorithm of molecular dynamics, adapted to DPD [21].

Since our aim is to model experiments performed with AFM, we have incorporated explicitly its curved tip into the system, constructing it from individual DPD particles. Additionally, we model the brush – covered cancerous cell as a flat surface on top of which there are grafted chains of three different lengths, as suggested by recent experiments [11].

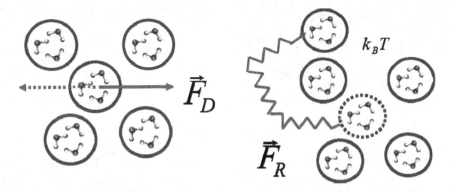

Fig. 2. Illustrative representation of the forces that make up the thermostat in DPD; F_D represents the dissipative force, which accounts for the local viscosity of the fluid, while F_R is responsible for the local Brownian motion. The perfect coupling between these contributions keeps the global temperature fixed. Adapted from [19].

These linear chains are made up of DPD particles, joined by freely rotating harmonic springs, which interact with particles on the same chain and with those on other chains according to the DPD rules given by the forces illustrated in Figs. 1 and 2. In addition to those interactions we have introduced a three – body harmonic potential that acts between neighboring bonds, whose purpose is to introduce rigidity to the chains. There are also monomeric solvent particles that permeate the brush, which are meant to represent the buffer used in AFM experiments with cells in vitro. Lastly, the cell's surface on which the brushes are grafted is subjected to a sinusoidal force along the x – direction with maximum amplitude $(2/w)$ and fixed frequency $(w = \pi/100\Delta t)$. The motivation for doing so arises from force measurements on oscillating polymer brushes using AFM [22, 23]. In Fig. 3 we present the system simulated in this work.

As seen in Fig. 3, the cell's surface and the brushes grafted onto it lay on the xy – plane, while the tip of the AFM exerts pressure along the z – axis, with the tip of the AFM probe being placed at a fixed distance, h, along the z – direction.

The interaction parameters a_{ij} for the conservative force between the i-th and j-th beads depend on the coarse-grained degree, i.e., the number of molecules grouped into a DPD bead. For these simulations, we considered a coarse-grained degree equal to three, which leads to the parameters a_{ij} shown in Table 1. We chose $\sigma = 3$ as the noise amplitude for the random force, and $\gamma = 4.5$ as the friction coefficient included in the dissipative force; the random and dissipative forces are coupled through the fluctuation-dissipation theorem, such that $\sigma^2/2\gamma = k_B T = 1$. The spring – like models for the distance- and angle-dependent interactions between neighboring beads (see the green beads in the inset of Fig. 3) are given by Eqs. (1) and (2), respectively:

$$F_{spring} = k_s(r_{ij} - r_0)\hat{r}_{ij}, \tag{1}$$

$$F_{angular} = k_a \sin(\theta_0 - \theta_{ijk}), \tag{2}$$

where k_s and k_a are the constants of two-body and three-body spring forces, respectively, $r_0 = 0.7r_c$ is the relaxation distance between two adjacent beads attached by a Hookean spring, θ_{ijk} is the angle between the bonds $\hat{r}_{ij}$ and $\hat{r}_{jk}$ formed by three adjacent beads (as if the bonds were attached by an angular spring) and $\theta_0 = 180$ ° is the relaxation angle between these bonds. We chose the spring constants as $k_s = 100 \left[k_B T/r_c^2\right]$ and $k_a = 100 \left[k_B T/r_c\right]$, as those values have been successfully tested before [24].

The system conformed by the solvent and the brushes is confined by two walls (see Fig. 3); the bottom wall (located at $z = -l_z/2$, where l_z is the length of the simulation box in the z direction) is an implicit wall that represents the cell's surface, and its inter-action with other beads is a linearly decaying short-range force, given by:

$$F_{wall}(z_i) = \begin{cases} a_{wi}(1 - z_i/z_c)\hat{z} & z_i \leq z_c, \\ 0 & z_i > z_c \end{cases} \tag{3}$$

where a_{wi} is the maximum interaction of the surface with the particle i (see Table 1), z_i is the distance of the particle i to the surface, z_c is the cutoff radius and $\hat{z}$ is the unit vector

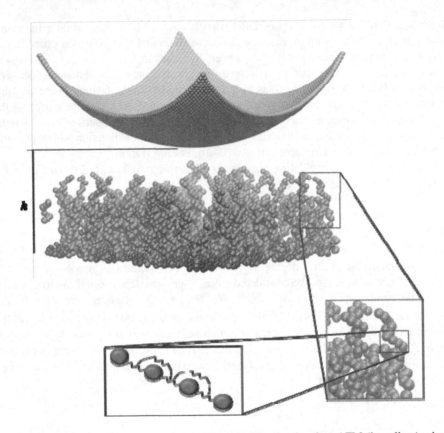

Fig. 3. Model for brushes on cancerous cells probed by the tip of an AFM (in yellow) whose curvature radius is R. The brushes have three different lengths and are represented by chains of different colors, with the blue ones representing the smallest, followed by the red ones, and the green chains are the largest. The beads that make up the chains are joined by harmonic springs and by angular harmonic springs (see insets). The number of beads that make up the chains (N), and the number of chains per unit area on the cell's surface (Γ) are $N_1 = 5, N_2 = 30, N_3 = 42$ and $\Gamma_1 = 1.76$ nm^{-2}, $\Gamma_2 = 0.49$ nm^{-2}, $\Gamma_3 = 0.20$ nm^{-2}. The subindexes 1, 2 and 3 refer to the blue, red and green chains, respectively. The cell lies on the xy – plane and the brush is placed at a fixed distance, h (Color figure online).

in the z direction. The top wall (at $z = l_z/2$) is an explicit surface that represents an AFM tip, formed by a set of DPD beads arranged on a surface with a curvature radius $R = 0.8l_x$, where l_x is the size of the box in the x - direction (this surface is represented in Fig. 3 by yellow beads). The beads on this surface interact with the other particles on the same surface through their conservative DPD interaction, but their dissipative and random forces are zero, and those beads remain at rest. The conservative interaction between the AFM beads and those of the fluid (solvent and brush beads) is more repulsive than that between AFM beads, so that the tip remains impenetrable to the fluid. The full set of interaction parameters a_{ij} is shown in Table 1.

Table 1. Table of all the interactions parameters a_{ij} in the system (*since the distance between the AFM's tip and the cell's surface is larger than the cutoff radius. **Because it is an implicit surface).

$a_{ij}[k_B T/r_c]$	Solvent	Chain's head	Chain's tail	AFM beads	Cell's surface
Solvent	78	79.3	79.3	140	100
Chain's head	79.3	78	78	140	60
Chain's tail	79.3	78	78	140	100
AFM beads	140	140	140	78	0*
Cell's surface	100	60	100	0*	0**

The brushes attached to the cancerous cell are modeled by linear chains of beads of three different sizes: $N_1 = 5$, $N_2 = 30$ and $N_3 = 42$. We set the number of chains per unit area to $\Gamma_1 = 1.76nm^{-2}$, $\Gamma_2 = 0.49nm^{-2}$ and $\Gamma_3 = 0.20nm^{-2}$ for the short, medium-sized, and large chains, respectively. The reason for choosing those values for the chains' length and grafting densities is because we want to model the relative differences in length and grafting density found in AFM experiments performed on cancerous human cervical cells [11]. In these simulations we introduced an oscillatory force along the x – axis acting on the beads attached to the cell's surface (the *heads* of the brushes, see Fig. 4). This force is given by:

$$F_x(\Delta t) = A \cos (wn\Delta t)\hat{x}, \qquad (4)$$

where $w = \pi/100\Delta t$ is the oscillation frequency, $A = 2/w$ is the oscillation amplitude, Δt is the time step, and n is the number of simulation step.

The dimensions of simulation box are $l_x = l_y = 20r_c$ and $l_z = 26r_c$, the occupied volume by the system is $V \approx 4933.77r_c^3$ and the total density $\rho \approx 3$. The simulations proceed in two stages. First, we perform a thermalization process that consists of simulations of 10 blocks of 10^4 time steps each, with a time step of $\Delta t = 0.01t_0$ where $t_0 = \left[\sqrt{m_0 r_c^2/k_B T}\right] \approx 3.072x10^{-12}s$ for a coarse-grained degree equal to three. Once the

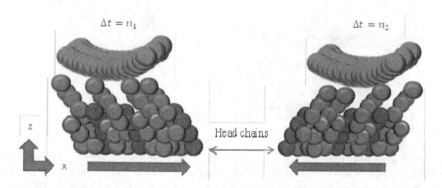

Fig. 4. Schematic representation of the oscillatory force, Eq. (4), acting on the chains' head beads "grafted" on the cell's surface. The oscillation period is $T = 200\Delta t$.

system reaches thermal equilibrium, we carry out the production phase, with 15 blocks of 10^4 time steps each; in this phase we use a time step of $\Delta t = 0.03 t_0$.

3   Results and Discussion

Let us start by considering the concentration profiles of the three types of brushes that make up the composite brush on the cancer cell's surface, when such brushes are moving under the influence of an external oscillatory force while being compressed by the tip of an AFM in the perpendicular direction. The results are shown in Fig. 5. In the snapshot shown in Fig. 5(a), one recognizes that some of the largest chains, i.e. those represented in red and green, have moved away from the tip of the AFM to relieve some pressure. Figure 5(b) shows the concentration profiles of each type of brush; the blue curve corresponds to the shortest chains, the red and green curves are the profiles of the medium – sized and largest chains, respectively. The oscillations are related to the ordering of the beads that make up the chains close to the surface of the cell; notice also how the solvent particles penetrate the brushes all the way down to the surface of the cell. The period of the oscillations is roughly the size of the DPD particles, as expected [25]. There is a local maximum in the profile of the solvent right about where the profile of the smallest chains (blue line) goes to zero, which is due to the fact that the global density of the system is kept constant, therefore if there is a deficit in the brush profile it is compensated by the solvent's concentration. The same phenomenon occurs where the concentration of the medium – sized brushes decays, close to the tip of the AFM (about $z = 10$ in Fig. 5(b)). Lastly, it is important to note that the largest chains and the solvent rub against the tip of the AFM, especially the latter.

In Fig. 6 we show the profile along the z – direction of the x – component of the velocity of the beads that make up the brushes shown in the previous figures. It must be recalled that there is an external oscillatory force applied to the surface of the cell along the x – axis, which means that, to obtain the profile in Fig. 6 we chose

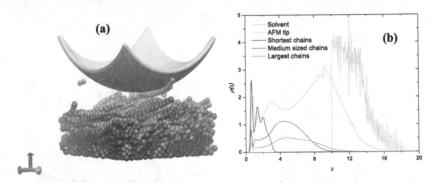

Fig. 5. (a) Snapshot of the brushes on a cancer cell as they are being compressed by the tip of the AFM. Notice how some chains relieve compression by moving sideways. The solvent particles are omitted, for simplicity. (b) Concentration profiles of each type of brush, in reduced DPD units. The profile of the solvent (in cyan) and that of the tip of the AFM (in yellow) are shown also (Color figure online).

the maximum values of $v_x(z)$ in every slice along the z – direction. The oscillations close to the surface of the cell are the result of the collective motion of the brushes, which are relatively close to the surface to respond to the oscillations imposed by the external force at $z = 0$. Since those correlations tend to disappear as one moves away from the surface of the cell, the second maximum seen in Fig. 6 is of smaller amplitude than the first. As we approach to the tip of the AFM the velocity decay, because the fluid is far enough from the oscillating surface, and once that particles are in contact with the tip of the AFM (yellow vertical line in Fig. 6) the decay are qualitatively different.

Since the complex fluid made up of solvent particles and brush chains is under the influence of an external flow, there is a shear rate, which is defined as:

$$\dot{\gamma} = \frac{v_{max}}{\Delta z},\tag{5}$$

which is not constant, as in Couette flow between flat, parallel plates [26]. Although in the present case the separation between the AFM and the cell's surface is fixed, the brush is moving under the influence of an external harmonic force, and we take the maximum velocity in each slice along the z - direction, which is lower as we move away from the

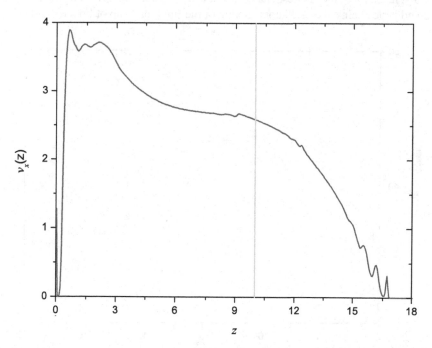

Fig. 6. Profile of the x – component of the velocity of the beads that make up the chains on the surface of the cancerous cell. Since the brushes are under the influence of an oscillatory external force, we used the maximum values of such component to obtain the averages in every slice used to make this profile. The vertical yellow line indicate the position where begin the tip of the AFM probe. The scales on the axes are expressed in reduced DPD units (Color figure online).

cell's surface, and that allows us to construct a profile of shear rate as shown in Fig. 7. The shear rate profile is qualitatively very similar to the velocity profile because they are proportional, see Eq. (5). One sees in Figs. 6 and 7 that close to the upper end of the AFM tip there appear oscillations with constant periodicity, which are due to the layering of particles.

Determining the shear rate is important because with it and with the response of the fluid to the average x – component of the external force applied one can obtain the shear – dependent viscosity of the fluid, according to the relation

$$\eta = \frac{\langle F_x(\dot{\gamma}) \rangle}{\dot{\gamma}}. \qquad (6)$$

The numerator in Eq. (6) is shown in Fig. 8 as one moves along the direction perpendicular to the surface of the cell, while the denominator is shown in Fig. 7. The oscillations present in Fig. 8 close to the surface of the cell are particularly informative; they have approximately the same period while their amplitude is reduced as z increases, effectively disappearing at distances larger than about $z = 3$ from the cell's surface. The oscillations are the collective response of the brushes to the externally applied oscillatory force on the plane of the surface, and their disappearance after $z = 3$ is consequence of the thickness of the brush made up of the shortest chains, see the blue line in Fig. 5(b). For the medium – sized and large chains, the oscillatory motion of the fluid made up of brushes and solvent

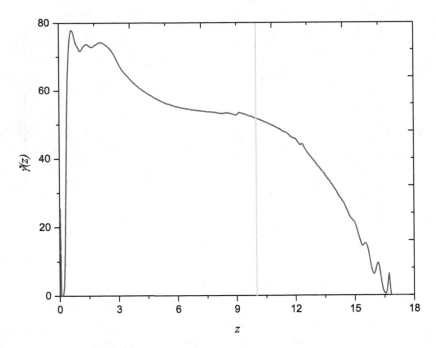

Fig. 7. Profile of the shear rate, $\dot{\gamma}$, experienced by the beads of all the brushes on the surface of the cancer cell. The vertical yellow line indicate the position where the tip of the AFM probe is placed. The axes are expressed in reduced DPD units (Color figure online).

particles is averaged out, and as we approach to the surface of the AFM tip (yellow line in Fig. 8), this force become lower. Once the brushes are beyond this point, the collisions between the brushes and the surface of the AFM probe decrease, as well as the number of particles (see Fig. 5(b)), and that is why the force experienced by DPD beads along the x – direction is lower. We can see an oscillatory behavior of $\langle F_x \rangle$ (see inset in Fig. 8) at the end of the AFM tip, which is in the same range ($z > 15$) as in the velocity profile and the shear rate profile, the reason is that beyond that point, the solvent particles are confined and arranged in layers.

Using Eq. (6) and the results presented in Figs. 7 and 8 we calculated the profile of the shear dependent viscosity, which is shown in Fig. 9. Clearly, the fluid displays non – Newtonian behavior, as expected for a fluid as complex as the present one. The viscosity has three maxima of comparable amplitude at $z \approx 0.7$, $z \approx 1.4$ and $z \approx 2.1$, which appear because the particles are arranged near the cell's surface and these variations have approximately the size of a DPD bead. After this point we have another maximum before the brushes reach the tip of the AFM, which is due to the fact that in that region ($z^* \approx 5$) we have mostly the medium-sized chains and their collisions increase the force in the x-direction, e.g. increase the viscosity (see Figs. 5(b), 8 and 9).

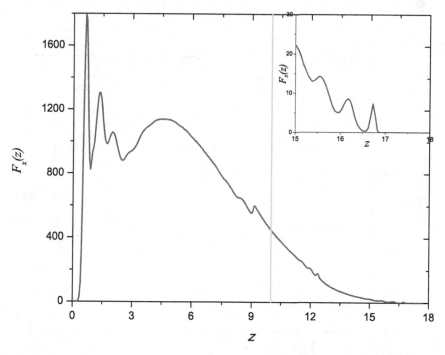

Fig. 8. Average profile of the force applied on the x – direction experienced by the brushes along the direction perpendicular to the plane of the cell on which the brushes are moving under the influence of an external oscillating force, the inset is a zoom of the same profile in the range $z > 15$. The meaning of the vertical line is the same as in the previous two figures. The scales on the axes are expressed in reduced DPD units (Color figure online).

Beyond $z = 10$, the viscosity decreases more or less linearly until $z \approx 13.5$; when $z > 13.5$ we see that the viscosity increases although the F_x decays. The reason is that as we move beyond that point, the projected area in the xy-plane of each slice along z-direction is smaller, e.g., the relation in the numerator of Eq. (6) increase as the value of z increases. This is the first report of a viscosity profile in an AFM system that we are aware of. At distances close to the cell's surface, the fluid experiences an almost undamped response to the applied external force, which translates into an almost inviscid fluid response. However, as the particles move away from the surface, the influence of the oscillatory external force is damped and the increase in viscosity results from increased collisions between beads and the AFM probe.

The z-component of the force whose profile is shown in Fig. 10 and it is qualitatively very similar to its x-component counterpart, shown in Fig. 8. The oscillations with decaying amplitude close to the cell's surface have the same origin as those in Fig. 8, i.e., they are the response of the shortest chains, mostly, which is why they disappear for $z > 3$. The maximum in $z \approx 4.5$, appears also in Figs. 8 and 10 because that is the thickness of the smallest brush on the cell's surface. The pressure exerted by the solvent particles and the displacement induced by the shear force increase the force in the region near this point ($z \approx 4.5$). As the fluid approaches the surface of the AFM tip the force decays like the AFM tip profile (yellow profile in Fig. 5(b)).

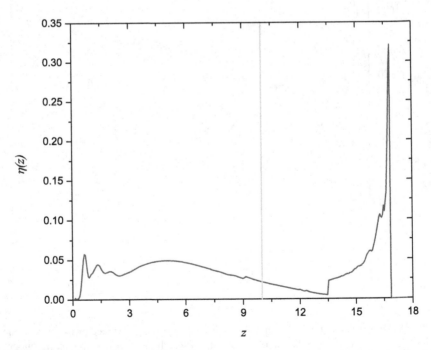

Fig. 9. Profile of the shear dependent viscosity of the fluid made up of brushes and solvent particles, see Eq. (6) and Figs. 7 and 8. The yellow and red vertical lines have the same meaning as in those figures. All quantities are expressed in reduced DPD units (Color figure online).

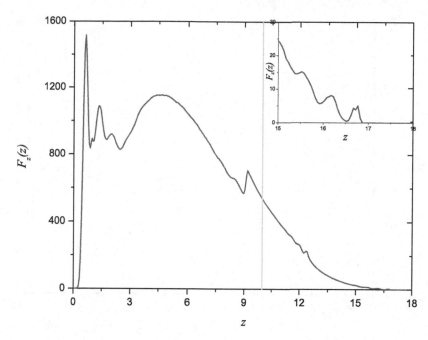

Fig. 10. Profile of the average z – component of the force experienced by the particles of the fluid as the distance from the surface of the cell ($z = 0$) is increased. The inset show the same profile in the range of $z > 15$. Both axes are expressed in reduced DPD units. The vertical colored line have the same meaning as in previous figures.

Finally, we calculate the friction coefficient along the z – direction. This coefficient is defined as the ratio of the average value of the x – component of the force on the chains, over the average value of its z – component counterpart, see Eq. (7):

$$\mu(z) = \frac{\langle F_x(z) \rangle}{\langle F_z(z) \rangle}, \tag{7}$$

where the numerator is the quantity related to the x – axis in Fig. 8 and the denominator corresponds to the z – axis of Fig. 10. It is, by definition, a dimensionless number, which can be measured in experiments carried out with AFM [22], therefore it constitutes a very useful characteristic that allows direct comparison of our model with those experiments. The friction coefficient profile shown in Fig. 11 displays low values close to the surface of the cell, because the fluid is almost inviscid in that region. After this minimum value, there appears oscillatory behavior due to the propagation of the oscillatory shear force applied in the cell's surface, but this behavior disappears at $z \approx 3$ and the coefficient of friction becomes equal to 1 until the fluid reaches the surface of the AFM tip. That is because both force components (F_x, and F_z) have approximately the same value in a region where the shortest brush ends and the tip of the AFM appears. Beyond the point $z = 10$, the friction coefficient shows almost constant but this time is lower, $\mu \approx 0.9$, because the forces are smaller, however $\langle F_z \rangle$ is larger than $\langle F_x \rangle$. Lastly, the oscillations

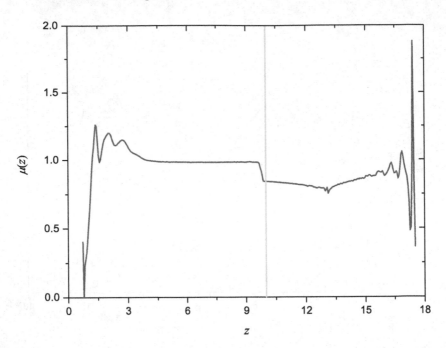

Fig. 11. Friction coefficient profile according to Eq. (7). The x – axis is expressed in reduced DPD units. The vertical colored line has the same meaning as in previous figures.

in the upper end of the AFM tip have the same origin as those shown in the insets of the Figs. 8 and 10. The values of the friction coefficient, seen in Fig. 11, are larger than those obtained with polymer brushes, using also DPD simulations [27, 28], because the proportion of solvent particles to brush beads is smaller in this work than in other reports. It is known that the solvent acts as a lubricant in polymer brushes [22, 23], and here we modeled a fluid formed predominately by brushes.

4   Conclusions

The influence of an external oscillatory force on the surface of epithelial cells covered by brushes of different lengths, such as those observed in experiments carried out on human cervical cells with AFM, appears to be stronger on the smallest brush, which responds to the oscillations with small damping. However, for the largest brushes at the amplitude and frequency used in this work, the response appears to be slower, allowing for the relaxation of the chains and their averaged interactions. The profiles of the viscosity and friction coefficient, which are the first of their kind reported in the literature as far as we know, show very similar behavior close to the surface of the cell. This is because the surface is subjected to an oscillatory force, and this oscillatory behavior permeates all of these profiles. Our results show that the interaction between the chains and the tip of the AFM is increased, as well as these rheological properties, not only because of their molecular characteristics such as density and length. But also, crucially, because the use of a three – body potential between bonds along the chains leading to an effectively larger persistence length of the brushes, which forces them to collide with the tip of the AFM, and with each other. We believe this work is useful as a guide in the interpretation of recent experiments in fluids as complex as those modeled here.

Acknowledgments. AGG would like to thank S.J. Alas, S. Hernández, J.L. Menchaca and I. Sokolov for helpful discussions. JDHV and AGG acknowledge also the hospitality of E. Pérez and the Polymer Group at the Instituto de Física (UASLP), where this work was conceived.

References

1. Franco, E., Villa, L., Sobrinho, J., Prado, J., Rousseau, M., Désy, M., Rohan, T.: Epidemiology of acquisition and clearance of cervical human papillomavirus infection in women from a high-risk area for cervical cancer. J. Infect. Dis. **180**, 1415–1423 (1999)
2. Guck, J., Schinkinger, S., Linconl, B., Wottawah, F., Ebert, S., Romeyke, M., Lenz, D., Erickson, H., Ananthakrishnan, R., Mitchell, D., Käs, J., Ulvick, S., Bibly, C.: Optical deformability as an inherent cell market for testing malignant transformation and metastatic competence. Biophys. J. **88**, 3689–3698 (2005)
3. Lekka, M., Dorota, G., Pogoda, K., Dulińska-Litewka, J., Gostek, J., Klymenko, O., Prauzner-Bechciki, S., Wiltowska-Zuber, J., Okoń, K., Laidler, P.: Cancer cell detection in tissue sections using AFM. Arch. Biochem. Biophys. **518**, 151–156 (2012)
4. Cross, S., Jin, Y., Rao, J., Gimzewski, J.: Nanomechanical analysis of cells from cancer patients. Nature Nanotech. **2**, 780–783 (2007)
5. Plodinec, M., Loparic, M., Monnier, C., Obermann, E., Zanetti-Dallenbach, R., Oertle, P., Hyotyla, J., Aebi, U., Bentires-Alj, M., Lim, R., Schoenenberger, C.: The nanomechanical signature of breast cancer. Nature Nanotech. **7**, 757–765 (2012)
6. Müller, D., Dufrêne, Y.: Atomic force microscopy: a nanoscopic window on the cell surface. Trends Cell Biol. **21**, 461–469 (2011)
7. Li, Q., Lee, G., Lim, C.: AFM indentation study of breast cancer cells. Biochem. Biophys. Res. Comm. **374**, 609–613 (2008)
8. Lekka, M.: Atomic force microscopy: a tip for diagnosing cancer. Nature Nanotech. **7**, 691–692 (2012)
9. Koch, T., Münster, S., Bonakdar, N., Butler, J., Fabry, B.: 3D traction forces in cancer cell invasion. PLoS One **7**, e33476 (2012)
10. Jonietz, E.: Mechanics: the forces of cancer. Nature **491**, S56–S57 (2012)
11. Iyer, S., Gaikwad, R., Subba-Rao, V., Woodworth, C., Sokolov, I.: Atomic force microscopy detects differences in the surface brush of normal and cancerous cells. Nature Nanotech. **4**, 389–393 (2009)
12. Gama Goicochea, A., Alas, S.: Computer simulations of the mechanical response of brushes on the surface of cancerous epithelial cells. Sci. Rep. **5**, 13218 (2015)
13. Yao, D., Shao, Y.: A novel technique of quantifying flexural stiffness of rod-like structures. Cell Mol. Bioeng. **1**, 75–83 (2008)
14. Hoogerbrugge, P., Koelman, J.: Simulating microscopic hydrodynamic phenomena with dissipative particle dynamics. Europhys. Lett. **19**, 155–160 (1992)
15. Allen, M., Tildesly, D.: Computer Simulation of Liquids. Oxford University Press, New York (1989)
16. Español, P., Warren, P.: Statistical mechanics of dissipative particle dynamics. Europhys. Lett. **30**, 191–196 (1995)

17. Gama Goicochea, A., Balderas, M., Lopez-Esparza, R., Waldo-Mendoza, A., Perez, E.: On the computational modeling of the viscosity of colloidal dispersions and its relation with basic molecular interactions. Eur. J. Phys. **36**, 055032 (2015)
18. Pastorino, C., Gama Goicochea, A.: Dissipative particle dynamics: a method to simulate soft matter systems in equilibrium and under flow. In: Klapp, J., Ruíz, G., Medina, A., López A., Sigalotti, L. (eds.) Selected Topics of Computational and Experimental Fluid Mechanics. Environmental Science and Engineering, pp. 51–79. Springer International Publishing Switzerland (2015)
19. Gama Goicochea, A., Balderas, M., Hernández, J., Pérez, E.: The role of the dissipative and random forces in the calculation of the pressure of simple fluids with dissipative particle dynamics. Comp. Phys. Comm. **188**, 76–81 (2015)
20. Murtola, T., Bunker, A., Vattulainen, I., Deserno, M., Karttunen, M.: Multiscale modeling of emergent materials: biological and soft matter. PCCP **11**, 1869–1892 (2009)
21. Vattulainen, I., Karttunen, M., Besold, G., Polson, J.: Integration schemes for dissipative particle dynamics simulations: from softly interacting systems towards hybrid models. J. Chem. Phys. **116**, 3967 (2002)
22. Klein, J., Kumacheva, E., Mahalu, D., Perahia, D., Fetters, L.: Reduction of frictional forces between solid surfaces bearing polymer brushes. Nature **116**, 634–636 (1994)
23. Eiser, E., Klein, J.: The effect of mobile polymers on the normal and shear forces between polymer brushes. Macromolecules **40**, 8455–8463 (2007)
24. Gama Goicochea, A., Romero-Bastida, M., López-Rendón, R.: Dependence of thermodynamic properties of model systems on some dissipative particle dynamics parameters. Mol. Phys. **105**, 2375–2381 (2007)
25. Velázquez, M., Gama Goicochea, A., González-Melchor, M., Neria, M., Alejandre, J.: Finite-size effects in dissipative particle dynamics simulations. J. Chem. Phys. **124**, 084104 (2006)
26. Macosko, C.: Rheology Principles, Mesurements, and Applications. Wiley-VCH Inc., New York (1994)
27. Goujon, F., Malfreyt, P., Tildesley, D.: Interactions between polymer brushes and a polymer solution: mesoscale modelling of the structural and frictional properties. Soft Matter **6**, 3472–3481 (2010)
28. Gama Goicochea, A., Mayoral, E., Klapp, J., Pastorino, C.: Nanotribology of biopolymer brushes in aqueous solution using dissipative particle dynamics simulations: an application to PEG covered liposomes in a theta solvent. Soft Matter **10**, 166–174 (2014)

A New Effective Potential for Colloidal Dispersions with Polymer Chains Emerging from Mesoscopic Scale Interactions

Ketzasmin A. Terrón-Mejía[1], Roberto López-Rendón[1], and Armando Gama Goicochea[2($\boxtimes$)]

[1] Laboratorio de Bioingeniería Molecular a Multiescala, Facultad de Ciencias, Universidad Autónoma del Estado de México, Av. Instituto Literario 100, 50000 Toluca, Mexico
[2] Tecnológico de Estudios Superiores de Ecatepec, Av. Tecnológico s/n, 55210 Ecatepec, Estado de México, Mexico
agama@alumni.stanford.edu

Abstract. A new potential of mean force is proposed for colloidal dispersions, which is obtained from coarse – grained, pair interactions between colloidal particles formed by the explicit grouping of particles that are themselves groups of atoms and molecules. Using numerical simulations, we start by constructing colloidal particles made up of 250 mesoscopic particles joined by springs and interacting with each other through short – range forces. Afterward we proceed to model several colloidal concentrations and obtain the colloidal particles pair correlation function, from which we derive the potential of mean force. In our second case study, we add linear polymer chains of the same length that attach by one of their ends to the colloids, at a fixed colloidal concentration, and carry out numerical simulations at increasing concentrations of polymer chains, from which we obtain the potential of mean force once again following the same procedure as in the previous case. For the last case study we fixed both the colloids' and the polymer chains' concentration, while increasing the length of the polymer chains and obtain again the potential of mean force. In all of these simulations, the solvent particles are included explicitly. Using these data we propose a new effective potential of interaction for colloidal dispersion whose parameters can be obtained from mesoscopic scale parameters and carry out standard molecular dynamics simulations with this new potential, thereby providing a route for more fundamentally obtained, coarse – grained approaches to model colloidal dispersions.

Keywords: Colloidal dispersions · Potential of mean force · Dissipative particle dynamics

1 Introduction

Colloidal dispersions have numerous applications in various fields such as chemistry, biology, medicine, and engineering [1, 2]. There is a need to obtain potential functions that are useful alternatives to the Lennard – Jones (LJ) and other competing potentials

© Springer International Publishing Switzerland 2016
I. Gitler and J. Klapp (Eds.): ISUM 2015, CCIS 595, pp. 447–460, 2016.
DOI: 10.1007/978-3-319-32243-8_31

for the modeling of colloidal dispersions in equilibrium, so that their characteristic parameters are not based on quantum ab initio simulations of experiments on isolated molecules, but on mesoscopic scale situations, for better comparison with experiments. Interaction forces between colloidal particles in all suspensions/emulsions play an important role in determining the properties of the materials, such as the shelf life, stability, rheology and flavor, the behavior of a number of industrial processes (e.g. mixings, membrane filtrations) as well as the formula of chemical and pharmaceutical products.

Theoretical studies on the equilibrium properties of colloidal dispersions by Derjaguin and Landau [3] as well as Verwey and Overbeek [4] focused on understanding the origins of interactions between colloidal particles. This resulted in the Derjaguin–Landau–Verwey–Overbeek (DLVO) theory, which describes forces of molecular origin between bodies immersed in an electrolyte, and can be used to quantify several key features of colloid aggregation. The colloid dispersion interaction components of the DLVO model are treated by summing the pairwise dispersion interactions between the constituent atoms/molecules in the particles.

The simplest potential model for non – electrostatic interactions in colloidal particles is the hard sphere potential, in which the particles are regarded as hard spheres that are elastically reflected on contact with other particles [5]. Another simple and popular potential model is the LJ potential [6], which is useful to mimic short range repulsion and medium range van der Waals attraction. On the other hand, Hamaker [7] and de Boer [8] investigated theoretically the dispersion forces acting between colloidal objects. They considered spherical bodies, assumed pairwise additivity of interatomic dispersion energies, and demonstrated the essential results that although the range of atomic forces was of the order of atomic dimensions, the sum of the dispersion energies resulted in an interaction range for colloidal bodies of the order of their dimensions.

The classic numerical approaches used for studying colloidal dispersions are Monte Carlo (MC) and Molecular Dynamics (MD) [9]. However, these methods are inappropriate for describing mesoscale properties, because they still require very long simulation times and exceedingly large computer memory. To obtain a better understanding of the unique phenomenon of ordering, which occurs in colloidal suspensions, reliable mesoscopic computational models are sorely needed [10]. For systems with colloidal beds of a similar size to the complex fluid microstructures (e.g., polymeric clusters, large blood cells) or not much larger, the bed–solvent particle interactions become important. These molecular interactions are responsible for creating colloidal microstructures, such as micelles and colloidal crystals, which can be simulated within the framework of dissipative particle dynamics (DPD). The true advantage of DPD over MD consists of the possibility of matching the scale of discrete-particle simulation to the dominant spatiotemporal scales of the entire system. In MD simulation the time scales associated with evolution of heavy colloidal particles are many orders of magnitude larger than the temporal evolution of solvent particles.

Several approaches have been proposed for coupling a DPD fluid to colloidal particles. In early works based on the DPD method, colloids were simulated by constraining clusters of DPD particles to move as a rigid object. Examples of the application of DPD methods to colloidal dispersions have been reported in many sources [11–15]. In most of these works, each colloidal particle was modeled as a group of dissipative particles. However, the interactions between colloidal particles and solvent molecules in a real dispersion ought to depend on the characteristics of the dispersion of interest. In other words, such interactions are strongly dependent on the mass and diameter ratios of colloidal particles to solvent molecules, the properties of the interaction potential between such particles, etc. If we take into account that dissipative particles themselves are just virtual particles, which is a cluster or group of solvent molecules, it may be possible to use a model potential for the interaction between dissipative particles, instead of regarding a colloidal particle as a group of dissipative particles [16].

A fundamental aspect for studying colloidal dispersions under the framework of DPD lies in the model interaction potential used. Although one is in principle free to choose any potential form, the conservative force is often chosen purely repulsive and linear to allow for large time-steps and hence make the DPD simulations as fast as possible. Such linear forces lead to a finite conservative potential, meaning that the centers of mass of the particles can actually overlap. This reflects the fact that effective interactions of soft objects often lead to a repulsive but finite potential [17]. An effective potential of a one-component model that accurately reproduces the colloid–colloid radial distribution function of a colloid–polymer mixture was proposed by Guzman and de Pablo [18]. Although this model was not made for studying colloidal systems at the mesoscopic scale, the particles of this effective model interact through an effective potential, obtained by inversion of the Ornstein–Zernike equation and a closure suited for fluids with repulsive cores. Pool and Bolhuis discussed the implication for the applicability of soft repulsive potentials for the study of micelle formation [19]. They compared results of two surfactant models: one based on LJ interactions and one based on the soft repulsive potential that is often used in dissipative particle dynamics (DPD). Meanwhile, Pan and Tartakovsky used a model where the interaction between particles is modeled by central and non-central DPD forces, which conserve both linear and angular momenta exactly [20]. Vincent et al. [21] derived an interaction potential between particles with grafted polymer chains in a solvent containing additional polymer molecules, which includes parameters such as the polymer χ-parameter, polymer adsorbed densities, molar volumes, etc. Satoh and Chantrell investigated the validity of the application of the dissipative particle dynamics (DPD) method to ferromagnetic colloidal dispersions by conducting DPD simulations for a two–dimensional system [16]. Its model interaction potential, based on LJ potential, gives rise to physically reasonable aggregate structures under circumstances of strong magnetic particle–particle interactions as well as a strong external magnetic field.

Despite the efforts that have been made to model colloidal interactions at the mesoscopic level, there is still a deficit of effective potential models to describe efficiently conservative forces, which is crucial for the understanding of colloidal systems. A good effective potential for studying colloidal dispersions must contain adjustable parameters that represent aspects such as the concentration of colloids, polymer concentration and size of the chains among others. To date, an effective potential with such characteristics for colloidal dispersions under framework of DPD has not yet been proposed. That is the central purpose of the present work.

2 Models and Methods

In MD [22], the molecules move under the action of the forces that are set up between them. These forces are pairwise, additive, and symmetric. The technique models reality on the molecular scale and could theoretically be used to accurately simulate a large macroscopic system. However, computational considerations limit the size of the system and the time during which it can be simulated. From Newton's second law of motion, the evolution of the position, r_i, and momentum, $p_i = mv_i$, of particle i with mass, m_i, and velocity v are described by

$$\dot{r}_i = \frac{p_i}{m_i} \text{ and } \dot{p}_i = F_i(t) = \sum_{j \neq i} F_{ij}^C,$$ (1)

where $F_i(t)$ is the force acting on particle i at time t and F_{ij}^C is the conservative force acting on particle i due to particle j. This conservative force is simply a central force, derivable from some effective potential ϕ_{ij} as follows

$$F_{ij}^C = -\frac{\partial \phi_{ij}}{\partial r_{ij}}.$$ (2)

As we can see, the conservative force is only a function of particle positions, and includes inter-particle forces as well as any effects from external forces. The physical basis of conservative interparticle interactions is typically a very short-range repulsion due to steric effects (i.e. volume exclusion/particle collision), a short-range attractive force that has its physical origins in dispersion interactions, and a long-range screened electrostatic force, which may be either attractive or repulsive. For multicomponent solvents, attractive depletion forces due to the presence of additional solutes can also be significant. Typically, surface chemistries of colloidal particles and solvent properties (pH, ionic strength) are modulated to balance the attractive van der Waals force with a repulsive electrostatic force and promote particle dispersion. Conservative inter-particle forces can often be approximated as a sum of pairwise two-body interactions, each of which depend only on the separation r_{ij} between particles i and j (as well as relative orientation for non-spherical particles). Determining the functional form of ϕ_{ij} for two particles in a solvent requires an averaging (or coarse-graining) of all degrees of freedom other than the inter-particle separation. In a rigorous statistical mechanical framework, ϕ_{ij} is the potential of mean force between colloidal particles [15].

The DPD method introduced by Hoogerbrugge and Koelman [23] treats a fluid using a collection of particles with 'soft' interactions, allowing for a much larger time step than atomistic MD. The characteristic dimension of DPD particles (i.e. the cutoff of the DPD interparticle interactions) is much larger than the molecular dimension of fluid molecules, but should be smaller than the relevant flow characteristic size (in the case of suspensions, the colloid particle diameter). The foundations of the DPD method can be found in various sources [24–28], therefore we shall only outline some general aspects of this technique. The idea behind DPD simulations is similar to a traditional molecular dynamics algorithm [22] in the sense that one must integrate Newton's second law of motion using finite time steps to obtain the particles' positions and momenta from the total force. A difference from atomistic molecular dynamics is that the DPD model involves not only a conservative force $\left(\mathbf{F}^C\right)$, but also random $\left(\mathbf{F}^R\right)$, and dissipative $\left(\mathbf{F}^D\right)$, components acting between any two particles i and j, placed a distance r_{ij} apart. In its traditional form, the DPD total force is the sum of these three components [24], as expressed by Eq. (3):

$$\dot{\mathbf{p}}_i = \mathbf{F}_i(t) = \sum_{j\neq i} \mathbf{F}_{ij}^C + \sum_{j\neq i} \mathbf{F}_{ij}^D + \sum_{j\neq i} \mathbf{F}_{ij}^R. \tag{3}$$

All forces between particles i and j are zero beyond a finite cutoff radius r_c, which represents the intrinsic length scale of the DPD model and is usually also chosen as $r_c \equiv 1$. The conservative force determines the thermodynamics of the DPD system and is defined by a soft repulsion:

$$\mathbf{F}_{ij}^C = \begin{cases} a_{ij}(1 - r_{ij})\hat{\mathbf{r}}_{ij} & r_{ij} \leq r_c \\ 0 & r_{ij} > r_c \end{cases}, \tag{4}$$

where a_{ij} is the maximum repulsion strength between a pair of particles i and j, and $\mathbf{r}_{ij} = \mathbf{r}_i - \mathbf{r}_j$, $r_{ij} = |\mathbf{r}_{ij}$, $\hat{\mathbf{r}}_{ij} = \mathbf{r}_{ij}/r_{ij}$. The dissipative and the random forces are given by

$$\mathbf{F}_{ij}^D = -\gamma\omega^D\left(r_{ij}\right)\left[\hat{\mathbf{r}}_{ij} \cdot \mathbf{v}_{ij}\right]\hat{\mathbf{r}}_{ij}, \tag{5}$$

and

$$\mathbf{F}_{ij}^R = \sigma\omega^R\left(r_{ij}\right)\xi_{ij}\hat{\mathbf{r}}_{ij}, \tag{6}$$

where γ is the dissipation streng, σ is the noise amplitude, ω^D and ω^R are distance dependent weight functions, $\mathbf{v}_{ij} = \mathbf{v}_i - \mathbf{v}_j$ is the relative velocity between the particles i and j, and $\xi_{ij} = \xi_{ji}$ is a random number uniformly distributed between 0 and 1 with variance $1/\Delta t$ where Δt is the time step of the simulation. The magnitude of the dissipative and stochastic forces are related through the fluctuation-dissipation theorem [24]:

$$\omega^D\left(r_{ij}\right) = \left[\omega^R\left(r_{ij}\right)\right]^2 = max\left\{\left(1 - \frac{r_{ij}}{r_c}\right)^2, 0\right\}. \tag{7}$$

At interparticle distances larger than r_c, all forces are equal to zero. The strengths of the dissipative and random forces are related in a way that keeps the temperature internally fixed, $k_B T = \frac{\sigma^2}{2\gamma}$; k_B being Boltzmann's constant. The natural probability distribution function of the DPD model is that of the canonical ensemble, where N (the total particle number), V, and T are kept constant. Additionally, polymers are modeled as linear chains formed by DPD beads joined by freely rotating, harmonic springs with a spring constant $K_0 = 100.0$ and an equilibrium position $r_0 = 0.7$ [29] as shown in the following equation:

$$\mathbf{F}_{ij}^{\text{spring}} = -K_0 (r_{ij} - r_0) \hat{\mathbf{e}}_{ij}. \tag{8}$$

The effective potential model proposed in this work for colloidal interactions acting only between colloidal particles is a combination of the classical LJ and Morse potentials. This effective potential model has the following form:

$$\phi_{ij}(r) = \left(\frac{\sigma}{r_{ij}} \right)^n - \alpha e^{-\beta (r_{ij} - \sigma)^2}. \tag{9}$$

This potential captures the essence of the short-range interactions of the LJ and Morse potentials. The first term in Eq. (9) captures the short – range repulsion between colloids as in the LJ potential, while the second is responsible for the attraction between colloids that arise from elastic attraction between the polymer coatings and van der Waals interactions, as in the Morse potential. The adjustable parameters of this effective potential are σ, n, α, and the purpose of this work is to relate them to more basic parameters such as colloid and polymer concentrations, and the polymerization degree. In the analysis performed in here, two fundamental properties were used namely, the radial distribution function, $g(r)$, and the potential mean force (PMF), $W_{PMF}(r)$. We focus here on the latter, which is an effective pair interaction that provides important thermodynamic information about many – body systems. It can be obtained from the colloids' radial distribution functions, $g(r)$, through the relation [30]:

$$W_{PMF}(r) = -k_B T \ln[g(r)]. \tag{10}$$

3   Simulation Details

Our procedure to make colloidal particles is very simple: one starts by putting a central DPD particle at a given site and bind other particles of the same type to it, using harmonic springs, see Fig. 1. This results in a larger, composed DPD particle. The total number of individual DPD particles that make up a colloidal particle is 250. Our simulations are performed under the following conditions: the quantities $k_B T = r_C = m = 1.0$, r_C is the cutoff radius and m is the mass of DPD particle, all particles have the same mass and size. The density is fixed for all simulations at 3.0 DPD units and the integration time step used is $\Delta t = 0.03$. The parameters σ and γ of the DPD forces are taken as 3.0 and 4.5 respectively, and the quality of solvent elected is theta solvent with a coarse-graining degree equal to 3; this means the parameter $a_{ij} = 78.0$ DPD units for every i and j. All simulations are carried out in the canonical ensemble. All the methodology and calculations described in this work have been performed using our

Fig. 1. Illustration of the construction of the colloidal model particle used in this work. The red particles represent DPD particles and the black lines represent the harmonic springs that bond these DPD particles to make up the colloidal particle (Color figure online).

simulation code, called SIMES, which is designed to study complex systems at the mesoscopic scale using graphics processors technology (GPUs) [31].

In the first case of study, we explore the structure of colloidal particles as a function of their concentration. For this purpose we put 16, 32, 64, and 128 colloidal particles in a cubic simulation box whose volume was $V = 27.51^3 r_c^3$, which corresponds to colloidal concentrations equal to $\chi_{C1} = 7 \times 10^{-4}$, $\chi_{C2} = 15 \times 10^{-4}$, $\chi_{C3} = 30 \times 10^{-4}$ and $\chi_{C4} = 60 \times 10^{-4}$, respectively. The total the number of individual DPD particles making up the colloids is $N = 62500$. For the second case study we fixed the colloidal concentration at $\chi_C = 7 \times 10^{-4}$ and we added polymer chains, which were grafted to the colloidal particles. The length of the polymer chains are fixed at $N_p = 6$ DPD particles, bonded with harmonic springs; the constants chosen of harmonic potential are $k_0 = 100.0$ and $r_0 = 0.7r_c$. For this case we study the impact of the polymer concentration over the structural properties of colloidal particles, the concentrations used in the simulations are $\chi_P = 0.02, 0.04$ and 0.07 in a cubic simulation cell of lateral size $L = 40.00$ DPD units with total number of particles $N = 192000$. The parameter $a_{c\text{-}ph} = 39.0$ is the interaction of the polymer heads with the colloidal particle, while the parameter $a_{c\text{-}pt} = 78.0$ controls the interaction of the polymer tail with the colloids; both are represented by a_{ij} in Eq. (4). Finally, in the third case we study the impact of the length of the polymer chains on the properties of the system. For this case we fixed the concentration of colloidal particles at $\chi_C = 7 \times 10^{-4}$, and the concentration of polymer molecules at $\chi_P = 0.02$, in a cubic simulation box whose volume is $V = 40^3 r_c^3$. The polymerization degrees of the chains tested in this case are $N_p = 6, 12$, and 24 DPD particles. We performed simulations of 10^2 blocks of 10^4 DPD steps for a total of 10^6 DPD steps, reaching a total simulation time of 4.8 μs. All quantities are expressed in reduced units unless otherwise noted. In Table 1 are summarized the parameters corresponding to Eq. (9) for the three case studies presented in this work.

Table 1. Parameters of the effective potential proposed in this work. χ_{cn}, χ_{pn} and N_{pn} correspond to the concentration of colloids, polymer concentration, and the size of the polymer chain respectively, subscript n indicates the three case studies presented in this paper.

Case	σ	η	α	β
χ_{c1}	5.40	16	0.40	0.80
χ_{c2}	5.40	16	0.60	0.60
χ_{c3}	5.30	16	0.80	0.50
χ_{p1}	8.20	4	1.00	0.10
χ_{p2}	8.50	7	1.00	0.10
χ_{p3}	8.75	9	1.00	0.10
N_{p1}	8.20	4	1.00	0.10
N_{p2}	9.60	4	1.25	0.08
N_{p3}	8.50	4	0.60	0.03

4   Results and Discussion

The results obtained for the first case study are presented in Fig. 2; in particular, Fig. 2 (a) shows the radial distribution functions of the colloidal dispersions at increasing concentrations. At all concentration except the largest one ($\chi_{C4} = 60 \times 10^{-4}$, blue line in Fig. 2(a)) the fluid behaves basically like an ideal gas with soft – core repulsion. Yet at the largest concentration modeled the fluid develops structure, with a large peak appearing at about $r = 5$, with periodic oscillations of about the same magnitude. The corresponding PMF in Fig. 2(b) shows the development of a shallow primary minimum at r close to 5, with a secondary one appearing at $r \approx 11$. What this means is that the fluid behaves like an ideal gas until the concentration is large enough that two – body interactions become important, leading to a colloidal dispersion that can be kinetically unstable at relatively large colloidal concentrations.

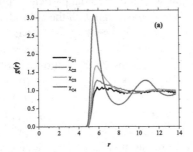 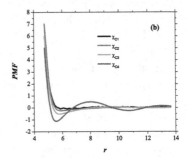

Fig. 2. (a) Radial distribution function of the colloidal particles made up of DPD particles, at increasing concentrations of colloidal particles. (b) The corresponding potential of mean force for each colloidal concentration shown in (a); see Eq. (10). See text for details. All quantities are expressed in reduced DPD units.

The snapshot of the system at the various colloidal concentration used to obtain the data shown in Fig. 2 are presented in Fig. 3.

Fig. 3. Snapshots of some typical cases of explicitly formed colloidal particles made up of DPD particles (in yellow), including the solvent monomeric particles (in cyan). These configurations correspond to colloidal concentrations χ_{C1} through χ_{C4}, from left to right respectively. See text for details (Color figure online).

The snapshots shown in Fig. 3 show how the simulation box looks like at the four different colloidal concentration model for this fist case. It is important to notice that, even at a relatively large colloidal concentration, such as the one corresponding to the third from left snapshot in Fig. 3, there are essentially negligible many – body inter-actions between the composed colloidal particles. This is a consequence of the short range of the DPD interaction defined in Eqs. (4)–(8).

The results of the simulations of the second case study, when the colloidal con-centration was fixed and the fixed – length polymer concentration was increased are presented in Fig. 4.

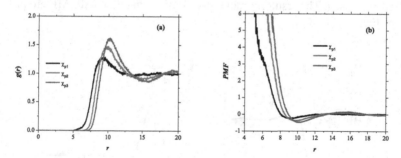

Fig. 4. (a) Radial distribution function and (b) potential of mean force (PMF) of colloids covered by fixed – length polymer chains of increasing concentration. The concentrations of polymers are $\chi_{p1} = 0.02$ (black line), $\chi_{p2} = 0.04$ (red line), and $\chi_{p3} = 0.07$ (blue line), and the size of chains is $N_p = 6$ beads. The colloidal concentration was fixed at $\chi_C = 7 \times 10^{-4}$ (black line in Fig. 2) (Color figure online).

It is remarkable that even for the smallest colloidal concentration, which behaves essentially as a soft – core ideal gas (see Fig. 2) there appears structuring even for the smallest polymer concentrations, as Fig. 4 demonstrates. The radial distribution function

(Fig. 4(a)), and hence the PMF (Fig. 4(b)) both show a weakly developing but measurable structuring for colloids at relatively short distances from each other. As Fig. 4(b) indicates, the major influence of the polymer brush coating on the colloidal particles is to increase the core repulsion between them, while at the same time developing a very shallow attractive well at relative distances close to two particle diameters ($r \approx 10$ in Fig. 4(b)). The snapshots corresponding to the simulations used to obtain the data presented in Fig. 4 are shown in Fig. 5.

Fig. 5. Snapshots of the simulations of DPD particle – made colloids (in blue) with grafted polymer chains (in red) of fixed length $(N_p = 6)$ at increasing polymer concentration on the colloids' surfaces. See text for details. The solvent particles are omitted for clarity (Color figure online).

Our last case study corresponds to the situation where colloidal and polymer concentrations are fixed, while the polymerization degree of the chains grafted to colloids is increased. The resulting radial distribution function and PMF are presented below, in Fig. 6.

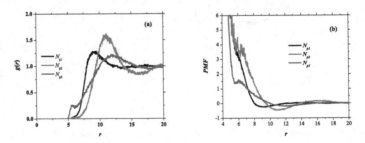

Fig. 6. (a) Radial distribution function, and (b) PMF for a colloidal dispersion at fixed colloid and polymer concentration, while varying the polymerization degree. The polymerization degrees studied are $N_{p1} = 6$ (black line), $N_{p2} = 12$ (red line) and $N_{p3} = 24$ (blue line) beads. The colloids' concentration is fixed at $\chi_C = 7 \times 10^{-4}$, and the polymers' concentration is $\chi_P = 0.02$ (Color figure online).

The influence of the polymerization degree on an essentially non – interacting colloidal dispersion (see black line in Fig. 2) when polymers of increasing polymerization degrees are added is quite noticeable in Fig. 6. The principal effect is the appearance of an effectively thicker colloid – particle repulsive diameter, as indicated by the red line in Fig. 6(b). Interestingly, increasing the polymerization degree up to $N_{p3} = 24$ (blue line in Fig. 6) yields incipient colloid agglomeration, as the first maximum in the blue line in Fig. 6(a) shows. This means that a fraction of the colloids has been joined through a "bridging" mechanism, which binds particles due to the association of the long polymer chains that cover them, as is shown by the snapshot in Fig. 7; see particularly the rightmost image. When the polymerization degree leads to a radius of gyration larger than the average distance between colloids (set by the colloid concentration), the dispersant nature of the polymers is hampered and the polymers begin to act as binders, as Figs. 6(b) and 7 show.

Fig. 7. Snapshots of simulations of particle – made colloids with constant grafted density of polymer chains on the colloids' surfaces ($\chi_P = 0.02$), while increasing the polymerization degree: $N_{p1} = 6$ (red chains, leftmost snapshot), $N_{p2} = 12$ (green chains, middle snapshot) and $N_{p3} = 24$ (yellow chains, rightmost snapshot). The colloids are shown in blue (Color figure online).

In Fig. 8 we show the comparison between the PMF obtained from the simulations of explicitly formed colloids with polymer coatings under the various conditions described in this work, with the effective potential proposed here.

We focused on only three cases for simplicity, and as Fig. 8 shows, the match between the PMF that emerges naturally from the simulations of explicitly formed colloids with mesoscopic scale interactions is remarkably well represented by the effective potential proposed here, in Eq. (9). Using the data in Table 1 we can relate the adjustable parameters of the effective potential (Eq. (9)) with specific properties of the dispersion modeled, such as colloidal or polymeric concentration, as well as polymerization degree. What this means is that one can then perform ordinary, i.e. not DPD simulations between bare particles that obey the new effective potential, Eq. (9), with the freedom to choose the adjustable parameters of such potential to model the colloidal concentration, the polymer concentration and the chain length by simply choosing those parameters accordingly to the trends presented here.

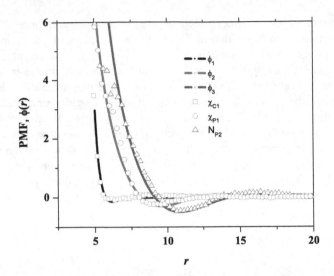

Fig. 8. Comparison of the PMF obtained from the simulations carried out in this work for explicitly made colloids coated with polymer brushes (data points), with the effective potential ($\phi(r)$) proposed here, see Eq. (9), indicated by the lines. The squares correspond to bare colloids at the concentration $\chi_{C1} = 7 \times 10^{-4}$; the circles represent the PMF for colloids at the same concentration $\chi_{C1} = 7 \times 10^{-4}$, coated with chains of constant length $N_p = 6$ beads with polymer concentration equal to $\chi_{p1} = 0.02$. The triangles represent the PMF of a colloidal dispersion whose colloidal and polymer concentrations are equal to $\chi_{C1} = 7 \times 10^{-4}$ and $\chi_{p1} = 0.02$, respectively, and the chains polymerization degree is $N_{p2} = 12$. The appropriate parameters used for the effective potential (lines) can be consulted in Table 1.

5 Conclusions

A new effective pair potential with adjustable parameters that represent various physical situations such as colloidal concentration, polymer concentration and chain length is proposed here as an alternative for the modeling of colloidal dispersions. The novelty of the new potential is its ability to predict correctly the potential of mean force of structured colloids at the mesoscale with explicitly included polymer chains grafted on the surfaces as dispersants. The protocol presented here describes a procedure to carry out efficient simulations with bare particles that interact with the new potential proposed here without losing physical information (such as particle concentration or polymerization degree), while at the same time saving up computational resources.

Acknowledgments. This work was supported by SIyEA-UAEM (Projects 3585/2014/CIA and 3831/2014/CIA). KATM thanks CONACyT, for a graduate student scholarship. All simulations reported in this work were performed at the Supercomputer OLINKA located at the Laboratorio de Bioingeniería Molecular a Multiescala, at the Universidad Autónoma del Estado de México. The authors are grateful to *Red de Venómica Computacional y Bioingeniería Molecular a Multiescala*. AGG would like to thank E. Blokhuis (University of Leiden) for several informative conversations.

References

1. Russel, W.B., Saville, D.A., Schowalter, W.: Colloidal Dispersions. Cambridge University Press, Cambridge (1989)
2. Hiemenz, P.C., Rajagopalan, R.: Principles of Colloid and Surface Chemistry, 3rd edn. Marcel Dekker, New York (1997)
3. Derjaguin, B.V.: Theory of the stability of strongly charged lyophobic sols and the adhesion of strongly charged particles in solutions of electrolytes. Acta. Physicochim. USSR **14**, 633–662 (1941)
4. Verwey, E.J.W., Overbeek, J.T.G.: Theory of the stability of lyophobic colloids. Dover, London (1999)
5. Kranenburg, M., Laforge, C., Smit, B.: Mesoscopic simulations of phase transitions in lipid bilayers. Phys. Chem. Chem. Phys. **6**, 4531–4534 (2004)
6. Kranenburg, M., Venturoli, M., Smit, B.: Phase behavior and induced interdigitation in bilayers studied with dissipative particle dynamics. J Phys. Chem. B. **107**, 11491–11501 (2003)
7. Hamaker, H.C.: The London–van der Waals attraction between spherical particles. Physica **4**, 1058–1072 (1937)
8. de Boer, J.H.: The influence of van der Waals forces and primary bonds on binding energy, strength and orientation, with special reference to some artificial resins. Trans. Faraday Soc. **32**, 10–37 (1936)
9. Kumar, A., Jianzhong, W.: Jamming phase diagram of colloidal dispersions by molecular dynamics simulations. Appl. Phys. Lett. **84**, 4565–4567 (2004)
10. Gibson, J.B., Chen, K., Chynoweth, S.: Simulation of Particle Adsorption onto a Polymer Coated Surface using the Dissipative Particle Dynamics Method. J. Colloid Interface Sci. **206**, 464–474 (1998)
11. Dzwinel, W., Yuen, W.D., Boryczko, K.: Mesoscopic dynamics of colloids simulated with dissipative particle dynamics and fluid particle model. J. Mol. Model. **8**, 33–43 (2002)
12. Dzwinel, W., Yuen, D.A., Boryczko, K.: Bridging diverse physical scales with the discrete-particle paradigm in modeling colloidal dynamics with mesoscopic features. Chem. Eng. Sci. **61**, 2169–2185 (2006)
13. Martys, N.S.: Study of a dissipative particle dynamics based approach for modeling suspensions. J. Rheol. **49**, 401–424 (2005)
14. Boek, E.S., Coveney, P.V., Lekkerkerker, H.N.W., van der Schoot, P.: Simulating the rheology of dense colloidal suspensions using dissipative particle dynamics. Phys. Rev. E **55**, 3124–3133 (1997)
15. Bolintineanu, D.S., Grest, G.S., Lechman, J.B., Pierce, F., Plimpton, S.J., Schunk, P.R.: Particle dynamics modeling methods for colloid suspensions. Comp. Part. Mech. **1**, 321–356 (2014)
16. Satoh, A., Chantrell, R.W.: Application of the dissipative particle dynamics method to magnetic colloidal dispersions. Mol. Phys. Int. J. Interface Between Chem. Phys. **104**, 3287–3302 (2006)
17. Louis, A.A., Bolhuis, P.G., Hansen, J.P., Meijer, E.: Can polymer coils be modeled as "soft colloids"? Phys. Rev. Lett. **85**, 2522–2525 (2000)
18. Guzmán, O., de Pablo, J.J.: An effective-colloid pair potential for Lennard-Jones colloid–polymer mixtures. J. Chem. Phys. **118**, 2392–2397 (2003)
19. Pool, R., Bolhuis, P.G.: Can purely repulsive soft potentials predict micelle formation correctly? Phys. Chem. Chem. Phys. **8**, 941–948 (2006)

20. Pan, W., Tartakovsky, A.M.: Dissipative particle dynamics model for colloid transport in porous media. Adv. Water Resour. **58**, 41–48 (2013)
21. Vincent, B., Edwards, J., Emmett, S., Jones, A.: Depletion flocculation in dispersions of sterically-stabilised particles (soft spheres). Colloids Surf. **18**, 261–281 (1986)
22. Allen, M.P., Tildesley, D.J.: Computer Simulation of Liquids. Clarendon, Oxford (1987)
23. Hoogerbrugge, P.J., Koelman, J.M.V.A.: Simulating microscopic hydrodynamic phenomena with dissipative particle dynamics. Europhys. Lett. **19**, 155–160 (1992)
24. Español, P., Warren, P.: Statistical Mechanics of Dissipative Particle Dynamics. Europhys. Lett. **30**, 191–196 (1995)
25. Groot, R.D., Warren, P.B.: Dissipative particle dynamics: Bridging the gap between atomistic and mesoscopic simulation. J. Chem. Phys. **107**, 4423–4435 (1997)
26. Maiti, A., McGrother, S.: Bead–bead interaction parameters in dissipative particle dynamics: Relation to bead-size, solubility parameter, and surface tension. J. Chem. Phys. **120**, 1594–1601 (2004)
27. Groot, R.D., Rabone, K.L.: Mesoscopic simulation of cell membrane damage, morphology change and rupture by nonionic surfactants. Biophys. J. **81**, 725–736 (2001)
28. Hoogerbrugge, P.J., Koelman, J.M.V.A.: Simulating microscopic hydrodynamic phenomena with dissipative particle dynamics. Europhys. Lett. **19**, 155–160 (1992)
29. Gama Goicochea, A., Romero-Bastida, M., López-Rendón, R.: Dependence of thermodynamic properties of model systems on some dissipative particle dynamics parameters. Mol. Phys. **105**, 2375–2381 (2007)
30. Roux, B.: The calculation of the potential of mean force using computer simulations. Comp. Phys. Comm. **91**, 275–282 (1995)
31. http://www.simes.uaemex-labs.org.mx/

Scaling Crowd Simulations in a GPU Accelerated Cluster

Hugo Pérez[1,2(✉)], Benjamín Hernández[3], Isaac Rudomín[2],
and Eduard Ayguadé[1,2]

[1] Universitat Politècnica de Catalunya, BarcelonaTECH, Barcelona, Spain
hperez@bsc.es
[2] Barcelona Supercomputing Center, Barcelona, Spain
[3] Oak Ridge National Laboratory, Oak Ridge, TN, USA

Abstract. Programmers need to combine different programming models and fully optimize their codes to take advantage of various levels of parallelism available in heterogeneous clusters. To reduce the complexity of this process, we propose a task-based approach for crowd simulation using OmpSs, CUDA and MPI, which allows taking the full advantage of computational resources available in heterogeneous clusters. We also present the performance analysis of the algorithm under different workloads executed on a GPU Cluster.

Keywords: Crowds · Simulation · Visualization · Parallel programming models · Accelerators · Heterogeneous architecture · GPU cluster · HPC

1 Introduction

Heterogeneous clusters provide various levels of parallelism that need to be exploited successfully to harness their computational power totally. At node-level, Pthreads, OpenMP directives, among other libraries, provide access to CPU level parallelism and OpenACC, CUDA or OpenCL libraries do the same for accelerators. Once node-level parallelism is achieved, additional scalability is accomplished by allocating computation in several nodes, using the message passing interface (MPI).

Programmers need to combine these programming models in their code and fully optimize it for each level of parallelism which turns into a complex task. These two processes also may suggest programming heterogeneous systems is an ad hoc activity.

During the last years, the Barcelona Supercomputer Center (BSC-CNS) has led a task-based approach to simplify code development efforts on these architectures. As a result, programmers can use OmpSs and MPI to leverage the computational power of heterogeneous clusters.

Our particular endeavors have been focused on the design, development and analysis of crowd simulations in these systems. Our first efforts [1] combined CUDA and MPI models for in-situ crowd simulation and rendering on GPU

© Springer International Publishing Switzerland 2016
I. Gitler and J. Klapp (Eds.): ISUM 2015, CCIS 595, pp. 461–472, 2016.
DOI: 10.1007/978-3-319-32243-8_32

clusters and recently [2] we have adopted OmpSs. We proposed a task-based algorithm that allows the full use of all levels of parallelism available in a heterogeneous node. OmpSs allowed us to analyze the simulation under different resource allocations.

In this article we present new techniques to scale the algorithm introduced in [2] to multiple nodes. We also introduce the analysis of the algorithm and provide scalability performance of the simulation running under different resource allocations on the Barcelona Supercomputing Center's Minotauro Cluster.

The rest of the work is organized as follows: the Background section introduces crowd behavior models and OmpSs as a task-based parallel programming model. The algorithm, implementation and results obtained from our case study are discussed in next sections. Finally, we present our conclusions and future work considering OmpSs requirements for visualization.

2   Background

2.1   Crowd Simulation

Microscopic and macroscopic modeling are the most important approaches to crowd simulation. While macroscopic modeling describes global interactions with the environment and the crowd itself, microscopic modeling exposes the interactions among the individuals within a group [3].

We are particularly interested in microscopic modeling of crowds using Agent-Based Models or ABM. An ABM simulates the actions and interactions of autonomous agents and promotes the progressive assembly of agents into groups resulting in global-scale behaviors, i.e. it provides macroscopic features on a large-scale. By applying ABM, the simulation can handle each agent individually and use general behavior rules in a single rule multiple agents fashion, which suits the Single Instruction Multiple Data (SIMD) model.

There is a large body of work in crowd simulation, below we present a brief description of the principal behavior models.

Boids. This method [4] is based on three basic rules: separation, alignment and cohesion. These rules maintain together and give a collision-free direction to a group of boids (bird-like objects).

Social Forces. This method follows a physics-based approach [5]. Agent behavior is modeled by attractive forces called social forces. Attractive forces lead the agent to a destination, and repulsive forces maintain the agent free of collisions. The method allows the introduction of various social interactions.

Predictive/Velocity-Based Models. In these methods, agents calculate the set of velocities that lead to a collision with an obstacle; to move on routes without collision, agents choose velocities out of this domain [6]. This concept is expanded by Van den Berg [7,8], introducing the notions of Velocity Obstacles (VO) and Reciprocal Velocity Obstacles (RVO) and the notion of Optimal Reciprocal Collision Avoidance (ORCA).

Synthetic Vision. It simulates the human visual system and uses the distance to obstructions and the possible lines of sight. It applies simple heuristics that enable agents to adapt their walking speed and direction [9,10].

We provide a detailed description of crowd simulation and rendering techniques that take advantage of GPUs and GPU Clusters in [1,11,12].

2.2 A Brief Introduction to OmpSs

Translating a sequential algorithm into one based on tasks consists in encapsulating the main steps into functions, changing these functions into tasks and defining data dependencies between them (Listing 1.1). Data dependencies definition is necessary to guarantee data locality and automatic scheduling. OmpSs also allows incremental code parallelization, and thus code testing can be performed during the migration process. We refer the reader to OmpSs specs for an in-depth description of each directive [13].

Listing 1.1. OmpSs syntax to define a task.

```
1  #pragma omp target device ({ smp | cuda | opencl })
2  {[ndrange(workDim, gworkSize, lworkSize)]}
3  [implements( function_name )]
4  {copy_deps | [copy_in( array_spec ,...)] [copy_out(...)]
       [copy_inout(...)] }
5  #pragma omp taskwait [on (...)] [noflush]
```

From Listing 1.1 (code line 1), the **target** directive indicates the device and programming model used to execute the task; the **ndrange** directive, in code line 2, is used to configure the number of dimensions (workDim), the global size of each dimension (gworkSize) and the number of work-items for each workgroup (lworkSize).

Directive **implements** (code line 3) allows the definition of multiple task implementations of the same function, for example, one in the CPU and one in the GPU; the runtime decides which is better during execution and can even execute both in parallel.

Directive **copy_deps** (code line 4) ensures that the device has a valid and consistent copy of the data. Therefore, the programmer does not need to do explicit memory allocations for the device or data transfers between the host and devices.

A synchronization point is defined by using **taskwait** (code line 5), and all data is copied from the device to the CPU memory. Similarly, **taskwait on**, synchronize the execution and transfers specific variables. With the **no flush** directive synchronization occurs but data is not transferred to CPU memory.

Using OmpSs with multiple GPUs offers the following advantages:

- It is not necessary to select the device for each operation.
- There is no need to allocate special memory in the host (pinned memory) or the device.

- It is not necessary to transfer data between host and devices, OmpSs maintains memory coherence efficiently and reduces transfers using data regions.
- Programmers do not need to declare streams, OmpSs implements them by default.
- All available devices are used by default, therefore, the application scales through all the devices.

OmpSs does all these operations automatically.

3   Algorithm Overview

Following our previous development and analysis efforts using different programming models and parallelism approaches, we use the wandering crowd behavior algorithm introduced in [1,2] where design and complexity details of the algorithm are discussed in detail. However for clarity sake, we describe the basic algorithm.

The sequential algorithm is composed of three primary tasks as shown in the following steps:

Step 1: Navigation space is discretized using a grid (Fig. 1(a)).
Step 2: Set up the agents' information (position, direction, and speed) randomly according to the navigation space size.
Step 3: Update position for each agent: calculate collision avoidance within a given radius. Evaluation of the agent's motion direction switches every 45° covering a total of eight directions counterclockwise (Fig. 1(b)).

The agent moves in the direction with more available cells or fewer agents within its radius.

Processing these tasks in parallel within a cluster, requires tiling and stencil computations. First, the navigation space (from now on it will be called the World)

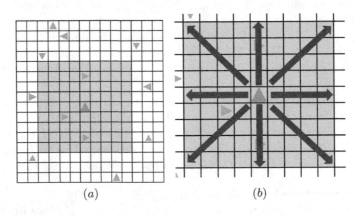

(a)   (b)

Fig. 1. (a) Navigation space discretization. (b) Search radius for collision avoidance.

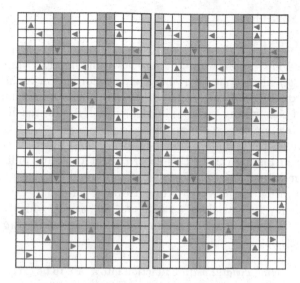

Fig. 2. Dividing the domain in tiles

and information for all the agents is divided into zones. Each zone is assigned to a node which in turn is divided into sub-zones (Fig. 2). Then, the tasks performed in each sub-zone can be executed in parallel by either a CPU or GPU. Stencil computations are performed on an inter and intra-node basis. A step by step description of the algorithm is included:

Step 1: Navigation space is discretized using a grid; then the resultant grid is discretized into zones. Each node will compute each zone.

Step 2: Divide each zone into tiles (sub-zones). A CPU or GPU will compute each sub-zone. Each CPU or GPU stores their corresponding tile of the world.

Step 3: Set up the communication topology between zones and sub-zones.

Step 4: Exchange borders (stencils).

Step 4a: (Intra-node) Exchange the occupied cells in the borders between sub-zones.

Step 4b: (Internode) Exchange the occupied cells in the borders between zones

Step 5: Update position for each agent in parallel: Calculate collision avoidance within a given radius. Evaluation of the agent's motion direction switches every 45° covering a total of eight directions counterclockwise. The agent moves in the direction with more available cells or fewer agents within its radius.

Step 6: Agents' Information Exchange.

Step 6a: (Intra-node) Exchange agents' information that crossed a border and moved to another sub-zone.

Step 6b: (Internode) Exchange agents' information that crossed a border and moved to another zone.

4   Implementation

OmpSs' advantages for code development in heterogeneous architectures were noted in our previous publication [2]. As shown in the algorithm from Sect. 3, a new level of stencil computation and agents' information exchange has been introduced to extend computations to additional nodes. OmpSs flexibility allows us to make MPI calls within tasks to implement internode stencils. Thus, incremental code development is still possible.

As an example, we include a code snippet of one function converted to a task illustrated in Listing 1.2. In this case, **target** directive indicates that the GPU will execute the *updatePosition* task. OmpSs will take care of the memory management by using the directive **copy_deps**. There is an explicit definition of data dependency for variables *agents*, *ids* and *world*, which are input and output of the task. Task execution is done by calling *updatePosition* as a regular language C function.

Listing 1.2. Converting *updatePosition* function into a task to be executed as a CUDA Kernel.

```
1
2   // Kernel declaration as a task
3   #pragma omp target device (cuda)
4   ndrange(2, (int) sqrt(count_agents_total),
               (int)sqrt(count_agents_total), 16, 16) copy_deps
5   #pragma omp task inout(
6   ([agents_total_buffer] agents ) [0; count_agents_total],
7   ([agents_total_buffer] ids ) [0: count_agents_total],
8   [world_cells_block] world )
9   extern "C" global void updatePosition(
10  float4 *agents, *ids, int *subzone, ...);
11
12  // Kernel execution
13  bool runSimulation ( )
14  {
15      ...
16      for ( int i = 0 ; i < subzones; i ++)
17      { ...
18          updatePosition(agents[i], ids[i], subzone[i], ... );
19          ...
20      }
21
22  #pragma omp taskwait
23      ...
24
25  //////////////////////////////////////////////////////////////////////
26  //Internode exchange of agents
27  //////////////////////////////////////////////////////////////////////
28  MPI_Send(agents_left_out_pos, ...);
29  MPI_Send(agents_left_out_ids, ..);
```

```
30      MPI_Send(&count_agents_left_out, ...);

31
32      MPI_Recv(agents_int_pos, ...);
33      MPI_Recv(agents_int_ids, ...);
34      MPI_Recv(&count_agents_right_in, ...);
35      count_agents_int += count_agents_right_in;

36
37  }
```

As noted in Sect. 3, we apply a second level of tiling, first dividing the domain(agents and world) between the nodes, assigning one tile (called zone) to each node, and inside each node the zone is divided into subzones. Then each subzone is processed as a task, and they are distributed between the computing resources (CPUs and GPUs) for parallel processing. At run-time, this information is exchanged within the nodes by OmpSs and between the nodes by MPI (code lines 31–38 from Listing 1.2).

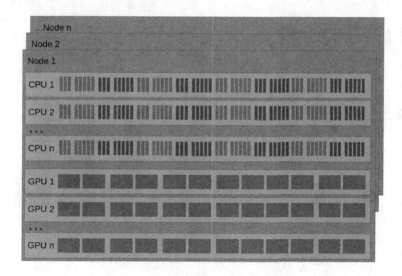

Fig. 3. Tasks processed in parallel in different nodes

Using run-time variables we can control the number of CPUs and/or GPUs that are used. By default, OmpSs uses all the available computing resources. If more hardware resources are added to one node, for example, more CPUs or GPUs, the simulation will use them without any code changes. Figure 3 shows a schema of how tasks are processed in parallel inside each node also it shows the triple level of parallelism, the first one at the node level, the second one at CPU core level and the third one at CUDA thread level.

5   Results

We conducted our tests on the Barcelona Supercomputing Center's Minotauro
Cluster. Each node has two CPU Intel Xeon E5649 6-Core at 2.53 GHz, 24 GB
of RAM, two NVIDIA Tesla M2090 GPUs with 512 CUDA Cores and 6 GB of
GDDR5 Memory. We used CUDA 5.0, Mercurium compiler version 1.99.9 [14]
and Nanos runtime system version 0.9a [15].

Our first test was to compare the execution time of one-node and multi-node
versions, for the multi-node version we use 4, 9 and 16 nodes. We simulated up to
126 million of agents, in a world of 27852×27852 cells. For the one-node version,
the world was partitioned into 16 tiles, i.e. a zone with 16 sub-zones, using two
GPUs and ten CPU cores. In the multi-node version the world was decomposed
into 4, 9 and 16 zones, according to the number of nodes, then each zone was
partitioned into 16 tiles (sub-zones) for all cases. In each node, both GPUs and
ten CPU cores were used, the remaining two cores control both GPUs. Figure 4
shows the results, comparing both versions.

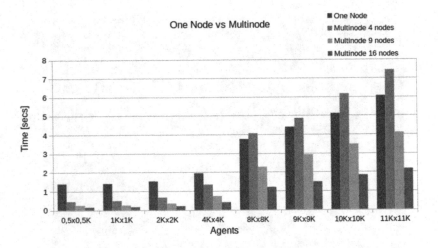

Fig. 4. Execution time one-node vs multi-node

Applying tiling in one node allowed us to simulate a large number of agents,
limited just by the host memory size. The bottleneck is the data transfer between
the host and the GPUs. Figure 5, shows the data transfers in one iteration for
both GPUs, for a simulation of 64 million of agents. Although we overlap with
other tasks performed in the CPU, at one point the data calculated by the GPU
is indispensable to continue with the simulation. For the multi-node version,
bottlenecks related to CPU-GPU data transfers are solved partially by distributing the data between nodes. Nevertheless, another type of bottleneck appears
as communication overhead between nodes. We minimize such bottleneck by
compacting data, i.e. when border information exchange occurs, only occupied
cells are transferred; and by overlapping computation with communication.

Fig. 5. Data transfer between the host and the GPUs. The pink color represents data transfer from the host to the devices, the green represents transfers from the devices to the host.

Each node of the Minotauro Cluster has a PCI Express 2.0 (8 GB/s) interface where more modern technology uses PCI Express 3.0 (16 GB/s) interface. Summit, the next cluster at Oak Ridge National Laboratory [16], will provide NVLink technology that is expected to be five to twelve times faster than current PCI Express 3.0. Thus, in the future these bottlenecks will be alleviated by hardware technology improvements. Meanwhile, it is important to keep applying different techniques to take advantage of all the cluster's computing power.

The achieved speedup for 4, 16, 64 and 126 million agents, using 4, 9 and 16 nodes is shown in Fig. 6. For 4 and 16 million we observe a linear speedup; however, for 64 and 126 million agents there is not any speedup at all using four nodes. This is due to the intensive communication within and between nodes for such large simulations.

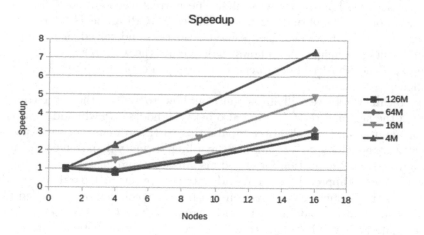

Fig. 6. Speedup

The second experiment consisted of testing the algorithm's workload. It can simulate up to 764 million of agents (Fig. 7) and is limited by the size of the world. The system can scale up to several hundred million agents by using multiple nodes. This is important because we are now developing the core modules of communication that will allow us to develop more complex simulations.

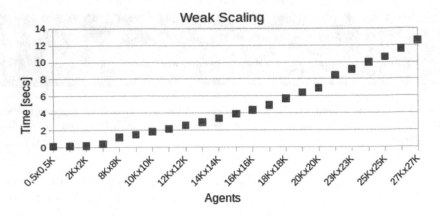

Fig. 7. Weak scaling

6   Conclusion and Future Work

We presented the development of a task-based scalable crowd simulation and analyzed how the simulation scales to a different number of nodes. The system can scale up to several hundred million agents by using multiple nodes, using all the computing resources available in the cluster.

Comparing with our previous work [1], which used MPI and CUDA programming models, we improved our results. The current version allows us to take advantage of the computing resources effectively (CPUs and GPUs) by using OmpSs. In addition, we identified some bottlenecks and solved them: applying a double tiling technique that allows to distribute the work between the nodes, minimizing the transfer of data between nodes and exploiting the triple level of parallelism.

As future work, we will investigate on how to reduce the data transfers between the host and the GPU and also between nodes. We will add task-based in-situ analysis and visualization capabilities to the system, i.e. we expect to take advantage of OmpSs' automatic scheduling, memory management, communication and synchronization for crowd visualization and analysis.

A task-based approach may have advantages over current parallel rendering techniques. For example, visualization can be easily coupled or decoupled from the simulation just by adding or removing rendering tasks. This also applies to crowd analysis. It will help in decomposing communication between the simulation, visualization and analysis into tasks while their execution may take advantage of OmpSs' synchronization and automatic scheduling. Also, synchronization and automatic scheduling will allow us to deploy the visualization system into immersive or large-scale tiled displays connected to GPU clusters. Finally, OmpSs can be seen as a bridge connecting data from simulation to visualization and analysis while maintaining the rendering algorithms intact.

This interaction is expected to be similar to the OmpSs-CUDA programs, where OmpSs is aware of the CUDA's context, memory, and GPU availability.

Nevertheless, the full interaction between OmpSs-OpenGL is not supported yet. Additional challenges such as OpenGL thread safety, OpenGL context creation and registration in OmpSs, OmpSs multiGPU compatibility for graphics or updating of the OmpSs scheduling system to support graphics load balancing have to be solved first.

Acknowledgements. This research was partially supported by: CONACyT doctoral fellowship 285730, CONACyT SNI 54067, BSC-CNS Severo Ochoa program (SEV-2011-00067), CUDA Center of Excellence at BSC, Oak Ridge Leadership Computing Facility at the Oak Ridge National Laboratory, under DOE Contract No. DE-AC05-00OR22725, the Spanish Ministry of Economy and Competitivity under contract TIN2012-34557, and the SGR programme (2014-SGR-1051) of the Catalan Government.

References

1. Hernández, B., Perez, H., Isaac, R., Ruiz, S., DeGyves, O., Toledo, L.: Simulating and visualizing real-time crowds on GPU clusters. Computación y Sistemas **18**, 651–664 (2014)
2. Perez, H., Hernández, B., Rudomin, I., Ayguade, E.: Task-based crowd simulation for heterogeneous architectures. In: Handbook of Research on Next-Generation High Performance Computing. IGI (2015, in progress)
3. Bonabeau, E.: Agent-based modeling: methods and techniques for simulating human systems. Proc. Nat. Acad. Sci. **99**, 7280–7287 (2002)
4. Reynolds, C.W.: Flocks, herds and schools: a distributed behavioral model. In: Proceedings of the 14th Annual Conference on Computer Graphics and Interactive Techniques, SIGGRAPH 1987, pp. 25–34. ACM, New York (1987)
5. Helbing, D., Molnár, P.: Social force model for pedestrian dynamics. Phys. Rev. E **51**, 4282–4286 (1995)
6. Paris, S., Pettré, J., Donikian, S.: Pedestrian reactive navigation for crowd simulation: a predictive approach. Eurographics 2007 Comput. Graph. Forum **26**, 665–674 (2007)
7. Van Den Berg, J., Patil, S., Sewall, J., Manocha, D., Lin, M.: Interactive navigation of multiple agents in crowded environments. In: Proceedings of the 2008 Symposium on Interactive 3D Graphics and Games, I3D 2008, pp. 139–147. ACM, New York (2008)
8. van den Berg, J., Guy, S.J., Lin, M., Manocha, D.: Reciprocal n-body collision avoidance. In: Pradalier, C., Siegwart, R., Hirzinger, G. (eds.) Robotics Research. STAR, vol. 70, pp. 3–19. Springer, Heidelberg (2011)
9. Ondřej, J., Pettré, J., Olivier, A.H., Donikian, S.: A synthetic-vision based steering approach for crowd simulation. ACM Trans. Graph. **29**, 123:1–123:9 (2010)
10. Moussaïd, M., Helbing, D., Theraulaz, G.: How simple rules determine pedestrian behavior and crowd disasters. Proc. Nat. Acad. Sci. **108**, 6884–6888 (2011)
11. Rudomin, I., Hernández, B., de Gyves, O., Toledo, L., Rivalcoba, I., Ruiz, S.: GPU generation of large varied animated crowds. Computación y Sistemas **17**, 365–380 (2013)
12. Ruiz, S., Hernández, B., Alvarado, A., Rudomín, I.: Reducing memory requirements for diverse animated crowds. In: Proceedings of Motion on Games, MIG 2013, pp. 55:77–55:86. ACM, New York (2013)

13. Duran, A., AyguadÉ, E., Badia, R.M., Labarta, J., Martinell, L., Martorell, X., Planas, J.: OmpSs: a proposal for programming heterogeneous multi-core architectures. Parallel Process. Lett. **21**, 173–193 (2011)
14. Balart, J., Duran, A., Gonzàlez, M., Martorell, X., Ayguadé, E., Labarta, J.: Nanos mercurium: a research compiler for openmp. In: Proceedings of the European Workshop on OpenMP, vol. 8 (2004)
15. Barcelona Supercomputing Center: Nanos++ runtime (2015). http://pm.bsc.es/nanox
16. NVIDIA: Summit and sierra supercomputers: an inside look at the U.S. Departmentof energy's new pre-exascale systems. Technical report, NVIDIA (2014)

A Template for Scalable Continuum Dynamic Simulations in Multiple GPUs

Julián Becerra-Sagredo[1]([⊠]), Francisco Mandujano[2], Carlos Málaga[2],
Jaime Klapp[1,3], and Irene de Teresa[4]

[1] "ABACUS" Centro de Matemáticas Aplicadas y Cómputo de Alto Rendimiento,
Departamento de Matemáticas, Centro de Investigación y de Estudios Avanzados
(CINVESTAV-IPN), Carretera México-Toluca Km 38.5, La Marquesa, 52140
Ocoyoacac, Estado de México, Mexico
juliansagredo@gmail.com
[2] Departamento de Física, Facultad de Ciencias,
UNAM, Ciudad Universitaria, 04510 Mexico, D.F., Mexico
[3] Departamento de Física, Instituto Nacional de Investigaciones Nucleares,
La Marquesa Ocoyoacac s/n, Ocoyoacac, Edo. de México, Mexico
[4] Department of Mathematical Sciences,
University of Delaware, Newark, DE 19716, USA

Abstract. In this work we present a programming philosophy and a
template code for achieving computational scalability when using multiple graphics processing units (GPUs) in the numerical solution of any
mathematical system of equations found in continuum dynamic simulations. The programming philosophy exploits the principal characteristics
of the GPU hardware, with emphasis in the delivering of threads with
massive memory fetches, intense calculations using local registers and
limited writes to global memory. The philosophy requires explicit formulas for calculations for which domain decomposition is trivial. The
domains are decomposed in regions that use the local central processing unit (CPU) to communicate common interfaces using the message
passing interface (MPI). A template code for the heat equation is established and tested for scalability. The novelty is that we show a series
of codes, constructed from the basic template, that solve all the basic
model equations found in continuum dynamics, and present illustrative
results. The model equations are the heat equation, the Poisson equation, the shallow-water equations, the flow in porous media equations
and the vorticity equations.

1 Introduction

The last decade has been witness to radical changes in number crunching hardware [1,2]. The graphics processing unit (GPU) has reached approximately an
order of magnitude in peak, double precision, floating point operations per second (FLOPS), compared to the central processing unit (CPU). Today, the GPU
can deliver more than 3000 GFLOPS, while the CPU delivers just above 500
GFLOPS. Additionally, the peak memory bandwidth, the velocity to fetch data

© Springer International Publishing Switzerland 2016
I. Gitler and J. Klapp (Eds.): ISUM 2015, CCIS 595, pp. 473–484, 2016.
DOI: 10.1007/978-3-319-32243-8_33

from memory, is around $500\,\mathrm{GB/s}$ for the GPU compared to under $80\,\mathrm{GB/s}$ for the CPU. And the trends are getting steeper for every new processor generation presented [3]. At the present time, the GPUs double their performance approximately every year while the CPUs do it almost every two years.

Supercomputers are increasingly relying upon the GPUs each year [2], mostly to increase the FLOPS delivered given a fixed monetary budget. Besides their highest performance, the GPUs bring savings because they deliver the best cost/operation and energy/operation ratios. Surprisingly, the transition to GPUs has been slow in the programming side and supercomputers are still dominated by distributed, multi-core applications. One of the main reasons behind the slow implementation of algorithms into the GPU is that the methodologies need to be adapted to the GPU architecture following a theoretical ideal GPU-programming philosophy [3]. Perhaps, the applied mathematics community has not paid sufficient attention to the changes in the hardware and has produced a series of methodologies that might be suited for some GPU acceleration [4,5], but not for exclusive, multiple GPU, scalable performance.

In the field of continuum dynamics, theoretical research has been mainly focused in weak formulations of partial differential equations and their discretization using finite elements [6–8] . The research groups in applied mathematics have produced a great variety of theorems and applications for this particular formulation [9–13]. The finite elements are highly attractive because complex geometries and a mixed systems of equations, including constrains, can be discretized and solved using implicit formulations, reducing stability constrains for the time steps. Once the numerical engine for the discretization and the inversion of the matrix has been implemented, the extension of the method to new applications is relatively simple, and new research can be directed to find the numerical convergence of the algorithms and the best choice for the preconditioning of the matrix. The finite element method produces a great sparse matrix with mixed entries that in most cases is solved using a General Minimum Residual (GMRES) algorithm [14].

The applied mathematician often overlooks the use of the GMRES algorithm as a black box and focuses mainly in establishing the weak formulation of the partial differential equations. Here is where we find the greatest obstacle for scalable simulations. The community argues that sooner or later they will have a general sparse matrix inverter, GMRES or else, working on multi-processors and they will be able to simply change the matrix inversion engine in their codes. The community had some success using domain decomposition for the inversion of the sparse matrix in systems of multiple processors but, to this date, this is still one of the most important open themes in the field [15,16].

Unfortunately for the domain decomposition of matrices, many-core architectures like GPUs are quite different than multi-cores. Multi-cores can assign a large region of elements in the sparse matrix to each core and use iterative matchings to achieve convergence. The GPU requires one code applied independently to each element, using massive memory fetches for the discretization and writing its result to memory, fully in parallel.

The use of methods like GMRES makes sense in GPUs for systems of linear or non-linear equations to be solved for every element, independently. That is, a local inversion of a small matrix per thread. But large matrix inversions are not easy to implement in parallel. The main problem is that GMRES was designed and optimized as a sequential algorithm. It requires matrix-vector multiplications, rotations and the creation of a basis using the Gram-Schmidt algorithm. Matrix-vector multiplications can be implemented in parallel, but the rotations and creation of the basis vectors is always sequential [17]. Additionally, the domain decomposition of matrices using iterative algorithms faces a fundamental problem, the slow transmission of the long distance components of the solutions. For example, when solving a Poisson equation, the potential has always local components due to sources located at very long distances. Numerically, the computation must be able to communicate those sources rapidly when solving for the corrections at the intersection of the domains. Given the algorithm in its current form, only partial accelerations can be achieved for a large number of cores, computing matrix multiplications in the GPUs and reductions in the CPUs [17].

Intensive research is being done in the field and the reader must not loose attention to new developments. Finite elements can adapt to the GPU programming philosophy with some modifications of the general matrix strategy. Some alternatives are to produce explicit finite element methods and to reduce the equations complexity to allow the use of multigrid. Successful implementations can be found in this direction [18–23].

Other methods have evolved under relative isolation during the fertile decade of finite elements, these include finite differences, finite volumes [24] and Lagrangian advection [25, 26]. The algorithms are popular among engineers but are ignored or regarded as low order by most mathematicians. In this direction, our team has been successful in producing new high-order numerical schemes that combine the best features of these methods, exploiting explicit integration, full multi-dimensionality, fast memory fetches and fine grain parallel processing, while avoiding memory latencies with a fixed memory model.

In this paper we show that the development of high-order, moment preserving, semi-Lagrangian schemes [27], combined with the explicit solution of diffusion equations and multigrid or multiscale algorithms [28], provide a high-order convergent framework for incompressible, compressible and constrained continuum dynamics, ideally scalable in an array of many-core architectures.

First, we present a general programming philosophy and a heat equation template for multiple GPUs, showing its scalability using a large number of units. After that, the programming philosophy is applied to a series of model equations that contain all the possible systems of equations found in continuum dynamics. These are pure hyperbolic systems like the shallow-water equations, elliptic-hyperbolic systems like the vorticity equations, and parabolic-hyperbolic systems like the porous media equations.

2 Programming Model

The programming model must exploit the hardware characteristics of the GPUs to achieve peak performance in each card, and communicate several GPUs efficiently to obtain scalability. It is possible that we obtain acceleration using several GPUs, but the main goal must be the run of very large problems with small time penalties. We must be able to run a multiple sized problem in the same multiple number of GPUs for approximately the same computing time as the unit problem run in one. Therefore, we need to observe how the computational time varies with the number of mesh points for a fixed problem size per GPU, known as weak scalability.

Each GPU has a very large memory bandwidth and a very large number of low power processors. The programming model for each GPU must encourage the massive parallelization of the work space into the maximum number of threads, each using of the maximum number of memory fetches, intense computations in local registers and a few memory writes. If global iterations are needed, the iterations are better implemented on top of the GPU routines, after full workspace operations are finished.

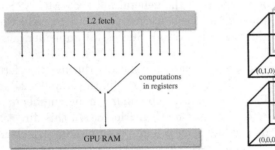
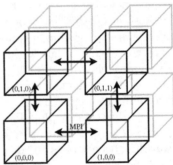

Fig. 1. Programming model for a single GPU (left) and message passing model for many GPUs (right). For each node in the numerical domain, massive L2 memory fetches are combined with intensive operations in registers and limited writes to global memory. The data missing in each face is transferred by the CPUs with MPI.

Figure 1 (left) shows the programming model for a single GPU. The run is carried out entirely on the GPU without large data transfers to the CPU. Inside the GPU, each thread represents a node of the numerical grid. For every thread, there are many memory reads using a read-only array, allowing the state-of-the-art compiler to assign a fast L2-memory transfer without the need to declare texture transfer arrays. This allows fast and massive memory transfers to local registers. Then the registers are used for the numerical operations and the results are written back to a write-only array in global memory. Every algorithm must be converted in every possible way to this philosophy in order to efficiently exploit the capabilities of the GPUs.

The multiple GPU model is based on domain decomposition of the computational domain and communication using the message passing interface MPI. Domain decomposition of continuum dynamics problems always involve communications between domains to update the domain border data. Depending on the approximation order of the algorithm, more than one line of border data can be communicated. The border data is stored in a special array that is transferred to the local CPU and communicated to the corresponding neighbor CPU using MPI. Once the data has been transferred between CPUs, each CPU loads the border data to their respective slave GPU.

Figure 1 (right) shows a three-dimensional domain decomposition and a sketch of the communication model using MPI. The domain decomposition can be done in one, two or three dimensions, as desired, but it must be kept in mind that it could be important to minimize the area to be communicated. A full three-dimensional domain decomposition provides the minimal area of communication.

Bounded irregular domains can be handled including the irregular domain in a bounding box and eliminating the unnecessary nodes. Infinite domains must be handled using adequate boundary conditions.

3   Template Code

We establish a template code for the chosen programming philosophy. A programmable building block, basis of all the algorithms presented here, used for diagnostics of performance and scalability.

The model problem chosen for the template is parabolic, known as the heat diffusion equation

$$\frac{\partial u}{\partial t} + \kappa \nabla^2 u = f, \tag{1}$$

where $u = u(x,t)$, $x \in [0, L_1] \times [0, L_2] \times [0, L_3]$, $t = [0, \infty]$, $u(x,0) = u_0(x)$, and the given source $f = f(x,t)$.

We use first order forward differences in time and second order, 27-point stencil finite differences in space. We obtain an explicit algorithm that reads the values of 27 nodes, operates the finite differences and writes the solution for the next time step.

This algorithm is stable for time steps $\Delta t < \frac{(\Delta x)^2}{2\kappa}$, with $\Delta x = max_i(\Delta x_i)$, and therefore has a strong time step restriction. We use two arrays to distinguish present and future and use them only for reading and writing, respectively, at every time step. Given the characteristics of the algorithm, threaded for every node in the domain, a single GPU achieves peak performance and the penalties of the time step are reduced in the overall computational time. The algorithm is also perfectly scalable for GPUs with different numbers of processors.

For multiple GPUs, the computational domain is partitioned in $N_1 \times N_2 \times N_3$ cubes or parallelepipeds, assigning a subdomain to every GPU. After a full mesh time iteration, the faces of the subdomains are loaded to the local CPU and communicated with MPI using send and receive commands. The corresponding neighboring CPU receives the data and loads it to its slave GPU. The transfer of the data is done in an ordered way for every direction.

We fix the spatial discretization and increase the number of nodes. The code is first run in one Tesla C2075 card and the results are shown in Fig. 2 with a light grey colored line. It shows a linear relation between the number of mesh points

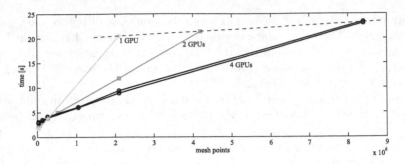

Fig. 2. Computational time against number of mesh points for one, two and four GPUs Tesla C2075. The dotted line shows the almost perfect scalability slope. Runs for 8 million mesh points can be performed by four GPUs almost in the same computational time than 2 million mesh points in one GPU. The small slope of the dotted line indicates the penalization of the message passing between GPUs.

and the computational time. Reaching approximately 20 s for 6400 time steps and two million mesh points. We run the code for two (grey line) and four (black lines) GPUs. We observe that for the same two million mesh points, two GPUs need almost half the computational time than one, accelerating the computation. But four GPUs are not able to do it in a fourth of the time. Accelerating computations using several GPUs is possible but it's not our main goal.

The use of several GPUs is needed to run problems with a large number of mesh points. In Fig. 2, the dotted line shows practically perfect scalability. The little slope shows the penalization time of the message passing to bind the subdomains. It means that we can run more than eight million mesh points in four GPUs, using the same computational time than two million points in one GPU. The slope of the dotted line could be used to estimate the computational time using many GPUs. The black line is double because the run in four GPUs is performed with one- (upper) and two-dimensional subdomain partitions, showing no considerable differences.

When using clusters with a large number of GPUs, we have observed perfect scalability as long as the GPUs share a motherboard. A large penalty can result of the message passing to distributed motherboards depending on the type of network. In such cases, perfect scalability is sacrificed against the possibility of a very large computation. Abacus I, an SGI cluster in Cinvestav, Mexico, achieves perfect scalability for two Tesla K40 cards that share motherboard. The computational time for the 20 s benchmark increases ten times for 27 cards in 14 nodes, computing 56 million points; and fifty times for 64 cards in 32 nodes, computing 134 million points.

4   Model Equations and Algorithms

We show a set of model equations that cover the whole range of the systems found in continuum dynamics simulations. The numerical algorithms are original and have been developed following the programming model presented for several GPUs. Therefore the algorithms have the same scalability properties of the heat equation template. The heat equation template was our model for parabolic equations. Here, we extend the programming philosophy to elliptic equations, using a multiscale method close to a multigrid [28]; to hyperbolic equations, using a moment preserving high-order semi-Lagrangian scheme [27]; and to mixed systems of equations with constraints.

4.1   Elliptic Equations

The chosen model for elliptic systems of PDEs is the three-dimensional Poisson equation

$$\nabla^2 u = f, \tag{2}$$

for $u \in [0, L_x] \times [0, L_y] \times [0, L_z]$, given $f = f(x, y)$.

This equation is solved using the multiscale algorithm described in [28], closely related to a multigrid. The multiscale algorithm consists of solving heat equations iteratively, using coarse nested discretizations, helped by interpolations to the rest of the mesh, in a descending cycle, until the heat equation is solved in the whole mesh. The process has been seen to converge to machine precision when full cycles are repeated a few more times for the residual function.

In Fig. 3, we show an illustration for the elliptic equation's solver constructed from the template. It shows the solution of the Poisson equation for a singular source with the shape of Mexico. Neumann boundary conditions are used because the solution is used to deform a mesh. The mesh is deformed using equations of motion for each mesh point, with a force computed from the potential found as solution to the Poisson equation.

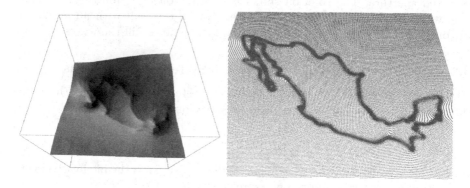

Fig. 3. Potential function, solution of the Poisson equation with Neumann boundary conditions and a singular one-dimensional source with the shape of Mexico. Illustrative for a multigrid, elliptic equation's solver constructed from the template. The solution is used as the potential of a force to move the mesh points of a regular grid and obtain adaptivity.

4.2 Hyperbolic Equations

The chosen model for hyperbolic equations are the two-dimensional shallow-water equations: the conservation of water volume

$$\frac{Dh}{Dt} = -h\nabla \cdot v, \tag{3}$$

and the acceleration of the water column

$$\frac{Dv}{Dt} = -\nabla h, \tag{4}$$

where h is the height of the water column, and v its velocity. The total time derivate, known as the material derivative $D/Dt = \partial/\partial t + v \cdot \nabla$, requires the solution of the trajectories $dx/dt = v$.

The equations are solved using a semi-Lagrangian, moment preserving, numerical scheme described in [27]. The scheme makes use of fluid elements that move and deform, starting from a Cartesian set, the corners of the elements are treated as movable nodes that travel in space following the given equations with total derivatives in time. As the points travel, the element that they describe deforms, and after a few time steps a non-linear exact map is performed to see the new element in a space where coordinates are orthogonal, where high-order, moment preserving interpolations are performed to restart the mesh points in a reference mesh.

The algorithm requires 216 neighbors. It uses arrays for the position of the nodes and computes trajectories and interpolations explicitly. It has a very relaxed CFL time step restriction, as long as the trajectory is well integrated.

In Fig. 4, we present the dynamic solution to the shallow water waves in a tank with variable floor. The floor has an obstacle, a transverse bump with a centered aperture. The solution shows the formation of a diffraction pattern. The waves are originated at the left face, moving the wall with an oscillating piston. The end of the channel has a dissipation zone to kill the waves.

4.3 Model for a Parabolic-Hyperbolic Systems of Equations

The chosen model for a parabolic-hyperbolic system of equations is the three-dimensional flow in porous media: the conservation of mass

$$\frac{Dn}{Dt} + n\nabla \cdot v = q, \tag{5}$$

for the effective density $n = \phi\rho$, where ϕ is the porosity, v is the intrinsic velocity, and q is a mass source; and the pressure equation

$$[(1 - \phi)C_r + \phi C_f] \frac{\partial P}{\partial t} = \phi\left(-\nabla \cdot v + \frac{q}{n}\right), \tag{6}$$

where C_r and C_f are the compressibiity of the solid and the fluid, respectively. The system is closed using Darcy's law for the intrinsic velocity

$$v = \boldsymbol{K} \cdot (-\nabla P + \boldsymbol{f}), \tag{7}$$

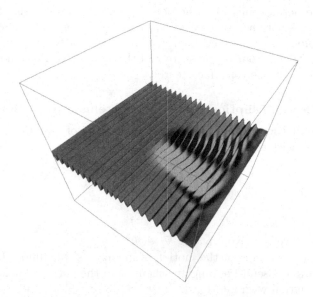

Fig. 4. Height of the water column for shallow water waves in a tank, illustrative of a hyperbolic system of equations' solver constructed from the template. The left wall is moved with an oscillating piston, and the opposite side has a dissipation zone to kill the waves. The floor has a transverse bump with a centered aperture. The waves show diffraction.

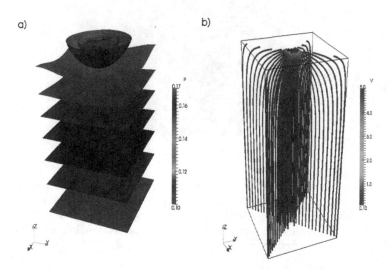

Fig. 5. Solution to the porous media equations for one fluid. (a) Graph of the contours of pressure for an extraction point in the top. (b) Graph of the streamlines colored with the velocity magnitude.

where K is the permeability over the porosity and f is an external force.

We solve the equations using a heat equation solver for the parabolic pressure equation combined with the semi-Lagrangian scheme for the hyperbolic part. In Fig. 5, we show the contours of pressure and the streamlines for a flow in porous media with a sink at the top's face center.

4.4   Model for an Elliptic-Hyperbolic Systems of Equations

The chosen model for an elliptic-hyperbolic system of equations is the two-dimensional vorticity equation

$$\frac{D\omega}{Dt} = 0, \tag{8}$$

coupled to the Poisson equation

$$\nabla^2 \phi = -\omega, \tag{9}$$

with the velocity vector given by $v = \nabla \times \phi\hat{k}$.

These equations represent the motion of incompressible fluids. The vorticity is advected using the semi-Lagrangian scheme and the potential is found solving the Poisson equation with multigrid.

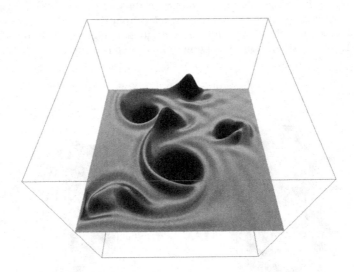

Fig. 6. Snapshot of the vorticity, illustration of the numerical solution of elliptic-hyperbolic systems of equations like those found in incompressible flow simulations, using a code based on the template. We solve the two-dimensional vorticity dynamic equations for an initial random distribution of Gaussian bell vortices with both signs. The box has slip wall boundary conditions.

In Fig. 6, we show a snapshot of vorticity, represented by the height of the mesh, starting from a random distribution of Gaussian bell vortices in positive and negative directions. The box has Dirichlet boundary conditions and therefore the walls have normal velocity equal to zero.

5   Conclusion

We presented a programming model using trivial domain decomposition with message passing for computations using multiple GPUs. The programming model has been proven to be perfectly scalable for GPUs that share a motherboard. In that case, the computational times remain in the same range for runs with increasing number of nodes using a large and fixed number of nodes in each GPU. For clusters of many GPUs in distributed motherboards, we have found a variable penalty associated to the message passings between nodes, dependent on the network. Problems of hundreds of millions of nodes can be solved sacrificing perfect scalability. The novelty of the work is that the programming philosophy is used to implement a diffusion equation solver for parabolic equations, a multiscale solver for elliptic equations, and a semi-Lagrangian advection scheme for hyperbolic equations. The three models are combined in schemes to solve systems of equations that model all the types of systems found in continuum dynamics, for incompressible, compressible and constrained flows.

Acknowledgements. This work was partially supported by ABACUS, CONACyT grant EDOMEX-2011-C01-165873.

References

1. Nickolls, J., Dally, W.J.: The GPU computing era. IEEE Micro **30**(2), 56–69 (2010)
2. Keckler, S.W., Dally, W.J., Khailany, B., Garland, M., Glasco, D.: GPUs and the future of parallel computing. IEEE Micro **31**(5), 7–17 (2011)
3. NVIDIA CUDA C Programming Guide, version 7.5. Nvidia (2015)
4. Göddeke, D., Strzodka, R., Mohd-Yusof, J., McCormick, P., Buijssen, S.H.M., Grajewski, M., Turek, S.: Exploring weak scalability for FEM calculations on a GPU-enhanced cluster. Parallel Comput. **33**(10–11), 685–699 (2007)
5. Lu, F., Pang, Y., Yin, F.: Scalability analysis of parallel algorithms on GPU clusters. J. Comp. Inf. Syst. **10**(14), 5947–5957 (2014)
6. Strang, G., Fix, G.: An Analysis of the Finite Element Method. SIAM, Wellesley Cambridge Press, Wellesley (1973)
7. Kuzmin, D., Hämäläinen, J.: Finite Element Methods for Computational Fluid Dynamics: A Practical Guide. Computational Science and Engineering. SIAM, Philadelphia (2014)
8. Löner, R., Morgan, K., Peraire, J., Zienkiewicz, O.C.: Recent developments in FEM-CFD. In: Fritts, M.J., Crowley, W.P., Trease, H. (eds.) The Free-Lagrange Method. Lecture Notes in Physics, vol. 238, pp. 236–254. Springer, Heidelberg (2005)
9. Yazid, A., Abdelkader, N., Abdelmadjid, H.: A state-of-the-art review of the X-FEM for computational fracture mechanics. Appl. Math. Model. **33**(12), 4269–4282 (2009)
10. Sukumar, N., Malsch, E.A.: Recent advances in the construction of polygonal finite element interpolants. Arch. Comput. Meth. Eng. **13**(1), 129–163 (2006)
11. Belytschko, T., Gracie, R., Ventura, G.: A review of extended/generalized finite element methods for material modeling. Modell. Simul. Mater. Sci. Eng. **17**(4), 1–24 (2009)

12. Schweitzer, M.A.: Generalizations of the finite element method. Cent. Eur. J. Math. **10**(1), 3–24 (2012)
13. Long, Y.Q., Long, Z.F., Cen, S.: Advanced Finite Element Method in Structural Engineering. Springer, Heidelberg (2009)
14. Saad, Y., Schultz, M.H.: GMRES: a generalized minimal residual algorithm for solving nonsymmetric linear system. SIAM J. Sci. Stat. Comput. **7**, 856–869 (1986)
15. Hamandi, L.: Review of domain-decomposition methods for the implementation of FEM on massively parallel computers. IEEE Antennas Propag. Mag. **37**(1), 93–98 (1995)
16. Kruzel, F., Banaś, K.: Vectorized OpenCL implementation of numerical integration for higher order finite elements. Comp. Math. Appl. **66**(10), 2030–2044 (2013)
17. Khodja, L.Z., Couturier, R., Glersch, A., Bahi, J.M.: Parallel sparse linear solver with GMRES method using minimization techniques of communications for GPU clusters. J. Supercomput. **69**(1), 200–224 (2014)
18. Turek, S., Göddeke, D., Becker, C., Buijssen, S., Wobker, H.: UCHPC - unconventional high performance computing for finite element simulations. In: International Supercomputing Conference, ISC 2008 (2008)
19. Płaszewski, P., Macioł, P., Banaś, K.: Finite element numerical integration on GPUs. In: Wyrzykowski, R., Dongarra, J., Karczewski, K., Wasniewski, J. (eds.) PPAM 2009, Part I. LNCS, vol. 6067, pp. 411–420. Springer, Heidelberg (2010)
20. Dick, C., Georgii, J., Westermann, R.: A real-time multigrid hexahedra method for elasticity simulation using CUDA. Simul. Model. Pract. Theory **19**(2), 801–816 (2011)
21. Banaś, K., Plaszewski, P., Maciol, P.: Numerical integration on GPUs for higher order finite elements. Comp. Math. Appl. **67**(6), 1319–1344 (2014)
22. Huthwaite, P.: Accelerated finite element elastodynamic simulations using the GPU. J. Comp. Phys. **257**(Part A), 687–707 (2014)
23. Martínez-Frutos, J., Martínez-Castejón, P.J., Herrero-Pérez, D.: Fine-grained GPU implementation of assembly-free iterative solver for finite element problems. Comput. Struct. **157**, 9–18 (2015)
24. LeVeque, R.J.: Finite Volume Methods for Hyperbolic Problems. Cambridge Texts in Applied Mathematics. Cambridge University Press, Cambridge (2002)
25. Oñate, E., Owen, R.: Particle-Based Methods: Fundamentals and Applications. Computational Methods in Applied Sciences. Springer, Heidelberg (2011)
26. Falcone, M., Ferretti, R.: Semi-Lagrangian Approximation Schemes for Linear and Hamilton-Jacobi Equations. Other Titles in Applied Mathematics. SIAM, Philadelphia (2013)
27. Becerra-Sagredo, J., Málaga, C., Mandujano, F.: Moments Preservind and high-resolution Semi-Lagrangian Advection Scheme (2014). arXiv: 1410.2817
28. Becerra-Sagredo, J., Málaga, C., Mandujano, F.: A novel and scalable Multigrid algorithm for many-core architectures (2011). arXiv:1108.2045

GPU Simulations of Fluid and Composition Dispersion in a Porous Media with Smoothed Particle Hydrodynamics

C.E. Alvarado-Rodríguez[1,3], J. Klapp[2,3(✉)], E. Mayoral[2],
and J.M. Domínguez[4]

[1] División de Ciencias Naturales y Exactas, Universidad of Guanajuato,
Noria Alta s/n, Guanajuato, Mexico
q_l_o@hotmail.com
[2] Departamento de Física, Instituto Nacional de Investigaciones Nucleares,
La Marquesa Ocoyoacac s/n, Ocoyoacac, Edo. de México, Mexico
jaime.klapp@inin.gob.mx
[3] "ABACUS" Centro de Matemáticas Aplicadas y Cómputo de Alto
Rendimiento, Departamento de Matemáticas, Centro de Investigación y de
Estudios Avanzados (CINVESTAV-IPN), Carretera México-Toluca Km 38.5,
La Marquesa, 52740 Ocoyoacac, Estado de México, Mexico
[4] Environmental Physics Laboratory (EPHYSLAB),
Universidad de Vigo, Vigo, Spain

Abstract. Fluid and composition dispersion in a porous media plays a relevant role in some industrial processes. The proper characterization of the porous media and the dynamics of the involved fluids are key parameters for the study of some industrial processes. This characterization is a challenge for the numerical methods community. The SPH open-source code named Dual-SPHysics is presented as a new tool for evaluating the fluid dynamics in porous media. The code was developed using CUDA, which can be used for solving the system of equations on GPU devices. In particular, we report the obtained performance for the DualSPHysics code and a comparison between the efficient implementations for CPU and GPU.

1 Introduction

Multiphase flow in porous media has a relevant role in the analysis of many industrial activities. The velocity, dispersion, and motion of fluids in a porous media are key parameters for processes such as pollutant transport, mobile reactive beds, oil recovery, etc. The proper characterization of the porous media properties, such as the permeability and dispersion, is crucial for this type of analysis. In order to predict the behavior of these processes, the numerical simulations (at proper scales) provide information of the flow which is almost impossible to obtain from other sources. Smoothed Particle Hydrodynamics (SPH) is a meshfree Lagrangian numerical method. This method was first proposed for astrophysical problems ([6], see also [11]), but nowadays it is widely used in computational fluid dynamics [7, 12, 13]. In the SPH method the fluid is discretized in a set of particles. Each of these particles is a nodal

© Springer International Publishing Switzerland 2016
I. Gitler and J. Klapp (Eds.): ISUM 2015, CCIS 595, pp. 485–494, 2016.
DOI: 10.1007/978-3-319-32243-8_34

point for which physical quantities (such as position, velocity, density, and pressure) are computed as an interpolation of the values of the neighboring particles. The fluid transport in porous media is a cutting edge topic in the CFD community, so a new set of equations should be implemented to satisfy all the peculiarities of the simulations. In order to properly represent these cases, the implementation of two phases with different properties (viscosity, density, wettability) is needed. One of the drawbacks of this method is its computational cost. This issue has been overcome thanks to the parallelized SPH code named DualSPHysics [2] that takes advantage of the rising new technology of the Graphic Processor Units (GPUs).

2 DualSPHysics

DualSPHysics is an open-source code developed by the University of Vigo (Spain) and the University of Manchester (UK) in collaboration with experts from all around the globe that can be freely downloaded from www.dual.sphysics.org. This project started with the need of improving the performance of SPH simulations with the use of High Performance Computing (HPC), and more precisely GPU devices. The GPU computing accelerates the serial codes by up to two orders of magnitude. DualSPHysics has proven its outstanding performance, reaching limits like being able to simulate more than 10^9 particles using 128 GPUs with an efficiency close to 100 % [4].

For multiphase flow simulations with the DualSPHysics code, we have implemented different formulation of the momentum equation coupled to the continuity and diffusion equations.

3 Implementation on GPU

Large simulations can be achieved with the promising GPU technology for problems that previously required CPU-based high performance computing (HPC). Moreover, the coming out of languages such as the Compute Unified Device Architecture (CUDA) made possible programming GPUs for general purpose applications. In the particular case of SPH, the first implementation of the method on GPUs were carried out by [8, 9].

The DualSPHysics governing equations are presented in Eqs. (1–5). The Eq. (1) was changed for Eq. (4) to model multiphase flows properly [1]. The equations can be written in the form

$$\frac{dv_a}{dt} = -\sum_b m_b \left(\frac{P_b}{\rho_b^2} + \frac{P_a}{\rho_a^2} + \Pi \right) \nabla_a W_{ab} + g, \tag{1}$$

$$\frac{d\rho_a}{dt} = \sum_b m_b v_{ab} \nabla_a W_{ab}, \tag{2}$$

$$P = B\left[\left(\frac{\rho}{\rho_0}\right)^{\gamma} - 1\right], \tag{3}$$

$$\frac{dv_a}{dt} = -\sum_b m_b\left(\frac{P_a + P_b}{\rho_a\rho_b} + \Pi\right)\nabla_a W_{ab} + g, \tag{4}$$

$$\frac{dr_a}{dt} = v_a + \varepsilon\sum_b \frac{m_b}{\rho_{ab}} v_{ab} W_{ab}, \tag{5}$$

where v is velocity, t is time, m is mass, P is pressure, ρ is density, Π is the viscous term, ∇W is the gradient of the kernel, g is the acceleration of gravity, B is a constant related with the velocity of sound, r is the position of the particle, $\gamma = 7$ and $\varepsilon = 0.3$.

For simulating dispersion by convection and diffusion we implemented the following equation [14]

$$\frac{DC_a}{Dt} = \sum_b^n \frac{(m_b\rho_a D_a + m_a\rho_b D_b)}{\rho_a\rho_b}\frac{r_{ab}\cdot\nabla_a W_{ab}}{r_{ab}^2 + \eta^2}C_{ab}, \tag{6}$$

where C is the concentration, D is the diffusion coefficient, $\eta^2 = 0.001h^2$, and h is the smoothing length.

The Eq. (6) was implemented using both the C ++ and CUDA programming languages. The program can then be executed either in the CPU or in the GPU. The code is organized in three main stages that are repeated each time step: 1 creating a neighbor list; 2 computing particle interactions from the momentum, concentration and continuity conservation equations, and 3 time integration.

The Eq. (6) was implemented in the most efficient option, according to [5], where all data is kept in the memory of the GPU where all process are parallelized and only output data requires transfers from the GPU to the CPU. The flow diagram is shown in Fig. 1.

Fig. 1. Flow diagram of GPU simulations.

The system update can be parallelized easily on the GPU. An example of the pseudocode, where the concentration values are update, is shown below.

```
template<...> __global__ void KerComputeStepVerlet (...)
{
        Unsigned        p=blockIdx.y*gridDim.x*blockDim.x        +
        blockIdx.x*blockDim.x + threadIdx.x;
        if(p<n){
                conc1[p] +=(0.5f*dt)*(dcdtm11[p] +dcdt1[p]);
                conc2[p] +=(0.5f*dt)*(dcdtm12[p]+dcdtr2[p]);
                conc3[p] +=(0.5f*dt)*(dcdtm13[p]+dcdtr3[p]);
        }
}
```

4   Validation Test

The validation test refers to a finite vertical strip of pollution tracer within a rectangular water tank. The concentration initial distribution is shown in Fig. 2 (left panel). The pollutant has an initial constant concentration $C_0 = 1$ kg/m^3 extending from $x_1 = 0.44$ m to $x_2 = 0.55$ m, and the initial water concentration is set equal to 0. The diffusion coefficient $\mathcal{D}$ is equal to 10^{-4} m^2/s.

Referring to the X-position ($x_0 = 0.5$ m) of the pollutant, the time evolution of the concentration field along the x coordinate using the SPH models is compared with the following analytical solution (Eqs. 8 and 9) derived from the classical diffusion equation (Eq. 7) as a function of the length and the initial constant distribution of the contaminant concentration, which can be written in the form

$$\frac{DC}{Dt} = \mathcal{D}\nabla^2 C \tag{7}$$

$$C(x,t) = \frac{C_0}{2} erfc\left(\frac{x_1 - x}{\sqrt{4\mathcal{D}t}}\right) for\, x \leq x_0 \tag{8}$$

$$C(x,t) = \frac{C_0}{2} erfc\left(\frac{x - x_2}{\sqrt{4\mathcal{D}t}}\right) for\, x > x_0 \tag{9}$$

where C is the concentration, C_0 is the initial concentration, $\mathcal{D}$ is the diffusion coefficient, x is the coordinate in the XY plane, and t is time.

In Fig. 2 (middle and right) we compare the analytical and SPH results for 1 and 2 s after the start of the simulation.

The SPH results show good agreement with the analytical solution. However, a convergence test was performed to ensure that the SPH results with different resolutions are still in agreement with the analytical solution. The validation test was simulated with different resolutions (number of particles) which was set as a function of the initial inter-particle spacing (dp).

Figure 3 shows the SPH results for the convergence test. The SPH results increase the agreement when the dp decreases, the better agreement was obtained with dp = 1 mm. This means that the error between the SPH results and the analytical solution decline with a better resolution. Nevertheless, a relative error between results was calculated.

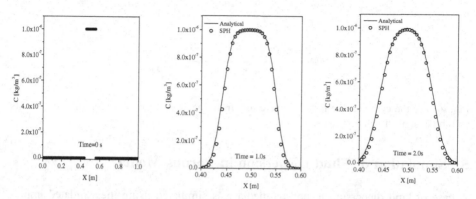

Fig. 2. Initial distribution of concentration in the validation test (left panel). SPH results are compared with the analytical solution for 1 s (middle panel) and 2 s (right panel).

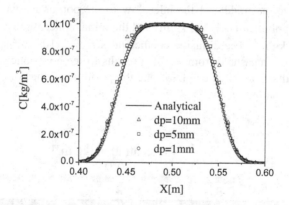

Fig. 3. Results from the convergence test with dp = : 10 mm, 5 mm 1 mm.

The relative error was calculated using the following equation [15]

$$\pounds = \sqrt{\frac{\sum\left(C_{SPH} - C_{analytical}\right)^2}{\sum C_{analytical}^2}},$$ (10)

where $\pounds$ is the relative error, C_{SPH} is the concentration from the SPH results and $C_{analytical}$ is the concentration from the analytical solution. As expected, the relative error decreases when the resolution increases. The Fig. 4 shows the relative error for different values of dp.

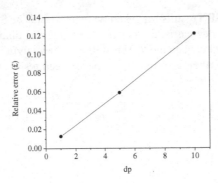

Fig. 4. For the convergence test, relative errors from the comparison between the SPH results and the analytical solution.

5 Simulation of Fluid Dispersion in Porous Media

A case of fluid dispersion in porous media was simulated using the validated implementations in DualSPHysics. In this case the porous media with a porosity of 0.5 was represented with circles of *radius* $= 0.4$ mm in a diagonal mesh. Fluid particles are moved by a piston with a constant velocity $v_x = 2$ mm/s. Fluid particles with a miscible pollutant are set at the middle of the inlet flow to the porous media, the initial concentration of the pollutant is $C_0 = 1$ kg/m^3 and the initial concentration of the saturated fluid is $C_f = 0.8$ kg/m^3. The diffusion coefficient is $D = 1x10^{-8}$ m^2/s. Three concentration profiles were measured from the SPH results to see how concentration changes in the porous media. The initial condition and the positions of the concentration profile measurements are shown in Fig. 5.

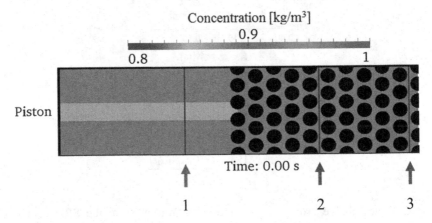

Fig. 5. Initial condition of the case of fluid dispersion in porous media. The arrows indicate the location of the concentration profile measurements.

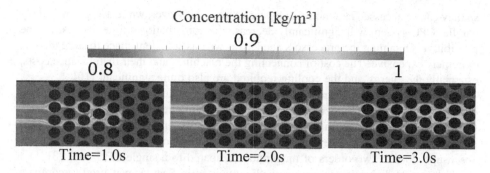

Fig. 6. Numerical solution of dispersion in porous media at 1, 2 and 3 s.

SPH results of the dispersion in porous media at different times are shown in Fig. 6. The results illustrate the pollutant dispersion in the porous media. From this type of simulations we can evaluate processes where the flow and dispersion in porous media have an important role.

The concentration profiles for the time of 3 s are shown in Fig. 7 for the different zones of the porous media shown in Fig. 5. The concentration profiles display the fluid dispersion change due to the porous media. The profile 1 shows the dispersion in the zone free of porous media. The profiles 2 and 3 shows how the dispersion changes when the pollutant flow through the porous media.

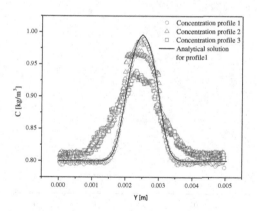

Fig. 7. Concentration profiles at 3 s for the sites shown in Fig. 5.

6   Run Time Comparisons

The first possible step in incorporating some form of parallelism is to fully use the cores available in a system. Most computer processors today possesses some degree of parallelism with the system memory available to each core simultaneously, so with parallel computing the processing power of each core can be assigned to creating multiple threads executing the code in parallel. The data are then uploaded in the shared memory so they can be accessed and modified by each thread. However, while using a massively parallel CPU system will significantly decrease the computational time, its cost can be prohibitive. Obtaining the processors needed, as well as sufficient space to store them is extremely expensive. The cost of connecting the machines and their maintenance costs, especially the energy and the cooling required are also quite significant [10].

GPUs are specialized hardware designed to process large quantities of data to be displayed on computer screens in real time. The unique architecture of GPUs makes them particularly suitable for computationally intensive simulations using Lagrangian methods such as SPH. The large number of multi-processors on a GPU enables speed-ups close to two orders of magnitude compared to a single CPU code [3].

The case of dispersion in porous media, reported in Sect. 5, was used to compare the runtime simulation using a CPU or GPU processor. The case was performed with different resolutions to evaluate the speed of simulations as function of the number of particles. The runtime comparison for simulations using a CPU or GPU processor are shown in Fig. 8. The difference in the simulation times for this case become important when the number of particles is higher than 2×10^5. The simulations were performed using a CPU Intel Core i7 with 8 cores and a GPU Titan Black with 2880 cores. The best speedup obtained in the simulation with 1 million of particles was about 25 times faster in the GPU than the CPU.

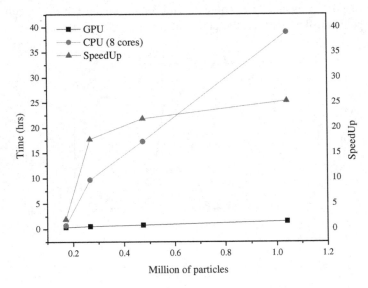

Fig. 8. Computational time for different number of particles using different units of processing.

7   Conclusions

The equation of diffusion implemented in DualSPHysics was tested to evaluate the accuracy of the simulations. Numerical results show good accuracy and convergence with different resolutions.

Simulations with high resolutions have better accuracy. This results evidence the necessity of the GPU's to simulate cases with high resolution in practical times.

The use of GPUs reduce the high resolution simulation computational time. The GPU used in this work was about 25 times faster than the CPU simulating 1 million of particles.

DualSPHysics has shown good accuracy at a reasonable computational time using GPU computing and provides reliable results according to the validation.

This new implementation allows the study of different options in order to choose the most optimal approach in fields like pollutant transport, mobile reactive beds, oil recovery, etc.

Acknowledgements. C.E.A.R. is grateful to CONACyT for a PhD grant. This work was partially supported by ABACUS, CONACyT grant EDOMEX-2011-C01-165873. The calculations for this paper were performed in the Cinvestav-Abacus supercomputer.

References

1. Colagrossi, A., Landrini, M.: Numerical simulation of interfacial flows by smoothed particle hydrodynamics. J. Comput. Phys. **191**, 448–475 (2003)
2. Crespo, A.J.C., Domínguez, J.M., Rogers, B.D., Gómez-Gesteira, M., Longshawb, S., Canelas, R., Vacondio, R., Barreiro, A., García-Feal, O.: DualSPHysics: open-source parallel CFD solver based on smoothed particle hydrodynamics (SPH). Comput. Phys. Commun. **187**, 204–216 (2015)
3. Crespo, A.J.C., Dominguez, J.M., Barreiro, A., Gomez-Gesteira, M., Rogers, B.D.: GPUs, a new tool of acceleration in CFD: efficiency and reliability on smoothed particle hydro dynamics methods. Plos One **6**, e20685 (2011)
4. Domínguez, J.M., Crespo, A.J.C., Valdez-Balderas, D., Rogers, B.D., Gómez-Gesteira, M.: New multi-GPU implementation for smoothed particle hydrodynamics on heterogeneous clusters. Comput. Phys. Commun. **184**, 1848–1860 (2013). doi:10.1016/j.cpc.2013.03.008
5. Domínguez, J.M., Crespo, A.J.C., Gómez-Gesteira, M.: Optimization strategies for CPU and GPU implementations of a smoothed particle hydrodynamics method. Comput. Phys. Commun. **184**, 617–627 (2013). doi:10.1016/j.cpc.2012.10.015
6. Gingold, R.A., Monaghan, J.J.: Smoothed particle hydrodynamics: theory and application to non- spherical stars. Mon. Not. R. Astr. Soc. **181**, 375–389 (1977)
7. Gómez-Gesteira, M., Rogers, B.D., Crespo, A.J.C., Dalrymple, R.A., Narayanaswamy, M., Domínguez, J.M.: SPHysics - development of a free-surface fluid solver- Part 1: theory and formulations. Comput. Geosci. **48**, 289–299 (2012)
8. Harada, T., Koshizuka, S., Kawaguchi, Y.: Smoothed particle hydrodynamics on GPUs. In: Proceedings of Computer Graphics International, pp. 63–70 (2007)
9. Kolb, A., Cuntz, N.: Dynamic particle coupling for GPU-based fluid simulation. In: 18th Symposium on Simulation Technique, Erlangen, Germany (2005)
10. Mcintosh-Smith, S., Wilson, T., Ibarra, A.A., Crisp, J., Sessions, R.B.: Benchmarking energy efficiency power costs and carbon emissions on heterogeneous systems. Comput. J. **55**, 192–205 (2012)
11. Sigalotti, L.D., Klapp, J.: Collapse and fragmentation of molecular cloud cores. Int. J. Mod. Phys. D. **10**, 115–211 (2001)

12. Sigalotti, L.D.G., Troconis, J., Sira, E., Peña-Polo, F., Klapp, J.: Diffuse-interface modeling of liquid-vapor coexistence in equilibrium drops using smoothed particle hydrodynamics. Phys. Rev. E **90**(1), 013021 (2014). doi:10.1103/PhysRevE.90.013021
13. Sigalotti, L.D.G., Troconis, J., Sira, E., Peña-Polo, F., Klapp, J.: SPH simulations of evaporation and explosive boiling of liquid drops in microgravity. Phys. Rev. E **92**, 013021 (2015). doi:10.1103/PhysRevE.92.013021
14. Tartakovsky, A.M., Meakin, P.: Pore-scale modeling of immiscible and miscible fluid flows using smoothed particle hydrodynamics. Adv. Water Resour. **29**(10), 1464–1478 (2006)
15. Xenakis, A.M., Lind, S.J., Stansby, P.K., Rogers, B.D.: An ISPH scheme with shifting for Newtonian and non-Newtonian multi-phase flows. In: Proceedings of the 10th International SPHERIC Workshop, pp. 84–91 (2015)

Numerical Modelling of the Laguna Verde Nuclear Power Station Thermal Plume Discharge to the Sea

Hermilo Ramírez-León[1]([envelope]), Héctor Barrios-Piña[2],
Franklin Torres-Bejarano[3], Abraham Cuevas-Otero[4],
and Clemente Rodríguez-Cuevas[5]

[1] Instituto Mexicano del Petróleo, Mexico City, Mexico
hrleon@imp.mx
[2] Tecnologico de Monterrey, Guadalajara, Mexico
hector.barrios@itesm.mx
[3] Universidad de la Costa, Barranquilla, Colombia
ftorres4@cuc.edu.co
[4] DEPFI-UNAM, Mexico City, Mexico
abraham.esiaz@gmail.com
[5] Faculty of Engineering, UASLP, San Luis Potosí, Mexico
clemente.rodriguez@uaslp.mx

Abstract. The coastal water pollution is a problem that responds to the over-population, natural resources exploitation and the increase of technologic development; this has led to an alteration of the physical, chemical and biological parameters of both continental and coastal waters. Among the main sources of pollution are those arising from industrial activities, this is the case of the electricity generation industry which requires large volumes of water for cooling systems. This work contributes to the knowledge of the behaviour of thermal discharges into coastal waters, and it requires solving the Navier-Stokes-Reynolds equations for shallow waters, using a numerical model formerly developed; water quality equations associated are solved too. The results obtained are satisfactory, since dispersion patterns of the thermal plume are well reproduced in accordance with the patterns measured for different climate scenarios in the zone.

1 Introduction

In this paper we carried out a study of the thermal dispersion at sea by implementing a numerical model. The case study is the thermal plume of Laguna Verde Nuclear Power Station (LVNPS), located on the coast of the Gulf of Mexico (GDM), in the state of Veracruz, Mexico as shown in Fig. 1. The circulating water system of the Power Station (PS) is an open system and provides a continuous supply of cooling water to the condenser from the Gulf of Mexico. The cooling water passing it through the condenser and then discharging to the sea via Laguna Salada. The combination of a channel in Laguna Salada with a breakwater around the intake structure tries to ensure that the discharged water will have a minimal effect on the temperature of the sea water at the intake structure.

© Springer International Publishing Switzerland 2016
I. Gitler and J. Klapp (Eds.): ISUM 2015, CCIS 595, pp. 495–507, 2016.
DOI: 10.1007/978-3-319-32243-8_35

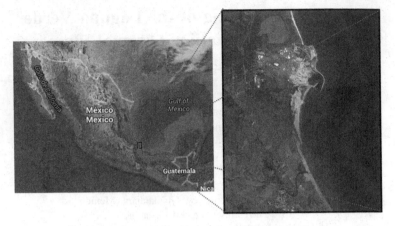

Fig. 1. Location of Laguna Verde Nuclear Power Station (LVNPS)

Thermal discharges from Power Stations into the sea at higher temperatures cause thermal pollution of water. It has been shown that a slight change in water temperature can have considerable impact on the environment. From an environmental perspective, this local variation in water temperature can significantly disturb aquatic ecosystems, causing alterations in organisms that grow there. On the other hand, from a technical-operational point of view, the problem of hot water recirculation in the PS occurs sometimes because of the wrong location of the intake of discharges, which results in a decrease in power generating capacity of the PS. Hence the need to study and monitor the dispersion of the thermal plume at sea and determine its orientation and its area of influence.

In this work, we show a very exhaustive comparison between the plume dispersion measured and the one simulated for 2012, although measurements were developed from 2011 to 2013. The use of numerical modeling to simulate the thermal plume dispersion can help to redesign the discharge structure in case of recirculating hot water to the intake and also to minimize environmental impacts. The Federal Electricity Commission of Mexico (CFE, for its acronym in Spanish) provided important information for flow and temperatures in the suction, temperatures and volumes in the discharge channel and some meteorological parameters. All this information allowed to feed the model with current information and this is reflected in the quality of the predictions, as it will be shown below.

2 Numerical Model

2.1 Governing Equations

The system of equations used to describe the velocity fields and the free surface variations are the shallow-water equations. In order to solve the equations, two approximations are used. The first one is the hydrostatic approximation (Eq. 1):

$$\frac{\partial P}{\partial z} = -\rho_0 g, \tag{1}$$

where P is the pressure (in Pa), ρ_0 is the reference density (in kg/m^3), g is the acceleration due to gravity (in m/s^2) and z denotes the reference vertical plane (in m). This approximation is valid when the horizontal length scale is much greater than the vertical length scale. This is the main condition for the shallow-water assumption. The second assumption is the Boussinesq approximation, where density is considered constant in all terms of the conservation of momentum equations with the exception of the gravitational term.

By considering the above approximations and after turbulent averaging, governing equations for the velocity U, V and W components have the following form (Eqs. 2, 3 and 4, respectively):

$$\frac{\partial U}{\partial t} + U\frac{\partial U}{\partial x} + V\frac{\partial U}{\partial y} + W\frac{\partial U}{\partial z} = -\frac{\rho g}{\rho_0}\frac{\partial \eta}{\partial x} + \frac{\partial}{\partial x}\left(2\nu_E\frac{\partial U}{\partial x}\right)$$
$$+ \frac{\partial}{\partial y}\left[\nu_E\left(\frac{\partial U}{\partial y} + \frac{\partial U}{\partial x}\right)\right] + \frac{\partial}{\partial z}\left(\nu_E\frac{\partial U}{\partial z}\right) + fV, \tag{2}$$

$$\frac{\partial V}{\partial t} + U\frac{\partial V}{\partial x} + V\frac{\partial V}{\partial y} + W\frac{\partial V}{\partial z} = -\frac{\rho g}{\rho_0}\frac{\partial \eta}{\partial y} + \frac{\partial}{\partial y}\left(2\nu_E\frac{\partial V}{\partial y}\right)$$
$$+ \frac{\partial}{\partial x}\left[\nu_E\left(\frac{\partial U}{\partial y} + \frac{\partial V}{\partial x}\right)\right] + \frac{\partial}{\partial z}\left(\nu_E\frac{\partial V}{\partial z}\right) - fU, \tag{3}$$

$$\frac{\partial W}{\partial z} = -\left(\frac{\partial U}{\partial x} + \frac{\partial V}{\partial y}\right), \tag{4}$$

where t is the time (in s), U, V and W are the time-averaged velocity components (in m/s), in the x, y and z-directions, respectively, ρ is the water density (in kg/m^3), η is the free surface elevation (in m) and ν_E is the kinematic eddy viscosity (in m^2/s) which consists of turbulent and molecular components, such that $\nu_E = \nu_t + \nu$. The parameter f is the Coriolis parameter defined by $f = 2\Omega \sin \phi$ (in s^{-1}), where Ω is the rotation rate of the Earth (7.2921×10^{-5} rad/s) and ϕ is the latitude. By integrating the continuity equation, Eq. 4, over the water depth and by using a kinematic condition at the free surface, leads to the free surface equation (Eq. 5):

$$\frac{\partial \eta}{\partial t} + \frac{\partial}{\partial x}\left(\int_{-h}^{\eta} U dz\right) + \frac{\partial}{\partial y}\left(\int_{-h}^{\eta} V dz\right) = 0, \tag{5}$$

where the water depth $h(x, y)$ and the free surface elevation $\eta(x, y)$ are measured from a reference level or from the undisturbed water surface as shown in Fig. 2.

2.2   Turbulence Modelling

The turbulent viscosity coefficient v_t is then computed through the mixing-length model given by [10], as shown in Eq. 6:

$$v_t = \left(l_h^4 \left[2\left(\frac{\partial U}{\partial x}\right)^2 + 2\left(\frac{\partial V}{\partial y}\right)^2 + \left(\frac{\partial V}{\partial x} + \frac{\partial U}{\partial y}\right)^2 \right] + l_v^4 \left[\left(\frac{\partial U}{\partial z}\right)^2 + \left(\frac{\partial V}{\partial z}\right)^2 \right] \right)^{1/2} \quad (6)$$

where the vertical length scale $l_v = \kappa(z - z_b)$ for $(z - z_b)/\delta < \lambda/\kappa$ and $l_v = \lambda\delta$ for $\lambda/\kappa < (z - z_b)/\delta < 1$, κ is the von Kármán constant typically 0.41, $(z - z_b)$ is the distance from the wall, δ is the boundary-layer thickness and λ is a constant, typically 0.09. In the case of shallow-water flows, due to a steady current, the boundary-layer thickness may be assumed to be equal to the water depth h. The horizontal length scale is usually different than the vertical length scale, and the simplest assumption is to assume direct proportionality defined by $l_h = \beta l_v$. The constant β has to be determined experimentally. For parallel flow cases (or near parallel), eddy viscosity reverts to its standard boundary-layer form. With $l_h = l_v$, it reverts to its correct mathematical three-dimensional form (with negligible vertical velocity).

2.3   Free Surface and Bottom Conditions

The shear stress at the free surface is specified by the prescribed wind stresses $\tau_{\omega x}$ and $\tau_{\omega y}$ (Eqs. 7 and 8, respectively):

$$v_t \frac{\partial U}{\partial z}\bigg|_{surface} = \tau_x^\omega, \quad (7)$$

$$v_t \frac{\partial V}{\partial z}\bigg|_{surface} = \tau_y^\omega, \quad (8)$$

where $\tau_x^\omega = C_\omega \rho_a \omega_x |\omega_x|$ and $\tau_y^\omega = C_\omega \rho_a \omega_y |\omega_y|$, ρ_a is the air density (in kg/m^3), and ω_x and ω_y are the time-averaged wind velocity components (in m/s). The wind-drag coefficient C_ω is computed by the Garratt's formula $C_\omega = (0.75 + 0.067\omega) \times 10^{-3}$, where ω is the main magnitude of the wind velocity vector at 10.0 m above the free surface.

The shear stress at the bottom is given by the bottom stress defined in terms of the velocity components by using the Manning-Chezy's formula such as:

$$v_t \frac{\partial U}{\partial z}\bigg|_{bottom} = \frac{g\sqrt{U^2 + V^2}}{Cz^2} U, \quad (9)$$

$$v_t \frac{\partial V}{\partial z}\bigg|_{bottom} = \frac{g\sqrt{U^2 + V^2}}{Cz^2} V, \quad (10)$$

where C_z is the Chezy friction coefficient (in $m^{1/2}/s$). The velocity components are taken from values of the layer adjacent to the sediment-water interface.

2.4 Transport Equations

A state equation is used to compute density variations and is defined as:

$$\rho(P, T, S) = \frac{\rho_0}{\left(1 - \frac{P}{k_P}\right)}, \tag{11}$$

where k_P is a coefficient function of pressure, temperature and salinity. The formulation to compute the value of k_P can be found in [11]. The transport equations to compute temperature and salinity fields are:

$$\frac{\partial T}{\partial t} + U\frac{\partial T}{\partial x} + V\frac{\partial T}{\partial y} + W\frac{\partial T}{\partial z} = \frac{\partial}{\partial x}\left(K\frac{\partial T}{\partial x}\right) + \frac{\partial}{\partial y}\left(K\frac{\partial T}{\partial y}\right) + \frac{\partial}{\partial z}\left(K\frac{\partial T}{\partial z}\right) + Q, \tag{12}$$

$$\frac{\partial S}{\partial t} + U\frac{\partial S}{\partial x} + V\frac{\partial S}{\partial y} + W\frac{\partial S}{\partial z} = \frac{\partial}{\partial x}\left(K\frac{\partial S}{\partial x}\right) + \frac{\partial}{\partial y}\left(K\frac{\partial S}{\partial y}\right) + \frac{\partial}{\partial z}\left(K\frac{\partial S}{\partial z}\right), \tag{13}$$

where T and S are time-averaged. The diffusion coefficient K (in m^2/s) is considered function of the turbulent viscosity as $K = v_t/Pr$, where the Prandtl number is $Pr = 0.9$.

Finally, the heat flow linearization proposed by [4] was used for the specific quantification of Q (Eq. 12), which quantifies the flow of heat between the water-air interface, with the following formulation:

$$Q = \frac{\Delta Q(\Delta A)}{\rho C_{pw}(\Delta V)} \Delta t \tag{14}$$

In summary, hydrodynamics is described by four unknowns, U, V y W and η, computed through Eqs. 2–5, respectively, and thermodynamics is defined by ρ, T and S, computed through Eqs. 12 and 13, respectively. Pressure is the hydrostatic one and can be estimated at any time by using Eq. 1.

All these equations are contained in the π-HYDRO numerical model formerly developed for this kind of industrial and environmental problems (www.pimas-consultores.com).

2.5 Numerical Solution

The numerical model is based on a second-order finite difference formulation. A spatial mesh which consists of rectangular cells with horizontal sizes Δx and Δy, and height Δz, is used. Scalars are located at the center of cells and velocity components are shifted at the middle of cell sides (staggered cell). Each cell is denoted at its center with indices i, j and k as shown in Fig. 2. The time accuracy is also second-order and the solution method is an adaptation of the semi-implicit Eulerian-Lagrangian scheme proposed by [1]. This method treats the advection and diffusion terms differently. The solution of the advection terms is given by a Lagrangian formulation through the characteristic method and the solution of the diffusion terms is obtained by an Eulerian formulation through the Adams-Bashforth scheme [3, 8].

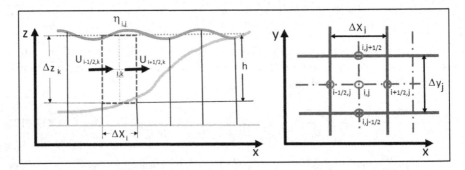

Fig. 2. Computational mesh and notation used

2.6   Numerical Model Validation

In 2008 the model developed was applied to the problem of the thermal plume dispersion of LVNPS. At that time, this model was calibrated and properly validated by means of an exhaustive work [9] for the local climatic scenarios required (dry, rainy and cold-front seasons, respectively). In Fig. 3 we show the model validation with measurements for a dry season; the comparison of the recirculation thermal plume with measurements inside of the inshore intake can be observed.

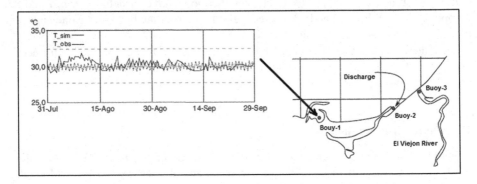

Fig. 3. Model validation obtained from Ramírez et al., 2013.

3 Thermal Plume Dispersion

3.1 Initial and Boundary Conditions

In Fig. 4 initial and boundary conditions, for the numerical simulations, are summarized. Coastal currents, oceanic temperatures and salinity where all obtained from the HYCOM oceanographic model (www.hycom.org), while the tidal cycles were generated with the aid of the CICESE software (www.cicese.edu.mx). The suction as well as the discharge flow rates, temperatures and salinity were provided by [2]. The wind patterns and atmospheric temperatures were processed from the hourly records measured and provided by [2]. The discharge of "El Viejón" river was calculated based on the corresponding hydrological study, which in turn was conducted from the analysis of the climatologic stations within the area of influence and the generation of the typical hydrographs. All of these conditions were obtained for three climatic periods in the area: dry season, rainy season and cold-front season during the years 2011, 2012 and 2013. The reader can be referred to [7] for further details about the analysis process herein described.

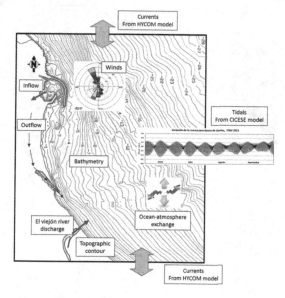

Fig. 4. Initial and boundary conditions definition

3.2 Results

Figures 5, 6 and 7 show the results obtained for the dry, rainy and cold-front seasons, respectively, during the year 2012. It can be observed that the simulated results showed good correspondence with the measured data provided by [2].

In order to quantify the recirculation of the thermal plume from the point of discharge to the suction of the LVNPS, a line following this path was defined. Then the

502   H. Ramírez-León et al.

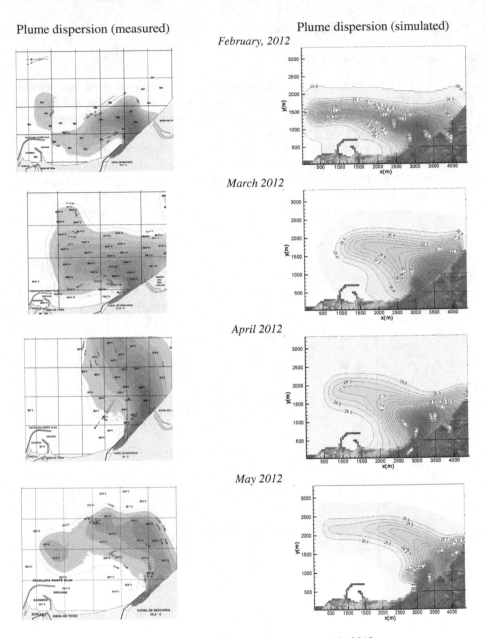

Fig. 5. Results obtained for the dry season in 2012

values for temperature were plotted along such line, at specific times of each one of the climatic scenarios simulated (see Fig. 8). The snapshots were defined by observing the evolution of both, the hydrodynamic and the temperature fields, paying special attention to those scenarios in which the thermal plume recirculates toward the intake

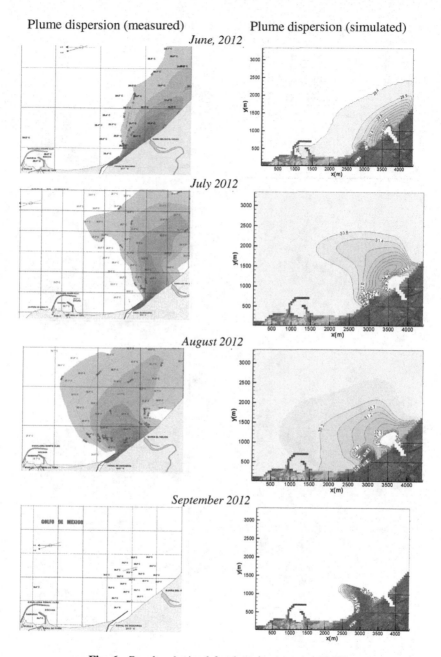

Fig. 6. Results obtained for the rainy season in 2012

structure, since this zone is the most critical operation stage of the LVNPS's cooling system. From a comparison between the three scenarios, it can be observed that the most important influence of the thermal plume takes place during the dry season,

504   H. Ramírez-León et al.

Plume dispersion (measured)   Plume dispersion (simulated)

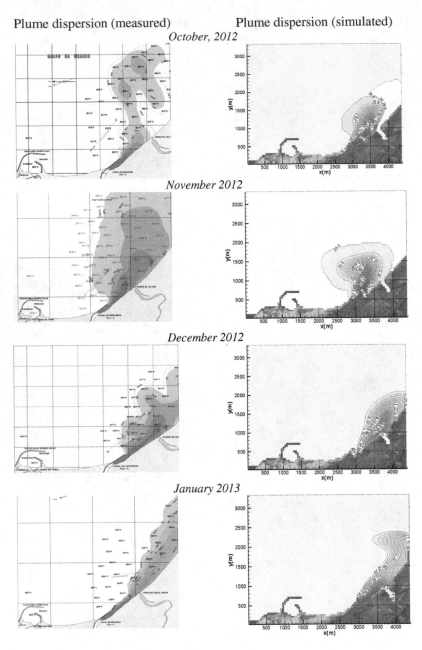

Fig. 7. Results obtained for the cold-front season in 2012

because the temperature decay only 2.3°C approximately, from the discharge to the intake. On the opposite, it was found a less influence during the rainy and the cold-front seasons.

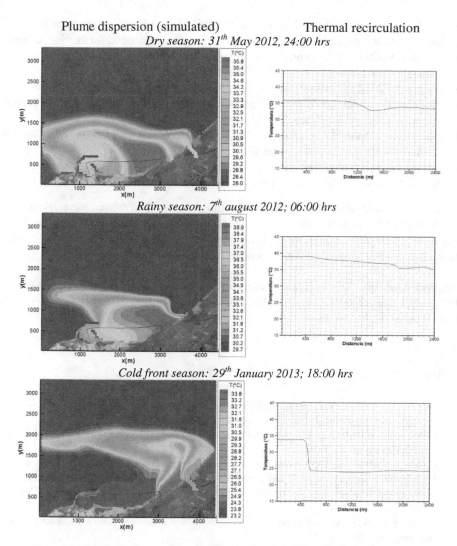

Fig. 8. Critical cases of recirculating thermal plume to the LVNPS

4   Conclusions

The present study shows the results of a numerical simulation conducted to study the behavior of the thermal plume discharge of the LVNPS. The study was based on available information provided by CFE, at the time it was complemented with the implementation of the HYCOM global oceanic circulation model within the domain under study. The results enable us to set the following conclusions:

- The hydrodynamics of the coastal zone in front of the LVNPS depends on the tidal patterns, so the direction and magnitude of the currents depend on the tide as well.
- The π-HYDRO model reproduces properly the behavior of the thermal plume dispersion for the different simulated scenarios.
- During the 2012 dry season, the thermal plume showed a slight tendency toward the intake work, which could alter the normal operation of the cooling system with a decrease in the performance.
- In the rainy season, the discharge of "El Viejón" river has a significant effect on the thermal plume dispersion into the sea.
- During the three years simulation period, the cold-front season is the stage in which the intake work of the LVNPS receives no influence of the discharge at all.

It's also remarkable that if the phenomena associated to waves were taken into consideration, better predictions of the thermal plume dispersion in the coastal zone might be achieved. Although these phenomena have been already studied in this area, their effect on the thermal plume dispersion has not yet been incorporated ([5, 6]).

Acknowledgements. This work was developed with the support of the Biological Institute of the National Autonomous University of Mexico, and by the Federal Electricity Commission of Mexico, who provided the plume dispersion measurements of the LVNPS.

References

1. Casulli, V., Cheng, R.T.: Semi-implicit finite difference methods for three dimensional shallow water flow. Int. J. Numer. Meth. Fluids **15**, 629–648 (1992)
2. CFE Comisión Federal de Electricidad, Departamento de Ingeniería Civil / Proyecto Laguna Verde, México D. F (2006)
3. Couder, C., Ramírez, H., Herrera, E.: Numeric optimization of the hydrodynamic model YAXUM/3D. In: Capítulo 342 Del Libro Numerical Modeling of Coupled Phenomena in Science and Engineering- Practical Uses and Examples. Publicado Por Springer Verlag (2008)
4. Haney, R.L.: Surface thermal boundary conditions for ocean circulation models. J. Phys. Oceanogr. **1**, 241–248 (1971)
5. Herrera, E., Ramirez, H.: Numerical modeling of wave phenomena (refraction diffraction) applied to breakwaters of the cooling water intake of Laguna Verde Nuclear Power Plant in Veracruz Mexico. In: Capitulo 12 del libro Numerical Modeling of Coupled Phenomena in Science and Engineering- Practical Uses and Examples. Publicado por Springer Verlag (2008)
6. Herrera-Diaz, I.E., Couder-Castañeda, C., Ramirez-Leon, H.: A fast simulation method for wave transformation processes in coastal zones. J. Appl. Res. Technol. **9**(2), 249–272 (2011)
7. PIMAS: Modelación numérica de la pluma térmica de la descarga del sistema de enfriamiento de la Central Nucleoeléctrica de Laguna Verde, Ver. Elaborado por PIMAS Proyectos de Ingeniería y Medio Ambiente S.C. para el Instituto de Biología, UNAM (2014)
8. León, H.R., Piña, H.B., Cuevas, C.R., Castañeda, C.C.: Baroclinic mathematical modeling of fresh water plumes in the interaction river-sea. Int. J. Numer. Anal. Model. **2**, 1–14 (2005)

9. Ramírez-León, H., Couder-Castañeda, C., Herrera-Díaz, I.E., Barrios-Piña, H.A.: Modelación numérica de la descarga térmica de la Central Nucleoeléctrica Laguna Verde. Revista Internacional de Métodos Numéricos para Cálculo y Diseño en Ingeniería **29**(2), 114–121 (2013)

10. Stansby, P.K.: A mixing-length model for shallow turbulent wakes. J. Fluid Mech. **495**, 369–384 (2003)

11. UNESCO: Background papers and supporting data on the international equations of state of seawater. Technical papers in marine science, vol. 38, p. 192 (1981)

Hydraulic and Environmental Design of a Constructed Wetland as a Treatment for Shrimp Aquaculture Effluents

Hermilo Ramírez-León[1](✉), Héctor Barrios-Piña[2], Abraham Cuevas-Otero[3],
Franklin Torres-Bejarano[4], and Jesús T. Ponce-Palafox[5]

[1] Instituto Mexicano del Petróleo, Mexico City, Mexico
hrleon@imp.mx
[2] Tecnologico de Monterrey, Guadalajara, Mexico
hector.barrios@itesm.mx
[3] DEPFI - UNAM, Mexico City, Mexico
abraham.esiaz@gmail.com
[4] Universidad de la Costa, Barranquilla, Colombia
ftorres4@cuc.edu.co
[5] Universidad Autónoma de Nayarit, Tepic, Nayarit, Mexico
jesus.ponce@usa.net

Abstract. Shrimp aquaculture has grown to the extent that pressure on natural ecosystems has greatly increased. The shrimp farms effluents usually discharge their wastes, with high nutrients load, into coastal water bodies without any previous treatment. This work presents a method to design a constructed wetland for handling these effluents. Our method is based on a first order equation model and a hydrodynamic numerical model as the main component for the design process. Numerical results showed consistency with the first order theory, when pollutants concentration were reduced to values accepted by the applicable regulations.

1 Introduction

In many Latin American countries, shrimp aquaculture is well known as being one of the highest boom economical activities over the last three decades. Although this activity is a significant source of employment and therefore of income in such countries, its impact on the environment is also irrefutable [8,9].

Because shrimp aquaculture is commonly developed in lowland areas, one of the main impacts of shrimp farming is precisely the destruction of mangroves and salt marshes for pond construction. Other adverse effects that can be mentioned are: eutrophication of water bodies, nutrient and organic enrichment of recipient waters resulting in accumulation of anoxic sediments, hydroperiod and salinity changes, biodiversity loss, land use changes, changes in benthic communities, etc. [4]. These in turn affect the shrimp farming productivity and in addition important ecosystems such as mangroves and estuaries, most of them protected areas. Accordingly, nowadays there are many efforts to make shrimp farming more sustainable, eco-friendly and profitable.

© Springer International Publishing Switzerland 2016
I. Gitler and J. Klapp (Eds.): ISUM 2015, CCIS 595, pp. 508–522, 2016.
DOI: 10.1007/978-3-319-32243-8_36

Some of the strategies being implemented include biological treatment, integrated management practices, biofilters, improved ponds design, enhanced residence time of water, reduction of water exchange; but the Food and Agriculture Organization of the United Nations still recognizes that increasing efficiency in resource use and minimizing adverse environmental interactions will be major goals for the next decades (FAO 2005). Proposing any alternative to mitigation involves describing in more detail the shrimp farming impact on the environment.

Intensive and semi intensive systems require fertilizers and high water exchange rates to increase their production, but these fertilizers are not absorbed entirely by the shrimp; instead, a lot of faeces are produced and shrimp pond water quality tends to deteriorate through the grow-out period, as the feeding rate increases with shrimp size and biomass. Major environmental impacts of shrimp aquaculture at the operation stage have been related to high input-high output intensive systems, including the aftermath of discharging large quantities of suspended solids and nutrients (phosphorus and nitrogen) once the harvest has been concluded.

Some research on this topic suggest that the use of mangroves and halophytes as biofilters of shrimp pond effluents is an effective tool for mitigating the impact in those regions where mangrove wetlands and appropriate conditions for halophyte plantations exist. This work is then aimed to describe the principles of computational fluid dynamics applied to a constructed wetland design as a proposal for treatment of shrimp farm effluents. A case study has been used to demonstrate the procedure [10], and its location in the State of Nayarit - Mexico is shown in Fig. 1.

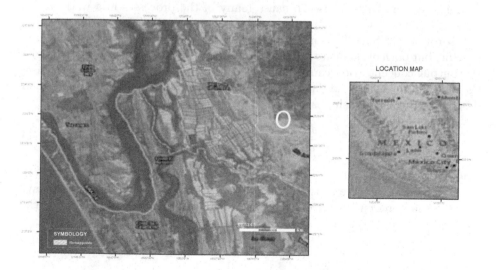

Fig. 1. Location of the shrimp farms sampled, Nayarit - Mexico

2   Environmental Design Criteria

Wetlands are terrains that are wet during part or all year round because of their location; they may be located either at topographic depressions or in areas with steep slopes and low permeability soils. The common factor in every wetland is their capacity to modify soil properties because of the chemical, physical and biological changes that occur during the flooding. This capacity is precisely what makes wetlands such unique ecosystems with higher rates of biological activity than many others among the major ecosystem groups on earth. Due to the high biological activity present in a wetland, many of the common pollutants that occur in conventional wastewaters can be transformed into harmless byproducts or essential nutrients that can be easily used by other organisms.

Currently, treatment wetlands are man-made systems that have been designed to achieve an improved treatment capacity by means of passive processes; they are the so called constructed wetlands. When compared to other treatment alternatives, constructed wetlands have proved to be a more economical option. Depending on the flow regime, there are currently three types of constructed wetlands: free water surface (FWS) wetlands, horizontal subsurface flow (HSSF) wetlands and vertical flow (VF) wetlands; each has different treatment capacities and space requirements. An HSSF wetland has been selected for the purpose of this work.

The environmental key aspects to be taken into consideration for the wetland sizing are related to the shrimp pond effluent water quality, which in turn depends on the operation conditions, more specifically whether the system is intensive, semi intensive or extensive. Among the sizing methods, first order models are still the most used because many of the processes in a wetland are basically first order, for instance mass transport, volatilization, sedimentation, and sorption [7]. Such first order models may be either area specific or volume specific, but both of them are primary input and output data based. Accordingly, the output concentration can be expressed in terms of the inlet concentration, the flow rate, and the wetland area or volume; and the differential equation describing this relationship is:

$$\frac{d\mathbf{C}}{dx} = -\frac{\mathbf{k}}{\mathbf{q}_w} * (\mathbf{C} - \mathbf{C}^*) \tag{1}$$

where C is the contaminant concentration (g/m^3), dx the wetland void fraction, k the areal removal rate constant (m/day), q_w the hydraulic load rate (m/day) and C^* the apparent background concentration (g/m^3). By solving Eq. 1, the wetland area (in this case) can be computed with Eq. 2:

$$\mathbf{A}_w = -ln[(\mathbf{C}_0 - \mathbf{C}^*)/(\mathbf{C}_i - \mathbf{C}^*)]\mathbf{q}_p\mathbf{A}_p/\mathbf{k}_z \tag{2}$$

where A_w is the wetland planar area (m^2) required to achieve a target concentration after the treatment C_0, q_p the hydraulic loading in the shrimp pond, A_p the shrimp pond planar area (m^2) and k the areal removal rate constant (m/day) for the contaminant under analysis.

At this stage, field work is essential to get all the required input data, such as total nitrogen (TN), total phosphorus (TP), biochemical oxygen demand (BOD), dissolved oxygen content (DO). These contaminants were selected because nitrogen and phosphorus are the main responsible for eutrophication in lakes. Both BOD and DO, act as indicators of the water pollution level and are commonly a regulatory parameter for discharges to water bodies; the second one is also an important participant in some contaminant removal mechanisms.

On the other hand, the target concentration after the treatment can be defined according to local or regional applicable regulations. Since the Mexican regulation is not specific about wastewater discharges to lakes or estuaries, the EPA (Environmental Protection Agency of the United States) recommended criteria for TP and TN [5] were applied to specify a numerical value of C_0 to be introduced in Eq. 2.

The wetland area was computed with Eq. 2 for the two pollutants (nitrogen and phosphorus). Finally, the two values were compared and the largest was selected, as defined by the phosphorus degradation. Once the wetland area was computed, a channel-wetland of 240 m length and 20 m width has been considered. The channel-wetland width was set according to the site conditions and the trajectory of it borders the shrimp ponds as shown in Fig. 2. With such design, artificial channels will drain waste water directly to the channel-wetland, to be finally disposed to local water reservoirs.

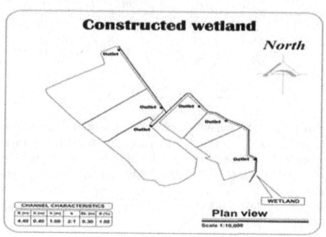

Fig. 2. Scheme of a constructed wetland system

3   Hydraulic Design Criteria

In Sect. 2 all the environmental criteria for the wetland sizing were presented using a first-order model approach (K-C*). However, this technique fails to address significant aspects of wetland performance, including effects of hydraulics [7]. Evidently, highly efficient wetlands cannot be designed if a better understanding of the governing processes in these systems is not achieved first.

This, coupled with the increasing application of constructed wetlands and increasingly strict water quality standards is a sufficient reason for developing better design tools. In that score, a depth averaged hydrodynamic model coupled with a water quality module have been used to study the wetland hydraulics.

3.1   Governing Equations

The hydrodynamic model π - **HYDRO** calculates the velocity fields using the Reynolds-Averaged Navier-Stokes equations for shallow water flows. But the presence of vegetation in a wetland has significant effects on flow and causes difficulties in hydraulic design, therefore a correction term is considered in the velocity equations in order to characterize the shear stress due to that presence [3]. After turbulent averaging, the governing equations for the velocity components have the following form:

$$\frac{\partial U}{\partial t} + U\frac{\partial U}{\partial x} + V\frac{\partial U}{\partial y} + W\frac{\partial U}{\partial z} = -\frac{\rho g}{\rho_0}\frac{\partial \eta}{\partial x} + \frac{\partial}{\partial x}\left(2\nu_E \frac{\partial U}{\partial x}\right)$$
$$+ \frac{\partial}{\partial y}\left[\nu_E\left(\frac{\partial U}{\partial y} + \frac{\partial V}{\partial x}\right)\right] + \frac{\partial}{\partial z}\left(\nu_E \frac{\partial U}{\partial z}\right) - \frac{1}{\rho_0}\frac{\tau_x^v}{\Delta z}, \qquad (3)$$

$$\frac{\partial V}{\partial t} + U\frac{\partial V}{\partial x} + V\frac{\partial V}{\partial y} + W\frac{\partial V}{\partial z} = -\frac{\rho g}{\rho_0}\frac{\partial \eta}{\partial y} + \frac{\partial}{\partial y}\left(2\nu_E \frac{\partial V}{\partial y}\right)$$
$$+ \frac{\partial}{\partial x}\left[\nu_E\left(\frac{\partial U}{\partial y} + \frac{\partial V}{\partial x}\right)\right] + \frac{\partial}{\partial z}\left(\nu_E \frac{\partial V}{\partial z}\right) - \frac{1}{\rho_0}\frac{\tau_y^v}{\Delta z}, \qquad (4)$$

$$\frac{\partial W}{\partial z} = -\left(\frac{\partial U}{\partial x} + \frac{\partial V}{\partial y}\right), \qquad (5)$$

where U, V and W are the mean velocity components in the x, y and z directions, respectively (m/s); g is the acceleration due to gravity (m/s^2); ρ is the water density (kg/m^3); ρ_0 is the water reference density (kg/m^3); η is the free surface elevation (m); ν_E is the kinematic eddy viscosity (m^2/s), which consists of turbulent and molecular components, such that $\nu_E = \nu_t + \nu$; Δz is the height of the vegetation layer (m); and τ_x^v and τ_y^v are the vegetation shear stresses in the x and y directions, respectively (N/m^2).

By integrating the continuity equation (Eq. 5) over the water depth, and by using a kinematic condition at the free surface, the equation used to calculate the free surface elevation is:

$$\frac{\partial \eta}{\partial t} = -\frac{\partial}{\partial x}\left(\int_{-h}^{\eta} U\,dz\right) - \frac{\partial}{\partial y}\left(\int_{-h}^{\eta} V\,dz\right), \qquad (6)$$

where $h(x,y)$ is the water depth (m).

In Eqs. 3 and 4, the latter terms characterize the shear stress due to vegetation, which causes a decrease in the velocity field. These terms are neglected in regions without vegetation.

3.2   Turbulence Modeling

The turbulence effects were accounted by the simple two-layer mixing-length
model presented by [11]. The defining characteristic of this model is that the horizontal mixing length is explicitly made a multiple of the vertical mixing length
within a general three-dimensional eddy-viscosity formulation. This means that
the horizontal mixing length and associated strain rates determine the magnitude of the eddy-viscosity, which determines the degree of vertical mixing. The
turbulent viscosity coefficient ν_t is then computed by means of the following
mixing-length model:

$$\nu_t = \left\{ l_h^4 \left[2 \left(\frac{\partial U}{\partial x} \right)^2 + 2 \left(\frac{\partial V}{\partial y} \right)^2 + \left(\frac{\partial V}{\partial x} + \frac{\partial U}{\partial y} \right)^2 \right] \right.$$
$$\left. + l_v^4 \left[\left(\frac{\partial U}{\partial z} \right)^2 + \left(\frac{\partial V}{\partial z} \right)^2 \right] \right\}^{1/2}, \tag{7}$$

where the vertical length scale $l_v = \kappa(z - z_b)$ for $(z - z_b)/\delta < \lambda/\kappa$, and $l_v = \lambda\delta$
for $\lambda/\kappa < (z - z_b)/\delta < 1$; κ is the von Kármán constant, typically 0.41; $(z - z_b)$ is
the distance from the wall; δ is the boundary-layer thickness; and λ is a constant,
typically 0.09 [3]. In the case of shallow-water flows, due to the steady current,
the boundary-layer thickness may be assumed to be equal to the water depth
h. The horizontal length scale is usually different from the vertical length scale,
and the simplest assumption is direct proportionality defined by $l_h = \beta l_v$. The
constant β must be determined experimentally. For parallel or near-parallel flow
cases, eddy viscosity reverts to its standard boundary-layer form. With $l_h = l_v$,
it reverts to its correct mathematical three-dimensional form (with negligible
vertical velocity).

3.3   Vegetation Shear Stress

When vegetation is present in the flow, the bottom stress in terms of the shear
law is defined, in the x and y directions, as:

$$\tau_x^b = \rho_0 C_D^b U \sqrt{U^2 + V^2}, \tag{8}$$

$$\tau_y^b = \rho_0 C_D^b V \sqrt{U^2 + V^2}, \tag{9}$$

where C_D^b is the bottom stress coefficient, which is a function of the bottom
relative roughness k_s/h and the Reynolds number, (Re), as:

$$C_D^b = \begin{cases} 0.2044 \left\{ \log \left[1.72/\,\text{Re} + (k_s/14.8h)^{1.11} \right] \right\}^2 & \text{if } k_s/h < 0.2. \\ 1.56 x 10^{-2} \, (k_s/h)^{\frac{1}{3}} & \text{if } k_s/h \geq 0.2. \end{cases} \tag{10}$$

Equation 10 is taken from [1]. If the bottom roughness, k_s, is known in terms of
the Manning coefficient, n, the following definition is used:

$$k_s = 0.3048 \, (n/0.031)^6. \tag{11}$$

The shear stress caused by the presence of vegetation is given by [3]:

$$\tau_x^v = \frac{A_x M C_D^v}{2} \rho_0 U \sqrt{U^2 + V^2} = \left(\frac{U^*}{U}\right)^2 \rho_0 U \sqrt{U^2 + V^2}, \tag{12}$$

$$\tau_y^v = \frac{A_y M C_D^v}{2} \rho_0 V \sqrt{U^2 + V^2} = \left(\frac{V^*}{V}\right)^2 \rho_0 V \sqrt{U^2 + V^2}. \tag{13}$$

where C_D^v is the vegetation stress coefficient; M is the vegetation density per unit area (m^{-2}); U^* and V^* are the shear velocity (m/s) in the x and y directions, respectively; and A_x and A_y are the effective plant blocking areas (m^2) in the x and y directions, respectively. For a two-dimensional simulation, the blocking areas of a plant are approximated by the product of the undeflected plant height and the effective width of the plant.

3.4 Numerical Model

In order to achieve good accuracy in the velocity calculation and to consider different vegetation heights, a multilayer model-based approach is used. Figure 3 depicts how the numerical model considers different vegetation heights within the water. A spatial mesh, which consists of rectangular cells with horizontal sizes Δx and Δy and height Δz, is used. Scalars are located at the center of cells, and velocity components are shifted to the center of cell edges. Each cell's center position is described using i, j and k. The computational mesh is shown in Fig. 4.

The numerical model is based on a second-order finite difference formulation. The time accuracy is also second-order, and the solution method is an adaptation of the semi-implicit Eulerian-Lagrangian scheme proposed by [2]. This method treats the advection and diffusion terms differently. The solution of the advection terms is given by a Lagrangian formulation through the characteristic method, and the solution of the diffusion terms is given by an Eulerian

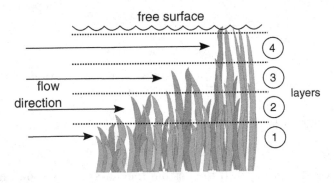

Fig. 3. The multi-layer approach in the presence of vegetation. An example showing four layers and different plant heights (taken from [3])

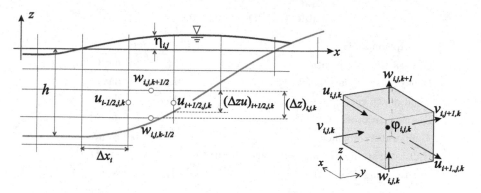

Fig. 4. Computational mesh and notation used, where φ represents a scalar quantity (taken from [3])

formulation through the Adams-Bashforth scheme. In the Lagrangian scheme of the advection terms the total derivative for velocity is used, providing a low numerical diffusivity and an unrestricted Courant condition. Advection accuracy is also known to be vital for realistic prediction of recirculating flows and must be second-order. These terms are treated explicitly and to maintain second-order temporal accuracy, a second-order interpolation formula has been chosen. In a one-dimensional case the interpolation gives:

$$U_{i-a}^n = \left(1 - p^2\right) U_i^n + \left(0.5p^2 + 0.5p\right) U_{i-1}^n + \left(0.5p^2 - 0.5p\right) U_{i+1}^n, \qquad (14)$$

where p is the Courant number. Vertical diffusion is treated semi-implicitly with first-order accuracy to enhance stability, and hence to get an overall robust scheme. The interested reader is referred to [3] for further details of the numerical model.

3.5 Water Quality Module

Conservation of mass for a chemical that is transported yields the Advection Reaction Dispersion (ARD) Eq. (15), which is the governing equation for the water quality module π-**WQ**. Once the hydrodynamics has been solved, the results are used as inputs to solve the transport equation for all the contaminants under study. As mentioned in Sect. 2, the chemical - biological variables simulated by the model are TN, TP, BOD and DO. π-**WQ** can be operated at various levels of complexity to simulate some or all of these variables and their interactions, while solving a state equation for temperature and salinity, since both have high influence in the mentioned processes.

$$\underbrace{\frac{\partial \mathbf{C}}{\partial t}}_{Temporal\ term} + \underbrace{\mathbf{U}\frac{\partial \mathbf{C}}{\partial x} + \mathbf{V}\frac{\partial \mathbf{C}}{\partial x}}_{Advection} = \underbrace{\frac{\partial}{\partial x}\left(\mathbf{E}_x \frac{\partial^2 \mathbf{C}}{\partial x^2}\right) + \frac{\partial}{\partial y}\left(\mathbf{E}_y \frac{\partial^2 \mathbf{C}}{\partial y^2}\right)}_{Dispersion} \pm \underbrace{\Gamma_c}_{Reaction}$$

$$(15)$$

Table 1. BOD reaction terms

Description	Notation	Units
Oxygen to carbon ratio	a_{OC}	mg O/mg C
Deoxygenation rate @ 20°	k_D	day^{-1}
Algal death rate	$k_1 D$	day^{-1}
Denitrification rate @ 20°	k_{2D}	day^{-1}
Temperature coefficient	Θ_D, Θ_{2D}	None
Half saturation constant for oxygen limitation	K_{BOD}	mg O_2/L
Fraction dissolved CBOD	f_{D5}	None
Organic matter settling velocity	V_{s3}	m/day

where C is concentration in water; E_h and E_v are the horizontal and vertical diffusion coefficient, respectively; and Γ_c is the reaction term. First, advective and diffusive transport are calculated, and then all the equilibrium and kinetically controlled chemical reactions.

The reaction term is specific for each contaminant or substance, and its modeling can be as complex as the biological - chemical - physical phenomena desired to consider for characterization. For instance Eqs. 17–20 are all the reaction term for the nitrogen cycle [12], four nitrogen variables are modeled: phytoplankton nitrogen, organic nitrogen, ammonia and nitrate; while Eq. 16 is the reaction term for the BOD. Different complexity levels can be distinguished from one another, and similarly, equations for all the state variables are solved.

$$\Gamma_{BOD} = \frac{d(BOD)}{dt} = \underbrace{a_{OC} \times k_{1D} \times N_1}_{death} + \underbrace{k_D \, \Theta_D^{(T-20)} \left(\frac{DO}{K_{BOD} + DO} \right) BOD}_{oxidation}$$

$$- \underbrace{\frac{V_{s3}(1 - f_{D5})}{D} BOD}_{settling} - \underbrace{\frac{5}{4}\frac{32}{14} k_{2D} \, \Theta_{2D}^{(T-20)} \left(\frac{K_{NO_3}}{K_{NO_3} + DO} \right) N_4}_{denitrification} \qquad (16)$$

where terms are as defined in Table 1.

$$\Gamma_{N_1} = \frac{d(N_1 a_{NC})}{dt} = \underbrace{G_{P1} \times a_{NC} \times N_1}_{growth} - \underbrace{D_{P1} \times a_{NC} \times N_1}_{death} - \underbrace{\frac{V_{s4}}{D} \times a_{NC} \times N_1}_{settling} \qquad (17)$$

$$\Gamma_{N_2} = \frac{d(N_2)}{dt} = \underbrace{D_{P1} \times a_{NC} \times f_{ON} \times N_1}_{death} - \underbrace{k_{71} \Theta_{71}^{(T-20)} \left(\frac{N_1}{K_{mpc} + N_1} \right) N_2}_{mineralization}$$

$$- \underbrace{\frac{V_{s3}(1 - f_{D7})}{D} N_2}_{settling} + \underbrace{K_{RON} \times a_{NC} \times C_{PR}}_{macrophytes\ death} \qquad (18)$$

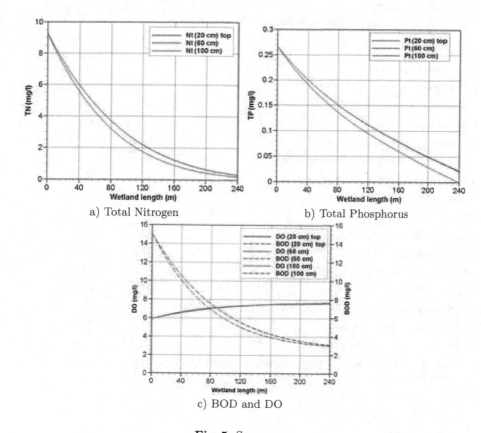

a) Total Nitrogen

b) Total Phosphorus

c) BOD and DO

Fig. 5. Sag curves

$$\Gamma_{N3} = \underbrace{k_{71}\Theta_{71}^{(T-20)}\left(\frac{N_1}{K_{mpc}+N_1}\right)N_2}_{mineralization} - \underbrace{G_{P1}\times a_{NC}\times P_{NH_3}\times N_1}_{growth}$$

$$-\underbrace{k_{12}\Theta_{12}^{(T-20)}\left(\frac{DO}{K_{NIT}+DO}\right)N_3}_{nitrification} + \underbrace{D_{P1}\times N_1 \times a_{NC}\times(1-f_{ON})}_{death} - \underbrace{K_{UAN}}_{macrophytes\ absorption}$$

$$(19)$$

$$\Gamma_{N4} = \frac{d(N_4)}{dt} = \underbrace{k_{12}\Theta_{12}^{T-20}\left(\frac{DO}{K_{NIT}+DO}\right)N_3}_{nitrification} - \underbrace{G_{P1}(1-P_{NH_3})N_1 \times a_{NC}}_{growth}$$

$$-\underbrace{k_{12}\Theta_{12}^{(T-20)}\left(\frac{K_{NO_3}}{K_{NO_3}+DO}\right)N_4}_{denitrification}$$ $$(20)$$

where terms are as defined in Table 2.

Table 2. Nitrogen reaction terms

Description	Notation	Units
Phytoplankton nitrogen	N_1	mg N/L
Organic nitrogen	N_2	mg N/L
Ammonia nitrogen	N_3	mg N/L
Nitrate nitrogen	N_4	mg N/L
Nitrogen to carbon ratio	a_{NC}	mg N/mg C
Organic nitrogen mineralization @ 20°	k_{71}	None
Temperature coefficient	Θ_{71}, Θ_{12}	None
Temperature	T	° C
Nitrification rate @ 20°	k_{12}	day^{-1}
Phytoplankton growth rate	G_{P1}	day$_{-1}$
Phytoplankton loss rate	D_{P1}	day$_{-1}$
Algal settling velocity	V_{s4}	m/day
Segment depth	D	m
Fraction of dead and respired phytoplankton recycled:		
to the organic nitrogen pool	f_{ON}	None
to the ammonia nitrogen pool	$(1 - f_{ON})$	None
Half saturation constant for phytoplankton limitation of phosphorus recycle	K_{mpc}	mg/L
Fraction dissolved organic nitrogen	f_{D7}	None
Macrophytes biomass in carbon units	C_{PR}	mg/L
Dissolved Oxygen	DO	mg/L
Preference for ammonia uptake term	P_{NH_3}	None
Organic matter settling velocity	V_{s3}	m/day
Half saturation constant for oxygen limitation of nitrification	K_{NIT}	mg O^2/L
Denitrification rate @ 20°	k_{2D}	day^{-1}
Michaelis constant for denitrification	K_{NO_3}	mg O$_2$/L
Absorption rate of nitrites nitrogen to the macrophytes	K_{UNN}	day^{-1}
Absorption rate of ammonia nitrogen to the macrophytes	K_{UAN}	day^{-1}

4   Results and Discussion

Decay curves for the contaminants and water quality indicators were obtained from the simulation. After the treatment, the concentration of TN and that of TP were reduced to values accepted by the applicable regulations as considered not harmful for ecosystems. The target concentration for the TN was 0.50 mg/l. Figures 5a and 6a show that concentration in the wetland decreased from an initial value of 9 mg/l to less than the desired concentration, at the outlet.

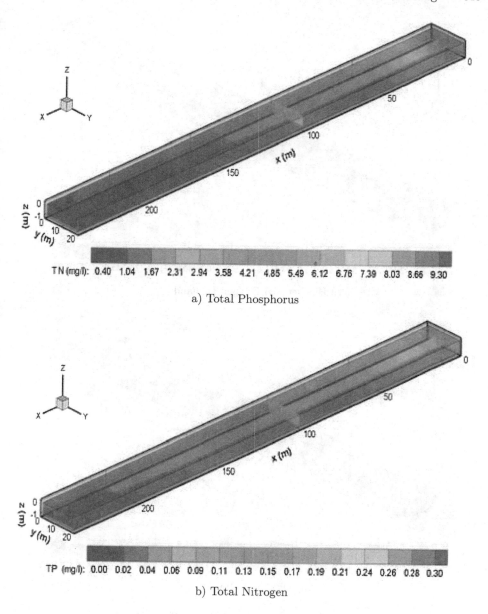

a) Total Phosphorus

b) Total Nitrogen

Fig. 6. 3D view for biodegradation in the wetland

Similarly, the initial concentration for the TP was reduced from $270\,\mu$g/l (see Figs. 5b and 6b) to a value below the target, $50\,\mu$g/l. Regarding BOD and DO, results show consistency since it is expected to have DO increased (see Figs. 5c and 7b) as the biological activity rate drops off (Figs. 5c and 7a).

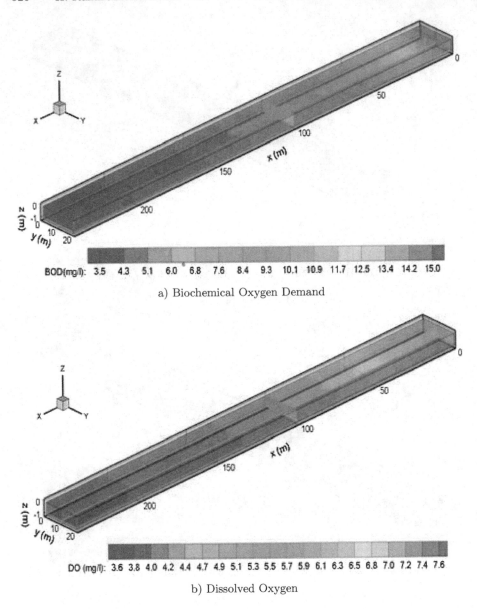

BOD(mg/l): 3.5   4.3   5.1   6.0   6.8   7.6   8.4   9.3   10.1   10.9   11.7   12.5   13.4   14.2   15.0

a) Biochemical Oxygen Demand

DO (mg/l): 3.6 3.8 4.0 4.2 4.4 4.7 4.9 5.1 5.3 5.5 5.7 5.9 6.1 6.3 6.5 6.8 7.0 7.2 7.4 7.6

b) Dissolved Oxygen

Fig. 7. 3D view for biodegradation in the wetland

It should be noted that each decay curve herein presented consists of three profiles, showing concentration against distance, at different depths. The first and the second profile (black and red lines), are located 20 cm and 60 cm below the free surface location, respectively; and they are very similar to one another. The third profile is located at 1 m depth and differences between the first two are not significant. This confirms that the shallow water approximation was appropriate since results don't exhibit a high depth dependence.

The wetland size was initially set using a first order equation to have an estimated length for the treatment, as described in Sect. 2. But the wetland modeling is based on more complex equations that not only solve the hydraulics but also all the chemical and biological cycles due to the bacteria's activity and their interaction with the vegetation. Consequently, the first calculated wetland length is validated by the hydraulic modeling performed since both methods arrive at the same result by different ways. However, the authors consider that more research is still required in the constructed wetland modeling field, especially that involving calibration of all the parameters and reaction constants.

5   Conclusions

A depth averaged hydrodynamic model coupled with a water quality module was implemented to study hydraulics within a wetland, which is a proposal for shrimp ponds effluents treatment. The model proved to be effective for simulating all the chemical and biological processes within the wetland, since all the sag curves, for the contaminants and water indicators considered, exhibited an exponential decay rate just as the literature describes them as first order ones.

References

1. Arega, F., Sanders, B.F.: Dispersion model for tidal wetlands. J. Hydraul. Eng. **130**, 739–754 (2004)
2. Casulli, V., Cheng, R.T.: Semi-implicit finite difference methods for three dimentional shallow water flow. Int. J. Numer. Methods Fluids **15**(6), 629–648 (1992)
3. Barrios-Piña, H., Ramírez-León, H., Rodríguez-Cuevas, C., Couder-Castaeda, C.: Multilayer numerical modeling of flows through vegetation using a mixing-length turbulence model. Water **6**, 2084–2103 (2014)
4. Chávez, E.A., Castro-Ortiz, J.L.: Impacto del cambio climático sobre las pesquerías de la zona de transición templado-cálida del Pacífico oriental mexicano. In: López-Martínez, J. (ed.) Variabilidad Ambiental y Pesquerías de México, pp. 70–83. National Committee of Aquaculture and Fisheries, Mexico (2008)
5. EPA: Summary Table for the nutrient criteria documents (2002)
6. FAO 2005–2015: World inventory of fisheries. Impact of aquaculture on environment. Issues Fact Sheets. Text by Uwe Barg. In: FAO Fisheries and Aquaculture Department, Rome, Updated 27 May 2005 (Cited 8 May 2015). http://www.fao.org/fishery/topic/14894/en
7. Kadlec, R.H., Wallace, S.D.: Treatment Wetlands, vol. 83, 2nd edn. CRC Press, Boca Raton (2009)
8. López-Martínez, J. (ed.): Variabilidad Ambiental y Pesquerías de México. National committee of aquaculture and fisheries, Mexico (2008)
9. Páez-Osuna, F.: Camaronicultura y Medio Ambiente, pp. 15–19. Mazatlán Academic Unit, Institute of Marine Sciences and Limnology - UNAM, Mazatlán (2001)

10. PIMAS: Diseño del sistema de canales de las granjas de cultivo acuícola para la disposición y depuración de las aguas residuales -Valle de la Urraca- Prepared by PIMAS (Proyectos de Ingeniería y Medio Ambiente S.C.) for The State of Nayarit Committee of Aquaculture Health (2014)
11. Stansby, P.K.: A mixing-length model for shallow turbulent wakes. J. Fluid Mech. **495**, 369–384 (2003). doi:10.1017/S0022112003006384
12. Wool, T.A., Ambrose, R.B., Martin, J.L., Comer, E.A.: Water quality analysis simulation program (WASP) version 6.0 draft: user's manual. US Environmental Protection Agency-Region 4, Atlanta, USA (2001)

Review of Coastal Modeling Using HPC and ADCIRC+SWAN to Predict Storm Surge, Waves and Winds, Produced by a Hurricane

Oscar Cruz-Castro[✉]

CONACyT Research Fellow, Facultad de Ingeniería,
Universidad Autónoma Del Estado de México, Toluca, Mexico
oscruc@gmail.com, ocruzca@conacyt.mx

Abstract. Scientists, engineers, universities, companies, and government agencies around the world, all of them related to coastal engineering issues, understand the importance that High Performance Computing (HPC) has brought to the way they approach larger and physically complex problems within this field. This technology is being used to predict the effects of large storms approaching the coast (near real time) and with this information help authorities to handle emergencies generated by a hurricane. This work will make a brief review, in its introduction, of the initiatives that have been developed in the Netherlands and USA by different research groups and universities to implement algorithms for storm-surge prediction. In Sect. 2 we will focus our attention on the implementation and progress made by a research group involving actors at government level, and universities to make ADCIRC a tool employed for the end mentioned above. In Sect. 3 entitled, ADCIRC+SWAN for the Mexican Pacific, we shall show how this tool is being used to hindcast storm-surge by expounding a newborn project that is being developed at UAEM to implement a similar approach for the Mexican Pacific. Finally in Sect. 4, Conclusions, we will indicate how the work developed so far has changed the perspective that we and other countries have for dealing with the effects of a hurricane impacting our coasts.

1 Introduction

Coastal modeling studies apply different algorithms to model the effects of astronomical tides, winds (wind driven setup and currents), wave setup, wave runup and atmospheric pressure changes on large bodies of water such as oceans, and coastal areas. Adding to these effects is the calculation of storm-surge (rising of coastal water levels) produced by a hurricane approaching the coast. Here the purpose of coastal modeling is to help authorities visualize high risk flooding areas caused by strong winds and waves. For them to take emergency evacuation decisions, it will require nearly real time calculations of these effects as a hurricane approaches the coast. On the other hand, simulation of scenarios related to different hurricane tracks heading to the coast, considering water levels associated to climate change, can be made beforehand within a design/risk analysis

I. Gitler and J. Klapp (Eds.): ISUM 2015, CCIS 595, pp. 523–534, 2016.
DOI: 10.1007/978-3-319-32243-8_37

approach. The aim is to determine the effects mentioned above in important areas along the coast, in order to improve our risk assessment and forecasting abilities of coastal storm surge [1]. This is one complex problem, where combination of various algorithms is required for calculating as close as possible to reality these effects, in real time and beforehand. In both cases the power required for computing is beyond the normal calculations made by workstations.

In general a coupling between a wave model and a circulation model (including a wind formulation, meteorological forcing) needs to be performed through a recasting of the wave model as a subroutine within the circulation model, or as a module with which it can interact; in order to avoid interpolation and to maximize efficiency. Moreover, the coupling of these models in a parallel fashion is visualized in order to take advantage of HPC. For the case of storm-surge prediction, there are algorithms (computational engines) developed to certain extent to work in parallel for CPU. The ones found in the literature with more impact in their applications are: Delft3D-FLOW using Delft3D-WAVE (Netherlands), FVCOM using SWAVE (USA), SELFE using WWMII (USA), and ADCIRC (USA) using SWAN (Netherlands), all of them open source algorithms.

Delft3D, developed at Delft Hydraulics, is a suite composed of several modules grouped around a mutual interface, capable to interact with one another. Delft3D-FLOW is the engine that can calculate tide and wind driven flows (storm-surge), and it is based in finite differences, using a curvilinear or rectilinear grid. They have made efforts to parallelize their code to work with MPI, although the current implementation does not allow yet parallel computing on distributed memory systems, such as on a cluster of PCs [2]. The surface wave model Delft3D-WAVE is used to implement the wave field of a hurricane [3].

The Finite-Volume, primitive equation Community Ocean Model (FVCOM) [4–7], is an engine used to simulate the circulation and ecosystem dynamics from global to estuarine scales, which has made progress in the implementation of parallel computing for hindcast, nowcast and forecast of storm-surge [8], among other processes. FVCOM is a prognostic, unstructured-grid, finite-volume, free-surface; 3-D primitive equation coastal ocean circulation model developed by the University of Massachusetts-Dartmouth (UMASSD) and Woods Hole Oceanographic Institution (WHOI) joint efforts [9]. It works together with SWAVE [9], which is an adaptation of SWAN to unstructured grids, to implement the wave field of a hurricane. More information about this algorithm and group of developers can be found at http://fvcom.smast.umassd.edu/FVCOM/index.html.

The Semi-implicit Eulerian-Lagrangian finite-element model (SELFE) [10], is an open-source community-supported code [11–13], which solves the Navier-Stokes equations (in both hydrostatic and non-hydrostatic form). It is based on unstructured triangular grids, and designed for the effective simulation of 3D baroclinic circulation. The numerical algorithm is high-order, robust, stable and computationally efficient, and it has developed their source code for parallel implementation. The Wind Wave Model II (WWM-II) [14], is used to implement the wave field of a hurricane. More information about this algorithm can be found at http://www.stccmop.org/knowledge_transfer/software/selfe.

The ADvanced CIRCulation model (ADCIRC) [15,16] is a two-dimensional depth integrated, barotropic time-dependent long wave, open source multi-scale, multi-physics hydrodynamic coastal circulation model. The code solves the equations of motion and moment of a moving fluid in conjunction with a rotating Earth, for long waves (astronomical tide and storm-surge), using an unstructured triangular mesh [16,17], and employing a parameterization of bottom friction through Manning formulation [18]. Equations are formulated using the traditional approaches hydrostatic pressure and Boussinesq approximation. The domain is divided in space using a continuous-Galerkin finite-element technique [17] and in time using the method of finite differences. It has been optimized by unrolling loops for enhanced performance on multiple computer architectures. ADCIRC includes MPI library calls to allow it to operate at high efficiency (typically better than 90 percent) on parallel computer architectures [19]. More information about this algorithm can be found at http://adcirc.org/. The Simulating WAves Nearshore (SWAN) [20,21], is a third generation model, which calculates random, short-crested wind-generated waves within inland waters, coastal regions, and open ocean. It is a finite difference model that solves the action balance equation and its solution represents the short waves.

ADCIRC is coupled with SWAN to determine efficiently and accurately the wave field associated with the hurricane including tides, and storm-surge that propagates from deep water to the coast, as explained in [22]. Both algorithms obtain the wind field using a parametric tropical cyclone model Holland [23] implemented in the ADCIRC code. These coupling of codes is maintained and actualized by the ADCIRC Development Group (ADDG), which has made significant progress for parallel implementation using HPC [19,22].

The last three combinations of models mentioned above are in operation and a better description of their capabilities and comparisons is carried on in [1,24]. One thing to emphasize is that with enough resolution and computational power either one of the three model combinations should converge to the same solution.

The next section will deepen in the ADCIRC basis and will indicate the work that has been developed by the group mentioned above with this algorithm at the time of being selected by government agencies in the USA to predict storm surge for the east coast and Gulf of Mexico in the USA.

2   ADCIRC Developments

There has been a significant effort carried in the USA to implement new strategies to deal with the effects of natural disasters related to hurricanes (tropical cyclones) and extra-tropical cyclones along its east coast. One of such events was Hurricane Katrine in 2005, which due to the extensive damage in infrastructure and lost of lives, made a deep impact about the conception of how to employ technologies available to hindcast and forecast the effects of such phenomena. Several studies followed after this event and others for hurricanes in later years, where researchers and universities made important advances in developing the methodologies to follow in order to study storm-surge and inundation through coastal ocean modeling capabilities available at that time. The following is a review of the work mentioned above.

The ADCIRC code was originally developed around 1993 by Joannes Westerink, a civil engineer at the University of Notre Dame, and Richard Luettich, a marine scientist at the University of North Carolina [25,26]. In the mid nineties the ADDG, parallelized the code which was scalable up to certain number of processors. Also at this time the biggest runs that could be accomplished were with about 20,000 nodes in a workstation that requires 3 days to run, before the parallelization. Then in the late nineties with the upgrade of the code (a couple of hours to run), the work accomplished by ADDG had more impact in reaching agencies which considered the use of this code to implement case studies as a first step to comprehend how to obtain meaningful data from hindcast simulations. This approach can be observed in the relationship that the U.S. Army Corps of Engineers (USACE) New Orleans District established with the ADDG in order to develop a storm-surge model for New Orleans and surrounding coastal areas [25,26]. From this initiative a series of models for the Louisiana south part were developed with an increasing level of resolution and detail that still continues nowadays.

By 2005 a mesh for the Gulf of Mexico, the Caribbean Sea, and a large portion of the western North Atlantic Ocean was in operation with about 314,442 nodes. The purpose of extending the domain was to model with more accuracy the storm-surge as it propagated from deep water to coastal areas, where characteristics were refined according to the new resolutions achieved (topography, bathymetry, land structures), that ranged from tens of kilometers in the open sea, to 50–100 m in the Louisiana areas around New Orleans. With this mesh a synthetic slow moving hurricane, Category 3 named Pam was run, which was the first attempt to visualize the effects of a storm like this before Katrina actually happened [25,26]. With the media attention received after Katrina, the USACE turned to the ADDG to help them understand what went wrong during this hurricane, which resulted in several studies that USACE used to redesign the levee system in New Orleans [25]. The next couple of years brought collaborations with other universities and agencies, some of the most important are mentioned below.

In 2006 the ADCIRC code was implemented at the Texas Advanced Computing Center (TACC) at The University of Texas at Austin (UT), which started the use of TACCs Dell HPC cluster, Lonestar, one of the most powerful computing systems for open academic research in the world, at that time [25]. From this point on, the use of ADCIRC became more relevant when implemented in other projects. The ADDG working collaboration with TACC allowed them to visualize how HPC and ADCIRC could be a tool employed by forecasters and emergency management people, since a high level of detail for the output can be achieved in real time. Later on, other institutions followed the lead of the ADDG, such as the Naval Research Laboratory [27], which in 2007 prepared a technical report about Katrina, where they notified the development of a grid with 375,479 nodes and a spatial resolution of 225 m in coastal and inland areas in Louisiana and Mississippi.

With this new approach other groups, agencies, and universities, as the Louisiana Sea Grant College Program at LSU (Sea Grant), the Renaissance Computing Institute (RENCI) at the University of North Carolina at Chapel Hill (UNC), Louisiana State University (LSU), the Computational Hydraulics Laboratory (CHL) at the University of Notre Dame, the U.S. Integrated Ocean Observing System (IOOS) at the National Oceanographic and Atmospheric Administration (NOAA), the Coastal Hazards Center, the University of Oklahoma, and TACC all of them in the U.S., have partnered through two initiatives that complement each other.

The first one is the ADCIRC Surge Guidance System (ASGS), that is based in the tight coupling of ADCIRC and SWAN, which primary function is to provide real time storm-surge guidance for updating emergency response groups during a tropical or hurricane event. The system works through a collection of THREDDS Data Servers, located in the City University of New York (CUNY), NOAA, RENCI, LSU and TAAC, that cover the Gulf of Mexico and most of the east coast of the U.S. The system also harvest THREDDS content into a master catalog. The second one is the Coastal Emergency Risks Assessment (CERA), which is a coastal modeling research and development effort that provides operational advisory services related to impending hurricanes in the United States. CERA is a component of the ASGS, and retrieves from the catalog available simulations and metadata. Both systems are being used to alert authorities and population of areas of high risk of inundation in the Gulf of Mexico and east coast of the U.S. More information about these systems can be located here: http://coastalemergency.org/#va.

Based on the relationships described above, during 2014 and 2015 these groups have been dedicated to improve the algorithms to revamp the ADCIRC code to take advantage of new developments for HPC. For instance a collaborative research project named Scalable Toolkit for an Open community supporting near Real time high resolution coastal Modeling (STORM), with National Science Foundation (NSF) support, focused in the new computing architectures available to HPC, is updating the ADCIRC base code and numerical algorithms so it can remain a cutting edge tool for coastal modeling applications. Information about this program can be found here: http://storm.stellar-group.org/.

Another important application of the ADCIRC code comes with the possibility of computing a considerable number of high-resolution runs, that would provide information on prediction uncertainty and, considering enough runs (at least 100), could allow the creation of extremely detailed probabilistic flood and wave-impact predictions to guide decision making during coastal storms. Recently the resolution employed depending of the area of study is in the neighborhood of around 3,500,000 nodes working with ADCIRC. For instance the USACE through the Engineer Research and Development Center (ERDC) is using the state of the art in HPC with ADCIRC, employing a suite called CSTORM-MS (Coastal Storm Modeling System) running on a Garnets Cray XE6, with 4,716 compute nodes and 32 cores/node = 150,912 processors. Here the suite is focused on production runs that will lead to preparation of risk maps, and quantification of risk for coastal communities to storm events.

The next section will describe the use that is being made in Mexico applying the ADCIRC+SWAN in a project supported by the Consejo Nacional de Ciencia y Tecnología (CONACYT) and the Universidad Autónoma del Estado de México (UAEM).

3 ADCIRC+SWAN for the Mexican Pacific

During the last 30 years Mexico has experienced an increase in hazards caused by hydro-meteorological phenomena associated with climate change, such as hurricanes, tropical storms and cold fronts, which usually produce extreme rainfall for both mainland and coastal areas. These weather events have occurred more frequently in Mexican coasts in recent years increasing risk disasters on population and in its vulnerability. One such event combined the power of hurricane Ingrid [28] which made landfall in Tamaulipas (Gulf of Mexico), and Hurricane Manuel [29] making landfalls in Guerrero (Pacific), as tropical storm, and in Sinaloa (Pacific), as hurricane. These hurricanes happened almost at the same time from 12 -19 September 2013, creating severe destruction (landslides) specially in Guerrero, extreme rainfall and flooding that spread well over 26 states. This event raised concern among academy and authorities about identifying the vulnerability of population in Mexican coasts.

The situation mentioned above would be of no concern if the population growth and migration trends to coastal areas were low in Mexico, this is more delicate if we consider the fact that many industrial parks are placed in low lying coastal areas; according to Gómez et. al, [30], just above one third of Mexican population lives in counties exposed to hydro-meteorological phenomena. The impact caused by these events ranges from minor flooding to natural disasters, where deaths and suffering of affected population occurs, in addition to socio-economic damages which might reach hundreds of millions of dollars.

In this work we analyze recent events that have occurred at Altata Port in Sinaloa Mexico, in 2013 (Hurricane Manuel), with direct impact over the region. Here the coupling of ADCIRC+SWAN [22,31], is employed to estimate conditions such as storm surge, flood levels, duration times, flow rates, streams damaging roads, as to identify areas with risk of property loss, and life. The purpose is to compare observed damages (where available) to the areas identified as hazardous in the model, to then simulate enough events employing EST (Empirical Simulation Technique) [32] that allows proper estimation of vulnerable areas based upon selected variables. The data obtained from numerical simulations will be employed to generate Hazard Maps of the region, that later on will be used in the preparation phase of the humanitarian logistic stream [33] in furthering an initiative to implement measures to increase population resilience in locations identified with certain degree of risk, for different areas along Mexican coasts.

The proposed work is being carried out through tests on a workstation that has (2) 8-core Intel Xeon Processor E5-2640 v3, with a total of 8 physical cores x 2 threads for a total of 16. Currently a mesh with 126,000 nodes with parallelized

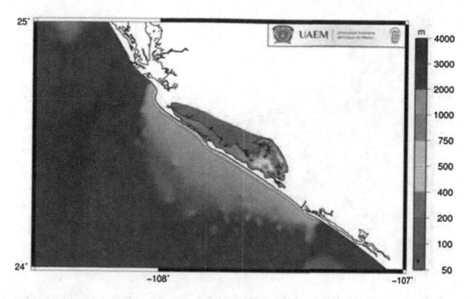

Fig. 1. Grid size as implemented for the area of Altata, Sin, colors indicate the range in size of the elements of the grid.

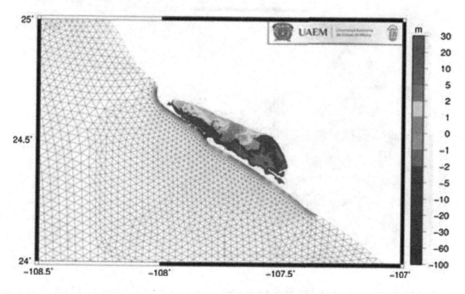

Fig. 2. Bathymetry employed for the area of Altata, Sin, colors indicate the range in size of depths for bathymetry and elevations for topography on the grid.

ADCIRC+SWAN model runs in about 28 hours, for a time in prototype of 7 days (4 hours per day of simulation in prototype). Most mesh density is in the study area in Altata, Sinaloa, with 80 % of the nodes. Here the limitation encountered is the number of nodes that can be used without the system be restricted by the

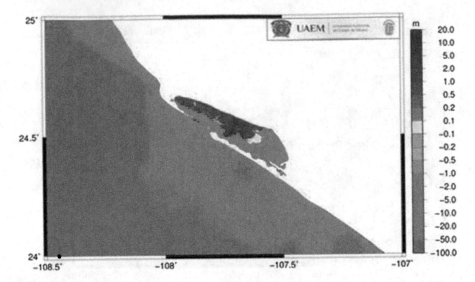

Fig. 3. Bathymetry employed for the area of Altata, Sin, colors in a scale of green-blue indicate the range of depths for bathymetry and elevations for topography on the grid.

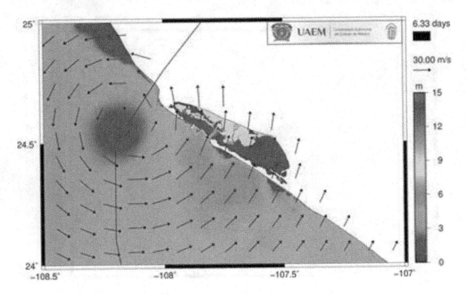

Fig. 4. Significant wave height, and wind speed at Altata, Sin. produced by hurricane Manuel.

amount of time to simulate, which precludes its use in real time as implemented. Figure 1 shows the surrounding area of Altata which is a small town connected to the Pacific Ocean, located about 45 miles west of Culiacan, Sinaloa in Mexico, the area shown is just part of the grid modeled that covers half of the Mexican Pacific Ocean, from Nayarit to Baja California Norte.

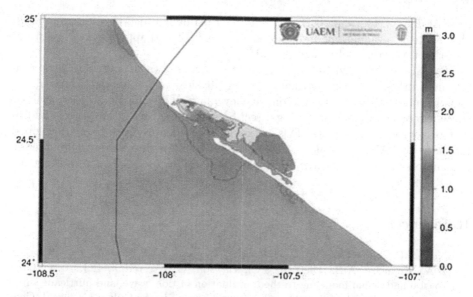

Fig. 5. Maximum Water Elevation at Altata, Sin. produced by hurricane Manuel.

Figures 2 and 3 show the bathymetry employed for the study with two different approaches to better understand the information. Figures 4 and 5 show the preliminary results obtained by running ADCIRC+SWAN. Figure 4 shows the trajectory of hurricane Manuel, wind speed and significant wave height as calculated just before it made land fall very near to Altata. Figure 5 shows the maximum water surface elevation as calculated for any time during the run.

4   Conclusions

The advancement of technology has propelled the application of specialized algorithms employed altogether with High Performance Computing (HPC), as they approach larger and physically complex problems. The cooperation among scientists, engineers, universities, companies, and government agencies, especially in the U.S.A, has allowed predicting the effects of large storms approaching the coast (near real time) and with this information helping authorities to handle emergencies generated by a hurricane. Mexico is now entering this arena with the purpose of performing such simulations that can generate flood hazard maps calculated by ADCIRC+SWAN as different hurricanes hit the Mexican Pacific.

The latter effort is seen as a long-term work; where several events simulated and analyzed statistically (Empirical Simulation Technique) have to be performed. Regarding flooding risk, it will be determined for several areas identified as likely to receive a hurricane, which will be initially modeled for different risk scenarios. Therefore, it is of great interest the use of numerical modeling under these scenarios, and to show the importance this approach has. It is by working on this fashion that institutions such as the Mexican Navy, CENAPRED,

CONAGUA, SMN, and SEDATU who share similar objectives for population alert systems, evacuation, and land use, will benefit and appreciate the information this type of modeling can provide.

The aforementioned institutions need accurate data, to evacuate people in a timely manner. Such information from physical and numerical data allows logistics models that result in contingency plans. These plans are essential for the safety of the country and bring direct benefit to the population when a hydrometeorological event occurs. This is exemplified with the work being developed for the area of Altata, Sinaloa, Mexico, where the main objective is to provide the parameters needed for the logistics models that will be used to create contingency plans.

References

1. Kerr, P.C., Martyr, R.C., Donahue, A.S., Hope, M.E., Westerink, J.J., Luettich, R.A., Kennedy, A.B., Dietrich, J.C., Dawson, C., Westerink, H.J.: U.S. IOOS coastal and ocean modeling testbed: evaluation of tide, wave, and hurricane surge response sensitivities to mesh resolution and friction in the Gulf of Mexico. J. Geophys. Res. Oceans **118**(9), 4633–4661 (2013). http://dx.doi.org/10.1002/jgrc.20305

2. Hydraulics, W.D.: Delft3D User Manual. Deltares, The Netherlands (2014). http://oss.deltares.nl/documents/183920/185723/Delft3D-FLOW_User_Manual.pdf

3. Thuy, V.T.T.: Storm surge modelling for vietnam's coast, IHE Delft, Technical report (2003)

4. Chen, C., Beardsley, R.C., Cowles, G.: An unstructured grid, finite-volume coastal ocean model (FVCOM) system. Oceanogr. Wash. DC Oceanogr. Soc. **19**(1), 78 (2006). http://dx.doi.org/10.5670/oceanog.2006.92

5. Chen, C., Beardsley, R.C., Cowles, G.W., Qi, J., Lai, Z., Gao, G., Stuebe, D.A., Xu, Q., Xue, P., Ge, J., et al.: An unstructured-grid, finite-volume community ocean model: FVCOM user manual, SMAST/UMASSD (2013). http://fvcomer.com/download/FVCOM_User_Manual_v3.1.6.pdf

6. Chen, C., Huang, H., Beardsley, R.C., Liu, H., Xu, Q., Cowles, G.: A finite volume numerical approach for coastal ocean circulation studies: comparisons with finite difference models. J. Geophys. Res. Oceans **112**(C3), c03018 (2007). http://dx.doi.org/10.1029/2006JC003485

7. Chen, C., Liu, H., Beardsley, R.C.: An unstructured grid, finite-volume, three-dimensional, primitive equations ocean model: application to coastal ocean and estuaries. J. Atmos. Oceanic Technol. **20**(1), 159–186 (2003). http://dx.doi.org/10.1175/1520-0426(2003)020⟨0159:AUGFVT⟩2.0.CO;2

8. Cowles, G.W.: Parallelization of the FVCOM coastal ocean model. Int. J. High Perform. Comput. Appl. **22**(2), 177–193 (2008). http://dx.doi.org/10.1177/1094342007083804

9. Qi, J., Chen, C., Beardsley, R.C., Perrie, W., Cowles, G.W., Lai, Z.: An unstructured-grid finite-volume surface wave model (FVCOM-SWAVE): implementation, validations and applications. Ocean Model. **28**(1–3), 153–166 (2009). The Sixth International Workshop on Unstructured Mesh Numerical Modelling of Coastal, Shelf and Ocean Flows. http://www.sciencedirect.com/science/article/pii/S1463500309000067

10. Zhang, Y., Baptista, A.M.: SELFE: A semi-implicit Eulerian-Lagrangian finite-element model for cross-scale ocean circulation. Ocean Model. **21**(34), 71–96 (2008). http://www.sciencedirect.com/science/article/pii/S1463500307001436

11. Bertin, X., Oliveira, A., Fortunato, A.B.: Simulating morphodynamics with unstructured grids: description and validation of a modeling system for coastal applications. Ocean Model. **28**(13), 75–87 (2009). The Sixth International Workshop on Unstructured Mesh Numerical Modelling of Coastal, Shelf and Ocean Flows. http://www.sciencedirect.com/science/article/pii/S1463500308001637

12. Cho, K.-H., Wang, H.V., Shen, J., Valle-Levinson, A., Teng, Y.C.: A modeling study on the response of Chesapeake Bay to hurricane events of Floyd and Isabel. Ocean Model. **4950**, 22–46 (2012). http://www.sciencedirect.com/science/article/pii/S1463500312000352

13. Pinto, L., Fortunato, A., Zhang, Y., Oliveira, A., Sancho, F.: Development and validation of a three-dimensional morphodynamic modelling system for non-cohesive sediments. Ocean Model. **5758**, 1–14 (2012). http://www.sciencedirect.com/science/article/pii/S1463500312001175

14. Roland, A., Cucco, A., Ferrarin, C., Hsu, T.-W., Liau, J.-M., Ou, S.-H., Umgiesser, G., Zanke, U.: On the development and verification of a 2-D coupled wave-current model on unstructured meshes. J. Mar. Syst. **78**(Supplement), S244–S254 (2009). coastal Processes: Challenges for Monitoring and Prediction. http://www.sciencedirect.com/science/article/pii/S0924796309001535

15. Luettich Jr., R., Westerink, J., Scheffner, N.W.: ADCIRC: an advanced three-dimensional circulation model for shelves, coasts, and estuaries. report 1. theory and methodology of ADCIRC-2DDI and ADCIRC-3DL. DTIC Document, Technical report (1992). http://oai.dtic.mil/oai/oai?verb=getRecord&metadataPrefix=html&identifier=ADA261608

16. Luettich, R.A., Westerink, J.J.: Formulation and numerical implementation of the 2D/3D ADCIRC finite element model version 44. XX (2004). http://www.unc.edu/ims/adcirc/adcirc_theory_2004_12_08.pdf

17. Dawson, C., Westerink, J.J., Feyen, J.C., Pothina, D.: Continuous, discontinuous and coupled discontinuous continuous Galerkin finite element methods for the shallow water equations. Int. J. Numer. Meth. Fluids **52**(1), 63–88 (2006). http://dx.doi.org/10.1002/fld.1156

18. Mayo, T., Butler, T., Dawson, C., Hoteit, I.: Data assimilation within the advanced circulation (ADCIRC) modeling framework for the estimation of Mannings friction coefficient. Ocean Model. **76**, 43–58 (2014). http://www.sciencedirect.com/science/article/pii/S146350031400002X

19. Luettich, R., Westerink, J.: A (parallel) advanced circulation model for oceanic, coastal and estuarine waters (ADCIRC). http://www3.nd.edu/~adcirc/manual/ADCIRC_manual.pdf

20. Booij, N., Holthuijsen, L., Ris, R.: The "swan" wave model for shallow water, Coastal Engineering Proceedings, **1**(25) (1996). http://citeseerx.ist.psu.edu/viewdoc/download?=10.1.1.471.104&rep=rep1&type=pdf

21. Holthuijsen, L., Booij, N., Ris, R.: A spectral wave model for the coastal zone. In: Ocean Wave Measurement and Analysis, ASCE, pp. 630–641 (1993)

22. Dietrich, J., Zijlema, M., Westerink, J., Holthuijsen, L., Dawson, C., Luettich Jr., R., Jensen, R., Smith, J., Stelling, G., Stone, G.: Modeling hurricane waves and storm surge using integrally-coupled, scalable computations. Coast. Eng. **58**(1), 45–65 (2011). http://www.sciencedirect.com/science/article/pii/S0378383910001250

23. Holland, G.J.: An analytic model of the wind and pressure profiles in hurricanes. Mon. Weather Rev. **108**(8), 1212–1218 (1980). http://dx.doi.org/10.1175/1520-0493(1980)108⟨1212:AAMOTW⟩2.0.CO:2

24. Chen, C., Beardsley, R.C., Luettich, R.A., Westerink, J.J., Wang, H., Perrie, W., Xu, Q., Donahue, A.S., Qi, J., Lin, H., Zhao, L., Kerr, P.C., Meng, Y., Toulany, B.: Extratropical storm inundation testbed: intermodel comparisons in Scituate, Massachusetts. J. Geophys. Res. Oceans **118**(10), 5054–5073 (2013). http://dx.doi.org/10.1002/jgrc.20397

25. Sera, W.: From katrina forward: producing better storm surge forecasts, TACC, Texas Advanced Computing Center, Ut at Austin, Technical report (2008). http://chg.ices.utexas.edu/news/fromkatrinaforward.pdf

26. Van Heerden, I., Bryan, M.: The Storm: What Went Wrong and Why During Hurricane Katrina-the Inside Story from One Loui siana Scientist. Penguin, New York (2006)

27. Blain, C., Massey, T., Dykes, J., Posey, P.: Advanced surge and inundation modeling: A case study from hurricane katrina, DTIC Document, Technical report (2007). http://www.dtic.mil/cgi-bin/GetTRDoc?Location=U2&doc=GetTRDoc.pdf&AD=ADA518508

28. Beven, J.: Hurricane ingrid, al102013, NATIONAL HURRICANE CENTER, Technical report (2014). http://www.nhc.noaa.gov/data/tcr/AL102013_Ingrid.pdf

29. Pasch, R., Zelinsky, D.: Hurricane manuel, ep132013, NATIONAL HURRICANE CENTER, Technical report (2014). http://www.nhc.noaa.gov/data/tcr/EP132013_Manuel.pdf

30. Gómez, C.A., Esquivel, J.C.H., Vázquez, A.R.: Migración interna, distribución territorial de la población y desarrollo sustentable (2009)

31. Sebastian, A., Proft, J., Dietrich, J.C., Du, W., Bedient, P.B., Dawson, C.N.: Characterizing hurricane storm surge behavior in Galveston Bay using the SWAN + ADCIRC model. Coast. Eng. **88**, 171–181 (2014). http://www.sciencedirect.com/science/article/pii/S0378383914000556

32. Scheffner, N.W., Clausner, J.E., Militello, A., Borgman, L.E., Edge, B.L.: Use and application of the empirical simulation technique: user's guide, DTIC Document, Technical report (1999)

33. Cozzolino, A.: Humanitarian Logistics: Cross-Sector Cooperation in Disaster Relief Management. Springer Science & Business Media, Heidelberg (2012)

Modeling the Blood Vessels of the Brain

Nathan Weinstein[1], Karla Gisela Pedroza-Ríos[2], Edgar Nathal[3],
Leonardo Di G. Sigalotti[4,5], Isidoro Gitler[1], and Jaime Klapp[1,6(✉)]

[1] Departamento de Matemáticas Centro de Investigación y de Estudios Avanzados
(CINVESTAV-IPN), "ABACUS" Centro de Matemáticas Aplicadas y Cómputo de
Alto Rendimiento, Carretera México-Toluca Km 38.5, La Marquesa,
52740 Ocoyoacac, Estado de México, Mexico
[2] Hospital Regional de Alta Especialidad de Ixtapaluca,
Km. 34.5 Carretera Federal México-Puebla, Pueblo de Zoquiapan,
56530 Ixtapaluca, Mexico
drakarlapedroza@gmail.com
[3] Instituto Nacional de Neurología y Neurocirugía 'Manuel Velasco Suárez',
Insurgentes Sur No. 3877, Tlalpan, La Fama, 14269 Mexico, D.F., Mexico
[4] Area de Física de Procesos Irreversibles Departamento de Ciencias Básicas,
Universidad Autónoma Metropolitana-Azcapotzalco (UAM-A),
Avenue San Pablo 180, 02200 Mexico, D.F., Mexico
[5] Centro de Física, Instituto Venezolano de Investigaciones Científicas, IVIC,
Apartado Postal 20632, Caracas 1020-A, Venezuela
[6] Departamento de Física, Instituto Nacional de Investigaciones Nucleares (ININ),
Carretera México-Toluca S/N, La Marquesa,
52750 Ocoyoacac, Estado de México, Mexico
jaime.klapp@inin.gob.mx

Abstract. The results described in this work are part of a larger project.
The long term goal of this project is to help physicians predict the hemodynamic changes, and associated risks, caused by different treatment
options for brain arteriovenous malformations. First, we need to build a
model of the vascular architecture of each specific patient. Our approach
to build these models is described in this work. Later we will use the
model of the vascular architecture to simulate the velocity and pressure
gradients of the blood flowing within the vessels, and the stresses on
the blood vessel walls, before and after treatment. We are developing a
computer program to describe each blood vessel as a parametric curve,
where each point within this curve includes a normal vector that points
in the opposite direction of the pressure gradient. The shape of the cross
section of the vessel in each point is described as an ellipse. Our program
is able to describe the geometry of a blood vessel using as an input a
cloud of dots. The program allows us to model any blood vessel, and
other tubular structures.

1 Introduction

The human brain is part of the nervous system, often described as the most
complex system in the human body, not only for its anatomical structure, but
also by the way it works.

© Springer International Publishing Switzerland 2016
I. Gitler and J. Klapp (Eds.): ISUM 2015, CCIS 595, pp. 535–554, 2016.
DOI: 10.1007/978-3-319-32243-8_38

The brain has a very high metabolic rate; although it usually weights between 1.3 and 1.5 Kg, which is about 2 % of the human body weight, it consumes about one fifth of the oxygen, and one fourth of the glucose required by the human body.

Its continued dependence on oxygen and glucose combined with its inability to store them, cause the brain to need a constant blood flow for proper operation. The brain receives, on average, a fifth of the cardiac output. If the heart pumps 5000 to 6000 ml per minute, the brain receives 1000 to 1200 ml every minute distributed by arterial sectors. The average regional blood flow is between 50 ml and 70 ml per 100 g of brain tissue per minute. It is higher in the gray matter than in the white matter [1].

The amount of blood in the cranial cavity is on average 75 ml and also contains the cerebrospinal fluid (CSF) in similar amounts. If we assume fluid incompressibility, the volume of blood and CSF combined with the volume of the brain itself must remain constant, a phenomenon known as the Monro-Kellie hypothesis [2,3], see Fig. 1.

The history of cerebral blood flow study started with the anatomy. In 1660, Willis and Lower demonstrated that an arterial circle, called the circle of Willis, allows communication between major brain arteries. Subsequently, they found that this polygon has anatomical variations in up to 48 % of brains. Currently, these variations can be identified not only with autopsies, as it was before, but also with neuroimaging studies [4].

In 1874, Duret made a description of the arterial vascular territories, one for each of the six main vessels supplying the brain, including the arteries that feed the face and scalp as they have anastomoses or communications with the intracerebral arteries [5]. Currently we can see the angioarchitecture statically with angio-computed tomography (CT) scan and also dynamically using digital subtraction angiography (DSA) and 4D magnetic resonance imaging (4DMRI).

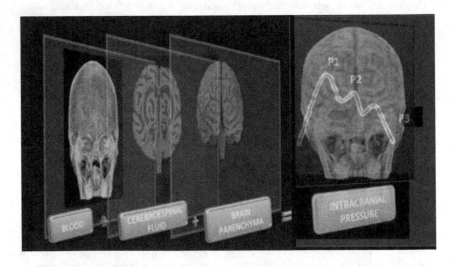

Fig. 1. The Monro-Kellie hypothesis.

Even the metabolic functioning of the brain can be evaluated with positron emission tomography (PET) and functional magnetic resonance imaging (fMRI).

Vascular modeling can help physicians predict changes of flow caused by the use of interventional therapies. In order simulate pathological conditions like atherosclerosis, aneurysms and vascular malformations and treatment interventions it is first necessary to define the shape and physical properties of a blood vessel graph and the blood flowing through it. In order to increase the accuracy of the model, it is important to consider the elastic properties of arteries and their reaction to changes in the concentration of vasoactive gases like CO_2 [25].

Knowledge of the angioarchitecture is essential; recognition of branching hierarchy, fractal tree models [26–29] and types of arterial flows is very helpful in the simulation of complex blood vessel graphs.

Blood circulation in the arteries and veins may be defined as a non-Newtonian fluid in an elastic tube with a cyclic and pulsatile movement. This means, that there is a periodic lengthening of the vessel wall in a circumferential direction. Cyclic radial stretching of vasculature is synchronized with the pulse and is defined as the tangential component of frictional forces generated at the surface by the blood. It is greater in the big arteries, laminar in arterioles and stationary in capillaries. The shear stress in the arteries is approximately 10–$70\,\mathrm{dyn\,cm}^{-2}$ and 1 to $6\,\mathrm{dyn\,cm}^{-2}$ in the veins as a result of flow velocity changes in the post-capillar venules [30]. Blood flow is susceptible to turbulence under physiological conditions where the arteries split or elsewhere in abnormal conditions like stenosis [31].

Because many blood cells are larger than the capillaries' diameter, blood flow modeling requires the integration of rheology [32–36].

The Navier-Stokes equations have been integrated into mathematical models in order to obtain pressure and flow gradients in arterial networks [28]. An interesting point to analyze, is the functional interrelation between velocity, vessel radius and shear stress, that determine flow characteristics. For example, the principle of minimum work establishes a balance between energy dissipation due to shear stress and the minimum volume of the vessel graph [16].

The challenges for doctors include the use of measuring instruments to obtain the variables needed to simulate the blood flowing through a certain blood-vessel graph. The tests may be non-invasive like trans-cranial Doppler ultrasound (TDU), the tonometer, and photoplethysmography [37] or as invasive as intra-operative measurement of flow with a micro vascular Doppler device [38–40] or intracranial pressure measurement through an intracranial device [41,42], see Fig. 2.

Many mathematical and computational modeling efforts, have allowed physicians to predict the rupture risk of an aneurysm; based upon the geometry of the aneurysm and certain hemodynamic parameters [43–48]. Modeling and simulation, has also been helpful to predict the effect of specific embolization stent or coil materials used in endovascular procedures [48–50]. Other models calculate the rupture risk of vascular malformations, [51,52] and the occlusive effect of radiosurgery [53].

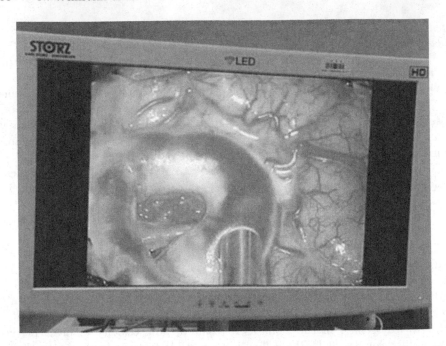

Fig. 2. Intraoperative assessment of blood flow during a brain arteriovenous malformation resection.

The evolution of computational modeling will allow the development of a translational medicine focused in the optimal use of basic research in clinical, surgical and interventional practice.

2   Vascular Anatomy

The brain is anatomically divided into three parts: both cerebral hemispheres, the brain stem and the cerebellum. Cerebral circulation is generally divided in two parts: anterior circulation and posterior circulation. Anterior circulation irrigates most cerebral hemispheres. Posterior circulation supplies the brain stem, cerebellum and the basal ganglia including the thalamus [6]. Cerebral vasculature is complex and its study is divided into arterial and venous segments. The arterial segment of anterior circulation is given by the right and left internal carotid arteries. The arterial segment of posterior circulation is given by the vertebrobasilar system that originates at the vertebral arteries. The internal carotid arteries are branches of the right and left common carotid arteries, respectively. The right common carotid artery is a branch of the brachiocephalic trunk, while the left is a direct branch of the aortic arch. The vertebral arteries are originated from the subclavian arteries, originated from the aortic arch.

Each carotid artery splits up into two terminal branches, the anterior cerebral artery and the middle cerebral artery, both supply most of the cerebral hemisphere including the frontal, parietal and temporal lobes. The vertebral arteries join together to form the basilar artery at the apex, it bifurcates in the two posterior cerebral arteries. The carotid artery joins the posterior cerebral arteries on each side through the posterior communicating artery. The arterial branches that originate at the vertebral and basilar arteries supply the brain stem, the cerebellum and the occipital lobe. As we mentioned before, there are anatomical variations in structure between hemispheres and vascular territories between individuals [6,7], see Fig. 3.

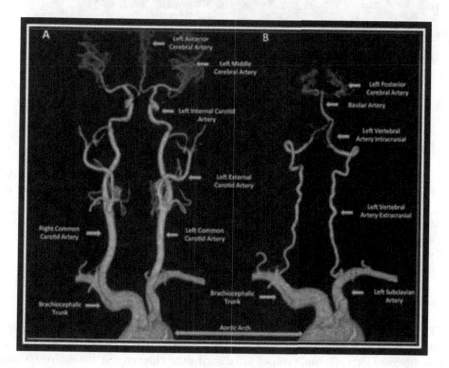

Fig. 3. Three-dimensional reconstructions of the brain arteries from CT scans: (A) Anterior circulation, showing the origin of the carotid arteries. (B) Posterior circulation, showing the origin of the vertebral arteries and its convergence at the brain.

Venous circulation begins at the end of the capillaries, with venules that become hemispheric veins, which drain into venous sinuses. Interestingly, venous drainage is bilateral until it converges in the midline in the superior sagittal sinus, inferior sagittal sinus and straight sinus which are on the midline of the head converge at the level of the occipital protuberance. Subsequently, the sagittal sinus splits up into two transverse sinuses at occipital level, which then converge through the sigmoid sinus which drains into the internal jugular veins located in the neck as shown in Fig. 4. These last veins reach the superior vena cava, which drains into the right atrium of the heart [1].

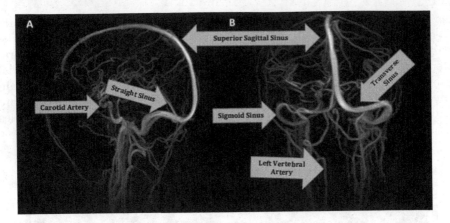

Fig. 4. Normal venous drainage and its relation with the main arteries observed in a MRI with 3D reconstruction: (A) Lateral view, and (B) Posterior-anterior view.

2.1   Structural Characteristics of the Blood Vessels

Arteries are the blood vessels that carry blood from the heart to the rest of the body. Three layers arranged concentrically comprise the wall structure of arteries:

– Tunica adventitia, also known as tunica externa, is a layer formed by connective tissue.
– Tunica media, is made up of smooth muscle cells and elastic sheets.
– Tunica intima, includes an elastic tissue called basal membrane and the endothelium, which is in contact with the blood.

There are differences in the arrangement of fibers and the thickness of each vascular layer in cerebral arteries compared to the extra cranial arteries. The elastic fibers of extracranial arteries are distributed throughout the entire arterial wall. After the arteries penetrate the duramater, the elastic fibers condense into a subendothelial elastic lamina [7]. The brain vessel walls are thinner than the extra cranial arteries (the tunica media is much thinner, and the arteries and arterioles in the subarachnoid space lack a tunica adventitia) [7] and the flow rate to diameter ratio is bigger. As the brain vessels have higher content of collagen and elastin, their distensibility is larger [8,9]. This differences added with the hemodynamic features of the brain blood flow predispose to different diseases, such as cerebral aneurysms, which are focal dilations of arteries caused by a weakened wall whose clinical manifestation can be catastrophic for the patient causing a cerebral hemorrhage [10,11].

The characteristics of the vascular wall vary not only in relation to arterial diameter in the same person; there are also structural differences according to sex and age [9,12,13]. Usually as time passes blood vessels loose elasticity. As we age, atheromatous plaques form [9].

Elastic arteries whose middle layer is thicker contain an elastic lamina and smooth muscle fibers. The aorta and its main branches and the carotid arteries are elastic arteries. Their average diameter is 15 mm with a wall thickness of about 1 mm.

Muscular arteries or distribution arteries are medium sized vessels with increased smooth muscle fibers in the middle layer, also characterized by limited internal and external elastic membranes. Their average diameter is 6 mm with a wall thickness of 1 mm.

Arterioles have an average diameter of 30 μm and an average wall thickness of 6 μm. Arterioles are composed of several layers of smooth muscle, because they are the sites of most resistance in the cardiovascular system, small changes in their size cause large variations in total peripheral resistance.

Capillaries are the smallest vessels; with a diameter of about 8 μm and a wall thickness of 0.5 μm [14]. The other difference with the general vasculature is that brain capillaries are covered by the foot processes of cerebral cells named pericytes that form an external layer.

The collateral circulation, or collateral flow, consists of connections between each vascular territory allowing the persistence of the cerebral flow despite the corresponding blood flow occlusion. These connections are normally developed or acquired after chronic hemodynamic changes.

Veins are low pressure vessels that return blood from the organs to the heart. Compared to arteries: the internal diameter of veins is larger, they contain fewer muscle and elastic fibers and they have thinner walls relative to their diameter. Veins are made up of the same three layers as the arteries. A notable feature of veins are the valves, folds of the tunica intima used to send blood reflux to vascular sites. However, intracranial veins do not have valves and the flow is by a gradient of pressure in favor of atmospheric pressure.

The veins are classified by size: The capillaries drain into venules, with an average diameter of 20 μm and an average wall thickness of 1 μm. The venules usually converge into medium veins that have a specific name according to their anatomical location. The average diameter of a medium vein is 5 mm and the average wall thickness is 0.5 mm. Large veins are those veins that drain directly into the heart and have an average diameter of 1.5 cm.

In the brain there exists the venous sinuses, which are folds of the covering of the brain called the duramater, and cerebral veins converge onto them. The venous sinuses are very important for intracranial pressure control, because they contain the arachnoid villuses that are necessary for cerebrospinal fluid absorption. Both hemispheres drain cerebrospinal fluid into the sagittal sinus. An occlusion or thrombosis of the sagittal sinus may cause severe brain damage.

2.2 Cerebral Auto-Regulation

Information about the regulation of intracranial pressure and cerebral blood flow can be derived from studies regarding the intracranial pressure taking into account the Monro-Kellie law. Normally there are changes in regional blood flow according to mental activity; with fMRI and PET we may identify changes in blood flow and even activity metabolism in awake patients.

The pressure inside the skull is constant and volume changes occur, mainly, at the expense of blood and cerebrospinal fluid flow. Cerebral vascular auto-regulation is the mechanism by which cerebral blood flow remains constant, in order to maintain proper central nervous system function. Despite changes in arterial resistance through neurogenic, chemical, metabolic and myogenic mechanisms. Vasoregulation phenomena balance skull content and brain function, for example: when the intracranial pressure increases, the first step is to increase venous drainage and the re-distribution of cerebrospinal fluid. Then the cerebral perfusion decreases and consequently, the production of cerebrospinal fluid is reduced. Even with changes in venous pressure, the system tends to maintain a constant cerebral perfusion pressure (CPP) in order to maintain the nervous system in a functional state. Adequate levels of CPP are 70–90 mmHg, intracranial pressure levels are 5–15 mmHg, and mean arterial pressure is 80–100 mmHg. Cerebral blood flow is directly proportional to the difference between the mean arterial pressure (MAP) and the intracranial pressure (ICP) and inversely proportional to the peripheral vascular resistance (PVR) [15]:

$$CPP = MAP - ICP. \tag{1}$$

$$CBF = CPP/PVR \tag{2}$$

These principles are important for understanding cerebral blood flow regulation. Simulating and monitoring these parameters is very helpful for critical care units. The ability of vascular cells to react to changes in transmural pressure, through CBF auto regulation, is called CVPR [17–20]. In order to predict brain damage, it is necessary to calculate the cerebrovascular pressure reactivity (CVPR), [16–18].

The balance between cerebral perfusion pressure and cerebrovascular resistance is what triggers self regulation. This balance depends on several elements such as the arterial concentration of gases, like O_2 and CO_2. CO_2, is the most important local vasodilator. Blood viscosity is essential to allow adequate exchange of these gases and arterial diameter regulation.

Blood density ρ is approximately $1.000 \, g \, cm^{-3}$ and the average blood viscosity μ is $(0.035 \, g \, cm^{-1} \, s^{-1})$. Viscosity is not the same in all people because it depends on many factors, such as the concentration of blood cells (hematocrit) and age [21]. Vascular diameter depends of several mechanisms: Neurogenic control, is mediated by neurotransmitters called vasoactive amines, like adrenaline. Myogenic control, is a response that regulates vessel distensibility and the ratio of stretching tension to the cerebrovascular pressure reactivity [17,22,23]. The vascular endothelium has receptors for substances such as: nitric oxide, electrolytes and elements released in inflammation that affect vascular diameter [23,24] (Fig. 5).

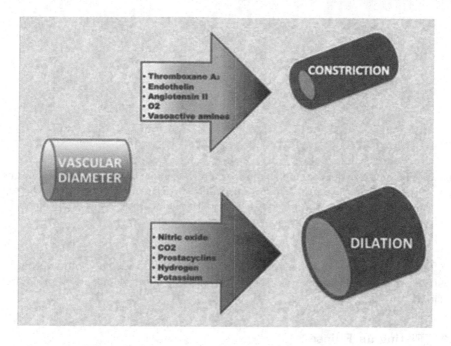

Fig. 5. Substances that affect the vascular diameter.

3   Describing the Geometry of the Arteries of the Brain

In order to describe the geometry of the main arteries and veins of the brain it is useful to think of every vessel as a parametric curve. Each point within this curve has a normal vector pointing away from the pressure gradient. The shape of the cross section of the vessel in the plane defined by the point and its normal is an ellipse. In addition, each parametric curve ends where it subdivides. The vessels that originate after the subdivision are also described as parametric curves with associated ellipses, and are considered children of the original vessel, forming a directed graph. This graph can be built for each individual patient and should be fairly easy to compare computationally. This approach has been used before [54–60].

The capillaries are very complex and it is better to describe them as a fractal, finding the relevant recursive properties. In order to model the geometry of the arteries based on the MIDA atlas [61], we have already implemented or adapted certain computational tools to achieve the following results:

3.1   Finding the Cross Sections of the Main Arteries

First, we locate where the main arteries begin. We note that the arteries are aligned with the y-axis. The cross section at $y = 138$ (Fig. 6) shows the cross sections of the carotid and vertebral arteries. The lines $z = 42$ and $x = -30$ separate

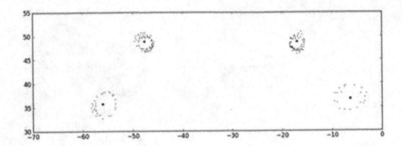

Fig. 6. The cross section around y = 138, where the main brain arteries begin. The right vertebral artery is on the top left quadrant, the left vertebral artery on the top left, the right carotid on the bottom left, and the left carotid on the bottom right quadrant.

the four cross sections of the arteries. We use these to divide the points into four clusters, each cluster is the cross section of an artery and it has an elliptic cross section.

3.2　Fitting an Ellipse

We needed a method to fit an ellipse to a set of points. Fitting an ellipse is not a trivial problem. There exist two main families of methods to solve this optimization problem: (a) algebraic approaches that minimize the sum of the squared distances between each point and the model ellipse, giving a direct solution [62–64]. (b) geometric approaches, such as a genetic algorithm [65], that vary parameters such as the location of the center, the size of the axes, the location of the foci and the angle of rotation of the ellipse, to make a maximum-likelihood fit. They usually require a starting fit and then iterate until they reach an acceptable solution.

We have used a Python class that wraps the functions written by Nicky van Foreest (http://nicky.vanforeest.com/misc/fitEllipse/fitEllipse.html) to implement the approach proposed by Fitzgibbon, Pilu and Fischer [63]. The approach is summarized below.

A general conic section can be defined as a set of points $X = (x, y)$ such that $f(a, (x, y)) = D \cdot a$, where the vectors D and a are: $D = (x^2, xy, y^2, x, y, 1)$ and $a = (a_{xx}, a_{xy}, a_{yy}, a_x, a_y, a_1)$.

In order for a conic section to be an ellipse, it must satisfy the following inequality: $4a_{xx}a_{yy} - a_{xy}^2 > 0$. This inequality may be rewritten as the following matrix equation: $a^T C a$, where C is a 6×6 matrix filled with zeros except for $C_{1,3} = C_{3,1}$ and $C_{2,2} = -1$. The sum of squared distances between a set of N data points $x_i, i = 1, ..., N$, is given by the following equation:

$$\Delta(a, x) = \sum_{i=1}^{N} (f(a, x_i))^2. \tag{3}$$

We then need to find the vector a for which the sum of squared distances is minimal, which can be rewritten as:

$$\Delta(a, x) = \sum_{i=1}^{N} a^T D_i^T D_i a = a^T S a, \tag{4}$$

where $S = \sum_{i=1}^{N} D_i^T D_i$ is a 6×6 matrix.

Since the conic condition is independent of the linear scaling in a we may therefore replace this condition by some positive number ϕ. We then state the constrained minimization problem as:

$$\text{argmin}_a \Delta | a^T C a = \phi. \tag{5}$$

To solve the above constrained problem, we introduce a Lagrange multiplier λ and the Lagrangian so that

$$L(a) = \Delta(a, x) - \lambda(a^T C a - \phi). \tag{6}$$

We need to minimize $L(a)$ as a function of a. $\partial_a L(a) = 0$, results in the equation $Sa = \lambda C a$. Now multiplying this from the left by a^T and using the constraint $a^T C a = \phi$ (resulting from the derivative of $L(a)$ with respect to λ), we obtain:

$$a^T S a = \lambda a^T C a = \lambda \psi, \tag{7}$$

where ψ is a constant. Thus, to minimize $\Delta(a, \mathbf{x}) = a^T S a$ we must look for the smallest λ that satisfies this equation. Finally, we note that $Sa = \lambda C a$ can be rewritten as the following generalized eigenvalue problem

$$\frac{1}{\lambda} a = S^{-1} C a. \tag{8}$$

We have to solve this eigenvalue problem. That is, we must solve for a and look for the eigenvector corresponding to the largest eigenvalue $1/\lambda$. In Fig. 7. we show an example application of the method described above, the number of points in the example, is similar to what we have found in a section of an artery. The method requires at least five points to fit an ellipse.

3.3   Following a Blood Vessel

After finding the ellipses and their centers at the four cross sections of the main arteries, we need to follow each artery, and then fit a new ellipse after each step. For the first points we assume a normal vector that is parallel to the y-axis. The normal we are storing for each point has a magnitude of 1, therefore $\vec{n_0} = [0, 1, 0]$.

For each successive step, we first guess the location of the next artery center assuming that the path does not turn: let the initial point $\vec{p} = [x, y, z]$ with a normal $\vec{n} = [n_x, n_y, n_z]$ and a the step size t, then the guesses, $\vec{g} = \vec{p} + t\vec{n} = [x + tn_x, y + tn_y, z + tn_z]$. The radius associated to the guess is the major semi

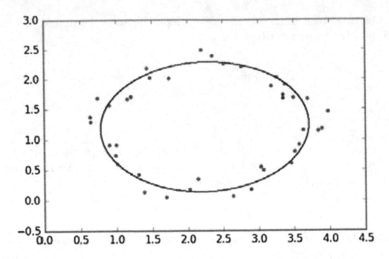

Fig. 7. Example of an ellipse fitted to the red points using the method described above (Color figure online).

axis of the ellipse of the previous point. Then we find the points in the input point cloud within a distance of four times the radius.

Next, we must find the equation of the plane that includes point $\vec{g}$ with the normal $\vec{n}$. The equation of the plane is found as follows: Let $\vec{q} = [x, y, z]$ be another point in the plane, the vector $\vec{q} - \vec{g} = [x - x_0, y - y_0, z - z_0]$ must lie completely on the plane and be perpendicular to $\vec{n}$, and the dot product of both must equal zero, $[n_x, n_y, n_z] \cdot [x - x_0, y - y_0, z - z_0] = 0$. The equation may be rearranged into the standard form of a plane equation:

$$n_x x + n_y y + n_z z - (n_x x_0 + n_y y_0 + n_z z_0) = 0. \tag{9}$$

The next step is to find, for each point $\vec{p}$ in the input point cloud within four times the radius, the nearest point $\vec{q}$ in the plane. Now let t be the signed distance between $\vec{p}$ and the normal plane. The point $\vec{q} = \vec{p} - t\vec{n}$. Remembering that $\vec{n}$ is a unit vector, we use the following equation to find t:

$$t = \frac{ax_p + by_p + cx_p + d}{\sqrt{a^2 + b^2 + c^2}} = ax_p + by_p + cx_p + d. \tag{10}$$

After that we form a rectangle of 200 by 200 points, where the sides are large enough to accommodate the points in the plane. Then we form a two dimensional image of the plane with the points in the plane by starting with a 200 by 200 array of zeros; then for each point in the plane, we find the nearest point in the rectangle, and set the corresponding element in the image array to 1 obtaining an image like the one shown in Fig. 8.

The next step is to decide how many artery cross sections the image contains. This is another nontrivial problem, that required developing, adapting and testing many imaging functions. The most important and useful are: *(a)* a function

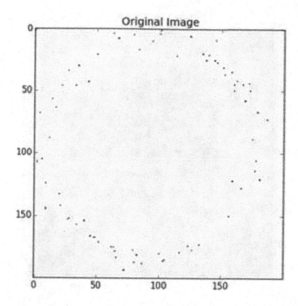

Fig. 8. An image obtained from projecting the points near a plane into the plane.

that finds for each pixel in the image its distance from the nearest point (Fig. 9) and *(b)* a function that finds the potential artery centers based on the results from *a* (Fig. 10). The imaging function in *b* first finds all the attractor regions, composed of pixels that have the same distance to the nearest point of the image, that are surrounded by pixels that have a smaller distance to the nearest point of the image. Then it filters the following attractor regions: *(i)* those that contact the border, *(ii)* the regions with a prominence (distance to another region that is also in contact with other regions that lead to another attractor region) smaller than a certain threshold, *(iii)* The regions that are not separated by any points from other more prominent attractor regions, or with the same prominence but a larger surface area, and *(iv)* the attractor regions that have a distance to the nearest point that is smaller then a certain fraction (about 1/3 works well) of the distance from the nearest point of another attractor region.

When the normal plane of the point contains more than one artery center, the current vessel ends. The program must follow each new center separately building another vessel for each center and then store them as children of the original vessel. When there are no more points in the direction of the normal, the function modeling the vessel must stop and return. The elipses obtained after modeling a section of an artery are shown in Fig. 11.

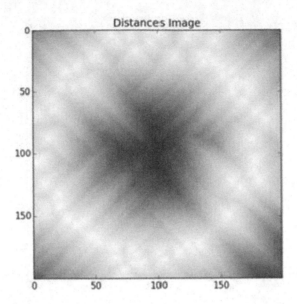

Fig. 9. An image of the distances to the points, white is nearer deep blue is farther (Color figure online).

3.4   Possible Problems for This Approach and Some Methods that May Help in Their Solution

Once an artery splits up (Fig. 12 A), the points in the image must be clustered by an artery center. A scatter plot of the distance from the center versus the angle may help (Fig. 12 B).

Some arteries may split so that the daughter artery is almost perpendicular to the artery from which it originates, and the analysis using only the normal plane may not detect the daughter artery. Therefore, it must be necessary to use a spherical view plane to detect all splitting arteries. Instead of having a normal plane we will have a sphere that may be implemented as a 2D wrapping matrix. Then, if for the section of space defined by the four angles $\Phi, \Phi+d, \Psi$ and $\Psi + d$ and a threshold radius that is larger than that of the sphere, that section contains a point, then the corresponding bit in the sphere matrix is set to 1.

If the runtime of the program becomes too long, the program must be parallelized, by exploring the arteries initially using 4 threads, and spawning a new thread each time an artery splits up. In addition, there are some methods to fit an ellipse, which are more efficient than the one we are using [65,66].

Another challenge will be to build the surface and volume meshes that will allow us to model the hemodynamics within the artery. The arteries are not very smooth and the automated methods that already exist may not work properly. Therefore we may either increase the linear density of the ellipses in the model, increase the number of points per ellipse, or use the model itself to weave the surface mesh ellipse by ellipse by connecting their borders with triangular faces.

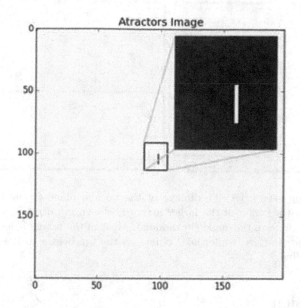

Fig. 10. The attractor region left after filtering the dubious attractor regions. On the top right corner, the enlarged region from the distances image that corresponds to the area in the rectangle with the attractor in white.

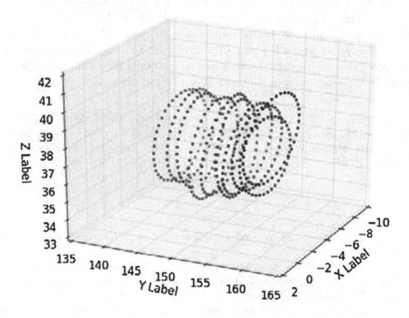

Fig. 11. The ellipses obtained after modeling a segment of the left carotid.

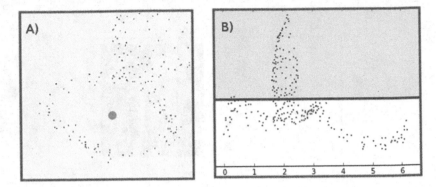

Fig. 12. Splitting artery: (A) The image of the normal plane at the location where the artery splits, the center of the larger artery is shown in purple. (B) A plot of the distance of the points vs the angle (in radians). Most of the points below the blue line belongs to the large artery, while those points on the top belong to the smaller artery (Color figure online).

4   Conclusion

In this work we have introduced a novel computational implementation of a method to model the geometry of a blood vessel graph. We presented the first model of the geometry of a blood vessel obtained using a program we are developing. Our program describes a blood vessel using a parametric curve, where each point within this curve includes a normal vector that points toward the direction of the blood flow. We use an ellipse to model the shape of the cross section of the vessel at each point of the curve. This is the first step in the process a tool development that will allow us to model the brain hemodynamics of specific brain arteriovenous malformations in patients.

Acknowledgement. We would like to thank Juan Carlos Cajas, Mariano Velazquez, Jazmin Aguado, Marina López, Alfonso Santiago and Abel Gargallo from the Barcelona Supercomputing Center for their valuable advice. This work was partially supported by ABACUS, CONACyT grant EDOMEX-2011-C01-165873.

References

1. Osborn, A.G.: Diagnostic cerebral angiography. Am. J. Neuroradiol. **20**(9), 1767–1769 (1999)
2. Kim, D.-J., Czosnyka, Z., Kasprowicz, M., Smieleweski, P., Baledent, O., Guerguerian, A.-M., Pickard, J.D., Czosnyka, M.: Continuous monitoring of the monro-kellie doctrine: is it possible? J. Neurotrauma **297**, 1354–1363 (2012)
3. Mokri, B.: The Monro-Kellie hypothesis: applications in CSF volume depletion. Neurology **5612**, 1746–1748 (2001)

4. van Laar, P.J., Hendrikse, J., Golay, X., Lu, H., van Osch, M.J., van der Grond, J.: In vivo flow territory mapping of major brain feeding arteries. NeuroImage **29**(1), 136–144 (2006)

5. Duret, H.: Recherches anatomiques sur la circulation de l'encéphale. Archives de Physiologie normale et pathologique **6**, 60–91 (1874)

6. Pérez, V.H.: Atlas del sistema arterial cerebral con variantes anatómicas. Editorial Limusa (2002)

7. Conn, P.M.: Neuroscience in Medicine. Humana Press, Totowa (2008)

8. Fontana, H., Belziti, H., Requejo, F., Recchia, M., Buratti, S., Recchia, M.: La circulación cerebral en condiciones normales y patológicas: Parte ii. las arterias de la base. Revista Argentina de Neurocirugía **21**(2), 65–70 (2007)

9. Gomes, CRdG, Chopard, R.P.: A morphometric study of age-related changes in the elastic systems of the common carotid artery and internal carotid artery in humans. Eur. J. Morphol. **41**(3–4), 131–137 (2003)

10. Canham, P.B., Talman, E.A., Finlay, H.M., Dixon, J.G.: Medial collagen organization in human arteries of the heart and brain by polarized light microscopy. Connect. Tissue Res. **26**(1–2), 121–134 (1991)

11. Rowe, A., Finlay, H., Canham, P.: Collagen biomechanics in cerebral arteries and bifurcations assessed by polarizing microscopy. J. Vasc. Res. **40**, 406–415 (2003)

12. Duvernoy, H.M., Delon, S., Vannson, J.: Cortical blood vessels of the human brain. Brain Res. Bull. **7**(5), 519–579 (1981)

13. Wright, S.N., Kochunov, P., Mut, F., Bergamino, M., Brown, K.M., Mazziotta, J.C., Toga, A.W., Cebral, J.R., Ascoli, G.A.: Digital reconstruction and morphometric analysis of human brain arterial vasculature from magnetic resonance angiography. NeuroImage **82**, 170–181 (2013)

14. Dobrin, P.B.: Mechanical properties of arteries. Physiol. Rev. **58**(2), 397–460 (1978)

15. Rosenberg, J.B., Shiloh, A.L., Savel, R.H., Eisen, L.A.: Non-invasive methods of estimating intracranial pressure. Neurocrit. Care **15**(3), 599–608 (2011)

16. Rossitti, S., Löfgren, J.: Vascular dimensions of the cerebral arteries follow the principle of minimum work. Stroke J. Cereb. Circ. **24**(3), 371–377 (1993)

17. Budohoski, K.P., Czosnyka, M., de Riva, N., Smielewski, P., Pickard, J.D., Menon, D.K., Kirkpatrick, P.J., Lavinio, A.: The relationship between cerebral blood flow autoregulation and cerebrovascular pressure reactivity after traumatic brain injury. Neurosurgery **71**(3), 652–661 (2012)

18. Kim, M.O., Adji, A., O'Rourke, M.F., Avolio, A.P., Smielewski, P., Pickard, J.D., Czosnyka, M.: Principles of cerebral hemodynamics when intracranial pressure is raised: lessons from the peripheral circulation. J. Hypertens. **33**(6), 1233–1241 (2015)

19. Chung, E., Chen, G., Alexander, B., Cannesson, M.: Non-invasive continuous blood pressure monitoring: a review of current applications. Front. Med. **7**(1), 91–101 (2013)

20. Lee, K.J., Park, C., Oh, J., Lee, B.: Non-invasive detection of intracranial hypertension using a simplified intracranial hemo- and hydro-dynamics model. Biomed. Eng. Online **14**(1), 51 (2015)

21. Simmonds, M.J., Meiselman, H.J., Baskurt, O.K.: Blood rheology and aging. J. Geriatr. Cardiol. **10**(3), 291–301 (2013)

22. Dolenska, S., Interpretation, A.D.: Understanding Key Concepts for the FRCA. Cambridge University Press, Cambridge (2000)

23. Faraci, F.M., Heistad, D.D.: Regulation of the cerebral circulation: role of endothelium and potassium channels. Physiol. Rev. **78**(1), 53–97 (1998)

24. Obrenovitch, T.P.: Molecular physiology of preconditioning-induced brain tolerance to ischemia. Physiol. Rev. **88**(1), 211–247 (2008)
25. Alastruey, J., Moore, S.M., Parker, K.H., David, T., Peiró, J., Sherwin, S.J.: Reduced modelling of blood flow in the cerebral circulation: coupling 1-D, 0-D and cerebral auto-regulation models. Int. J. Numer. Meth. Fluids **56**(8), 1061 (2008)
26. Perdikaris, P., Grinberg, L., Karniadakis, G.E.: An effective fractal-tree closure model for simulating blood flow in large arterial networks. Ann. Biomed. Eng. **43**(6), 1432–1442 (2014)
27. Cymberknop, L.J., Armentano, R.L., Legnani, W., Pessana, F.M., Craiem, D., Graf, S., Barra, J.G.: Contribution of arterial tree structure to the arterial pressure fractal behavior. J. Phys: Conf. Ser. **477**, 012030 (2013). IOP Publishing
28. Aslanidou, L., Trachet, B., Reymond, P., Fraga-Silva, R., Segers, P., Stergiopulos, N.: A 1D model of the arterial circulation in mice. ALTEX **33**, 13–28 (2015)
29. Reymond, P., Vardoulis, O., Stergiopulos, N.: Generic and patient-specific models of the arterial tree. J. Clin. Monit. Comput. **26**(5), 375–382 (2012)
30. Chiu, J.-J., Chien, S.: Effects of disturbed flow on vascular endothelium: pathophysiological basis and clinical perspectives. Physiol. Rev. **91**(1), 327–387 (2011)
31. Sáez-Pérez, J.: Distensibilidad arterial: un parámetro más para valorar el riesgo cardiovascular. SEMERGEN-Medicina de Familia **34**(6), 284–290 (2008)
32. Pries, A., Neuhaus, D., Gaehtgens, P.: Blood viscosity in tube flow: dependence on diameter and hematocrit. Am. J. Physiol. Heart Circ. Physiol. **263**(6), H1770–H1778 (1992)
33. Sochi, T.: Non-Newtonian Rheology in Blood Circulation (2013). arXiv preprint arxiv:1306.2067
34. Liu, Y., Liu, W.: Rheology of red blood cell aggregation by computer simulation. J. Comput. Phys. **220**(1), 139–154 (2006)
35. Ouared, R., Chopard, B.: Lattice Boltzmann simulations of blood flow: non-newtonian rheology and clotting processes. J. Stat. Phys. **121**, 1–2 (2005)
36. Fedosov, D.A., Caswell, B., Karniadakis, G.E.: A multiscale red blood cell model with accurate mechanics, rheology, and dynamics. Biophys. J. **98**, 2215–2225 (2010)
37. Epstein, S., Vergnaud, A.-C., Elliott, P., Chowienczyk, P., Alastruey, J.: Numerical assessment of the stiffness index. In: 2014 36th Annual International Conference of the IEEE Engineering in Medicine and Biology Society (EMBC), pp. 1969–1972. IEEE (2014)
38. Akdemir, H., Oktem, I.S., Tucer, B., Menkü, A., Başaslan, K., Günaldi, O.: Intraoperative microvascular Doppler sonography in aneurysm surgery. Minimally Invasive Neurosurgery, MIN **49**(5), 312–316 (2006)
39. Hui, P.-J., Yan, Y.-H., Zhang, S.-M., Wang, Z., Yu, Z.-Q., Zhou, Y.-X., Li, X.-D., Cui, G., Zhou, D., Hui, G.-Z., Lan, Q.: Intraoperative microvascular Doppler monitoring in intracranial aneurysm surgery. Chin. Med. J. **126**, 2424–2429 (2013)
40. Badie, B., Lee, F.T., Pozniak, M.A., Strother, C.M.: Intraoperative sonographic assessment of graft patency during extracranial-intracranial bypass. AJNR Am. J. Neuroradiol. **21**, 1457–1459 (2000)
41. Steinman, D.A.: Computational modeling and flow diverters: a teaching moment. Am. J. Neuroradiol. **32**(6), 981–983 (2011)
42. Hawthorne, C., Piper, I.: Monitoring of intracranial pressure in patients with traumatic brain injury. Front. Neurol. **5**, 121 (2014)
43. Balakhovsky, K., Jabareen, M., Volokh, K.Y.: Modeling rupture of growing aneurysms. J. Biomech. **47**, 653–658 (2014)

44. Meng, H., Feng, Y., Woodward, S.H., Bendok, B.R., Hanel, R.A., Guterman, L.R., Hopkins, L.N.: Mathematical model of the rupture mechanism of intracranial saccular aneurysms through daughter aneurysm formation and growth. Neurol. Res. **27**, 459–467 (2005)

45. Utter, B., Rossmann, J.S.: Numerical simulation of saccular aneurysm hemodynamics: influence of morphology on rupture risk. J. Biomech. **40**(12), 2716–2722 (2007)

46. Xiang, J., Tutino, V.M., Snyder, K.V., Meng, H.: CFD: computational fluid dynamics or confounding factor dissemination? the role of hemodynamics in intracranial aneurysm rupture risk assessment. AJNR Am. J. Neuroradiol. **35**, 1849–1857 (2013)

47. Russin, J., Babiker, H., Ryan, J., Rangel-Castilla, L., Frakes, D., Nakaji, P.: Computational fluid dynamics to evaluate the management of a giant internal carotid artery aneurysm. World Neurosurg. **83**(6), 1057–1065 (2015)

48. Jeong, W., Rhee, K.: Hemodynamics of cerebral aneurysms: computational analyses of aneurysm progress and treatment. Comput. Math. Meth. Med. **2012**, 782801 (2012)

49. Morales, H.G., Larrabide, I., Geers, A.J., San Román, L., Blasco, J., Macho, J.M., Frangi, A.F.: A virtual coiling technique for image-based aneurysm models by dynamic path planning. IEEE Trans. Med. Imaging **32**, 119–129 (2013)

50. Babiker, M.H., Chong, B., Gonzalez, L.F., Cheema, S., Frakes, D.H.: Finite element modeling of embolic coil deployment: multifactor characterization of treatment effects on cerebral aneurysm hemodynamics. J. Biomech. **46**, 2809–2816 (2013)

51. Raoult, H., Bannier, E., Maurel, P., Neyton, C., Ferré, J.-C., Schmitt, P., Barillot, C., Gauvrit, J.-Y.: Hemodynamic quantification in brain arteriovenous malformations with time-resolved spin-labeled magnetic resonance angiography. Stroke **45**(8), 2461–2464 (2014)

52. Telegina, N., Chupakhin, A., Cherevko, A.: Local model of arteriovenous malformation of the human brain. In: IC-MSQUARE 2012: International Conference on Mathematical Modelling in Physical Sciences (2013)

53. Andisheh, B., Bitaraf, M.A., Mavroidis, P., Brahme, A., Lind, B.K.: Vascular structure and binomial statistics for response modeling in radiosurgery of cerebral arteriovenous malformations. Phys. Med. Biol. **55**(7), 2057–2067 (2010)

54. Nowinski, W.L., Thirunavuukarasuu, A., Volkau, I., Baimuratov, R., Hu, Q., Aziz, A., Huang, S.: Informatics in Radiology (infoRAD): three-dimensional atlas of the brain anatomy and vasculature. Radiographics: Rev. Publ. Radiol. Soc. North Am. Inc. **25**, 263–271 (2005)

55. Volkau, I., Zheng, W., Baimouratov, R., Aziz, A., Nowinski, W.L.: Geometric modeling of the human normal cerebral arterial system. IEEE Trans. Med. Imaging **24**(4), 529–539 (2005)

56. Volkau, I., Ng, T.T., Marchenko, Y., Nowinski, W.L.: On geometric modeling of the human intracranial venous system. IEEE Trans. Med. Imaging **27**, 745–51 (2008)

57. Nowinski, W.L., Thirunavuukarasuu, A., Volkau, I., Marchenko, Y., Aminah, B., Puspitasari, F., Runge, V.M.: A three-dimensional interactive atlas of cerebral arterial variants. Neuroinformatics **7**, 255–264 (2009)

58. Nowinski, W.L., Volkau, I., Marchenko, Y., Thirunavuukarasuu, A., Ng, T.T., Runge, V.M.: A 3D model of human cerebrovasculature derived from 3T magnetic resonance angiography. Neuroinformatics **7**, 23–36 (2009)

59. Nowinski, W.L., Chua, B.C., Marchenko, Y., Puspitsari, F., Volkau, I., Knopp, M.V.: Three-dimensional reference and stereotactic atlas of human cerebrovasculature from 7 Tesla. NeuroImage **55**, 986–998 (2011)

60. Nowinski, W.L., Thaung, T.S.L., Chua, B.C., Yi, S.H.W., Ngai, V., Yang, Y., Chrzan, R., Urbanik, A.: Three-dimensional stereotactic atlas of the adult human skull correlated with the brain, cranial nerves, and intracranial vasculature. J. Neurosci. Methods **246**, 65–74 (2015)
61. Iacono, M.I., Neufeld, E., Akinnagbe, E., Bower, K., Wolf, J., Vogiatzis Oikonomidis, I., Sharma, D., Lloyd, B., Wilm, B.J., Wyss, M., Pruessmann, K.P., Jakab, A., Makris, N., Cohen, E.D., Kuster, N., Kainz, W., Angelone, L.M.: Mida: a multimodal imaging-based detailed anatomical model of the human head and neck. PLoS ONE **10**, e0124126 (2015)
62. Halĭr, R., Flusser, J.: Numerically stable direct least squares fitting of ellipses. In: Proceedings of 6th International Conference in Central Europe on Computer Graphics and Visualization, WSCG, vol. 98, pp. 125–132 (1998)
63. Fitzgibbon, A., Pilu, M., Fisher, R.: Direct least square fitting of ellipses. IEEE Trans. Pattern Anal. Mach. Intell. **21**, 476–480 (1999)
64. Watson, G.: Least squares fitting of circles and ellipses to measured data. BIT Numer. Math. **39**(1), 176–191 (1999)
65. Ray, A., Srivastava, D.C.: Non-linear least squares ellipse fitting using the genetic algorithm with applications to strain analysis. J. Struct. Geol. **30**, 1593–1602 (2008)
66. Kanatani, K., Rangarajan, P.: Hyper least squares fitting of circles and ellipses. Comput. Stat. Data Anal. **55**(6), 2197–2208 (2011)

Author Index

Printed in the United States
By Bookmasters